INDUSTRIAL RELATIONS IN IRELAND

INDUSTRIAL RELATIONS IN IRELAND

THEORY AND PRACTICE

SECOND EDITION

Patrick Gunnigle, Gerard McMahon
and
Gerard Fitzgerald

GILL & MACMILLAN

Gill & Macmillan Ltd
Hume Avenue, Park West
Dublin 12
with associated companies throughout the world
www.gillmacmillan.ie

0 7171 2837 7
Index compiled by Helen Litton
Print origination in Ireland by Carole Lynch

*The paper used in this book is made from the wood pulp of managed forests.
For every tree felled, at least one tree is planted, thereby renewing natural resources.*

A catalogue record is available for this book from the British Library.

Contents

Acknowledgments

For helping us complete this text we would like to acknowledge the support and contribution of a number of individuals and organisations.

Various external organisations and individuals provided data and assistance. In particular we would like to thank the following:

- Professor Phil Beaumont, University of Glasgow
- Professor Bill Roche and Teresa Brannick, Smurfit Graduate School of Business, University College Dublin
- Maurice Cashell, Ed Crean, Padraig Cullinane, Joe McLoughlin and Martin Territt, Department of Enterprise, Trade and Employment
- Michael McDonnell, Frank Brennan and Gaye Hand, Institute of Personnel and Development in Ireland
- Kieran Mulvey and Jim Palmer, Labour Relations Commission
- The library staff at the Dublin Institute of Technology, Aungier St, and at the Central Statistics Office
- Noel Harvey, Galway-Mayo Institute of Technology
- Jacq Ashmore, National Centre for Partnership
- Dr Brendan McPartlin, National College of Ireland
- Paul Joyce, Labour Law Practitioner, Free Legal Advice Centre
- Tom Wall, Assistant General Secretary, Irish Congress of Trade Unions

Colleagues at the University of Limerick were most helpful. In particular we would like to acknowledge the contribution of Tom Dalzell, doctoral student, University of Limerick, for his assistance with the material on industrial relations negotiations, and Fergus Walsh, now Personnel Officer, Shannon Aerospace, for his assistance with material on employer associations. Noreen Heraty, Mike Morley and Tom Turner provided much information and advice. Joe Wallace, Tom Turner, Daryl D'Art, Tom Garavan, Patrick Flood, Sarah Moore and Sarah MacCurtain all helped in various ways, not least through their own research and publications. Professors Noel Whelan and Donal Dineen have always been most helpful and encouraging of our work while Geraldine Floyd provided the necessary administrative support and direction.

We would also like to mention the contribution of Ailbhe O'Reilly and Gabrielle Noble of Gill & Macmillan in helping to bring this work to fruition.

Finally, we would like to mention our families — Theresa, Eoin, Sean and Tadhg (Gunnigle); Monica, Laura, Alison and Kevin (McMahon) and Sarah, Eoghan and Stephanie (Fitzgerald) — and thank them for their patience and good humour.

PG, GMcM & GF, October 1998.

List of Figures and Tables

TABLES

CHAPTER ONE

Industrial Relations: A Contextual and Theoretical Overview

1.1 INTRODUCTION: WHAT DO WE MEAN BY INDUSTRIAL RELATIONS?

The subject area of industrial relations is one of the most discussed specialist areas of organisational and national economic management. The public prominence of the topic is primarily attributable to its headline making capacity — when in the throes of industrial action, mass redundancy and wage bargaining type activities. These events materialise at plant, industry and national level, commanding extensive media coverage and widespread public interest and concern (e.g., the nurses' dispute, the Garda Síochána 'blue flu' strike, the Ryanair trade union recognition strike). However, the subject is largely shrouded in confusion and anxiety, at the expense of insightful analysis — a factor contributing to the ongoing public pronouncements urging dramatic (and often ill-conceived) policy changes (e.g., to outlaw strikes). Frequently, states of 'moral panic' consume the nation, when other more pervasive and injurious work-related phenomena, like health and safety issues, absenteeism levels or a new European Directive might be adjudged more consequential. Of course issues of conflict and disharmony, allied with workers' exposure to aspects of industrial relations during their working lives, do give the subject considerable public appeal.

Industrial relations does not easily lend itself to definition. However, the primary focus of the subject is on the employment relationship of about one and a half million employees in the Republic of Ireland, working across all employment sectors and entity types. These include national or local government, private companies extending from multinational subsidiaries to local corner shops, semi-state companies, single domestic employers and co-operatives, spanning both union and non-union enterprises. Even the term 'industrial relations' itself has connotations of the traditional unionised blue collar working environment in the manufacturing sector, whilst the term 'employee relations' conjures up images of the non or less unionised white collar services sector. In this text, for ease of classification, the terms are assumed by the authors to be synonymous.

As with most subjects, a narrow conception does not facilitate genuine understanding. Therefore, the subject of industrial relations can best be understood and interpreted in the wider context of the historic, political, social and economic processes which have shaped the regulation of working lives. The broad base of the subject therefore draws upon a range of disciplines to facilitate the development of an understanding of both individual and collective relationships, in white and blue collar work environments, and at plant, sector, national and international levels. The complexity of the area has necessitated the adaptation of a vast array of other specialist subject areas — like labour law and labour market economics — to accommodate a comprehensive analysis of all the issues which affect people at work.

Traditionally, the subject-matter has been preoccupied with considerations about trade unions. This emphasis, whilst understandable, fails to appreciate the importance of contextual matters and contrasting (non-union) perspectives on the same phenomena. Both issues, of the context and perspectives on industrial relations, are addressed in this opening chapter, and the centrality of the institutions and entity types, role players, procedures, processes and products of the subject area. Accordingly, in addition to developing an appreciation of the main contextual influences and theoretical perspectives, familiarity with the following range of institutions and issues is warranted to enable the student to develop an informed view of the nature and scope for change and development in our industrial relations system:

Institutions: trade unions, trade union section and branch committees, union confederations/national affiliations, the Irish Congress of Trade Unions (ICTU), employers' organisations, the Irish Business and Employers' Confederation (IBEC), trades councils, the Labour Relations Commission (LRC), the Labour Court, the Employer Labour Conference (ELC), the Employment Appeals Tribunal (EAT), the law courts, the European Commission (EC), European Parliament and European Union (EU), Joint Labour Committees (JLCs), Joint Industrial Councils (JICs), Government Departments, the Employment Equality Agency (EEA), Health and Safety Authority (HSA), specially appointed commissions (e.g., on industrial relations, health and safety), relevant educational and research institutes etc.

Role players: shop stewards and shop steward organisation, full-time trade union and employer organisation officials, personnel or human resource specialists, arbitrators, conciliators, adjudicators, Equality Officers, human resource consultants, other third party actors, Government Ministers, etc.

Processes/Procedures: third-party referrals, strike and other industrial actions, union recognition, establishing and maintaining closed shops and non-union entities, disciplinary, grievance and dispute handling procedures, consultation, involvement, participation and negotiation processes and skills etc.

Issues: the roles of the State, the European Commission, Parliament and Union; the role of collective and individual labour law, the future roles of trade unions and employer organisations, political decision making and national level economic and social bargaining; economic (including industrial and employment) policy, strikes, lockouts, picketing, pay levels and payment systems, terms and conditions of employment, union recognition and avoidance phenomena, health and safety, new technology, employee flexibility, total quality management and world class manufacturing, employee involvement/participation, management styles or approaches to employee relations etc.

In so far as is possible this text outlines and analyses the various dimensions of the subject listed above, attempting to adopt a factual and unbiased approach to the study of industrial relations. The very nature of the subject-matter inevitably means that many aspects of the topic are contentious. Accordingly, an effort is made to steer a middle line, whilst outlining the central strands of the main differing viewpoints that have been expressed on the various aspects of the subject. Of course a most attractive aspect of the topic is that it allows students to develop their own opinions and to make up their own minds as to the merits of the contrasting perspectives outlined. The text therefore endeavours to facilitate this process by producing a general overview of the more significant contextual, theoretical, institutional, substantive and procedural aspects, whilst reviewing what are generally adjudged in the literature to be the more salient trends in this labour relations arena. Therefore, more contentious or debatable dimensions of the subject, including the range of political arguments and the plethora of factual data, which lend themselves on occasion to a number of possible interpretations, are reviewed in as objective a manner as is possible, with a view to encouraging students to establish their own position on the matters in question.

However, it is important that the development of particular viewpoints and perspectives be embedded in an appreciation of the many central features and facts in and around which the system of industrial relations operates. Accordingly, this text endeavours to provide a balanced and comprehensive treatment of the topic without an undue emphasis on any specific area. By maximising the descriptive and minimising the analytical or academic orientation, the text opts for a practical approach to the subject-matter. Where students wish to further explore particular aspects of a theme an extensive referencing system has been adopted by the authors to facilitate same. The structure of the text was designed to address the subject in an orderly fashion, by linking each chapter to its successor and proceeding, where possible, by a block building process. By dividing all of the chapters into a series of sections and subsections it is intended to make the material more manageable and to appropriately differentiate the various topics rather than allow one topic merge into the next without any indication of a change.

In Figure 1.1 an attempt is made to present a working model or overview of the Irish system of industrial relations. Each component of this model is outlined and critically evaluated at an appropriate point in the text. In this opening chapter the main contrasting theoretical perspectives and contextual factors which have determined the current — and which will influence the future — shape of the industrial relations system are reviewed. The system itself can be viewed from many different angles or perspectives. However, no one view can yield a perfect understanding, but each can add to our insights. The location of five theoretical perspectives on the outer perimeter of Figure 1.1 is designed to convey the potential of each and all of these theories to provide their own insights on the whole system, or aspects of same. That is, these theoretical perspectives or frames of reference offer contrasting explanations of the same phenomena or various parts of the industrial relations system. Despite the academic orientation of these theories, their relevance should not be underestimated. The decision to support one or other of the theories may well be reflected in, for example:
– the nature of legislation introduced by the politician or his/her party;
– the approach to union recognition adopted by the general manager or his/her board of directors;
– the intransigence and preparedness to recommend industrial action by the worker representative and his/her union.

The prevalence of dual direction arrows attempts to depict the relationship between the various components of the system. This may be reflected in a vast array of exchanges, such as trade union opposition to legal intervention on grounds of history or tradition, the reform of third party dispute-settling agencies owing to the nature and volume of (conflict) cases coming before them, the impact of the terms of a collective agreement reached at national, industrial or organisational level by employees and employer(s) (or their representative organisations) on the state of the economy, or even the content of a plant level procedural agreement on disciplinary action resulting from national and international political influences, culminating in legislative decisions as to what constitutes an unfair dismissal.

Chapter 2 exposes the reader to the most significant societal regulator of trade union, employer and employee relationships — the law. This chapter is divided into two main sections to accommodate the contrasting objectives of collective labour law and its preoccupation with trade unions and their operations, and individual labour law which is primarily concerned with the rights of workers *vis-à-vis* their employers (and vice versa).

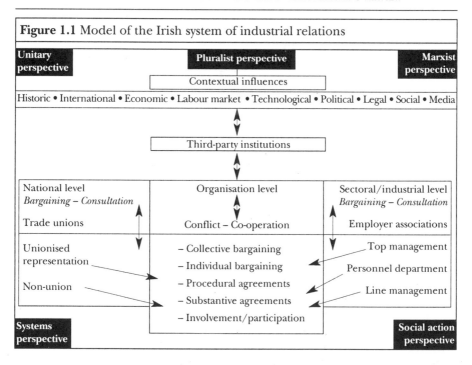

Figure 1.1 Model of the Irish system of industrial relations

Chapters 3, 4 and 5 examine the main components of the system's institutional framework i.e., the State, trade unions and employer organisations. Industrial relations has evolved many different organisations and institutions to act as the machinery or vehicle for the management of the human factor at plant, industry and national levels. The State's influence has always been a dominant one — particularly in the context of its legislative role — and in recent decades as a provider of fora for the resolution of issues on which employees and employers (or their respective representative organisations) fail to agree amongst themselves. Indeed, given that about one in four of all persons engaged in non-agricultural employment operates in the public sector, it would be remiss not to review the State's own internal industrial relations mechanisms. The main parties to the institutionalised relationship are of course the trade unions and employer organisations. The formation of these groups, their relative power and respective values and interests, exert a fundamental impact on the way employment relationships are managed and develop, and are therefore examined in detail in this text.

In chapters 6 and 7 the collective bargaining process, which is so central to industrial relations, is reviewed. For the student of industrial relations an understanding of the nature, development and skills associated with the collective bargaining and negotiation process at all levels of the economy is crucial. It is through this process that those economic, social and political issues which structure and are inherent to the employment relationship are accommodated and resolved. In chapter 6 the commonplace differentiation between the substantive and procedural products of the bargaining process is recognised. The substantive products span the various details of the effort-reward relationship (e.g., pay and conditions), whilst the procedural dimensions are concerned with how the substantive issues are addressed (i.e., who has the right or power to negotiate via what administrative or bargaining arrangements). Given the extensive scope provided by the employment relationship for conflict over both substantive and procedural issues, chapter 7 also provides a descriptive and analytical overview of the nature of conflict, with particular emphasis on strikes. In the face of the public's preoccupation with industrial action, its impact on our international reputation, together with the trade union movement's insistence upon the retention of the 'fundamental right' to withdraw labour in the event of total disagreement with their negotiating counterparts, this topic warrants detailed consideration.

Chapter 8 examines the principles and practices associated with employee participation or involvement. Given the emergence of 'partnership' based approaches to industrial relations, this chapter serves to explain the attempted transition from conflictual to co-operative strategies at the workplace.

In chapters 9 and 10 an attempt is made to broadly distinguish between the varying business environments and organisational approaches or styles to the management of the labour relations function. Particularly with the influx of multinational subsidiaries to the Republic of Ireland over the past thirty-five years, one can distinguish significant differences in the style of employee or human resource management policies being pursued e.g., single or dual union pre-production agreements, non-union policies.

In chapter 11 emerging trends and likely developments or influences on the future shape and nature of the industrial relations system are considered. These include the extent and impact of flexibility initiatives (e.g., part-time work, multi-skilling), technological developments, total quality and world class manufacturing initiatives and international (including European Union) influences, trends and developments.

1.2 THE CONTEXTUAL SETTING OF INDUSTRIAL RELATIONS

Any initiative designed to analyse and prescribe in the area of Irish industrial relations requires some familiarity with those prominent influences which have helped or forced the system to adopt its present shape and character. Hence Salamon's (1998) definition of 'industrial relations' as '. . . a set of phenomena, operating both within and outside the workplace, concerned with determining and regulating the employment relationship'.

The structure and nature of trade unions, employer organisations, specialist Government-funded institutions in the area, workplace practices and managerial styles, legislative initiatives and the plethora of voluntary arrangements in place can be more gainfully assessed from a knowledge base spanning two centuries which have thrown up a vast range of economic, political and social changes. Whilst there has been an astonishing array of such interrelated influences, in this section of the opening chapter an attempt will be made to accommodate the more salient of such influences under the interrelated headings of history, economics, the labour market and politics. Of course, such coverage does not purport to be either comprehensive or detailed, but to provide some limited insight into the more salient influences shaping the nature and development of the contemporary Irish system of industrial relations.

1.2.1 HISTORY AND INDUSTRIAL RELATIONS

Historical factors are of particular relevance in developing an understanding of industrial relations, and particularly trade unionism, in Ireland today. As the Industrial Revolution swept Britain in the nineteenth century, with the advent of factory-cum-machine type production and the further concentration of population in the large industrial cities and towns, trade unions emerged and grew. This was an attempt to give redress to the perceived imbalance wrought by private enterprise capitalism and the prevalent *laissez-faire* economic orthodoxy. At the time this orthodoxy or economic system was underpinned by the belief that the market was the only means by which all prices, including wages, profits and economic priorities should be determined.

Therefore, trade unions were identified as a real threat to the prevalent economic, social and political order. In fact, the unions of Britain and Ireland are among the oldest institutions of the modern world. Defining a trade union as a 'continuous association of wage earners for the purpose of maintaining and improving the conditions of their working lives', Sidney and Beatrice Webb have identified the earliest such union as an association of London hatters in the reign of Charles II. In the opinion of the Webbs — some of the very first writers on the subject of industrial relations — the Journeymen Hatters' Trade Union of Great Britain and Ireland could trace its origins back to that early association of London hatters (Boyd, 1984). The first Irish trade union to be identified by name was the Regular Carpenters of Dublin, which, it is estimated, was founded in 1764.

There is also evidence that there were several unions or 'combinations' active in the Cork area in the middle of the eighteenth century. Their activities included organising strikes, picketing, destroying tools, materials and machinery, and ostracising employers who would not give in to their demands. Eventually Parliament declared that anyone in Cork city found guilty of being a member of an unlawful trade union should be 'imprisoned not above six months, whipped in public and released only on giving recognisance of good behaviour for seven years' (Boyd, 1972). From 1770 there is an account of two weavers who were found guilty of 'combination', and were whipped through the streets of Dublin from Newgate Prison to

College Green. In 1780 the Irish Parliament passed further legislation for the suppression of all trade unions, an initiative which predated similar legislation in Britain by twenty years. The debate in Parliament was marked by a demonstration of 20,000 trade unionists in Dublin city. Even members of the Irish clergy had condemned unions as 'iniquitous extortions' (Boyd, 1972). However, despite the legal and social pressures, unions maintained their influence, as individual employers disregarded the legal scenario and negotiated with them. The State's role at this time was deemed to be one of facilitating the unfettered operations of the free market and to confront and control any challenge which was considered to be in 'restraint of trade' e.g., trade unions. Consequently, with the emergence of unions, by the beginning of the nineteenth century a series of statutory and judicial decisions (dating back to 1729) had served to make them illegal under a variety of headings.

The official hostility toward trade unions may be primarily attributed to the *laissez-faire* economic 'religion' of the time. This debarred any interference with the laws of supply and demand in the market-place. However, the minority ruling class also feared the onset of civil disturbance. This had already been witnessed in the Irish rural context with such secret societies as the Whiteboys and the Ribbonmen, and had been central to the outbreak of the French Revolution of 1789, and the ideas of democracy and republicanism which subsequently spread throughout Europe.

Nevertheless, Irish craft workers' trade unions continued to surface, to a large extent as a branch of their unions in the United Kingdom — of which Ireland was a part at that time. In a society plagued by unemployment, destitution and illness the skilled tradesmen enjoyed a relatively privileged place in society by virtue of their relatively high wages and permanent employment. For the purpose of maintaining that position they sought to increase the value of their trade by restricting access to it via an apprenticeship system. Such apprenticeships were generally confined to relatives. In addition, the craft unions endeavoured to increase the security of their members by providing mutual unemployment and sick benefits.

Inter-union co-operation in Ireland formally emerged for the first time in the shape of Trades Councils i.e., organisations representing trade unionists in individual towns and cities. Such Trades Councils were founded in Belfast in 1881, and in Dublin in 1884, and though primarily concerned with the interests of craft workers, their unification was a significant step in the overall development of the Irish trade union movement. With the growing disenchantment of Irish representatives at the lack of priority accorded their business by the British Trade Union Congress, in 1894 the Irish Trade Union Congress (ITUC) was established. By 1900 a total of 60,000 workers were in membership of the ITUC.

Over the 1871 to 1906 period a series of key enactments was passed by the British Parliament. These granted legality to trade unions, protected union funds from court action, recognised collective bargaining and legalised peaceful picketing. Around this time the first real efforts to organise unskilled workers began. At the end of the nineteenth century Ireland was in the throes of the Land League disturbances — a mass movement designed to elevate tenants to land owners. Together with the lessons learned from the experiences of their British general worker counterparts, and from their rural counterparts via the Land League, mass organisation, solidarity and organised struggle arrived on the trade union agenda at the behest of unskilled general workers. Unlike the craft unions, the general workers' unions were open to all, charged low subscription rates, provided no mutual benefits, had no control over access to work, were more inclined toward frequent and aggressive industrial action and retained quite explicit and radical political links.

However, the struggle to extend union membership and recognition beyond the relatively privileged craft workers was a bitter and often bloody affair, on occasion involving the police and army in a series of repressive measures taken on behalf of employers. Major confrontations occurred, for example, in Belfast in 1907, Dublin 1908, Cork 1909 and Wexford 1911. Directly related to these events was the establishment of the Irish Transport and General Workers' Union (ITGWU) in 1909 by James Larkin. Probably the most renowned confrontation which this union became involved in was the 1913 Dublin lockout. On 21 August 1913, 200 tramway workers who had refused to leave the union were sacked. This was the first significant event in a bitter five-month conflict between the ITGWU, led by Larkin, and the Dublin Employers' Federation, established by the prominent businessman William Martin Murphy. Within a month of the lockout or strike starting, over 400 employers and 25,000 workers were in the throes of a violent confrontation. In the face of police assaults the workers established a self-defence group, called the Irish Citizens' Army. A key tactic of the employer grouping was effectively to starve the strikers and their families into submission — a tactic which was eventually to prove successful. In the strike's immediate aftermath, however, the union was reorganised and eventually grew to become the largest trade union in the country (Larkin, 1965). The strike failed primarily because there were too many workers chasing too few casual jobs, and they weren't in a position to bring any big or crucial industry to a permanent standstill. However, the strike marked a seachange in workers' attitudes and the union was to grow rapidly afterwards. The employers' federation involved in this dispute had actually been established in 1911, two years after its Cork counterpart, on which it was modelled. It subsequently played a major role in the 1942 founding of the Federated Union of Employers (FUE) (later to merge with the Confederation of Irish Industry (CII) to become the foremost Irish employers' representative organisation, the Irish Business and Employers' Confederation (IBEC)).

The emergence of general unions was a slow process, as the lack of extensive secondary industry in rural Ireland discouraged the formation of large groups of organised workers in the towns, and those which existed

9

seldom extended beyond a single town. Yet by 1920 the ITGWU could boast a membership of 130,000 members, of whom nearly 50,000 were newly recruited farm labourers. Furthermore, affiliation levels to the Irish TUC jumped from 110,000 in 1914 to 300,000 by 1921.

By this time the central objectives of trade unionism had been clearly established: to secure recognition, to procure collective agreements covering the terms and conditions of employment of their members, and to influence the State's legislative and policy making process in such areas as employment conditions, housing, health care, social welfare and education. Effectively, the labour movement was accepting the emerging industrial society, though exerting its effort to mould it to its advantage. Such developments were inevitably accompanied by a significant change in the State's attitude toward trade unionism — from one of hostility, intransigence and legal suppression to one of recognition and accommodation — subject to its deference to the main economic, political and social structures of society.

The Trade Union Act of 1941 sought to reorganise the union movement and rationalise bargaining structures. It had the tacit support of the ITGWU, which stood to benefit from it. However, it was opposed by James Larkin's newer Workers' Union of Ireland and a large number of British-based unions. The long-standing acrimony between the charismatic firebrand Larkin, and the more conservative William O'Brien, treasurer of the ITGWU, which was part ideological and part personal, came to a head in 1944–45. The union movement and the Irish Labour Party split in two. Just as the 'national question' and related tensions have played, and continue to play, a central role in Irish political matters, so also was it inevitable that such considerations would affect the operation and current shape of the industrial relations system right up to the present time. Nevertheless, by 1959 the ITUC split was resolved and the Irish Congress of Trade Unions (ICTU) was established to represent the vast majority of trade unions operating in this country. Furthermore, union membership almost doubled between 1945 and 1959, peaking in 1980 at over half a million. The key determinant of union membership levels in Ireland is the level and nature of economic activity.

1.2.2 ECONOMICS AND INDUSTRIAL RELATIONS

The policies and practices adopted by Irish trade unions over the years have been characterised by constant adaptations to the reality of political, economic and industrial life in the country. Changes in these spheres have primarily prompted a reactive and pragmatic response, as the trade union movement adjusts its priorities, postures and principles in what is perceived to be in the best interests of its membership and potential membership (i.e., the unemployed) at the time. However, this adaptability also reflects an inability on its part to hugely influence or determine the nature and consequent shape of the Irish economy. It tends to resign itself to a practical role of persuasion within the accepted political and economic framework. Whilst such pressure group type persuasion may adopt various guises, the more significant stakes are primarily pursued through ICTU's influence on Government policies e.g., on job creation, pay determination and labour law.

Though individual trade unions may participate in this process, either through ICTU or in an independent capacity, their primary preoccupation inside the prevalent economic parameters is to protect and improve the pay and conditions of their membership at plant, industry and national levels, via collective bargaining, and similarly to secure the best deal for their clientele in the face of an entity's economic efficiency drive. It is no surprise then that some authorities to the right of the political spectrum have little hesitation in ascribing the rampant inflation of the 1960s and 1970s, together with subsequent unemployment levels, to the unreasonable pay demands and labour market rigidities respectively sought, secured and imposed by trade unions.

The relatively slow growth of Irish trade unionism in the nineteenth and earlier part of the twentieth centuries may be attributed to the somewhat belated onset of the Industrial Revolution. The absence of high grade coal and iron ore, at least in comparison with Great Britain, was a contributory factor in this tardy development. However, one cannot disregard the historical determinants, such as the colonisation of Ireland by England, which proceeded from the middle of the sixteenth century onwards, and undoubtedly prevented the growth of industry well before the Industrial Revolution. Such restrictions, which included a spell of tariff impositions and export restrictions, prevailed up to 1922 as Ireland was perceived as not just a political, but also an economic threat. By the time British policy had adjusted to one of free trade, in the earlier part of the nineteenth century, years of colonial exploitation had so severely weakened Irish industry that it was generally incapable of competing internationally. Consequently, throughout the nineteenth and early twentieth centuries Ireland remained primarily an agricultural economy. In fact, the Cumann na nGaedheal Government of 1922 had no industrial policy, believing agriculture to be the mainstay of the economy. Half the workforce was in agriculture, food and drink made up most exports and there was a huge market 'next door' in Britain. The belated transition to a modern industrial economy was a hesitant and slow process.

Over the 1914–20 period trade union membership increased from 110,000 to 250,000 (Roche and Larragy, 1989), but declined again with the depression in agriculture and trade during the 1920s. This was inevitably accompanied by declining money wages and rising unemployment. Enjoying the legal tolerance secured by their British counterparts, (which had been incorporated into the new State's legislature), trade unions surfaced hesitantly, addressing themselves to issues of growth, consolidation and adaptation to the prevalent and primarily hostile economic order. Indeed, such was the stagnant nature of society and the related lack of vision amongst the nation's leadership, that considerable trade union energy was devoted to the establishment and maintenance of

11

differentials, rather than the attainment of any wider economic and social goals. That is, a status, rather than a class, consciousness prevailed.

Throughout the 1930s significant moves toward economic development were taken inside protectionist economic policies. These were designed to promote greater national economic self-sufficiency, and proved effective in securing the development of new industries and the expansion of older ones. However, the onset of the Second World War and the consequent material supplies shortage contributed to a decline of over a quarter of industrial output during this period. In fact, as late as 1946 agriculture accounted for 47 per cent of total employment, services for 36 per cent and industry for just 17 per cent. Even that 17 per cent was predominantly characterised by small establishments so that by 1958 only forty concerns outside the public service employed more than 500 workers (Lee, 1980). Over the 1945–50 period a short post-war recovery was experienced, which was accompanied by an increase of about 70 per cent in both strike frequency and union membership levels. However, the recovery of the late 1940s concealed the limitations of the protectionist strategy adopted in 1932. Unlike the remainder of Europe, the 1950s proved to be a miserable decade for the Irish economy. Economic performance was disappointing — marked by emigration, balance of payments difficulties and virtual stagnation — with an actual decline in national output in the last half of the decade. In O' Hagan's (1987) assessment:

> . . . at Government level and at civil service level, there were serious deficiencies in the quality of economic policy making, and a lack of purpose, of energy and of leadership, which was all too readily reflected at other levels of society. . . . There was in fact a policy vacuum, which was all too readily filled by short-term and short-sighted measures to preserve or bolster up uneconomic employment.

Whilst the level of trade union membership increased by over 7 per cent during the 1950s, as it undoubtedly benefited from State intervention in the economy, the level of strike frequency dropped significantly from its post-war heights, as trade unions resigned themselves to the economy's stagnation or lack of growth. The fact that by 1960 there were 123 operative trade unions — of which eighty-four had an enrolled membership of less than 1,000 — yields some insight into the priority still being accorded status and relativity factors in the mind of the Irish worker, in preference to class consciousness or solidarity type considerations (Lee, 1980).

In the late 1950s there was a change, and Ireland entered a period of sustained economic growth. The 1960s and 1970s were periods of sustained and unprecedented improvements in living standards and of considerable growth in the Irish economy. By 1964 advertisements placed by the Industrial Development Authority (IDA) in *Fortune* magazine in America featured a small Irish boy scrawling 'Yanks please come over' on a brick wall. Significant emphasis was placed on attracting direct foreign investment and foreign owned companies were given generous incentives to locate new facilities in Ireland. Commenting upon the changing social climate of the 1960s McCarthy (1973) famously suggested that it was:

> . . . a decade of upheaval. We are probably as yet too close to it to recognise its uniqueness. It was a period of national adolescence. The old structures of society were breaking down, the Second Vatican Council had shattered the timeless authoritarian image of the Roman Catholic Church. New attitudes were being painfully developed and new structures and institutions to reflect them. Television mirrored and magnified all that we did.

Indeed, this period witnessed the demise of 'the deferential worker', as previously accepted values, attitudes and institutions came under challenge. The expansion of educational opportunities and media influences increased awareness of the outside world and facilitated a greater preparedness to question previously sacrosanct practices. Allied to this awakening was an opening up of educational and social possibilities which were previously denied or non-existent.

By 1978 total output had reached two and a half times its 1926 level. It was a time of unprecedented rapid wage increases and an approximation to nearly full employment for craftsmen. Trade union membership levels rose by nearly 70 per cent over the period, whilst strike frequency more than doubled. The barriers of pay relativity which had been established were now being reinforced, as both white and blue collar workers engaged in some of the most notorious industrial actions in the history of industry relations, as they clamoured to preserve their differentials and position on the social ladder (McCarthy, 1973; McCarthy et al., 1975). Two of the main influences on this dramatic turnaround were the increased level of Government expenditure and a revised industrial development policy, which encouraged overseas companies to set up base in Ireland. By 1983 almost 1,000 such foreign operations, with a labour force of 87,600, had set up in Ireland.

Over the 1960s and 1970s, following in the path of its main trading partners, the Irish Government opted to relegate the *laissez-faire* approach to economic affairs, and adopt a Keynesian approach to economic growth management and planning. This involved the Government in the stimulation of demand through budgetary deficits and increased expenditure, yielding higher levels of economic activity (via the multiplier effect), and reduced levels of unemployment. Successive Governments over this period pursued this strategy of manipulating aggregate demand, public spending and budget deficits for the attainment of full employment levels.

However, this route to the idyllic economy brought with it a new set of ills. Chief amongst these was the spiralling level of inflation, which the social partners attempted to halt via a series of national level pay agreements for the nation's workforce, which came into effect from the beginning of 1971. In addition, the surge in economic confidence brought with it a drift of power to the workplace, with shop stewards dominating the collective bargaining scene at plant level. An upsurge in unofficial strike action materialised as workers seized upon the boom climate created by economic expansion, demand buoyancy and high employment levels.

However, by the 1980s two problems of significance had materialised. Firstly, the accumulated foreign debt had grown (from £126 million in 1972) to £7,900 million by 1985 bringing with it an increase of over £730 million in annual debt interest payments. Secondly, unemployment levels had escalated from about 6 per cent to 17 per cent over the 1971 to 1986 period — with worse to follow. Once again, following on international trends, the Government opted for 'fiscal rectitude' through monetarist policies, primarily designed to tackle the balance of payments deficit and the attainment of international competitiveness. The policies of particular relevance in the industrial relations context included moderate pay rises and reduced Government spending — with consequences for welfare benefit levels, Government subsidisations and public sector employment. In effect this constituted a *neo-laissez-faire* economic route, involving reduced State intervention in an economy left largely to the devices of the market-place.

The advent of this 'new realism' in the 1980s and early 1990s was accompanied by reduced trade union bargaining power and membership levels, spiralling unemployment and an upsurge in managerial confidence, together with instances of 'macho management' practices. As the international recession heightened coming into the 1990s, a persistent balance of payments problem, further increased unemployment and rising interest rates combined to create real constraints and tensions. A consequence of this downturn in economic prosperity was the intensification of divisions within society, as unemployment spiralled and public expenditure on welfare benefits and services declined — just at the time when the need for them was greatest. Nevertheless, the various indices used to measure industrial action or strike levels reveal a general downward trend, accompanied by sharp declines in trade union membership levels.

For example, the proportion of the workforce in trade union membership fell from a high of 55 per cent in 1980 to about 43 per cent by 1997. The decline in trade union density in the 1980–87 period is generally attributed to economic factors, particularly recession, increased unemployment and structural changes in the distribution of employment (decline/stagnation of employment in traditionally highly unionised sectors such as 'traditional' manufacturing and the public sector), and growth in the service and foreign industry sectors, some of which have traditionally posed difficulties for union penetration (see Roche and Larragy 1989, 1990 and chapter 4 for greater detail). On the industrial action front, an atmosphere of harmony was evident, reflected in the 1996 quarterly returns which reveal the lowest ever figure for days lost due to strike action. Reflecting on the social and political impact of the crisis which liberal capitalism found itself in, Bew et al. (1989) observed upon:

> . . . the relative lack of class conflict. The profound changes in social and economic life . . . were not reflected in the emergence of radical politics, industrial militancy or in any fundamental change in the nature of Irish society. Ireland remained a conservative society imbued with the values of Catholicism, nationalism and ruralism, although less stridently so than in earlier periods.

However, by the late 1990s the 'Celtic Tiger' was in vogue, reflecting a new economic confidence and era. This was reflected in such factors as the fastest growth rates in the EU, equivalent to twice the OECD rate, the lowest inflation rate in Europe, the healthiest Exchequer returns ever, a large balance of payments and current budget surplus, low mortgage interest rates, declining unemployment, booming profits and incomes and the lowest crime rate for nearly twenty years. No economic model had predicted such a reversal of fortune. For example, in 1993 the Bank of Ireland's Chief Economist pessimistically observed that: '. . . perhaps Ireland's misfortune is to be a small and peripheral part of a structure that is, historically speaking, pretty useless at creating jobs for its people' (O'Grada, 1987). The timing of such pronouncements couldn't have been worse, with aggregate employment rising by 7 per cent between 1989 and 1995, and Central Statistics Office predictions of a rise of between 7.2 and 12.9 per cent in employment levels between 1996 and 2006. Indeed, the evidence presented in Tables 1.1 and 1.2 indicates an overall rise of about 25 per cent in employment levels over the 1985 (recession) era to the 1997 boom era. The Economic and Social Research Institute's (ESRI) Medium Term Review for the Irish economy for the 1997–2003 period warns that the biggest domestic danger to economic growth is an excessive rise in expectations. These would feed into wage inflation or insupportable demands on the Exchequer. If the notion of 'pay-back time' were to become the dominant spirit of pressure groups, then the economy and society may have to pay for it in the future — by way of higher unemployment and lower real incomes. Sweeney (1998) has also identified this type of break up of the 'national partnership approach' to pay determination as a serious threat to the 'Celtic Tiger's' health. Whether such a development could herald another 'boom-and-bust' cycle in the imminent EMU environment, with disappearing structural funds, remains to be seen. Time will tell whether this 'Celtic Tiger' is to grow and prosper or to become the 'Celtic Titanic'.

1.2.3 THE LABOUR MARKET AND INDUSTRIAL RELATIONS

Though a central component of the economic framework, such is the impact of the labour market on the evolution and operation of the Irish industrial relations system that it warrants separate consideration. In 1997, out of a population of about 3.6 million, the Irish labour force numbered approximately 1.5 million. Over the 1971–96 period there was an increase of over one-third in the size of the labour force (see Table 1.3). This is attributable to a combination of the underlying growth in the population aged fifteen years and over, and increasing female participation in the workforce. Until recently, despite the proliferation of Government sponsored training and education schemes, the out-of-work figure has risen steadily. For example, in 1971 unemployment stood at 6.7 per cent, but by 1986 it had risen to 17.9 per cent. In fact over the 1979–93 period unemployment jumped by about 230 per cent. By early 1993 unemployment had peaked at over 300,000 — or approximately 20 per cent of the labour force. The main causal factors giving rise to this 1980s decline were the impact of the long-running international recession and the increasing size of the labour force. Recent years have witnessed very significant improvements on this front though many of the jobs created are less secure, more lowly paid, part-time, fixed-term or based on fixed-term contracts.

The three key influences on the size of the labour force are the numbers in the population in each age group, the percentages in each age (and sex) group that are active in the labour market and levels of emigration or immigration. The size of the labour force has been constantly increasing over the past twenty-five years — and despite the significant decline in the birth rate since 1980 — this trend is set to continue into the early years of the next century, albeit at a decelerating rate. For decades the Irish unemployment problem has been masked by high emigration rates. However, when this option narrowed in the 1980s, unemployment rates rose, even when total employment levels were rising. On the matter of activity rates there is evidence that: the youth (i.e., fifteen to twenty-four year olds) are increasingly opting to remain inside the educational system; males over fifty-five years are opting for early retirement; and there is a significant increase in the participation rate of (primarily married) females in the twenty-five to forty-four years of age bracket. Leddin and Walsh (1990) attempt to explain these phenomena which: '. . . can be understood as responses to economic factors. High unemployment undoubtedly encouraged young people to postpone entry into the labour force, while many older people were offered early retirement by firms that were anxious to reduce their labour force.' The relatively low participation rates for both sexes in the fifteen to nineteen year age group (at less than 25 per cent) is explained by high participation in education, while the steep rise between this age group and those aged twenty to twenty-four years (at about 75 per cent), marks the transition from education to the labour force.

Table 1.1 Labour force classification by males, females and married females, 1977–97 (in thousands, % in parentheses)

Year	Males (as a % of total employed)	Females (as a % of total employed)	Married females (as a % of total females)
1977	755 (72)	288 (28)	84 (29)
1981	816 (71)	335 (29)	113 (34)
1985	743 (69)	331 31)	135 (41)
1989	738 (68)	352 (32)	156 (44)
1992	740 (65)	399 (35)	200 (50)
1997	826 (62)	513 (38)	249 (60)

Source: Labour Force Surveys and Census of Population, Central Statistics Office

The increasing number of married women in the paid labour force (see Table 1.1) reflects more complex factors, including the fall in the birth-rate and higher levels of educational attainment among women. It also seems that more job opportunities have been available in the occupations where women are traditionally employed. There have also been changes in legislation making it harder to exclude women from employment. The relative decline in male employment levels, together with the associated expansion in female employment is also evident from Table 1.1. The level of female participation in the labour force has escalated from 28 per cent in 1971 to approximately 40 per cent in 1996. This trend is mainly evident in retail distribution, insurance, financial/business, professional and personal services.

Related to this trend is the substantial shift in employment levels from the agricultural to the services sector (see Table 1.2). The seventy year period since 1926 has witnessed major changes in the relative employment shares of the three broad sectors of economic activity: agriculture, industry and services. The diminishing importance of agriculture is clearly evident — as is the growth of the services sector since 1971.

According to Gunnigle and Morley (1993): '. . . the most notable changes in the Irish labour market over the past twenty years have been the dramatic fall in numbers employed in agriculture and the consistent growth in employment in the services sector which now accounts for almost 60 per cent of all employees.' In fact, in contrast with trends elsewhere, the Irish industrial sector has grown in recent years. After large job losses in the 1980s, numbers grew again during the 1990s (see Table 1.2). However, the composition of industrial type employment has altered significantly, with contractions in many of the older, labour-intensive, indigenous style sub-sectors such as construction, textiles, clothing and footwear and expansions in more

Table 1.2 Employment changes by sector, 1961–97 (in thousands, % in parentheses)

Year	Agriculture	Industry	Services
1961	380 (36)	257 (25)	414 (39)
1975	238 (22)	337 (31)	498 (47)
1979	221 (19)	365 (32)	559 (49)
1985	171 (16)	306 (28)	602 (56)
1989	163 (15)	306 (28)	621 (57)
1992	153 (13)	318 (28)	668 (59)
1997	134 (10)	386 (29)	818 (61)

Source: Census of Population and Labour Force Surveys, Central Statistics Office

technology-related, export-oriented and foreign-owned type employments (e.g., chemical and engineering).

Consequently, the occupational structure of those at work has also altered, with the demise of traditional industry and its associated skills, and their replacement through the emergence and growth of newer ones. Most striking in this context is the overall decline of male manual type jobs in the manufacturing sector — job types which have traditionally provided rich pickings for trade union organisers. This relative decline in the potential market of the trade union movement is also reflected in the fact that between 1988 and 1995 the number of full-time jobs increased by 8 per cent, while at the same time the number of part-time jobs increased by 80 per cent and the number of occasional jobs by nearly 76 per cent. The number of jobs held by women increased by over 31 per cent, whereas the number held by men only rose by 6 per cent. Taking a wider picture, over the 1971–96 period, participation by males in the labour force declined steadily from 82 per cent to 70.7 per cent. Historically, male labour force participation rates have greatly exceeded those of females, peaking at 87.4 per cent in 1946, but declining thereafter to stand at 70.7 per cent by 1996 (see Table 1.3).

Related to this trend is the effect of technology on such matters as the size, spread, location and duration of employment. The quickening pace of technological change is having a dramatic impact on the structure and nature of the labour market and all job types therein. A key dimension of this trend is the aforementioned move away from manual work. However, the creation of replacement job opportunities, resulting from the 'electronics' revolution of microchips, lasers, computers and new technical systems is too low, volatile and of the wrong type to compensate for the attrition rate in the other industries.

Table 1.3 Main labour market indicators

Census Year	Persons in the labour force	Labour force participation rate		Unemployment rate
		Male%	Female%	
1971	1,125	82	28.2	6.7
1981	1,271	76.4	29.7	10.5
1986	1,330	74.0	32.2	17.9
1991	1,383	71.7	35.9	16.9
1996	1,534	70.7	40.7	14.8

Source: Census of Population, Central Statistics Office

In summary then, the most significant implications to emerge from this overview of labour market trends are rising employment levels, diminishing but still significantly high unemployment, together with increases in the size and changing composition of the active labour force. The prime beneficiaries of these changes are (mainly married) female part-time workers in the services sector of the economy. The decline in male manual full-time employment in recent years is also notable. In chapter 11 we review these developments including the related phenomenon of increased 'atypical' employment patterns (e.g., part-time, temporary and self-employment). From an industrial relations perspective these changes have had their fall-out in terms of 'atypical' work patterns, trade union recognition disputes, changes in such matters as working methods, job content, wage differentials and skill protection practices. The impact on industrial relations is also evident in the growth in part-time work, which is primarily a female phenomenon. During 1997 there was an increase of about 60,000 in the number of part-time workers. Women now outnumber men by a ratio of over 2:1 in this category. This has implications for the rising incidence and extent of low pay, minimal job security and decreasing union membership-cum-collective bargaining strength, as trade unions continue to find it difficult to penetrate this market segment.

In recognition of these trends and the 'reality' of the market-place, ICTU(1996) has sought comparable treatment for full-time and part-time workers, a national minimum wage for atypical workers, the elimination of 'zero-hour' contracts and the extension of existing protective legislative provisions to this 'atypical' category. Indeed, it is also argued that a 'new realism' wrought by the 1980s recession and political developments, has been recognised by a trade union movement prepared to repeatedly commit itself to relatively modest pay increases, agreed at national level since 1987, in anticipation of a beneficial return in the form of greater employment generation efforts and lower levels of taxation on income. Since the late 1980s pay settlements (and arguably as a consequence inflation levels), have been at appreciably lower levels than during the 1960s or 1970s. During the 1960s and 1970s unemployment figures were significantly lower and trade union density and negotiating strength were greater. Recent economic and labour market developments, however, raise new issues for trade unions, like the increased prominence of non-union policies. These are particularly evident amongst the newer industrial 'high tech' and service sector employments — many of which are attributed with sophisticated human resource management practices which pre-empt the need for a trade union among employees (Mc Govern, 1989). Furthermore, the reality of these changes has also forced unions to expand their range of services and to focus more upon the needs of part-time and female workers in negotiations with management and Government, for the purpose of maintaining their authority, influence and membership levels.

By the middle of the 1990s the Irish economy began to experience skill shortages in the labour market, the likes of which had not been witnessed for nearly twenty years. For example, in 1998 the Government-appointed Expert Group on Future Skills forecast a shortfall of 2,200 technologists annually to 2003. This severely affected information technology sector claims that it has been forced to award average salary increases of up to 31 per cent in some areas (Higgins, 1997). Almost three-quarters of firms in Dublin's International Financial Services Centre claim that a scarcity of the type of labour they require in Ireland forces them to look abroad for the requisite skills. Furthermore, nearly two-thirds of small firms claim that they have vacancies that they cannot fill.

Whether this pressure on the labour market can be eased in the future remains to be seen. The availability of young people to the jobs market is set to be squeezed over the coming years, by both increasing education and a general fall in the number of young people in the population. We have seen that the numbers of women workers in the labour market accelerated in the 1990s, to almost four times the speed of increase in the two previous decades. Women now account for almost 40 per cent of those in work — a rise very much in tandem with employment growth in the services sector. Recent years have also seen a growth in the number of non-Irish people attracted to this country. These include not just the much publicised asylum seekers, but a large number of skilled European Union (EU) and non-EU nationals sought by companies eager to fill shortages — particularly in information technology and language areas. Ultimately, however, the principle of neo-classical economics suggests that the impact of a tightening labour market serves to increase the relative power of the employee in the employment relationship. This has an inevitable impact on the industrial relations system.

1.2.4 POLITICS IN INDUSTRIAL RELATIONS

The role of the State in the industrial relations arena has been most significant over a century which has seen it adjust from the casting of trade unions as illegal entities, to an accommodation in a social partnership or neo-corporatist type model, with union involvement in the national level decision-making processes covering the whole gamut of economic and social affairs.

Though the State aspires to the role of independent referee and regulator of labour relations matters, as it addresses the worst excesses of liberal capitalism, it would be inappropriate to evaluate its role as that of an impartial facilitator. In any democratic society the State reflects the differences in power between capital and labour and endeavours to side with whomever yields the greatest political influence. In effect then, through their various powers and agencies, successive Irish Governments have upheld the established norms, values and culture of liberal capitalism.

Nevertheless, over time the State has been cautious to refine the extremes of *laissez-faire* ideology and concede the more modest demands of trade unions, so long as they are peacefully presented and pursued, constitutional and maintain due deference to property rights and industrial capitalism e.g., freedom of association (as provided for under the Constitution of 1937), rights to collective bargaining and to take industrial action. However, the first Free State Government did display some disdain for entitlements granted by their British predecessors, as it proceeded to alienate most working class voters and reject the application of Whitley procedures to Ireland i.e., the provision of arbitration machinery for the Civil Service. In 1922 Michael Collins, as Minister for Finance, received (and denied the requests of) a delegation of staff representatives urging the retention of arbitration in the Free State. In fact, it was not until 1950 that advances of any significance were made in this regard. It is also argued that the policies of this Cumann na nGaedheal Government in the 1920s increased the gap between rich and poor (O'Grada, 1997). When it was eventually succeeded by Fianna Fáil in 1932, the new Government's policy was adjudged to be far more indulgent and populist in its attitude to welfare matters.

In line with the eventual adherence to an 'auxiliary' or accommodative strategy, the State largely supported the voluntarist principle in labour relations, by mainly confining legal interference to the provision of mediation services. Such a strategy, whilst successfully isolating trade union militancy and dampening popular support for the route to revolutionary socialism, has forced the trade union movement to (generally) separate and seek its ideologically driven aspirations through a political wing i.e., the Labour Party or via tripartite or corporatist structures.

The Irish Labour Party was established in 1912 at the initiative of James Connolly and James Larkin at the Trade Union Congress. However, between a preoccupation with the burning 'national' question, which has consumed the overwhelming majority of political thought and action over many centuries, and a negligible industrial base (at least until the 1960s), the scope for the development of strong working class communities and culture was severely restricted. Of some further relevance to the relatively modest

influence of the Labour Party is the fact that the party, together with the Irish Trade Union Congress, decided not to contest the 1918 General Election. This decision has been attributed to the party's lack of funds, interested candidates, political organisation and political direction. There was also a very definite reluctance among trade union and labour leaders to oppose the Sinn Féin candidates — who secured seventy-three of the 105 parliamentary seats in the eventual election. However, it is now argued that: '. . . this policy of abstention removed Labour from centre stage in Irish politics for many years, as it sidestepped the great issue of the time which was the struggle for independence' (Kavanagh, 1987). In fact, as Fitzpatrick (1977) suggests, attempts to examine Labour's efforts to remain distinct from the mainstream of Republican politics becomes a review of 'the process whereby Labour and the Republican movement were sucked together', so prominent has the national question been.

In any case, a working class consumed by sacrosanct relativities and occupational status was unlikely to fill the ranks of a vibrant left wing opposition along Western European lines. A striking consequence of this void is that there has been little substantial difference in policy stances between successive Governments on economic and social issues. Given the ideological similarities across the main political parties and Governments, there has been relatively mild opposition to the directions, policies and actions of the govermental process.

The absorption of working class demands into the existing industrial and political structures has also facilitated the maintenance of widespread support for those parties representing the values and beliefs of liberal capitalism. Indeed, for the larger part of this century the State has adopted such an 'auxiliary' role as it avoided direct coercive interference in the industrial relations process, leaving the parties to resolve their own differences via free collective bargaining. Furthermore, following on the British example, the Government addressed itself to the social problems arising from the deficiencies of industrial capitalism, opting for greater intervention to protect and improve the quality of people's existence. The progressive creation of a welfare state in the decades succeeding the Second World War reflected a belief within society that the State should accept responsibility for the provision of education, health and related social services — as effectively the 'haves' support the weak or 'have nots', with equality rather than ability of access dominating public policy. This perspective also dominated the economic arena, as the Government maintained and persisted with the nationalisation of essential industries and manipulated the economic levers at its disposal to create unprecedented high levels of employment. Of course, the gradual creation of a welfare state facilitated the maintenance of political consensus, stability and legitimacy. The emergence of a corporatist or interventionist ideology was accompanied by an integration of political, economic and social decision making. From the 1960s onwards the State's policy of corporate control came into evidence as trade union representatives were invited on to consultative bodies with a role in economic planning e.g., the National Industrial and Economic Council, the Committee on Industrial Organisation. The advent of tripartite consultations was adjudged important, given the need for economic adaptation, restructuring and the establishment of appropriate and realistic planning targets. The Government therefore had to fall back on those interests involved on the ground, in order to acquire the necessary information and understanding, as well as to secure their co-operation in the implementation of policy. The relegation of plant/entity-wide free collective bargaining and the emergence of national level tripartite bargaining, involving Government, employers and trade unions, marked a new phase in the State/trade union movement relationship.

The decision to enter the European Economic Community (EEC) with effect from 1973 was another important development in the political environment of industrial relations. An immediate impact was felt in areas of industrial development and individual labour law. The influx of multinational enterprises is commonly accredited with a greater level of professionalism in the area of personnel or human resource management, together with an increase in both trade union membership cum pre-production employment agreements, and non-union establishments (McMahon, 1990). Significant revisions were also prompted in such areas as dismissal, employment equality, mass redundancy and worker participation legislation. This development has certainly facilitated the emergence of prominent players on the industrial relations pitch in the form of the EU and the European Parliament. Furthermore, few doubt that the Community will play a key role in shaping the political agenda of the future. The passage of the Single European Act and the 'Amsterdam Treaty' has focused the minds of most pressure groups in society on the implications of greater economic and political union across the Member States. Amongst the range of influences on the industrial relations environment considerable attention is being devoted to the 'social dimension', or Social Charter, which spans a range of social and employment rights including health and safety, equitable remuneration, equality, information and consultation entitlements, and freedom of movement.

The advent of contemporary national level partnership arrangements — covering a host of economic (including pay) and social issues — can be traced back to the maintenance men's dispute of 1969–70. This was, according to the Dublin Chamber of Commerce, 'the greatest crisis in industrial relations ever experienced in the history of the State', producing a 20 per cent wage rise over eighteen months(O'Grada, 1997). The expectations sparked by this settlement promptly raised industrial relations on the Government's agenda. Such a large settlement threatened the Government's economic management aspirations in the desire to control incomes and inflationary pressures, thus eventually giving rise to the national tripartite arrangements. Prior to the suspension of such arrangements, over the 1982–87 period, they had expanded in scope to accommodate a plethora of economic and social affairs under the title of 'national understandings'. The temporary demise of the consensus approach at national level during the 1980s can be primarily attributed to a hardened negotiating stance on the part of both employers and State. Related to this was a change in Government, with the more populist or pragmatic Fianna Fáil party being replaced by a Fine Gael/Labour Coalition. A subsequent change of Government facilitated the resurgence of the social partnership type approach from 1987 onwards, with representative national level agreements again embracing the range of economic and social issues. Furthermore, it is interesting to contrast the fact that whilst their British counterparts were left out in the cold during the 1980s and most of the 1990s, the Irish trade union movement played a central role in decisions on not just pay increases, but national economic and social strategy and planning. Effectively, the economic recession of the 1980s served to direct Ireland further down the road to corporatism, establishing a pattern which has endured to date. In the opinion of Von Prondzynski (1988), however, the progress down this road — the price of participation (in the 1987 Programme) ought be costed against:

> ... every evidence that the Programme was designed as a back-up to the Government's programme of expenditure cut-backs and income restraint; the intention was primarily to tie the hands of the trade unions in particular and make difficult any serious militancy in opposition to these policies ... this approach is working rather well.

The participative model therefore, initiated by Sean Lemass in the late 1950s, now appears to be accepted in principle by, at least, the upper echelons of the trade union and employer organisations, as reflected by their involvement in a variety of industry and national level tripartite fora. However, this commitment to a participative approach is less evident at firm level. The focus of attention on both sides of the industrial relations process at this level tends to be the size of the wage settlement — an element well capable of exposing the fragility of interest group solidarity.

In the early 1990s then, the sad state of many important national economic indicators, pressures exerted by a persistent international recession and constraints on remedial initiatives imposed by membership of, and adherence to, the EU and Single European Market respectively, combined to apparently signal a new era in the management of industrial relations. Political developments in many industrialised economies — including the resurgence of *laissez-faire* individualism in Britain over the 1979–97 period, with its emphasis on monetarism, free enterprise, open markets, deregulation, and privatisation — and the demise of socialist economies in Eastern Europe, forced the recall and revision of many left wing and trade union ideological aspirations. This helped reinforce the merits of operating inside the neo-corporatist model for the trade union movement and the furtherance of its more immediate demands under the auspices of the prevalent liberal capitalist political system. Indeed, it may be argued that the status of the trade union movement, in a centralised, corporatist state has cushioned it from the trends visible elsewhere in recent times.

By the late 1990s however, it is apparent that industrial relations may have reached another crossroads. Whilst the resurgent national economic and labour market environment depicted above has contributed to this, the British and French general elections in 1997, the re-election of the Democrats' nominee in the US presidential election and the increasing 'Europeanisation' of industrial relations make it an ever-changing melting pot for subjects and observers alike.

1.3 THE ROLE OF THEORY IN INDUSTRIAL RELATIONS

The role of theory in industrial relations is intended to facilitate the analysis and appraisal of the subject's processes, structures and institutions in as objective a manner as is possible with any of the social sciences. This section of the text attempts therefore to outline and evaluate the main academic theories which have been developed in an effort to provide a logical and consistent means of understanding and interpreting industrial relations realities. Particularly over the past twenty years, there has been a series of prescriptions for change designed to improve the conduct of industrial relations in this country e.g., changes in strike laws, worker participation/ involvement schemes, trade union rationalisation. Such proposals can often be highly contentious and the theoretical bases upon which they are founded rarely enunciated. Accordingly this section of chapter 1 introduces and assesses the main theoretical perspectives and related value judgments on the nature of the world of work.

As each theory originates from a different base or set of assumptions, it would be inappropriate to insist upon a single 'best' theory of industrial relations, or to force the student down a 'pick and choose' road in the construction of an analytical framework to fit with their own particular values, perspective or insight. Whilst insisting upon this discretionary prerogative it would be remiss not to acknowledge the primacy of the pluralist analysis in Irish industrial relations practices and debates. This is reflected in the high levels of union density together with the central role of, and preoccupation with, collective bargaining — and its institutions — at establishment, industrial and national levels.

1.3.1 PLURALIST ANALYSIS
The pluralist and related analyses of industrial relations systems in Western societies have been in pole position for over thirty years now. This framework or model is based upon the existence of a 'post-capitalist' society, where

industrial and political conflict have become institutionally separated, ownership is distinguished from management, and authority and power in society more widely distributed. In effect, such an analysis acknowledges that society is comprised of a range of individuals, interest and social groups, each in pursuit of their own objectives. As in society, the employing entity is comprised of an accommodation or alliance of different values and competing sectional interests. So it is only through an accommodation that work organisations can attempt to operate with any degree of continuity and success. Just as the political system is institutionalised and regulated through a party political and parliamentary process, so also is the industrial system institutionalised and regulated through representative organisations and appropriately structured processes. The existence of these competing organisational values and interests then facilitate 'a complex of tensions and competing claims which have to be "managed" in the interests of maintaining a viable collaborative structure' (Fox, 1973).

Hence the emergence of a succession of temporary compromises — or collective agreements — as the opposing aspirations for higher profits and productivity or efficiency are aligned with improved pay and working condition type demands. As Dubin (1954) summarises: 'Collective bargaining is the great social invention that has institutionalised industrial conflict. In much the same way that the electoral process and majority rule have institutionalised political conflict in a democracy, collective bargaining has created a stable means for resolving industrial conflict.'

Such a perspective acknowledges the legitimacy of trade union organisation, interests and the right to contest the managerial prerogative. In any case: '. . . greater stability and adaptability is given to industrial relations by collective bargaining than by shackling and outlawing trade unions' (Clegg, 1975). The structures, formats and processes of labour relations are perceived as the manifestation of the power relations and conflict between employers, managers and trade unions. Accordingly, conflict is viewed as a logical and inevitable feature of the world of work and consequently requires management by a variety of role players or representatives, procedures, processes and specialist institutions.

A central feature of this post-capitalist perspective is that the class conflict by-product of the industrial revolution has now abated. The Marxist analysis of the powerful capitalists and weak wage earners — of the socially elite and the socially weak — is no longer an appropriate model. Contemporary society, it is argued, is more open and mobile, with the franchise extended for the further democratisation of politics, greater accessibility of educational opportunity opening hitherto closed occupational routes and the advent of the welfare state serving to alleviate the worst extremes of deprivation and inequality. Such societal developments have combined to effectively undermine and point to the need for a replacement of the Marxist prognosis. Furthermore, the spread and diffusion of property ownership, status and authority in the post-capitalist society has irretrievably removed the sharp divisions between those who were once industrially and politically powerful and their counterparts, who were weak and powerless in both these crucial spheres. With the opening up of routes to a vast array of prized positions in society therefore — whether it be in the political, industrial or professional arenas — the 'superior' and 'subordinate' classes in the employment context need no longer be synonymous with the political or social classes, either generally or through successive generations.

Accordingly, with the separation of industrial and political conflict, collective bargaining has become the focus of attention at the workplace for the regulation of relations. With the emergence, structuring and regulation of representative organisations on both sides of industry, appropriate fora have now been established to address the tensions and conflicts arising at all levels between these sectional interest groups e.g., ICTU and IBEC at national level. In the event of failure to resolve differences at plant level an array of third party institutions provide a generally acceptable route for the resolution of contrasting objectives and conflict. In conjunction with this system it is argued that the development of employee involvement or participative practices serves to emphasise the distribution or diffusion of power and authority in industry. According to Dahrendorf (1959) these developments are well reflected in: '(1) the organization of conflicting interest groups itself; (2) the establishment of 'parliamentary' negotiating bodies in which these groups meet; (3) the institutions of mediation and arbitration; (4) formal representations within the individual enterprise; and (5) tendencies towards and institutionalization of workers' participation in industrial management.' Pluralists then acknowledge the inevitability of conflict, but point to the relative stability of a society which institutionalises, manages and contains any differences via collaboration, negotiated compromises and mediation.

1.3.2 UNITARY ANALYSIS

The basic premise of the unitary perspective on the employee relations system is that all employment units are, or should be, cohesive and harmonious establishments with a total commitment to the attainment of a common goal. Being unitary in structure and purpose, with shared goals, values and interests, and one source of (managerial) authority the staff relations are set upon a plinth of mutuality and harmony. That is, there is no conflict between those contributing the capital (i.e., the owners) and the contributors of labour (i.e., the employees). Consequently, all staff members agree unreservedly with the aspirations of the organisation and the methods and means deployed to give effect to these targets. Through this team, or complementary partnership, approach it is assumed that both sides of the equation can satisfy their common goals of high profitability and pay levels, job security and efficiency. Notwithstanding same, it is implicitly acknowledged that — as with any team approach — competent and strong leadership or management are a prerequisite to the pursuit of organisational effectiveness. In practice this may give rise to elements of paternalism and/or authoritarianism on the part of management in their approach to employee relations matters.

Paternalism may be reflected in a managerial concern for staff needs, together with a rejection of union recognition and collective bargaining practices. Authoritarianism may also materialise in a dominant managerial value system, characterised by a minimal concern for employee welfare and outright opposition to union recognition and collective bargaining initiatives (e.g., Ryanair). In either scenario trade unionism is opposed as a threat to the organisation's unity of purpose and the (legitimate and rational) managerial prerogative as it competes for employee loyalty and commitment. The consequent rejection of collective bargaining is therefore based upon managements' perceived legitimate prerogative to proceed without the incumbency of negotiation to attain consent to their decision-making initiatives and responsibility. In such a setting it is assumed that management will insert an appropriate communications structure to alert staff to organisational priorities and to management expectations of staff in respect of same. In response, staff give effect to these instructions as they display their loyalty to the entity for the realisation of their common goals (e.g., job security).

In essence the unitary theory rejects the concept of enduring conflict or organisational factionalism as such collision, competition or opposition distracts from what are assumed to be non-competing, co-operative initiatives. The existence of conflict is not perceived to be a structural feature of organisational life but:

> ... is either (a) merely frictional, e.g., due to incompatible personalities or 'things going wrong', or (b) caused by faulty 'communications', e.g., 'misunderstandings' about aims or methods, or (c) the result of stupidity in the form of failure to grasp the communality of interest, or (d) the work of agitators inciting the supine majority who would otherwise be content. (Fox, 1966)

The unitary philosophy is therefore predominantly managerial in that it legitimises their authority under the heading of commonality, largely attributes the source of conflict to subordinates and serves as a means of justifying their decisions to any interested parties — whilst explaining opposition to same as either ill-informed or perverse. The undoubted increase in levels of opposition to trade union recognition and the associated rise in the number of non-union establishments has significantly strengthened the prevalence and validity of this particular analytical model on the national scene.

1.3.3 MARXIST ANALYSIS

Though Marxist analyses of industrial relations are more a by-product of a theory of capitalist society and social change than of the labour relations system itself, they do have considerable implications and provide a useful framework for the interpretation of the relationship between capital and labour. That is, Marxism is more concerned with the structure and nature of society, than with the actual workplaces which that society accommodates. Of course when the original Marxist analysis of the nature and structure of society was conceived the phenomena of trade unionism and collective bargaining were barely established. Consequently, the application of the original Marxist analysis to contemporary labour relations institutions and phenomena is primarily the product of neo-Marxist theoreticians.

These sources attribute the industrial relations system with a limited role (via the resolution of pay and condition issues and the delineation of the boundaries of managerial prerogative) rather than with any central role in the Marxist prognosis. Marxism envisages a fundamental change in the distribution of power and wealth in society. However, under this theory conflict in the industrial relations arena has at least a symptomatic value, in its reflection of the opposing economic interests engendered by capitalism.

This body of theory is then essentially an analysis of the evolution of society — of which the capitalist (or bourgeois state) is only one phase. That is, Marxism depicts a series of developments, or phases of social change, from the initial state of primitive communism through an era of feudalism to capitalism which it is predicted would give rise to a class war (between the 'Bourgeoisie' and the 'Proletariat'), culminating in a dictatorship of the proletariat before progressing to socialism and eventually a Utopian classless society.

In essence the Marxist perspective is based upon the premise that class (i.e., capital and labour) conflict is at the root of societal change. This conflict is not a simple consequence of contrasting demands and tensions at the workplace, but is the product of an inequitable distribution of power and wealth in wider society. Such inequity is also reflected in society's social and political institutions which serve to maintain the position of the dominant establishment group i.e., the owners of the means of production. Therefore, social and political conflict — and social change — is the result of these central economic inequities and divisions within society, between the owner or capitalist and labouring classes. Accordingly, conflict reflects the difference between these social classes with their diametrically opposed economic and political interests. Class and political conflict are therefore inextricably linked with industrial conflict — which the Marxist perspective adjudges to be a permanent feature of capitalism. This persistent and unavoidable conflict is the result of these competing interests seeking to consolidate and advance their relative positions in the economic power structure as they contest the distribution of the entity or society's power, wealth and 'surplus value'.

In effect, then, the industrial relations system is a marginal forum for the conduct of a class war, which will ultimately spill out and over into a more fundamental political revolution initiated by the working class. Trade unions are viewed in this context as a collective response to the exploitation of the capitalist system and may perform a central role in the wider political process, for the attainment of significant alterations to the economic and social system on behalf of the proletariat.

The operation of (national, industrial and enterprise-based) bodies of joint regulation, however, with their agreed procedures and processes are adjudged by Marxists to accommodate, consolidate, legitimise and effectively enhance the managerial prerogative and power position, whilst projecting an image or veneer of power sharing. That is, the whole collective bargaining process is perceived to at least temporarily accept, facilitate and ultimately support the inherent contradictions of capitalism. Furthermore, the State's legislative framework is perceived by Marxists to be a related piece of armoury designed to support managements' interests (Hyman, 1975).

In summary then, when evaluating prescriptions arising from other perspectives, the Marxists would argue that economic and political issues cannot be separated. Marxists place great emphasis on the antagonistic interests of capital and labour, and, in sharp contrast with alternative analytical frameworks, focus on the importance of assessing the power held by opposing interests. For an insightful appreciation of the industrial relations system, focus on the relative 'power' positions of competing (or conflicting) interests, should not be underestimated.

1.3.4 SOCIAL ACTION ANALYSIS

The social action perspective on industrial relations 'stresses that the individual retains at least some freedom of action and ability to influence events' in the manner they adjudge to be most appropriate or preferable (Jackson, 1982). This theory emphasises the role players' or actors' definitions, perceptions and influences on reality. It is these definitions and perceptions which determine their relationships, behaviour and actions. Therefore, with this frame of reference, social and industrial relations actions are best understood in terms of their subjectively intended meanings. Concentration on observed behaviour at the workplace restricts the value of any interpretation, as it would overlook the deeper intent of the actors. The actors' decisions are determined not just by the specific work situations they find themselves in, but by a plethora of wider and underlying influences such as the attitudes, values, experiences and expectations developed over a lifetime both inside and outside of the workplace. The central relevance of this particular perspective is that it attributes to the individual actors some prerogative or discretion to shape the actual workplace and society in which they exist along (their) desired lines. In this context, however, they are restricted by their own perception of reality. Thus, the social action analysis accords some control or priority to the individual over the structure or system in which they find themselves. It offers a frame of reference which concentrates on the range of industrial relations system outputs as being as much the end result of the actions of its constituent parts as of the structure of the system itself. The social action theory is in fact rooted in a well developed sociological school of thought which argues that just as 'society makes man . . . man makes society' (Silverman, 1970). The impact on Irish industrial relations of individuals like James Larkin and William Martin Murphy arguably supports this perspective.

1.3.5 SYSTEMS ANALYSIS

The systems theory of industrial relations originated in the late 1950s in the United States when John Dunlop proposed that: 'An industrial relations system at any one time in its development is regarded as comprised of certain actors, certain contexts, an ideology which binds the industrial relations system together, and a body of rules created to govern the actors at the workplace and work community' (Dunlop, 1958).

Dunlop's construction of an integrated model is based upon a view of the industrial relations system as one which, though overlapping and interacting with the economic and political decision-making systems, is nevertheless a societal subsystem in its own right. This subsystem's output or product is comprised of a set of rules pertaining to the employment relationship, which spans their design, application and interpretation. Accordingly, the industrial relations system is primarily concerned with an output of rules covering all pay and condition type matters, together with the installation of procedures for their administration and application. The systems theory of industrial relations is therefore based upon the standard input-process-output model which Dunlop argues can be applied regardless of the economic or political system in place.

Under the input heading Dunlop identifies three sets of influences: actors, environmental contexts and ideology, which combine in the bargaining, conciliation and legislative processes yielding a body, network or web of rules. The actors include the different worker categories (whether organised or unorganised), the various layers of management — together with their respective representatives — and the range of third party agencies. The environmental context impinging on the state of the industrial relations system is comprised of technological, market/budgetary and societal power location and distribution variables. The technological impact is reflected in such factors as the size, skill and sexual breakdown of the workforce, its concentration or distribution, and the location and duration of the employment. The market or budgetary constraints, whether applied locally, nationally or internationally, affect all enterprise types, not just the entity's management, but also ultimately all of the system's role players. The 'power' input relates to the structural context of, or degree of autonomy afforded the industrial relations system by wider society. This will, of course, be significantly

31

influenced by the distribution of power in that society. The third, the ideological input recognises that whilst each group of actors in the system may have their own set of ideas, these are sufficiently congruent for a level of mutual tolerance, common belief or unifying ideological compatibility to prevail.

1.3.6 CONCLUSION AND CRITIQUE OF MODELS

As evidenced by their contrasting premises and prognoses all of the models of industrial relations outlined above have been subjected to critical evaluation. The pluralist analysis, for example, despite its prevalence and robustness, has been criticised for its ready acceptance of the social and political status quo and a fundamental conservatism which assumes an illusory balance of power between the various interest groups (Fox,1973; Goldthorpe,1974). Unlike both the unitary and Marxist theories, the pluralist analysis avoids making moral value judgments — a factor which actually both enhances and detracts from its standing. Similarly, the unitary perspective is cautioned for its unrealistically Utopian outlook, limited applicability (e.g., to non-union entities) and a paternalistic, management orientation which assumes a generally accepted value system. The Marxist analysis is adjudged in this 'post-capitalist' era to be anachronistic given that, among other things, the nature of class conflict has substantially changed and contemporary society with its mixed economy and welfare state is now more open and socially mobile. Beyond the subjectivity of Marxism, it is also argued that the distribution of power, property and social status in society is perceived to be more widely diffused today than it was in the nineteenth century, and consequently undermines the theory's simplistic classifications.

In regard to social action theory critics point to its neglect of those structural features which influence the action of its actors. This oversight, it is argued, really reflects the theory's own inability to explain the very nature of the wider system inside which these actions occur. Systems theory has also been subjected to considerable criticism, refinement and modification. For example, it is contended that the model's narrow focus omits the reality of and mechanisms for the distribution of wealth and power in society.

In effect its convenient unifying ideology-cum-status quo inclination — which takes society as given — merely accords the industrial relations system some functional role in the maintenance of stability and overlooks a range of issues including industrial relations change, the source of conflict and the system's interrelationship with the 'outside' political, economic and social scene. It is also argued that its structural emphasis leads to an output or rules focus at the expense of the actual decision- or rule-making processes. Additionally, it fails to explain the important behavioural variables i.e., why actors act as they do. It is also suggested that the system's model ought accommodate the significant role of the owners of business, who warrant inclusion in both an actor's and contextual capacity. Wood et al. (1978/79) also recommend that a modifying distinction be made in the model 'between the system which "produces" rules (i.e., the industrial relations system) and the system which is governed by such rules (i.e., the production system)'. Therefore, the revised approach recommends focusing upon both the narrower rule-making processes and the wider contextual influences e.g., political, legal and social contexts.

In conclusion, then, far from being a descriptive subject based upon common sense, a single analytical framework or a set of incontrovertible facts and statistics, political and theoretical controversy is inherent in the topic of industrial relations. There are a vast array of ways of interpreting what is going on, and a multitude of opinions about what ought be happening in this subject area. However, the fact that there is no universally accepted global theory is unavoidable and ought be accepted by the student as an attractive dimension of a topic which easily lends itself to contrasting perspectives, opinions and debate. In recognition of this fact, this text attempts, as far as is possible, to present a factual and unbiased account of the various institutions, processes and issues. It is for the student to make up his/her own mind on these matters as the book endeavours to take a neutral line, presenting the different sides of the various arguments.

CHAPTER TWO

The Role of the Law

2.1 INDIVIDUAL EMPLOYMENT LAW

OVERVIEW

The principal purpose of labour law is to regulate, to support and to restrain the power of management and the power of organised labour (Kahn-Freund, 1977). One may trace this process of legislative intervention in the employment relationship as far back as the 1349 Ordinance of Labourers. This initiative was designed to impose wage ceilings for both artisans and labourers in the 'Black Death' era of severe labour shortages. However, it wasn't until the nineteenth century that a range of protective statutes were enacted covering such matters as health and safety and the form that wage payments should take. Over the past thirty years there have been significant developments, particularly in the area of individual employment law. Each of these legislative initiatives may be viewed as a countervailing force, giving redress to the unequal bargaining power of the individual *vis-à-vis* the employing organisation. Of course, at the root of the employment relationship is the common law contract of employment, with its power to command and duty to obey. Thus, it may be argued that statute law is accorded a marginal role, in its attempts to regulate and co-ordinate this relationship. For example, though management retain the power to 'hire and fire' this prerogative is somewhat restrained by dismissal, redundancy and equality legislation. In an attempt therefore to cover the more salient and relevant aspects of 'individual' labour law this section of chapter 2 reviews the role of the employment contract, dismissal law, equality legislation and, finally, summarises other statutes of particular relevance to industrial relations at work. Accordingly, little attention is paid to those areas of the law which have had little usage, or have not given rise to controversy of any magnitude, in recent years.

2.1.1 THE CONTRACT OF EMPLOYMENT

The contract of employment is the legal basis of the employment relationship and is central to the interpretation and application of statutory rights. As with the basic law of contract it requires that there be an offer from the employer which is accepted by the employee, that there be consideration — or remuneration — from the employer for work done, and that there be an intention to create a legal relationship. The contract may be concluded on an oral or written basis. However, the passing of the Terms of Employment (Information) Act 1994 has, in effect, brought the completely oral contract to an end. Basically, any employee normally expected to work not less than eight hours per week and who has one month's service is entitled to a written statement of his/her basic terms and conditions of employment including hours of work, rates of pay, provision in relation to overtime, sick pay, holidays, etc. This statement must be received within two months of taking up employment. Existing employees at the time the Act was passed (i.e., in May 1994), must request the statement. A complaint lies to a Rights Commissioner in the event of failure to comply with the Act. Common law attempts to distinguish between a contract of service (i.e., with an employee) and a contract for service (i.e., with an independent contractor) (see Table 2.1). This is of some relevance given that it is only the 'employee' who can avail of the protection afforded under labour law. Case law indicates that three tests may be applied to differentiate between these contract types:

– Control: can the employer tell the employee what to do and how to do it?

– Integration: is the employee's work integrated into the business, or is it a case of the independent contractor working for the business?

– Multiple: what is the nature of the entire arrangement between the employer and the worker? This would be reflected in answers to the following types of questions:

– Are there wages, sick and holiday pay? Who pays them?

– Are income tax and social security deducted under the PAYE and PRSI systems respectively by the employer?

– Does the worker share in the profits/losses?

– Who provides the tools and equipment for the job?

– Are there specific provisions relating to termination?

– Is the employer entitled to exclusive service?

– Is it a genuine case of self-employment or is there an attempt to avoid protective legislation?

| **Table 2.1** | Key differences between contracts of service and contracts for service |

Of Service	For Service
Employer-employee relationship	Employer-independent contractor relationship
Usually a continuous relationship	A once-off piece of work relationship
Duty of care owed to employees	Duty of care arising from occupier's liability
Generally liable for the vicarious acts of employees	Generally not liable for the vicarious acts of independent contractors
Protective legislation applies to contract	Protective legislation does not apply (excl. Safety, Health and Wel. at Work Act 1989)
Wage/Salary payment method	Fee payment method
Subject of contract is to carry on continuous work	Subject of contract is once-off job.

Source: Gunnigle et al., 1992

Despite the variety of tests or issues which may be addressed when dealing with this matter Fennell and Lynch (1993) conclude that though '. . . the substitution and/or supplementation of the control test by one more attuned to modern employment conditions is . . . warranted under Irish law; . . . a certain measure of confusion is evident from the decisions of the Irish courts as to what formulation should be preferred'.

Accordingly, the application or otherwise of individual labour law enactments to specific employees remains somewhat uncertain. Lord Wedderburn (1986) has concluded that the variety of legal 'tests' have come asunder on the judiciary and it is 'not practicable to lay down precise tests' or a 'hard and fast list'. Indeed, he suggests, most courts now appear to apply the 'elephant test' for the employee i.e., an animal which is too difficult to define but easy to recognise when you see it!

2.1.2 DISMISSAL AND THE LAW

The Unfair Dismissals Act 1977–93 was an important development in Irish labour law given the restriction it places on the employer's right to fire. Whilst employer organisations chide its alleged impact on job creation initiatives, this allegation is strongly contested (Department of Labour, 1986), and some even argue that the Act has had major beneficial consequences for the conduct of industrial relations in the country. According to Murphy (1989):

> The Act has been a considerable success and has contributed to more effective management in notoriously problematic areas of management

decision making . . . in many areas of personnel administration and disciplinary control . . . [it] has strengthened collective bargaining at workplace level by creating a closer harmony between employer and trade union views of what constitutes a fair dismissal.

Following a review of anomalies and difficulties with the Act, an amendment Act was passed in 1993, with the changes principally favouring employees.

ACT'S PROVISIONS

It is estimated that the Act applies to most employees in Ireland. Under its provisions, once an 'employee' has been continuously employed for one year, and is normally expected to work not less than eight hours per week, he/she has a right of action for an unfair dismissal. Prior to the passing of the 1991 Part-Time Employees legislation, an employee needed to have worked eighteen hours per week in order to claim. In the event of a perceived unfair dismissal a case may be brought before either a Rights Commissioner, or the Employment Appeals Tribunal (EAT) within six months of the date of dismissal. Under the 1993 amending Act, however, either the Tribunal or the Rights Commissioner may extend this time limit by six months in exceptional circumstances. The option of going directly to the Tribunal only applies in the event of either party objecting to a Rights Commissioner hearing. It is estimated that between both the Rights Commissioners and the Tribunal, over 1,000 claims of dismissal arise annually (Mulligan, 1993). In fact, in 1995 and 1996 there were 1,180 and 1,133 respectively, appeals and claims under the Unfair Dismissal Acts to the EAT. Either party may appeal the Tribunal's decision to the Circuit Court within six weeks from the date on which the determination is communicated to the parties, and where an employer fails to carry out a determination an employee may also bring enforcement proceedings in the Circuit Court. Of course, if the employee has taken the matter to the Labour Court, or has instituted proceedings for damages at common law for wrongful dismissal, he/she would not also be entitled to redress under the Act.

All employees are covered by the Act's provisions, with a number of exceptions, which include those:
– with less than one year's continuous service with the same employer (unless the employee is alleging the dismissal took place on grounds of pregnancy (or related matters) or trade union membership or activities);
– over the normal retiring age;
– close relatives of the employer who are members of his/her household and work in a private dwelling house;
– employed by the Defence Forces and the Garda Síochána;
– employed by, or under, the State (excluding those provided for under section 17 of the Industrial Relations Act 1969);

– serving apprenticeships/trainees with FAS;
– officers of local authorities or health boards (excluding temporary officers), and of vocational educational committees and committees of agriculture; and
– persons normally working outside the State.

The Act provides that a dismissal will automatically be deemed to be unfair if it can be attributed to:
– trade union membership or activities (including industrial action);
– religious or political opinion;
– involvement in civil or criminal legal proceedings against the employer;
– race or colour;
– sexual orientation;
– age;
– being a member of the travelling community;
– pregnancy; or
– the exercise of maternity, adoptive leave or holiday entitlements.

The burden of proof in dismissal cases normally resides with the employer. Yet the employee must show that he/she is actually covered by the Act's provisions and that a dismissal actually took place. In general then, employers bear the brunt of the Act's regulatory force in so far as the onus of responsibility is on them to show that they have acted reasonably. The Tribunal then attempts to evaluate the employer's (re)action and sanction with a view to determining whether it lies within the range of responses which a 'reasonable' employer might make. A common determinant of the Tribunal's decisions on the status of a dismissal is whether the employer followed fair and proper procedures prior to the dismissal. This requirement of procedural fairness is rooted in the common law concept of natural justice and in the provisions of the 1937 Constitution. In addition, a Code of Practice on Disciplinary Procedures was issued by the Labour Relations Commission in 1996. This Code is admissible in proceedings before, amongst others, the EAT. The amendment Act of 1993 also provides that the existence or otherwise of a dismissal procedure is a factor the Tribunal can take into account in making its determinations. The four basic obligations in regard to disciplinary procedural arrangements identified from case law by Fennell and Lynch (1993) are:

(1) *Investigation*: an inadequate investigation of the situation on the part of the employer may give rise to a dismissal being deemed unfair. Accordingly a reasonable and fair investigation of the matter should be undertaken by the employer.

(2) *Hearing*: the employer must put the relevant case before the employee, thus allowing him/her to respond. A refusal to allow trade union representation at such meetings is likely to render the dismissal unfair.

(3) *Warning*: prior to dismissal for misconduct or poor performance the employee should be given a warning, thus providing him/her with an opportunity to improve.

(4) *Proportionate Penalties*: a dismissal will be adjudged to be unfair where the employer is seen to over-react. That is, if a lesser penalty would have been more appropriate in the circumstances.

The normal reaction of the EAT to a failure to follow fair procedures, especially those laid down in a collective agreement, is to adjudge the dismissal to be unfair. However, the extent of the contribution on the employee's part to the circumstances resulting in the dismissal will be taken into account when the Tribunal decides upon the appropriate remedy. Consequently, even if the Tribunal concludes, for whatever reason, that a dismissal was unfair, it might consider it appropriate to make a 100 per cent deduction from the compensation which the employee would otherwise be entitled to! It is also notable, however, that the Circuit Court has concluded, in instances, that an otherwise 'fair dismissal' does not automatically become unfair due to its procedural defects. Nevertheless, a direct result of this 'procedural fairness' ingredient is that there have been widespread changes in companies' procedures, practices and decision-making processes, with disciplinary and dismissal procedures now commonplace (O'Connor, 1982).

FAIR DISMISSAL

Those areas where a dismissal may be justified can largely (but not exclusively) be categorised under the following headings: (1) conduct, (2) capability/competence and (3) redundancy:

(1) *Conduct*: This may take the form of a single act of gross misconduct or a series of such minor acts where the employee disregards relevant warnings. Dismissal arising out of alleged employee misconduct is the most common case type coming before the Tribunal. A fair dismissal under this heading normally occurs where the essential employer-employee relationship of trust is undermined. It generally applies to matters of sick leave abuse, substance or alcohol abuse, criminal convictions, dishonesty, disobedience, breach of the duty of loyalty and fidelity, and violence or intimidation (see Madden and Kerr, 1990). The Tribunal has not, however, established any objective standard of 'unacceptable conduct' which justifies dismissal. Instead, it opts to evaluate the dismissal decision on the grounds of 'reasonableness', given the particular circumstances of each case. Consequently, one cannot construct a comprehensive and rigid checklist of conduct types which will be adjudged by the Tribunal to be unacceptable and warrant dismissal. The 'reasonableness' parameters inside which it will evaluate each case relate to the nature and extent of the investigation undertaken prior to the dismissal and the conclusion reached on the basis of the information yielded. Accordingly, the employer is obliged to carry out a fair and full investigation, whilst adhering to the aforementioned principles of natural justice (see above). It is also relevant under this heading that 'off-duty' conduct — where it has implications for the employer — has been adjudged by both the Tribunal and the courts to constitute grounds for fair dismissal.

(2) *Capability/Competence*. Dismissal pertaining to the capability, competence or qualifications of the employee for performing work of the kind which he/she was employed to do may be justified. Of course capability or competence driven dismissals often require the employer to advise the employee in advance of the relevant failure, thus enabling him/her to improve. Competence-related dismissals tend to arise where the employee is alleged to demonstrate a sub-standard work rate. Capability-related dismissals normally surface under the guise of attendance at work. Employees who are persistently late, or fail to attend work regularly, are commonly adjudged by the Tribunal to be incapable of performing the work which they were employed to do. Indeed, even in those cases of persistent or extensive absence due to illness the furnishing of medical certification will not normally protect one from a dismissal where the employer has satisfied him or herself that a return to work is not imminent.

(3) *Redundancy*: Dismissals on the grounds of redundancy usually constitute fair dismissals. Accordingly, dismissal attributed to the employer ceasing business, reducing workforce size or no longer requiring the employee's kind of work is not unfair. The onus of proving that a genuine redundancy situation exists, however, resides with the employer, and the claimant/employee can certainly question the validity of the redundancy. However, even if there is a genuine redundancy situation, an employee can argue that he/she was unfairly selected. In such circumstances the employee must show that the same scenario applied to one or more other employees who were not made redundant and that the redundancy procedure (e.g., last in first out (LIFO)) was unjustifiably breached, or that the selection was driven by any of the unfair reasons to dismiss set down on p.38. Effectively, then, the employer is precluded from using arbitrary criteria when selecting staff for redundancy, though he/she may successfully plead special reasons for departing from an agreed or traditional procedure. He/she also needs to be careful that in carrying out the selection for redundancy, fair procedures are followed.

CONSTRUCTIVE DISMISSAL

The term 'constructive dismissal' relates to those cases where the employee terminates the contract on account of the employer's conduct. For example, the employee would be entitled to terminate the contract where the employer's conduct constitutes a significant breach, going to the root of the contract, or in the event of the employer indicating that he/she no longer intends to be bound by one or more of its essential terms. Even in those cases where the employee is not legally entitled to terminate the contract a constructive dismissal may be identified if the employer has acted unreasonably. The reasonableness of the employee in refusing to accept changes in the terms or conditions of employment will be considered by the Tribunal in the light of the circumstances and of good industrial relations. However, the onus of proof, that there was an act or omission on the employer's part, constituting a breach of contract, resides with the employee. Case law precedent, however, has led some authorities to conclude that this concept of constructive dismissal was somewhat meaningless, and that the relevant criteria to be applied remain something of a mystery (Von Prondzynski, 1989). What is clear is that each case will turn on its own facts and that a hasty decision to resign on the employee's part, without attempting in some way to resolve the problem, may make it difficult to discharge the onus of proof that is upon them.

UNFAIR DISMISSAL REMEDIES

The Act provides for three remedial options in the event of a dismissal being deemed to have been unfair: reinstatement, re-engagement and compensation. It is interesting in this regard to note that of the 1,061 claims disposed of by the Tribunal in 1996, 474 were withdrawn during hearing, 223 were withdrawn prior to the hearing, 145 were dismissed and 219 were allowed.

Reinstatement enables the employee to resume in the same position, on the same contractual terms, as those applying prior to the dismissal event. A practical implication of this award is that the dismissal is effectively deemed never to have occurred. Accordingly, the relevant back-pay must be awarded, the employee's seniority maintained and pension rights restored. Furthermore, if there have been any changes in the interim in the terms and conditions of employment that would have been applicable to that employee they must also now be enforced (e.g., pay rise). Reinstatement is only awarded where the employee is adjudged not to have contributed to the dismissal in any way. Of the 219 claims allowed by the Tribunal in 1996, reinstatement was ordered in just nine cases. Re-engagement entitles the employee to resume in the same or in a reasonably suitable different position, on contractual terms which are deemed reasonable in light of prevailing circumstances. Such awards do not normally date back to the date of dismissal. As a result, though the unfairly dismissed employee's continuity of service is not affected, the period elapsing between the dismissal and the engagement effectively constitutes suspension without pay. Of the aforementioned 219 claims, re-engagement was ordered in sixteen. When deciding between a reinstatement or a re-engagement award the Tribunal tends to take account of the extent, if any, to which the employee contributed to the unfair dismissal. However, over the years 1988 to 1991 it is estimated that out of 3,502 claimants only 202 (6 per cent) were re-employed (Mulligan, 1993). Compensation or payment is therefore the most common remedial option, but may only be awarded up to a maximum of 104 weeks' net remuneration (including bonus payments) in respect of the employment from which the employee was dismissed. The size of payment was determined, up to 1993, by taking into account the estimated future loss, pension loss and the actual net loss of remuneration incurred by the employee as reduced by tax, (sometimes) social welfare and any alternate employment earnings. Arising from the 1993 legislation, however, compensation calculations must disregard income tax rebates made by reason of the dismissal and unemployment, sickness and occupational injury payments to an employee under the Social Welfare Acts 1981–93. Deductions are also likely to be made from the compensation figure awarded where it is adjudged that the employee's conduct contributed to the dismissal, or that the employee failed to take adequate steps to secure alternate employment. The practical consequence of these calculations is that, for example, over the four-year period 1988–91 the average compensatory award was £3,149 (Mulligan, 1993). However, arising from the aforementioned compensation calculation changes, together with the other provision under the 1993 amendment, whereby a basic award of up to four weeks' remuneration is payable to claimants held to be unfairly dismissed where no financial loss has been incurred, this average award level has increased. In fact, in 1996, the average compensation awarded by the Tribunal was £5,354.05.

Of course the Tribunal retains the prerogative to select whichever remedy it deems appropriate in the particular circumstances. Though the views of the parties to the case ought to be elicited by the Tribunal it may still choose to overlook same and issue an alternate remedy. According to Madden and Kerr (1990) the factors which appear to drive this decision are '. . . the poor nature of the relationship between the parties, the fact that the employee has made serious allegations about the employer, the fact that the employee is not fit to return to work, [and] the fact that changes in the work situation means that no suitable job is available'.

Where the Tribunal issues a reinstatement or re-engagement award it would appear to assume that the relationship between the parties is not beyond repair. Fennell and Lynch's (1993) review indicates, however, that whilst the 'Pyrrhic victory' of compensation is the preferred remedy, re-employment is ordered where the employer acted extremely badly or the claimant is in great hardship.

2.1.3 EMPLOYMENT EQUALITY AND THE LAW

As with many of the legislative initiatives pertaining to employment matters taken in recent years, the introduction of equality legislation was primarily prompted by our membership of the European Community, and the necessity to comply with its Directives. Under this heading, legal provisions in relation to equal pay and equal treatment in employment, as well as maternity rights, are of particular relevance. Each of the original pieces of domestic legislation in this area has actually been repealed and amended. The Anti-Discrimination (Pay) Act 1974 and the Employment Equality Act 1977, were passed to implement the equal pay and equal treatment directives respectively in the 1970s. They have recently been consolidated into one Act, the Employment Equality Act 1998, and as a result the law in this area has been significantly altered. The Maternity (Protection of Employees) Act 1981 has given way to the Maternity Protection Act 1994, in order to give effect to the so-called

'Pregnant Workers' Directive of 1992. The details of these initiatives are considered below.

EQUAL PAY

The Anti-Discrimination (Pay) Act 1974 entitled men and women to equal pay for equal work. As well as gender, the 1998 enactment also allows a claim to be made where the complainant is alleging he/she is performing equal work but is being paid less on grounds of marital status, family status, sexual orientation, religion, age, disability, race, or membership of the traveller community.

For the purposes of an equal pay claim, pay is interpreted as basic wages, together with all direct and indirect financial benefits and incentives (excluding pension benefits). Under the new Act, the person or persons claiming — group claims are common — must compare themselves with an actual comparator. The comparator need not be a current employee, but can be someone employed in the three years prior to the complainant or, it would appear, three years after him/her. The complainant must also satisfy the following conditions:
– he/she must be working under a contract of service;
– he/she must be working for the same or an associated employer. A significant change here is that the requirement to work in the same 'place' is removed in the new Act;
– he/she must be performing 'like work' with the comparator. That is, either (a) his/her work is identical, (b) job differences are insignificant in relation to the job as a whole or (c) his/her work is 'equal in value' in terms of criteria like responsibility, skill, physical or mental effort.

If the complainant can establish these requirements, the onus shifts to the employer to show that there are grounds other than gender (or marital status, age, disability, etc.) for the difference in the respective rates of pay. Standard grounds in this respect include qualifications, experience, service or grading. For details of methods of complaint see the section on 'Remedy Routes' below.

Undoubtedly the 1974 enactment has contributed to the improved relative position of female workers in the national wage structure. For example, over the 1970–80 period average hourly female earnings rose by 11 per cent against the equivalent male rate (McMahon, 1987). However, with the average hourly female rate standing at 73 per cent of the male rate in 1997, it is apparent that there remains considerable scope for improvement. According to Fennell and Lynch (1993), the 1974 Act was 'fraught with difficulties'. These included, in their view, 'the failure to specifically guarantee a remedy for indirect pay discrimination' (see below), together with the 'requirement of a male comparator' when pursuing claims. In the new Act, the latter requirement remains, despite calls for a 'hypothetical comparator' to be introduced. However, specific definitions of indirect discrimination (see below) have been introduced in this area for the first time. Whether this will lead to an increase in claims remains to be seen. There were only eighteen claims in total heard by Equality Officers and the Labour Court in 1997. Of these, only four were successful, with some of the claimant group enjoying success in a further two of these cases.

EMPLOYMENT EQUALITY

The Employment Equality Act 1977 was designed to protect against discrimination in relation to access to employment (i.e., recruitment and selection) and terms and conditions of employment, as well as access to promotion and training schemes, benefits, facilities and services. There were a limited number of situations where sex constituted an occupational qualification for a job — where the Act did not apply — such as physiology (excluding physical strength or stamina), or authenticity for the purpose of entertainment, e.g., sperm donor or model. These still apply in the new Employment Equality Act 1998.

As with equal pay, a range of potentially discriminatory grounds has been introduced in the new legislation, including family status, sexual orientation, religion, age, disability, race (including colour, nationality, ethnic or national origins) and membership of the traveller community. However, a number of detailed qualifications and exceptions exist, that make it difficult to forecast how some of the new grounds will operate. The new Act also makes it unlawful to victimise an employee for exercising his/her rights under the legislation.

Unlawful discrimination may be termed direct or indirect. Direct discrimination occurs where a person is treated less favourably than a person with or without the relevant characteristic (i.e., gender, age, disability, etc.) is, or would be, treated in similar circumstances. Claims in relation to discrimination at the recruitment and selection stage seem to be the most common and often revolve around alleged discriminatory questions or treatment at the interview. The definitions of indirect discrimination have been reshaped in the new Act, as a result of a Supreme Court judgment. Basically, indirect discrimination involves an apparently neutral practice or requirement which effectively serves to discriminate against a particular category, because fewer of its members are able to comply with it. The practice or requirement must not be objectively justifiable for the employment in question. For example, a minimum height requirement for a job where height was not a relevant factor might operate to indirectly discriminate against women as a group, as opposed to men.

REMEDY ROUTES

Under the 1998 Act, a new system of complaints has been introduced, although it retains many of the features of its predecessor. The Employment Equality Agency is renamed the Equality Authority, to reflect its wider remit. It is still charged with providing information on the legislation and advising potential complainants, as well as taking proceedings on someone's behalf where it is not reasonable to expect the person in question to take a case themselves. It is also empowered to conduct enquiries and to issue non-discrimination notices, and ultimately to apply for an injunction in the Circuit or High Court to prevent discrimination continuing. An interesting new feature is the power to invite employers to carry out 'Equality Reviews' and/or 'prepare and implement equality action plans'.

Complaints will now be referred under the Act to a new office of 'the Director of Equality Investigations', who may appoint Equality Officers, or 'Equality Mediation Officers', to hear these complaints. As with the previous legislation, if the complaint results in an alleged dismissal, the matter must be brought directly to the Labour Court. In addition, gender-based complaints or claims in relation to the infringement of the equal pay or equal treatment directives may be brought to the Circuit Court. The Circuit Court is empowered to award unlimited compensation in this regard, although with an equal pay claim the period of compensation is limited to the six years before the date of referral. The Director of Equality Investigations may award up to three years' arrears of equal pay, or compensation of up to 104 weeks' remuneration, in an equal treatment case. The Labour Court has the same powers, with an additional power to order reinstatement or re-engagement (with or without compensation) in a dismissal case.

Potential appeals lie from the Director to the Labour Court, and from the Labour Court to the Circuit Court. The Circuit Court may also enforce decisions of the Director or the Labour Court and lastly, points of law may be referred to the High Court.

SEXUAL HARASSMENT
Successive Labour Court decisions (since 1985) have determined that sexual harassment, though not specifically alluded to, was actually prohibited under the Employment Equality Act 1977, as less favourable treatment in relation to conditions of employment. Clearly, the Act did not define sexual harassment and so it was a matter for the Labour Court to determine. Again, the new Act tackles this issue and defines sexual harassment as acts of physical intimacy, or requests for sexual favours, or other acts such as words, gestures or the display of pictures or other material that are unwelcome to the recipient and could reasonably be regarded as sexually offensive, humiliating or intimidating on grounds of gender. Included in the list of potential harassers are employers, fellow employees or clients, customers or other business contacts of the employer. Sexual harassment at the place where the recipient is employed or 'otherwise in the course of her/his employment', is covered by the Act. It is, however, a defence for the employer to show that he/she took 'such steps as are reasonably practicable' to prevent or reverse the harassment. In practice, this will necessitate having the appropriate complaints procedure in place to deal with the problem and ensuring that it is implemented.

MATERNITY LAW

As noted in the introduction to this section, the 1981 Maternity legislation was replaced by the Maternity Protection Act 1994, in order to comply with the 'Pregnant Workers' Directive. Most of the provisions in the directive were already covered by the 1981 Act, but some additions such as health and safety leave entitlements were necessitated.

The Maternity Protection Act 1994 entitles female employees to a period of maternity leave of at least fourteen weeks, where the employer is notified in writing at least four weeks prior to the expected 'confinement', and a medical certificate establishing the fact of pregnancy is supplied. In addition to this leave period an important addition in the 1994 Act is the right to time off, without loss of pay, for ante- and post-natal medical visits. This entitlement is dependent on the provision of both medical evidence of pregnancy and the appropriate notification to the employer concerned. There is no qualifying service or minimum weekly working hours requirement to secure the right. The exact dates of the maternity leave can be chosen by the employee, but the period must cover the four weeks prior to and post confinement. Whilst on maternity leave the employee's continuity of service is not broken. She is entitled to return to her job after the birth, provided she notifies the employer of her intentions in writing at least four working weeks in advance of the envisaged date of return. The requirement to provide a second notification two weeks prior to the date of return has been dropped in the 1994 Act. It is worth noting that the EAT has held, in some unfair dismissal cases prior to the 1994 Act, that written notification of return to work is a mandatory requirement. As a result, a new provision in the Act allows the EAT, or a Rights Commissioner, to extend the time for giving the notification where there are 'reasonable grounds' for the failure or the delay in providing it. However, the procedural requirements for the exercise of the right to take maternity leave and the right to return to work have been adjudged to be 'unnecessarily complex' (Kerr, 1987). The 1994 Act appears to have done little to remedy this problem. In 1996 the Tribunal disposed of twenty-four claims under the Act. Of these, one was allowed, nine were dismissed and fourteen were withdrawn prior to or during the hearing.

A new potential right to health and safety leave from work has been introduced for pregnant workers, workers who are breast-feeding or who have recently given birth. This leave exists independently of maternity leave, and can occur from the beginning of pregnancy up to twenty-six weeks after the birth. To be entitled, the worker must be at risk, as a result of exposure to specific physical, chemical or biological agents which the employer is unable to eliminate, and where suitable alternative work cannot be found. In addition, if a doctor certifies that night-work is unsuitable and the worker cannot be moved to day work, she may become entitled to such leave.

An assessment as to whether a medical risk exists appears to be a matter for the Health and Safety Authority to decide. Disputes as to leave entitlements are heard by a Rights Commissioner with an appeal to the EAT. Dismissal-related disputes may be brought to either a Rights Commissioner or the EAT.

2.1.4 Health and Safety at Work

The relevance of the health and safety topic is reflected by the fact that in 1991 a total of 2,779 accidents — of which seventy-three were fatal — were reported to the Health and Safety Authority. By 1996 this figure had risen to 4,805 — of which 59 were fatal. In 1992, a survey conducted by the Federation of Irish Employers (FIE — now IBEC) indicated that, on average, member companies had thirty accidents per year, resulting in the loss of 139 working days per company. The total cost of claims in 1989, for the survey group, was over £4.5 million (FIE, 1991). Total employers' liability insurance — another indicator of the magnitude of the problem — is estimated to run at over £100 million per annum (Carroll and Byrne, 1992). Over the 1991–96 period an average of 8,187 employers liability claims were allowed by the Irish Insurance Federation per annum. Health and safety has been an important part of the EC's social policy agenda since the late 1970s and by the end of 1992 — the European Year of Safety, Hygiene and Health Protection at Work — over twenty directives concerned with the subject had been adopted as Community law.

Legislation pertaining to health and safety at work is quite complex as, in addition to common law, it spans some twenty enactments together with approximately 200 regulations. Barrington (1982) has classified these provisions as follows:
– legislation which deals exclusively with the health and safety of workers;
– statutes concerned with the regulation of work hours;
– statutes not designed as worker protection measures exclusively, but nevertheless providing varying degrees of protection; and
– statutes on the border line between issues of general environmental pollution and those of occupational health and safety.

Safety at work is the responsibility of everyone at the workplace, both employer and employee. The primary responsibility, however, rests with the employer. Most claims for personal injury following a work accident contend that the employer failed in one or more of his/her common law duties. Under common law the Irish courts have decided that employers are obliged to exercise reasonable care toward employees in relation to health and safety matters. Common law takes effect after the event, and its primary function is to compensate staff for injuries received at work. The implications of common law are that employers must:
– provide a safe system of work;
– ensure the provision of competent fellow workers;
– provide safety equipment and effective supervision; and
– provide a safe place of work.

The provision of a safe system of work obliges the employer to show that the protection or system provided is in accord with the general practice of that trade. Accordingly, an employer would not be responsible solely because an accident occurred in the course of the job. The failure to provide competent fellow workers (including subordinates and supervisors) may, but rarely does, constitute the basis of a claim. According to Gunnigle et al. (1992) this duty obliges an employer to:

– clarify the personal qualities and skills required to do the particular job;

– ensure the existence of a systematic recruitment and selection procedure; and

– provide the necessary training to do the job and special remedial training where required.

Furthermore, the employer may be found to be liable for the careless action of one employee which causes injury to another employee (i.e., vicarious liability). The common law obligation to provide proper safety equipment, for the purpose of avoiding staff exposure to risk and injury, includes a requirement that management take reasonable steps — up to and including disciplinary action — to ensure the use of that equipment. The provision of a safe place of work demands that the workplace be organised in the interests of health and safety. This obligation also extends to a customer's premises. Consequently, if staff are injured whilst working on a customer's premises they may successfully claim against their own employer.

The most recent statute law of significance in this area, the Safety, Health and Welfare at Work Act 1989, is applicable to all employment types. It sets down major principles which all employers and employees must observe. According to Gunnigle et al. (1992) it is the most significant piece of legislation within the employment sphere in the last ten years as:

– it is the first attempt to codify the law on safety, health and welfare in over twenty-five years;

– it established the National Authority for Occupational Safety and Health for the purpose of providing integrated co-ordination and monitoring of safety, health and welfare at work;

– it introduces flexibility in the area of employee representation and consultation;

– it emphasises the preparation of pro-active safety, health and welfare policies within the organisation;

– it changes the emphasis of the inspectorate system from one with a punitive focus to a facilitative one. It also strengthens the powers of the inspectorate where companies refuse to conform with the legislation; and

– it emphasises the formulation of voluntary codes of practice and regulations, and it broadens the scope from one with a safety bias to consideration of occupational health and welfare issues.

In effect then, it is essentially a 'framework Act' with a guiding philosophy and direction to be supplemented by way of regulations and codes of practice. The National Authority which develops these regulations and codes is primarily responsible for enforcing, advising, promoting and undertaking research in the area. The Authority's inspectorate has wide-ranging enforcement powers, which extend to the right to serve a prohibition notice — requiring that work should stop when there is a risk of imminent and serious injury to workers — and to prosecute employers. Over the 1992–96 period, for example, an average of 11,315 visits took place annually, of which 10,169 were workplace inspections (on average per annum).

The Authority has also issued guidelines on the formulation of a Safety Statement. Under the 1989 Act, a Safety Statement — which details the manner in which the health, safety and welfare of staff will be ensured at the workplace, is obligatory on all employers. However, a survey carried out by the Authority in 1991 revealed that only 16 per cent of workplaces had satisfactory safety statements. Overall then, the Act obliges employers 'in so far as is reasonably practicable to':
– design and maintain a place of work which is safe and without risk to health;
– provide safe means of access to and egress from a place of work;
– provide and maintain plant and equipment which is safe and without risk to health;
– provide necessary information, instruction, training and supervision for safe and healthy working;
– provide and maintain suitable protective clothing or equipment where hazards cannot otherwise be controlled;
– prepare adequate emergency plans;
– prevent risks to health and safety in relation to use of articles or substances;
– provide welfare facilities; and
– acquire the services of a competent person when necessary to ensure the safety and health of employees at work.
From the employees' perspective there is an obligation that they:
– take reasonable care to ensure the safety of themselves and others;
– co-operate with their employer in relation to compliance with statutory requirements;
– use protective equipment, clothing or other means for securing safety, health and welfare; and
– report potential risks to the employer in the event of their becoming aware of any.

The Act also entitles staff to be consulted for the purpose of making arrangements for co-operation in promoting and developing health, safety and welfare at work. Furthermore they have the right to make representations to their employer on such matters, and their views must be taken into account 'in so far as is reasonably practicable'. If the workforce so decide, they may appoint a safety representative to act on their behalf. Amongst other entitlements, the safety representative may inspect the workplace at an agreed frequency and may accompany a Health and Safety Authority inspector on a tour of inspection.

As noted above, European influences in this area have been considerable. In 1989, the same year as the Safety, Health and Welfare at Work Act was enacted, the EC agreed the so-called 'Framework' Directive on Health and Safety, and in some respects, our domestic legislation was influenced by its passage. Indeed, the power to issue regulations to develop the 1989 Act was used to implement the framework and six other Health and Safety Directives together by way of the Safety, Health and Welfare at Work (General Application) Regulations (S.I. 44/93). From 1980 on, Health and Safety Directives have been implemented in Ireland on such diverse and technical subjects as safety signs, exposure to chemical, physical and biological agents, noise, manual handling of loads, visual display screens, lead, asbestos and protective equipment at work.

2.1.5 OTHER EMPLOYMENT LEGISLATION

Table 2.2 Summary of other employment legislation in Ireland	
Act	**Scope**
Organisation of Working Time Act 1997	Working hours, rest breaks, rest periods, annual leave, public holidays, Sunday working, zero hour contracts
Protection of Young Persons (Employment) Act 1996	Working hours and age limits for young persons at work
Minimum Notice Act 1973–1991	Minimum notice periods on dismissal
Terms of Employment (Information) Act 1994	Written statement on terms and conditions of employment
Payment of Wages Act 1991	Methods of payment and deductions from wages
Worker Protection (Regular part-time Employees) Act 1991	Extension of Protective Employment Legislation to part-time workers
Pensions Act 1990	Administration of pension schemes
Redundancy Payments Acts 1967–1991	Lump sum payment on redundancy
Protection of Employment Act 1977 (as amended)	Consultation prior to collective redundancies
Transfer of Undertaking Regulations 1980	Protecting employees' rights in cases of change of ownership
Protection of Employees (Employers' Insolvency) Act 1984–91	Payments due to employees in case of employer insolvency
Adoptive Leave Act 1995	Rights to leave from work in the event of adoption
Data Protection Act 1988	Access to automated/computer data

ORGANISATION OF WORKING TIME

Again, as a result of the necessity to implement an EC measure — the 'Working Time' Directive, the area of working hours and holidays has been codified in new legislation — the Organisation of Working Time Act 1997. In the process, a number of pieces of legislation have been repealed (including the Conditions of Employment Acts 1936 and 1944 and the Holidays (Employees) Act 1973). In addition, the part-time workers legislation of 1991 (see below) required amendment in the area of holiday entitlements.

The new Act is long and complex, and like its predecessors, full of exemptions and exceptions in the area of working hours, rest periods and breaks. Some of its salient points are:
– a maximum working week of forty-eight hours by March 2000, over a reference period of four, six or twelve months, depending on the category of worker;
– minimum rest breaks of fifteen minutes per 4.5 hours worked and thirty minutes per six hours worked;
– minimum rest period of eleven hours per twenty-four hours and twenty-four hours per week (i.e., a consecutive weekly rest period of thirty-five hours);
– minimum annual leave entitlements of four weeks for full-time workers by 2000 and 8 per cent of hours worked in the case of part-time or casual employees;
– entitlement to some form of compensation, whether by way of payment or time off in lieu of Sunday work;
– entitlement to a minimum payment should a worker be engaged on a zero hour contract and not be provided with any or the requisite amount of work;
– special restrictions on hours worked at night, in particular night-work involving particular hazards.

Complaints under this Act are made to a Rights Commissioner, with a right of appeal to the Labour Court.

YOUNG PEOPLE AT WORK

The Protection of Young Persons (Employment) Act 1996 prohibits the employment of children under sixteen years of age. However, a child over fourteen years may be permitted to do light non-industrial work during school holidays, provided it is not harmful to health, development or schooling. The Act further provides for the setting of limits to the working hours of young people, for rest intervals and the prohibition of night-work.

MINIMUM NOTICE LAW

The minimum notice legislation entitles employees to a minimum period (or to accept pay in lieu) of notice prior to dismissal. Those employees covered by the Act, with thirteen weeks' service, are entitled to statutory minimum notice. This applies on a sliding scale basis to employees, whereby the longer the

service the longer is the notice period entitlement (i.e., up to a statutory maximum of eight weeks). An employer is also entitled to at least one week's notice from an employee with thirteen or more weeks' service. A study of the Act by Gunnigle et al. (1992) reveals that the EAT has determined that:
– notice given must be sufficiently certain and precise, leaving no room for ambiguity or uncertainty;
– the precise expiry date must be specified; and
– employees to whom the notice provisions apply are entitled to the same rights during the minimum notice period as they would enjoy but for the notice.

The minimum notice right does not, however, preclude either side from terminating the contract without notice on account of what the EAT would adjudge to be 'severe misconduct' by the other party (Von Prondzynski, 1989a). During 1996 the Tribunal dealt with 2,296 claims under the Minimum Notice and Terms of Employment Acts 1973–91. Of these 1,618 were allowed, 212 were dismissed, 299 were withdrawn during hearing and 167 were withdrawn prior to hearing.

TERMS OF EMPLOYMENT

As noted in section 2.1.1 on the contract of employment, an employer is now obliged to furnish any employee who has one month's continuous service, working not less than eight hours per week, with a written statement outlining basic terms of employment. The minimum notice legislation referred to above used to be called the Minimum Notice and Terms of Employment Act 1973 and provided for a similar statement, as the Terms of Employment (Information) Act 1994 now does.

The essential differences are firstly, that the employee (if employed since May 1994) is automatically entitled to the statement and does not have to request it. Secondly, there is a direct method of complaint for an aggrieved employee to a Rights Commissioner, whereas under the 1973 Act, it was up to the Department of Labour to take proceedings. This led to a widespread lack of compliance. The information required in the statement includes:
– names of employer and employee and the address of the employer in the State;
– the place of work and the employee's job title and nature of work;
– the date of commencement of employment;
– details of pay, including overtime, commission and bonus and the methods of calculating them;
– whether pay is to be weekly, monthly or otherwise;
– conditions about hours of work and overtime;
– holiday entitlements;
– sick pay arrangements and pension schemes if any; and
– periods of notice or, if the contract of employment is for a fixed time, the date when the contract expires.

The changes outlined above were once again necessitated by the obligation to implement an EC directive. There were just four such cases dealt with by the Tribunal in 1996, of which one was upheld, one was upset and two were withdrawn.

WAGE PAYMENT LAW

Under the Payment of Wages Act 1991 seven legal wage payment methods are provided for, including payment by cheque, bank draft, credit transfer or similar method, postal order and, of course, cash. Provision is also made for those situations in which financial institutions are affected by industrial action. Where the employee is paid on a non-cash basis and the cash is not readily available, subject to the employee's consent, the employer must pay wages by another non-cash method. Should the employee not agree, the employer must pay the wages in cash. The circumstances in which deductions, in particular those relating to acts or omissions of the employee, can legally be made from wages and payments made by employers, are also set down. Effectively, deductions must be provided for in the contract or other written form, the employee must be made aware in advance that a deduction will be made and the deduction must be reasonable in relation to the employee's wages. In 1996 the Tribunal dealt with twenty-two cases under this Act, with five being upheld and the remainder being withdrawn.

PART-TIME WORKERS' PROTECTIVE LAW

Arising from the growth of the secondary labour market or the 'peripheral' workforce, the Worker Protection (Regular Part-Time Employees) Act came into operation with effect from April 1991. All part-time workers are covered by the Act if they work at least thirteen weeks (not necessarily consecutive) with the same employer and are normally expected to work not less than eight hours a week for that employer. The Act provides for the application to regular part-time workers of the redundancy, minimum notice, worker participation (see chapter 8), unfair dismissals , maternity and employers' insolvency legislation. During 1996 the Tribunal disposed of seventy-one cases under this Act. Of these six were allowed, thirteen were dismissed, thirty-five were withdrawn during hearing and seventeen were withdrawn prior to hearing.

PENSIONS PROVISIONS

The Pensions Act of 1990, whilst not making occupational pension schemes compulsory, does attempt to regulate those schemes already in existence, and those which will come into operation after 1990. Effectively the legislation (Gunnigle et al., 1992):
– establishes a Pensions Board to monitor and supervise the new requirements under the Act;

– provides for the compulsory preservation of pension entitlements for employees who change employments;
– introduces a minimum funding standard for certain funded schemes;
– provides for the disclosure of information to scheme members;
– clarifies the duties and responsibilities of scheme trustees; and
– implements the principle of equal treatment for men and women in occupational benefit schemes.

DATA PROTECTION LAW

The Data Protection Act 1988 entitles individuals to establish the existence of automated personal data, to have access to such data in relation to them and to have inaccurate data rectified or erased. The Act also obliges the Data Controller (i.e., the organisation which uses automated personal data) to adhere to a number of obligations including the accuracy, relevance, use etc. of such data. Furthermore, a Data Protection Commissioner is provided with a legal basis for intervening where an individual complains that the principles have not been observed. The relevant principles provided for in the Act are:
– that the Data Controller fairly obtains and processes the data;
– that the automated data be factually accurate and, where necessary, up-to-date;
– that the data is kept for one or more specified and lawful purposes;
– that the data shall not be used or disclosed in any manner incompatible with the specified and lawful purposes;
– that the data retained be attainable, relevant and not excessive in relation to the specified and lawful purposes;
– that the personal data shall not be kept for longer than is necessary for the specified and lawful purposes; and
– appropriate security measures should be taken by data controllers and processors against unauthorised access to or attention, disclosure or destruction of the data, and against its accidental destruction or loss.

A new EC directive (for implementation in October 1998) extends the duties of employers and the entitlement of employees in this area. Basically, an employee would be entitled to request details of all data, including manual files kept in relation to them.

Furthermore under the 1998 Freedom of Information Act one has the right of access to official records held by Government departments or other specified public bodies. This includes the right to have personal information held on one corrected or updated, and the right to be given reasons for decisions taken by public bodies that affect one. This legislative initiative has been deployed by job applicants and interviewees to gain access to the reasons for their failure both to be shortlisted for interview and called for interview.

REDUNDANCY AND OWNERSHIP CHANGES

The subject of statutory redundancy entitlements constitutes a fertile area for disputes. During 1992 for example, 687 cases under the Redundancy Payments Acts 1967–91 were dealt with by the EAT. This legislation entitles workers with at least two years' continuous service, who have not reached retirement age, to a redundancy payment in the event of being made redundant. The legislative provisions pertaining to redundancy are too numerous and detailed to document here, however, suffice to note that the payment itself is calculated as follows:

– a sum equivalent to the employee's normal weekly working remuneration; plus

– half of the normal weekly remuneration for each year of continuous employment between the date on which the employee turned sixteen years old and the date at which they turned forty-one (or up to the termination of the contract of employment); plus

– full weekly remuneration for each year of continuous employment from the date of the employee's forty-first birthday until the dismissal, i.e., up to the termination of the contract.

A week's pay in such circumstances is subject to a statutory ceiling of £300 per week (£15,600 per annum), though it is adjusted from time to time.

Where collective redundancies arise, the provisions of the Protection of Employment Act 1977 come into force. These require the employer to supply the employees' representatives with specific information regarding the proposed redundancies and to consult with those representatives at least thirty days before the first dismissal takes place, to see if they can be lessened or avoided. The employer is also obliged to advise the Minister for Enterprise, Trade and Employment at least thirty days in advance of the first dismissal. Despite the apparent stringency of these requirements, however, the legislation is adjudged to be of limited value. Von Prondzynski (1989a) and Gunnigle et al. (1992) suggest that the wide exceptions provided for in the Act mean that its enforcement is least possible where it is most necessary. In the event of the employer becoming insolvent the Protection of Employees (Employers' Insolvency) Act 1984–91 comes into play. Subject to certain limits and conditions, monies due to workers by way of pay arrears (including holiday and sick pay), entitlements under the minimum notice, equal pay, unfair dismissals and employment equality enactments, and monies due from court orders in respect of wages, sick pay, holiday pay or damages at common law for wrongful dismissal may be paid out of the Redundancy and Employers' Insolvency Fund. Outstanding employee contributions to an occupational pension scheme up to a year prior to the insolvency date, which the employer deducted but did not pay over, are also protected. In 1992 the EAT had to deal with 276 cases under this Act. By 1996 this had decreased to nineteen complaints — of which all were allowed.

The Transfer of Undertaking Regulations 1980, again based on the EC 'Acquired Rights' Directive, are designed to protect employees' jobs in the event of a change in their employer's identity, where the business in question resumes its activities having been sold as a going concern. Subject to the employer's right to effect redundancies for economic, technical or organisational reasons involving changes in the work force, employees are entitled to continue working under the same terms of employment with service and contractual rights maintained. Both the outgoing and incoming employer are also obliged to keep employees informed of developments — though this requirement is often ignored in practice.

These regulations have attracted criticism in recent years due to the increasing number of transactions in which the European Court of Justice has held them to apply, including contracting out or in, and change of contractor situations. An employee whose rights are infringed under the legislation, resulting in dismissal, may bring an unfair dismissal claim to the EAT in the normal manner. There is some evidence at present of a slight row back at European level in the scope of this directive.

2.2 COLLECTIVE LABOUR LAW

OVERVIEW

Collective labour law establishes the legal framework under which industrial relations takes place. Collective labour law is distinguished from individual labour law in that its concern is to regulate the relationship between employers and collectivities of employees (normally trade unions). Individual labour law, as we have seen, is concerned with the conferring of positive employment rights on workers and as such concentrates on the relationship between the individual worker and the employer or management (Fennell and Lynch, 1993). Von Prondzynski (1989) and Kerr (1989) note that collective labour law in Ireland is largely governed by legislation which can be classified into two categories. The first category covers statutes which were enacted prior to Irish independence in 1922. Article 50 of the Irish Constitution of 1937 provides that, subject to its provisions, the laws in force prior to 1937 should continue unless repealed or found to be repugnant to the Constitution. The pre-1922 Westminister legislation largely regulated the legal status of trade unions and the taking of industrial action. The second category describes the statutes which were enacted by the Oireachtas since 1922, which were in the main designed to deal with the perceived problem of trade union multiplicity and others to provide for the establishment of industrial relations institutions such as the Labour Court.

The most significant development in Irish collective labour law in recent years has been the enactment of the Industrial Relations Act 1990. This Act represents the most comprehensive revision of industrial relations, trade dispute and trade union law in the history of the State and its development and provisions will be discussed in later sections. The following sections aim to give a brief overview of the evolution of collective labour law in Ireland from its pre-independence Westminster heritage to its present framework.

2.2.1 THE EVOLUTION OF IRISH COLLECTIVE LABOUR LAW

In the last century, the emergence of trade unions was hindered and restricted by an openly hostile State and legal system which, as Kerr (1989) suggests, often viewed trade unionists as 'rebels and revolutionists'. Up until 1871 with the enactment of the Trade Union Act of that year, the British common law doctrine of criminal conspiracy was the commanding influence in the relationships between employer and employee. Trade unions were regarded by the courts as criminal conspiracies and were judged to be in restraint of trade. By 1870, however, a growing acceptance of the trade union movement, facilitated by its ability to harness its members' voting power, enabled the unions to gain a concession from the Conservative Government of the day. The Trade Union Act of 1871 which resulted gave trade unions the first seeds of legal respectability. The Trade Union Act legalised the existence of trade unions but carefully refrained from giving them the status of corporate entities, that is, entities capable of suing and being sued in their own name. The Act declared that the mere fact that a trade union's aims are in restraint of trade is not sufficient to render any union member liable for the offence of criminal conspiracy. The Act also provided that contracts entered into by a trade union were contracts which the law would enforce. However, the courts were debarred from directly enforcing, or recovering damages for breach of any agreement between one union and another, agreements between unions and employers, or agreements between unions and their members. Another objective of the Act as Von Prondzynski (1989) points out was to encourage the trade unions to register with the Registrar of Friendly Societies. Wallace (1994) suggests that the practical effect of the provisions of the Act was to allow trade unions to exist within the law but to prevent legal regulation of their affairs. The 1871 Act, as subsequently amended, governs the legal status of trade unions in Ireland today.

The attempt of the Trade Union Act of 1871 to legitimate trade unions within the law was largely unsuccessful as it became evident from judicial decisions that even though the existence of trade unions was legal, many of their activities were illegal. This arose because of the underlying common law concept of criminal conspiracy. For example, if two or more union members combined to threaten to withdraw their labour this was held by the courts to be a criminal conspiracy. Furthermore, picketing of any description was held to be illegal. The effect was to significantly frustrate the operation of trade unions in their efforts to improve the pay and conditions of workers through collective action. Following a successful campaign, which saw the trade union movement again support the Conservative party of Disraeli in return for a promise to amend the legislation, the remit of the criminal law was considerably restricted by the introduction of the Conspiracy and Protection of Property Act 1875. The Conspiracy and Protection of Property Act 1875 provided:

(1) that no one was liable for any act committed 'in contemplation or furtherance of a trade dispute' unless the act would also be a crime if committed by one person;

(2) that a breach of contract by workers of gas or water supply was to remain a crime in certain circumstances;

(3) immunity to peaceful picketing in connection with a trade dispute (that is, picketing that does not entail violence or intimidation);

(4) that a breach of contract by any person which endangered human life, risked serious bodily injury or exposed valuable property to destruction, continued to be a crime.

The Trade Union Amendment Act of 1876 strengthened the legal position of trade unions by ensuring that trustees could be held accountable for union funds. The net effects of these legislative changes was to remove the taint of illegality from trade unions. The Acts of 1871 and 1875 virtually excluded the law of conspiracy from the field of trade disputes. Kerr and Whyte (1985) argue that the reaction of employers and the courts, when denied the use of criminal liabilities was to develop the notion of civil conspiracy under the law of tort, which provided remedies against conduct deliberately aimed at causing financial loss. The new threat posed to trade unions was that their ability to take effective industrial action was hampered by the prospect of employers seeking awards of damages and orders of injunctions. The crime of conspiracy had been succeeded as an anti-union weapon by the tort of conspiracy. This significant threat to the unions was bolstered by a number of important decisions. In the case of *Quinn v Leathem* (1901), initially heard in Belfast, it was established that if two or more persons combine together without legal justification to injure another, they are liable for damages for conspiracy. In this famous case it was held that an official of a trade union was liable for combining to injure an employer by threatening to withdraw labour from one of his customers unless the latter ceased to do business with him. While no unlawful act had been committed by any of the defendants individually, the combination to injure was an unlawful conspiracy, entitling the plaintiff to recover civil damages for the loss he had suffered. The Conspiracy and Protection of Property Act 1875 was judged to afford no protection since it gave immunity only from criminal conspiracy. However, the judgment was against the union official Leathem and not the union.

From the trade union perspective an equally disturbing development was the decision of the House of Lords in the case of *The Taff Vale Railway Company v Amalgamated Society of Railway Servants* (1901). The trade unions had been reluctantly accepting civil actions against union officers and members as in the *Quinn v Leathem* case, but unionists did not believe that the trade union as an entity could be sued to meet the liabilities for torts committed by its officers. Until 1901 it was assumed that because a registered union was an unincorporated association having no legal identity distinct from that of its individual members, this placed the union's funds beyond the reach of the judicial process. The decision which emanated from the lawlords in the *Taff Vale* case was that the union's funds were not immune from suits of damages. The case itself arose as a result of a strike by members of the Amalgamated Society of Railway Servants in August 1900. Richard Bell, the union's general secretary had persuaded 'blackleg labour' not to work, thus inducing them to breach their contract with the Taff Vale company. The company sought an injunction and damages against the union. The case was heard on appeal in the House of Lords, where it was held that a registered trade union, as constituted under the Trade Union Act of 1871, was a legal entity possessing sufficient attributes of corporate personality to enable it to be sued in its registered name for the torts of its servants or agents.

This decision was a tremendous blow to the unions as it seemed likely to reduce them to impotence, since if they declared a strike they ran the risk of their funds being attacked by the law. In the *Taff Vale* case the union had to pay £35,000 in total as a result of the case found against it (£23,000 damages was awarded to the company).

During the subsequent five years it has been estimated that unions lost £200,000 in similar actions. The effect of the decision in the *Taff Vale* case was to destroy the legal rights of trade unions as established by the Acts of 1871 and 1875, and to make strikes illegal. The trade union movement in response to these and other cases again looked to the political arena for redress (Wallace, 1988b). It campaigned vigorously for parliamentary reform to overturn this judge-made law. In the 1906 elections the election of a Liberal Government led to the passing of the Trade Disputes Act 1906. The Trade Disputes Act 1906 provided protection to trade unions and their members by granting them immunity from the tort of civil conspiracy, legalising peaceful picketing and providing immunity against actions which would otherwise have been illegal at common law. Section 4 of the Act also provided that trade unions could not be held liable for any act under the law of tort. The Act in effect conferred a 'blanket immunity' on trade unions by prohibiting any actions in tort against them in their registered name. This meant that the decision in the *Taff Vale* case had been reversed and union funds were immune from awards of damages. The immunities conferred in the Act are restricted to persons 'acting in contemplation or furtherance of a trade dispute', (dubbed the 'golden formula' by Wedderburn (1965)). Von Prondzynski (1989) suggests that the Trade Disputes Act 1906 adopted a very simple technique, that is, it identified the main judicial decisions which had disabled trade unions and gave unions an immunity from legal action under these judicial precedents.

It is important to note that the Act did not give a positive right to strike. Kerr and Whyte (1985) report that the trade unions opposed the enactment of a comprehensive labour law code with positive rights and obligations and opted for the more pragmatic immunities approach. The immunities approach adopted in the Trade Disputes Act gave a distinctly voluntarist orientation to British and Irish industrial relations, characterised by the essentially abstentionist role of the State in the system.

The final piece of Westminster collective labour legislation enacted before we achieved independence is the Trade Union Act 1913. The Act amended the definition and registration provisions for trade unions. Its most important provision was to allow the funds of a trade union to be applied for political purposes. The Act arose because of the decision of the House of Lords in the case of *Osborne v Amalgamated Society of Railway Servants* (1911) which held that unions were not entitled to raise or expend funds for political purposes. The Act reversed this position, provided that political purposes were included in the union's objects and separate political funds set up from which members could opt out.

Table 2.3 Collective labour legislation enacted by the Oireachtas

Statute	Provisions
Trade Union Act 1935	Trade unions allowed to own unlimited amount of land
Trade Union Act 1941	Negotiation licences, sole negotiation rights
Trade Union Act 1942	Exemptions from negotiation licences, appeals in sole rights situations
Industrial Relations Act 1946	Establishment of the Labour Court
Trade Union Acts 1947–52	Six Acts extending power to reduce deposits of Irish unions by 75 per cent
Industrial Relations Act 1969	Enlargement of the Labour Court, Office of Rights Commissioners
Trade Union Act 1971	New negotiation licence rules: £5000 deposit, 500 members, 18 month wait
Trade Union Act 1975	Encouraged tne amalgamation of trade unions
Industrial Relations Act 1976	Allowed agricultural workers access to the Labour Court
Worker Participation (State Enterprises) Act 1977–1988	Elected worker directors
Trade Disputes (Amendment) Act 1982	Extended immunities of the 1906 Act to all except the police and the army
Industrial Relations Act 1990	Labour Relations Commission, pre-strike secret ballots, immunities/injunctions curbed, trade union rationalisation

Source: McGinley, 1990

Table 2.3 summarises the legislative developments in Irish collective labour law since 1922. After independence the Oireachtas was relatively slow to augment the collective labour framework that it had inherited. The eighteen years between 1922 and 1940 saw a period of legislative inaction with only one statute enacted — the Trade Union Act of 1935. This Act essentially enables trade unions to hold an unlimited amount of land. The trade union movement was largely happy with the protectionist legislation that existed and as McGinley (1990) suggests its main concern was to preserve its Victorian legacy embodied in the Acts of the UK Parliament to which we have referred.

The Trade Union Act of 1941 was enacted against the backdrop of great concern over the perceived structural defects in the trade union movement. The proliferation of trade unions was seen to be a significant catalyst in the creation of industrial unrest. Von Prondzynski (1989) suggests that there was also a widespread belief at the time that the large number of trade unions, fragmented and unco-ordinated, and the substantial number of British-based unions operating here were hostile to the best interests of the State. The Trade Union Act of 1941 obligated trade unions who wished to engage in collective bargaining to have a negotiating licence and in so doing introduced for the first time the concept of an 'authorised trade union'. The Act confined the immunities contained in the Trade Disputes Act of 1906 to such 'authorised trade unions'. A number of conditions were specified for a trade union to qualify for a licence which essentially entailed depositing a sum of money with the High Court.

The second essential feature of the Act provided for the establishment of a Trade Union Tribunal which could give sole negotiating rights to one or more unions. This second feature posed a significant threat to the British-based unions who could not get sole negotiating rights on their own. Both features of the Act were designed to exclude certain trade unions from operating by regulating the function of negotiation, licensing some unions for the purpose and excluding others (Von Prondzynski, 1989). The aim of the Act was to discourage the formation of new unions and to cut down the number of existing ones.

The Trade Union Act of 1941 was the focus of much criticism when debated in the Dáil, particularly from Fine Gael TDs who questioned the constitutionality of the Act. Prior to enactment, it was the subject of an intense campaign by the trade union movement which culminated in a large protest march in Dublin. A Trade Union Bill was drafted in 1942 designed to address some of the concerns expressed at the Trade Union Act of 1941 and mindful of the fact that certain exemptions to the general provisions must exist. The Bill was passed without debate, with the Trade Union Bill of 1942 providing certain exemptions from holding negotiating licences and providing appeals machinery in sole negotiation rights situations.

The Trade Union Act of 1941 was to become the subject of a constitutional test case in 1946 when the ITGWU applied for sole negotiating rights in the road passenger and tramway services of CIE where the British-based National Union of Railwaymen (NUR) also operated. The NUR challenged the constitutionality of Part III of the Act which dealt with the issue of sole negotiation rights and in July 1946, the Supreme Court on appeal ruled that it was repugnant to the Constitution. Part III was struck down, all that remained of the 1941 Act were the provisions for negotiating licences.

The Trade Union Act of 1971 amended many of the provisions for negotiating licences under the 1941 Act, as the Government continued to pursue its policy of discouraging the formation of new unions. The 1971 Act provided that a union must notify the Minister for Labour and ICTU of its intention to apply for a negotiation licence eighteen months beforehand. The Act also required that the union have 500 members in the State at the date of application for a licence and eighteen months beforehand. The appropriate deposit held with the High Court, which varied depending on the size of the union, was now to be at a minimum of £5,000. The Trade Union Act of 1975 extended the policy of promoting trade union rationalisation by encouraging amalgamations between unions, essentially providing financial assistance to trade unions which successfully merged.

The Worker Participation (State Enterprises) Acts of 1977 and 1988 were a limited attempt to give employees a formal say in the decision-making processes of the bodies that employ them. The Acts provide for one-third of the directors of the bodies concerned to be elected for a fixed period by the employees from candidates nominated by trade unions or other representative bodies. Von Prondzynski (1998) contends that the experience of some of the worker directors elected under the provisions of the Acts demonstrates the limited extent to which the idea of participation has taken root in Ireland. The issue of employee participation is covered in chapter 8.

The Industrial Relations Acts of 1946 and 1969 established certain third party institutions namely the Labour Court and the Rights Commissioners whose function is principally to assist employers and trade unions in the conduct of industrial relations, particularly in the case of trade disputes. The development and the provisions of these Acts will be described in chapter 3.

2.2.2 THE REFORM OF COLLECTIVE LABOUR LAW — THE DEBATE
The Industrial Relations Act 1990 passed into law on 18 July 1990 and is now the definitive piece of legislation governing relations between employers and employees and their representatives in this country. The Act is the most comprehensive revision of the law governing trade unions, trade disputes and industrial relations generally in over eighty years, since the Trade Disputes Act 1906.

The Act is the culmination, however, of over fifty years of debate on the general role of the law in industrial relations and more specifically on the need for reform of existing trade disputes legislation. Wallace (1991a) argues that the lack of legislative activity from Government up to 1990 masks a recurrent and persistent interest in legal reform of industrial relations. Since the late 1940s successive Governments identified the need to reform and update the existing legislation but until 1990 none had achieved anything substantial. McCall (1988) notes that Lemass made considerable progress in the late 1950s but his efforts were to no avail. Reform of Irish industrial relations and trade disputes law has been high on the agenda of the Department of Labour since its establishment in 1966 (Department of Labour, 1991b; Kerr, 1991a). Kerr (1991a) suggests that the persistence of the reform debate can be understood by the fact that the general state of industrial relations was perceived throughout the 1950s, 1960s and 1970s to be in serious disorder — unofficial strikes were widespread, there were frequent disruptions to essential services and there were a significant number of inter-union disputes, all of which were afforded immunities under the Trade Disputes Act. One of the very first initiatives of the newly established Department of Labour was to draft a Trade Union Bill in 1966 which proposed to remove immunities to liability under the Trade Disputes Act from trade union members who engaged in unofficial action, and required the holding of a secret ballot before a strike. The Bill was subject to severe criticism from the trade union movement and did not receive a second reading. The Government chose not to pursue the Bill because of the lack of consensus, the Minister for Labour conceding that legislation in this regard could only be effective if it had the co-operation of the trade unions (Dáil Debates, 1969).

In May 1978, the Government, faced with employer calls for action over the increasing incidence of industrial action, appointed a Commission of Inquiry on Industrial Relations. The Commission was charged with examining industrial relations generally, and specifically to report on the relevance of statute law to industrial relations. Since the early 1970s employers had been advocating radical reform of the law applicable to trade disputes. Kevin Duffy (1993) suggests that the demand for reform was also coming from the Industrial Development Authority who argued to the Government that the perceived poor industrial relations record in Ireland was a deterrent to the attraction of foreign investment.

The Commission's trade union participants withdrew in protest at the delay in bringing forward legislation to extend the coverage of the Trade Disputes Act to the public service. The Commission which reported in 1981, maintained that there were serious defects in Irish trade union structure. Essentially, their view was that trade union multiplicity was a major problem, with too many small unions giving poor service to members. Inadequate levels of service then led to disaffection among members and frequently to unofficial action (Report of the Commission of Inquiry on Industrial Relations, 1981). The Commission concluded that voluntary means alone were incapable of governing Irish industrial relations. The Report of the Commission made a number of controversial recommendations in relation to collective labour legislation including:

(1) the immunities trade unions enjoyed under the 1906 Act be limited;

(2) the withdrawal of immunities from disputes of rights, that is, disputes concerning dismissal, equality, union recognition and inter-union disputes;

(3) the introduction of a mandatory disputes procedure;

(4) the establishment of a Labour Relations Board and a Labour Relations Court which would determine whether industrial action complied with the trades disputes provisions. While none of these recommendations was implemented, Wallace (1988b) argues that the report provided a central focus for the debate on reform which continued throughout the 1980s.

The Report of the Commission was subject to much academic criticism. For example, McCarthy and Von Prondzynski (1982) condemned the Commission's lack of original work and argued that it selectively used secondary data to support its conclusions. Kelly and Roche (1983) maintained that in advocating greater legalism the Commission ignored countries that had a great deal of legal regulation and a high strike record. Wallace and O'Shea (1987) argued that the Commission had incorrectly identified the cause of unofficial strikes. On a more general note, the serious problem with Irish industrial relations as identified by the Commission related to trade union structure, yet the prescriptions were to do with trade disputes.

The 1980s saw a decade of discussions between the Department of Labour, the ICTU and the FIE. These discussions were led by various publications which emanated from the Department. There were four sets of proposals throughout the 1980s, the final set of proposals by the Minister for Labour of the day, Bertie Ahern, in 1988, formed the basis of the provisions found in the Industrial Relations Act 1990. The 1983 discussion document rejected most of the Commission's recommendations, particularly the removal of immunities, and concurred with the academic criticisms of the Commission's report (Department of Labour, 1983). In the view of the Department any increase in the incidence of strikes indicated inadequacies in the industrial relations dispute-settling machinery rather than defects in the law (Kerr, 1991a). A discussion document published in 1985 by the Department of Labour and expanded upon in 1986, proposed the establishment of a Labour Relations Commission charged with the statutory responsibility to promote good industrial relations. More fundamentally, the proposals advocated a radical move away from the immunities-based system to a 'positive rights' approach (Department of Labour, 1985). This approach opted for a positive right to strike instead of the immunity from liability in the event of a strike. A complete defence was to be afforded when the right was used. These proposals were met with criticism from the trade union movement because of the feared limitations which would have been placed on the right to strike. For example, it was envisaged that the right would not apply in workmen versus workmen disputes, in the event of secondary picketing, in the case of industrial action involving one worker, a strike by a minority of workers where there had been a recent ballot against such an action, and occupation of or damage to property, personal injury or trespass. It was also feared that more restrictive conditions might later be imposed on the exercise of the right to strike.

The publication of the Industrial Relations Bill 1989 was preceeded by another discussion document in 1988 which, as mentioned, bore a remarkable similarity to the eventual Act (Department of Labour, 1988). The immediate origins for the 1988 discussion document are to be found in the Programme for National Recovery which committed the Minister for Labour to holding discussions with the social partners about changes in industrial relations which in the words of the Programme, 'would provide a better framework for collective bargaining and dispute settlement and help to create conditions for employment generating investment' (Department of Labour, 1991b). The 1988 proposals reverted to an immunities-based approach, but the exceptions to the complete defence outlined in the 1985 proposals survived. Bonner (1987) explains that the primary reason for reverting to the immunities system was the unenthusiastic response of ICTU to the positive rights approach. Wallace (1991a) argues that the consistency in proposals for reform is probably indicative of a number of inter-related factors: firstly, the influence of the Commission of Inquiry in setting the agenda for reform, secondly, a certain continuity of thinking on the topic of reform within the Department of Labour, and thirdly, the influence of British legislation on Irish thinking. The proposals were put to both sides of industry as the Minister sought to achieve a balance which would reflect the rights and responsibilities of both employers and trade unions. Various modifications were made to the proposals during the detailed negotiations which took place and a number of changes were also made in the text of the Bill during its passage through the Oireachtas. The Bill was generally well supported across all political parties when debated in the Dáil. The Workers' Party (Rabbitte and Gilmore, 1990) however, were unhappy with the Bill and were of the view that it would lead to more intervention in industrial relations matters by the courts.

2.2.3 THE INDUSTRIAL RELATIONS ACT 1990

A number of more immediate factors may help to understand the rationale for the introduction of the Act. While undoubtedly the problems of perceived disorder (for example, unofficial strikes, inter-union disputes, strikes in essential services etc.) which had persistently haunted the Irish industrial relations system, were very infrequent in the late 1980s, the Department of Labour felt it was no time to be complacent. In the light of the national consensus secured under the Programme for National Recovery the Department of Labour felt it was an appropriate time to press ahead with changes to the existing labour law designed to maintain the relatively good record of industrial peace.

The law in relation to trade disputes had become extraordinarily complex (Department of Labour, 1991b; Kerr, 1991b). A considerable volume of case law had arisen from the judicial construction of the Trade Disputes Act 1906.

Indeed, so much case law surrounded the 1906 Act that the usefulness of the legislation in providing a guide as to what was or was not permissible in a trade dispute was considerably diminished.

A threat of a constitutional challenge to the Trade Disputes Act 1906 had also long existed. It was feared that the constitutionality of the blanket immunity in the Act might be tested in relation to Article 34 which guaranteed access to the courts. The Department of Labour anticipated that the Industrial Relations Act 1990 would address this situation.

The policy of encouraging trade union rationalisation initiated under the Trade Union Act of 1941 and extended under the Trade Union Acts of 1971 and 1975 was believed to have played a significant role in promoting trade union mergers and amalgamations. It was hoped that the new legislation would further promote this process.

The purpose of the 1990 Industrial Relations Act as outlined by the then Minister for Labour, Bertie Ahern, 'is to put in place an improved framework for the conduct of industrial relations . . . [with the] . . . overall aim of maintaining a stable industrial relations climate' (Department of Labour, 1991). The longer title of the Act sets out that the aim of the Act is 'to make further and better the provision for promoting harmonious relations between workers and employers'. Bertie Ahern (1991) maintained that the 'Act was aimed at tightening and clarifying the situation in relation to trade disputes'.

THE PROVISIONS OF THE ACT

The provisions of the Act can be broadly divided between trade union law and industrial relations legislation.

I Trade Union Law Provisions

A. TRADE DISPUTES

The approach adopted in the area of trade disputes law was to repeal the Trade Disputes Acts of 1906 and 1982 and to reintroduce the main provisions of these Acts with amendments. The main features of the provisions relating to trade disputes are outlined below.

(1) *Individual disputes*: The Act withdraws immunities from one-person disputes where agreed procedures have not been followed.

(2) *Secondary action*: This is now restricted unless the union can show that the secondary employer directly sought to frustrate the aims of the dispute.

(3) *Picketing*: Workers may now only picket their own employer at the employer's place of work. Where it is not practical to picket the employer's place of business, the picket may be placed at the approaches to the employer's place of business.

(4) *Immunities*: The Act places limitations on the blanket immunity which existed under section 4 of the Trade Disputes Act 1906 in respect of tortious acts. The immunity now only exists for acts 'committed in contemplation or furtherance of a trade dispute'.

(5) *Worker versus worker disputes*: These no longer fall within the definition of a trade dispute.

(6) *Injunctions*: In trade dispute situations where a secret ballot has been held and one weeks' notice given, the granting of injunctions, particularly ex-parte injunctions is restricted.

B. Secret Ballots

As of 18 July 1992 union rules must contain provisions for the holding of secret ballots before any form of industrial action can be taken. No injunction will be granted to an employer in the event of a secret ballot being held.

The Act specifies that trade union rules should provide that:

(1) the union shall not organise, participate in, sanction or support a strike or other industrial action without a secret ballot, entitlement to vote on which shall be accorded equally to all members whom it is reasonable to believe will be called upon to engage in the strike or other industrial action;

(2) the union shall take reasonable steps to ensure that every member entitled to vote in the ballot votes without interference from, or constraint imposed by, the union or any of its members, officials or employees and, so far as is reasonably possible, that such members shall be given a fair opportunity of voting;

(3) the committee or management or other controlling authority of a trade union shall have full discretion in relation to organising, participating in, sanctioning or supporting a strike or other industrial action notwithstanding that the majority of those voting in the ballot, including an aggregate ballot, favour such strike or industrial action;

(4) the committee or management or other controlling authority of a trade union shall have full discretion in relation to organising, participating in, sanctioning or supporting a strike or other industrial action against the wishes of a majority of those voting in a secret ballot, except where, in the case of ballots by more than one trade union, an aggregate majority of all votes cast, favours such strike or other industrial action;

(5) where the outcome of a secret ballot conducted by a trade union which is affiliated to the Irish Congress of Trade Unions or in the case of ballots by more than one such trade union, an aggregate majority of all the votes cast is in favour of supporting a strike organised by another trade union, a decision to take such supportive action shall not be implemented unless the action has been sanctioned by the Irish Congress of Trade Unions;

(6) as soon as practicable after the conduct of a secret ballot the trade union shall take reasonable steps to make known to its members entitled to vote in the ballot (i) the number of ballot papers issued, (ii) the number of votes cast, (iii) the number of votes in favour of the proposal, (iv) the number of votes cast against the proposal and (v) the number of spoilt votes.

C. TRADE UNION RATIONALISATION

The Act makes a number of amendments to existing trade union law designed to encourage mergers and to discourage formation of new or breakaway unions. The Act essentially increases the minimum membership level required for a negotiating licence to 1,000 and alters the sum of money required to be held on deposit with the High Court. The amount required varies according to the size of the union but the minimum deposit now stands at £20,000. The Act also amends the Trade Union Act of 1975 by offering grants towards the expenses incurred in a two-year period prior to a merger attempt even if the attempt fails.

II Industrial Relations Legislation

The Act provides for the establishment of the Labour Relations Commission and divides functions between it and the Labour Court. The Act also makes changes in the procedure for the referral of disputes to the Labour Court and amends procedures in relation to the operation of Joint Labour Committees, employment regulation orders and registered employment agreements. The industrial relations provisions of the 1990 Act will be described in the discussion of the role of third parties in chapter 3.

THE EXPERIENCE TO DATE

It may still be too soon to give a complete assessment of the wider implications of the legislation and of its impact on the general conduct of industrial relations, in light of the relatively short period of time that the Act has been in existence. Moreover, two fundamental sections of the Act which deal with balloting and injunctions have only been in place since July 1992. Throughout the 1990s, we have experienced a period of relative industrial peace with few strikes to test the Act's provisions. However, there have been some significant developments in relation to the trade disputes provisions and recently to the balloting provisions. Despite the limited number of cases aired in the courts arising from the Act, a number of them have given rise to particular concern amongst trade unionists. Especially worrying has been the interpretation of the provisions on individual disputes and picketing by the judiciary. The 1990 Act withdraws immunities fom one-person disputes where agreed procedures have been broken. In the case of *Westman Holdings v McCormack and Others* (1991) the question arose as to whether a dispute involving seven employees was seven individual disputes. As there were no agreed procedures in the company the question was left undecided. In *Iarnród Éireann v Darby and O'Connor* an injunction was granted in a dispute in which the court held that an individual worker who was supported by his fellow workers had not complied with agreed procedures. What seems particularly disturbing from the trade union perspective is that disputes with a strong collective element to them, for example, the dismissal of a shop steward, have immunity withdrawn from them until procedures are exhausted (Wallace, 1991a).

In the case of *Westman Holdings v McCormack and Others* the question of picketing also arose. The *Westman Holdings* case is one of the most significant cases to be heard involving the trade disputes provisions of the Act to date. The case involved the sale of a licenced premises, where the workers who were dismissed by the original owner sought work with the new owner of the premises. Section 11 of the Act provides that workers may only picket their employer. Westman Holdings was able to obtain an interlocutory injunction restraining the employees from picketing the premises after establishing a fair case that he was not their employer. This decision was confirmed on appeal to the Supreme Court. The case was ultimately settled out of court during the trial and as such no definitive decision had been taken on whether the picketing was lawful under the circumstances. Kerr (1991b) describes the alarming possibility which the decision seems to offer employers, that is, by dismissing employees during a trade dispute, the employees would no longer be covered by the 1990 Act. Thus, in dismissing the employees and terminating their contract of employment the employer could claim that the employees were no longer his employees. However, the Department of Labour have asserted that if employers began to use the Act in this manner the Act would have to be amended.

A number of other provisions of the Act may cause trade unions some difficulties. For example, secondary action though allowed under the Act is more restricted. Meenan (1991) describes the requirement that the secondary employer had directly sought to frustrate the strike as a 'very high onus' of proof. Meenan (1991) has also drawn attention to the complicated rules in respect of secret ballots, the need for ballots for secondary action and the complex provisions for the aggregation of votes in a multi-union ballot as among the multiplicity of factors which could be used to challenge the legality of the ballots. There have already been calls for the amendment of the secret ballot provisions, particularly those relating to the provisions for aggregation of votes in a multi-union ballot, in response to the controversy surrounding the ballots in the Irish Steel dispute in 1993. Indeed, there have been a number of recent high profile cases which have brought the potential difficulties of the balloting provisions into sharp focus for the trade union movement. A Supreme Court ruling in the case of *BATU v G & T Crampton* in late 1997 looks set to impose far more onerous obligations on unions than were initially envisaged under the legislation. The case involved the building trade union, BATU, which appealed a High Court decision imposing an interlocutory injunction restraining the union and workers from picketing builders G & T Crampton. The Supreme Court was satisfied that the union had not discharged the onus of showing that an effective ballot was held and awarded the injunction. In the light of the ruling it now appears that trade unions will have to be able to prove that they have properly held a secret ballot, that all workers were afforded an opportunity to vote and clearly indicate the nature of any action to be taken if they are to bring into effect the provisions of section 19 of the Act. The outcome of the recent Supreme Court judgment in the case of *SIPTU v Nolan Transport* also sends a clear message to trade unions to ensure that they conduct secret ballots properly.

The judgment resulted from an appeal of a High Court decision in 1994 when SIPTU was ordered to pay more than £1.3 million in damages and costs to the company after Nolan Transport had instigated proceedings against SIPTU. The main issues in the case revolved around whether or not a trade dispute existed and whether or not the union was entitled to authorise strike action, having regard to the manner in which the secret ballot was conducted and the manner in which those voting actually voted. The union had organised a picket at Nolan Transport in protest at the dismissal of its members. The nature of the dispute was contested by the company who argued that the dispute was part of the union's overall strategy of compelling all the drivers at the company into union membership. The Supreme Court overturned the High Court decision and found that the union had engaged in a *bona fide* dispute and that as such the statutory immunities conferred by the 1990 Industrial Relations Act should apply. In its judgment the Supreme Court reaffirmed its decision in the *BATU v G & T Crampton* case in stating that the onus lies on the party resisting an application for an interlocutory injunction (the union) to prove that a secret ballot had been held properly. The wider implications of the *Nolan Transport* judgment are still being assessed, particularly in respect of the vexed issue of trade union representation and recognition.

The loss of injunctive relief was universally welcomed within the trade union movement. The injunctive remedy was the most frequent legal recourse used by employers. Duffy (1993) suggests that in the years prior to the enactment of the 1990 Act, the situation had got to the point where an injunction would be granted in almost every case in which it was applied for. The Act now provides that an interlocutory injunction will not be granted where, in addition to holding a secret ballot and giving due notice, the union establishes a fair case that it was acting in furtherance or contemplation of a trade dispute. Kerr (1997) contends that this was illustrated to good effect in the case of *Bus Éireann v SIPTU* where an application for an interlocutory injunction to restrain a strike was refused in 1993.

The trade union response to the operation of the Act so far has been on balance largely favourable. There was some initial disquiet as evidenced by two motions put down at the 1991 ICTU Annual Delegate Conference condemning the Act. One of those motions submitted by the Irish Distributive and Administrative Trade Union committed ICTU to 'lobby extensively to have the Act amended so that an equitable balance between the interests of employees and trade unions is achieved' (*Industrial Relations News*, 1991). This may be seen as a knee-jerk reaction to the uncertainties which some of the initial cases may have created in trade union circles. Duffy (1993) the Assistant General Secretary of ICTU, however, claims to be unaware of any situation in which a union has found it impossible to deal with a dispute because of the provisions of this legislation, nor is he aware of any industrial action taken by a union which was less successful than it might otherwise have been because of the provisions of the legislation. On the whole, to date it would appear that the Act has had little impact on the long established way of conducting industrial relations in this country. Wallace (1991c) argues that a continuation of the strict judicial interpretation of the Act would mean that the employers would have the opportunity to use the law in a wide range of circumstances. However, to date there has been little evidence of employers having increased their recourse to the law in industrial relations matters. Wallace (1991) suggests that a more fundamental uncertainty is to what extent employers will use the law, even if the opportunities arise, considering the traditional voluntarist nature of the Irish industrial relations system.

CHAPTER THREE

The Role of the State

3.1 INTRODUCTION

It should be evident from the discussion in chapter 1 that the primary responsibility for the conduct of industrial relations rests with management, employees and their representatives. Indeed, the bulk of everyday industrial relations is conducted by these parties. Employer associations and trade unions will be discussed respectively in the succeeding chapters. In this chapter, our concern centres on the role of the State, the third major actor on the industrial relations stage, or the 'third force' as Poole (1986) describes it. The involvement of the State in industrial relations may not be as obvious as that of trade unions and employers but in some respects its impact may be more potent. The State sets the framework within which industrial relations exist and it is the State alone which has the law-making powers which may substantially change the rules affecting the employment relationship (Crouch, 1982). Salamon (1992) defines the State as the 'politically based and controlled institutions of government and regulation within an organised society'. When we speak of the State in Ireland we refer to members of the Dáil, the Government, civil service, judiciary, Garda Síochána and the defence forces. However, as Salamon points out, the Government of the day (the party or parties in power) is the most important element within the State as it 'determines the directions, policies and actions of the State machinery'.

The primary responsibility of the State is the management of the national economy in a manner conducive to economic growth and the furtherance of national prosperity. It tries to accomplish this by pursuing four objectives which may not always be compatible, namely, to maintain a high level of employment, to ensure price stability, to achieve a favourable balance of payments and to protect the exchange rate (Crouch, 1982). The State also has social objectives which emanate from the ideological perspective and general view of the nature of society of the party in Government. The industrial relations strategies adopted by the State are then designed with general reference to the attainment of these twin economic and social aims, and the methods the State chooses to pursue these objectives are largely determined by the ideological perspective of the Government of the day. The State's role in industrial relations is more pronounced in certain countries than in others, depending to a large extent on the context, circumstances and traditions within each country. The role of the State in a particular country may also be more pronounced from one administration to another because of the political beliefs and differences of the various parties in power.

An individual's perceptions, assumptions and expectations about how the State should be involved in industrial relations and the degree to which the State's intervention in industrial relations is considered legitimate or otherwise, largely depends on the individual's frame of reference. For example, viewed from the Marxist and radical perspectives, the State is seen historically as serving class interests, i.e., those of the capital class, irrespective of the party in power. Marx exemplifies this in suggesting that 'the executive of the modern State is but a committee for managing the common affairs of the whole bourgeoisie'. Thus, Marx argues that the State's role in the industrial relations sphere is seen as protecting and supporting capital and its workplace representatives i.e., management. The function of the State is to preserve the capitalist system and to preserve the dominance of capital over labour. Similarly, Hyman (1975) argues that public policy is 'nothing more than the ideal expression of the dominant material relationships' in industry.

The contrasting pluralist perspective views the State as a neutral party, or indeed in many respects, as a referee between the divergent interests of employers and employees. Central to this viewpoint is the notion of 'voluntarism' that is, minimal legal interference by the State in the conduct of industrial relations matters, leaving employers and trade unions free to develop work rules and procedures to suit particular organisational and industrial contexts. From this standpoint if the State is to intervene in industrial relations matters it should be to impose certain minimum standards and to protect individual rights in the employment relationship and to protect the 'national interest' if the Government of the day regards it as threatened.

Although advocating a non-interventionist, generally passive role for the State and promotion of a *laissez-faire* economic philosophy, the unitarist perspective sees an increased role for the State's law-making powers in regulating certain areas of industrial relations. Fox (1973) argues that unitarists believe that 'increased legal intervention in industrial relations matters can and should take the form of regulating ... behaviour directly and embracing this regulation by direct punitive legal sanctions'.

The aim of this chapter is firstly, to consider the approaches or strategies that the State may pursue in industrial relations and secondly, the four main methods by which the State may intervene in industrial relations, namely (1) as an industrial relations policy maker, (2) as a provider of dispute resolution machinery, (3) as a legislator and (4) as an employer.

3.2 STATE APPROACHES TO INDUSTRIAL RELATIONS

A useful analysis of the policy alternatives or approaches which may be pursued by the State in industrial relations has been suggested by Crouch (1982). Crouch identifies four alternative approaches which may be adopted by the State in industrial relations, namely (1) market individualism, (2) liberal collectivism, (3) corporatism and (4) bargained corporatism. Crouch sees these alternative approaches as expressions of the inter-relationship between the dominant ideology in the industrial relations system (be it liberal or corporatist) and the relative power and autonomy of trade unions (be they strong and autonomous or weak and regulated). These varying options obviously entail very different social, political and economic implications. These ideal State approaches to industrial relations are summarised in Table 3.1 below and are discussed in the subsequent sections.

Table 3.1 State approaches to industrial relations

	Political ideology	Trade unions relationships	Employer-employee
Market Individualism	*laissez-faire*	weak and regulated	exploitative or paternalistic
Liberal collectivism	liberal	strong and autonomous	voluntarist, free collective bargaining
Corporatism	corporatist	weak and regulated	subordinated and controlled, trade unions agents of control
Bargained corporatism	interventionist	strong and autonomous	voluntarist and tripartite

Source: Adapted from Rollinson, 1993

3.2.1 MARKET INDIVIDUALISM

The dominant economic philosophy in market individualism is *laissez-faire*. This philosophy sees the market forces of supply and demand as the ultimate arbitrator of the competitive interests of capital and labour. Thus, labour is seen as a commodity to be bought or sold at a price to be determined by the market mechanism. Trade union interventions in the form of collective bargaining are seen as distorting the operation of the market and are treated with open hostility by employers favouring such a strategy. The *laissez-faire.* option means mitigating trade union strength other than by means of compromise and agreements, typically by increased legislation aimed at placing legal limitations on trade union freedoms. Hence trade unions under market individualism tend to be weak and regulated. Thus, as Crouch (1982) points out, market individualism subordinates employees to the control and authority of the owner and the relationship between them is at best paternalistic but at worst exploitative. In keeping with the *laissez-faire.* doctrine, direct involvement by the State in industrial relations matters is avoided. Roche (1989) refers to this State approach as the 'market control' strategy which sees the Government's role as supporting the reconstruction of competitive labour markets and controlling inflation and hence wage settlements by managing the money supply.

3.2.2 LIBERAL COLLECTIVISM

Liberal collectivism describes a framework which sees the co-existence of a liberal political ideology and the development of strong autonomous trade unions. Such an accommodation sees the acceptance of autonomous trade unions (by management) which represent, bargain and reconcile conflicting interests with management through the collective bargaining process. However, as Salamon (1992) points out, the dominant interests of management are protected through the establishment of a boundary between issues to be decided by collective bargaining and issues to be determined by managerial prerogative. The concepts of 'voluntarism' and 'pluralism' are central to this State approach. In this approach the parties to industrial relations insist on settling their own affairs without State interference. Roche (1989) classifies this State approach as 'auxiliary State control'. The role of the State is primarily facilitative, confined to providing dispute resolution institutions to aid the reconciliation of conflicts of interests which arise, and legislating to provide employees with a 'floor of rights', or minimum standards, which, of course, can be improved upon through the collective bargaining process.

3.2.3 CORPORATISM

The theory of corporatism has its origins in a concept or idea about society which was common in the late nineteenth century. The classical idea of corporatism was a model of social organisation which sought to provide a blueprint for society where the State would function in co-operation with organised social interest groups. Corporatism was intended to chart a middle ground between liberal capitalism and State totalitarianism. The classical corporatists argued that liberal capitalist societies were characterised by rugged individualism and endemic social conflict, whereas totalitarianism was intrinsically repressive.

Roche (1989) defines corporatism 'as a strategy or model of public policy-making in which the State seeks to co-opt the leadership of social interest groups into policy formulation in return for assurances that the latter will seek to deliver their respective constituencies when it comes to the implementation or execution of policies developed in central talks or agreements'.

Lehmbruch et al. (1982) argue that the following statements would character-istically define a fully corporatised system:

(1) Interest organisations are strongly co-opted into governmental decision making.

(2) Large interest organisations (in particular unions) are strongly linked to political parties and take part in policy formation.

(3) Most interest organisations are hierarchically structured and membership tends to be compulsory.

(4) Occupational categories are represented by non-competitive organisations enjoying a monopoly.

(5) Industrial relations are characterised by strong concertation of unions and employer associations with the Government involved.

Corporatism then, as Poole (1986) suggests, denotes heavy involvement of the State, usually taking the form of general legal regulation of industrial relations and the incorporation of trade unions into the State apparatus. Crouch (1982) argues that such incorporation weakens trade union power and finds employees subordinated with trade unions operating as agents of State control.

Two variants or types of corporatism have been identified, namely (1) State or pure corporatism and (2) bargained corporatism.

State or pure corporatism, is facilitated by a concentration of powers in Government, monopoly forms of capital, the absence of associations of labour and political systems with a single party. This form of corporatism either involves massive State coercion or sufficient societal unity to make coercion unnecessary. In particular a unity of view must exist among employers, the State and the trade union leadership. As Poole (1986) contends: 'Corporatism is nurtured by a commitment to harmony and identity of interests at a cultural or ideological level reflected in a range of ethical and political philosophies that include Catholicism, conservatism and social democracy.'

The corporate State is one which is often associated with totalitarian regimes of Fascist Italy and Germany in the 1930s and 1940s and the former Eastern-bloc Communist countries.

3.2.4 BARGAINED CORPORATISM

Bargained corporatism, often referred to as societal or liberal corporatism, describes a State approach to industrial relations which evolves in the presence of a dominant interventionist political ideology and strong autonomous trade unions. It represents the outcome of centrally organised interest groups and of open political systems. Such an approach involves increased Government consultation, negotiation or political exchange with both employers' associations and organised labour through established tripartite corporatist forums at national level. This approach involves the Government, in effect, becoming a third party to the collective bargaining process, interposed between the trade union movement and employer associations.

It is the voluntary nature of bargained corporatism and the consequent lack of compulsion and independence of trade unions which differentiates it from pure corporatism. In totalitarian Communist or Fascist regimes non-cooperative trade unions are often disbanded and membership of co-operative ones made compulsory. Co-operative trade unions are often granted a deliberate representational monopoly. Centrally derived policies on industrial relations matters are enforced on affiliated organisations and in turn on the general body of members. Bargained corporatism, however, entails trade union acceptance and commitment to strategies which may restrain the pursuit of their members' sectional interests. This restraint may take the form of voluntary wage controls to aid the Government's efforts to manage inflation, relaxation of restrictive practices in the interests of improving productivity, a commitment to avoid industrial conflict etc. In a bargained corporatist regime, the trade unions endeavour to deliver their constituents' consent to such restraint in return for Government concessions. These concessions will usually give the trade union movement political influence in the policy formulation process of social and economic issues which normally cannot be attained through free collective bargaining, for example, increased investment and job creation. Employers are similarly enticed into participation in the process in return for such political influence and Government commitments to control inflation, taxes etc.

Roche (1989) has also identified two variants of corporate State involvement i.e., a legislative variant and a social contract variant. His legislative variant is more akin to State corporatism where the State defines and controls the operations of the corporate bodies by statute, including the corporate bodies' ascendency over their members. The social contract variant essentially equates to what has been described as bargained corporatism.

O'Shea (1983) contends that corporatist systems differ from liberal collectivist or pluralist ones by virtue of their more orderly and planful structure and their more intimate and more dependent relationship with the State. O'Shea argues that a central hypothesis of the theory of corporatism is that corporatist systems are more governable and better able to absorb fundamental industrial change.

3.3 THE CHANGING NATURE OF IRISH STATE STRATEGIES

The dominant State approach to industrial relations in Ireland at the beginning of this century was market individualism. More widespread collectivisation and a greater degree of trade union organisation prompted the State to alter its stance to one of liberal collectivism or what Roche terms 'auxiliary State control'. In discussing Irish State strategies since the Second World War, Roche (1989) argues that there has been a drift from auxiliary State control to attempts at corporate control which can be best understood in terms of two phases. Roche suggests that the first phase, during the 1960s, saw the trade unions becoming involved in a number of largely consultative bodies such as the Employer Labour Conference and the National Industrial and Economic Council. Throughout this period, however, liberal collectivism and 'collective bargaining remained inviolate' with any attempt by the State to intervene in pay determination being perceived as hostile by the trade unions who used the threat of withdrawing from these consultative bodies as a means of repelling such corporatist advances. Roche suggests that it was during this phase that the strategic and institutional basis for further State intervention into industrial relations was established. Roche argues that the second phase in the movement towards attempts at corporate control of the bargained or social contract variety entailed the repeated negotiation of National Wage Agreements and two tripartite National Understandings in the 1970s and early 1980s. This period was characterised by active State involvement in the process of collective bargaining together with trade union participation in the process of government. Liberal collectivism or the auxiliary State resurfaced during the period 1982–87 with a return to decentralised bargaining. The sequence of national agreements which have been negotiated since 1987 — the Programme for National Recovery (PNR), the Programme for Economic and Social Progress (PESP), the Programme for Competitiveness and Work (PCW) and the current Partnership 2000 for Inclusion, Employment and Competitiveness — have seen a recommitment by the State and the social partners to pursuing a strategy of bargained corporatism. In comparative terms, Ireland would appear to be weakly corporatised, when compared to the highly corporatised systems of Austria, Sweden or Norway. The issue of politics and the development of State policy in Irish industrial relations has been addressed in depth in chapter 1, and the role of the State in collective bargaining in Ireland is discussed in greater detail in chapter 6.

3.4 THE STATE AS A PROVIDER OF DISPUTE RESOLUTION FACILITIES

A second major role for the State in industrial relations is that of provider of dispute resolution facilities. The voluntarist nature of the Irish system of industrial relations ensures that the parties are free to settle their disputes through the process of collective bargaining by negotiation and compromise. In the event of their failing to resolve any differences they may prefer to avoid resort to industrial action and refer the matter to an independent third party for conciliation, adjudication or arbitration. The State has provided for the settlement of trade disputes in this manner by the establishment of a number of specific institutions. Indeed, from the time of independence in 1922, the State has provided third party assistance in industrial relations. As Forde

(1992) notes, the establishment of State sponsored specialised bodies to resolve trade disputes is a feature of most advanced industrial societies.

A policy of non-intervention by the State will not always extend to the point where it can completely opt out of industrial relations matters. The 'public interest' (which in some sense the Government has to represent) and electorate opinion may often pit the State in the role of industrial peacemaker with the settlement of damaging and socially disruptive disputes seen as a direct responsibility of the State (Farnham and Pimlott, 1990).

In the area of dispute resolution then, the State has established the following institutions: the Labour Court, the Employment Appeals Tribunal, the Labour Relations Commission, Rights Commissioners, Employment Appeals Tribunal and Employment Equality Officers. Figure 3.1 below charts the framework under which these institutions operate in the industrial relations field.

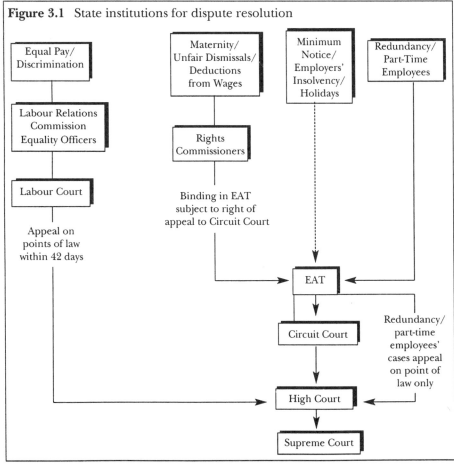

Figure 3.1 State institutions for dispute resolution

Source: Adapted from Wallace 1987

3.4.1 THE LABOUR COURT

The Labour Court is the principal institution in Ireland which facilitates the resolution of trade disputes. Article 37 of the Irish Constitution authorises the establishment of tribunals outside the court system with limited functions and powers of a judicial nature in non-criminal matters (Forde, 1992). The Labour Court was established by the Industrial Relations Act of 1946, with the aim as outlined in the Act's longer title 'to make further and better provisions for promoting harmonious relations between workers and their employers and for this purpose to establish machinery . . . for the prevention of trade disputes' (Industrial Relations Act 1946). Provisions of that Act relating to the Court's constitution and operations were amended by the Industrial Relations Act of 1969 and by the Industrial Relations Act 1976. The effect of these Acts was to significantly expand the role of the Court in the industrial relations system. The role of the Labour Court changed significantly with the introduction of the Industrial Relations Act of 1990 which assigned many of its previously held functions to the Labour Relations Commission, which was established under the 1990 Act.

The principal role of the Labour Court in the Irish industrial relations scene is to investigate and make recommendations on cases referred to it by parties in dispute. These are normally issues where the parties have failed to reach agreement or compromise at local level. The Court has a number of other functions including:

– the registration and variation of certain agreements;
– the establishment and servicing of Joint Labour Committees and the ratification of conditions of employment by these committees;
– the provision of chairpersons and/or secretaries for Joint Industrial Councils; and
– hearing appeals against a Rights Commissioner's recommendations and appeals against an Equality Officer's decision.

Figure 3.2 Labour Court referral procedure

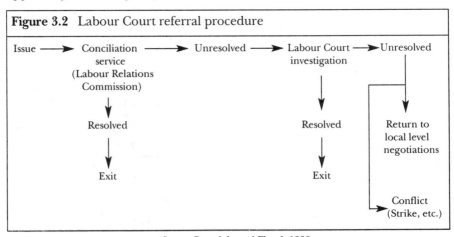

Source: Gunnigle and Flood, 1990.

The Labour Court's referral procedure requires that in the first stage the parties in dispute are obliged to avail of the services of the conciliation service of the Labour Relations Commission. Should an issue remain unresolved after conciliation, it may be then referred to the Labour Court for investigation. The Industrial Relations Act 1990 provides that the Court may normally investigate a dispute in only one of the following situations:

– if it receives a report from the Labour Relations Commission that no further efforts on its part will help resolve the dispute, or

– if it is notified by the Chairperson of the Commission that the Commission has waived its function of conciliation in the dispute.

The Court may also investigate a dispute:

– if it is hearing an appeal in relation to a recommendation of a Rights Commissioner or an Equality Officer, or

– if it decides after consultation with the Commission that exceptional circumstances of the case warrant a Labour Court investigation, or

– if it is referred to under Section 20 of the Industrial Relations Act 1969.

In addition the Court may investigate a dispute at the request of the Minister for Enterprise and Employment.

The Court at present consists of a chairman, three deputy chairmen and nine ordinary members, all of whom are appointed by the Minister for Enterprise and Employment. The ordinary members are nominated for appointment by organisations representative of trade unions and employer associations. The ordinary members are required to always be available to the Court and are not permitted to hold any other employment which would prevent them from fulfilling their responsibilities to the Court.

For the speedy dispatch of business the Court may sit by division. At present there are three divisions of the Court. The operation of a fourth division was suspended in 1992. A division is comprised of a chairman or deputy chairman and two ordinary members, one of the latter being a workers' representative and the other an employer representative. A Labour Court hearing is normally presided over by such a division.

The title 'Labour Court' has often been noted as something of a misnomer, indeed, Von Prondzynski and McCarthy (1989) suggest that the title is misleading. The Labour Court itself has asserted that 'the procedure and general atmosphere prevailing at a hearing by the Court, for the purpose of the investigation of a trade dispute, bears little resemblance to the formalities of a court of law'. Hearings are generally held in private, unless one of the parties concerned requests a public hearing.

Formalities are reduced to a minimum. Written submissions are normally made by both parties, before the Court investigation commences. These written submissions are read at the Court hearing by the main spokesperson for each side but the fact that certain aspects of the dispute may not be covered in the written submission does not prevent a party from covering these additional aspects by the way of a supplementary oral submission. Any points on which clarification or elaboration is required will be dealt with by way of questions by members of the Court. The more fully facts and arguments are given in the written and oral submissions the less need there will be for members of the Court to put questions. Written submissions are required to be in the hands of the Court a few days before the hearing (Labour Court Explanatory Handout).

Witnesses may be summoned before the Court and be examined under oath, and may be required to produce to the Court any document in their possession or control. However, these provisions are rarely used. When the Court feels it has adequately investigated a dispute it will conclude the hearing and set about issuing a recommendation. Section 19 of the 1969 Industrial Relations Act outlines that 'the Court having investigated a trade dispute may make a recommendation setting forth its opinions on the merits of the dispute and the terms on which it should be settled'. Prior to the enactment of this piece of legislation the Court under section 68 of the 1946 Act was obliged to have regard to the public interest, the promotion of industrial peace, the fairness of the terms to the parties concerned and the prospect of the terms being acceptable to them. This section was repealed in 1969 as from very early in the operation of the Court it became clear to the Court that it was almost impossible to reconcile all of these criteria (Kerr and Whyte, 1985). This was highlighted by R. J. Mortished the first Chairman of the Court in commenting that 'a settlement acceptable to the parties might be against the public interest and one which was not acceptable to the parties would not promote industrial peace' (Labour Court Third Annual Report).

An example of a recommendation issued by the Labour Court is contained in the appendices to this book. A recommendation normally takes the form of a summary of the case submitted by each party to the dispute followed by the Labour Court deliberations with regard to the basis for settlement. The Court occasionally makes an oral recommendation at the end of the hearing or from time to time it may issue its recommendations by letter.

The recommendations of the Court are generally not legally binding on the parties to the dispute. They are merely recommendations not judgments which may be accepted or rejected by the parties. McCarthy (1984) described a Labour Court recommendation as 'essentially a third view' for the parties in dispute to consider and that the Court was established 'as a body whose purpose was to promote accommodation . . . to act as an honest broker, neither to apply law nor to create it'. Despite the Court's recommendations only having a morally binding force, the acceptance rate has traditionally been high. A survey conducted by the Court in 1995 found that 84 per cent of recommendations were accepted by both sides to a dispute (Hourihan, 1996).

However, in the event of the Court hearing an appeal of the decision of a Rights Commissioner or an Equality Officer, or where workers or their trade unions refer a dispute to the Court for investigation under section 20(i) of the Industrial Relations Act 1969 (i.e., where the trade union refers the dispute on its own and agrees to be bound by the Court's recommendation) the recommendations of the Court are legally binding. This, in the eyes of the Court 'is in complete accord with the principle of free collective bargaining which underlies the establishment of the Labour Court. The Court's duty is to give a considered opinion as to the terms on which a particular dispute should be settled but the responsibility for the settlement rests at all times with the parties themselves' (Labour Court Explanatory Handout).

Bearing in mind the voluntary nature of its recommendations, the Court has had a very satisfactory record with on average over three-quarters of its recommendations accepted by both parties. Even when Labour Court recommendations are rejected their terms may often form the basis for a solution on return to local level negotiations. Table 3.2 below lists the numbers of recommendations issued by the Court each year since 1971.

Table 3.2	Labour Court recommendations		
Year	No. of Recommendations Issued	Year	No. of Recommendations Issued
1971	162	1985	963
1972	n/a	1986	839
1973	326	1987	837
1974	365	1988	708
1975	403	1989	646
1976	474	1990	529
1977	462	1991	603
1978	546	1992	640
1979	575	1993	652
1980	866	1994	533
1981	766	1995	624
1982	975	1996	522
1983	1,045	1997	501
1984	941		

Source: Labour Court Annual Reports

The number of industrial disputes referred to the Labour Court rose dramatically throughout the 1970s, increasing from 162 cases in 1971 to 862 cases in 1980 and reaching a peak level of activity in 1983 when it issued 1,045 recommendations. This greatly contrasts with the situation in the previous decade when the Court heard on average 100 cases per year. The Court itself attributed this enormous increase in caseload to a general over-dependence on the Court and in many cases the failure of the parties to conduct full and meaningful negotiations at local level, the Court no longer being perceived as the 'court of last resort' (Labour Court Thirty-first Annual Report). John Horgan, a former Chairman of the Court concluded that the increased reliance may have been due to 'negotiators losing the art of compromise' (Horgan, 1989).

In commenting on this trend Wallace (1991b) suggests that:

> . . . it seems largely unacknowledged the extent to which the greater proceduralisation of workplace industrial relations following the influence of the Donovan Commission 1965 to 1968 has contributed to this trend. Dispute procedures in Ireland now almost invariably contain a clause which restrains industrial action prior to referral to the Labour Court. This means that employers and unions can end up referring disputes to go to the Court, not because of any desire on the part of both parties to go to the Court, but because they must do so in order to comply with procedures.

Another telling factor in the dramatic rise of usage may have been the terms of the National Wage Agreements and National Understandings in the 1970s. Bonner (1991) suggests that these agreements contributed to increased reference to the Court. However, the significant decline in the activity of the Court since 1986 was felt by the then Department of Labour 'to be reflective of the improved industrial relations of recent years' (Department of Labour Annual Report 1991). But it would be foolhardy to ignore the high levels of unemployment and the economic downturn experienced during the period as a significant factor.

The number of recommendations issued has continued to decline throughout the 1990s. Murphy (1997) attributes this to fewer referrals to the Court because of the more vigorous policy towards the settlement of disputes at the conciliation stage in recent years.

The Court was seen to depart from its broad role of promoting collective bargaining and resolving industrial conflict when it was given the role as determinant of disputes under the Anti-Discrimination (Pay) Act 1974 and the Employment Equality Act of 1977. Fennell and Lynch (1993) note that surprise was expressed in many quarters with the granting of such jurisdiction to the Court rather than to the Employment Appeals Tribunal. Despite initial reservations by Von Prondzynski and McCarthy (1989) and the Employment Equality Agency among others as to the quality of its early decisions, the general consensus is that the Court has discharged its functions well and has developed an expertise with regard to equality claims. A determination of the Court in relation to claims of discrimination may be appealed on points of law only within six weeks to the High Court. There has been a noticeable downward trend in relation to the number of Court determinations regarding equal pay, being as low as two in 1990. This may be due to a number of factors, but, as Wallace (1991b) argues, most probably to the greater familiarity industrial relations practitioners have with the Act. The number of Labour Court determinations in relation to the Employment Equality Act

1977 has traditionally been very low. Since its enactment there have never been more than ten such determinations a year.

Table 3.3 below provides a brief analysis of the 624 recommendations and decisions of the Labour Court in 1995 as a means of illustrating the range of the current functions of the Court.

Table 3.3 Cases completed by the Labour Court in 1995	
Category of dispute	**No.**
Cases referred to the Court by the L.R.C.	305
Appeals against Rights Commissioners' Recommendations	102
Issues arising from Registered Employment Agreements	72
Other disputes referred directly to the Court	107
Appeals against Equality Officers' Recommendations on pay and employment issues or claims for implementation of such recommendations	17
Cases involving time limits under Equality Acts	11
Direct reference of claims for dismissal under 1977 Equality Act	10
Total	624

Source: Employment Equality Agency, various annual reports

3.4.2 THE EMPLOYMENT APPEALS TRIBUNAL

The Employment Appeals Tribunal (EAT) was initially established under section 39 of the Redundancy Payments Act 1967 as the Redundancy Appeals Tribunal. Its initial role was to adjudicate in disputes about redundancy and to administer the system of redundancy compensation introduced by the 1967 Act. The Minimum Notice and Terms of Employment Act 1973 extended the jurisdiction of the Tribunal to hearing applications brought under that Act by dismissed employees for compensation for loss sustained by them by reason of their employers' failure to give them the statutory period of notice. The Tribunal's jurisdiction was further extended by the Unfair Dismissals Act 1977 with regard to hearing claims for redress for unfair dismissals. It was re-titled the Employment Appeals Tribunal under section 18 of the Unfair Dismissals Act 1977. The EAT currently also adjudicates upon and interprets a number of other Acts, namely the Maternity (Protection of Employees) Act 1981, Protection of Employees (Employers' Insolvency) Acts, 1984 to 1991, the Payment of Wages Act 1991 and the Worker Protection (Regular Part-Time Employees) Act, 1991. The EAT also hears appeals of the decisions of Rights Commissioners.

Table 3.4 sets out the workload in terms of referrals and the outcome of claims and appeals heard by the EAT in 1995 and as such is illustrative of the current functioning of the Tribunal. As can be seen, 5,136 claims and appeals were referred to the Tribunal during the year, 671 under the Redundancy Payments Acts, 3,204 under the Minimum Notice and Terms of Employment Acts, twenty-seven under the Maternity (Protection of Employees) Acts, thirty-five under the Protection of Employees (Employers' Insolvency) Acts, eighty-two under the Worker Protection (Regular Part-Time Employees) Act 1991, and 1,117 under the Unfair Dismissals Acts. In addition the Tribunal heard eighty-nine appeals against Rights Commissioners' recommendations in 1995.

Table 3.4 Summary of appeals referred in 1995 and the outcome of the appeals disposed of in 1995

Act	Number of appeals referred*	Allowed	Dismissed	Withdrawn during hearing	Withdrawn prior to hearing	Total number of appeals disposed of
Redundancy Payments	671	257	128	151	72	608
Minimum Notice and Terms of Employment	3204	2345	330	293	140	3108
Unfair Dismissal	1117	174	162	378	177	891
Maternity Protection	27	–	7	9	6	22
Protection of Employees (Employers' Insolvency)	35	59	12	1	2	74
Worker Protection (Regular Part-Time Employees) Act	82	3	16	19	12	50
Total	5136	2838	655	851	409	4753

* Some appeals disposed of in 1995 were referred in 1994.
Appeals against recommendations and decisions of Rights Commissioners are excluded.

Source: Department of Enterprise and Employment, 1996

The composition of the Tribunal consists of a chairman and twelve vice-chairmen. The chairman is required under statute to have at least seven years' experience as a practising barrister or solicitor. This statutory requirement does not apply to the serving vice-chairmen but in practice they tend to have similar legal experience. These members are appointed by the Minister for Enterprise and Employment. The Tribunal also consists of a panel of thirty-eight ordinary members, drawn equally from nominees of employer associations and the Irish Congress of Trade Unions. The EAT, in similar fashion to the Labour Court, operates in divisions consisting of a chairperson or vice-chairperson and one member from the trade union and employer sides, in accordance with section 39(ii) of the Redundancy Payments Act of 1967. A clerk attends each EAT hearing whose function is to offer mainly administrative support to the Tribunal.

Applications to the EAT are made on special forms (RP51A) available from the Tribunal or the Department of Enterprise and Employment. Employees must give their names and addresses, the name and address of the employer, the names of the Acts under which they are claiming, the grounds of the application and the redress sought (Von Prondzynski and McCarthy, 1989). Employees must also give the name and address of their representative (if any). With regard to representation, an applicant to the EAT may present their case in person, may be represented by counsel or a solicitor or by a representative of a trade union or employers' association (Fennell and Lynch, 1993). Of the 683 claims and appeals heard under the Unfair Dismissals Act 1977–1991, 598 employees (87.6 per cent) were represented (ninety-six by trade unions and 502 by solicitor or counsel) and 566 employers (82.9 per cent) were represented (seventy-six by employer organisations and 490 by solicitor and/or counsel) (EAT Twenty-fifth Annual Report). Employees must observe the time limits specified under the Act that they apply — otherwise they may lose their right to bring a claim.

The procedures adopted by the EAT are similar to court proceedings but there is less informality. Fennell and Lynch (1993) describe the approach of the EAT when hearing an applicant as 'legalistic, individualistic, rights based, heavily reliant on common law notions of fair procedure and assessment of reasonableness'. Rules of procedure for the EAT are outlined in the Redundancy (Redundancy Appeals Tribunal) Regulations 1968, the Unfair Dismissals Act 1977, and the Maternity Protection (Claims and Appeals) Regulations 1981. These Regulations, however, are accompanied by and subject to the principles of 'constitutional' or 'natural justice' (Forde, 1992). Under the various Regulations it is possible for a party to make an opening statement, call witnesses, cross-examine any witnesses called by any other party, give evidence and address the Tribunal at the close of the evidence. Evidence is normally given on oath. Hearings of the EAT are usually held in public, but may be held *in camera* at the request of either party.

The decision of the EAT (called a determination) can be given at the close of the hearing but more usually it is issued some time later in written form. A sample EAT determination is included in the appendices. The EAT maintains a register of its decisions, which may be inspected free of charge by any employer or employee.

Should an employer fail to carry out the terms of an EAT determination, proceedings may be taken by the Minister for Enterprise and Employment to the Circuit Court in order to ensure compliance. EAT determinations are not subject to the principle of precedence as in a court of law. Table 3.5 below highlights the number of cases referred to the EAT since 1978.

Table 3.5   Number of EAT referrals 1978–96

Year	No. of Cases Referred	Year	No. of Cases Referred
1978	1,506	1987	8,537
1979	1,410	1988	6,099
1980	2,478	1989	4,474
1981	2,658	1990	5,938
1982	4,029	1991	4,921
1983	5,357	1992	6,590
1984	5,654	1993	5,710
1985	9,741	1994	4,480
1986	8,019	1995	5,225
		1996	4,097

Source: EAT Annual Reports, and Department of Enterprise and Employment Annual Report 1996

For applicants under the unfair dismissals and maternity protection legislation the Tribunal issues determinations which may be appealed to the Circuit Court within six weeks. At the Circuit Court the case is heard *de novo* that is, there is a full re-hearing of the case. Appeals in relation to the other acts such as redundancy, protection of employees, minimum notice and part-time workers, falling under the jurisdiction of the Tribunal can only be made to the High Court on a point of law.

An examination of the effectiveness of the Tribunal cannot ignore its value as a forum which endeavours to provide a speedy and inexpensive method for individuals who wish to seek remedies for alleged infringements of their statutory rights. Hence the approach of the EAT 'is one concerned with the vindication of a worker's rights rather than the conciliation of conflicts of interests' (Fennell and Lynch, 1993). A perceived difficulty (particularly in trade union circles) with the operation of the Tribunal as a forum of dispute resolution, is that it often translates labour disputes which may have a high collective validity e.g., the dismissal of a shop steward, into individualistic rights-based claims.

3.4.3 THE LABOUR RELATIONS COMMISSION

As discussed in the previous chapter, the enactment of the Industrial Relations Act 1990 heralded the first significant institutional reform in the dispute resolution machinery in Ireland since the Industrial Relations Act of 1969. The Act provided for the establishment of a new body, namely the Labour Relations Commission, which took over many of the functions previously performed by the Labour Court. It is a tripartite body with trade union, employer and independent representation (see appendices), and has been given the overall responsibility for promoting good industrial relations in this country. To this end the Commission provides a range of services which are designed to help prevent and resolve disputes. Apart from taking over the management, co-ordination and policy direction of the existing conciliation, Rights Commissioners and equality services (roles previously discharged by the Court), the Industrial Relations Act 1990 also charged the Commission with some newly established functions:

– to provide an industrial relations advisory service;
– to prepare codes of practice relevant to industrial relations matters;
– to offer guidance on codes of practice and help to resolve disputes concerning their implementation;
– to conduct or commission research into matters relevant to industrial relations;
– to review and monitor industrial relations developments;
– to assist Joint Labour Committees and Joint Industrial Councils in the exercise of their functions.

The then Minister for Labour when speaking of the rationale for the establishment of the Commission referred to the need to have a body with primary responsibility for promoting better industrial relations. Thus, the Commission was expected to highlight examples of good practice and encourage others to adopt similar practices (Dáil Debates, 1989). Kevin Bonner, Secretary at the Department of Labour, and a key architect of the 1990 Act, argued that 'a body such as the Labour Court with responsibility for investigating and issuing recommendations is constrained from adopting a more forceful role in the promotion of good industrial relations' (Bonner, 1989). Bonner also cites the support of some prominent academics for the establishment of a new independent body with this mission. McCarthy (1982), in criticising the previous institutional arrangements, urged the creation 'of a system by which better practices would be promoted'. Hillery (1979), in a similar vein, suggested the establishment of a new institution which he believed 'could play an important role in improving the quality of industrial relations acting as an agent of change'.

Another reason for the reform of the institutional structures (and continuing to be a major objective of the Commission) was 'to encourage and facilitate a more active approach to dispute prevention and resolution' thus placing a new emphasis on the settling of disputes at local level. Another related objective of the Commission was 'to restore the original purpose and status of Labour Court investigations and recommendations' (Dáil Debates, 1989). The stated rationale for the separation of the roles of the Commission and the

Labour Court was to restore the role of the Labour Court as a 'court of last resort'. Kieran Mulvey, Chief Executive of the Commission, argues that the setting up of the Commission had the clear intent of changing 'the almost automatic reference (of disputes) to the Court' (Mulvey, 1991). In debating the 1990 Act in the Dáil, the then Minister for Labour noted the central role which the Court had developed in the 1970s in the resolution of disputes which arose from the terms and the interpretation of national wage agreements. The Minister contended that the industrial relations actors had developed the habit of referring disputes to the Court and had found it difficult to revert to settling their own problems. Relatively trivial matters were being heard by the Court which had assumed the mantle of 'court of first resort'. It was intended that the Court would revert to its original function i.e., 'the final authoritative tribunal in industrial relations matters whose recommendations would once again be documents with great moral authority with the main responsibility for dispute resolution being shifted back to the parties themselves' (Kerr, 1991a). Kevin Duffy (1992) argued that 'in the past the conciliation service was often used as a formality in order to advance to the Labour Court, and the real negotiation took place after the Court had issued its recommendation'.

The establishment of the Labour Relations Commission was not greeted enthusiastically by all. Brian Hillery, Fianna Fáil TD and UCD Professor of Industrial Relations, expressed the concern that the Commission may, far from becoming a significant agent in the promotion of good industrial relations, become 'just another layer of bureaucracy' (Hourihan, 1990). Wallace (1991) speculated that should the Labour Relations Commission become successful in promoting high levels of settlement at local level (at conciliation or in the workplace) the cases coming to the Court will be those to which management were unwilling or unable to give concessions, in other words, hopeless cases. This, he felt, might lead the Court to fall into disrepute with the trade unions in the likely event of them losing a high proportion of these cases.

The Labour Court itself was highly critical of the establishment of the Commission, when the Department of Labour first published proposals for the body in 1988. In a published response to the Minister's proposals, the Court expressed difficulty in understanding:

> ... how the effectiveness of the conciliation service or the quality of its work could be better achieved under the proposed Labour Relations Commission than is possible under the Court. The same staff would be involved, their terms of reference would be the same and the outcome of their work would be unchanged — either the case would be resolved or referred to the Court. (Labour Court Forty-second Annual Report)

The Court concluded that it could not 'envisage the setting up of a Labour Relations Commission as establishing an improved dispute settling service to the constituents of the social partners on either qualitative or administrative grounds'. In fact, the Court asserted that the proposed Commission 'would profoundly diminish the effectiveness of the Court by divorcing from it the right to determine the cases it will hear and separating from it the conciliation service which has always been regarded as an integral part of the Court' (Labour Court Forty-second Annual Report).

THE CONCILIATION SERVICE

The Labour Relations Commission's most public and arguably most important function, and, as Mulvey (1991) suggests, the major ongoing area of the demand for services of the Commission, is the conciliation service. As mentioned earlier, the conciliation service was formerly provided by the Labour Court.

The origins of conciliation in the UK and Ireland trace back to 1860 when A.J. Mundella persuaded both parties to a dispute to set up a permanent conciliation and arbitration board (Farnham and Pimlott, 1990). Official conciliation has been in operation since 1896, with the enactment of the Conciliation Act of that year. Kelly (1989) reports that during the 1920s and 1930s the Department of Industry and Commerce contained a small staff of conciliators whose purpose was to aid employers and trade unions in dispute. The Conciliation Act was repealed in 1946 by the Industrial Relations Act of which section 16 empowered the Labour Court to appoint individuals to act as Conciliation Officers. The Industrial Relations Act of 1969 retitled these officers as Industrial Relations Officers and provided that they 'shall assist in the prevention and settlement of trade disputes and in the establishment and maintenance of means for conducting voluntary negotiations between employers and workers either generally or in particular industries or particular areas or between particular employers and their workers'.

Conciliation has been described as the involvement of an independent third party in the negotiation of the settlement to a dispute (Kerr and Whyte, 1985). The conciliator has no power to compel the parties to reach agreement. Conciliation, as opposed to adjudication, does not entail the offering of proposals by the conciliator as to how the dispute should be settled.

This voluntary nature and the informality of the conciliation service has led to its considerable appeal with both employers and workers. It is best viewed as an extension of the direct negotiations at local level. The efficiency of the service depends almost entirely on the measure of co-operation which is forthcoming from the parties themselves.

The normal procedure at a conciliation conference is for an Industrial Relations Officer (IRO) to preside over a meeting of the conflicting parties as a means of learning each side's point of view. Having listened to both parties, the IRO may hold separate meetings (known as side conferences) with both parties to get a better idea of the basis for the dispute and what is required to resolve the issue. The IRO acts as a facilitator and will try to guide the parties along certain lines in the search for an acceptable solution.

Table 3.6 Conciliation service referrals, 1971–97

Year	No. of disputes in which conciliation conferences were held	No. of disputes settled at conciliation (% in parentheses)	Year	No. of disputes settled at conciliation (% in parentheses)	No. of disputes settled at conciliation (% in parentheses)
1971	628	429 (68)	1985	2,021	1,355 (67)
1972	713	443 (62)	1986	1,892	1,268 (67)
1973	855	487 (56)	1987	1,787	1,151 (64)
1974	951	646 (68)	1988	1,571	1,064 (68)
1975	1,108	576 (52)	1989	1,450	1,019 (70)
1976	1,071	581 (54)	1990	1,552	1,143 (74)
1977	1,175	638 (54)	1991	1,880	1,598 (85)
1978	1,288	651 (51)	1992	1,935	1,451 (75)
1979	1,301	633 (49)	1993	1,844	1,309 (71)
1980	1,375	693 (50)	1994	1,551	1,028 (66)
1981	1,582	766 (48)	1995	1,692	1,184 (70)
1982	1,855	927 (50)	1996	1,487	1,204 (81)
1983	2,090	1,114 (53)	1997	1,588	1,318 (83)
1984	1,750	1,037 (59)			

Source: Labour Court and Labour Relations Commission Annual Reports

There has been a perceptible fall-off in the numbers of referrals to conciliation in recent years. The Labour Relations Commission attributes this to a number of factors including:
– the Commission's continuing efforts to encourage employers and employees to resolve their own disputes through direct negotiation;
– a response to the activities of the Commission's advisory service;
– the increased use of informal intervention such as telephone networking with the parties concerned (Labour Relations Commission, 1997).

As can be seen from Table 3.6 above, success rates in resolving issues at conciliation have fluctuated over the years. The conciliation service had an average success rate of approximately 50 per cent for much of the 1970s. The settlement rate increased to over 65 per cent for the latter half of the 1980s. The settlement rate throughout the 1990s averaged 76 per cent. The 1997 figures from the Labour Relations Commission suggest that the success rates at conciliation are continuing to improve with 83 per cent of cases in 1997 settled at the conciliation stage.

The relocation of the conciliation service under the auspices of the Labour Relations Commission was designed to give a new impetus to the role of conciliation, and to encourage the parties to take more responsibility for the resolution of disputes (Department of Labour, 1990). One possible reason for the increasing success rates is that because of this increased emphasis on the settling of disputes at conciliation, Industrial Relations Officers are now less willing to allow unions or management to use the conciliation service as a stepping stone to full Labour Court investigations. There had been frequent criticisms over the years of both employers and trade unions abusing the system through their unwillingness to settle at conciliation. The gate-keeper role assigned to the Commission by the Industrial Relations Act 1990 is expected to ensure that only issues of substance proceed to the Labour Court, where they are not settled at conciliation.

The on-the-ground evidence of this change in the process of conciliation is evident in the increased number of conciliation conferences held. Prior to the establishment of the Commission, Duffy (1992) contends, parties to a dispute 'may have expected to attend one or maybe two conciliation conferences on a dispute, after which the dispute, if not resolved would be referred to the Labour Court. We are now finding that conferences are being adjourned and re-convened until the Commission is satisfied that every effort has been made to resolve the dispute.'

THE ADVISORY SERVICE

The Industrial Relations Act 1990 made provision for an 'industrial relations advisory service'. The legislation states that 'the Commission may if it thinks fit, on request or on its own initiative provide for employers, employers' associations, workers and trade unions such advice it thinks appropriate on any matter concerned with industrial relations'. This is arguably the most innovative feature arising from the formation of the Commission and is an innovation which has been advocated by academic commentators in the past (Wallace, 1991). Wallace suggests that the rationale for the advisory service is as follows: 'A small number of companies are responsible for a disportionate number of the difficulties which arise in the area of industrial relations. By focusing on these organisations and conducting industrial relations audits and providing expert advice, it should be possible to lower the incidence of industrial action at a national level.'

Disputes are often merely a symptom of a greater underlying problem in the workplace and such problems often remain after a dispute has been settled. The main focus of the conciliation service is to deal with the immediate dispute. The brief of the advisory service, however, is to help identify the underlying problems giving rise to recurring industrial relations unrest where impartial advice from a third party acceptable to management and unions could help to resolve such issues (Department of Labour, 1991). In the past the Labour Court was not always able to examine underlying problems at workplace level which can give rise to frequent disputes.

The conception of an advisory service operating in such a manner is undoubtedly to be commended. However, Wallace (1991) draws attention to a number of possibly significant problems and limitations in operationalising the idea. He notes that persistent problems which arise in organisational settings are more likely to be associated with structural factors e.g., relating to the nature of the work, size of the organisation, economic or financial pressures, the place in the product life-cycle where a product may be located, etc. Many such structural factors are likely to be outside the scope of the advisory service's influence. He also questions the criteria which the advisory service will use in approaching its investigations. Wallace argues that the envisaged mode of operation of the service presupposes that 'good' industrial relations can be objectively defined and can be brought about by a 'set of techniques'. Most industrial relations theorists would challenge these notions. Wallace also points to the fact that in-depth studies have been undertaken in the past with, at best, mixed results. For example, the inquiry into the banks' dispute in 1971, and the 1972 investigations into the ESB did not prevent further disputes arising in these industries in the 1970s.

CODES OF PRACTICE

One of the principal new functions of the Labour Relations Commission is to prepare codes of practice on an unspecified range of matters in industrial relations. It can do so at the request of the Minister for Enterprise and Employment or of its own volition. Codes such as these have long been a feature of industrial relations in Britain and Northern Ireland. Under the terms of the Industrial Relations Act 1990 the Commission is charged with drafting codes of practice in consultation with employer and trade union organisations and other interested parties. When approved by the Commission the draft is then submitted to the Minister for Enterprise and Employment who can make a statutory instrument declaring the code to be a code of practice for the purposes of the 1990 Act. While codes of practice are set in a statutory framework they are not directly enforceable in that a breach of the code will not attract any civil or criminal sanction. The codes of practice are intended to give guidance to employers and trade unions on particular issues, and are intended to have strong moral authority but no more. Thus, the drafting of the codes of practice under the terms of the Act is unlikely to address the problem raised by the Commission of Inquiry on Industrial Relations in their report in 1981 namely 'that voluntary codes possess the serious disadvantage of being least likely to be adopted in the very circumstances where they are most needed'. Codes of practice can, however, be admissible in evidence and can be taken into account by the courts or the dispute settlement agencies in determining any issue to which they may be relevant. Duffy (1992) claims that there is some confusion as to what is intended by allowing codes to be 'admissible in evidence'. Much will depend on the manner in which the Labour Court and other bodies apply the right to take codes into account when determining cases that come before them.

To date one code of practice has been prepared dealing with disputes procedures and procedures for resolving disputes in essential services. That code of practice sets out the type of procedures which should be followed in processing disputes on all collective and individual issues. The code in the essential services proposes the use of arbitration systems so as to avoid the likelihood of the service being disrupted by an industrial dispute.

The Minister has also suggested the following areas to the Commission to be possibly covered by codes:

- protection and facilities for worker representatives in the company;
- provision of information to and consultation with employees on the activities of the undertaking and on decisions likely to affect employees.

The Industrial Relations Act 1990 also assigned the Labour Relations Commission with responsibility for assisting Joint Industrial Councils (JICs) and Joint Labour Committees (JLCs) in the discharge of their functions. The Commission's role is essentially to provide Industrial Relations Officers to act as chairpersons to a number of JICs and JLCs.

Joint Industrial Councils are permanent voluntary negotiating bodies whose task is to facilitate collective bargaining at industry level in certain industrial sectors (Gunnigle and Flood, 1990). They are composed of representatives of employers and trade unions within the industry. Joint Industrial Councils may be registered with the Labour Court. However, Kerr and Whyte (1985) contend that registration only offers marginal advantage to the JIC as accommodation in the premises of the Labour Court and secretarial services are made available to both registered and unregistered JICs alike. At present there are three registered JICs in existence for the footwear and construction industries and one for the Dublin wholesale fruit and vegetable trade. Of these the Construction Industry Joint Industrial Council has been suspended since July 1982, due to an unresolved difference between employer and union representatives. The Joint Board of Conciliation and Arbitration for the Footwear Industry has been suspended since October 1983. The JIC for the Dublin Wholesale Fruit and Vegetable Trade has not formally met since the early 1970s.

In addition to these registered councils, there are eleven unregistered JICs. They exist in respect of the following industries: bacon curing, bakery and confectionery trade, banks, electrical contracting, flour milling, grocery provision and allied trades, hosiery and knitted garments manufacture, printing and allied trades in Dublin, State industrial employees, woollen and worsted manufacture, and telecom. Approximately 83,000 workers are represented by these councils (Labour Relations Commission Annual Report, 1992).

Joint Labour Committees are statutory bodies comprised of employer and trade union representatives and independent members which regulate wages and conditions of employment in areas where collective bargaining is poorly established (Gunnigle and Flood, 1990). There are currently fifteen Joint Labour Committees (JLCs) in existence covering approximately 88,000 workers (Labour Relations Commission Annual Report, 1992). Joint Labour Committees exist in respect of the following industries: aerated waters, agriculture, brush and broom, catering (excluding Dublin), contract cleaning

(Dublin), hairdressing (Cork), hairdressing (Dublin), handkerchief and household goods, hotels (excluding Dublin and Cork), law clerks, provender milling, shirtmaking, tailoring, women's clothing and millinery. A JLC for the catering industry in the County Borough of Dublin and the Borough of Dun Laoghaire was the most recent addition to this list, in November 1992. JLCs are charged with determining the legally binding minimum wages and conditions of employment for those workers represented by them. The JLC submits proposals to the Labour Court for fixing minimum wage rates or for regulating conditions. If the Court accepts the proposals then it makes an Employment Regulation Order (ERO) giving statutory effect to the proposals. Employment Regulation Orders are enforced by inspectors appointed by the Minister for Enterprise and Employment.

3.4.4 RIGHTS COMMISSIONERS

The office of the Rights Commissioner was created by section 13 of the Industrial Relations Act 1969. The Rights Commissioners' service was originally attached to the Labour Court, and its function was to intervene in, and to investigate, industrial disputes with the view to promoting settlement. Rights Commissioners were primarily established to reduce the workload of the Labour Court and to provide a 'prompt adjudication service for what may be regarded as the less major industrial relations issues' (Kelly, 1989). The clear intention at the time was that the Rights Commissioners would be a more informal avenue for dealing with industrial disputes than a full Labour Court investigation. The rationale for the establishment of an office which appeared to duplicate the functions performed by Conciliation/Industrial Relations Officers is still unclear. Forde (1992) argues that they played a valuable role in resolving disputes which were caused by incidents with one or a small group of employees. Since the enactment of the Industrial Relations Act of 1990 the Rights Commissioners' service has operated as part of the Labour Relations Commission but is totally independent in the performance of its functions. Rights Commissioners are appointed by the Minister for Enterprise and Employment from a panel submitted by the Commission and under the terms of the Industrial Relations Act 1969 may investigate a trade dispute provided that:
– it is not a dispute connected with the rates of pay, hours or times of work, or annual holidays of a body of workers;
– it is not a dispute concerning persons who do not have access to the Labour Court;
– a party to the dispute does not object in writing to such an investigation; and
– the Labour Court has not made a recommendation about the dispute.

There are five Rights Commissioners currently in office. They are available to parties in dispute provided both agree to such a hearing and to accept the Commissioner's decision. In practice, Rights Commissioners mostly investigate disputes concerning individual employees. They follow their own procedures and adopt their own practices, having no statutory guidelines to direct their activity and operate individually (Von Prondzynski and McCarthy, 1989). Investigations are held in private with Rights Commissioners obliged to issue a written recommendation outlining their opinions on the merits of the dispute. The Industrial Relations Act 1990 provides that an objection to an investigation by a Rights Commissioner must be notified in writing to the Commissioner within three weeks.

The role of the Rights Commissioners has significantly expanded since 1969 with the enactment of further employment legislation giving them additional functions. They now have a statutory role in investigating cases under the Unfair Dismissals Act 1977, the Maternity (Protection of Employees) Act 1981, since 1992 the Payment of Wages Act 1991 and more recently under the Terms of Employment Act 1994.

A recommendation by a Rights Commissioner is not legally binding but in practice they tend to be observed by employers and trade unions. However, disputes heard under the Industrial Relations Act 1969 may be appealed to the Labour Court, which results in an order which is binding on the parties to the dispute. An appeal against a Rights Commissioner's recommendation must be notified in writing to the Labour Court within six weeks from the date of the recommendation. Cases in relation to the other Acts in which they have a role can be appealed to the Employment Appeals Tribunal. Similarly, an appeal against the recommendations of the Rights Commissioner under these Acts must be made within six weeks.

Table 3.7   Rights Commissioner activity 1979–90

Year	Disputes referred	Recommendations issued by Rights Commissioners	Appeals to Labour Court (% in parentheses)
1979	1,699	506	36 (7.1)
1980	2,025	661	86 (13)
1981	2,057	639	73 (11.4)
1982	1,931	531	63 (11.9)
1983	1,637	583	100 (17.2)
1984	1,445	687	118 (17.2)
1985	1,431	679	109 (16.1)
1986	1,708	603	107 (17.7)
1987	1,732	630	98 (15.6)
1988	1,477	550	76 (13.8)
1989	1,149	455	91 (20)
1990	1,202	43	64 (14.7)

Source: Department of Labour and Labour Court Annual Reports

Table 3.7 outlines the activity of the Rights Commissioners between 1979 and 1990. The number of disputes referred to the Rights Commissioners has tended to far exceed the number of recommendations issued in any given year. This is accounted for by the fact that many cases investigated do not result in a recommendation. Kelly (1989) argues that this is a testimony to the success of the Rights Commissioners in resolving disputes upon intervention.

There was a dramatic growth in the number of cases disposed of by the Rights Commissioners in the early 1980s reaching a peak level of activity in 1981 of some 2,057 cases. The activity of the Rights Commissioner service from 1991–96 is presented in Table 3.8 below. The service has averaged approximately 1,100 investigations in recent years.

Table 3.8 Rights Commissioner activity 1991–96

Category of dispute	1991	1992	1993	1994	1995	1996
Industrial Relations Acts 1969–90	980	965	823	705	618	521
Unfair Dismissal Acts 1977–93	124	110	216	225	247	202
Maternity Protection 1981–94	2	1	3	–	3	3
Payment of Wages Act 1991	–	115	264	279	274	29
Terms of Employment Act 1994	–	–	–	–	12	15
Total	1106	1191	1306	1209	1154	1030

Source: Labour Relations Commission Annual Reports

In 1996, Rights Commissioners investigated 1,030 disputes. These investigations were referred to the service under the various pieces of legislation which have assigned a statutory role to the Rights Commissioners. The bulk of the cases investigated in any year make reference to the Industrial Relations Act 1969–90 — 521 in 1996 — but cases under the Unfair Dismissals and Payment of Wages legislation also represent a significant proportion of the service's workload.

The Rights Commissioner service has been received favourably by all sides of industry, by practitioners and industrial relations experts alike. Kelly (1989) reports that academic analysis of the service tends to be complimentary, with little adverse comment. Noted advantages of the service are its perceived impartiality, flexibility and accessibility, providing a quick and efficient mechanism for dealing with problems which have proved intractable at local level.

3.4.5 EQUALITY OFFICERS
Section 6 of the Anti-Discrimination (Pay) Act 1974 created the Office of the Equal Pay Officer attached to the Labour Court. The title was subsequently changed to Equality Officer under the Employment Equality Act of 1977. Equality Officers deal with issues relating to discrimination on the grounds of sex or marital status arising under the Anti-Discrimination (Pay) Act 1974 and the Employment Equality Act 1977. The Anti-Discrimination Act entitles

women to equal pay for 'like work' while the Employment Equality Act prohibits discrimination against women on the grounds of sex or marital status in non-pay areas like recruitment, training, promotion and working conditions.

Equality Officers operate within the scope of the Labour Relations Commission but are independent in the performance of their functions. When a dispute is referred to an Equality Officer, he/she will carry out an investigation and issue a recommendation, based on the merits of the case. During the course of an investigation the Equality Officer examines written submissions made by the parties, meets the parties and visits premises to inspect work in progress. Equality Officers are empowered to enter premises, examine records or documents, seek information and inspect work in progress in the premises. To impede an Equality Officer in his/her investigation is an offence subject to a substantial fine. If either party is dissatisfied with this recommendation, they may appeal to the Labour Court within forty-two days. The Court's determination in such circumstances is final and legally binding on the parties. There is also a right to appeal the determination of the Labour Court to the High Court on a point of law.

Table 3.9 below highlights the number of Equality Officer recommendations issued from 1978 to 1996. During 1996 the Equality Officer service issued twenty-five recommendations in cases under the Employment Equality Act 1977. This is a little above the average in recent years. A noticeable downward trend can be seen in the number of recommendations issued by the Equality Officer in relation to the Anti-Discrimination (Pay) Act 1974, which stood at eleven in 1996.

Table 3.9	Equality Officer recommendations 1978–96			
	Employment Equality Act 1977		Anti-Discrimination (Pay) Act 1974	
Year	No	In favour of claimant	No	In favour of claimant
1978	5	2	52	n/a
1979	14	8	52	38
1980	14	9	65	48
1981	20	9	55	42
1982	12	2	27	18
1983	22	11	28	12
1984	28	10	27	7
1985	18	7	17	2
1986	8	3	19	8
1987	11	8	14	7
1988	11	5	16	9
1989	12	8	12	5
1990	35	11	13	5
1991	22	16	8	4
1992	22	12	14	4
1993	19	11	11	4
1994	20	9	7	2
1995	17	4	9	1
1996	25	7	11	2

Source: Employment Equality Agency and Labour Relations Commission Annual Reports

Table 3.10 Equality Officer referrals 1991–96

Year	Employment Equality Act 1977	Anti-Discrimination (Pay) Act 1974
1991	67	38
1992	37	20
1993	26	12
1994	32	15
1995	44	19
1996	54	37

Source: Employment Equality Agency Annual Reports

The Employment Equality Act 1977 also provided for the establishment of another institution of the middle ground, the Employment Equality Agency. This Agency is responsible for the promotion of equality of opportunity, the elimination of discrimination between men and women, married and single, in relation to employment and for keeping the two pieces of equality legislation under review. The Employment Equality Agency is also empowered to offer guidance to claimants who bring a case to the Labour Court. The Agency also has the sole right to initiate proceedings in cases of discriminatory advertisements and where there is a general policy of discriminatory practices.

3.5 THE STATE AS A LEGISLATOR

One of the key functions of the State is to pass laws regulating the conduct of the people and organisations it controls (Brewster, 1989). Labour law in Irish industrial relations falls into two broad categories, namely, collective labour legislation and individual employment legislation. Both have been discussed in detail in the previous chapter, therefore this section aims to revisit the topics by means of a summary of the salient points to describe each category.

COLLECTIVE LABOUR LEGISLATION

Collective labour legislation deals with the relationship between employers and collectivities of employees (normally through trade unions) and until recently was almost entirely based on earlier British legislation. Article 50 of the Irish Constitution of 1937 provides that, subject to its provisions, the laws in force prior to 1937 should continue unless repealed or found to be repugnant to the Constitution. Consequently, Irish Trade Union and Trade Disputes law, until the introduction of the Industrial Relations Act of 1990 had remained largely similar to that which applied in 1922 in Britain and Ireland.

The most significant development in the area of collective labour legislation in recent years has been the enactment of the Industrial Relations Act 1990. This piece of legislation has been described as an important benchmark in trade union law. As well as the subject of institutional reform, the Act deals with trade disputes, immunities, picketing, secret ballots, injunctions and trade union rationalisation. A detailed account of this Act can be found in chapter 2.

INDIVIDUAL EMPLOYMENT LEGISLATION
Some of the personal fundamental rights of the citizen are outlined in Article 40 of the Constitution and include the right of citizens to freely express their opinions and convictions, and to form associations and unions. The citizen's right to form associations and unions is qualified by the State's right to enact laws in the public interest governing its exercise. The citizen's right includes that of not being forced into joining or leaving, or being dismissed because of trade union membership. The Unfair Dismissals Act 1977 additionally provides that the dismissal of an employee because of trade union membership or activity shall be deemed unfair. The constitutional guarantee does not preclude employers and employees (or their trade unions) from making agreements specifying which union, or one of a number of unions, workers in the particular employment will join. However, the constitutionality of such closed shop arrangements remains open to question.

The contract of employment, through its common law provisions, constitutes the legal basis of the employer-employee relationship. More recently, legislation has had a significant impact on this relationship with the passing of a number of Acts affecting individual employee rights at work. Since the 1970s several important Acts have been passed and a large number of regulations and statutory instruments introduced under existing employment legislation. Much of this change has been in the area of dismissals and sex discrimination. These pieces of legislation were dealt with in detail in the preceding chapter.

There is a considerable body of employment protection legislation in Ireland providing a basic floor of rights to individual employees. This legislation is marked by several inconsistencies particularly the differing periods of service required to qualify and the different adjudicating mechanisms. A summary of employment law in Ireland is outlined in Table 3.11.

3.6 THE STATE AS AN EMPLOYER — INDUSTRIAL RELATIONS IN THE PUBLIC SECTOR

Apart from its legislative and facilitatory functions, the State plays a significant role as the country's major employer. It employs 188,700 people and its annual pay and pensions bill amounts to £4,806 million. It spends 38 per cent of each year's national output, and its staff make up 18 per cent of those employed outside of farming (Kiberd, 1996). Obviously, the way the public sector is managed will have a critical impact on the whole economy. The State provides employment in a range of areas including the Civil Service proper, education, local authorities and health boards, security forces, and State-sponsored bodies. The public sector is highly unionised having a trade union density of approximately 80 per cent in contrast to less than 40 per cent in the private sector (McGinley, 1997).

In some public sector areas, distinctive industrial relations features have developed but, as Cox and Hughes (1989) note, it would be inappropriate to view public sector industrial relations as inherently different from that pertaining in the private sector. Indeed, the Report of the Commission of Inquiry on Industrial Relations (1981) suggests that personnel problems in both the public and private sectors are similar although differences tend to occur in the procedural responses made.

Table 3.11 Access to adjudication bodies in the public sector

	Arbitration Boards		Labour Court	
	Category	No. (approx.)	Category	No. (approx.)

Civil Service:
  non-industrial
  industrial
	Grades up to
	assistant secretary
	–
		30,800
		
		–
			–
			
			All categories
				–
				
				8,000

Gardaí	All ranks excl. commissioners	11,400		
Teachers (1st and 2nd level, and RTCs)	All categories	43,000	–	–
Other educational groups	VEC clerical, etc., staff	1,000	Other categories	8,000
Health Boards (a)	Officer grades (incl. general nurses)	23,500	Manual and craft grades, psychiatric nurses	16,000
Voluntary hospitals (b)	–	–	All categories	16,000
Local authorities	Officer grades	10,000	Non-officer grades	25,500
Non-commercial State bodies	–	–	All categories	9,000
Commercial State bodies: ESB An Post Telecom Éireann	– – Temporary voluntary C&A scheme for most grades, civil service arbitrator	– 8,500 18,000	All categories in theory, seldom used (b) Legal entitlement to go to Court waived temporarily	12,000
Others	–	–	All categories	49,200
Total		146,200		143,700

Source: Cox and Hughes, 1989

In relation to the negotiation of pay and conditions of employment, a notable distinction may be drawn between those public sector areas subject to agreed Conciliation and Arbitration (C and A) schemes and those which come within the scope of the Labour Court/Labour Relations Commission. The Conciliation and Arbitration schemes which are peculiar to the public sector date from the 1950s and currently different schemes operate for categories such as the (non-industrial) civil service, teachers, gardaí, local authorities and health boards and the Vocational Educational Committees. Approximately 50 per cent of the public sector are covered by the Conciliation and Arbitration schemes. A unique feature of the civil service scheme is the network of staff panels which evaluate any claims from recognised unions or staff associations before these are forwarded to conciliation. Conciliation consists of joint councils of management and employee representatives which consider claims before them and issue an agreed report. The composition and specific role of conciliation councils differ between schemes, and only specific issues may be referred to conciliation. These issues include pay, allowances, working hours, overtime, grading, and policies on recruitment, promotion, discipline, pensions and sick pay. Most claims exclude issues relating to individual employees. The vast majority of issues are resolved at conciliation but those which are not may proceed to arbitration provided they are arbitrable under the terms of the appropriate Conciliation and Arbitration scheme. An Arbitration Board normally consists of an agreed chairman (often legally qualified) and two representatives from both the management and staff side. Detailed written submissions are made by both sides and these are supplemented by oral submissions and witnesses as appropriate. The finding of the Board is sent to the Minister for Finance and the other appropriate Minister, who have one month to approve the report or submit it to the Government. The Government has the option of accepting the report or moving a Dáil motion to reject or amend it — a course of action which is normally seen as exceptional. The local authority and health board scheme differs from the above format in that the management or staff side have the option of rejecting the decision of Arbitration.

In addition to the specific grades in the public sector discussed above, employees in most State-sponsored bodies have access to the Labour Court. Exceptions are An Post and Telecom Éireann who have a separate Conciliation and Arbitration scheme.

A notable characteristic of public sector industrial relations is the role of the Department of Finance (previously this role was executed by the Department of the Public Service). It acts as the Government's adviser on matters relating to public sector pay and employment related matters. It will critically review pay claims, lay down appropriate policy guidelines and oversee their implementation through direct and indirect negotiations. The Department represents the State as employer at the Employer Labour Conference and is involved in many of the Conciliation and Arbitration hearings.

Another important actor on the management side in the public sector is the Local Government and Staff Negotiations Board (LGSNB) whose role is to assist local authorities and health boards in industrial relations. Representatives of the Board act on behalf of management on the appropriate Conciliation and Arbitration scheme and in major negotiations with non-officer grades.

CHAPTER FOUR

Trade Unions

4.1 INTRODUCTION

This chapter considers the nature and role of trade unions in Irish industrial relations. The types of unions, their objectives and their governing structures are reviewed. The chapter subsequently examines the issues of trade union density, recognition and influence using recent research evidence. The pattern of trade union membership is normally evaluated through the utilisation of some measure of trade union density, that is the actual level of trade union membership expressed as a percentage of the potential 'unionisable' workforce. The two common measures of union density are as follows: (1) workforce density: the percentage of the workforce (including the unemployed) who are trade union members; (2) employment density: the percentage of employees who are trade union members (see later discussion on trade union membership). This chapter reviews the changing pattern of union membership in Ireland, and, in so doing, addresses some of the critical challenges facing the Irish trade union movement.

4.2 ROLE AND OBJECTIVES OF TRADE UNIONS

Trade unions have traditionally been seen as the most effective means of countering employer power and achieving satisfactory pay and working conditions for employees. Their role is well established in the Irish context with legislation dealing with the legal recognition of trade unions dating back to pre-independence days. Partly as a consequence of the perceived inadequacies of both individual bargaining and staff associations many workers have come to view trade unions as the best mechanism of representing their interests to employers (through collective bargaining), and to Government and employer organisations on a broader political level.

Essentially, unions are organisations which aim to unite workers with common interests while seeking to define those interests, express them, safeguard and advance them through their interactions (particularly collective bargaining) with individual employers, employer associations, Government, Government agencies and other parties. The basic strength of a union, therefore, lies in its ability to organise and unite workers. By joining trade unions employees provide themselves with the collective means to redress the imbalance in bargaining power which is often perceived to exist between individual workers and their employer. The Webbs, who wrote the first comprehensive history of trade unions and early collective bargaining, came up with what was long accepted as the most comprehensive definition of a trade union: 'A continuous association of wage earners with the objective of improving or maintaining conditions of employment' (Webb, S. and B., 1920:1). While this description aptly describes the workplace collective bargaining role of trade unions it fails to explicitly address the broader societal role of trade unions in advancing worker interests in the political arena. Salamon (1998:85) provides a more comprehensive definition of a trade union as 'any organisation, whose membership consists of employees, which seeks to organise and represent their interests both in the workplace and society and, in particular, seeks to regulate the employment relationship through the direct process of collective bargaining with management'.

This description captures the essence of a trade union's role, namely as a permanent association of organised employees whose primary objectives are to:
– replace individual bargaining by collective bargaining thereby redressing the balance of bargaining power in favour of employees and reducing management prerogative in employment related matters;
– facilitate the development of a political system where worker interests have a greater degree of influence on political decisions and resulting in an economic and social framework which reflects the interests of wage earners and the working class; and
– achieving satisfactory levels of pay and conditions of employment and providing members with a range of services.

4.2.1 LEGAL POSITION
The legal position of trade unions, particularly in relation to their operation and formation has been an issue of some debate in the context of Irish industrial relations (see chapter 2). The main pieces of legislation dealing with the formation and operation of trade unions in Ireland are the Trade Union Acts of 1941 and 1971 and the Industrial Relations Act 1990. Trade unions are defined under the 1941 Trade Union Act as bodies carrying on negotiations for fixing wages or other conditions of employment. This legal definition of trade unions is very broad ranging and extends to employer organisations (Kerr, 1989, 1997; Kerr and Whyte, 1985). The legislation stipulates that, apart from certain 'excepted bodies', only 'authorised' trade unions holding a negotiating licence are permitted to engage in collective bargaining on pay and working conditions. This legislation also specifies the conditions which a union must

fulfil before it can be issued with such a licence. Trade unions may only gain a negotiating licence where they register with the Registrar of Friendly Societies and meet specified criteria, particularly the following:

– Notification: unions must notify the Minister for Enterprise and Employment and the Irish Congress of Trade Unions at least eighteen months before applying for a licence.
– Membership: a minimum of 1,000 members.
– Financial deposit: ranging from £20,000 for up to 2,000 members to £60,000 for 35,000 or more members.

It should be noted that financial deposits are not required where a new trade union is formed as a result of the amalgamation of two or more unions. Trade unions with headquarters outside the Republic of Ireland need not register as outlined. However, they must be legally recognised trade unions in their country of origin and meet some prescribed guidelines in relation to their controlling authority. Otherwise, such unions must meet the notification, membership and deposit requirements set out above. The legislation also provides for the operation of a number of 'excepted' bodies. These 'excepted' bodies are not required to hold a negotiating licence to engage in collective bargaining and include workplace ('staff' or 'house') associations/unions, some civil service associations and teachers' associations (Kerr and Whyte, 1985). Examples of excepted bodies include the Irish Hospital Consultants' Association and the Irish Dental Association. A number of organisations which now hold a negotiation licence and operate as a trade union were originally 'excepted bodies', such as the Irish Nurses' Organisation (Von Prondzynski and Richards, 1994).

The major piece of legislation governing trade union operation is the Industrial Relations Act 1990. This Act deals with trade disputes, immunities, picketing, secret ballots, injunctions and trade union rationalisation. The Act provides for the protection of persons who organise or engage in trade disputes from civil liability. The Act further provides for the protection of trade union funds against actions for damages and the legalisation of peaceful picketing in trade dispute situations. The Act requires trade unions to conduct secret ballots of all members of the union who could be reasonably expected to take part in the strike, prior to engaging in industrial action. The Act only provides for secondary picketing (i.e., picketing an employer other than the primary employer involved in the dispute) where it is reasonable for workers to believe that the second employer was acting to frustrate the industrial action by directly assisting the primary employer (see chapter 2 for more detail).

4.2.2 ALTERNATIVES TO TRADE UNION ORGANISATION
While trade unions have historically been the most prominent means of representing worker interests to employers, Government and other parties, it is useful to consider other means of representing worker interests in industrial relations. There are a number of alternative approaches which workers may

adopt in this respect. For example, workers may deal with employers on an individual basis (individual bargaining). This may be attractive to workers who are in a strong bargaining position such as those in possession of particular skills or knowledge which is highly valued by employers. This may especially be the case when particular categories of labour are in short supply and these workers can command favourable terms and conditions of employment through direct dealings with employers. Individual bargaining may also be attractive in organisations where management place a high priority on individual employee needs and provide attractive pay and conditions of employment. More generally, however, it is felt that individual workers are at a severe disadvantage in bargaining terms *vis-à-vis* employers and, consequently, individual bargaining is not an optimal approach for most workers. This is largely due to the widely perceived inequality in bargaining power between employers and individual workers.

Another alternative for workers is to form work-based 'staff associations' or groups to represent their interests to employers. Staff associations have traditionally comprised white collar employees such as professional and managerial staff, who are not trade union members. The officers of a staff association usually represent their members through consultation with the company's senior management on collective as well as individual issues and have several characteristics of trade unions. They have been viewed by some managers and employees as an alternative to traditional trade unionism. Joining a staff association is often seen as an improvement on individual bargaining since by joining together workers can present a united front to employers and redress some of the bargaining imbalance inherent in individual bargaining. Another related perceived advantage of staff associations is that they provide a collective voice for employees without the introduction of a third party (trade union) into management-employee relations. Some employees may prefer to join staff associations for particular reasons. For example, the traditional perception of trade unions as catering for blue collar workers may create a 'snob' value which encourages employees to join/ remain in staff associations. From an essentially employer perspective staff associations are often perceived as less difficult to deal with and less likely to engage in confrontational/adversarial bargaining approaches. However, work-based associations have been criticised because of their lack of independence from the organisation. Another disadvantage is the absence of an external organisational structure and resources with which to provide bargaining expertise or legal advice. Traditional trade unionists generally take a cynical view of staff associations, regarding them as a poor apology for real trade union organisation. These factors may often combine to limit the bargaining power of staff associations in their interactions with management. Some of the major contrasts between trade unions and staff associations are summarised in Table 4.1. It is important to note that these generalisations may not characterise all trade unions or staff associations.

Table 4.1 Trade unions and staff associations: contrasts

	Trade unions	Staff associations
Objectives	1. Replace collective bargaining with collective bargaining	Similar but less ideological commitment
	2. Pay and employment conditions	Yes
	3. Political	No
Controlling authority	Union headquarters; normally	No external authority strong role for ICTU
Rules/ procedures	Detailed constitution; often with strong political dimension	None or brief constitution; oriented to firm
External resources	Access to external expertise and resources; influence on national issues (e.g., centralised agreements on pay and other economic and social issues)	None except by contracting in
Methods	Collective bargaining: often with adversarial orientation	More consultative orientation
Use of sanctions	Prepared to use strike weapon	Most unlikely
Services to members	May have range of services	Limited

4.2.3 A SUMMARY OVERVIEW OF THE DEVELOPMENT OF TRADE UNIONS

The historical development of trade unions is inextricably linked to the development of industrial relations. The current nature of the trade union movement in Ireland has its origins in the dramatic changes brought about by the Industrial Revolution beginning in Britain in the eighteenth century and later spreading to Europe and North America. Developments in technology, particularly the use of steam power, improved machinery and greater sources of raw materials allowed for the production of goods in larger quantities for wider consumer markets. These developments heralded a gradual change from a largely peasant society based on agriculture and craft production to an industry-based society with new social divisions where greater numbers of people worked in the 'factory system' and relied on wages for their existence. In this new order people now worked together in much larger numbers and on much more tightly defined tasks. This scenario led to the emergence of modern management as a result of the need to plan, control, direct and organise the use of equipment, capital, materials and people in the factory system.

By and large the early factory owners adopted quite authoritarian approaches to workers. Working conditions were very poor and the term 'sweated labour' has come to characterise the conditions under which the early wage labourers worked.[1] Workers themselves could do little about this situation as they had little or no economic or political power. The legal system favoured the owners of capital and it was not until the growth of organised labour through the trade union movement that employee concerns could command the attention and action of factory owners and management.

The trade union movement had become well established in Ireland by the early 1900s, mostly in the larger cities of Dublin, Belfast, and Cork (Mc Namara et al., 1988; also see chapter 1). The growth in influence and power of the 'new unionism', which primarily sought to organise unskilled workers was most obviously manifested in the leadership skills of Jim Larkin and the Irish Transport and General Workers' Union. The festering conflict between employer and worker interests came to a head in the lockout of 1913 (see chapter 1 for greater detail). An important effect of this turbulent period was that it served to accelerate the organisation of employees into trade unions, and employers into employer associations, and thus placed an ever increasing emphasis on industrial relations. After the difficulties and confrontation of 1913, labour relations moved slowly towards a more constructive approach based on negotiations and bargained agreement. The union movement had arrived and employers had to take steps to accommodate it. This was done through multi-employer bargaining via employer associations, and through the employment of labour relations officers to deal with personnel and industrial relations matters at organisation level. Roche and Larragy (1986) estimate that union membership[2] rose from 110,000 in 1914 to 250,000 in 1920 leading Roche (1997a:54) to label this period the 'first phase of rapid mass union membership growth in Ireland'.

However, the period from the early 1920s saw a reversal of this trend with union membership falling in the face of economic recession. This trend reflected developments in Britain where the 1920s were characterised by a prolonged period of trade depression and industrial conflict. Employers found themselves in the driving seat, with little pressure to show any great concern for employee needs. The dominance of an autocratic management style, combined with poor pay and working conditions, led to poor industrial relations. Strikes were common with the unrest culminating in the General Strike of 1926 in Britain. In this period workers and their trade unions became increasingly suspicious of management motives in introducing welfare initiatives in the workplace. The unions became particularly anti-welfare as they saw it as a managerial strategy to prevent worker organisation. Now, with the demise of welfare, trade unions — particularly the new general unions — stepped up their organisation drives and, helped by the numerous grievances of industrial workers, saw their membership increase gradually throughout the 1930s. As unemployment began to fall, the position of the unions was reinforced and collective bargaining became more widespread. In many organisations this period saw establishment of a personnel function but with the emphasis on industrial relations rather than welfare. While the industrial relations aspect of management has its roots much farther back in the early attempts to organise workers in the new factories of eighteenth and nineteenth century Britain, it was not until the inter-war years that management-union relations became an established element of the managerial role. The position of the trade union movement as a significant actor in the industrial relations framework was firmly established in Britain by the end of the Second World War.

In Ireland too, trade union membership increased steadily from the early 1930s. Between 1930 and 1940 trade union membership increased from 99,500 to 151,600, representing an increase in employment density from 20 per cent to 26 per cent over the decade (Roche, 1997a). This trend reflected an acceleration in the level of industrialisation and economic activity. The rate of growth in union membership slowed during the Second World War, a development which Roche (1997a) attributes to a cyclical downturn in economic activity (and employment) as a result of the war, combined with the effects of wage tribunals which controlled the level of wage rises and thus restricted union influence on wage movements over the period.

This phase ended in 1946 and marked the start of a new era for Irish industrial relations with the establishment of the Labour Court under the terms of the Industrial Relations Act of that year. The removal of mandated restrictions on wage movements led to a rapid increase in trade union membership in the post Second World War period. Union membership rose from 172,000 in 1945 to over 449,000 in 1975. This represents more than a doubling of employment density over the thirty-year period 1945–75: in 1945 the level of employment density was just under 28 per cent but by 1975 this figure had risen to 59 per cent (see Roche, 1997a).

The period of fastest growth in union membership was during the immediate post-war period from 1945 until the early 1950s. Aggregate union membership increased from 172,000 in 1945 to 306,000 in 1955, representing an increase in employment density of 18 per cent (from 28 per cent in 1945 to 46 per cent in 1955). One reason for this growth was the greater cohesion of the union movement in negotiating increases in pay and improvements in employment conditions in the post-war period. The advent of the 'wage round' system (see chapter 6) became an important means by which the Irish trade union movement could exert its influence on Irish economic affairs. Wage rounds broadly represented general pay increases negotiated among most organised workplaces and workforce categories over the period from the end of the Second World War until 1970, (see chapter 6 for greater detail). Roche (1997a:56) further notes the significance of a change in State strategy towards industrial relations in helping the development of trade unions in Ireland, notably in establishing the Labour Court and in establishing a new framework for public sector industrial relations:

... the setting up of the Labour Court in 1946 symbolised the advent of a more tolerant or supportive approach to trade unions on the part of the Irish State. A similar change in State strategy was responsible for the granting of recognition to public service unions and the establishment of the civil service conciliation and arbitration schemes between 1946 and the early 1950s. The Labour Court actively sought to encourage union recognition in sectors where it had hitherto been opposed by employers — adding further institutional support to the expansion of trade union membership.

The decade of the 1950s witnessed a continued but much less rapid increase in trade union density. A drag on the pace of unionisation was economic recession, especially in the mid-1950s. The economic climate of the 1960s was quite different and marked by significant economic expansion and employment growth. The decade of the 1960s saw continued steady growth in union membership and density. This so-called 'decade of upheaval' also witnessed a great upsurge in union activity and, particularly, industrial conflict. As discussed in chapter 7, the 1960s were characterised by a marked increase in levels of industrial conflict. The increased industrial unrest experienced over the two decades since 1960 may be partially explained by the huge increase in the pace of industrialisation. Ireland moved in a relatively short period from being a primarily rural, agriculture-based economy to one which experienced a rapid increase in levels of urbanisation, industrial and commercial employment, living standards and education. Inevitably, such dramatic change will create difficulties for a rapidly evolving economy and similar difficulties have been encountered in many other countries.

Behind the picture of steady growth in union membership through the 1960s, a number of other developments in the nature of Irish trade unionism are significant. While not nearly as well developed as in Britain, the emergence of shop stewards as a significant factor in establishing and expanding plant level bargaining represented an important development in both workplace industrial relations and in the nature of trade union organisation (Marsh, 1973; McPartlin, 1997). Another important development which can be traced to this period is the growth in white collar trade unionisation since the 1960s (Bain, 1970; Hillery and Kelly, 1974; Kelly, 1975). Increasingly, workers in administrative, supervisory and other 'staff' categories joined trade unions and demanded bargaining rights with their employers. An important catalyst in this regard was the apparent success of craft and general unions in negotiating improvements in pay and working conditions. Many white collar workers increasingly viewed unionisation as an important means of replicating or improving on the gains of their counterparts in general or skilled job categories. Of particular note here is the growth in union membership in areas such as banking and education.

The 1970s saw a further slowing of the pace of unionisation with only modest growth in levels of union membership. In retrospect this levelling off in the pace of union growth was a precursor to a significant decline in union membership and density during the early 1980s. An important factor impacting on the role of Irish trade unions over this period was the national wage agreement 'era' in 1970–82. The development of national wage agreements marked a transformation from the rather unclear system of wage rounds which had existed since the end of the Second World War. National wage agreements involved centralised negotiations between trade unions and employers on pay and employment conditions which, once agreed, applied to all organised workers (see chapter 6 for greater detail). A key effect of national wage agreements was to move major pay bargaining issues away from the level of the enterprise. Initially this was seen as freeing management from complex negotiations with trade unions and giving them more certainty in corporate planning. At a time of relative economic prosperity and growth in union membership, the key role for the trade union in the workplace — pay bargaining — was removed. However, union officials still needed to justify their role to the membership. With the expectation that pay increases would be derived via national agreements, attention was increasingly focused on matters that could be negotiated at local level, such as employment conditions, pay anomalies and productivity. Far from eliminating workplace bargaining, national agreements merely changed its focus. Various types of productivity deals were negotiated throughout the period. In fact, productivity became an important means for work groups to gain pay increases above the stated maxima in national wage agreements. These contributed to a high level of wage drift during the national agreement, i.e., actual levels of wage increases exceeded the maximum levels set down in national agreements (Mc Carthy, 1977; O'Brien 1981, 1989). Indeed, the emphasis on industrial relations continued to expand throughout the era and one of the great advantages claimed for national agreements, namely, reduced levels of industrial conflict, failed to materialise. Indeed, the incidence of strike activity continued to increase in the 1970s (see chapter 7).

Another development in the post Second World War period which had a significant impact on the Irish trade union movement was the growth of investment by multinational companies (MNCs). Although Ireland had a multinational presence prior to the 1950s, the significant growth of MNC investment in Ireland came from a reversal of previous Government policy of protectionism and movement towards an open market economy in the late 1950s. The increase in MNC investment took off in the 1960s and mushroomed for much of the 1970s. O'Malley (1983) estimated that the foreign industry sector grew at an average rate of 21.4 per cent per annum in the 1960–74 period compared with a rate of 5.6 per cent for all industry (O'Malley, 1983). For many of the newer MNCs operating here — especially those of US origin, the Irish industrial relations framework represented something of a new experience. High levels of unionisation and union recognition, reliance on voluntary collective agreements and non-binding arbitration, multi-unionism and differing employment legislation represented new challenges for such organisations. Of particular concern was the question of unionisation. For many US companies in particular, the prospect of dealing with trade unions was a new departure. Many such organisations had a clear preference for non-union status (Murray, 1984). Even companies who had dealt with unions before were often unhappy about the prospect of dealing with a number of unions representing different categories of workers. Thus, where unions were recognised, this was generally achieved through what became known as 'sweetheart deals' whereby newly established firms agreed to recognise a particular union, or limited number of unions. Such agreements were based on post-entry closed shop arrangements, whereby workers were required to become and remain members of a particular union while in that firm's employment (Kelly and Brannick, 1984; Enderwick, 1986; Fennell and Lynch, 1993). Up to the late 1970s such so-called 'sweetheart deals' represented the conventional pattern of industrial relations among inward-investing foreign companies.

While the two oil crises of the 1970s temporarily affected union membership during the decade, the start of the 1980s witnessed a much more significant decline in unionisation. Employment density reached a record level of 62 per cent in 1980. However, the next seven years saw a steady decline in membership and density so that by 1987 employment density had fallen to 57 per cent. This figure represented a decrease in union membership of approximately 70,000 (from 528,000 in 1980 to 458,000 in 1987). The major reasons posited for this decline were deep economic recession, a rapid increase in unemployment and changes in employment structure involving decline/stagnation of employment in traditionally highly unionised sectors (such as 'traditional' manufacturing and the public sector) and growth in sectors which have traditionally posed difficulties for union penetration (electronics/computing and private services) (see Roche and Larragy, 1989, 1992; Roche, 1992, 1994, 1997a). The harsh economic climate of the early to mid-1980s dramatically changed the industrial relations environment. This period, which was characterised by widespread company rationalisations and redundancies, significantly altered the bargaining environment with adverse consequences for unions. Increasingly, employers sought to address issues such as payment structures and levels of wage increases, the extent of demarcation and, ultimately, the erosion of managerial prerogative by trade unions. Restrictive trade union legislation in Britain and hard line management approaches in many firms indicated a more offensive approach to dealings with trade unions. The negative outcomes for unions of strikes by miners in Britain and air traffic controllers in the US reflected the changed climate of the early 1980s. Trade union membership began to fall in many Western countries. Many of the newer and apparently successful companies had evolved a management style and a corporate culture which rejected collective dealings with trade unions. The term *employee relations* gradually gained acceptance in the management vocabulary signifying the subtle but significant change from 'collectivist' management-union to 'individualist' management-employee interaction (see, for example, Gunnigle, Morley and Turner, 1997). Unions themselves had to adapt to their changing environment. Merger activity increased dramatically throughout the 1980s as unions attempted to both rationalise their activities and improve service to members (Roche, 1988). The most significant merger was that between the Federated Workers' Union of Ireland (FWUI) and the Irish Transport and General Workers' Union (ITGWU) to form the Services Industrial Professional and Technical Union (SIPTU). There is conclusive evidence of increased employer opposition to union recognition since the 1980s and of significant growth of non-union firms, especially among the US multinational sector (McGovern, 1987, 1989; Gunnigle, 1995). Overall, the decade of the 1980s saw a combination of factors combine to create a very difficult environment for trade unions, and contribute to a decline in union penetration in Irish organisations. These issues are considered in greater depth later, in our consideration of patterns of union density and recognition.

The period from the late 1980s to the present seems to have witnessed some stabilisation in the levels of union membership. However, we have limited statistical data for much of the 1990s. Nevertheless, it is plausible to argue that the participation of trade unions which the series of tripartite agreements negotiated since 1987 (see chapter 6) has given unions a much greater influence in decision making on key economic and social issues. Looking at trends in union membership, data based on returns from unions affiliated to the Irish Congress of Trade Unions suggest that trade union membership rose from approximately 460,000 in 1990 to some 491,000 in 1996 (ICTU, 1997; Department of Enterprise and Employment, 1997). This increase seems largely related to the huge growth in the numbers of people at work in the Irish economy. However, in spite of this growth in aggregate membership, it appears that union density continues to fall. Roche and Ashmore (1998) estimate that employment density stood at approximately 53 per cent in 1995. Thus, while unions are gaining somewhat from increased employment, the rate of growth in union membership is less than the rate of employment growth, leading to a decline in union density. Other important trends noted by Roche and Ashmore (1997) are the increase in the proportion of women who are trade union members and the increasing proportion of union members employed in the public sector. Again, we return to many of these issues later in this chapter.

4.3 TYPES OF TRADE UNION

Irish trade unions have traditionally been organised on an occupational basis. This means that workers tend to join a specific union because of the particular job or trade in which they are employed. Trade unions in Ireland have traditionally been grouped into three broad categories, namely, craft unions, general unions and white collar unions. It should be noted that it is extremely difficult to categorise unions as 'pure' craft, general or white collar since many unions deviate from a tight definition of their union category in some dimension. For example, general unions may have white collar and craft workers in membership and not all 'craft' unions operate a recognised apprenticeship system. Thus, the categorisation of trade unions as craft, general or white collar should be interpreted as broadly indicative of union types in Ireland. Other countries may be characterised by different union classifications. In Japan, for example, one finds a proliferation of so-called 'enterprise unions'. These are company-based unions comprised of different employee categories (manual, administrative, etc.) whose sole membership comes from the enterprise in which they operate. Even in the UK, which has a similar union classification to Ireland, Turner (1962) suggests that a more appropriate categorisation of union types is one based on whether union membership is 'open' to employees regardless of occupation or 'closed' to all employees except those working in a defined trade requiring a prescribed apprenticeship or training period. However, the craft, general, white collar categorisation provides a convenient benchmark upon which to analyse Irish trade unions as discussed below.

4.3.1 CRAFT UNIONS

Craft unions cater for workers who possess a particular skill in a trade where entry is restricted to workers who have completed a prescribed apprenticeship programme or equivalent. Prominent examples of occupational categories which are organised in craft unions are electricians and fitters. Craft unions represent probably the earliest form of union organisation and have their origins in the early unions which emerged in Britain at the start of the nineteenth century. These 'model' unions, as they became known, confined their membership to skilled categories such as printers and carpenters who had served a recognised apprenticeship in their particular trades. The first British craft union to organise in Ireland was the Amalgamated Society of Engineers (Boyd, 1972). It established five Irish branches in 1851 and by 1858 it had ten branches here with a membership of 1,300. These early craft unions represented a relatively small proportion of the labour force. In Ireland it is estimated that by 1890 there were only about 17,500 trade union members in total, all of whom were skilled workers (Boyd, 1972). However, the significance of the 'model' unions was that by becoming accepted as important actors in the industrial relations system they created a vital bridgehead in ensuring the acceptance of trade unions as part of the political and organisational framework.

Craft unions have traditionally been protective of their trade by ensuring that only people holding union cards are permitted to carry out certain types of skilled work. It is suggested that such unions, by controlling entry to the craft, have traditionally held considerable negotiating power. This strategy is often criticised as being a source of restrictive work practices and demarcation disputes. Increased mechanisation and consequent de-skilling has had a detrimental impact on the membership and power of craft unions as reflected in the reduction of their share of union members from a high of 17 per cent in 1940 to approximately 10 per cent in the mid 1990s (Roche and Larragy, 1989). Indeed, some older craft unions have ceased to exist as their traditional craft was rendered obsolete by developments in technology and work practices. However, craft unions remain an important part of Ireland's industrial relations system. Figures from the Irish Congress of Trade Unions suggest that the three main engineering craft unions (Amalgamated Engineering and Electrical Union (AEEU), Technical, Electrical and Engineering Union (TEEU) and the National Union of Sheet Metal Workers of Ireland (NUSMWI)) have 6 per cent of ICTU members while the major building unions (Union of Construction and Allied Trades and Technicians (UCATT), Building and Allied Trades Unions (BATU) and the Operative Plasterers' and Allied Trades' Society of Ireland (OPATSI) account for just under 4 per cent of total ICTU membership (ICTU, 1990; Gunnigle et al., 1995).

4.3.2 GENERAL UNIONS

Unlike the restrictive recruitment strategies of craft unions, general trade unions adopt an open approach, taking into membership all categories of worker, regardless of skill or industry. Despite this open recruitment approach, however, general unions have traditionally catered for semi-skilled and unskilled workers. In more recent years, some general unions have attracted white collar and some craft categories into membership.

The origins of general trade unions are rooted in the increased number of unskilled or general workers employed in the large factories and other large organisations which characterised late nineteenth and early twentieth century Britain. These new unions tended to be more militant than the more traditional craft unions of the period. They initially organised categories such as general labourers and dock workers and were noted for both their aggressive bargaining style in attempting to improve the pay and working conditions of their members, and for their greater political consciousness in attempting to advance working class interests. While general unions catering for unskilled workers (such as labourers and dockers) existed in Ireland from the 1860s, these unions only began to play a more active role in Irish industrial and political life in the early 1900s, most particularly as a result of the emergence of Jim Larkin as key figure among Irish trade unionists:.

> The years 1907 and 1913 are outstanding in Irish trade union history for they are the years in which the unskilled labourers, at first in Belfast and then in Dublin, asserted their right to belong to trade unions. In each city this right was bitterly contested by employers ... on the workers' side

was Jim Larkin .... He led the struggles for free trade unionism and will be remembered as long as there is a Labour movement in Ireland. (Boyd, 1972:74)

Jim Larkin was involved with the National Union of Dock Labourers (NUDL) in Liverpool and moved to Belfast as a union organiser in 1907. He subsequently extended his organising activities to Dublin and other Irish cities. After a dispute with the NUDL, Larkin left the union and established the Irish Transport and General Workers' Union (ITGWU) in 1909. When James Connolly returned from the US in 1910 he soon became active in the labour movement, joining the ITGWU as an organiser in Belfast. The ITGWU and other general unions catered for categories such as dockers, carters and railway workers. They became engaged in series of strikes in 1911 and 1912 culminating in the Dublin lockout of 1913. While the fall-out from this bitter dispute initially dealt a severe blow to the general unions they slowly recovered and reorganised and by the early 1920s membership had recovered dramatically (Boyd, 1972; Mc Namara et al., 1988). Larkin left for the US in 1914, and later, after his return, founded another general union, the Worker's Union of Ireland (WUI), having had some dispute with former colleagues in the ITGWU.

Today, general unions tend to be among the largest unions in the country. They are common in all types of organisations and industrial sectors, the best known example being the Services, Industrial, Professional and Technical Union (SIPTU), which is by far the largest trade union in Ireland with a membership of 199,000 (Department of Labour, 1993). SIPTU was created in 1990 as a result of the merger of the then two largest trade unions in the country, the Irish Transport and General Workers' Union (ITGWU) and the Federated Workers' Union of Ireland (FWUI). Overall, general unions account for approximately 46 per cent of trade union members with SIPTU itself accounting for around 40 per cent of the membership (Roche and Ashmore, 1998).

4.3.3 WHITE COLLAR UNIONS
White collar unions normally cater for professional, supervisory, technical, clerical and managerial grades. These unions experienced significant growth in membership, particularly in the period from the late 1960s until the early 1980s. The share of union members in white collar unions increased from 24 per cent in 1940 to approximately 42 per cent in the mid 1990s (see Roche and Ashmore, 1998). In the ten-year period 1966–76 white collar unions increased their membership by 71 per cent as compared to a growth in union membership generally of 30 per cent (Roche and Larragy, 1989). The dramatic growth in the services sector, particularly in the public sector, was a significant factor facilitating the growth of white collar unionisation. While traditionally white collar workers were generally reluctant to join trade unions, Kelly (1975) identified a number of factors which served to increase

the propensity of white collar workers to unionise. In particular, he noted the impact of negative circumstances at work, especially poor job design and general quality of working life, as important factors encouraging white collar unionisation. One can also point to changing attitudes of white collar workers to trade unions, a development accelerated by the emergence of unions designed to cater for the specific needs of white collar workers. The British-based Association of Scientific Technical and Managerial Staffs (ASTMS) attracted a large number of Irish insurance workers and other professional staffs into its membership. The Irish Transport and General Workers' Union became the first general union to explicitly develop a white collar section under Pat Rabbitte, now TD. Another important factor in white collar unionisation was the significant advance in pay and conditions secured by blue collar unions which encouraged hitherto more conservative white collar workers to unionise. White collar categories thus represented a relatively 'greenfield' opportunity for union membership drives in the 1960s and 1970s.

In evaluating union membership statistics it is difficult to differentiate between white collar and blue collar workers. However, the major areas of concentration of white collar workers are the public sector and in financial/professional services. Recent figures from the Irish Congress of Trade Unions (ICTU) suggest that the five largest public sector unions (Irish Municipal Public and Civil Trade Union (IMPACT), Communications Workers' Union (CWU), Irish Nurses' Organisation (INO), Civil and Public Services Union (CPSU) and the Public Services Executive Union (PSEU)), account for almost 17 per cent of ICTU members, while the three major teachers' unions (Irish National Teachers' Organisation (INTO), Association of Secondary Teachers of Ireland (ASTI), Teachers' Union of Ireland (TUI)) account for over 8 per cent of ICTU members. Turning to the financial services sector we find that the two major unions here (Irish Bank Officials' Association (IBOA) and the Manufacturing Services and Finance Union (MSF)) account for another 8 per cent of ICTU membership. As noted earlier, many white collar workers are also members of general unions such as SIPTU.

4.3.4 INDUSTRIAL UNIONS

Pure industrial unions in the sense of unions catering for all workers in a particular industry are not part of the Irish union structure. However, there are some trade unions whose membership is comprised only of workers in particular industries or industrial sectors. Many of these unions operate in the State or semi-State sectors notably the National Bus and Rail Workers' Union (NBRU), Irish National Teachers' Organisation (INTO) and the ESB Officers' Association (ESBOA). The Irish Bank Officials' Association (IBOA), which recruits members at every level within the banking sector, is a union confined to one particular segment of the private sector. Some older unions whose membership was confined to traditional industrial sectors have been absorbed into the larger general unions, e.g., the Irish Shoe and Leather Workers' Union.

4.4 TRADE UNION STRUCTURE AND GOVERNMENT

While it is always difficult to generalise about the structures of different organisations, it is possible to identify a number of general characteristics in the organisation structure of the majority of Irish trade unions. A basic characteristic of the governing structure of most Irish trade unions is that ultimate decision-making authority is vested in the membership and executed through resolutions passed at the Annual Delegate Conference (ADC). It is then the job of the union executive to carry out policy thus decided. The union officials' primary task is to carry out the operational aspects of the union's role, servicing the membership through assistance and advice. The branch is the basic organisational unit in the union structure and it may be organised on either a geographic (catering for several enterprises) or individual enterprise basis. A typical union structure is outlined in Figure 4.1. The structure and personnel of trade unions in Ireland can be described at three levels, namely, the workplace, branch and national level.

Figure 4.1 Model workplace trade union structure

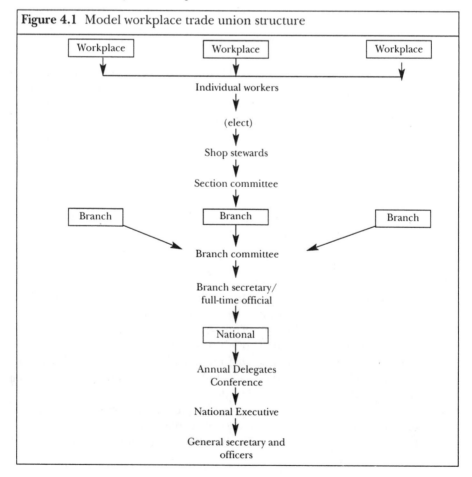

A. WORKPLACE LEVEL

At workplace level the *shop steward* is the key union representative. Their role is to represent employee interests on workplace issues, liaise with union officials, and keep members *au fait* with union affairs. In practice shop stewards may become involved in much workplace bargaining involving local grievances or disputes. On more major issues, their role is to support the trade union official and give feedback to the membership. Salamon (1998:175) describes the role of the shop steward as 'an employee who is accepted by management and union as a lay representative of the union and its members with responsibility to act on their behalf in industrial relations matters at the organisational level'.

An employee's first personal contact with a trade union will normally occur in the workplace. This usually happens when a shop steward invites a new employee to become a union member. The shop steward is the main trade union representative in the workplace. They are elected by fellow trade union members at elections which normally take place once a year. A number of shop stewards may be elected to represent different sections/employment categories within an organisation.

Shop stewards are also employees of the organisation and, as such, must perform their normal job. It should be noted that the Code of Practice (under the Industrial Relations Act 1990) issued in 1993 in respect of Employee Representatives states that such representatives should be afforded 'reasonable' time off to perform their representative duties. Equally, trade union representatives are charged with representing their members in a fair and equitable manner. It has become custom and practice in a number of organisations for shop stewards to be given time off to perform their union role and have access to requisite facilities (e.g., secretarial and telephone). However, these are often minimal and it is extremely rare for shop stewards to be given substantial leave to perform their union duties. This may be because the small scale of most Irish organisations does not facilitate such resources being afforded to shop stewards. However, there have been exceptions in this regard. For example, Krups Engineering, the former Limerick-based manufacturing company, provided for a full-time union representative and a union office within the plant.

In the context of the operation of trade unions, the shop steward performs a number of important tasks. These include:
(1) recruiting new members into the union;
(2) collecting union subscriptions from members in the absence of automatic 'check-off' arrangements;
(3) negotiating with management representatives on behalf of members;
(4) acting as a channel of communication between members and the union central office;
(5) defending and advancing the interest of members at all times.

The number of shop stewards has grown considerably over the last thirty years and particularly in the period from the mid 1960s to the 1980s. This growth is probably due to a number of factors, particularly, (1) the increased acceptance of shop stewards by management; (2) the increase in plant level collective bargaining; (3) the increase in employment legislation and consequent attention to 'policing' employee rights in the workplace and (4) the heavy demands of union officials and associated reluctance of some unions to appoint more full-time officials.

It is suggested that the vast majority of shop stewards may spend about an hour during the working day on their union activities, paid by their employers, and perhaps as much again, unpaid. Research suggests that a considerable number of shop stewards take on the job because they feel they would be good at it, think it is important, or feel it would help them 'get on' (Marsh, 1973; Flood, 1988; Salamon, 1998). A considerable number, however, are persuaded into it. Despite their initial reluctance, they later become highly motivated, finding the role satisfying. Sometimes managers may perceive shop stewards as the source of grievances. However, they are more often seen as the ones whose role is to articulate grievances felt by members. Because of their role they may be more attuned to problems, and likewise they may 'squash' grievances which they feel are not worth progressing. Shop stewards have a difficult situation in that they have to maintain the support of their members while at the same time maintaining a position with management from which they can negotiate effectively. Furthermore, they often perform their shop steward role with little training and/or direction from their union.

The *Section Committee* normally comprises an elected group of shop stewards. The section committee allows stewards representing various sections/groupings in the organisation to meet regularly, discuss common problems and decide on policy. Such a committee is generally called a Shop Stewards' Committee. All of the shop stewards are members of the same trade union, and if the shop stewards are members of different trade unions the committee is called a Joint Shop Stewards' Committee. Joint Shop Stewards' Committees can regulate conflict between unions, and support and if necessary sanction individual stewards. They also constitute a more powerful and unified body for negotiating with management.

B. BRANCH LEVEL

The branch is the fundamental element of trade union organisation and provides the means by which the ordinary 'rank and file' can participate directly in the affairs of the union (Salamon, 1998; also see McPartlin, 1997). The branch comprises a group of trade union members. Sometimes all the members of a branch work in one large organisation but, as is more often the case in Ireland, a branch is made up of people from different organisations who work in a particular geographical area. Figure 4.1 indicates how individual trade union members and their elected representatives are grouped together into a trade union branch. The union branch carries out two important functions:

– it manages the internal affairs of the union;

– it strives for improvements of the terms and conditions of branch members.
The branch is thus the basic unit of trade union organisation and is usually divided up into several broad sections according to the grade or type of worker: 'The branch plays a pivotal role in internal union affairs, as a channel of communication, disseminating policy and instructions downward and the views of the membership upwards' (McPartlin, 1997:82).

Branch policy is decided by the branch at ordinary general meetings and at the branch Annual General Meeting (AGM). The affairs of the branch are managed by a Branch Committee which is normally part time. This committee is elected at the AGM which also elects delegates to attend the Annual Delegate Conference of the union. The Branch Committee and all branch members are served by a Branch Secretary. In larger unions the Branch Secretary will have assistance, and they are all permanent employees of the union. If this is the case then they are known as Full-time Branch Officials whose primary functions are (a) the administration of branch affairs and (b) negotiating terms and conditions for all branch members with management representatives.

C. NATIONAL LEVEL

The election of union officers takes place at the Annual Delegate Conference (ADC). Motions concerning the union and its policies are also discussed and voted upon. The motions are usually branch resolutions and a motion that is approved at the ADC becomes a resolution of the conference and so the policy of the union. As illustrated in Figure 4.1, the ADC is comprised of branch delegates, the union's National Executive Council (NEC) and the union's General Council. McPartlin (1997:82) summarises the role of the ADC as

> . . . to debate motions put by the members through their branches or put by the National Executive Council. If the motions are adopted they are called resolutions and become the policy of the union. A second function of the Conference is to act as a controlling body to which the NEC and the general officers of the union are accountable. The Delegate Conference represents the lay membership of the union.

The National Executive Council is responsible for carrying out the decisions of the ADC. In particular it appoints the union's full-time branch officials and appoints staff employed by the union. The general officers of a union are usually full-time employees of the union and they do not have another job. In some unions they are appointed to their position by the National Executive Council and in others they are elected at the Annual Delegate Conference or by a ballot of union members. The general officers usually consist of a general president, a general secretary, a general vice-president and a general treasurer.

4.4.1 IRISH CONGRESS OF TRADE UNIONS (ICTU)

The Irish Congress of Trade Unions (ICTU) is the central co-ordinating body for the Irish trade union movement. Currently it is estimated that some 97 per cent of trade unionists are in membership of unions affiliated to Congress (ICTU, 1993; Irish Industrial Relations Review, 1993; Roche and Ashmore, 1998). The role of ICTU is aptly summarised in a 1996 IDS/IPD publication as follows:

> The function of the ICTU is to 'represent the collective will and purpose of the Irish trade union movement'. Its main task is to co-ordinate trade union activity by representing unions in national collective bargaining, overseeing inter-union relations, representing the unions on various national agencies as and to act as the voice of the trade union movement internationally through membership of the European Trade Union Confederation and involvement in the work of other international institutions. (IDS/IPD, 1996:162)

While Congress acts as a representative of the collective interests of the Irish trade union movement, individual unions retain a large degree of autonomy and ICTU relies on the co-operation of affiliated unions in promoting its overall goals.

The Irish Congress of Trade Unions was established in 1959 as a result of a merger between the Irish Trade Union Congress (ITUC) and the Congress of Irish Unions (CIU). This merger served to heal a long standing rift in the Irish union movement which was partially related to personality differences and also based on tensions between Irish- and British-based unions (IDS/IPD, 1996). The CIU had primarily represented Irish-based unions while the older ITUC's membership comprised mostly British-based unions (see McPartlin, 1997).

The ICTU is an all-Ireland body with the presidency and vice-presidency alternating in two-year terms between officials from the Republic and from Northern Ireland. The main governing authority of ICTU lies in the Annual Delegate and Special Delegate Conferences. The Annual Conference decides on key policies and the ICTU executive is responsible for policy execution as well as general administration. Ultimate decision-making power within Congress is vested in the Annual Delegate Conference (ADC). Here delegates from affiliated unions consider various resolutions presented by union delegates and those adopted become ICTU policy. Both trade unions and trades councils (see below) are allowed to send delegates to these conferences and to vote on motions. Voting rights are based on membership size so that, for example, larger trade unions have greater voting rights than small unions. The ICTU Executive Council is elected at the ADC and is responsible for policy execution as well as general administration and management. The General Purposes Committee has responsibility for dealing with urgent matters between executive council meetings while a system of sub-committees is used to deal with a range of particular issues as discussed below.

The ICTU plays a particularly important role at national level, representing and articulating union views to Government and other institutions. Its role is particularly significant in centralised pay negotiations. Along with the other social partners (Government, employer and farming representatives), it is party to national negotiations on pay and other aspects of social and economic policy. It is the vehicle through which trade unions decide on participation in centralised pay bargaining, approve any agreement thus concluded, and ensure affiliated unions adhere to the terms of such agreements. ICTU also represents trade unions on several national bodies and provides union nominees for conciliation and arbitration services.

Various committees operate under the auspices of ICTU. As noted above, the general purposes committee deals with urgent business between executive council meetings. Other key committees include the Disputes Committee, the Industrial Relations Committee and the Demarcation Committee. The *Disputes Committee* deals with inter-union disputes, most of which tend to revolve around jurisdiction over membership (McPartlin, 1997). Much of this work concerns interpretation of rule 47 of the ICTU Constitution which regulates procedures for the transfer of members between unions. The *Demarcation Tribunal* deals with inter-union disputes in relation to the demarcation of work. Such disputes normally concern issues such as work boundaries and job content (e.g., disputes between different craft unions or between a craft union and a general union as to whose members should carry out certain tasks). The *Industrial Relations Committee* has the particularly important responsibility of dealing with applications for an 'all-out' picket in disputes. Such a picket obliges all union members, employed in the organisation in dispute, not to pass the picket. This does not impact on the right of an individual union to engage in strike activity and place a picket which requires its own members to obey (i.e., a single union picket). A trade union requesting an all-out picket must apply to the Industrial Relations Committee which must then meet with the striking union, other consenting and/or objecting unions and any other union which establishes its right to be consulted because of its members' involvement.

4.4.2 TRADES COUNCILS

These are voluntary groupings of unions on a regional or local basis. They are made up of officials and members of local unions who meet regularly to consider matters of common interest. They can be extremely influential in determining union policy and are sometimes perceived to relate more closely to membership needs than Congress. Trades councils may become particularly active in relation to certain political issues and were very much to the fore in the PAYE protests of the early 1980s. In 1993 there were some thirty-five trades councils affiliated to ICTU.

In the remaining sections we consider patterns of trade union membership in Ireland, paying particular attention to changing membership trends and developments in the area of trade union recognition.

4.5 TRADE UNION MEMBERSHIP IN IRELAND

In the previous sections we reviewed the nature, objectives, structure and government of trade unions. Clearly, such factors play a key role in influencing the extent to which workers join and remain in membership of trade unions. In this section we focus especially on the issue of trade union membership. We review in greater detail the pattern of trade union membership with considerable emphasis on developments at the level of the enterprise, particularly the issues of trade union recognition and influence.

As noted in the introduction to this chapter, the most widely used indicator of trade union penetration in a country is union density. The two commonly used measures of union density are:

– *workforce density*: the percentage of the total civilian workforce (i.e., including those employed and those seeking employment) who are trade union members;
– *employment density*: the percentage of civilian employees who are trade union members.

The Republic of Ireland is characterised by relatively high levels of trade union density. The number of trade unions in Ireland totals some fifty-two unions. These unions cater for a total membership of approximately 504,000. Using 1995 figures, workforce density was approximately 41 per cent while employment density stood at 53 per cent (see Roche and Ashmore, 1998; also see Roche, 1997a).

As illustrated in Table 4.1, trade union density in Ireland reached record levels in 1980 but has since fallen with the most dramatic decreases occurring over the period 1980–88 (Roche, 1989, 1997a; Roche and Ashmore, 1998). Workforce density fell from a high of 55 per cent in 1980 to its current level of approximately 43 per cent. As noted earlier, this decline in union density in the 1980s is principally attributed to macro-economic factors, particularly economic depression, increased unemployment and changes in employment structure involving decline/stagnation of employment in traditionally highly unionised sectors, and growth in sectors which have traditionally posed difficulties for union penetration (Roche, 1992, 1994, 1997a; Roche and Larragy, 1989; Roche and Ashmore, 1998). In addition to these factors, it is also likely that developments at enterprise level have also contributed to this decline, most notably changes in management approaches to industrial relations. Of particular significance in this respect was the growth in union avoidance strategies on the part of employers and the increased adoption of so called 'individualist' human resource management (HRM) practices (Beaumont 1995; Gunnigle 1995a and b; Gunnigle, Morley and Turner 1997a; McGovern 1989; Roche and Larragy 1989). This issue is discussed in greater depth in chapters 9 and 10.

Table 4.2. Trade union membership, 1945–95

Year	Membership	Employment Density	Workforce Density
1945	172300	27.7	25.4
1955	305620	45.7	41.6
1965	358050	52.4	48.8
1975	449520	60	53.2
1980	527960	61.9	55.3
1985	485050	61.3	47.5
1986	471740	58.6	45.3
1987	458050	57	43.6
1988	440890	55.1	42.4
1989	459920	57.4	44.5
1990	474590	57.1	45
1991	484730	57.1	44
1992	487320	57.3	43
1993	485700	56.4	42
1994	492820	55	41.8
1995	504450	53	41

* Employment Density = Trade union membership/civilian employees at work x 100
** Workforce Density = Trade union membership/civilian employee workforce x 100

Source: Figures are derived from the UCD DUES Data Series [Business Research Programme, University College Dublin and University of Mannheim Centre for European Social Research, Germany] (Roche and Ashmore, 1998; also see Roche, 1992, 1997a).

Looking at trends in union membership in the 1990s, we find that figures from the DUES data series indicate an overall increase in union membership but a significant downward trend in union density. Table 4.2 indicates that union membership rose from 440,000 in 1988 to over 504,000 in 1995 (Roche and Ashmore, 1998). This increase in membership appears to reflect the fact that more people are now at work than ever before. However, if we consider trends in union density the picture is not so sanguine for trade unions. It appears that while aggregate union membership is increasing, levels of trade union density are falling. Roche and Ashmore (1998) estimate that employment density now stands at approximately 53 per cent, representing a fall in union density of approximately 9 per cent since 1980 and almost 4 per cent since 1990. Reasons for growth and decline in trade union membership are discussed later in this chapter. It is important to note that figures for Irish trade union membership do not include the estimated 25,000 members of the Garda and Army representative associations. Clearly, the inclusion of these figures would increase the levels of trade union density in Ireland. Neither do these figures include a number of organisations with 'excepted body' status granted under the terms of the 1941 Trade Union Act.

In comparison to other countries, however, we find that levels of union density in Ireland are quite high. As illustrated in Table 4.2, the level of trade union density in Ireland compares favourably with union density in the UK which is currently some 40 per cent, and is considerably higher than in the US where employment union density as a proportion of the non-agricultural workforce stands at approximately 16 per cent and is confined to a small number of industrial sectors.

Table 4.3	International employment union density			
Australia	42%		Italy	40%
France	12%		Sweden	85%
Germany	34%		United States	16%
Canada	35%		Netherlands	25%
Great Britain	40%		Japan	27%
Austria	46%		Luxembourg	50%
Belgium	53%		Norway	57%
Finland	71%		New Zealand	42%
Denmark	73%			

Source: Visser, 1991

Turning to the distribution of trade union membership by size of union we find considerable imbalance as illustrated in Table 4.3. What we find is a small group of quite large unions which cater for the great majority of Irish trade union members. The remaining unions are quite small in membership terms. Indeed, taking a longer term perspective we see a trend whereby a few larger unions have come to dominate union membership in Ireland: smaller unions are losing members while significant growth in trade union membership is occurring mostly among these larger unions. This may be a vindication of Government policy in the Industrial Relations Act 1990 to encourage the reduction of small unions.

Table 4.4	Trade union membership by size of union * (1996)	
No. of members	**No. of unions**	**% of Total membership**
1,000 or less	16	1.2%
1,001 — 5,000	19	7.5%
5,001 — 10,000	5	7.7%
10,001-15,000	2	4.6%
Over-15,000	10	79%

* This table only refers to trade unions holding negotiating licences under the Trade Union Acts and exlcudes a number of other representative bodies who do not hold such a licence but who operate as trade unions

Source: Department of Enterprise and Employment, 1998

A related and important development in Irish trade union structure since the 1980s has been the significant increase in trade union mergers. Union mergers clearly facilitate some rationalisation in the trade union movement but can also be a source of discontent due to the potential loss of identity and influence of individual trade unions, particularly where a small union merges with a much larger one. The aggregate number of trade unions has declined dramatically in recent years, falling from over 100 unions at the turn of the 1960s to some fifty-two unions at the latest count (Table 4.4). The merger of the two largest trade unions in the country, the ITGWU and FWUI, in 1990 to form SIPTU was probably the most significant trade union merger in Ireland.

Table 4.5   Numbers of trade unions in Ireland holding negotiation licences 1987–96

Year	Number of Unions
1987	67
1989	63
1990	63
1991	58
1992	55
1996	52

Source: Department of Enterprise and Employment, 1998 (Note: figures presented here are based only on trade unions holding negotiation licences and differ from previously published figures which included a number of Civil Service Staff Associations which did not hold negotiation licences)

Table 4.6   Large trade unions in Ireland (1996)

Name of Union	Membership
1 Services, Industrial, Professional and Technical Union, (SIPTU)	226,522
2 The Union of Retail, Bar and Administrative Workers, (MANDATE)	31,308
3 Irish Municipal, Public and Civil Trade Union, (IMPACT)	31,000
4 Technical Engineering and Electrical Union, (TEEU)	26,031
5 Irish National Teachers' Organisation, (INTO)	20,579
6 Manufacturing, Science and Finance Union, (MSF)	20,386
7 Irish Nurses' Organisation, (INO)	19,628
8 Amalgamated Transport and General Workers' Union, (ATGWU)	17,867
9 Communications Workers' Union, (CWU)	15,794
10 Association of Secondary Teachers, Ireland, (ASTI)	15,345

Source: Department of Enterprise and Employment, 1998

The ten largest trade unions in terms of membership are outlined in Table 4.6. As noted above, these ten unions have a combined membership of some

424,500 and account for almost 80 per cent of all trade union members. From this table we can also see that SIPTU, the largest union in the State, caters for over 40 per cent of total trade union membership.

4.6 TRADE UNION DENSITY AT ORGANISATION LEVEL

While national statistics provide us with an overall picture of trade union density, it is necessary to look at union membership levels at organisation level to gain insights into the operational role and impact of trade unions. The levels of trade union membership and the extent of trade union recognition are key indicators of the nature of enterprise level industrial relations.

In examining levels of trade union density at organisation level (the number of employees in a given organisation who are trade union members) the Cranfield-University of Limerick Study (CUL) provides a useful source of information.[3] This study is based on a postal survey of human resource management and industrial relations practice in Ireland's largest organisations and currently has data from 1992 and 1995 (Brewster and Hegewisch, 1994; Gunnigle et al., 1994; Gunnigle, Morley, Clifford and Turner, 1997). In this study respondents were asked to indicate the proportion of the workforce in their organisation which was in membership of a trade union. These findings are summarised in Figure 4.1. As we can see, the level of trade union density in the organisations surveyed is very high, with 64 per cent of organisations reporting that 50 per cent or more of their employees are members of a trade union. These findings indicate that levels of trade union density in Irish organisations are quite high and consistent with the aggregate national statistics discussed earlier. However, as we shall see below in our discussion on union recognition, newer organisations appear to have lower levels of union density and many are opting for a non-union approach.

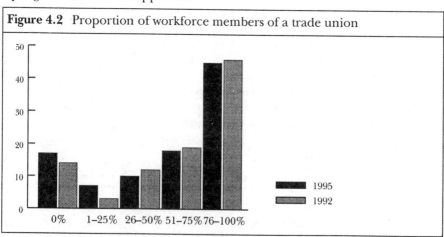

Figure 4.2 Proportion of workforce members of a trade union

Source: Cranfield-University of Limerick Study 1992, 1995 [n=261 (1995); n=228 (1992)]

4.6.1 TRADE UNION RECOGNITION

A number of commentators have identified changes in the extent and nature of collective employee representation as a critical dimension of a shift in employer approaches to industrial relations (see, for example, Kochan et al., 1986). Of particular significance in this regard is the trend in union recognition and the role of collective bargaining. Collectivism in industrial relations incorporates the extent to which management acknowledges the right of employees to collective representation and the involvement of the collective in influencing management decision making (Purcell, 1987; Gunnigle, 1995b). Trade union recognition is, therefore, a critical barometer of 'collectivism' in industrial relations since, in Ireland, the granting of such recognition remains largely an issue of management prerogative. This is not to say that trade union(s) action or the decision of the Labour Court may not convince employers to accede to union recognition, but rather to acknowledge the reality that currently the decision to concede recognition is largely an issue of management discretion. Salamon (1998:175) defines trade union recognition as 'the process by which management formally accepts one or more trade unions as the representative(s) of all, or a group, of its employees for the purpose of jointly determining terms and conditions of employment on a collective basis'.

Salamon (1998:175)goes on to suggest that trade union recognition is '. . . perhaps the most important stage in the development of an organisation's industrial relations system . . . it confers legitimacy and determines the scope of the trade union's role'. By securing recognition an employer acknowledges the right of a trade union to represent and protect its members' interests in the workplace and to become jointly involved in regulating key aspects of the employment relationship. As Torrington and Hall (1991:504) specifically comment, trade union recognition represents '. . . an almost irrevocable movement away from unilateral decision making by management'.

In the Irish Constitution (1937), the State guarantees liberty for the exercise of the 'right of citizens to form associations or unions'. This amounts to an effective constitutional guarantee of freedom of association, embodied in article 40.6.1.iii of the Irish Constitution, and confers the right on workers to form or join associations or unions. The Constitution guarantees this right subject to 'public order and morality', and goes on to provide that laws may be enacted for the 'regulation and control in the public interest' of the exercise of this right. However, beyond this constitutional guarantee of freedom of association, there is no statutory provision to govern the process of trade union recognition. This means that although workers have constitutional support to join trade unions, there is no legal obligation on employers to recognise or bargain with such unions (Commission of Inquiry on Industrial Relations, 1981). In a case of dispute in relation to trade union recognition, the Labour Court may issue a recommendation. However, this does not have legal effect. It should be noted that constitutional support for the concept of freedom of association has also been interpreted to include an implied right not to join trade unions or associations where individuals do not wish to do so. This was demonstrated in a Supreme Court case of 1961 involving industrial action by a section of a company's workforce to enforce a 'closed shop' (i.e., compulsory union membership for all employees). In this case it was held that while the Constitution conferred on employees the right to join trade unions it also included an implied right not to join and on this basis the court found against the union and its actions (*Educational Company of Ireland v Fitzpatrick and others* IR 323 1961).

Historically, this lack of statutory provision in relation to trade union recognition has not been a major problem in Irish industrial relations: most medium and large employers have traditionally recognised and concluded collective agreements with trade unions. However, the issue of trade union recognition has more recently become an extremely contentious issue. Of particular note has been the desire of the Irish Congress of Trade Unions to secure some form of mandatory union recognition where a trade union has organised a proportion of an organisation's workforce. We address this issue below. Before doing this, however, it is useful to look at recent research evidence on trade union recognition in Ireland.

If we firstly look at evidence from the Cranfield-University of Limerick (CUL) study, we find quite a healthy picture of trade union recognition in Ireland. As we can see, from Table 4.6, almost 80 per cent of the organisations surveyed recognised trade unions for collective bargaining purposes (Gunnigle, Morley, Clifford and Turner, 1997). As was the case in relation to union density, these findings present a very positive picture of trade union recognition.

Table 4.7 Trade union recognition		
	1992(n=224	1995
Trade Union Recognition	83%(186)*	80%(205)
No Trade Union Recognition	17%(38)	20%(50)

Source: Cranfield-University of Limerick Study, 1995

However, it should be noted that the CUL study draws on data from Ireland's largest organisations. Clearly, trade unions have been successful in securing recognition in such organisations. However, the picture is not quite so positive when we look at more recently established firms. It is widely accepted that trade union penetration tends to be strongest in the public service and 'traditional' manufacturing (see, for example, Roche, 1997a). It may therefore be useful to look outside these sectors for a more reliable indicator of the changing role of trade unions. The next section therefore considers empirical findings from two recent studies of industrial relations in newly established firms. The first study focused on companies which established 'greenfield' site facilities in the period 1987–92 (Gunnigle, 1995a and b). The second study looked at overseas firms who had expanded employment or established new firms in the period 1994–95 (Hourihan, 1996).

Union recognition in 'newer' organisations
Information on the industrial relations strategies and practices of 'greenfield' companies is a useful barometer of change in industrial relations and, particularly, trade union penetration. Greenfield companies are less constrained by established practice and thus possess greater scope to choose what they feel are 'appropriate' industrial relations approaches and to establish policies and practices which will develop and reinforce their chosen approach. It is therefore reasonable to suggest that if approaches to industrial relations are changing, such change should be most evident in greenfield sites. The study on greenfield site companies found a high incidence of non-unionism, with over half (53 per cent) of these new firms not recognising trade unions (as opposed to approximately 20 per cent in the Cranfield-University of Limerick Study) see Table 4.7. The incidence of non-unionism was mainly related to ownership and industrial sector. Indeed non-unionism was predominantly confined to US-owned firms in 'high technology sectors'. Only four (15 per cent) of the twenty-seven US firms studied recognised trade unions. No US-owned firm operating in a 'high technology' sector recognised trade unions. Interviews among non-union firms revealed that, for the great majority, the decision to pursue the non-union route was determined at corporate headquarters. In general, it seemed that the impact of corporate headquarters in influencing establishment level industrial relations was greater in non-union firms that in unionised firms.

In contrast to their US counterparts, most Irish and European companies recognised trade unions. Indeed senior management in other foreign-owned companies seemed less concerned than their US counterparts with the issue of union recognition. An interesting theme to emerge in interviews with three of the Japanese companies was their preference for single union recognition or 'one grieving voice' as stated by the general manager of a large Japanese company (Gunnigle, 1995a).

Union		OWNERSHIP			
Recognition	Irish	US	European	Other	total
Yes	82% (9)	15% (4)	100% (8)	57% (4)	25 (47%
No	18% (2)	85% (23)	0	43% (3)	28 (53%)

Table 4.8 Trade union recognition in greenfield sites by country of ownership

Source: Gunnigle, 1995b

Hourihan's (1996) study entailed a review of union recognition trends among overseas firms which announced at least 100 new jobs over a twenty-three month period, January 1994 and November 1995, see Table 4.8. Out of a total study population of fifty companies, only twelve (24 per cent) recognised trade unions. When the population is disaggregated into 'new' (thirty-two) and 'expanding' (eighteen) firms, an even starker picture emerges. Of the twelve firms which recognised trade unions, ten were expanding companies. Thus, only two (6 per cent) of the thirty-two new companies recognised trade unions. These findings reinforce our earlier evidence on union avoidance in greenfield site companies. In a period when direct foreign investment in Ireland is at an all-time high, it is clear that these new companies are overwhelmingly choosing the non-union route.

Table 4.9   Overseas companies and union recognition by country of ownership 1994–95

Ownership	Union Recognition in 'New' Companies (n=32)	
	Yes	*No*
USA	0	20
UK	1	5
Other EU	12	
Other	0	3
	Union Recognition in 'Expanding' Companies (n=18)	
	Yes	*No*
USA	7	7
Other EU	1	0
Other	2	1

Source: Hourihan, 1996

FACTORS IMPACTING ON TRADE UNION DENSITY AND RECOGNITION

A number of variables have been advanced to account for variations in union membership and recognition between organisations (see, for example, Bain and Price, 1983; Hirsch and Berger, 1984). Turner et al. (1994) suggest that in general the factors which were found to be determinants of inter-establishment variations in the level of union membership are similar to those that account for the presence or absence of union recognition in an organisation. Green (1990) distinguishes between the supply of an available union to each workplace and the demand for a union, that is, the decisions of individuals as to whether to join. The presence of a union at a workplace acts as a 'gateway', enabling workers to become union members. On the supply side the structural factors associated with the job itself determine whether there is a recognised union available, and on the demand side, individual characteristics also determine whether an employee joins an available union. His analysis pointed to the importance of such structural factors as industry, sector, occupation, firm size, gender and proportion of part-time workers in determining union status (Turner, 1994; Turner et al., 1994; see also Beaumont and Harris, 1991).

Roche (1997a) encapsulates these influences by identifying three sets of factors which impact on employee decisions on joining and remaining in membership of a trade union, namely (1) cyclical; (2) institutional and (3) structural factors, as outlined in Table 4.9.

Table 4.10 Influences on trade union growth and decline

Type of influence	Examples	Nature of effect on union growth
Cyclical	Rate of change in wages; prices, employees at work; unemployment; profits and productivity	*Short-run* change
Institutional	Legislative initiatives; changes in bargaining levels; political composition of Governments; employer ideologies/strategies	May accelerate or retard growth during *particular periods* (shorter term) or on a *long-term* basis
Structural	Changing sectoral/occupational/gender composition of workforce; level of employment concentration; general social attitudes towards trade unionism	*incremental and long-term* effects

Source: Roche, 1997a

Cyclical factors relate to the general business cycle. For example, it might be expected that people will be less inclined to join trade unions when the economy is in recession and unemployment high (and vice versa). Roche further argues that union membership will be positively associated with growth in wage levels ('credit effect') and the level of inflation ('threat effect'). Institutional factors relate to the impact of various institutions (such as trade unions) on industrial relations. Key issues here include the role of Government in regulating the operation of labour markets and industrial relations interactions through, for example, employment legislation (see chapter 2) and the operation of specific industrial relations agencies/institutions, such as the Labour Court and the Labour Relations Commission. An issue of particular importance and one considered later in this chapter is Government approaches to trade unions and, particularly, trade union recognition. Clearly, such factors can act as a spur or an impediment to trade union growth. Another important institutional influence is the nature and level of collective bargaining. Since the mid-1980s we have seen the development of broad-ranging centralised agreements between the 'social partners'. The model clearly facilitates a high level of union influence on major economic and social policy decisions. However, they may also result in the senior echelons of the union hierarchy being perceived as remote and out of touch by the 'grass roots' membership. *Structural influences* relate to the changes in the structural composition and distribution of the workforce as well as to broader social divisions in society at large (Roche, 1997a:45). It is widely accepted that union membership tends to be higher in the public than the private sector. And within the private sector, certain industries or industrial segments have proved more receptive to union penetration than others. For example, traditional manufacturing sectors in Ireland, such as the food and drink sector have much higher levels of unionisation than the computer/electronics sector — an area where unions have encountered severe difficulties in achieving membership and recognition. Employment category, gender and the nature of employment contracts are also influential. Blue collar workers have traditionally been more receptive to union membership than white collar workers; men have been more inclined to join than women and permanent employees more likely to join than part-time or temporary workers. Some recent research evidence on the impact of these various factors on union membership, with particular focus on Ireland, is considered below.

Looking at the broader international literature we find that size, sector, industry and the proportion of white collar, part-time and female workers have all figured prominently as significant explanatory variables in empirical studies on union penetration (Bain and Price, 1983; Bain and Elsheikh, 1979; Booth, 1986; Deery and Cieri, 1991).Variations in union membership levels are associated with shifts in the gender, occupational and industrial composition of potential union membership (particularly shifts in employment in the public/private and manufacturing/services sectors) and changes in industrial structure such as employment concentration, single or multi-establishment status, product markets and capital intensity.

It has been suggested that *single independent establishments* are more likely to have a negative impact on unionisation than establishments which are owned or controlled by a large firm or multinational corporation (Bain and Elsheikh, 1980). It is argued that a single establishment is more likely to relate to its employees in a paternalistic manner in how terms and conditions of employment are determined, and in a personal and informal way rather than by formal rules applied impersonally to all — an approach which may facilitate collective organisation. It has also been suggested that unionisation is affected by the *nature of the market* in which the product or service of the establishment is sold or delivered (Bain and Elsheikh, 1979). In this regard it is argued that union penetration is less likely among firms which operate in highly competitive product markets.

Turning specifically to the Irish context, Turner et al. (1994) found that the level of unionisation was positively related to *establishment size* (number of employees): larger organisations are more likely to recognise trade unions and tend to have a greater proportion of their workers in union membership. As the authors point out, this finding is consistently supported by most of the empirical research on the determinants of unionisation. In their most recent analysis based on the Cranfield-University of Limerick (CUL) study, the impact of *sector* (public versus private sector) emerged as a significant factor (Gunnigle, Morley, Clifford and Turner, 1997). Here we find that the level of union density is highest in the public sector. While making up just over one-fifth of the organisations studied, the public sector accounted for some 40 per cent of the most highly unionised establishments (i.e., 76–100 per cent of the workforce unionised). This finding is supported by other studies, most notably that of Hourihan (1996) who estimated that union density in the public service is approximately 80 per cent but only around 36 per cent in the private sector. In Turner's (1994) analysis of union penetration in Ireland he identified three particular industrial sectors which were positively related to union density: 'traditional' manufacturing had the strongest effect, as perhaps could be expected, while the 'transport and communications' and 'banking' sectors were also positively associated with union penetration. Transport and communications is a traditionally highly unionised sector while banking in the Republic of Ireland is also highly unionised, with the employees in the four largest banks covered by a single trade union.

A factor considered particularly influential in explaining variations in trade union membership is *country of ownership* (also see Beaumont, 1985; Gunnigle, 1995b). In particular, US-owned companies in the electronics industry are reputed to pursue an active strategy of union avoidance or union marginalisation through the use of human resource management (HRM) practices such as individual employment contracts, direct employee communication and the prompt handling of grievances (McGovern, 1989c; Gunnigle, 1995a and b). The CUL study found that country of ownership had a significant impact on the proportion of an organisation's workforce which were trade union members. Irish and other European-owned organisations tended to have the highest levels of union membership while US-owned organisations tended to have significantly lower levels of union recognition and density. On the issue of trade union recognition, the CUL study also found a significant variation between different organisations. US-owned organisations were less likely to recognise trade unions: some 69 per cent of US-owned organisations recognised trade unions while the corresponding figure for Irish and other foreign-owned organisations was more than 80 per cent. We have seen earlier that recent studies of newly established firms in the manufacturing and internationally traded services sectors point to an even higher incidence of non-union approaches by US-owned firms (Gunnigle, 1995a and b; Hourihan, 1996). Country of ownership is widely used as a proxy measure of the impact of managerial values on variations in the extent of trade union recognition. This approach is based on the assumption that decisions on trade union recognition will closely reflect underlying managerial values associated with country of ownership (Poole, 1986; Guest and Rosenthal, 1992). These findings bear out the suggestion that US-owned organisations are more likely to pursue a strategy of union avoidance (Beaumont, 1985; Kochan et al., 1986).

In concluding our analysis of patterns of trade union density and recognition in Ireland we can see that national statistics and information from larger, and older organisations indicate that trade union penetration in Ireland remains quite robust with high levels of union recognition and union density characterising most of Ireland's larger organisations. However, evidence from more recently established organisations, particularly those in the manufacturing and internationally traded services sectors, is less sanguine for trade unions. Here we find a significant trend towards union avoidance, especially among greenfield site companies. This issue is considered further in subsequent chapters and in our consideration of recent developments in the area of union recognition, discussed below.

4.6.2 TRADE UNION INFLUENCE AND THE NATURE OF MANAGEMENT-UNION RELATIONS
While analyses of trade union density and recognition are relatively straightforward and objective, assessing trade union influence is an altogether more complex task. Firstly, and unlike 'hard' measures such as membership and recognition, influence is largely perceptual. Secondly, influence can differ depending on the nature and type of influence we are talking about. For example, it is generally accepted that the existence of centralised agreements on pay and related matters since 1987 has greatly facilitated high levels of union influence on national affairs, particularly in areas of economic and social policy. In attempting to more accurately assess union influence at enterprise level, trade union recognition and density are useful proxies for union influence. We have seen earlier that the available data on trade union density and recognition point to some decline in union representativeness. However, we have also noted that union penetration in Ireland remains comparatively high by international standards.

Alongside the 'hard' indicators of trade union penetration, the CUL study explored management perceptions of the changing influence of trade unions (Gunnigle, Morley, Clifford and Turner, 1997). The CUL study asked respondents to indicate whether they felt the influence of trade unions had increased, decreased or remained stable in their organisation over the past three years. The results are summarised in Figure 4.2 and provide a relatively stable picture of union influence. Over seven in ten of respondents reported that trade union influence in their organisation had remained stable over recent years. Looking only at those organisations where respondents reported a change in union influence, we find that over three times as many firms report a decrease (22 per cent) as opposed to an increase (7 per cent) in union influence. As we can see from Figure 4.2, there were no significant differences between 1992 and 1995. Looking at potential explanatory factors impacting on perceived levels of union influence, the CUL study found that the decline in union influence was positively associated with *large organisations*, being in the *private sector* and with *European ownership*.

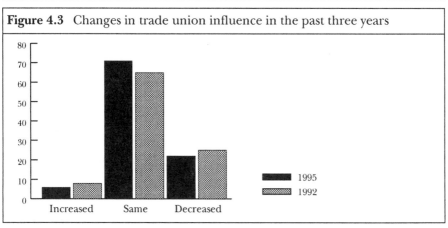

Figure 4.3 Changes in trade union influence in the past three years

Source: Cranfield-University of Limerick Study, 1995

The greenfield site study, discussed earlier, provides some additional insights into union influence at the enterprise level. This study considered the impact of trade unions on workplace level employee relations and found that a majority of companies (56 per cent) which recognised trade unions felt that unions had either a major or considerable impact on workplace employee relations; see table 4.10. However, it appears significant that respondents in 44 per cent of unionised firms felt that trade unions had either a 'minor' or little impact on workplace employee relations.

Table 4.11 Impact of trade unions in workplace employee relations

Impact of trade unions on workplace employee relations	As % of firms recognising trade unions
Major impact	8% (2)
Considerable impact	48% (12)
Minor impact	36% (9)
Little/no impact	8% (2)
Total	100% (25)

Source: Gunnigle, 1995a

In terms of management-union relations, it was significant that senior management representatives in all of the companies with union recognition reported that they had very good relations with their trade unions(s). Indeed, in all but one company, management respondents suggested that unions had a generally positive impact on both employee relations and organisation performance generally. The only company where management felt that trade unions inhibited company performance 'to some extent' was the single company which recognised a large number of trade unions. This company was a subsidiary of an older Irish company which had established a greenfield site in an effort to implement more 'innovative and flexible work practices'. Here, management felt that multi-unionism and some demarcations and other work practices impinged on its competitiveness, particularly in relation to new entrants to the industry (aircraft maintenance) who were implementing more flexible work practices and had lower unit labour costs.

4.6.3 CURRENT ISSUES AFFECTING TRADE UNIONS — THE DEBATE ON UNION RECOGNITION
A particular issue in the context of changing patterns of industrial relations concerns trade union recognition and the future role of collective bargaining. We have already seen that the 1980s witnessed a most serious decline in trade union density. We have also noted that this decline has principally been attributed to macro-economic factors, notably economic depression and increased levels of unemployment during the 1980s and changes in employment structure and developments (Roche and Larragy, 1989; Roche, 1992). However, there is also widespread evidence of increased employer opposition to union recognition (McGovern, 1989; Gunnigle, 1995b; Hourihan, 1996). Our earlier analysis of trends in trade union density and recognition have highlighted these developments, which are considered further in chapters 9 and 10.

The decline in trade union penetration in new firms, particularly in 'high technology' sectors is clearly an issue of concern for trade unions. Indeed, the Irish trade union movement, principally through the Irish Congress of Trade Unions, has been to the fore in evaluating means of increasing union influence, legitimacy and representativeness at both enterprise and national level (ICTU, 1993, 1995; Beaumont, 1995a; Sparrow and Hiltrop, 1994). A critical part of this strategy involved raising the issue of union recognition in discussions on centralised agreements. Most recently, it was agreed, under the terms of Partnership 2000, (see chapter 6) that a 'high level working group' be established to consider the issue of trade union recognition disputes. This working group comprised a broad membership representative of Government departments, Irish Congress of Trade Unions, Irish Business and Employers Confederation and the Industrial Development Agency. It submitted its report in late 1997 and the text of its draft recommendations is outlined in Table 4.12.

The gist of these proposals is that disputes in relation to union recognition should be dealt with in the context of the current system of voluntary collective bargaining. The proposals suggest that disputes in relation to union recognition should be dealt with through a series of steps, involving the Labour Relations Commission and its Advisory Service, the use of a 'cooling-off' period for intractable disputes and, ultimately, for a recommendation on the case by the Labour Court, with these general principles being incorporated into a voluntary code of practice. As outlined earlier, the present situation in relation to trade union recognition disputes is that the Labour

Table 4.12 Draft agreement on trade union recognition proposed by high level group established under terms of Partnership 2000

The parties to *Partnership 2000* are agreed that where negotiating arrangements are in place, the most effective means of resolving differences which arise between the employers and trade unions representing employees is by voluntary collective bargaining. Where collective bargaining fails to take place the following process should be put in place with which management and unions should fully co-operate in seeking to resolve the issue(s) in dispute effectively and expeditiously.

1. In the first instance the matter should be referred to the Labour Relations Commission who will appoint an Officer from its Advisory Service to assess the issues in dispute.
2. The Labour Relations Commission Officer will work with the parties in an attempt to resolve the issues in dispute.
3. In the event that the issues in dispute are not capable of early resolution by the Labour Relations Commission intervention, an agreed cooling-off period shall be put in place.
4. During the cooling-off period, the Labour Relations Commission Advisory Service will continue to work with the parties in an attempt to resolve any outstanding issues. The Commission may engage expert assistance, including the involvement of ICTU and IBEC, should that prove helpful to the resolution of any differences.
5. If after the cooling-off period all issues have been resolved, the Labour Relations Commission will disengage. Before disengaging, the Commission may make proposals to the parties for the peaceful resolution of any further grievances or disputes.
6. In the event of issues remaining unresolved after the cooling-off period, the Labour Relations Commission shall make a written report to the Labour Court on the situation, the Labour Court shall consider the position of the employer and the Union and shall issue recommendations on outstanding matters.

The High Level Group established under Paragraph 9.22 of Partnership 2000 believes that the general principles outlined above should be incorporated in a Code of Practice under section 42 of the Industrial Relations Act 1990. Further, the Group believes that the Code of Practice, once established, should have the full support of all parties concerned.

Court may issue a recommendation on cases referred to it but there is no compulsion on either party to accept such recommendation. We have also seen that in such cases the Labour Court generally recommends in favour of union recognition (Gunnigle, 1995a; 1998c). Based on the proposals of the High Level Working Group, any Labour Court recommendation would be similar to that which the Court already recommends today, namely a non-binding recommendation but with, perhaps, greater moral force than heretofore (*Industrial Relations News*, 1998a).

In evaluating the extent of union avoidance, the report identified two major areas where non-recognition of unions was common: small indigenous firms and the multinational sector. In the multinational sector the report suggests that non-union approaches are particularly common among US-owned firms and are generally associated with the adoption of well developed human resource management policies and systems. The report further suggests that because of the 'generally high value-added nature of the enterprises concerned' and the presence of 'generally good' terms and conditions of employment, employees in this sector do not generally seek to join trade unions to protect or advance their interests. In the Irish context, there is some empirical evidence both in support of and against this argument. Toner's (1987) findings in the electronics sector pointed to the presence of good terms and conditions of employment among the non-union firms studied (also see Flood and Toner, 1997). However, Gunnigle's (1995a and b) study of greenfield firms does not support the thesis that non-union firms provide pay and benefits which are above either the regional or sectoral norms or better than those provided by similar unionised firms.

From a trade union perspective, a critical element of this report is its lack of support for any mandatory system through which union recognition would be imposed upon recalcitrant employers. The high level group clearly opposed this approach, apparently on the grounds of its incongruity with Ireland's tradition of voluntary collective bargaining: 'A requirement for mandatory trade union recognition would represent a shift from the current largely voluntary system of industrial relations which has demonstrated a capacity to adapt to changing circumstances and which is generally seen as very valuable.'

In evaluating the international experience on mandatory union recognition, presumably based on the US context, the group argued that mandatory approaches can bring about a more adversarial and legalistic industrial relations system.

Looking at the broader context within which this report was formulated, a number of issues should be borne in mind. Of primary significance is the fact that much of Ireland's economic growth since the 1980s has been fuelled by the multinational sector, a substantial proportion of which are US non-union firms. Union avoidance is often a core value in many such firms. In seeking to attract more direct foreign investment and encourage firms already here to increase investment, Governments are acutely aware that imposition of mandatory union recognition mechanisms would act as a severe disincentive to such investment. The IDA, as members of the high level group, would clearly have articulated the implications of mandatory union recognition as a significant disadvantage in their efforts in selling Ireland as a site for direct foreign investment (Gunnigle, 1995a and b; 1998c). From the employers' perspective it is also likely that they sought to ensure that the report did not recommend approaches which would have a negative impact on multinational investment. Given that a considerable proportion of IBEC membership is comprised of non-union firms it is unlikely that their representatives would agree to any legally binding system of dealing with trade union recognition disputes. Indeed, from an employer perspective, these proposals may represent a considerable improvement on the pre-existing situation, since they recommend that both parties become 'locked in' to voluntary procedures until a Labour Court recommendation is issued and considered (*Industrial Relations News*, 1998b).

As noted in the *Industrial Relations News* (1998a) report on this issue, it is likely that these draft proposals will encounter considerable opposition and criticism from trade union members and officials. It is clear that these recommendations fall some way short of the mandatory trade union recognition called for by many trade union officials and activists over the past decade (*Industrial Relations News*, 1998a and b).

4.7 OTHER ISSUES FACING TRADE UNIONS

In concluding this chapter, it is useful to briefly address some other important issues facing trade unions at the start of a new millennium.

TRADE UNION RATIONALISATION

A common criticism of Irish trade union structure is that there are too many unions relative to total membership. It has been suggested that this causes problems for management who have to deal with a number of unions and also leads to inter-union rivalry and conflict as unions compete with each other for membership. At an aggregate level Ireland does have a large number of unions dealing with a small membership (some fifty-two unions cater for a total membership of approximately 504,000). However, as noted earlier, a closer examination of aggregate union membership statistics indicates that the vast majority of trade unionists are members of a small number of quite large trade unions leaving a large number of small unions which cater for a very small proportion of total union membership (see Table 4.3). Rationalisation of trade union structure in Ireland has been high on the agenda of successive Governments. McPartlin (1997) found a major increase in the number of union mergers from 1985 onwards. In 1990 the merger of the ITGWU and the FWUI, the then two largest trade unions in the country, to form SIPTU, heralded a wave of negotiations by trade unions on possible mergers and amalgamations. As a result, the number of trade unions in the Republic has declined dramatically in recent years. The total number of trade unions in Ireland has fallen from over ninety unions in the 1960s to just over fifty unions today leading McPartlin (1997:95) to conclude that '... Irish trade unionism is no longer the fragmented and conflicted movement that has so often been criticised in the past'. However, one possible downside of this rationalisation in the Irish trade movement is that we may also concurrently experience some dissatisfaction with merger activity due to a loss of identity and influence of some unions as a result of union mergers, particularly those involving the merger of small unions with much larger ones.

BRITISH AND IRISH UNIONS

A unique characteristic of Irish trade union structure is the fact that a number of British-based unions operate in the Republic of Ireland. Figures from the Irish Congress of Trade Unions (ICTU) suggest that there are some thirteen British-based unions operating in the Republic of Ireland (*Irish Industrial Relations Review*, 1993). Roche and Ashmore (1998) estimate that in 1995

British-based unions accounted for approximately 11.5 per cent of total union membership in Ireland. These include major unions such as the Amalgamated Transport and General Workers' Union (ATGWU) and the Manufacturing Science and Finance Union (MSF). Because trade unions rely primarily on current income from membership subscriptions, these unions are often in a strong financial position to service their Irish membership. However, major policy decisions in such unions are often taken in Britain and there has been some debate on the priority accorded to the concerns of the Irish membership in such decisions. Roche and Larragy (1989) note the declining trend in the share of union members catered for by British unions but attribute this to changes in the structural composition of the workforce rather than any factors deriving from their national base.

TRADE UNION DEMOCRACY

A common criticism of trade unions is that they fail to exercise adequate control over their membership or that militant minorities exercise undue influence over union affairs. These criticisms often refer to situations where it is alleged that a particular group of trade union members pursue a course of action which is at odds with the wishes of either the majority of the membership or the union officialdom. An implication of this line of thought is that unions can exert a type of autocratic control over the membership. This interpretation fails to appreciate the internal structure and operation of trade unions within our voluntary tradition. The very existence of trade unions is centred on meeting the needs of the membership. If they fail to do this then their very *raison d'être* diminishes. Trade union discipline and control is based on a moral set of acceptable practices and the union hierarchy will be keen to ensure these are upheld through persuasion rather than compulsion in order to retain membership confidence (Brannick and Kelly, 1989). While it is true that unions do have power to decide on issues it seems that control works in both directions (Marchington, 1982; Flood, 1988, 1991). A union can exert a certain degree of control over its members in deciding an appropriate line of action and it also has a disciplinary role in certain circumstances. However, the membership also has the right to decide on policy and it can exert control over the union to get it to serve the needs as perceived by that membership (e.g., by withholding subscriptions or threatening to join another union). In a multi-union environment trade unions must be very circumspect in meeting those needs lest they experience an exodus of membership.

4.8 CONCLUSION

In this chapter we have considered the issues of trade union membership and penetration in Ireland. Our review suggests that union strength in Ireland remains quite substantial. However, we have also seen that recent research evidence points to some decline in trade penetration. Of particular significance is the growth of union avoidance strategies, particularly in the multinational sector. A related issue of interest in this area is the impact of human resource management (HRM) practices on trade union penetration. This theme is further considered in chapters 9 and 10. However, in the next chapter we turn to the issue of employer organisation, particularly the role of employer associations in industrial relations.

NOTES

1. It is noteworthy that the origins of our current Joint Labour Committee system (outlined in chapter 3) lie in concerns about the use of 'sweated labour' at the turn of the century, resulting in the establishment of Trades Boards to enforce minimum pay rates in certain occupations. See, for example, McMahon (1987b, 1989).

2. Based on figures for membership of trade unions affiliated to the Irish Trade Union Congress: for greater detail, see Roche and Larragy (1986); Roche (1997a).

3. *The Cranfield-University of Limerick Study of Human Resource Management in Ireland* forms part of the 'Price Waterhouse-Cranfield Project on International Strategic Human Resource Management', first established in 1989 and currently involving twenty participating countries. The Irish node of this study is located at the Employment Relations Research Unit, University of Limerick and is directed by Patrick Gunnigle, Michael Morley and Tom Turner. The 1992 analysis was based on 222 respondent organisations while the 1995 study had 261 respondents. For a summary of data emanating from the international study see Brewster and Hegewisch. 1994. *Policy and Practice in European Human Resource Management: The Price Waterhouse Cranfield Survey.* London: Routledge. For a review of the 1992 Irish data see Gunnigle, Flood, Morley, and Turner. 1994. *Continuity and Change in Irish Employee Relations.* Dublin: Oak Tree Press, and for the 1995 data see Gunnigle, Morley, Clifford, Turner. 1997. *Human Resource Management in Irish Organisations: Practice in Perspective.* Dublin: Oak Tree Press.

CHAPTER FIVE

Employer Associations[1]

5.1 INTRODUCTION

As with worker organisations, employers are also likely to combine for purposes associated with employment and labour matters (Smith, 1970). This chapter considers the role of employer associations in Irish industrial relations. In particular, we examine the operation and structure of employer associations, the legal definition of employer associations in Ireland, employer association membership and the range of services provided by such associations. We begin, however, by considering the objectives of employers in industrial relations. This helps crystallise the reasons why employers join associations for industrial relations and other purposes, and the objectives and structure of such associations.

5.2 EMPLOYER OBJECTIVES IN INDUSTRIAL RELATIONS

The primary concern for organisations operating in a competitive environment is to maximise organisational effectiveness and generate satisfactory returns for the owners/stakeholders. Such returns are often expressed in terms of cost effectiveness and, for the commercial organisation, profitability. Management's primary role is to organise the factors of production, including labour, to achieve these objectives. Consequently, it must make decisions in a variety of areas to facilitate the achievement of corporate goals. Industrial relations is one such area where management must decide on optimal structures and practices.

It is difficult to assess the degree to which employers have specific industrial relations objectives or adopt related workplace strategies. Organisations vary so greatly in terms of structure and philosophy that it would be impractical to suggest a comprehensive set of industrial relations objectives. Indeed, it is clear that a particular organisation's industrial relations priorities and approach are heavily influenced by a combination of internal and external variables such as product market conditions and business goals which differ considerably between organisations. This theme is further developed in chapter 10 which considers management approaches or styles in industrial relations. Nevertheless, it is worthwhile considering some general beliefs common among employers. Thomason (1984) identifies a number of generic employer objectives in industrial relations as follows:

(1) *Preservation and consolidation of the private enterprise system*: This has larger political overtones and relates to employer desires to develop and preserve a 'business friendly' political and economic environment conducive to achieving business objectives at enterprise level. They will be particularly concerned that principles such as private ownership, the profit motive and preservation of authority and control in decision making are maintained and fostered.

(2) *Achievement of satisfactory returns for the owners*: This relates directly to the organisations' primary business goals. For commercial organisations to survive in the long term satisfactory profit levels must be achieved. Managerial approaches and strategies will always be influenced by this primary concern. Non-profit making organisations will be equally concerned with cost effectiveness and the quality of their products or services.

(3) *Effective utilisation of human resources*: Human resources are a key management resource and their effective utilisation is central to the management process.

(4) *Maintenance of control and authority in decision making*: Employers will strive to ensure effective control and authority in executing their management role, particularly in strategic decision making.

(5) *Good employer-employee relations*: Employers will also strive to maintain good working relations with employees but this must be achieved within the operational constraints of the organisation. The scope to agree attractive remuneration levels and conditions of employment, for example, will vary according to the organisation's market position and profitability as well as its personnel/human resource philosophy. Good industrial relations will be a priority since it constitutes an important ingredient in ensuring the organisation achieves its primary business goals (as well as being laudable in itself).

To help achieve such objectives particular employers have found it beneficial to combine with other employers into permanent organisations. At the outset it is necessary to distinguish between *employer associations,* which are concerned with industrial relations issues, and *trade associations,* which are primarily concerned with trade or commercial matters. Oechslin (1985) defines employer associations as:

> . . . formal groups of employers set up to defend, represent or advise affiliated employers and to strengthen their position in society at large with respect to labour matters as distinct from commercial matters.

This chapter considers the role of such employer associations, with particular emphasis on the Irish context.

5.3 THE HISTORICAL DEVELOPMENT OF EMPLOYER ASSOCIATIONS

Employer organisations of a sort undoubtedly existed before the emergence of modern trade unionism and some possibly had connections with the guilds of the Middle Ages. As Adam Smith observed as far back as 1776, employers are likely to combine into associations for purposes related with employment and labour matters generally.

However, the major impetus for the growth of employer associations was undoubtedly the perceived need to react to and deal with the 'new unionism' and counter growing union power. This helps distinguish between employer organisations whose precise *raison d'être* was to deal with labour matters (employer associations) and those where trade and commercial reasons were the main reason for their existence and development (trade associations). Another traditional reason why employers have formed representative associations is to prevent harmful economic competition with each other, particularly in relation to pay and to working conditions. Other reasons for the growth of employers' associations include the increased complexity of collective bargaining, the growth of employment legislation and the important role of employer associations in providing a forum for the exchange of views between employers.

In their early attempts to grapple with organised labour and employment matters, employers, after initially dealing with such issues on an individual enterprise basis, soon found it opportune to combine either on an *ad hoc* or temporary basis or to form permanent associations. The reasons behind the formation of such associations were largely functional. Most of the early business enterprises were owner-managed by the traditional entrepreneur/master. It has been argued that entrepreneurs have a weaker spirit of association than other social groupings and therefore any attempts at combination would need to have a solid rationale (Oechslin, 1985). Consequently, many of the early employer organisations and associations were forums for exchanging views and opinions and this role later developed into one of joint strategy formulation. Such organisations mostly operated on a regional/industry-wide basis. Central umbrella associations were a later development. Thus, the early employer organisations were largely masters' associations for particular industrial sectors and/or regions which had combined for a variety of reasons not necessarily related to labour matters. While some of these exist today, the more important contemporary employer associations are those of corporate employers with specific employment-related objectives.

5.4 EMPLOYER ASSOCIATIONS IN IRELAND

As discussed above, employer organisations in Ireland are classified into two categories — employer associations and trade associations — both of which must register with the Registrar of Friendly Societies. Employer associations are involved in industrial relations and must hold a negotiating licence under the terms of the Trade Union Act 1941. This distinguishes them from trade associations, which are not required to hold such a licence. Employer associations are in effect trade unions of employers and fall within the same legal definition as a trade union. While this may not initially seem significant it can have important implications for the role and membership of employer associations. In particular, it suggests an approach to industrial relations which emphasises the role of collectives or combinations as opposed to individuals (see later in this chapter and also chapter 10).

In 1998 the Department of Enterprise and Employment records indicated that there were eleven employer associations as defined above (shown in Table 5.1).

Table 5.1. Employer associations holding negotiation licences in Ireland 1998

Association	Membership
Construction Industry Federation	2,181
Cork Master Butchers' Association	24
Dublin Master Victuallers' Association	143
Irish Business and Employers' Confederation	3,376
Irish Commercial Horticultural Association	292
Irish Hotels' Federation	768
Irish Master Printers' Association	38
Irish Pharmaceutical Union	1,275
Irish Printing Federation	67
Licensed Vintners' Association	619
Society of the Irish Motor Industry	1,537

Total: Eleven Associations with 10,320 members

Source: Department of Enterprise and Employment, 1998

While the number of employer associations is much lower than their trade union counterparts, there is considerable diversity in membership composition. One can find within this listing examples of traditional masters' associations, industry-based associations, and a general association which is national in scope. It is interesting that in evaluating the role of employer associations in European countries, Traxler (1997) identifies a trend whereby countries are characterised by single employer associations and suggests that there has been a gradual erosion of task-based employer associations. In the Irish context, the Irish Business and Employers' Confederation (IBEC) has over recent years come to be the major employer force in both labour and trade matters. We first consider the role of IBEC in Irish industrial relations.

5.4.1 THE IRISH BUSINESS AND EMPLOYERS' CONFEDERATION (IBEC)

By far the largest employer association in Ireland is the Irish Business and Employers' Confederation (IBEC). IBEC was formed on 1 January 1993, as a result of the merger of the then largest employer association, the Federation of Irish Employers (FIE — formerly the Federated Union of Employers) and the then dominant trade/commercial association, the Confederation of Irish Industry (CII). IBEC represents business and employers in all matters relating to industrial relations, labour and social affairs. Based on figures in their most recent annual report, IBEC claims to have over 4,000 firms in membership (IBEC, 1998). These firms employ some 300,000 people or approximately 60 per cent of the country's labour force excluding agriculture, the public service and the self-employed. Some 75 per cent of member firms employ 100 people or less and approximately half employ fifty people or less. As the country's major representative of business and employers, IBEC seeks to shape national policies and influence decision making in a manner which protects and promotes member employers' interests. In 1996 IBEC developed a strategic policy framework which outlined IBEC's mission and vision (see Table 5.2), its strategic objectives and policy objectives up to the year 2005. The major strategic issues identified include competitiveness, enterprise, State involvement in industry, employee relations, social policy and income development, European Union, education and training, the environment, innovation and research and development, and employment.

Table 5.2 Mission Statement — Irish Business and Employers' Confederation
To vigorously pursue the development of a competitive and innovative economy; and be valued by its members as enhancing, to a significant extent, the overall climate in which business operates. To promote the achievement of constructive management/industrial relations, building on the improvements already made in recent years.   and To provide and market a portfolio of value for money services, available centrally through the confederation's regional and sectoral networks, that assist the efficiency and effectiveness of individual members and groups of members in a variety of ways and enhances the attractiveness of confederation membership.

Unlike the old FIE, IBEC's role is not confined solely to industrial relations. IBEC represents industry in matters of trade, economics, finance, taxation, planning and development. IBEC develops and reviews policy on this wide range of topics through consultation with members, research, and expert advice and opinion. A major role of IBEC is the representation of employer interests on these issues to Government and the public at large. It also maintains employer representation on various national and international bodies.

In all, the Confederation represents business and employers on over eighty separate organisations, institutions and committees. Representatives are chosen from the National Executive Committee elected by members, managers with particular experience and expertise, and senior executives from the confederation. IBEC also acts as Ireland's business and employer representative within UNICE, the European employer representative body; the International Organisation of Employers (IOE) and the International Labour Organisation (ILO). In this role IBEC evaluates European and international developments and their effect on its affiliated membership.

IBEC's industrial and employee relations, advisory and consultation services are organised on a regional basis. The Industrial Division and the Distribution and Services Division both operate from its Dublin headquarters while the five regional offices operate independently with back-up facilities provided from Dublin. Designated executives are often assigned to deal with individual company needs. Particularly important among these services is IBEC's role in representing member firms at mediation, conciliation and arbitration hearings. IBEC also provides a range of specialist services in areas such as management training, health and safety, and legal advice and representation.

The Small Firms Association (SFA) is an independent association within IBEC which represents and supports small business. The association has 4,000 members and provides business, economic and regulatory advice to its membership.

5.4.2 Construction Industry Federation (CIF)

The Construction Industry Federation (CIF) is the second largest employer association in Ireland. Unlike IBEC, which represents employers from a range of industrial sectors, the CIF is essentially an industry-based association dealing with both trade/commercial and industrial relations matters affecting the construction industry. Its affiliated membership totals just over 2,000, representing some 46 per cent of all firms in the construction industry. Firms in membership of the CIF employ around 50,000 workers or three-quarters of all workers in privately owned construction firms.

In the area of industrial relations, the main role of the CIF involves monitoring and handling industrial relations on all large sites, dealing with any matters referred to it by member organisations, negotiation of national registered agreements, representing members at conciliation and arbitration, and providing information and advice to member firms (Pollock and O'Dwyer, 1985).

5.4.3 Irish Small and Medium Enterprises (ISME)

ISME is an employer organisation which represents commercial small and medium sized organisations. It was established by a group of small and medium sized enterprises (SMEs) which broke away when the FIE and CII amalgamated to form IBEC (Traxler, 1998). While ISME does not hold a negotiating licence and thus does not meet the established definition of an employer association, it has been very prominent in commenting on economic and social affairs, including industrial relations. ISME's primary function is to represent the interests of its members to Government, Government bodies, and other major organisations impacting on competitive business. Direct membership consists of over 1,500 companies with a further 1,500 in the twelve organisations affiliated to ISME. Its literature suggests that 95 per cent of members have started and developed their own businesses and employ approximately 65,000 people. ISME distinguishes itself from other larger employer organisations by highlighting the fact that its members are entrepreneurs and not professional managers. ISME notes that its main strength lies in the fact that small and medium enterprises represent well over 90 per cent of businesses and it therefore aims to represent a very significant force in Irish business. ISME aims at harnessing that political influence and using it for what it perceives as the betterment of competitive business. ISME points out that 'independence enables it to speak out fearlessly on behalf of competitive and entrepreneur driven business. It maintains and strengthens that independence through a growing membership base' (ISME, 1997). Beyond seeking to influence opinion on broad policy level issues (e.g., centralised agreements and the minimum wage) ISME does not appear to have a strong industrial relations dimension but rather appears to concentrate primarily on trade and commercial matters.

A number of organisations operate under the umbrella of ISME: the Alarm Association of Ireland, the Association of Landscape Contractors of Ireland, the Association of Pharmaceutical Manufacturers of Ireland, Flour Confectioners' and Bakers' Association, Irish Cold Storage Federation, Independent Irish Security Companies, National Union of Security Employers and the Jewellers' Association of Ireland. ISME has often been viewed as something of a maverick employer organisation and has not been involved in centralised pay negotiation. Over recent years this situation seems to be changing with the organisation publicly supporting the concept of centralised pay agreements and actively seeking a place at the 'social partnership' table. This development may in part reflect a recognition that for ISME to effectively influence debate and decisions at a national level it needs to be involved in the 'social partnership' process.

5.4.4 OTHER EMPLOYER ASSOCIATIONS IN IRELAND

Most of the other employer associations are primarily concerned with trade and commercial issues although some are quite involved in industrial relations. The industrial relations role of the Irish Hotels' Federation is largely confined to representing employer interests on the Hotel Joint Labour Committee and providing general industrial relations advice to members. It does not involve itself in local bargaining. Similarly the Society of the Irish Motor Industry is mostly concerned with trade and commercial issues but does provide a personnel/industrial relations advisory and assistance service. The Licensed Vintners' Association provides a range of services to Dublin publicans, one of which involves labour relations. It conducts negotiations on pay and working conditions with the Irish National Union for Vintners and Allied Trades Assistants and also provides affiliated members with a personnel advisory service covering areas like personnel policy, discipline/dismissal and redundancies. The involvement of the remaining employer associations in industrial relations is limited.

5.4.5 OTHER EMPLOYER GROUPINGS

While this chapter is primarily concerned with formal employer associations operating in the area of industrial relations, it is also important to note, as discussed earlier, that employers may also establish and combine in less formal groupings. Such associations or groups are generally used by employers as a forum for the exchange of views and information on industrial relations matters and also as a mechanism for co-ordinating employer approaches to specific industrial relations issues. Such groupings have the advantage of informality and cohesiveness while conferring none of the obligations or costs attached to formal association membership. Such associations may be formed on a regional (e.g., the Limerick/Shannon Personnel Managers Group) or industrial basis (e.g., the Electronics Sector) and may meet on either a semi-permanent basis or only when a significant issue arises. The Institute of Personnel and Development (IPD) in Ireland, which is the major professional association for management practitioners in industrial relations, may also act as a forum for the exchange of opinion, debate and comment on industrial relations matters.

5.5 OBJECTIVES OF EMPLOYER ASSOCIATIONS

Some common employer objectives in industrial relations were outlined above and include:
– support for the private enterprise system;
– achievement of satisfactory returns for the owners of the organisation;
– effective utilisation of human resources;
– maintenance of management prerogative in decision making and ensuring good employer-employee relations.
Most employers would subscribe, with varying degrees of commitment, to these general objectives and many have found that through combination they can provide a common front and more effectively achieve employer goals at both the micro and macro level.

However, beyond these common objectives, Windmuller (1984) argues that it is inappropriate to refer to the views and approaches of employer organisations as constituting a specific ideology and suggests that employer organisations, unlike trade unions, do not subscribe to some ideal economic and social system and are not part of a quasi-political movement. While it may be valid to say that employer associations do not affiliate to a particular political party (as trade unions often do), employer associations do have broad economic, social and political objectives which they pursue and their role is not just confined to micro-level issues but is also concerned with larger societal level matters such as political control, economic and social policy. This is particularly the case with national level associations. At enterprise level employer associations will seek to provide members with a range of services to help them more effectively deal with industrial relations issues. A summary classification of broad employer association objectives is outlined in Table 5.3.

Table 5.3 Objectives of employer associations
1. *Political:* To effectively represent employer views to Government, the general public and other appropriate bodies so as to preserve and develop a political, economic and social climate within which business objectives can be achieved.   2. *Economic:* To create an economic environment which supports the free enterprise system and ensures that managerial prerogative in decision making is protected.   3. *Social:* To ensure any social or legal changes best represent the interests of affiliated employers.   4. *Industrial relations:* To ensure a legislative and procedural environment which supports free collective bargaining and to co-ordinate employer views and approaches on industrial relations matters and provide assistance to affiliated employers.

In a political era when lobby groups are becoming increasingly important, employer associations have assumed a significant role in representing employer interests on national issues. They provide a mechanism through which Governments can solicit employer views on areas such as employment and labour legislation, and are important vehicles for influencing public opinion on more general political issues. This political role of employer associations is most clearly associated with their desire to influence broad economic decision making. Employer organisations will generally support what could be termed conservative economic policies which serve to protect the interests of capital and minimise the extent of Government intervention in business and economic matters. In the area of social policy, employer associations will generally attempt to prevent, or at least lessen, the effects of protective labour or social legislation such as legal moves towards extending industrial democracy or information disclosure. However, they may accept some degree of social and legislative reform provided its perceived effects on the interests of capital are not adverse.

Turning to the specific industrial relations role of employer associations, these may be categorised into five broad areas:

EXCHANGE OF VIEWS

We have already suggested that many of the early employer organisations were traditional masters' associations which had initially combined to discuss labour relations and related issues. Such associations provided a useful forum for opinion exchange and discussion. As the impact of trade unions increased and the State became more active in economic and social affairs, the role of such associations became even more important. Employers now came together not only to exchange information but to agree common policies and strategies. This led to a greater formality in the organisational structure of employer associations. This role is still important today. However, it is practically difficult to get a wide input into any general discussions on policy issues of national significance although such opportunities can possibly be afforded at regional level. For larger associations, policies and positions are generally decided by a limited representative body of employer opinion.

REPRESENTATION OF EMPLOYER VIEWS TO GOVERNMENT AND ITS AGENCIES

As the political philosophy of *laissez faire* receded and Government became more active in economic and social affairs, employers saw a need for their views to be effectively represented to Government. We see this development most clearly in countries such as the UK as a result of the growth of the welfare state in the post-war era and increased social and employment legislation. As Munns (1967) remarked in his research paper on employers' associations to the Donovan Commission:

> All of the national organisations regard the representation of members' views to Government as an important and growing part of the function. The general importance arises from the fact that much legislation has a direct bearing on industrial affairs and associations take very seriously their responsibility to seek amendments to existing or proposed legislation which would have a harmful effect on their members, or to improve the practical execution of the Government's intentions.

Employers' associations, particularly at central level, will therefore seek to influence the direction and nature of labour legislation and Government policy generally so that the position of affiliated employers is adequately protected. Such efforts have been most obvious on issues such as industrial democracy and financial disclosure and have contributed to either the dropping or dilution of such legislation (see chapter 8).

This representative role in Ireland is largely filled by IBEC. IBEC plays a particularly prominent role in representing business and employer views on bodies such as the National Economic and Social Council, which was established by the Government as a forum for the discussion of the principles relating to the efficient development of the national economy; the Central Review Committee which monitors issues arising from nationally agreed arrangements (such as the PESP, PCW and Partnership 2000); FAS, the industrial training authority; the Employer-Labour Conference which was established to allow the various interest groups to deal directly with industrial relations issues; the National Authority for Occupational Safety and Health which controls the operation and enforcement of occupational health and safety legislation in Ireland; and the Employment Equality Agency which is the statutory authority with responsibility for the promotion of equality between men and women in employment.

This political representation role of employer organisations is now well established in many countries. Consequently, when Government seeks the views of employers, it will generally approach the appropriate employer organisation. As Oechslin (1985) suggests, such a practice is both a recognition of the technical expertise and representative character of the employers' association. Thus it is important that employer associations present a representative front so that Government can readily identify its source of advice and also identify representatives of employer interests for appropriate bipartite or tripartite bodies such as arbitration councils, Government commissions, international organisations, etc. In Ireland IBEC plays the lead role in nominating employer representatives to such bodies as the Labour Court and the Labour Relations Commission and the Employment Appeals Tribunal.

REPRESENTATION OF EMPLOYER INTERESTS TO THE PUBLIC

Allied to the political representation role of employer associations is their role in representing employer views to the public at large on relevant issues. This will usually be achieved through the general media or the association's own fora and publications. It is increasingly important that employer opinion on issues be adequately represented and this public relations type function is particularly relevant for central employer organisations. Relations with the media are an important element of this role as is a competent research and publications section.

PROVISION OF SPECIALISED SERVICES TO MEMBERS

Employer associations will provide a range of specialised industrial relations and related services for their affiliated membership. Sisson (1983) suggests that the main industrial relations services provided by employer associations are: (1) negotiation of pay and conditions of employment; (2) operation of disputes procedures; (3) advisory and consultancy services and (4) representation.

The issue of employer association membership is discussed below while the nature and utilisation of the industrial relations services of employer association services is considered later in this chapter.

5.6 MEMBERSHIP OF EMPLOYER ASSOCIATIONS

While the distinction between trade associations and employer associations is useful, it does not fully cater for situations where some organisations play a dual role in dealing with both trade and labour issues. Also some countries may have a central organisation which represents employer interests in both commercial and labour areas, for example, the Irish Business and Employers' Confederation in Ireland and the Confederation of British Industry in Britain. We earlier noted that an apparent European trend is that countries are characterised by single employer associations and a gradual erosion of task-based employer associations (Traxler, 1997). In the Irish context, IBEC has, over recent years, become the major employer force in both labour and trade matters. This section considers issues relating to membership and structure of employer organisations. In particular, it focuses on factors influencing membership and structure such as industry/regional issues, ownership and organisation scale, and then considers the government of employer associations.

Employer associations are comprised of a regionally, industrially and structurally diverse membership. Such regional and industrial diversity was manifested in the establishment of traditional masters' associations, which were particularly common in the building and butchering trades and whose objectives were largely confined to local trade and employment-related matters. While some such associations still exist today many have amalgamated with larger national associations. Although not a prerequisite for the representation of employer views at national level, the formation of a central representative confederation is an important mechanism for more effectively co-ordinating and articulating employer views. Of course, the role of such a confederation is dependent on numerous factors — not least the locus of collective bargaining. In countries dominated by industry-wide bargaining, such as Germany, the role of industry-wide associations may be dominant. However, a co-ordinated employer voice may also be necessary and this is generally provided by a central confederation. In Ireland this role is provided by IBEC and is particularly prominent during periods of centralised pay agreements which have now characterised Irish industrial relations for the best part of three decades.

Turning to the specifics of membership of employer associations, Thomason (1984) differentiates between *entrepreneurs* who essentially own (at least partly) and run their businesses and abstract *corporate entities* which are run by professional managements. He argues that the change in composition of employer association membership from entrepreneur owner-managers to corporate business firms run by professional management partly explains the changing role of employer associations. The corporate business firm has replaced the older entrepreneurial type firm as the prevalent type of organisation in membership of employer associations. Thomason suggests that this mix partly explains the different philosophies and roles of different employer associations.

There are also some tentative indications that ownership may influence employer association membership (Brown et al. 1981). A study of newly established companies in Ireland found that US-owned firms were less likely to join employer associations (Gunnigle, 1995b). This may be related to the corporate approach to trade unions and collective bargaining. Where this involves a preference for non-union status, such organisations may be reluctant to join an employer association (also see Purcell and Sisson, 1983; Oechslin, 1985). This issue is discussed in greater depth later in this chapter.

The issue of public sector organisations becoming members of an employer association is a relatively recent phenomenon. While initially it might seem incompatible for public sector organisations to join an employer association (traditionally a bastion of free enterprise), many have adopted a pragmatic approach by utilising employer association services in certain areas (Oechslin, 1985). In Ireland the Department of Finance and the Local Government Staff Negotiations Board fulfil the key advisory and assistance role for management in many parts of the public sector. However, some public sector organisations, particularly those in the semi-State sector, have taken up membership of employer associations as a result of an increase in the levels of unionisation in the public sector and the consequent need for expertise and advice on industrial relations issues.

As was the case in relation to trade union recognition, it is argued that organisation size is a key determinant of membership and utilisation of employer associations. For example, it has been suggested that small firms have more to gain by joining employer associations (ILO, 1975). The major reasons are related to cost and resources. When a small organisation reaches the stage where it becomes involved in formalised collective bargaining it may be particularly attractive to join an employer association. Such firms are not generally in a position to employ personnel/HR specialists and owner/ managers may not have either the necessary time or expertise to effectively handle such matters. Since the cost of joining an employer association is generally related to the size and/or profitability of the individual firm it may be relatively inexpensive for small firms to join. However, despite the apparent validity of this line of argument there is no conclusive evidence to support the view that small firms are more likely to join employer associations (Government Social Survey, UK 1968). In fact the research evidence on workplace industrial relations suggests that employer associations are not more frequently used by smaller organisations (Brown, 1981; Daniel and Millward, 1983; Gunnigle, 1992). Brown (1981) suggests that: '. . . one theory that can be dismissed is that employers' associations are primarily used by the smaller establishments who lack specialist resources'.

Thus the available literature seems to indicate that larger firms are more likely to join and utilise the services of employer associations and that employer association membership is positively correlated with organisations' size, ownership, trade union recognition, and the presence of specialist personnel/HR function.

5.6.1 ADVANTAGES AND DISADVANTAGES OF EMPLOYER ASSOCIATION MEMBERSHIP
We have already considered some of the factors influencing an organisation's decision to join an employer association for industrial relations purposes.

Clearly a key factor influencing employer association membership and utilisation is the desired managerial approach and philosophy towards workforce management. Contextual factors such as industry, size, market position, and history/ownership also impact upon decisions on employer association membership. It is clearly a decision for the senior management of a particular enterprise to critically evaluate its own position and decide if membership of an employer association is appropriate to its own particular circumstances. However, at a general level it is useful to outline the main advantages and disadvantages of employer association membership for individual organisations. These are summarised in Table 5.4.

Table 5.4 Advantages and disadvantages of employer association membership

Advantages	Disadvantages
* Collective approaches and uniform policy	* Cost of membership
* Advice on trade union matters	* Loss of autonomy
* Technical advice and information	* Loss of flexibility
* Skilled negotiators	* Comparisons with other firms
* Expert advisory and consultancy services	* Greater acceptance of role for trade unions
* Standardised pay and employment conditions	* Greater formalisation in industrial relations.
* On par with regional/industry norms	
* Assistance in industrial relations difficulties	
* Influence on Government/national affairs	

The next section reviews the services provided by employer associations and these correlate closely with the advantages of employer association membership. Below, some of the reasons why organisations may choose not to join an employer association are considered.

One of the disadvantages of employer association membership is a potential reduction of *autonomy* in decision making for the individual organisation. Employer associations will be keen that members maintain a standard line in negotiations on pay and conditions of employment through the development of agreed policy guidelines (e.g., member firms will be expected to keep pay increases within the terms of centrally negotiated agreements). These guidelines will reflect the needs of a diverse membership (in terms of organisation size, profitability, etc.). The individual organisation must decide if such norms are appropriate to its particular needs. For example, an organisation may wish to award a pay increase which breaches the guidelines laid down by an employer association.

Comparability is also an important factor. By virtue of association membership a particular organisation's pay and conditions will generally be compared to those pertaining in other member firms. Trade unions will use the terms of collective agreements struck with some member firms as 'leverage' to secure similar terms with other organisations.

The issues of autonomy and comparability reflect the difficulties employer associations face in developing common policies for a diverse membership. They also highlight the difficulties employer associations face in enforcing policy guidelines and raise the issue of control over affiliates. Breaches of agreed policy guidelines by individual member organisations can detrimentally affect the credibility of such guidelines and may incur the wrath of sections of the affiliated membership. This has occasionally resulted in firms withdrawing from membership or being disaffiliated by the association. Such breaches of discipline are almost inescapable in associations where membership is voluntary and general policies are laid down for a diverse membership. Like trade unions, employer associations will strive to ensure maximum organisation of their potential members and, in practice, exercise a more informal authority over members, relying on persuasion and peer pressure to secure adherence to common policies. Employer associations are generally reluctant to punish non-conforming members and particularly so where expulsion is considered. Should a large number of enterprises or even a few significant employers not join an employer association its representativeness is clearly called into question. Sisson (1983) notes some important British organisations which have either withdrawn from membership or never joined employer associations (e.g., Esso, Daily Mirror, British Leyland and Ford). Here, too, there is some evidence of notable enterprises not in association membership. These are often major employers and exert considerable influence on local pay trends and general industrial relations matters. An important factor in such decisions seems to be related to the degree of influence such organisations believe they might have on association policy and the restrictions that membership would place on their capacity for manoeuvre.

It is also important to evaluate how association membership fits in with the *corporate personnel philosophy*. This issue is also discussed below in assessing employer association membership and utilisation in new ('greenfield') companies. Employer associations are in effect trade unions of employers and have traditionally sought to deal with their employee counterparts through collective bargaining. However, some firms have a clear preference for non-union status. In recent years Ireland has seen considerable growth in the 'high technology' sector. This has largely been the result of foreign firms (particularly US-based) establishing manufacturing plants here. Non-union US companies such as Digital, Dell, Motorola and Microsoft are now an integral part of the manufacturing scene. Some of these firms have brought with them a particular corporate approach to industrial relations which places emphasis on dealing with employees on an individual basis rather than through trade unions. For some such firms membership of an employer association (i.e., a trade union of employers) is seen as incompatible with a management approach based on direct contact with the individual worker. IBEC seems acutely aware of the need to attract into membership employers who have an explicit preference for greater individualism in management-industrial relations. Consequently we have seen the creation of special status membership categories such as those which allow such affiliates maintain flexibility in decision making while retaining association membership and engaging in less formal policy co-ordination. Employee Relations Services Limited (ERS) is a fully owned subsidiary of IBEC which seems in part designed to attract into its membership companies which might not otherwise become members of IBEC. ERS provides a range of specialist services in areas such as management strategies and payment systems (e.g., performance-related pay). It also provides an industrial relations auditing service designed to furnish senior managers with an evaluation of industrial relations in their enterprise. ERS members pay a similar joining fee to IBEC members and have free access to IBEC's other services. IBEC members may use ERS services at a preferential rate. Many non-union companies may be more comfortable with membership of ERS as it maintains their 'non-union' stance. Such special status arrangements avoid the apparent stigma of joining a 'trade union of employers' and are clearly perceived as an important mechanism in attracting such companies, which are often US owned and non-union, into membership.

Table 5.5	IBEC subscription rates in respect of employee relations services (1998)
First Year Minimum Payment	IR£650.00
Minimum Subscription per annum	IR£520.00
and/or	
First 200 Employees	IR£21.82
next 800 Employees	IR£20.81
next 1000 Employees	IR£10.48
Remaining Employees	IR£5.17

A more pragmatic reason for non-membership is related to *cost* (see Table 5.5). An important issue here may be that firms pay the full cost of membership regardless of services used. By contrast an organisation which uses management consultants normally pays on the basis of services rendered. Most employer association subscriptions are related to size of firm (number of employees) and costs can be substantial for larger organisations (Ridgely, 1988). For example, based on the most recent membership costs available from IBEC, a company's annual subscriptions are typically as follows: £1,637 for a company with seventy-five employees; £6,445 (300 employees); £15,810 (750 employees); and £26,252 (1,500 employees). A number of large Irish organisations such as the major banks, some of the bigger public sector organisations and a number of other larger private sector employers have subscription costs in the region of £100,000 per annum.

Related to the issue of costs may be the perception among firms with a highly developed and well resourced personnel/human resource (P/HR) function that they do not need the services provided by employer associations.

This is based on the premise that such services can be adequately provided by the company's own P/HR function and, as such, the subscription paid for employer association membership does not represent good value for money. The suggestion that larger firms with well developed P/HR functions may not need many of the services provided by employer associations is alluded to in Reynaud's (1978) suggestion that employer associations may become '. . . an organisation of services for the small undertakings paid for by the big ones'. We have seen above that the research evidence does not support this view and it seems that large firms use employer associations as much, and often more than small ones (Brown, 1981; Daniel and Millward, 1983).

5.7 THE GOVERNING STRUCTURE OF EMPLOYER ASSOCIATIONS

In general, employer associations are organised so that ultimate decision-making power resides with the affiliated membership. However, there is a high degree of complexity in the structural arrangements of employer associations with various models of internal government in evidence and we can merely generalise on common themes with respect to the governing structures of employer associations. Windmuller (1984) suggests that the governing structures of the major employer associations will be composed of three to four levels:
(1) assembly or general meetings;
(2) general or executive council;
(3) executive board or management committee;
(4) presiding officer (president/general secretary/chairman).
Windmuller suggests that this structure attempts to cater for membership participation while allowing day-to-day management to be carried out by full-time staff. He argues that general assemblies or meetings, because of their large and unwieldy nature, will rarely meet more than once year and are largely a vehicle through which the membership influence and communicate with the central administration of the association. They help decide upon general policy issues and elect the various committees. Windmuller in commenting on their role suggests that '. . . hardly anywhere do general meetings exercise real power beyond the election of executive bodies'.

In contrast, the executive or general council tends to be much smaller. It normally comprises elected representatives and some office holders and will often be representative of various industrial, regional or sectional interests, and will meet with greater frequency (possibly four to five times a year). Its main role is to monitor and give general direction. The executive or general council is generally responsible for the appointment of the various committees and monitors their work and the general running of the association. Again, Windmuller comments that 'councils carry some weight but still lack the continuity and compactness to be the decisive element in policy formulation'.

Possibly the most important layer in the governing structure of employer associations is the management or executive committee/board. This is normally much smaller and meets regularly (possibly on a monthly basis). Its membership consists of representatives normally elected on a regional basis, from the various branch/industrial divisions, from the major enterprises, and some office holders of the association. Such bodies may also elect the various standing committees (finance, industrial relations, law, etc.) depending on whether there is a general council or not. Such committees often have the power to co-opt members which is often used to bring in prestigious and influential people from the business community who can make a valuable contribution to committee work. The executive board or general council exerts considerable influence on association policies and approaches, and, together with the association president and the senior staff, is primarily responsible for policy formulation and execution.

For many associations the position of chairman or general secretary is a part-time position held by a senior manager from an affiliated enterprise. However, with the increasing demands of association work this often creates a dilemma for the incumbent as this job requires considerable time away from their employer. Depending on the demands of the position, the relationship between the president and full-time senior manager of the association (director general/managing director) is a crucial one. Generally the director general is expected to administer all the association's affairs according to the policy guidelines laid down by the general assembly, the general council and/or the executive committee. The post holder is expected to work closely with the association president and take their advice on general policy matters. A primary role for the director general will be to manage the professional staff of the association. The number of staff working in employer associations — particularly national 'peak' associations — has increased considerably over recent years, both in scale and areas of specialisation, and now covers areas such as labour law, health and safety, negotiations, research, and administration.

It appears that while employer association structure presents an image of active participatory democracy, this may be somewhat misleading. For pragmatic purposes, control and direction of association affairs is generally vested in the hands of a small number of affiliated members who together with the president and full-time staff oversee the general running of the association. That is not to say that employer association affairs take little account of the wishes of the membership. On the contrary, since affiliation to employer associations is voluntary and because associations continually strive to be the authentic representative voice of their constituency, such associations must be very circumspect to take on board the needs and wishes of their membership.

Like trade unions, the primary source of revenue for employer associations is membership subscriptions. These subscriptions are used to cover the main costs of running the association — principally wages and salaries. We have seen that the membership subscriptions of member firms are usually related to some measure of profitability and/or company size. The most common measures are the wage bill, number of employees, sales/output, or value added. Other sources of revenue are training programmes, publications and payments for specialist services. However, given the general lack of hard information on employer association finances it is difficult to estimate the value of such sources or the break-down of association expenditure.

We have seen earlier that in deciding to join an employer association an individual enterprise is in effect agreeing to delegate some of its decision-making autonomy in industrial relations to that association. Since it is the role of an employer association to represent the collective interests of its affiliated membership it must by definition seek to exercise authority and — ultimately — discipline on those members whose actions are perceived as detrimental to the needs of the general membership. While in some countries (especially in Scandinavia) central employer associations have extensive power and influence to control the activities of member firms, the more widespread situation is that the control and influence exercised by employer associations over their memberships is becoming ever more tenuous. Probably the most difficult issue related to the running of employer associations is the question of authority and control over member firms. We have seen that most employer associations comprise a varying and diverse membership and will attempt to service and assist firms of differing size, profitability, management structure and philosophy. Consequently, there may be various factors which serve to inhibit the association's goal of common policies and approaches. For instance, particular firms may seek to gain competitive advantage through the labour market, which will affect common pay strategies. Also, trade unions will use their bargaining power to secure 'above the norm' deals with stronger companies which they can then use as precedents in later negotiations with other firms. Some companies may indeed be willing to strike 'above the norm' agreements with unions rather than incur industrial unrest. However, such agreements may be in breach of the policy guidelines of the employer association and incur the wrath of the broader membership. This has sometimes resulted in some significant firms withdrawing from membership or being disaffiliated by the association. Such breaches of discipline are almost inescapable in associations where membership is voluntary and general policies are laid down for a diverse membership. It would seem that more and more associations are attempting to circumvent this problem by offering a non-conforming membership status entitling firms to use the services of the association but not obliging them to strictly adhere to policy guidelines on issues like pay negotiations and conditions of employment (see earlier discussion on disadvantages of employer association membership). In general, therefore, employer associations exercise a more informal authority over members. They rely on persuasion and peer pressure to secure adherence to common policies and approaches. Employer associations are generally reluctant to explicitly punish non-conforming members and the last resort of expulsion from membership is a step associations are very reluctant to take.

5.7.1 THE GOVERNING STRUCTURE OF THE IRISH BUSINESS AND EMPLOYERS' CONFEDERATION (IBEC)

Within the organisational structure of IBEC, the role of the general membership of affiliated organisations is to elect a National General Council comprising 250 representatives who then determine general policy and appoint the National Executive Council. The council itself is comprised of office holders and nominees from the various regions and branches totalling fifty in all. It is primarily responsible for overseeing policy formulation and implementation, appointing the key specialist committees and the permanent secretariat in conjunction with the director general and federation secretary.

Figure 5.1 Organisational structure of IBEC

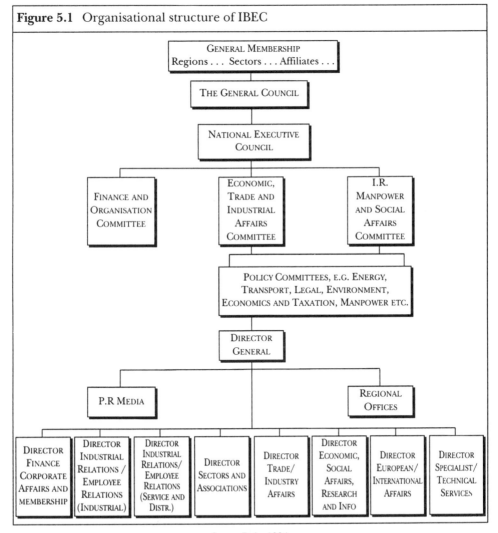

Source: Daly, 1994

165

The director general and the full-time staff are responsible for carrying out the primary activities and services of the association (see Figure 5.1).

5.8 EMPLOYER ASSOCIATION MEMBERSHIP AND MANAGEMENT APPROACHES TO INDUSTRIAL RELATIONS

Membership of employer associations is also seen as a useful indicator of preferred management approaches to industrial relations (also see chapter 10). Membership of employer associations has traditionally been associated with the pluralist industrial relations model. A recent study of industrial relations in new 'greenfield' companies in the manufacturing and traded services sectors found that the majority of firms surveyed were employer association members (see Table 5.6), in all but one instance, of the Irish Business and Employers' Confederation (Gunnigle, 1995a and b).

Table 5.6 Membership of employer associations		
Membership of Employer Associations	**Frequency (n=53)**	**%**
Yes	33	62
No	20	38

Source: Gunnigle, 1995a

The decision to join an employer association was positively associated with country of ownership and trade union recognition (also see Brown, 1981). While just over half of US- and Irish-owned organisations were employer association members over 86 per cent of other foreign-owned organisations were association members. It was also interesting to note that, in contrast to US-owned organisations, all of the European organisations were members of employer associations. As outlined in Table 5.7, greenfield companies which recognised trade unions were significantly more likely to join employer associations. Twenty-two of the twenty-five unionised firms (88 per cent) were employer association members while only eleven of the twenty-eight non-union (39 per cent) firms were members. Organisations recognising trade unions were also more likely to use employer associations directly in

Table 5.7	Employer associations' membership and utilisation by trade union recognition (n=33)				
	EMPLOYER ASSOCIATION MEMBERSHIP		**UTILISATION OF EMPLOYER ASSOCIATION SERVICES**		
			Direct involvement in establishment level industrial relations	**Industrial relations advice**	**General Personnel/ HR advice**
	Yes	**No**			
Union recognition	88% (22)	12% (3)	56% (14)	84% (21)	84% (21)
No union recog.	39% (11)	61% (17)	0	100% (11)	100% (11)

Source: Gunnigle, 1995a

workplace industrial relations. In contrast, non-union firms which were members of employer associations tended to use employer associations predominantly as a source of advice and information but did not generally involve them directly in workplace industrial relations.

We have already noted that the extant literature indicates that employer associations are most relevant in the private sector and that membership is positively related to trade union recognition, increased company size and the presence of a specialist personnel/HR function (Brown, 1981; Daniel and Millward, 1983). Indeed trade union recognition appears to be a key factor. Formalised collective bargaining arrangements, procedural agreements, and developed shop steward system (all characteristics of the traditional pluralist industrial relations model) appear to be positively related to employer association membership and extensive utilisation of employer association services (Brown, 1981). Even in smaller organisations the prospect of employer association membership may become increasingly attractive when such firms reach a stage of development where trade union recognition has been granted and there is a move towards formalising the company's approach to industrial relations management (Gunnigle and Brady, 1984; Gunnigle, 1989). The evidence from greenfield firms sheds some further light on the role of employer associations in Irish industrial relations. Here we find the more general pattern of utilisation was for firms to use the employer association primarily as a source of information and advice across a range of personnel/HR issues including industrial relations (see Table 5.8).

Table 5.8	Pattern of utilisation of employer associations (n=33)		
Utilisation of Employer Association Services	Direct Involvement in Establishment Level Industrial Relations	Employee Relations Advice	General P/ HR Advice
Yes	36%(12)	97%(32)	97%(32)
No	64%(21)	3%(1)	3%(1)

It is argued later, in chapter 10, that this evidence in relation to employer associations may be indicative of change in the role of collectivism in enterprise level industrial relations in Ireland (also see Gunnigle, Morley and Turner, 1997). Employer associations have traditionally been integral to the pluralist industrial relations model. However, growth of the non-union sector, particularly in greenfield sites, and a related expansion of individualistic human resource management (HRM) type policies means that, for such companies, membership of an employer association (in essence a trade union of employers) is often perceived as incompatible with a management approach based on individual dealings with employees. We have seen how Ireland's foremost employer association has responded to this development in part by establishing an advisory and consultancy service (ERS, discussed above) which provides particular services but does not confer the normal status of employer association member.

5.9 EMPLOYER ASSOCIATION SERVICES

It was suggested earlier that employer associations provide a range of industrial relations services for their affiliated membership particularly in the area of negotiations, research and advice, and representation. These various services are discussed below.

5.9.1 RESEARCH AND ADVISORY SERVICES

In reviewing the UK context, Sisson (1983) suggests that the major expansion in the work of employer associations has been in the provision of various advisory and consultancy services (also see Commission on Industrial Relations, 1972; Gladstone, 1984). These advisory and consultancy services fall into three broad categories, namely, (1) legal, (2) pay and (3) specialist consultancy.

The growth of both collective industrial relations legislation and protective employment legislation since the early 1970s has led to a significant increase in employer demand for specialist legal advice on these matters. Employer associations are expected to provide specialist legal advice and assistance to members in areas such as dismissal, redundancy, employment conditions, employment equality and industrial disputes. It is now usual for larger employer associations to have a specialist legal section which provides such advice and assistance in addition to publishing information guidelines on legislation for the general membership. In Ireland, we find that IBEC publishes a range of material on a wide variety of topics to keep its members abreast of legislative developments in industrial relations.

A more traditional employer association service concerns the provision of information and advice on both basic wage rates and levels of pay increases to member firms. Most employer associations carry out various surveys and analyses of wage rates and fringe benefits for differing occupations, regions and sizes of organisation. Consequently, they are able to provide member firms with up-to-date information on local, regional and national pay trends and advise such firms on reward issues. IBEC's research and information service gathers data on all aspects of work and employment (e.g., annualised hours, absence figures, etc.). It interprets information it collects — through, for example, the IBEC/ESRI monthly industrial survey — and also provides opinion on the likely impact of particular findings or initiatives for employers (e.g., the likely impact of European Works Council legislation, see chapter 8).

In addition to legal and pay advice, many employer organisations will also provide members with specialist advice and assistance on particular issues. This role is a general one and varies between associations. However, areas of specialist assistance include job evaluation, productivity schemes, work study, bonus schemes and recruitment. In an Irish pilot study, Butler (1985) found that advisory and consultancy services are seen by members as the most useful function of employer associations and found that those dealing with legislation, pay and redundancy were most widely utilised. These findings are summarised in Table 5.9.

Table 5.9 Utilisation of the advisory and consultancy services	
Services	**Percentage of Companies Utilising Services**
Recruitment	7.7%
Education and Training	32.5%
Labour Legislation	100%
Work study, Bonus Schemes	15.4%
Job Evaluation	0%
Redundancy Policy	77%
Local Pay Levels	100%
National Pay Levels	84.5%
Incomes Policy	38.5%
Others	7.7%

Source: Butler (1985)

5.9.2 REPRESENTATION

Apart from providing member firms with information and advice, employer associations may directly assist members by acting on their behalf in industrial relations negotiations. This role can be important at several levels. Employer associations can represent members in workplace level negotiations on, for example, the introduction of new technology. They can also play a more extensive role in representing their affiliates in either industry level or national level bargaining. This function of representation will also apply to mediation and arbitration where employer associations can represent affiliates at tribunal hearings, conciliation meetings and arbitration hearings. Given the growth in employment legislation and the greater complexity of industrial relations negotiations this role is likely to increase in significance.

The representational role of employer associations involves both a political dimension and third-party representation. Representing employer views to Government, State institutions, trade unions, the general public and other interested parties is a key role of employer associations. In general, one often finds a clear distinction between employer representation on trade/ commercial issues and employer representation on industrial relations matters. Indeed, this was the case in Ireland until 1993. Up to this time the Confederation of Irish Industry (CII) operated as the national organisation representing employer interests in matters of trade, economics, finance, taxation, planning and development. However, the CII did not involve itself in industrial relations. This latter role was primarily executed by the then Federation of Irish Employers (FIE, previously the FUE). The merger of the CII and FIE in 1993 consolidated these dual roles into one employer body, namely IBEC, which is consulted by, and makes representations to, Government on both industrial relations and general business/commercial matters. While IBEC represents employer interests on various national committees and institutions, it also provides employer representation on various mediation and arbitration bodies such as the Labour Court and the Employment Appeals Tribunal. Apart from IBEC, industry-based associations, such as the Construction Industry Federation, also carry out representative functions related to their own sectors.

An equally important representational function of employer associations occurs at conciliation and arbitration fora. Representing member firms at the Labour Relations Commission, Labour Court, Employment Appeals Tribunal and other third-party hearings is a valued and important service of employer associations as is evident from the extent of such activities, demonstrated in the annual reports of employer associations such as IBEC, CIF and those of the Labour Court and Labour Relations Commission (see Table 5.10). Affiliated firms will normally call on the services of their employer association if involved in third-party proceedings, although the extent of such utilisation may only involve obtaining advice and direction. At Labour Court hearings in particular, it is common for the employer case to be presented by an employer association official. This may also occur at Employment Appeals Tribunal hearings although there is an increasing tendency for employers to opt for legal representation at this forum.

The industrial relations arm of IBEC is involved in providing industrial relations advice and assistance to members. The provision of such advice/assistance may involve direct IBEC participation in negotiations with trade unions and would also cover research and specialist advisory services as well as assistance with the preparation of employment agreements, consultation on particular personnel/HR issues and the provision of premises and facilities for consultation and negotiation. The industrial relations functions of IBEC essentially encapsulate the previous roles of the Federation of Irish Employers (FIE). IBEC staff provide advice in response to membership enquiries and also engage in direct consultation with members on all aspects of employment such as pay, contracts, conditions of employment, recruitment, discipline, and dismissal. This includes direct negotiation and bargaining on behalf of members and representation before hearings of the Labour Court, the Labour Relations Commission, Rights Commissioners, and the Employment Appeals Tribunal.

Table 5.10 FIE/IBEC involvement in mediation, arbitration and negotiations

				(Cases per year)				
	1986	*1987*	*1988*	*1989**	*1992**	*1995*	*1996*	*1997*
Labour Court Investigation	538	488	386	394	217	159	169	170
Labour Court/Labour Relations Commission Conciliation	1,470	1,146	874	1,014	684	486	556	546
Employment Appeals Tribunal	396	190	n/a*	216	258	165	159	225
Rights Commissioner	586	429	n/a*	346	266	204	173	247
Equality Officer	28	35	n/a*	72	18	11	6	2
Consultation with Members	6,400	6,919	6,726	5,864	4,804	4,218	4,048	3,917
Trade Union Negotiations	2,928	2,842	2,702	2,540	1,286	797	764	1,040

(* = some figures not available; 1990, 1991, 1993. 1994 data not available in IBEC annual reports).

Source: IBEC annual reports

5.9.3 EDUCATION AND TRAINING

It is common for larger employer associations to provide training and development programmes for their members. Particular emphasis is often placed on training personnel/industrial relations specialists. Associations generally attempt to keep the membership up to date on current developments in areas such as employment law, working conditions, and EU level matters. Employer associations may also run joint training and development programmes with national or regional management training centres which eases the demand on resources while meeting the needs of the membership. An example here is IBEC's joint training initiatives with the Irish Management Institute (IMI).

5.9.4 COLLECTIVE BARGAINING

By far the most obvious service provided by employer associations for their affiliated memberships is in the actual conduct of collective bargaining. The role of employer associations in representing members in collective bargaining is important at two levels: multi-employer bargaining at industrial, regional or national level, and enterprise level bargaining (also see chapter 6). The issue of bargaining levels is significant in determining the role of employer associations in collective bargaining. Traditionally, the major role of employer associations has been in the conduct of multi-employer bargaining, especially at industry or national level. In the UK context, the Donovan Commission (1968) remarked that 'The practice of industry wide bargaining is closely bound up with the existence of employers' associations.'

It went on to conclude that a major reason why firms continued to remain members of employers' associations was their support for multi-employer bargaining '. . . membership of employers' associations is a consequence of unquestioning commitment to maintain the formal system of industrial relations. The system provides for industry-wide bargaining; employers' associations are essential for this; therefore companies belong to employers' associations.'

While this argument has some foundation it is clear that where the focus of bargaining has shifted upwards to national level or downwards to enterprise level, the role and importance of employer associations in collective bargaining has remained prominent. Multi-employer bargaining on an industry-wide basis has traditionally meant a key role for the appropriate employer association in conducting negotiations over pay and related issues on behalf of their affiliated membership. This form of bargaining was particularly common in Britain up to the 1980s but now seems to be on the wane with greater emphasis on enterprise level bargaining (Brown, 1981). It still remains a common format for collective bargaining in other countries such as Germany and is practised in some industrial sectors in Ireland. The Construction Industry Federation, for example, continues to play an important role in collective bargaining in the general building sector.

The apex of multi-employer bargaining involves negotiations at national level involving central employer association(s), trade unions and, possibly, Government. This form of collective bargaining gives a very prominent role to 'peak level' employer associations. During periods of centralised pay agreements in Ireland (1970–82, 1987 to date), employer associations, particularly IBEC, play a pivotal role in representing employer opinion to the other social partners. In effect, this means that individual affiliated members delegate bargaining responsibilities to their employer associations, thus making the employer association, and not the individual employer, the main actor on the employer side in industrial relations negotiations on pay and associated issues.

As we shall see in the next chapter, collective bargaining in Ireland in the post Second World War period was characterised initially by the wage-round system and later by a series of national agreements. Between 1946 and 1970 we had twelve wage rounds, five of which were negotiated centrally between employer representatives and trade unions, giving a prominent role to employer associations. The remainder were characterised by periods of intensive collective bargaining at either industry or enterprise level with wage increases permeating through to most organised employees (Roche, 1997b).

In the 1970–82 period, employer associations, largely through the Irish Employers' Confederation and the Federated Union of Employers (now IBEC), played a major role in the negotiation of a series of centralised pay agreements (Gunnigle, McMahon and Fitzgerald, 1995). When this system ended in 1982 there was a return to so called 'free' collective bargaining in the private sector (see chapter 6). This changed the role of employer associations from being the key employer actors in pay negotiations to a more supportive role in providing advice and assistance to individual enterprises and co-ordinating approaches to pay negotiations. The pattern of centralised national agreements on pay and related issues was re-established through the Programme for National Recovery, negotiated by the 'social partners' in 1986 and helped restore the then FUE (now IBEC) and, to a lesser extent the CIF, to their pivotal position in national pay bargaining. Since then we have had three further centrally negotiated agreements, some of which made for provision for some degree of local (enterprise level) bargaining, which also facilitated a significant role for employer association involvement in the conduct of enterprise level industrial relations on pay and related matters.

It is therefore apparent that while enterprise level collective bargaining was sometimes thought to leave little for employer associations to do this is demonstrably not the case in the Irish context. Where the focus of pay bargaining has shifted to enterprise level, as in 1982–86 in Ireland, there was little evidence of a dramatic reduction in the role of employer associations. Indeed, it appears that employer associations have an important role to play in single-employer bargaining. This role incorporates the co-ordination of policy on pay and employment related issues, formulating general guidelines for affiliated employers, supplying research data and information for use in negotiations, and providing expert personnel to either conduct the negotiations or advise and assist local management. This supportive and co-ordinating role at enterprise level is an important one from an employer viewpoint. By giving advice on pay trends and related issues, employer associations provide the basic information with which the individual organisation enters the bargaining process. By co-ordinating employer approaches, it establishes a framework for the conduct of such negotiations and by providing negotiating personnel it may either conduct the negotiations or advise/assist management in such negotiations.

5.9.5 DISPUTES PROCEDURES AND ADJUSTMENT

Closely associated with the prevalence of multi-employer bargaining is employer association involvement in the operation of disputes procedure. This role seems particularly important in some sectors of industry in the UK but is a significantly less prominent function of employer associations in Ireland. However, employer associations do tend to actively promote the use of workplace grievance and disputes procedures which cater for dispute referral to third-party conciliation and arbitration. Unlike in the UK, however, the operation of external disputes procedures at industry or national level by employer associations never played a significant role in the Irish industrial relations framework. Here, disputes procedures are normally negotiated at enterprise level. The role of employer associations is primarily to assist and advise members on the formulation and operation of such procedures.

The provision of strike insurance or other types of mutual defence schemes for employers involved in an industrial dispute has been a traditional function of employer associations. Again practice varies widely from informal commitments of support, through mutual aid agreements, to standard insurance schemes.

5.10 SUMMARY

This chapter has considered the role of employer associations in industrial relations. Particular emphasis has been placed on the nature and role of Irish employer associations such as IBEC and the CIF. The chapter also reviewed the main advantages and disadvantages of employer association membership for individual organisations and considered the main industrial relations services provided by such associations. Employer associations clearly play a very significant role in both national and enterprise level industrial relations. Of course, individual employers are responsible for the development and implementation of industrial relations policies and practices within their own individual organisations and workplaces. The issues of management approaches to industrial relations and related developments such as the increased interest in developing linkages between business strategy and industrial relations and impact of so-called human resource management (HRM) approaches is considered later, in chapters 9 and 10. However, the next chapter deals with what has traditionally been seen as a core activity in industrial relations, namely collective bargaining.

NOTE
1. The authors would like to acknowledge the assistance of Fergus Walsh in compiling this chapter. Fergus is Personnel Officer with Shannon Aerospace.

CHAPTER SIX

Collective Bargaining

6.1 WHAT IS COLLECTIVE BARGAINING ?

Collective bargaining refers to the process through which agreement on pay, working conditions, procedures and other negotiable issues is reached between organised (unionised) employees and management representatives (Gunnigle and Flood, 1990). Collective bargaining represents a mechanism through which divergent interests in organisations, namely, the interests of employees and employers, are reconciled through an orderly process involving negotiation and compromise.

The principal features of collective bargaining are that employees do not negotiate with their employers on their own behalf but do so collectively through representatives, and that various aspects of a worker's contract of employment are determined not individually but collectively. Clearly, then, a number of prerequisites must be fulfilled for collective bargaining to function successfully, namely:

(1) employees must have the freedom to associate, enabling workers to join together in trade unions which are not in any way under the control or influence of employers; and

(2) employers must·be prepared to recognise trade unions and accept the constraints placed upon their ability to deal with employees on an individual basis.

The process is called 'bargaining' because both employers and employees can apply pressure on the other. Clegg (1976) contends that this element of pressure is vital to collective bargaining and argues that mere representation of views or appeal for consideration is not bargaining. The requirement that collective bargaining is conducted with the view to reaching agreement does not exclude from the definition negotiations that may break down and result in a strike or lockout, provided of course, there was a genuine attempt to reach agreement.

The industrial relations systems of most industrialised countries are founded upon collective bargaining arrangements which act as the primary mode of union-management interaction and industrial relations government. However, many variations are apparent in the collective bargaining systems of any organisations, industries or countries chosen for examination. The conduct of collective bargaining may vary considerably between organisations but will remain essentially voluntary in nature, that is, it relies on the moral commitment of the participants.

Collective bargaining is by no means the only method of determining conditions of employment or regulating industrial relations. Even in countries where it is most dominant it nearly always exists side by side with other mechanisms, including individual bargaining between employer and employee, regulation by the Government (legislation), the unilateral imposition of terms of employment by management or similarly the imposition of terms unilaterally by trade unions. While these other methods do exist as realistic and sometimes successful alternatives to collective bargaining, there is a strong view that collective bargaining is in fact the most satisfactory way for employers and employees to determine conditions of employment. For example, the Donovan Commission clearly expressed its preference in stating that 'collective bargaining is the best method of conducting industrial relations' (Donovan, 1968).

Individual bargaining refers to the situation which arises when an individual negotiates with an employer in the classically contractual sense over the conditions of his or her employment. It is not considered unusual for an individual employee to be able to negotiate their own contract of employment. For example, employees at management or executive levels might negotiate their own terms or conditions as individuals. In the event of an employee individually bargaining the terms and conditions of his or her employment, it is often found that the features of the contract agreed have been influenced by the terms laid down in agreements reached between the organisation's management and unions. For the majority of employees, however, rates of pay, hours of work etc. are predetermined by company union agreements and cannot be haggled over to suit individuals.

In this chapter we are initially concerned with some of the different perspectives taken on the nature of collective bargaining and with the issue of structure in collective bargaining, but the chapter will centre on the development of the institution of collective bargaining and pay determination in Ireland.

6.2 THE NATURE OF COLLECTIVE BARGAINING

The credit for coining the expression 'collective bargaining' belongs to Beatrice Webb who first used it in her study on the co-operative movement of Great Britain (Webb, 1897). Of course, it has long since become firmly established in the vocabulary of industrial relations and trade unionism. The practice itself, however, had existed well before the term came into existence, with the earlier forms of collective bargaining erroneously being known as 'arbitration' or 'conciliation' (erroneous as no independent third party took part in the proceedings; Jensen, 1956). The precise nature of collective bargaining, however, has been the subject of much debate in academic circles over the years. Put simply, this debate has centred on whether collective bargaining may be best described as an economic or as a political activity. Farnham and Pimlott (1990) argue that in practice this theoretical distinction between collective bargaining as an economic or political activity has little conceptual or empirical validity. However, the following sections aim to briefly highlight some of the arguments central to this debate.

It is the Webbs who may also take credit for the first attempt at developing a comprehensive theory and definition of collective bargaining in their seminal work *Industrial Democracy* first published in 1897. The Webbs saw collective bargaining as one of the means utilised by trade unions in pursuing their objective of 'maintaining and improving the conditions of their members' working lives'. Collective bargaining is one category of three observed activities of trade unions which the Webbs identified in their research in nineteenth century Britain. The other activities were identified as mutual insurance and political activity. As Flanders (1968) later commented 'for the Webbs collective bargaining was exactly what the words implied: a collective equivalent and alternative to individual bargaining'. The Webbs saw collective bargaining as basically a process by which the individual contract is replaced by the collective agreement. The Webbs argued that collective bargaining can fundamentally best be seen as an economic activity because collective bargaining in their view is essentially a means of contracting for the sale of labour. Its purpose is to determine under what terms labour will continue to be supplied to a company by its existing employees and by those newly hired.

The Webbs' description of collective bargaining has been challenged, most notably by Alan Flanders (1968). Flanders argued that in dealing with collective bargaining the Webbs inaccurately defined the practice as 'a collective equivalent and alternative to individual bargaining'. Quite simply, Flanders' belief is that when discussing individual and collective bargaining, the Webbs were not 'comparing like with like'. Flanders (1968) argued that in essence collective bargaining is a rule-making activity (with no proper counterpart in individual bargaining) whose function is to regulate, but not replace, individual bargaining. In other words, the end product of the individual bargain is a contract while the outcome of collective bargaining is a set of rules. Flanders' description of collective bargaining as being essentially a rule-making process concurs with the views of other authors. For example, the International Labour Organisation (ILO) sees collective bargaining's over-riding purpose to be 'the negotiation of an agreed set of rules to govern the terms of the employment relationship, as well as the relationship between the bargaining parties themselves' (ILO, 1971). Flanders concedes that collective bargaining often replaces individual bargaining but suggests that they are not, however, complete alternatives (that is mutually exclusive) as the Webbs inferred, and he suggests that collective bargaining and individual bargaining can co-exist.

Flanders' second point of departure from the Webbs' view of collective bargaining surrounds their belief that collective bargaining is primarily an economic process. Flanders differed by suggesting that collective bargaining is in essence a political activity. He agrees with Harbison (1966) who proposed that an essential characteristic of collective bargaining is that it is 'a power relationship between organisations', and as such sees collective bargaining as best described 'as a diplomatic use of power'. The strike is seen to represent a strategic use of the power relationship between the organisation and union members and as such is seen as a bargaining ploy. In Flanders' eyes, there is no equivalent in the individual bargaining situation.

Flanders' view of collective bargaining as primarily a power relationship between organisations has found support in the work of many authors from varying perspectives throughout the literature. For example, Stevens (1963) defines collective bargaining as a 'social control technique for reflecting and transmitting the basic power relationships which underlie the conflict of interests in an industrial relations system'. Perlman (1936) proposes that collective bargaining is not just a means of raising pay and improving conditions of employment but 'above all a technique whereby an inferior social class or group carries on a never slackening pressure for a bigger share in the social sovereignty', highlighting the power struggle which he feels is in essence collective bargaining. Indeed, Perlman does not see collective bargaining as being confined to the industrial arena but manifesting itself 'equally in politics, legislation, court ligitation, government administration, religion, and education'. On a similar note, Hyman (1975) argues that collective bargaining is merely a means of social control and an institutionalised expression of the class struggle between those owning capital and those selling labour in industry. An obvious but important point highlighted by these definitions and others is that much of the debate on the nature of collective bargaining will be coloured by the theoretical perspective or frame of reference on industrial relations adopted by the author.

More recently, Alan Fox (1975) has come to the defence of the Webbs and tried to rehabilitate their perspective by attempting to answer many of the criticisms levelled by Flanders. Put briefly, Fox takes issue with Flanders' claim that collective bargaining can be differentiated from individual bargaining in that it is a rule-making activity. Fox argues that the individual bargain defines the rules which will be observed by both parties if the contract is entered into and these are reviewed during the course of the continuing relationship and as such 'the individual contract is just as much a rule-making instrument as its collective counterpart'.

Anthony (1980) argues that the notion of collective bargaining as fundamentally a rule-making process (as Flanders views it) may be problematic in that it suggests that there is an equal distribution of power between employer and union as a precondition for the existence of collective bargaining. Anthony admits that relationships encompassing a rough balance of power between the parties to collective bargaining are often found in industrial situations, however, 'collective bargaining also exists in different circumstances, where power is unevenly distributed, where control is more unilateral, where responsibility is barely jointly exercised'.

Fox feels Flanders' contention that collective bargaining is distinguished from individual bargaining by being a 'diplomatic use of power' is equally unacceptable. Fox asserts that the individual bargain can also embody a diplomatic use of power as evidenced by an employer or an employee who may temporarily have a bargaining advantage choosing to bring or not to bring their superiority of bargaining power to bear in the individual bargain for reasons of expediency. Fox (1975) argues that since both collective and individual bargaining involve a rule-making process and diplomatic use of power they are in fact similar, and 'that the former is indeed a collective version of the latter'. Fox disagrees with the major conclusion of Flanders' line of reasoning, that is, that the main function of collective bargaining and trade unionism is political rather than economic. Fox argues that the major bargaining preoccupation of trade unions relates to securing increased financial reward and improved conditions. Indeed, it is in this economic activity that trade unions find their major justification in their members' eyes.

6.3 THREE THEORIES OF COLLECTIVE BARGAINING

Chamberlain and Kuhn (1965) adopt a more holistic approach in attempting to develop a generic definition of collective bargaining. In reviewing the various theories of collective bargaining, they concluded that collective bargaining is (1) a means of contracting for the sale of labour, (2) a form of industrial government and (3) a method of management. This conception of collective bargaining Chamberlain and Kuhn defined as the marketing theory, the governmental theory and the managerial theory of collective bargaining.

The marketing theory is essentially similar to the classical view of the Webbs, which sees the individual contract as being replaced by the collective agreement Collective bargaining's purpose is to determine the terms and conditions under which labour will be supplied to an organisation by its employees. Central to the marketing theory is the belief that collective bargaining is necessary to redress the inequity of bargaining power between employer and employee.

The governmental theory views collective bargaining as a form of industrial government, similar to that described by Leiserson (1922) who argued that collective bargaining's principal function 'is to set up organs of government, define and limit them, provide agencies for making, executing and interpreting laws for industry and means for enforcement'.

The managerial theory stresses the functional relationship between union and company, suggesting that they combine 'in reaching decisions on matters in which both have vital interests'. The theory emphasises 'mutuality', namely that those who are integral to the conduct of an enterprise should have a voice in the decisions which affect them. So collective bargaining is viewed as a method of management, serving the interests of both parties. Collective bargaining serves employer interests of controlling the labour market and facilitating greater managerial control. From the trade union perspective, collective bargaining serves the interests of union members by regulating or checking the making of managerial decisions.

Chamberlain and Kuhn did not suggest that these three theories were mutually exclusive or incompatiable alternatives, but rather they may be seen as reflecting different stages in the development of collective bargaining. As Flanders (1968) suggests:

> Early negotiations were mainly a matter of fixing terms for sale of labour. . . . Later came the need for procedures for settling disputes on these and other issues between the parties. . . . Only when eventually agreements were made on subjects that entered into internal decision making processes of a business enterprise was there a basis for the managerial theory of collective bargaining.

Chamberlain and Kuhn (1965) also emphasise that collective bargaining is essentially a collaborative relationship, describing it as requiring 'that some agreement be reached . . . some agreement must ultimately be forthcoming if collective bargaining continues. Thus neither party is independent under collective bargaining. Neither can perform its function without the other.'

The notion of consensus or agreement is central to many of the definitions of collective bargaining found in modern textbooks. For example, Hawkins (1975) describes collective bargaining as 'the resolution of conflict through compromise', (compromise inferring that the process is based on agreement). The ILO has referred to collective bargaining as 'negotiations about working conditions and terms of employment between an employer, a group of employers, or one or more employer organisations on one hand, or one or more employee organisations on the other with a view to reaching agreement' (ILO, 1960). The definition offered at the beginning of this chapter echoes this view in describing collective bargaining as 'the process through which agreement on pay, working conditions, procedures and other negotiable issues is reached between organised employees and management representatives', Green (1991) discusses collective bargaining as fundamentally consisting 'of an employer, or a group of employers negotiating the terms and conditions of employees with the representatives of one or several worker organisations and reaching agreement on these issues'.

6.4 THE STRUCTURE OF COLLECTIVE BARGAINING

Bargaining structure refers to the stable or permanent features that help to distinguish the collective bargaining process in any particular system (Parker et al., 1971). It refers to the framework in which negotiations between employers and organised workers takes place. Parker et al. submit that variations in the bargaining structure of industrial relations systems can be accounted for by the differences which arise in respect of four aspects, namely, bargaining levels, bargaining units, bargaining forms and bargaining scope. Bargaining structure in any particular system is dynamic and variations in one or more of these dimensions will alter the structure of collective bargaining, from time to time.

6.4.1 BARGAINING LEVELS

By definition collective bargaining requires collective action on the part of employees. However, it does not necessarily require collective action on the part of employers. Individual employers as well as employer associations may form a bargaining group with trade unions. Trade unions may bargain with one employer, a group of employers or with representatives of an employer association. Hence, collective bargaining may take place at multi-employer or single employer level. Multi-employer bargaining can take place at national or regional level, or at the level of the particular industry. Single employer bargaining can also take place at a number of levels depending on the structure of the organisation. The individual employer can be involved in bargaining both at establishment level (largely referred to as workplace bargaining) and at a multi-establishment level (if the organisation is a multi-site operation). In addition collective bargaining at the level of the single employer might involve negotiations either with an individual union or in a multi-union environment with representatives from a group of unions. Frequently an employer may be involved in collective bargaining at both single-employer and multi-employer levels. For example, in certain industries agreements may be negotiated at several levels to determine different elements in the employment package (Farnham and Pimlott, 1990), for instance, pay increases may be negotiated through multi-employer bargaining at national level between employer associations and trade union federations, with hours of work being handled through single-employer negotiations at establishment level.

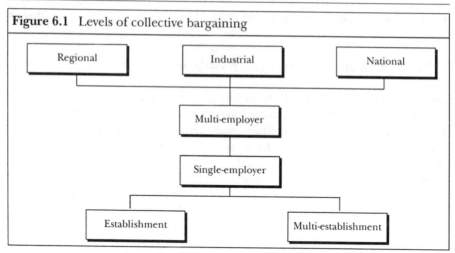

Figure 6.1 Levels of collective bargaining

Source: Gunnigle, Garavan and Fitzgerald, 1992

Some efforts have been made to explain why an employer may have a preference for either single or multi-employer bargaining. There are certain benefits of multi-employer bargaining which may help to explain its attractiveness to some organisations. For example, multi-employer bargaining relieves employers of the need to deal with annual wage negotiations, leaving members of the management team free to devote their time to other areas of importance. The standardising of rates of pay and conditions amongst a group of employers avoids pay competition between organisations, regulating an important aspect of the competitive market. Gunnigle and Flood (1990) argue that at a more strategic level multi-employer bargaining concentrates union attention at trans-company level, thereby separating the locus of management decision making from the locus of collective bargaining, effectively denying unions access to key management decision makers at the organisational level.

Gunnigle and Flood also suggest that for organisations in comfortable trading positions multi-employer bargaining is a relatively painless way of dealing with industrial relations. These advantages associated with multi-employer bargaining may, however, involve certain trade offs. While standardising rates of pay can be seen as beneficial in some ways, it may cause organisations to miss out on some important opportunities, for example, the capacity for single-employer bargaining to allow management negotiators to more closely relate wage rates to establishment level issues like increased productivity, cost reductions, regional norms and so on. In addition, if organisational members are directly involved in the negotiation process it can be argued that it increases the likelihood there will be a greater commitment to observe the terms of any agreements reached.

Pierson (1961) tries to throw light on the choice of level by reference to industrial structure. He observed that in the US 'multi-employer bargaining appears to thrive in those industries in which employers tend to be small relative to their union counterparts, product competition either on a national or local basis is intense, capital requirements relative to labour requirements are low, and profit margins are narrow'. Multi-employer bargaining may offer significant economies of scale to the smaller employer in sharing the costs of trained experts (employer associations) to deal with trade unions and to give advice on industrial relations issues. He also identifies the circumstances which in his view lead to single employer bargaining, 'production units tend to be large, capital constitutes an important part of total costs and is relatively immobile, and product competition is less intense'.

Similar studies in the UK by Deaton and Beaumont (1980) suggest that multi-employer bargaining is associated with high regional concentration of organisations, operating within a similar labour market, having a high union density with many unions operating within the same industry. Single-employer bargaining is associated with larger establishments, multi-site organisations, foreign ownership, organisations operating within non-competitive product markets, and the existence of specialist industrial relations managers at a senior level.

A multi-establishment organisation must also address itself to the issue of whether to negotiate at multi-establishment (corporate level) or at the level of the establishment (individual enterprise). Kinnie (1986) suggests that competitive pressures have led to two possible employer responses. On the one hand, corporate management may seek to exert central control over costs and work practices through greater centralisation in industrial relations management. On the other hand, many employers wish to decentralise control to create individual cost centres and delegate responsibility for increased efficiency. Kinnie (1986) argues that while the trend in managerial control is for greater centralisation, this does not necessarily involve a move away from establishment bargaining, suggesting that organisations are trying to strike a balance between pressures for centralisation and decentralisation recognising the need to co-ordinate strategic decision making at corporate level while allowing greater operational discretion at local level.

6.4.2 BARGAINING UNITS, FORM, SCOPE

A bargaining unit refers to the group of workers to be covered by a particular bargained agreement. A bargaining unit may cover a narrow group, e.g., all supervisory staff in one company or it may cover a larger group, say, all manual employees in an industry or all unionised workers in a country. A bargaining unit may also involve a single union, a group of unions or, for that matter, an association of unions who act as bargaining agents at the negotiating table for employees. Bargaining units will vary according to the bargaining level at which the negotiation takes place. For example, a single union may negotiate at establishment level, whereas an association or federation of unions is more likely to negotiate at national level.

Bargaining form describes the degree of formality of an agreement. This may vary from an informal approach which relies on unwritten agreements to a very formal approach which utilises comprehensive written agreements. It appears that the higher the bargaining level within a country, industry or organisation, the higher the degree of formality.

Bargaining scope relates to the range of issues to be covered, such as: basic pay, shift premiums, overtime rates, holidays, hours of work, disciplinary procedures etc., and may be comprehensive or restrictive in its range. A comprehensive scope implies that scope of bargaining covers the entire range of employment issues affecting employees while a restrictive scope suggests a focus on particular or problematic issues.

The end product of the collective bargaining process is the collective agreement. Collective agreements are frequently regarded as covering two different kinds of arrangements, those that deal with *substantive* issues and those that are *procedural* in nature. The scope of substantive agreements will obviously vary widely from company to company, but substantive terms usually concern pay, work quantity and quality specifications, hours of work, overtime premiums, shift allowances, holiday entitlements, sick benefits and allowances. However, this list is by no means exhaustive. Anthony (1980) describes procedural arrangements as determining the ways in which terms and conditions of employment are arrived at and the ways in which differences over the application of agreed terms and conditions are settled. Such procedural arrangements may cover discipline, grievances, disputes, rule changes, how wage claims are to be processed and other constitutional matters.

6.5 COLLECTIVE BARGAINING — AN APPRAISAL

The International Labour Organisation (ILO) has argued that collective bargaining offers a number of advantages which the ILO believes explains its prevalence and broad acceptance in many countries (ILO, 1973).

The first of these advantages lies in its flexibility. It is suggested that collective bargaining is far more flexible than other methods of industrial relations government, for example, statutory control. This is clearly evident from the diversity of agreements which can emerge from collective bargaining negotiations. Collective bargaining may be adopted to cope with the varying requirements of many different organisations and industrial sectors.

It has also been argued (particularly by pluralists who are the main advocates of collective bargaining) that collective bargaining redresses the undoubted disparity in bargaining power which exists between the individual employee and the organisation which is his or her employer. Collective bargaining is portrayed as an instrument which contributes to an approximate balance of power between organisations and their employees. The existence of collective bargaining arrangements can protect the individual worker against possible exploitation which may arise through individual dealings with an organisation because of the employer's superior bargaining position.

Collective bargaining allows workers to participate in the setting of the terms under which they are to work by ensuring their involvement in organisational decision making. The collective bargaining process also involves eliciting the consent of those who live under the terms of any agreement. This consent ensures stability between the parties thus reducing the potential for problems to arise which may cause conflict in the workplace. A related advantage of collective bargaining lies in its potential usefulness for solving problems arising from conflicts of interest over the distribution of scarce resources. Collective bargaining arrangements can be seen as a means of airing grievances and differences of opinion on contentious issues through orderly negotiation aimed at securing eventual agreement. It can be argued that the absence of such mechanisms for processing and resolving potential disputes would be detrimental to any notions of good industrial relations.

Whatever its potential advantages, the institution of collective bargaining has been criticised by individuals from varying theoretical perspectives and shades of opinion. Beaumont (1990) has highlighted some of these negative commentaries. For example, those viewing industrial relations from the unitarist frame of reference have long contended that collective bargaining arrangements are totally unnecessary, as they emerge from an employer's failure to satisfy his/her employees' job needs. Unitarists believe that collective bargaining will inevitably result in undesirable conflict and also introduces a competing focus of loyalty for employees within the workplace, that is, a union.

Those supporting the radical school of industrial relations have attacked collective bargaining for its inherent conservatism in that it promotes consensus and discourages social change. They see collective bargaining (with its emphasis on negotiation and compromise more often than not in relation to substantive issues) operating to reinforce the prevailing status quo and not challenging the structures of ownership and control in society. Beaumont suggests that radical scholars, for example, Hyman (1975), Fox (1974) and Hutchinson (1974), believe that collective bargaining has the effect of (1) producing only marginal improvements in the terms and conditions of employees, (2) lowering union members' expectations with regard to what is realistically negotiable, (3) makes industrial conflict more manageable through the process of procedural regulation, and (4) constrains the development of a cohesive working class consciousness orientated towards larger political and economic change.

The economic efficiency of collective bargaining has also been called into question. A view often advanced is that collective bargaining is inflationary in that rising wage settlements contribute to an increased overall level of prices which is damaging to society in general. Flanders (1967) argues that collective bargaining at particular periods took inadequate account of the public interest in having a relatively low rate of inflation and suggests that collective bargaining arrangements should be designed to minimise wage inflationary pressures. Phelps Brown (1971) argues that wages under collective bargaining may be 20 to 25 per cent higher than they otherwise would be but this advantage to the worker is not financed by the employer — it is achieved at the expense of the consumer, that is, other workers, through increased prices.

Beaumont (1990) reports that collective bargaining has been criticised for being 'too strike prone' in particular systems at particular periods of time. It has been argued that collective bargaining produces an unacceptable level of conflict and industrial disputes. This view is often advanced by those who believe that an optimal level of strike activity should exist in the public interest, that is a level that is socially tolerable and acceptable.

Collective bargaining has also received criticism because of its voluntary nature (particularly in Ireland and the UK) which renders collective agreements legally unenforceable. This, at least in some people's eyes, coupled with the extent of the legal immunities granted to trade unions, is seen to contribute to an overly adversarial system of collective bargaining.

6.6 COLLECTIVE BARGAINING IN IRELAND

Collective bargaining has been described as the central institution regulating behaviour between unions, employees and employers in Ireland (Turner, 1988). The Irish system of collective bargaining is characterised as being essentially a voluntaristic system. There is no legal obligation on trade unions and employers to engage in collective bargaining on pay or any other issue at any level. The system relies on the moral commitments of the participants, with collective agreements regarded as being 'binding in honour only'. The Commission of Inquiry on Industrial Relations (1981) noted that the Irish system reflects the view that collective bargaining and not the law should be the primary source of regulation in the employment relationship and should be based on the assumption by all parties that recourse to the law will be avoided. Von Prondzynski (1998) remarks that the voluntarist nature of the Irish system not only led trade unions to avoid the law but also persuaded successive Governments to avoid legal intervention where possible, and most employers were willing to embrace an alternative regulatory framework based on collective bargaining. Wallace (1997) argues that although voluntarism continues to be the predominant characteristic of the system, individual employment legislation is now highly legalistic and there has been some encroachment of legalism into collective industrial relations. He cites the intention to introduce a legally binding national minimum wage as well as the possible introduction of compulsory adjudication in the area of union recognition and other disputes that affect the public interest as evidence of the likelihood of this legal intrusion into industrial relations matters being extended further.

Employers are not legally obliged to recognise trade unions at the workplace. However, the high degree of unionisation has meant that employers have accepted collective bargaining with unions if they are representative of the workplace (Incomes Data Services, 1992). Union density is still relatively high and has not sustained the sharp decline experienced in other countries in the 1980s and 1990s, although there is evidence of a significant decline in trade union penetration in new multinational companies, especially those of American origin (Gunnigle, 1998).

Collective bargaining arrangements in Ireland are still strongly grounded in the pluralist tradition, that is, they are based on the assumption that a conflict of interests exists in the workplace between management and employees, with a primary reliance on adversarial collective bargaining to resolve temporarily the conflicting interests. The adversarial nature of the Irish model of collective bargaining has been exposed to certain pressures, in particular, the arrival of a greater number of multinational enterprises which rely on human resource management practices and have a strong preference for non-union environments (Roche and Geary, 1996).

Another characteristic of the Irish model is the tendency towards centralised bargaining. Calmfors et al. (1989) define centralised bargaining as 'the extent of inter-union and inter-employer co-operation in bargaining with the other side'. Centralised bargaining essentially describes institutionalised negotiation between representatives of trade union confederations (in Ireland, ICTU) and employer associations (in Ireland, primarily IBEC) about wages and other issues. Since achieving independence in 1922, there has been a changing emphasis on different levels of bargaining essentially oscillating between national and enterprise level which will be discussed in later sections. In more recent times, centralised bargaining in Ireland has been typified by attempts to adopt a corporatist approach to collective bargaining. Corporatist arrangements are distinguished from centralised bargaining in that corporatism integrates (1) Government intervention in collective bargaining so that negotiations become tripartite, (2) a debate over broader issues such as macro-economic concerns, and (3) the existence of consensus in the national interest. As evidence of this corporatist experimentation, pay determination in Ireland since 1970 has predominantly been negotiated with reference to some centrally bargained wage agreement between employer associations and the trade union movement (excepting the period of decentralised bargaining between 1982 and 1987), with varying degrees of Government involvement up to and including direct negotiations as evidenced by the Programme for National Recovery, the Programme for Economic and Social Progress, the Programme for Competitiveness and Work, and the most recent Partnership 2000 for Inclusion, Employment and Competitiveness.

Even in the presence of centralised bargaining, collective bargaining in Ireland is largely conducted at company level. The function of the national agreements is to set out agreed national level guidelines for wage increases and other related issues. The national agreement may also allow scope for supplementary productivity bargaining at establishment level. However, these guidelines are always subject to the outcome of negotiations at company level. Though, admittedly, the experience since 1987 has been that local level settlements have largely complied with the norms set out in the centralised agreements.

Industry-wide bargaining, though widespread in the 1960s is no longer a major factor in Irish industrial relations, as many of the industry-wide bargaining groups have since disbanded.

6.7 THE DEVELOPMENT OF COLLECTIVE BARGAINING AND PAY DETERMINATION IN IRELAND

The development of the institution of collective bargaining in Ireland can be traced with reference to a number of distinct temporal spans, namely:
- the late nineteenth century to 1941;
- 1941–46;
- the wage rounds from 1946–69;
- the sequence of national wage agreements from 1970–81;
- the period of decentralised bargaining between 1982, and 1987; and
- the current period of national bargaining which was initiated by the Programme for National Recovery in 1987 and continues under Partnership 2000 for Inclusion, Employment and Competitiveness.

6.7.1 THE BEGINNINGS

The emergence of the institution of collective bargaining in Ireland is inextricably linked to the economic and social developments which took place at the end of the last century. It is also undoubtedly closely associated with the growth of trade unions and (to a lesser extent) with the subsequent and often consequential growth of employer associations. The historical development of trade unions has been discussed in an earlier chapter.

The process of collective bargaining grew slowly from the first signs of its emergence in the 1890s. The early evidence of such bargaining was practised by members of the craft unions, which at the turn of the century were the only organisations capable of surviving the adamant resistance of employers and the open hostilities of the State. The forerunner to what we now understand as collective bargaining often involved organised skilled workers trying to regulate their wages by unilateral action. They would devise union standard wage rates ('price lists') and present them to employers as a demand and oblige their members not to work for less. They would also undertake to strike if their demands were not met. This bore little resemblance to what we now understand as collective bargaining but represented a kind of ultimatum (ILO, 1960). Faced with such an ultimatum, employers had either to accept the union rates or risk a strike.

Some employers chose to negotiate with the emergent trade unions, especially in times of prosperity, and conclude collective agreements with them as a means of avoiding industrial action. However, they would not necessarily agree to bargain in all circumstances particularly in times of poor performance or depression, when in fact wages were often reduced without consultation. The existence of structures for collective bargaining were therefore often dependent on the vagaries of the business cycle or the goodwill of the employer (ILO, 1960).

The passing of the Trade Disputes Act in 1906 reiterated the legality of trade unions, provided immunity from actions in tort to trade unions and legalised peaceful picketing. This key piece of legislation saw the trade union movement gain an increased foothold in many industries in Dublin, Belfast and Cork particularly with the foundation of (what was to become) the Irish Transport and General Workers Union in 1909.

The process of recognition of the developing 'new unions' was gradual, the initial reaction of employers being to resist this new wave of trade unionism as they had resisted the craft unions before them. The resistance was both ideological and philosophical, unions were seen to be interfering with the employers' freedom to run their businesses as they pleased, contrary to the principles of economic liberalism.

The first decade of this century also saw the emergence of the first employer associations, the Cork Employers' Organisation in 1909 and the Employers' Executive Committee in Dublin, whose explicit purpose was to put up a common front in the resistance to trade unionism. The issue of union recognition, of course, eventually resulted in confrontation in 1913 with the Dublin Lockout.

After the problems and trauma of this six-month strike, relations between employers and trade unions moved on to a more constructive approach based on negotiations and mutual agreement. The employers' systematic resistance to trade unionism and to the notion of joint dealings led to the frequent use of the strike. The heavy losses experienced by both sides heralded the gradual abandonment of resistance as an employer strategy in favour of collective bargaining. Employers had come to the realisation that the union movement had arrived and employers had to take steps to accommodate it.

The acceptance of the trade unions' role was reinforced in Britain by the Whitley Reports (1917–18) which favoured strong management-union relations and helped to establish permanent joint consultation procedures for various industrial sectors. At this time there was a notable 'about turn' in public policy which 'swung around to at least a benevolent tolerance of collective bargaining, and increasingly to its active promotion' (ILO, 1973). By 1920, two important prerequisites for the effective functioning of collective bargaining were fulfilled in Ireland, namely freedom of association (which was later strengthened by the Constitution of 1938) and trade union recognition (which to this day continues to be voluntary).

The period between the two World Wars saw collective bargaining still in its infancy in this country. Wages and conditions were still generally fixed by individual bargaining. Trade union density being relatively low, the majority of collective bargaining that did occur was carried out at the level of the individual firm, with less taking place through multi-employer bargaining via employer associations. O'Brien (1989) referred to this phase of collective bargaining as being 'unco-ordinated and rather haphazard'.

6.7.2 THE WAGE ROUNDS

The onset of the Second World War brought a temporary cessation of collective bargaining in Ireland, wage determination being governed by the Wages Standstill Order (No. 83) of 1941 which was issued under the Emergency Powers Act of 1939. Prices rose steadily during the war period which led to an erosion of purchasing power. The suspension of this order upon the ending of the war led to bargaining groups throughout the country lodging claims for substantial wage increases. The Government, in anticipation of the potential problems which might arise, set up the Labour Court to adjudicate on disputes that developed in relation to wage claims. The subsequent negotiation of these wage increases resulted in a general upward movement of wages which came to be known as the first wage round. McCarthy et al. (1975) define the notion of a wage round as 'a general upward movement in wages and salaries which (a) is usually completed in an active bargaining period of between 3 to 12 months, (b) recurs at regular intervals, (c) typically covers all bargaining groups and (d) results in wage increases of the same general order of magnitude'.

Collective bargaining during the period 1946–69 was to be dominated by a series of wage rounds which were negotiated at fairly regular intervals, approximately every two years. The duration of the round was largely dependent on economic conditions and the bargaining power of respective groups, but a time frame was not generally specified. There were twelve principal bouts of collective bargaining over the period, the majority of which were decentralised in format. Eight of these wage rounds were negotiated at either plant or industry level, that is, they represented periods of free collective bargaining where the parties negotiated their own agreements without interference. The remaining four were bipartite agreements negotiated between the Federated Union of Employers and the Irish Congress of Trade Unions at national level. Hardiman (1988) suggests that these centralised agreements were 'quite rudimentary and unsophisticated' and bore little resemblance to the national agreements which were to emerge in the 1970s. The first three of these centralised agreements were negotiated in the late 1940s and 1950s, (1948, 1952 and 1957) and were evaluated as being little more than 'ad hoc responses to particular economic circumstances' (O'Brien, 1981).

As already mentioned, the wage rounds were open-ended and thus no specific termination date was set for the round. Open-ended agreements persisted until the mid-1960s when fixed-term agreements became standard, and generally consisted of flat rate cash increases. Termination dates of individual agreements varied widely between different bargaining groups. As a result, the negotiating procedures became quite complicated, with wage rounds often overlapping each other. The termination dates differed by up to twenty-one months or more by 1970.

Wage rounds were by no means synchronised, being largely unplanned but, as Hillery (1989) contends, they became institutionalised into the Irish model of collective bargaining. The terms of wage rounds were usually accepted relatively quickly by industry, particularly if the Labour Court issued a recommendation upholding the level of the wage round increase.

Table 6.1   The bargaining level for wage rounds 1946–70

Year in which Implementation Commenced	Wage Round Number	
	Local level or decentralised bargaining	National level or centralised bargaining
1946	1	
1948		2
1951	3	
1952		4
1955	5	
1957		6
1959	7	
1961	8	
1964		9
1966	10	
1968	11	
1970	12	

Source: Adapted from O'Brien, 1981

The following are the characteristics reported by McCarthy et al. (1975) in their study of the wage round experience in Ireland during the period 1959–70:
(1) Wage rounds involved virtually every bargaining group. However, the increases took longer to filter through to some groups.
(2) The process did not result in identical settlements in each case, but it did result in the establishment of a minimum rate of increase (usually defined in money as opposed to percentage terms). The effect was to compress the overall wage structure. Thus in 1959 the highest paid bargaining group received approximately four times as much as did the lowest, but by 1970 this ratio was cut in half (OECD, 1979).
(3) In addition to the primary round a supplementary process was identified. Some groups were able to gain additional increases which were aimed at

restoring differentials, that is, the difference between different rates of pay for different types of labour. The supplementary process being a response to specific labour market pressures and exceptional status claims.

(4) Another feature of the system was that the level of settlements rose during the period whilst their duration fell.

(5) Less 'important' or powerful groups in the round waited for the results of others before lodging their claims.

McCarthy et al.'s study also notes that some 'key wage bargains', that is, the settlements of the more powerful bargaining groups (wage leaders) were the motive force of the wage rounds. When such claims were met this led to a chain reaction by competitive unions seeking to restore relativities. For example, the maintenance craft workers' agreement of October 1966 set the pattern for the eleventh round. The wage leaders in each round, because of their relatively powerful bargaining position, established a high norm for the round, which contributed to a high general level of wage increases through comparability claims.

THE EVOLUTION OF THE WAGE ROUNDS

The earlier wage rounds of the 1940s and 1950s were described by one commentator as 'sprawling untidy affairs, typical teenagers, one might say. Collective bargaining was little better than horse trading. Some union officials fought their way through rounds with the same mind set reminiscent of the late nineteenth century' (O'Brien, 1989).

In the early 1960s the Irish economy advanced at an average 4 per cent growth rate per annum. In the five-year period between 1958–63 industrial exports rose by 46 per cent. This new found prosperity, however, led to an 'intensification of distributive bargaining' (Hardiman, 1988) and an increase in wage competition between bargaining groups. Self interest and sectional interest as O'Brien (1989) suggests, were pushed to the fore at the expense of the national interest. The 1960s brought changed attitudes and increased expectation for Irish people which inevitably manifested itself in increased pressure for higher wages. The threat to the national interest was that the upward thrust to wage claims created inflationary pressures in the economy which threatened economic growth.

These economic fears prompted the Government of the day to review options aimed at modifying the system of wage rounds. The Government published a White Paper entitled *Closing the Gap* which proposed wage controls and implied that they might be enforced by the Employer Labour Conference (ELC) (a bipartite employer-employee consultative forum established in 1962). The trade union representatives of the ELC withdrew from the body in protest.

In December 1963 Sean Lemass proposed in the Dáil that future wage rounds should 'be based on an intelligent understanding and interpretation of the national interest (through national wage agreements) rather than through the procedures of horse trading and strikes as in the decentralised wage rounds' (Dáil Debates, 1963).

Lemass's efforts secured the fourth centralised wage agreement of the wage round era, the 1964 National Wage Recommendation (NWR). The NWR was innovative in that it introduced for the first time the idea of a particular wage round increase for a fixed term (two and a half years). Because of imprecise drafting and the issue of admissibility of non-wage claims (specifically the issue of the forty-hour week) the recommendation floundered and to quote the Minister for Labour of the day ended 'in a shambles' (O'Brien, 1989).

The first Maintenance Craftsmen's Agreement in 1966 was also for a fixed term and set a precedent which has bound bargainers at every level since, namely, agreements of fixed-term duration. The introduction of fixed terms into the wage rounds between 1966–70 did nothing, however, to combat competitive wage bargaining which was particularly prevalent in the craft sector, protection of relativities and differentials being deeply embodied in Irish collective bargaining, no more so than in craft unions. The decade culminated with the Maintenance Craftsmen's dispute. The dispute between the Federated Union of Employers and the maintenance craft unions centred on efforts to establish a national level multi-employer agreement covering craft workers and largely concerned an unsuccessful attempt by the Federated Union of Employers to break the relationship between contract craft and maintenance craft workers. The strike which resulted was historic, it lasted for six weeks, and, as Breen et al. (1990) argue, damaged the reputation of the trade union movement both internally and externally. It was unprecedented in its bitterness, and relations between craft and general unions were strained to virtual breaking — a split in the Irish Congress of Trade Unions at the time became a real possibility.

The chief lesson emerging from the operation of collective bargaining in the 1960s was that decentralised wage rounds as they operated were by their nature unstable and prone to inflation. The Irish system of wage determination had reached something of a crisis in its evolution — high levels of wage settlement and industrial action in pursuance of wage increases in the 1960s adding to the perception of disorder in collective bargaining, problems which were apparent to both sides of industry.

6.7.3 THE EMERGENCE OF NATIONAL WAGE AGREEMENTS

From the mid-1960s the National Industrial and Economic Council (a body established in 1963 which consisted of employer and employee representatives, senior civil servants and academics, whose brief was to give its views on the principles which ought to be applied for the development of the national economy) produced a series of reports which argued that one of the main tasks of the Government was to control domestic inflation. In its twenty-seventh report published in April 1970 (Report on Incomes and Prices Policy) they proposed the establishment of a bipartite body to interpret national policy guidelines for wage increases.

The Government responded quickly to this proposal and reconstituted the Employer Labour Conference (ELC), which at its inaugural meeting appointed a working committee to draft proposals which might initiate national level negotiations. Although the terms of reference for the reactivated ELC were approved by ICTU, the debate on the move at the following annual delegate conference of ICTU withheld approval from the concept of an incomes policy. An impasse on the question of a national wage agreement had been reached, despite threats of drastic action from the Government.

Again, the response of the Government was almost immediate. On 16 October it published a Prices and Incomes Bill which proposed statutory control of all incomes, limiting increases to 6 per cent or £1.80 per week until the end of 1971. In announcing the Bill the then Minister for Finance made reference to the 'truly staggering' claims already submitted at industry level e.g., 30 per cent for maintenance craftsmen, 40 per cent for builders, 66 per cent and 93 per cent from competing electricians' unions (Dáil Debates, 1970). The prospect of statutory control of Irish collective bargaining would have been a dramatic divergence from all that had come before it.

The threat was effective and the First National Wage Agreement was painfully hammered out, which gave 10 per cent for twelve months and 4 per cent for a further six months. The Government made a number of concessions to ICTU and agreed to withdraw the Bill (Breen et al., 1990). This process of moral persuasion and threats to legislate was to form an integral part of Government industrial relations strategy throughout the 1970s.

THE NATIONAL WAGE AGREEMENTS

The National Wage Agreement (NWA) of 1970 was a watershed in the evolution of Irish collective bargaining. It marked the departure from the traditional method of decentralised collective bargaining and saw the 'beginning of a prolonged suspension of free collective bargaining' (Roche, 1989).

The NWAs set the agreed rate of wage increase for the entire national workforce in all industries and sectors. The initial agreements (1970–76) were bipartite employer union agreements with the Government represented only in its capacity as public sector employer. As the decade progressed the Government came to become more directly involved in the negotiation of agreements. In all, between 1970 and 1978 seven NWAs were negotiated followed by two National Understandings in 1979 and 1980. The National Understandings differed from the NWAs in that they included two elements: a union-employer pay agreement and an agreement between the unions and Government on non-pay issues. The principal clause of each agreement was the clause governing the basic norm for pay increases, the amount payable and the phasing of the implementation of the agreement. The substantive terms altered from one agreement to the next. The basic pay increase, of course, was subject to the greatest variation. Virtually every NWA norm was biased in favour of the lower paid. However, no lasting improvements were made in their position over the course of the agreements.

Each NWA set out the conditions by which a bargaining group could pursue above-the-norm cost increasing claims, that is, claims which represented increases above and beyond the levels specified in the NWAs. These essentially related to anomaly (equity based), productivity based claims and improvements in the conditions of employment. O'Brien (1989) suggests that these anomaly and productivity clauses 'were tried and tested to the point of exhaustion'. Such claims contributed to a high level of wage drift in the period where actual levels of wage increases exceeded the maximal levels in individual agreements. Claims under these clauses were particularly prevalent in the public sector. Indeed, the Minister for Finance in his budget statement in 1981 remarked that the cost to the Government of anomaly awards had outrun the costs of the agreement norms (Dáil Debates, 1981).

The second and subsequent agreements allowed employers to claim inability to pay, in what became known as the below-the-norm clause. Employers thought that they might have a wide variety of grounds for such pleas, however, the criteria for the use of the clause were very restrictive and little use was made of it.

All the centralised agreements of the 1970s were negotiated through the offices of the Employer Labour Conference. The ELC was also charged with monitoring the implementation of the agreements. The Steering Committee of the ELC initially heard any problematic cases which arose. The ELC then referred the case to either its Interpretation Committee whose function was to clarify the meaning of the terms of the agreements or to its Adjudication Committee (since 1974) whose task was to rule on issues deemed to be in breach of the agreements.

Disputes which arose as a result of the agreements were required to be referred to the Labour Court. Each agreement with the exception of the 1978 agreement prohibited the taking of industrial action in pursuance of above-the-norm claims.

THE EVOLUTION OF THE NATIONAL WAGE AGREEMENTS

The 1970 NWA set the pattern for subsequent national bargaining in Ireland. The ratification of the 1970 NWA was considered no less than miraculous given the background of some of the claims from the more militant bargaining groups and the complexities and tensions that had to be overcome. The agreement ran for eighteen months and provided for two payments or phases of twelve- and six-month duration, the first being £2 a week for all adult male workers and the second on a percentage basis.

Table 6.2 below summarises the terms and conditions of the NWAs.

Table 6.2   The terms and conditions of the National Wage Agreements

Year	Round No.	Phase	Details
1970	13	1	£2 a week for men, £1.70 for women
		2	4% plus cost of living escalator of £33 a year
1972	14	1	9% on first £30 a week, £2.50 minimum for men, £2.25 for women; 7.5% on next £10 a week and 4% on the remainder
		2	4% plus cost of living escalator supplement of 16p for each 1% increase in the CPI
1974	15	1	9% on first £30 a week; 7% on next £10 a week; 6% on next £10 a week — minimum £2.40 a week.
		2	4% plus 60p a week; cost of living escalator 10%
1975	16	1	8% — minimum of £2 a week plus a quarter of 2nd phase of 14th round
		2	5% — minimum increase of £1 a week
		3	No increase except one quarter of 2nd phase of 14th round
		4	2.8%
1976	17	1	3% of basic pay plus £2 a week, subject to a maximum of £5 a week or £3 a week if greater
1977	18	1	2.5% plus £1 a week, minimum increase of £2 a week, maximum increase £5 a week
		2	2.5% plus £1 a week, minimum increase of £2, maximum increase of £4.23 a week
1978	19	1	8% minimum increase £3.50 a week
		2	2%

Source: Adapted from OECD, 1979 and McGinley, 1989

Even though there was no formal commitment to enter into discussions for a further agreement, both employer and trade union representatives negotiated a second agreement in 1972 which was ratified on similar lines to that of the agreement of 1970. It provided for improved increases for women and the lower paid, who had not fared particularly well during the period of decentralised bargaining (Hillery, 1989). The agreement was also for an eighteen-month duration.

At the conclusion of the Second National Wage Agreement average rates of pay had risen by 19 per cent compared to 17 per cent under the first NWA. This increase, coupled with lower rates of productivity and price increases, saw the Second NWA as being more inflationary.

The Second NWA, as already mentioned, saw the introduction of an inability to pay clause, for employers who could not meet the terms of the agreement because of their particular economic circumstances. This clause was to be replicated in all subsequent agreements.

Both sides of industry again voluntarily agreed to enter into negotiations for a third agreement in 1974. This agreement proved to be more difficult to negotiate than its predecessors given the background of the aforementioned inflationary pressures. A draft agreement drawn up by the ELC was rejected at a special delegate conference of ICTU, largely because of dissatisfaction with the level of the pay increase on offer. It was only with the intervention of the employers who increased their offer by 3 per cent and the securing of agreement from the Government to alter income tax relief, reform taxation and increase social welfare spending in the coming budget that the deal was finally ratified.

This Third NWA was for the shorter duration of twelve months. It included the principle of indexation (that is linking the level of pay increase directly to movements in official prices) which was to prove very costly. The period of the agreement saw inflation rise to unforeseen levels mainly as a result of 'imported inflation' caused in the main by the oil crisis following the Arab-Israeli War in 1973. The rate of inflation rose from 11.4 per cent in 1973 to 17 per cent in 1974. The pay agreement accorded pay average increases in the region of 30 per cent (OECD, 1979).

The Third NWA, in 1974, also saw the initiation of a successful attempt to narrow the spread of termination dates which had varied greatly because of the legacy of the wage round system. The range of termination dates fell from twenty-one months to about three months. This was achieved by a system of so-called 'substitution payments'.

The negotiation of the Fourth NWA in 1975 saw the Government of the day make an explicit input into the terms of that agreement. The Government's influence on previous NWA negotiations was limited to efforts to indirectly influence the level of settlements through the budgets. An agreement, which was essentially an indexation agreement was ratified in April of 1975. However, it soon became apparent that the terms of the agreement would cause considerable difficulties for employers, and would also pose significant cost to the Government in the light of the Public Sector Pay Bill.

In response to the situation and in addressing the mounting pressure from the FUE for discussions on integrating pay, taxation and social policy, and union concerns over income tax, the Government suggested having tripartite discussions on these issues.

In June of that year the Government introduced a supplementary budget which removed Value Added Tax from certain items and introduced price subsidies as a package aimed at breaking the inflationary spiral. The Government, using the supplementary budget as bargaining leverage, threatened to revoke these price reliefs if the Fourth NWA was not re-negotiated. It was, and the eventual agreement was a turning point in that a 'standstill agreement' was negotiated. The previous agreements had afforded larger increases than their predecessors and the rates of inflation of the day.

The renegotiation established the new sequence of having the budget precede the NWA negotiations and as Hardiman (1988) suggests 'created a degree of expectation that NWAs and budgets might be closely linked again in the future'.

Talks on a Fifth NWA in 1976 opened in March again under the auspices of the ELC, amidst widely disparate views. The Government had made an appeal for a voluntary pay pause, which understandably was supported by the employers who suggested a nine-month pay pause followed by a flat rate increase of £2.40 a week. The unions wanted an agreement to run back-to-back that is, they did not want a pay pause. In any event, a draft agreement was achieved which was to be for a thirteen and a half month duration, with an annualised increase of 14 per cent and which restricted special increases in the public sector. A special delegate conference rejected the proposals essentially because of the restrictions placed on special pay increases. In the light of this rejection the FUE proposed more favourable terms, namely, 3 per cent plus £2 a week and the inclusion of a two-month pay pause and was notably less restrictive on the issue of special pay increases. These proposals by the employers were contingent on the Government and ICTU partaking in tripartite discussions to work out a framework for a total pay policy for 1977–78 within the context of a general economic and social programme for the development of the economy. The Minister for Labour responded positively to the proposals and an interim agreement was worked out which would be for seven months' duration. As well as the above-mentioned substantive terms it also included a clause indicating that a further national agreement be agreed subject to tripartite discussions and be essentially budget linked.

The Sixth NWA, in 1977, was the first in which a pay agreement was explicitly negotiated with reference to budgetary provisions. In January 1977 the Minister for Finance, in the course of his budget announced a variety of tax concessions and measures to improve employment. All of these provisions were contingent on the NWA being ratified (Dáil Debates, 1977). This was a clear example of bipartite talks on pay increases being conducted against a background of a tripartite arrangement involving the Government, and involving issues other than pay. At the tripartite conferences the Government outlined its willingness to give £50 in tax concessions in return for moderate increases.

The terms of the agreement ratified were for 2.5 per cent of basic pay plus a £1 a week increase in phase one and phase two. The agreement was to last for fourteen months with a three-month pay pause between the expiration of the Fifth and the beginning of the Sixth NWAs.

Although the text of the Sixth NWA makes no specific reference to the budget, it was generally accepted that the tax concessions were integral to its acceptance (Breen et al., 1990; O'Brien, 1989).

The round of negotiations for a Seventh NWA in 1978 also had tax inducements and Government commitments central to its acceptance. Again, these concessions were contingent on the negotiation of an acceptable pay agreement. This, however, looked very unlikely as negotiations had reached deadlock by the time of the February budget in 1978. The new Fianna Fáil Government confirmed its commitment to the process of centralised bargaining when, as an inducement to ensure the ratification of a new agreement, it withdrew its strict limit of 5 per cent which it had put on pay increases.

The ensuing talks were difficult but an agreement was reached in March 1978 and involved a basic norm of 8 per cent. The agreement was accepted by ICTU by a slender margin. Hardiman (1988) suggests that the unions were generally unhappy with the above-the-norm clauses which were stricter than before at a time when most sectors were doing quite well. As a concession to the unions, the 1978 agreement introduced a new feature which provided for the negotiation of pay increases up to 2 per cent extra at local level. It also permitted for the first time industrial action in certain circumstances in pursuance of above the norm increases.

6.7.4 THE NATIONAL UNDERSTANDINGS

By 1978 there was growing disillusionment within the trade union movement with the system of NWAs. In particular, trade unions felt that they were enduring excessively strict limitations and not getting not enough in return. As Von Prondzynski (1992) points out, some unions had always seen centralised bargaining as a mechanism which inhibited trade unions from realising their full bargaining potential. At a special delegate conference in November 1978 ICTU rejected the opening of talks on a national agreement for 1979. The prospect of a return to decentralised 'free for all' bargaining loomed. The Government responded with a budgetary package aimed at renewing the unions' interest and invited the trade unions to discuss a 'National Agreement for Development' which included increasing tax free allowances, modifying tax bands and extra public spending on employment creation. ICTU again convened a special conference to discuss the Government's intentions and to construct some policy proposals which they would use as the basis for negotiation with the Government. Their prinicipal concerns dealt with the nature of taxation which they perceived to be inequitable but also included proposals on employment and participation.

In March 1979 negotiations got underway which eventually resulted in a first National Understanding called the 'National Understanding for Economic and Social Development'. ICTU's executive council, mindful of the fact that they had no mandate to openly engage in talks for a new national agreement, 'explained that they were simply engaged in talks on trade union policy proposals' (Roche, 1989). These talks involved a series of working parties. The trade union and employer talks centred on pay, and trade union representatives met with ministers on a variety of non-pay issues including taxation, employment, health and education.

A package of proposals resulted from these tripartite working parties, which were placed before a special delegate conference in May 1979, and surprisingly were rejected. The proposals failed to gain acceptance because the ITGWU felt that the arrangements for tripartite consultation were not far reaching enough (ICTU, 1975).

The Government felt that securing a national agreement was essential to the economic development of the country and threatened to introduce statutory pay guidelines for the interim period (in effect a 7 per cent pay limit). The FUE who feared a return to the 'nightmares' of 'free for all' bargaining increased their pay offer, and with other minor revisions, ensured the acceptance at an ICTU special delegate conference in July.

The National Understanding of 1979 represented something of a new departure in Irish collective bargaining. For the first time the Government became involved in national pay talks as a Government where previously it had been involved in its capacity of public sector employer. The NU of 1979 also for the first time introduced a major non-pay element into national agreements.

Table 6.3 The terms and conditions of the National Understandings

Year	Round No.	Phase	Details
1979	20	1	9% minimum increase of £5.50 a week
		2	2% plus amount related to CPI movement, minimum increase £3.30 a week
1980	21	1	8% plus £1 a week
		2	7%

Source: McGinley, 1989

The First NU covered a period of fifteen months in two phases. Phase one provided for a basic increase in pay of 9 per cent subject to a minimum of £5.50 a week. Phase two provided for a 2 per cent increase in basic pay and included provision for changes in the Consumer Price Index during the period (which, as it transpired, meant an actual increase paid under phase two of 7 per cent plus £2.40 a week).

A second NU was negotiated in 1980. This time around ICTU received an overwhelming mandate to pursue another national agreement. However, the FUE which had previously been an enthusiastic supporter of the central agreements, began to express dissatisfaction with their performance. A number of factors helped to explain the FUE's new found reluctance. They believed that an unsatisfactory balance had been achieved between the central norms of the agreements and local level bargaining. They were also disturbed by the high level of industrial disputes and became increasingly critical of the cost of the non-pay elements of the agreements (Fogarty et al., 1981).

Nevertheless, a series of bipartite and tripartite talks ensued, through different institutional channels from the first NU. The pay talks used the offices of the ELC and non-pay elements were taken up directly with the Taoiseach and members of the Cabinet. These talks were only completed successfully after the intervention of the Government with guarantees to the employers on the contents of the 1981 budget. The Second NU was therefore completed with as Roche (1989) suggests the FUE were 'openly resentful of undue political pressure' which they felt was brought to bear on them.

The Second NU was ratified in October 1980 and like its forerunner had a pay and a non-pay element It provided for increases in two phases: phase one granted an increase of 8 per cent of basic pay and £1 a week for eight months. The second phase granted an increase of 7 per cent for a period of six months after the end of phase one.

The expiration of the Second NU heralded the suspension of centralised bargaining in Ireland. Although formal talks opened towards negotiating a new understanding, an impasse was soon reached on the pay terms between ICTU and the FUE, and the newly elected Fine Gael-Labour Coalition Government was unwilling to intervene to avert a breakdown. What followed was a return to decentralised bargaining.

6.7.5 THE PERFORMANCE OF CENTRALISED BARGAINING 1970–81

The National Wage Agreements and National Understandings were generally accepted as being unsuccessful attempts at centralised bargaining. Admittedly, they attempted to address many of the shortcomings of the wage rounds in the 1960s. In particular, they were a much more structured system, levels of pay were set in specific terms, the duration of the agreements was fixed and machinery was provided to deal with disputes arising out of the terms of such agreements and to deal with any anomalies. As Von Prondzynski (1992) suggests 'they had basically stabilised what had become a chaotic picture'. However, the system was felt to be unsuccessful in that the principal objectives of each of the social partners were not achieved. The agreements were seen by the Government as opportunities to pursue national economic objectives. However, on this criterion it would appear that little success was achieved. In spite of Government and employer assurances to the trade union movement, unemployment rose sharply. In 1969 unemployment stood at 4 per cent of the labour force, but by 1982 it had reached 10.7 per cent (Conniffe and Kennedy, 1984). Another objective of all parties in the process of centralised bargaining was the reduction in the levels of industrial unrest. Although a claimed advantage of national agreements, this objective was not achieved. While the agreements contained procedures to promote industrial peace the level of working days lost through matters covered by the NWAs climbed in the second half of the 1970s. After some success in the early stages of national agreements, Ireland's strike record continued to deteriorate throughout the 1970s with mandays lost up by 30 per cent on the previous decade. The annual average number of days lost per year rose from 353,769 in the period 1960–69 to 430,759 in 1970–79 (Fogarty et al., 1981). Another associated and worrying development was the increased tendency for unofficial action, which over the period accounted for over two-thirds of all strikes (Wallace and O'Shea, 1987). A phenomenon which also reflected increased workplace organisation and the power of trade unions.

In spite of the reports that national agreements were anti-inflationary by nature, the Government was unable to deliver on its commitments and inflation actually rose throughout the 1970s, reaching 20 per cent by 1981. The perception of the Government's ability to honour its commitments was severely damaged as evidenced by John Horgan's (while still Chairman of the Labour Court) reference to the National Understandings as 'Notional Understandings' (McGinley, 1989).

ICTU pressed throughout the period for changes to the system of taxation, however, at the end of the period of national agreements there had been little change in the overall burden of taxation on wage and salary earners (which in fact rose from 30 per cent in 1979 to 45 per cent in 1981). Also, the proportion of personal taxation to personal income rose from approximately 7 per cent in the mid-1960s, to 12 per cent in 1974 and over 15 per cent in 1976 (Conniffe and Kennedy, 1984). From the employer perspective, calls for wage moderation were unsuccessful. Wage rises were seen as being higher than appropriate for the period, and employers were particularly aggrieved at what they called the excessive use of the above-the-norm clause.

6.7.6 THE EXPERIENCE OF DECENTRALISED BARGAINING 1982–87
When the long series of centralised national agreements finally ended in 1982 it was to be replaced with a short period of decentralised bargaining at enterprise level. The collapse of centralised bargaining, however, did not involve a return to the system of collective bargaining which pre-dated it and, indeed, bore little resemblance to that which took place before 1970. Collective bargaining throughout the wage round era has been described as amounting to little more than 'splitting the difference between initial offers and claims' (O'Brien, 1989). The function of trade union claims being to impress members and potential members. The claims were more often concerned with notions of equity or comparability, than with the companies' financial performance and ability to pay.

Gunnigle and Foley (1994) argue that the return to decentralised bargaining, however, saw viability and economic performance become the key criteria shaping wage increases. Wage increases now had to be earned through better company or individual performance. Hence, settlements varied widely throughout industries, with no wage round norm being established, indeed, many commentators questioned the existence of the wage round concept in the private sector between 1982 and 1987 (McGinley, 1989). The FUE sought to shift collective bargaining away from the notion of a specific norm in each wage round, and from the idea that wage rounds ought to follow each other automatically. Their position was that pay increases should be closely tied to what the individual firm could bear (Hardiman, 1988). The Government attempted at times to impose a norm through pay guidelines but these were largely ignored by private sector negotiators and as Von Prondzynski (1985) argues were best seen as the Government's opening position in the public sector pay negotiations. Table 6.4 below highlights the reported average increases achieved in the private sector over the period.

Table 6.4 Private sector pay increases 1981–87		
Round	**Average cumulative increase (%)**	**Average length (months)**
22	16.4	14.9
23	10.9	13.5
24	9.3	12.75
25	6.8	12
26	6.0	12
27	6.5	15.4

Note: It is important to bear in mind that these figures may disguise large disparities within and between rounds.

Source: McGinley, 1989

O'Brien (1989) suggests that the return to decentralised bargaining saw industry and trade agreements which were prevalent in the 1950s and 1960s become less fashionable in many areas. During the 1960s there were sixty industrial bargaining groups which covered the country. Many of these groups fell into disuse during the period of centralised bargaining and were disbanded and failed to be reactivated during the 1980s. No new industry/trade groups were formed, with the notable exception of a new Joint Labour Committee for contract cleaners. The focus of bargaining activity was quite clearly fixed at the level of the individual firm.

A notable feature of the period was the reduction over the rounds in the number and the range of supplementary cost-increasing claims (above-the-norm claims). Irish wage costs per unit rose by only 7 per cent between 1980 and 1985 compared with an average 37 per cent increase in competing countries (Hardiman, 1988). There was also consistent support by both employers and trade unions for one-year agreements and a progressive movement towards single phase agreements. This came about possibly in response to the uncertain economic conditions which prevailed and employers' needs to tie wage bargaining to the annual budgetary process.

The union negotiating agenda lengthened with non-wage conditions of employment taking on a greater significance in negotiations than before. The content of union claims changed with a shift away from pure pay claims to claims in relation to hours of work, bonuses, leave and general working conditions (Incomes Data Services, 1992). Employers countered with equally pressing demands, particularly in relation to working practices and methods, in which there seemed amongst trade union ranks 'to be a growing willingness to accept the need for changes' (FUE Annual Review, 1986).

The return to decentralised bargaining coincided with a dramatic rise in the unemployment rate, ever increasing redundancies (standing at over 30,000 per annum by 1984), falling trade union membership, coupled with recessionary conditions. All of these factors led to a much weakened trade union movement. Indeed, it has been argued that the deteriorating economic circumstances introduced a 'new realism' into employer/employee relationships which was to transcend all facets of organisational activities including collective bargaining (Gunnigle and Foley, 1993). The capacity of unions to engage in industrial militancy was reduced and the period saw a notable drop in the level of strikes.

Management during the period clearly regained the initiative with productivity improving strongly, often as a result of rationalisation. Overall, private sector employers did much better than they had hoped when local level negotiations resumed in 1982. In successive wage rounds pay norms followed falling inflation downwards. There was certainly no private sector employer push for a return to national agreements — indeed, as O'Brien (1989) argues, in the light of the advantageous bargaining position of employers there were very considerable doubts about it.

6.7.7 THE PROGRAMME FOR NATIONAL RECOVERY

The prime motivating factor for the reactivation of the process of national bargaining in 1987 was, undoubtedly, the growing crisis in the public finances. The three principal elements in current Government expenditure were foreign debt service, social welfare and the public sector payroll. At the end of 1986 the national debt of £24 billion was three times larger than it had been in 1980, and represented 148 per cent of annual GNP. Unprecedented levels of unemployment saw Government expenditure in social services increase from 28.9 per cent of GNP in 1980 to 35.6 per cent in 1985 (NESC, 1986). Many commentators warned that the country appeared to be heading for economic and financial disaster. Because of the perceived difficulties in tackling debt service and social welfare, the public sector payroll became the central focus of Government action. The experience of decentralised bargaining from 1982 saw more modest pay increases negotiated in the public sector. Also, in an attempt to contain the Government's paybill a career break scheme and an embargo on recruitment (designed to reduce numbers through natural wastage) were introduced.

The National Economic and Social Council (NESC), a consultative forum comprised of representatives of the main interest groups in the economy, the trade unions, employers and farmers, produced a report entitled A Strategy for Development 1986–1990. This report emphasised the need for cogent action to address the 'twin problems of mass unemployment and chronic fiscal imbalance' and was to become central to future Government thinking on the nature of national bargaining and incomes policy (NESC, 1986). The NESC report did not make any explicit recommendations on pay because the employer representatives on the council expressed the view that negotiation at the level of the firm was the most appropriate means of determining pay.

The beginning of 1987 brought the election of a Fianna Fáil Government whose economic strategy was to be broadly guided by the principles and priorities established in the NESC report. The Government in its initial budget announced a number of measures to improve the position of the public finances including restrictive measures in relation to public sector pay. During the course of a number of consultative meetings with the Government after the general election it became apparent that it was interested in attaining a three-year pay agreement.

In April of 1987 ICTU proposed to the Government that there should be discussions about a national plan for growth and economic recovery, public finances and social services. Interest in returning to a national agreement was expressed by a number of prominent trade union leaders throughout 1986 (such as John Carroll of the ITGWU and Bill Attley of the FWUI). A number of factors may help to explain ICTU's interest in the negotiation of a new national agreement. Issues such as employment, tax reform and social welfare were now central to the ICTU's agenda as it would appear that the political and economic objectives of trade unions had long since converged. Congress were now particularly concerned for the plight of low paid employees, who were suffering most in the recessionary conditions of decentralised bargaining in the 1980s because of their weak competitive bargaining position. The trade union movement was also mindful of the situation which had developed in the UK, where unions had suffered under the premiership of Thatcher and repressive Tory legislation. Bill Attley, the general secretary of the FWUI, warned at the ICTU annual delegate conference that the trade union movement was in serious danger of being marginalised (ICTU Annual Report, 1987). The trade unions looked to the prospect of a new national agreement to 'beef up' their role and status in Irish society. They had feared that the trade union movement might go the way the unions had gone in the UK and be excluded from the national scene. Dineen and Wallace (1991) argue that the decision of the trade unions to participate in the negotiation of the Programme for National Recovery must be seen in the light of falling membership levels between 1980 and 1987. This decline focused the attention of unions on the threat that unemployment posed to membership levels. By collaborating with Government policy and entering into a national agreement the unions would be seen to be getting wage increases, albeit modest ones, which they hoped would help to retain and attract new members.

ICTU was also troubled by the state of the public finances and the Government's need to control the public sector payroll which could only be achieved by either cutting numbers employed or by freezing sector pay rates, or indeed by both. The prospect of having a pay freeze in the public sector, which represented approximately half of the trade union membership, while the private sector locally negotiated even moderate increases posed a serious threat to the unity of the trade union movement.

On the employer side, the FUE were initially less than favourable towards the idea of a further national agreement. They were especially concerned about the proposed reduction in working hours and that a national agreement would be too rigid. They, however, 'had been gradually wooed into support of the government's wider economic policies in general .... the cuts in public spending were the kind the private sector employers have been urging for years' (*Business and Finance*, 1987). It would be accurate to suggest that the employers were under an amount of political pressure to negotiate a new agreement. However, in the final analysis their support for such an agreement was secured by their recognition that the likely terms of any proposed agreement would be advantageous to their affiliated companies. Indeed, the view expressed was that little was to be achieved by abstaining from the process, and, at least, participation had some potential.

The negotiations that followed were eventually concluded in October 1987 and resulted in the Programme for National Recovery (PNR). The programme was to cover the period up to the end of 1990 and entailed the following provisions:
– the creation of a fiscal, exchange and monetary climate conducive to economic growth. This included a commitment that the ratio of debt to GNP should be reduced to between 5 per cent and 7 per cent;
– movement towards greater equity and fairness in the tax system;
– measures to generate employment opportunities. Notably no extra expenditure was to be committed to this;
– reduction of social inequalities.

The PNR covered proposals for pay agreements in both the public and private sectors. The public sector agreement provided for a six-month pay pause and for increases in basic pay for the three-year programme of 3 per cent on the first £120 of basic weekly pay and 2 per cent on the balance. A minimum increase of £4 per week in basic pay for full-time adult employees was also agreed.

The private sector agreement provided for the same substantive terms. The £4 minimum, however, was to be subject to local negotiations. It also committed bargaining groups to not advancing any further cost-increasing claims on employers for the duration of the agreement. The minimum cash increase was aimed at benefiting low paid employees. It was also agreed, to facilitate an objective of the trade unions, that discussions would take place between the Government, the FUE and CIF and ICTU on the development of a general framework for reducing working time by one hour for those working forty or more hours per week.

The PNR was markedly different from the earlier centralised agreements. O'Brien (1989) argues that 'a whole host of old conventions were ditched and new conventions forged'. These included the following:

– a three-year agreement — previously unheard of;
– a pay increase at or even slightly below inflation — previously unheard of;
– no provision for below-the-norm or above-the-norm payments;
– a national commitment to pursue the reduction of working hours — previously unknown;
– no institutional monitoring of the agreement as the ELC had in the 1970s.

The pay terms were not fixed norms but guidelines which in the private sector had to be agreed through local level bargaining. This met a major employer concern on the flexibility of the pay arrangements. The PNR also differed from its predecessors of the 1970s in that the terms concerning economic and social policy were expressed as specific targets and not as binding commitments.

The PNR was generally viewed as a considerable success in that the terms of the agreement were largely satisfied. Wage increases which were achieved at local level ran roughly parallel to those suggested by the PNR. During the three years covered by the programme, manufacturing output and exports grew steadily creating a major balance of trade surplus. There was an advancement in economic growth of more than 4 per cent per annum on average and inflation reached its lowest level in thirty years in 1988. The debt-GNP ratio was stabilised, falling from 131 per cent in 1987 to 111 per cent in 1990 and net job gains were achieved, reversing the trends of the early 1980s. Strike levels declined considerably, with a particularly significant fall off in the level of unofficial strikes. Some questions have been raised by economists as to whether the success of the Irish economy experienced between 1987–90 was due to the PNR or to the generally buoyant international economy. As with most macro-economic issues the nature of the causation is difficult to ascertain.

Amongst the trade unions there was continuous criticism that the resources being generated were not being sufficiently channelled into employment creation. For example, the 1988 ICTU annual delegate conference saw three motions debated, all largely critically of the PNR. However, two years into the programme ICTU voted to continue to support it and, with the end of the three-year PNR in sight, decided in favour of entering talks on a new agreement.

6.7.8 THE PROGRAMME FOR ECONOMIC AND SOCIAL PROGRESS

In October 1990 ICTU again took the initiative and proposed that the Government, the employers, the farming organisations and trade unions should agree on a ten-year development strategy for the country. The result of the subsequent negotiations was the Programme for Economic and Social Progress (PESP).

The PESP covered the period from the expiration of the PNR to the end of 1993. The key objectives of the PESP were:
– sustained economic growth and the generation of greater income;
– a substantial increase in employment;

– a major assault on long-term unemployment;
– the development of greater social rights within our health, education, social welfare and housing services;
– the promotion of social responsibility in relation to discharge of tax liabilities;
– the development of worker participation, women's rights and consumer rights.

The agreement set out that increases were to be awarded annually for three years on the basis of:
– 4 per cent of basic pay in the first year of the agreement;
– 3 per cent of basic pay in the second year of the agreement;
– 3.75 per cent of basic pay in the third year of the agreement.

Where the application of this formula resulted in increases in basic pay for full-time employees of less than £5 per week in the first year, £4.25 per week in the second year or £5.75 in the third then the percentage increase could be adjusted by local level bargaining. These increases were to be negotiated through the normal industrial relations machinery with regard to the economic and commercial circumstances of the particular firm.

The PESP also provided for local bargaining in 'exceptional cases'. In such circumstances employers and trade unions could negotiate further changes in the rates of pay or conditions of employment which were up to but not exceeding 3 per cent of the basic pay of the group of employees concerned.

As was the case with the PNR, the PESP provided that no cost-increasing claims, in addition to the ones outlined above, could be made on employers during the course of the agreement. Unions were not precluded under the agreement from making claims for the introduction of pension or sick pay schemes where none existed. The PESP committed employers, trade unions and employees to promoting industrial harmony. Where the parties could not reach agreement on any issue covered by the PESP it was agreed that they could jointly refer the matter to the Labour Relations Commission/Labour Court or to some other agreed dispute resolution machinery.

The publication of the PESP was met with critical commentary from some quarters. Barret (1991), for instance, argued shortly after its negotiation that the PESP represented a continuation of the Government's 'slide back to borrowing and wasteful public expenditure', and marked an abandonment of the expansionary fiscal rectitude which appeared to have bolstered the economy under the PNR.

The public sector unions experienced some problems in the operation of the PESP, most notably the Government hinted that it was considering reneging on the pay aspects of the programme as a result of lower than expected growth at the beginning of 1992. A concerted protest strike throughout the public sector resulted from the Government's attempt to demand a flat rate increase of £5 instead of the 3 per cent under the programme (Von Prondzynski, 1992).

Perhaps the most significant critical aspect of the PESP, however, was its performance in relation to some of the objectives or targets outlined in the agreement. For example, the PESP had a substantial increase in employment as an objective, this did not occur, in fact, an ESRI analysis suggests that employment reduced by 5,000 between 1990 and 1993 (Barret, 1993). A major assault on long-term unemployment was promised. However, in September 1992 there were 49,000 more long-term unemployed than in 1990 (Barret, 1993). Under the terms of the PESP the standard tax rate was to be reduced to 25 per cent by 1993 but in fact was 27 per cent plus a 1 per cent 'temporary' income levy. The public sector pay bill which increased by over 27 per cent between 1990 and 1993 was also the source of much discontent. In hindsight it can be argued that the Government may have been a bit ambitious in its forecasts for the programme. Maurice Doyle, the Governor of the Central Bank, criticised the Government for not renegotiating the PESP when circumstances such as weak growth and rising unemployment required it. The attainment of the targets in the programme was undoubtedly hindered by such unforeseen developments as the currency crisis at the end of 1992, which would have been almost impossible to plan for.

The PESP was undoubtedly accompanied by more positive aspects. The fundamentals of the economy, that is, interest rates and inflation were still relatively good. The national consensus developed under the PNR was continued. The relative industrial peace, a feature of the PNR, also continued under the PESP. However, as Sheehan (1991) points out, 'there is no firm evidence one way or the other that centralised bargaining helps to secure industrial peace'. The Government has also argued that a significant number of jobs were saved during the term of the PESP through our improved competitiveness in wage costs relative to our main trading partners.

In making an assessment of its impact, it would be fair to say that the performance of the Irish economy for the duration of the PESP compares unfavourably to the relative success of the economy for the duration of its immediate predecessor the PNR. It would be rash, however, to suggest that the PESP was responsible for the economic problems that the country experienced subsequent to its negotiation. The performance of the PESP must be seen in the light of a depression in the international economy which was experienced for the duration of the programme. Indeed, given that the PNR was in effect when international conditions were favourable and that the results of the PESP were much less impressive when the international situation was less favourable, there would appear to be a strong argument that the success of such national agreements is contingent upon external factors.

6.7.9 THE PROGRAMME FOR COMPETITIVENESS AND WORK

Prior to the expiration of the PESP in December 1993, the parties to the programme set out their positions regarding the negotiation of a further national agreement. The unions advanced some preconditions for a renegotiation of a follow-on agreement, principally that the Government remove the 1 per cent 'temporary' levy and certain limitations placed upon social welfare payments, both introduced in the budget of 1993. Mr Edmund Browne, a joint president of SIPTU, argued that by introducing these measures the 'Government had diminished the status of the social partnership' and added that the Government was presiding over, and precipitating, the end of the social consensus process. Initially, the Government was unwilling to accept these preconditions and the prospect of a return to decentralised bargaining was on the cards. In the final analysis, however, it seemed unlikely that these preconditions would necessarily prevent the trade unions from taking a place at the negotiating table, and the preconditions may best be viewed as bargaining tactics on ICTU's behalf. It appears evident that ICTU would have found it more advantageous to be party to a new agreement than to stay out of any new arrangements. An analysis completed by SIPTU in 1992 showed that take-home pay for the average worker had increased in real terms in the years since 1987 after a decline in the years 1980–87 (IRN 36, 1992). Sheehan (1993) contends that many union leaders believed that their best interests would be served within the context of an overall national agreement similar to the PESP. There were some outspoken members of the trade union movement, for example, Michael O'Reilly the Secretary of the Amalgamated Transport and General Workers Union who condemned the PESP and its forerunner the PNR as 'having laid the basis of marginalisation of the whole trade union movement', and argued that the 'new right' had prompted sections of ICTU 'to advocate collaboration with employers and Government in controlling workers in order to create stability'.

The Government for its part had made it very clear that it wanted another national agreement to replace the PESP. The then Minister for Finance, Bertie Ahern, stressed that pay moderation would have to be part of any new deal and expressed interest in securing a no-strike guarantee until the year 2001. The Government had been reported as saying that it was willing to offer a number of concessions to the unions as part of any new agreement including the following:
- electing workers to company boards;
- increasing the nine annual public holidays;
- introducing a uniform working week of less than forty hours;
- greater equality for women workers;
- better health, welfare and housing services.

The private sector employers were relatively happy with the PESP. Some may have complained about the level of pay rises involved, though they were thankful for the certainty it offered. Pay bargaining at local level in the private sector produced increases which largely complied with the pay terms suggested by the PESP. The Incomes Data Services (1992) report that 90 to 95 per cent of companies surveyed adhered to the pay guidelines outlined by the PESP. The local level bargaining clause went well from the employers' point of view as it was conceded in less than 50 per cent of workplaces. However, many did regard the process of negotiating these local rises as 'difficult and troublesome' (*Business and Finance*, 1993). According to a survey carried out by the Institute of Personnel Management (IPM), 95 per cent of senior personnel managers were in favour of a further PESP type agreement (*Irish Times*, 1993). The IPM stressed the positive effects that centralised agreements had on improving competitiveness in the private sector and saw considerable prospects for obtaining low pay increases in the light of low levels of inflation. Some employers argued for the need for greater flexibility to be built into any new agreement, as it was clear from the experience of the currency crisis at the beginning of 1993 that the external environment of many organisations had the capacity to change so rapidly that a moderate increase under a national agreement may become unsustainable in a relatively short space of time.

An accommodation was reached between the Government and ICTU in relation to the unions' preconditions, and the outcome of the negotiations which ensued was the Programme for Competitiveness and Work which was negotiated within the context of the long-term development strategy for the country. Table 6.5 below sets out the pay terms agreed for the private sector and the public service for the duration of the programme which ran from 1994 to 1997.

Table 6.5 Pay terms of the Programme for Competitiveness and Work

Category	1994	1995	1996	1994-97
Private sector employees, basic increases*	2% for 12 months on basic pay from 1 January	2.5% for 12 months on basic pay from 1 January	2.5% for first 6 months; extra 1% in second 6 months	Increase of 8% in basic pay over three years
Building sector, basic increases	5-month pay pause, then 2% for 12 months	2% for 12 months from 1 June	2% for 4 months; 1% for next 3 months; 1% for final 3 months	5-month pay pause, then 8% increase over 33 months; deal lasts 39 months
Public-service employees, basic increases	Freeze to 1 June, then 2% for 12 months	2% for 12 months from 1 June	1.5% from 1 June; 1.5% from 1 October; 1% from 1 January 1997; deal to expire June 1997	5-month pay pause, then 8% rise in basic pay over 3 years to June 1997
Public service awards local/special awards	1% rise payable from 1 April as down payment prior to completed negotiation	0.75% rise payable from 1 June after negotiation	0.75% rise payable from 1 June after negotiation; final 0.5% payable from 1 June 1997	Maximum of 3% rise in pay for productivity increases under this carry-over from PESP

Source: Tansey, 1994

6.7.10 PARTNERSHIP 2000 FOR INCLUSION, EMPLOYMENT AND COMPETITIVENESS

In the year preceding the expiration of the PCW there had been a significant amount of media coverage on the future of centralised bargaining, with many analysts questioning whether the 'social partnership' which had commenced under the PNR in 1987 was coming to an end. The trade unions in particular, went through what seemed to become the standard ritual, involving the expression of serious misgivings about the centralised bargaining process, and with the idea of yet another national agreement. The doubts about the prospects for a new pact after the PCW were largely driven by critical comments in early 1996 from the SIPTU leadership, on the one hand, and because of a number of high profile disputes which had emerged in the public service, on the other.

SIPTU's reservations, which led Bill Attley and other leaders of the union to declare that the 'era of partnership is over', centred on the unions' insistence on the need for a significant move to relieve the burden on the PAYE sector. With more than ten months of the PCW remaining the then SIPTU vice president, Jimmy Somers, stated that the PCW's two priority goals in relation to personal income tax had not yet been met by the Government. These goals were firstly, alleviating the burden of taxation on workers with low income, particularly those with families, and secondly, raising the income threshold at which the higher rate of tax came into play. Somers asserted that unless workers could be convinced that commitments which had been given in previous agreements were honoured, they would not buy into any new arrangement (see IRN Report, 1996, 9:18-19).

The unions' view was supported by the then leader of the opposition, Bertie Ahern, who was highly critical of the Government's performance and warned that the national consensus was in danger of collapse. He argued that the trade unions were angry, 'specifically because the Government had sabotaged the partnership approach' and 'failed to honour the commitments of the PCW' (Sheehan, 1996a).

The unions also pointed to other significant stumbling blocks to their continued participation in the national consensus. They complained about lack of progress in regard to the extension of the partnership approach to the level of the workplace. There had been consistent criticism from the trade unions over many years that the consensus needed to be extended downwards to the level of the individual firm. It was widely felt that the agreements to date had been too focused on macro-economic issues and ICTU argued that a greater sense of ownership or involvement in the social partnership by employees at the level of the firm was required.

The vexed issue of union recognition and the denial of representational rights had rarely left the top of the trade union agenda. The unions had attempted to introduce a provision on trade union recognition as part of the PCW. The attempt was unsuccessful as the employers strongly resisted the move. Jimmy Somers, addressing the issue, argued that 'it should not be necessary, in an era of partnership, that groups of workers should have to strike in order to establish their constitutional right to join and to be represented by a trade union' (IRN Report, 1996, 9:18–19). For the unions the question of trade union recognition would have to be a central issue in any future negotiations with the other social partners.

A deep dissatisfaction with the PCW had been displayed at the Easter conferences of many unions in 1996 — most notably the teachers' unions. Apart from the concerns outlined above, many contributors at these conferences cited the tight nature of the terms negotiated under the PCW, particularly in the context of a buoyant economy, as an impediment to grassroots support for the concept of further national agreements.

Many commentators also questioned the future of the national consensus by reference to the rising industrial unrest in the public sector as evidenced by disputes which had occurred throughout the term of the PCW involving nurses, teachers, health board workers and lower paid civil servants (Croke, 1996). This unrest had seen the first national public service stoppage in ten years organised by 10,000 CPSU members in February 1996, and the narrowly avoided disruption at Dublin hospitals and health centres. There had been much speculation about the extent to which the stresses and strains which the PCW was under in the public service was both undermining the existing agreement and jeopardising the prospects for a new pact. As Sheehan (1996b) put it, rows between the Government and public service workers had certainly exposed 'the public sector as the "Achilles' heel" of national agreements yet again'.

The Government was anxious for any difficulties which would endanger the national consensus to be resolved. In the months prior to the expiration of the PCW the then Taoiseach, John Bruton, made a strong case for the continuation of the centralised bargaining process. He warned that a return to free-for-all pay bargaining would damage real living standards and hurt the most vulnerable members of society. He argued that the national programmes since 1987 had helped create a climate where companies could be confident of industrial peace, stable interest rates, low inflation and clarity about the evolution of wage costs.

The Secretary of the Department of Finance, Paddy Mullarkey, restated this view when he asserted that, based on pay moderation, the PCW along with the previous agreements had contributed to improving competitiveness and strong economic growth and job creation. Mr Mullarkey argued that although nominal pay increases had been moderate, there had been real benefits to employees in take-home pay as a result of changes in taxation and PRSI, combined with real improvements in the level and quality of social spending. During the lifetime of the PCW, employment had grown by 130,000 — against a background of generally declining employment in the rest of Europe — and increases in take-home pay had been in the order of between 4 per cent and 6.5 per cent. Social spending had risen by 5.8 per cent in a two-year period (Sheehan, 1996c).

The Government welcomed the publication of reports from both the ESRI and the NESC in 1996 which were roundly supportive of the continuation of the concept of social partnership. The ESRI quarterly report published in February 1996 argued that the maintenance of modest pay expectations facilitated by the national agreements played a major role in the robust recovery of the Irish economy in the early 1990s, at a time of recession in other European countries, saying that this broad national consensus

> ... on a fiscally responsible, low inflation and competitiveness-conscious economic strategy has yielded great benefits in terms of substantial employment growth, the stabilising of the public finances and a steady, but moderate, improvement in living standards for the majority of the population.

But it warned that the re-emergence of 'unrealistic public expectations' in relation to pay was the major threat to continued economic progress (ESRI, 1996).

The NESC report, *A Strategy into the 21st Century*, concluded that social partnership programmes are the most effective mechanism for developing competitiveness and social cohesion (NESC, 1996).

In an attempt to boost the prospects of trade union involvement in talks on a new agreement, the Government conceded that many of the unions' concerns would have to be discussed as part of any negotiation on a new arrangement and that a commitment to cut taxes — in particular — would be of central importance in securing a new national deal. The Government's own priority issue in any talks on a renewal of the social partnership would be controlling public spending and, obviously, wage restraint in the public service was seen to be a central issue in this regard. The Government was concerned with a spate of pay deals and offers under the restructuring clause of the PCW which were in process. The Government was conscious of the fact that its ability to make and fulfil tax pledges depended on its ability to control public expenditure.

The private sector employers were pleased with the generally positive experience of the PCW. Brian Geoghegan, a leading IBEC economist, strongly defended the performance of the PCW and argued that the national programme had delivered on jobs, kept inflation and interest rates low and delivered 'additional disposable income to an average employee with a mortgage on top of the net mix of pay and tax gains' (Geoghegan, 1996). Geoghegan estimated that 'the net (after tax, PRSI etc.) take home gain over the three years of the PCW for a married worker amounted to 11.8% and for a single worker to 13.9%'.

IBEC had their concerns, particularly in relation to the question of public expenditure and taxation, but largely welcomed the prospect of talks on a further agreement. The employers, however, as John Dunne, director general of IBEC states, did not see any disaster if national agreements were to be abandoned as they would have been relatively comfortable about the outcome in a 'free for all' (Dunne, 1996). In the absence of nationally agreed pay terms, IBEC perceived that the maintenance of pay discipline at the level of the workplace would be easier to achieve as a result of greater employee acceptance of the significance of external factors, such as competitive pressures and globalisation. IBEC had generally reacted cautiously to the trade union movement's demands for increased partnership at the level of the firm, and insisted that there could be no overall prescriptive solution to this issue, but accepted that the parties could agree a formula of words which would address partnership in aspirational terms.

Following this period of uncertainty, negotiations on a successor to the PCW opened in October 1996. The negotiations opened with a one day summit style forum which was addressed by nineteen different groups. This was the first occasion on which the Government had allowed for the involvement of organisations other than the more established social partners such as IBEC and ICTU in the centralised bargaining process. In the negotiations there was to be a much larger role for bodies representing socially disadvantaged groups and those representing a number of voluntary organisations. Groups such as the Irish National Organisation of the Unemployed (INOU), the National Youth Council, the Conference of Religious of Ireland (CORI) and Protestant Aid all made their representations at the negotiations. Von Prondzynski (1998) comments that many of the groups took an increasingly assertive approach in defending the interests of the disadvantaged and the socially excluded.

By mid-December 1996 the parties to the talks agreed on a new programme entitled Partnership 2000 for Inclusion, Employment and Competitiveness. The agreement outlined a detailed programme of social, economic and fiscal policies, accompanied, as had become the custom, by a separate pay agreement between the employers' organisations and ICTU in an appendix to the programme. The programme is to last for three years, with phased increases in pay during that period. As in previous agreements, the low paid are specifically catered for through the provision of minimum amounts of increases for each phase.

Partnership 2000 provides for pay increases of up to 9.25 per cent over a thirty-nine month period. The basic deal involves phased basic increases which total 7.25 per cent plus an additional local bargaining element of up to 2 per cent. The terms of the private sector agreement are set out in Table 6.6 below.

Table 6.6	Private sector pay terms of Partnership 2000 for Inclusion, Employment and Competitiveness
First phase	2.5% for 12 months
Second Phase	2.25% for 12 months
	(Local bargaining element: 2% in the second half of phase 2)
Third Phase	1.5% for 9 months
Fourth Phase	1.0% for 6 months

Source: Partnership 2000 for Inclusion, Employment and Competitiveness, 1996

The agreement provides for an opening basic rise of 2.5 per cent for the first twelve months followed by a 2.25 per cent increase in the second twelve-month period. The negotiable local bargaining element of 2 per cent comes into operation in the second half of the second phase. The third phase allows for an increase of 1.5 per cent of basic pay for the next nine months, and the final phase for an increase of 1.0 per cent over the final six months. The agreement provides for minimum increases of £3.50 per week in the second phase, £2.40 per week in the third phase and £1.60 per week in the fourth phase.

The public sector agreement which was finalised shortly after its private sector equivalent, includes the same basic phased increases, albeit with a slightly adjusted phasing. As a concession to the Exchequer the public sector agreement was subject to a later implementation of the first phase.

The provision dealing with the local bargaining element stipulates that employers and unions must, not earlier than the second half of the second phase of the agreement, negotiate at the level of the firm or at industry level — whichever is appropriate — 'for adjustments in pay and/or conditions of employment, the cost of which shall not exceed 2.0% of the basic pay cost' (Partnership 2000, 1996). Negotiations under the clause must also have regard to the costs involved and to the ability of the firm or industry to meet these costs. Therefore, arrangements can include 'appropriate cost off-setting measures and phasing arrangements, where necessary'. It was also agreed that disputes arising out of the negotiation of the local bargaining clause will be dealt with by the Labour Relations Commission, the Labour Court or other agreed machinery.

Partnership 2000 provides for a package of tax relief of close to £900 million. The taxation elements approved include a cut in the standard rate of tax of 27 per cent by 1 per cent and in employees' PRSI by 1 per cent, and an increase in the tax bands over the duration of the programme. The programme commits £100 million to a business tax package which is to provide for progressive reductions in the standard rate of corporation tax and improvements in the position of small firms over the three years.

Partnership 2000 sets down a number of financial targets — including a pledge that the general Government deficit will be held to at most 1.5 per cent of national output in each of the three years, and forecasts of growth in GNP of 5.5 per cent in 1997 and 4.5 per cent in 1998 and 1999. It also includes predictions of employment growth of on average 38,000 a year with inflation remaining relatively low at 2 per cent.

Apart from the central pay and tax elements, Partnership 2000 also includes a chapter on partnership at enterprise level and a specific commitment to the development of employee share ownership and profit sharing. These issues will be discussed at length in chapter 8 of this book. The long awaited chapter on partnership states that the parties have set out 'principles and definitions to develop this process, including best practice, proposed monitoring arrangements, and recommendations which should form the basis for discussions initiated at enterprise level between management, employees/trade unions' (Partnership 2000, 1996:9). The chapter entitled 'Partnership for Competitive Enterprises', notes that the social partners have agreed to establish a national framework to develop partnership at enterprise level. This framework, however, is not prescriptive and the parties agreed that there is a need to 'tailor the approach to fit different employment settings'. A National Centre for Partnership and Change is also to be set up, involving ICTU, IBEC, the Labour Relations Commission and other State agencies. The Centre will provide joint training for trade union officials and human resource managers.

Partnership 2000 agreed a series of measures which are aimed at tackling social exclusion. Similar measures had been a feature of the previous agreements since 1987. On this occasion, however, the provisions attempt to satisfy the concerns of those groups which were for the first time part of peripheral negotiations — groups such as the INOU and CORI — which make up what is often referred to as the 'social pillar' or the 'second strand' of social partnership. The Programme provides for £525 million for social inclusion measures. The measures outlined seek to bring more long-term unemployed people back into the workforce through improving their access to education, training and, ultimately, jobs. This is to be achieved by extending existing programmes and by developing new initiatives.

ICTU were successful on this occasion in getting the issue of trade union recognition addressed in the Partnership 2000 agreement. It was agreed that a high level group consisting of ICTU, IBEC, the IDA, Forbairt and representatives of the Department of the Taoiseach and of the Department of Enterprise and Employment would be charged with reporting back to the social partners within a year on how the issue of union recognition could be addressed.

The publication of Partnership 2000 was hailed as a success by the social partners. In welcoming the programme, ICTU stressed their view that the agreement was a 'new-style deal'. ICTU general secretary Peter Cassells said Congress's objective was to 'deepen and broaden' the process of national agreements beyond programmes to genuine partnership, and, from their perspective, Partnership 2000 marked a first, though significant, step in this direction (Hastings, 1996). IBEC were satisfied that the proposals for pay in the private sector took into account the requirements of competitiveness and the need for labour cost certainty over the thirty-nine month duration of the programme. They were also pleased that the programme deals with a number of issues which IBEC had argued strongly for, namely, the alleviation of the burden of personal taxation, progressive reduction in corporation tax and a strategic emphasis on competitiveness. Employers were also particularly pleased with the proposals contained in the programme for the development of the small firms sector. The Government was also pleased with the renewal of the social partnership and summarised the deal as reflecting the shared understanding of the strategy required for improved living standards based on moderate pay increases and full adherence to the terms of the Maastricht criteria for EMU.

Partnership 2000 was ratified by a special delegate conference of ICTU in January 1997. The vote by the trade union delegates was the closest since the acceptance of the PNR in 1987 (see IRN Report 6, February 1997). In the weeks preceding the vote and at the conference itself, the programme was subject to much debate. Those unions which called for rejection of the pact argued that workers will end up just 1 per cent better off after inflation at the end of the programme and that figures produced by ICTU showed large disparities between the respective positions of those on high and low incomes under the deal. There was also much criticism that nothing concrete had been achieved on the issue of union recognition.

Many unions which represented the low paid, for example, Mandate, voted for rejection of the Programme. The general secretary of Mandate, Owen Nulty, argued that under the programme low-paid, casual workers will receive around 10 per cent (including tax concessions) over thirty-nine months compared with 14 per cent or more for higher paid workers (Yeates, 1997). Jimmy Somers of SIPTU conceded that although the union recommended acceptance of Partnership 2000 many SIPTU members in low paid employments were swayed by these arguments. Mandate also expressed disappointment that the programme did not hold out any prospect of legislation to control the spread of unsocial hours and increased casualisation.

The Irish secretary of the ATGWU, Mick O'Reilly, advocated rejection of the new national agreement. He argued that a rejection of the package would allow unions to gain better pay rises for their members through creative local bargaining. He cited the example of the early 1980s when national agreements broke down after trade unions failed to push employers and the Government of the day beyond 12 per cent and where subsequently workers won increases of between 12.5 per cent and 20 per cent in local bargaining (Yeates, 1997). He also rejected the notion that the unemployed and other socially excluded groups would suffer if there were no agreement. Trade unions had a historic commitment to the unemployed and that would remain, whether or not there was an agreement.

Carolann Duggan, a SIPTU member in Waterford typified the feelings of many trade unionists when she said: 'The country is booming, the employers and the banks are making a fortune in profits, up 45% according to Bill Attley. Yet the workers who created all the wealth are being told to take a rise of 7.4% over three years and three months.'

Partnership 2000 is without doubt the most ambitious national agreement to date. It continues the established pattern of bargained national agreements for socio-economic policies but extends this pattern considerably. It sets out to create a new and wider social contract. Von Prondzynski (1998) views Partnership 2000 as representing something of a change of direction when compared with the previous national agreements since 1987. He contends that unlike the previous programmes, its emphasis is not as single-mindedly on economic competitiveness. In this regard, he believes that the reference to 'inclusion' and 'employment' before 'competitiveness' in the title is significant. Von Prondzynski suggests that 'the emphasis has shifted, at least slightly, from containing costs and combating inflation to protecting livelihoods and promoting employment', and argues that in this respect the corporatist tendencies of the Irish industrial relations system have been given a significant boost after the ambiguities of the previous agreements.

6.7.11 THE PERFORMANCE OF CENTRALISED BARGAINING FROM 1987

Gunnigle (1997) proposes that the achievement of a high level of national consensus through a model of 'bargained co-operation' is undoubtedly the most significant contemporary development in Irish industrial relations. Since 1987, collective bargaining in Ireland has been conducted within the framework of a sequence of national level agreements negotiated between trade unions, employers and the State — the so-called 'social partners'. It would almost be glib to say that this social partnership has paid off handsomely. While the four national agreements since 1987 have enjoyed varying degrees of success, it is widely held that they have laid the foundation for the recent revival of the Irish economy. By and large, the centralised agreements negotiated since 1987 have been associated with beneficial outcomes for the social partners involved. The years of social partnership have been marked by sustained high rates of economic growth, which have shown the Irish economy as one of the fastest growing economies in Europe or the OECD in the 1990s. This period has also been characterised by moderate wage increases, low levels of inflation, record employment growth and low levels of industrial conflict. Given the difficulties that exist in ascertaining the causation of macro-economic and industrial relations trends, it would be bold to claim the improved economic environment as a direct consequence of the continuing social partnership. However, there is general agreement that the recent achievements in the economy have been underpinned by the national consensus which has developed through the centralised bargaining process. While the centralised bargaining process was not the only contributor to the economic boom, it has helped to create the climate of stability which has led to unprecedented levels of investment in the economy. Tables 6.7–6.9 below summarise both the wage and non-wage elements of the four national programmes since 1987.

Table 6.7   Summary of percentage wage increases under centralised wage bargaining, 1987–2000

Programme	Years	Terms
Programme for National Recovery (PNR)	1987–1991	Average 2.5% per annum wage increase
Programme for Economic and Social Progress (PESP)	1991–1994	Yr. 1 — 2.5% increase Yr. 2 — 3% increase* Yr. 3 — 3.75% increase (* plus 3% local bargaining clause)
Programme for Competitiveness and Work (PCW)	1994–1997	Yr.1 — 2.5% increase Yr.2 — 2.5% increase Yr.3 — 2.5%
Partnership 2000 for Inclusion, Employment and Competitiveness (Partnership 2000)	1997–2000	Yr.1 — 2.5% Yr.2 — 2.25% increase* Yr.3 — 1.5% first 9 months plus 1% in the last 6 months. (* plus 2% local bargaining clause)

Source: Turner and D'Art, 1998

Table 6.8   Non-wage elements under centralised wage bargaining, 1987–2000

Programme	Years	Non-Wage Elements
PNR	1987–1991	Government commitments to reduce taxation burden on PAYE worker — improve social policy provisions — increase employment (mainly aspirational)
PESP	1991–1994	Government commitment as above — some tax reductions — unemployment continues to rise
PCW	1994–1997	Government commitment as above — drop in unemployment — some tax reductions
Partnership 2000	1997–2000	Government commitment as above — additional commitment on social inclusion and equality and extension of partnership arrangements at enterprise level

Source: Turner and D'Art, 1998

The social partnership arrangements since 1987 have corresponded with the recovery of the Irish economy from the disastrous early and mid-1980s and have seen a continuous period of economic growth since then. Despite the downturn in the world economy in the early 1990s, average real GNP growth of 4.1 per cent was achieved in the period 1988–94. The economy is currently growing almost three times as fast as the EU average and more than twice as fast as the OECD average. Economic growth is forecast to continue at a rate of between 7.5 per cent and 8 per cent for 1998 and 1999.

In their review of the performance of centralised bargaining since 1987, Turner and D'Art (1998) have completed an analysis of the changes in a number of key economic indicators for the period 1980–96 (see Table 6.7). This analysis is presented in Table 6.9 below and indicates a significant improvement in these economic variables since the return to the social partnership model in 1987. Real national income increased by 54 per cent between 1987 and 1996 compared to an increase of 7 per cent between 1980 and 1987. National income grew by 8 per cent alone in 1996.

The period has also seen a steady decline in the Debt/GDP ratio. The Debt/GDP ratio dropped significantly to stand at 73 per cent in 1996 from its 1987 rate of 131 per cent. The Debt/GDP ratio is forecast to drop to 61 per cent in 1998 (Wallace et al., 1998).

Table 6.9 Economic indicators 1980–96 (all figures reduced to base year 1968)

Years	National Income % change	Debt / GNP ratio	Average earnings % change*	Wage bill % change **	Company profits % change	Number employed % change	Unemployment % change
1980–1987	+7.1%	+38%	0%	+0.3%	+93.9%	-5.7%	+155%
1987–1996	+54.2%	-30% (1994)	+12.7%	+45.2%	+77.7%	+17.9%	-18.1%

*Average industrial earnings. **The entire wage bill for all PAYE workers minus agricultural workers

Source: Turner and D'Art, 1998. Compiled from Labour Force Survey and CSO Data Bank, National Accounts Data

While it is undoubtedly true that the level of job creation under the PNR and the PESP was disappointing, the PCW showed a marked improvement. The numbers employed increased by 248,000 from 1987 to 1997 and this has coincided with a significant fall in the numbers unemployed. The annual rate of unemployment stood at 17 per cent in 1987 but had decreased to 10.2 per cent in 1997 and for the first six months of 1998 has dropped below 10 per cent (Wallace et al., 1998). Martin Territ of the Department of Enterprise, Trade and Employment recently predicted that the real rate of unemployment for 1998 is expected to be 5 per cent or even less (Irish Times, 2 October 1998). He anticipates that analysis of the latest Labour Force Survey would record the lowest rate of unemployment since the survey was introduced in 1988 and that unemployment will be shown to have declined by over 65 per cent in the past decade.

The sequence of national wage agreements since 1987 has coincided with a period of low and predictable inflation. The rate of inflation has remained significantly below the EU average. The economy has also benefited from a prolonged period of relatively low interest rates which are set to decrease further in the run in to European Monetary Union.

Real wages have grown progressively since 1987 in sharp contrast to the situation which had persisted under decentralised bargaining in the 1980s. It is estimated that actual average disposable income increased by 17 per cent between 1987 and 1996 largely as a result of Government tax concessions agreed under the terms of the various programmes. This contrasts pointedly with the estimated drop of between 8 per cent and 10 per cent in actual average disposable income between 1980 and 1987 (Turner and D'Art, 1998). The expansion of the Irish economy since 1987 has not only seen real increases for wage earners but employers have also enjoyed large increases in company profits, 78 per cent between 1987 and 1996 (see Table 6.9).

Despite the fact that national pay agreements since 1987 provided for levels of wage increases significantly lower than those historically agreed in the preceding twenty-five years, they have been remarkably stable in pay terms and largely maintained — or unaffected by isolated breaches. Undoubtedly there have been cases where the strict terms of the national deals have not been adhered to, but these have been the exception rather than the norm. This is in stark contrast to the situation that existed under national wage bargaining in the 1970s.

The influence that a sharp decline in membership levels of approximately 13 per cent between 1980 and 1987 had on the decision of the trade unions to participate in centralised bargaining has already been discussed. Since 1987, membership levels have revived, with trade union membership increasing by 10.4 per cent between 1987 and 1996. Union density, however, has continued to decline (see chapter 4).

It can be argued that the advent of the centralised bargaining in 1987 has yielded considerable benefits in terms of industrial peace. The Irish system of industrial relations, noted throughout the 1970s for its strike proneness, is now characterised by a low level of industrial conflict. The incidence of strikes and the number of working days lost in strike actions has fallen considerably. In 1980, a total of 404,000 working days were lost in 132 strikes; by 1988 working days lost were down to 130,000, and in 1989, the number of recorded strikes fell to thirty-eight, and days lost to 50,000. The trend has continued throughout the 1990s and in 1994 there were thirty-two strikes with 24,000 days lost (Von Prondzynski, 1998). Turner and D'Art (1998) argue that while the decline in the 1980s occurred during a period of economic recession and conforms to economic explanations of strike patterns, the continued decline in all the indicators of industrial conflict after 1987, despite the emergence of an increasingly buoyant economy represents a surprising trend. This, Von Prondzynski (1998) argues, is an indication of the growing impact of centralised concertation. The nature of many of the disputes during the experience of social partnership has tended to focus on issues such as union recognition and the restructuring of enterprises rather than on pay.

6.7.12 THE FUTURE OF SOCIAL PARTNERSHIP

It is interesting to note that in 1987, centralised agreements were regarded as something of an anathema by the employers, a majority of politicians and a large section of trade unionists. Now after four consecutive programmes, it would seem that there is an unprecedented level of support — both at peak organisation level and politically — for the notion of social partnership. The economic success which has accompanied the national agreements has led to general support for their continuation. There is a general political consensus that national agreements bring beneficial outcomes. Even parties with an ideological orientation which would normally be opposed to centralised agreements, such as the Progressive Democrats, have no difficulty in engaging this new political consensus. It is not difficult to understand why most politicians favour the social partnership model or why policy makers would be reluctant to abandon a policy which has been associated with so much success. The programmes are seen to have played a role in delivering favourable economic outcomes such as increases in real take-home pay, low inflation and low interest rates, increasing profitability, employment growth, the maintenance of social spending and an industrial relations peace dividend.

Despite the centralised agreements appearing to be beneficial to all those involved, it would be wrong to underestimate the challenges in negotiating a new agreement on the expiry of the current programme, Partnership 2000. The partnership model has come under a great deal of pressure recently and it is evident that the pay terms set down under Partnership 2000 are under considerable strain. With the economy growing at unprecedented levels, public expectations have also grown, as well as union unrest over wage restraint. It is not surprising that high growth rates in the economy should be expected to translate into higher pay levels. The economic circumstances that now pertain are completely different to those existing at the time of negotiation of any of the recent wage agreements and undoubtedly will make it harder to maintain pay discipline. There was a large minority within the trade union movement that rejected Partnership 2000 and there continues to be a considerable level of disenchantment regarding the terms of the agreement. Underlining this resentment is the already mentioned increase in public expectations in the light of the economic boom but also the fact that public sector workers have been seen to benefit from agreements which are clearly in breach of the terms of the national agreements.

Once again, the issue of public sector pay has emerged to threaten the stability of the national pay agreements and could conceivably serve to undermine the process which commenced in 1987, and eventually weaken support for the partnership model. Many industrial commentators have long contended that a review of public sector pay determination is long overdue and will need to be addressed in any negotiations on a future agreement. The Government is currently under a great deal of pressure on the pay front. The recent spate of disputes in the public sector has seen pay increases well in excess of the formal terms of the agreements being claimed by a number of key groups of workers including the nurses and gardaí. Many other public sector unions have warned that they will pursue a number of relativity claims on the back of settlements in these high profile disputes. For the Government the issue is whether it can hold the line in advance of these 'knock on' claims and not set in train a pay spiral which would weaken the wage restraint in the current Partnership 2000 agreement. Roche (1998) argues that we may now be witnessing the re-emergence of trends which ultimately proved fatal for national pay bargaining in the 1970s. He believes that the 'critical thing is whether claims based on old style relativities, which were eclipsed in the 1980s, will reassert themselves'. In an attempt to defuse the prospect of unrest over wage restraint the Government has recently offered a number of concessions including further tax concessions, the introduction of a minimum wage and further efforts at resolving the issue of trade union recognition.

In any analysis, the social partnership model which has persisted since 1987 will only be abandoned if one of the social partners feels strongly enough that opting out of the model would better serve their strategic interests. Despite the strains that the model is currently enduring, it appears that, on balance, centralised wage agreements continue to suit the strategic interests of the main actors in the national bargaining process. From the Government's perspective, the political benefits of the tripartite deals which have been outlined seem compelling. It would also be surprising if there was any significant move to oppose centralised programmes from the private sector employers. Private sector employers have enjoyed the certainty which modest pay rises negotiated under the agreements have provided, but equally there is no evidence to suggest that a return to decentralised bargaining would cause them any great concern. Given the sort of competitive pressures that firms are under, which are acting as a significant restraining factor on pay demands, they would most probably be able to resist wage pressures at local level.

From the perspective of the trade unions, while workers in some sectors or individual firms might fare marginally better than others with a return to decentralised bargaining, the sort of headline deals which occurred in the 1980s would be less likely at the end of the 1990s. One possible consequence of the trade unions' continuing support for the social partnership may be the weakening of workplace union organisation and solidarity due to the restricted role for pay bargaining at the level of the firm since 1987. This may serve to undermine their ability to negotiate effectively on behalf of their members at local level.

Apart from pay, non-pay issues, like trade union recognition, commitments on health and welfare spending, labour legislation and programmes to combat unemployment and encourage greater social inclusion would be largely removed from the trade union sphere of influence were they to opt out of the centralised bargaining process. With the trade union movement continuing to be under pressure to retain and recruit members, particularly in incoming multinationals, the threat of marginalisation — which many trade unions feared in the 1980s — could arise again. Many trade union leaders who put the case for continuing trade union involvement in tripartite programmes express the view that the arguments that had influenced them to enter centralised bargaining in 1987 had not changed fundamentally, indeed, some see the arguments as even more compelling now.

If the social partnership is to continue into the next millennium, a further agreement will have to be negotiated within the context of the challenges and uncertainties posed by EMU. A recent survey carried out by Wallace, Turner and McCarthy (1998) considered the perceptions of employers and trade unions on the future of centralised bargaining in Ireland. One of the most significant findings is that 73 per cent of those surveyed feel that the most appropriate method for dealing with the challenges posed by EMU is to continue national centralised bargaining.

CHAPTER SEVEN

Conflict and Conflict Resolution

7.1 INTRODUCTION

Industrial conflict is one of the most emotive aspects of industrial relations and a major reason why the field often achieves headline status in the popular media. Given the potential differences of interest which can arise on employment matters, it is not surprising that some degree of conflict is inherent in organisations. As a number of commentators point out, the structure of the employment relationship, which emphasises employer needs for productivity, cost-effectiveness and change, is often at odds with employee needs for security, adequate rewards and opportunity for personal growth (see, for example, Allen, 1971; Jackson, 1987; Hyman, 1989; Huczynski and Buchanan, 1991). It is therefore to be expected that in this 'labour for pay' exchange, interests will clash and, on occasion, result in overt conflict (e.g., pay disputes). Indeed, such conflicts of interest are not just confined to the 'financial exchange' dimension but relate to other aspects of the employment relationship. The operational management of organisations requires the ongoing exercise of employer/managerial authority over employees on dimensions such as working time, work flow and task allocation (Reed, 1989; Morley et al., 1998). Again, some degree of conflict here is inevitable as differing interests clash and seek to establish their positions (e.g., disputes over demarcation or work loads).

However, as Salamon (1998:397) points out, the existence of such conflicts of interest is not 'synonymous with the use of overt collective industrial action', such as strikes or go-slows. Generally, conflicts of interest in industrial relations are resolved through interactions between the participants, particularly industrial relations negotiations, and through the use of established procedures. As such, the bulk of these conflicts are resolved without resort to industrial action. Industrial conflict is thus an inherent aspect of the employment relationship as a result of the differences that will inevitably arise between management and workers or their representatives. Industrial conflict is therefore 'normal' in organisations although excessive levels of conflict are generally undesirable. The resolution of conflicts of interest between employers and workers is a core concern of the parties involved in industrial relations. Edwards (1986) has termed this conflict of interest 'structured antagonism' and notes that while the 'actors' involved in industrial relations have 'divergent wants', they also depend on each other and so need to co-operate across a range of issues. Thus conflict and co-operation co-exist in organisations, and various industrial relations processes and practices have evolved to address these varying dimensions of the employment relationship (Watson, 1987).

It is also important to note that conflict in organisations is not necessarily harmful and can, indeed, have positive effects. Positive aspects of conflict include its capacity to facilitate articulation of individual or group grievances, the identification and review of discriminatory or unfair employment practices, positive changes in work arrangements or management regulation and a 'pressure release' mechanism which allows parties to vent opinions and positions which are a source of concern (Morley et al., 1998). From a management perspective it is critical that conflict be managed effectively and that is is not dysfunctional and damaging for the organisation.

7.2 PERSPECTIVES ON INDUSTRIAL CONFLICT

In attempting to analyse and explain industrial conflict it is useful to consider the various analytical frameworks commonly used to evaluate industrial conflict and industrial relations. Differing management perspectives are acknowledged as a critical factor, particularly in impacting on how the parties to conflict (particularly management) behave in situations of industrial conflict (see, for example, Fox, 1966; Marchington, 1982). A widely accepted framework for evaluating differing approaches to industrial conflict is that which identifies four alternative perspectives on conflict in organisations: (1) unitarist perspective; (2) pluralist perspective; (3) interactionist perspective and (4) radical perspective (Fox, 1966, 1973; Edwards, 1986; Huczynski and Buchanan, 1991; Morley et al., 19ᵣ These four perspectives are summarised in Table 7.1.

In chapter 1, the unitarist and pluralist frameworks were posited as useful models for explaining employee relations, interactions and industrial conflict (Fox, 1968, 1974; Marchington, 1982). In the *pluralist perspective*, organisations are seen as comprising a range of individuals and groups with different interests and priorities. It suggests that the interaction of these competing interests and groups necessitates the development of institutional arrangements which help manage these competing interests and achieve a level of bargained compromise, which allows the organisation to conduct its normal business. Thus, the pluralist framework accepts that conflict in

Table 7.1 Perspectives on industrial conflict

The Unitarist Perspective: The unitarist perspective on conflict in organisations essentially views conflict as an aberration which occurs because 'something has gone wrong'. Harmony and unity are seen as the natural state, with conflict an abnormal phenomenon which occurs as a result of some failure in the normal functioning of the organisations, such as poor communications, poor management or the work of 'troublemakers'. While viewing conflict as abnormal, the unitarist perspective also sees conflict as essentially negative and damaging the normal harmonious, productive state of the organisation. Thus conflict is viewed as something which can and should be avoided. Where it does occur, management should take appropriate steps to eradicate it, most probably by addressing the source: i.e., improve communications or organisation design, train managers or get rid of troublemakers.

The Pluralist Perspective: In contrast, the pluralist perspective views conflict as a naturally occurring phenomenon in organisations. It is accepted as an inherent characteristic of organisations arising from the differing perspectives and interests of all the groups and individuals who make up the organisation. Since conflict is seen as inevitable, management should therefore expect it to occur and plan for this eventuality so that it can be handled successfully and not endanger the achievement of the organisation's primary objectives. This pluralist perspective is consistent with the view that conflict is not necessarily negative but can have beneficial effects. Efforts should therefore be concentrated on channelling functional conflict to realise such organisational benefits. The emphasis is therefore on the management of conflict as opposed to its elimination.

The Interactionist Perspective: While the pluralist perspective accepts the inevitability of conflict, the interactionist perspective goes further by actually stimulating conflict and also instigating means for its resolution. This approach is based on the view that harmony and unity may serve to dull initiative and innovation. It is therefore seen as appropriate to maintain a certain level of conflict to stimulate creativity and innovation. Thus an 'acceptable' level of conflict is seen as both positive and necessary, particularly in creating a work environment which stimulates change and 'new' thinking.

The Radical Perspective: The radical perspective is essentially grounded in Marxist theory of capitalist society and social change. Conflict in capitalist societies is seen as a symptom of the structural enmity which exists between capital and labour, employer and employee. Such enmity arises from the organisation of work in capitalist societies and the unequal distribution of power between the dominant establishment group which own the means of production (employers, shareholders) and those whose labour is required to produce goods and services (workers). Therefore, conflict in organisations is simply a manifestation of broader class conflict in relation to the distribution of power in society. Organisations are therefore simply a microcosm of a broader class conflict between the 'bourgeoisie' (who control economic resources and political power) and the 'proletariat', with managers representing the interests of capital. In the radical perspective conflict is seen as a means of instigating revolutionary change designed to dismantle the capitalist system, redistribute power in favour of workers and the working class and, ultimately, achieve a classless society.

Source: Morley, Moore, Heraty and Gunnigle, 1998:263–4

organisations is inevitable because the needs and objectives of various interest groups will clash on occasion. The *unitarist perspective* is based on the premise that organisations are essentially cohesive and harmonious units and that all members of the organisation (management and employees) should share common goals (Fox, 1968, 1974; Marchington, 1982). Management and employees are seen as having the same interests with conflict occurring only as a result of misunderstandings or due to the efforts of troublemakers. In this perspective industrial conflict is not seen as inevitable and there is no perceived need for institutional arrangements to deal with conflict. The *interactionist perspective* is based on the premise that it is actually necessary to ensure a 'prescribed' level of industrial conflict in organisations since the absence of conflict inhibits initiative and innovation (Robbins, 1983; De Vliert, 1985). The *radical perspective* argues that it is the alienation caused by the organisation of work within the capitalist framework, involving divisions along labour, ownership and hierarchical lines, which makes conflict between labour and management endemic to industrial organisations (Hyman, 1976). Industrial conflict is therefore seen as part of a broader class-based conflict designed to dismantle capitalism.

These different perspectives on conflict are particularly significant in explaining the actions and behaviour of individuals and groups who are involved in conflict situations. Of particular significance in industrial relations is the impact of differing conflict perspectives on the actions and behaviour of managers in dealing with industrial conflict. Since line managers and supervisors or their equivalent play a key role in dealing with most conflict situations which arise in organisations, it is important to consider how differing conflict perspectives can help explain managerial behaviour and, particularly, why managers' approach and behaviour may differ in similar conflict situations. Depending on the particular conflict perspective which a manager holds, individual managers may behave differently in broadly similar conflict situations. The contrast most often used to illustrate this point is that between the unitarist and pluralist manager as illustrated in Table 7.2 (Fox, 1966).

The perspectives on industrial conflict outlined above represent dominant orientations which may be present in particular managerial and worker/trade union approaches, and offer a useful framework for evaluating behaviour in conflict situations. Depending on their particular conflict perspective, individuals and groups involved in industrial relations may adopt particular approaches and behaviour in conflict situations. In Ireland and elsewhere there is considerable evidence to suggest the dominance of a unitary perspective among owner/managers in small firms (Gunnigle and Brady, 1984; McMahon, 1996). The unitarist perspective is also considered characteristic of the value system of many American managers (see, for example, Bendix, 1956; Kochan et al., 1986). This rationale is often used to explain the vehement managerial opposition to trade union recognition in many US companies and also their preference for more individualist human resource management approaches which emphasise direct communications, regular appraisals and merit-based rewards (McGovern, 1989; Gunnigle, 1995, a and b; Gunnigle, Morley and Turner, 1997). This issue is addressed in greater detail in chapters 9 and 10.

Table 7.2 Dealing with industrial conflict: the unitarist and pluralist managers
The *Unitarist Manager* views the organisation in a unified 'team/family' mould, with everyone working together to achieve company objectives. Industrial conflict is not seen as inherent in workplace employee relations, but rather as a symptom of a breakdown in the employee relations framework (e.g., due to a misunderstanding) or introduced by people who do not have the company's interests at heart. The unitarist manager feels that such conflict can be eradicated: for example, by clarifying misunderstandings or dismissing troublemakers.   The *Pluralist Manager* sees a certain degree of industrial conflict as inevitable because of the differing objectives held by different interest groups in the organisation. Since the pluralist manager views industrial conflict as inevitable he/she tends to focus on developing institutional arrangements (such as collective bargaining) to ensure that such conflict is handled in a functional reasonable fashion and does not have a detrimental impact on the overall employee relations fabric.

Source: Adapted from Marchington, 1982; also see Gunnigle, McMahon and Fitzgerald, 1995

7.3 NATURE AND FORMS OF INDUSTRIAL ACTION

Having acknowledged that while conflict is a normal aspect of organisational life it need not necessarily lead to overt industrial action and also that workers and management co-operate across a range of areas, it is clear that the use or threat of industrial action is an intrinsic aspect of the employment relationship (Hyman, 1989). Salamon (1998:395–7) provides a comprehensive explanation of industrial action as:

> Any temporary suspension of normal working arrangements which is initiated unilaterally by either employees (whether through their union or not) or management with the objective of exerting pressure in the determination of the employment relationship (particularly within the collective bargaining process.

At a general level we can identify two broad categories of industrial action: (1) explicit and organised collective industrial action, and (2) unorganised and more implicit individual industrial action (Bean, 1976; Salamon, 1998). *Organised, collective action* encompasses systematic, collective efforts in pursuing a conscious strategy through co-ordinated action designed to achieve specified objectives. The most common examples of organised industrial action are strikes, go-slows, overtime bans and the withdrawal of co-operation. In contrast, *unorganised, individual action* tends to represent spontaneous, reactive and random responses which do not form part of a conscious strategy on behalf of its proponents. Common types of unorganised conflict include absenteeism, turnover, theft and many forms of industrial sabotage.

However, this distinction tends to be less clear-cut in practice, most particularly with respect to the actual randomness and spontaneity of unorganised conflict. A recent example in Ireland was the decision by the Garda Representative Association to request their members to 'call in sick' and thus not report for duty on one particular day (in May 1998). This so called 'blue flu' phenomenon is not new and indeed its use in the New York Police Department was cited by Blyton and Turnbull (1994) to illustrate the difficulty in differentiating between organised and unorganised industrial action. It is plausible to argue that such co-ordinated forms of traditionally 'unorganised' conflict are likely to become increasingly common as increased competitiveness and job insecurity renders more organised methods, especially strikes, less attractive to workers due to loss of income and possibility of dismissal (Morley et al., 1998). It is also clear that certain forms of apparently organised, collective action can be quite reactive and spontaneous in nature. For example, so called 'wildcat' strikes can occur when workers walk off the job in reaction to a particular incident. Such action often represents a predominantly spontaneous, reactive decision and does not tend to form part of any broader conflict strategy (Hyman, 1989).

The main forms of industrial action are summarised in Table 7.3. These forms are discussed below with particular focus on strike action including the pattern of strike activity in Ireland.

We have already noted that the basis for industrial conflict is felt to be rooted in the structure of the employment relationship in capitalist economies (see, for example, Blyton and Turnbull, 1994). It is argued that this creates a fundamental antagonism between employers and workers which becomes manifest in differences over issues such as working conditions and terms of employment. Although more appropriately viewed as a 'natural' phenomenon in organisations, industrial action is commonly perceived as extremely negative and damaging for organisations. Rollinson (1993) identifies three principal reasons why industrial action is seen in such negative terms:

(1) Industrial action is normally vertical in nature and therefore challenges the legitimacy of management authority/prerogative in decision making.

(2) Industrial action tends to be highly visible, both within and outside the organisation and can often involve large numbers of workers.

(3) The objective of industrial action tends to be misunderstood: such action is commonly seen as 'irrational' and/or dysfunctional with most conflict situations viewed as capable of resolution by discussions and negotiation, and therefore should not result in industrial action.

Table 7.3   Forms of industrial action

Strike: Collective in nature, involving temporary withdrawal of labour.

Withdrawal of Co-operation: Collective in nature, involving the withdrawal of representatives from joint institutions, strict interpretation of, and rigorous adherence to, procedure, absence of flexibility.

Work to Rule: Collective in nature, involving working only in accordance with the strict interpretation of written terms and conditions of employment, job description or other rules such as those concerning safety or hygiene.

Overtime Ban: Collective in nature, involving refusal to work outside normal contractual hours of work.

Go-Slow: Collective in nature, involving working at a lower than average level of performance.

Work-in/Sit-in: Occupation of the workplace or section thereof; denial of access to management. This approach is often used to prevent movement of plant and equipment (often associated with plant closures).

Sabotage: Individual in nature, involving conscious action to damage goods, equipment or other aspects of the work environment.

Pilfering and Theft: Individual in nature, involving stealing items owned by the organisation.

Absenteeism: Absenteeism tends to be generically defined as all absences from work other than paid holidays. As such it is reckoned that only a small proportion of absenteeism may represent a form of industrial action. Where it does, it tends to represent individual response to perceived problems in the workplace.

Labour Turnover: Labour turnover refers to the rate at which people leave the organisation. As with absenteeism, only a proportion of labour turnover in organisations represents a form of industrial action.

Lockout: The major form of industrial action instigated by employers which involves preventing the workforce, or a proportion thereof, from attending at work.

Source: Salamon, 1992; Gunnigle, McMahon and Fitzgerald, 1995; Morley et al., 1998

Rollinson (1993) suggests that the argument that industrial action is irrational/dysfunctional is a fundamentally flawed perspective. While negotiation and compromise are capable of resolving much industrial conflict, it is inevitable that at some stage and in some organisations, either party will not modify its position but rather utilise some form of industrial action to achieve its aims. Thus, as Rollinson (1993) specifically comments, industrial conflict is 'simply a rational extension of the negotiation process' (also see Morley et al., 1998).

In evaluating the different forms of industrial action outlined in Table 7.3 a number of factors are worth noting.

Looking firstly at *strike action*, we find that this is widely perceived as the most powerful and visible form of industrial action and a significant means through which trade unions have sought and secured improvements in pay and conditions of employment. As Salamon (1998:402) notes: 'The strike is often depicted as the ultimate and most favoured form of collective action in that, by stopping work and leaving the workplace, the employees clearly demonstrate both the importance of the issue in dispute and their solidarity.'

Strikes can also represent a means of mobilising collective interests in the broader social and political sphere. In the late nineteenth and early twentieth centuries a number of landmark industrial disputes paved the way for changes in labour legislation and increased protection for trade unions and freedom of association. In countries as diverse as Poland, Indonesia and Zimbabwe we know strike action has, in recent decades, provided a focus for those committed to greater democratisation in these countries. The following quote captures the broader political and social dimensions of strike activity:

> Some industrial disputes rock the world. A shipyard strike in Poland in 1980 was the match that lit the fire that eventually consumed communism and led to the phoenix of democratic institutions rising from the ashes. An air traffic controllers' strike in the US and a coal miners' strike in the UK produced massive union defeats which dramatically altered the social climate. Subsequent to those setbacks union membership and influence receded like ice cubes in a hothouse. (Adams, 1998)

Other forms of industrial action, such as overtime bans and working to rule are often more common than strikes themselves. These other forms of overt action can provide an effective means of achieving employee objectives while not entailing the potential hardships of strike action. In particular, actions such as *go-slows* or *overtime bans* can place considerable pressures on employers to move towards resolution while not jeopardising employee income and job security to as great a degree as might be the case as a result of strike action (Gunnigle et al., 1995). Of course, the effectiveness of such measures is heavily influenced by the particular organisational context within which such action is initiated. Clearly, an overtime ban is unlikely to meet with much success when order-books are empty and production requirements are low.

Industrial sabotage is described by Watson (1986:306) as the 'deliberate disruption of work flows within an organisation or the undermining of the conditions whereby dominant management purposes are readily achieved'. There is a dearth of information on the incidence of industrial sabotage as a form of industrial conflict. However, it appears that industrial sabotage has been and remains an important, if comparatively little used, form of industrial conflict (for greater detail see Brown, 1977). A far less obvious result of poor industrial relations is a lack of *commitment* to the organisation and lack of *trust* in management which can have far reaching long-term effects, for example, changes in work practices may be bitterly resisted; if other jobs are available labour turnover may be high; recruitment may be difficult; productivity may fall and absence may be high.

As noted above, a particular problem with what appears to be unorganised, individual action is the difficulty in differentiating between action taken as a form of industrial conflict and that which may occur for some other reason.

Particular cases in point are absenteeism and labour turnover. *Absenteeism* has been defined by IBEC as incorporating all absences from work other than paid holidays. It affects the internal supply of labour to the firm in the sense that an organisation which has an absenteeism problem finds itself understaffed and unable to cope with demands made upon it. Absenteeism is a serious cost factor in Irish industry. Data from the Irish Management Institute (IMI) estimate that average absenteeism rates range from 7 to 13 per cent across industry sectors and its cost in terms of money lost is higher than for total time lost due to official and unofficial strikes. Absenteeism derives from a range of factors which include: (1) ability to attend work (affected by illness, sex role responsibilities, age and transportation difficulties) and (2) the motivation to attend (see Gunnigle et al., 1997). The motivation to attend is generally seen as a function of satisfaction with the job situation (job content, variety, autonomy and discretion inherent in the tasks performed), internal and external pressures to attend. Internal pressures to attend include a 'sense of duty' to always attend wherever possible (despite sickness in some cases). External pressures to attend include the organisation's incentive system, the extent to which discipline or dismissal is likely to follow repeated absences, and the extent to which there are other job opportunities available in the local labour market.

Labour turnover refers to the number of persons who leave an organisation within a specified time period. Clearly, employees leave organisations for a variety of reasons, many of which have little to do with industrial relations. Bowey (1974) classifies the factors generating wastage into 'pull' and 'push' factors. 'Pull' factors are those factors which attract employees to another organisation while 'push' factors cause employees to leave involuntarily. 'Pull' factors identified include moving for higher earnings, moving to further one's career and the attraction of alternative job opportunities. 'Push' factors identified include leaving to avoid strains arising from interpersonal or other forms of conflict at work, 'running down' (reducing headcount) of an organisation and problems in relation to the induction/socialisation of new employees.

Finally, we have noted that employers also instigate industrial action. The major form of industrial action by employers is the *lockout*, which means that employers prevent the workforce, or sections thereof, from attending at work. It is often seen as the equivalent of strike action by employers.

We now turn more specifically to the Irish context and consider the nature and pattern of strike activity here.

7.4 STRIKE ACTIVITY IN IRELAND

Strikes may take different forms and arise for a variety of reasons. *Official strikes* are defined as those which have been fully sanctioned by the union executive. Such strikes normally take place after a series of negotiations and meetings have failed to resolve the issue and when all due procedures have been exhausted (Gunnigle et al., 1995). Official strikes may involve large numbers of workers and last for a prolonged period. However, *unofficial strikes* are those which have not been sanctioned by the trade union. Unofficial strikes tend to be quite reactive in nature and are often sparked off by a particular event or incident at workplace level, such as the dismissal of a worker or changes in work practices. Unless subsequently granted official approval by the trade union, unofficial strikes normally last for a shorter time and involve fewer workers than official strikes (Wallace and O'Shea, 1987; Wallace, 1988a and b).

A decision to engage in strike action will be based on a combination of factors. Particularly significant will be the issue at hand, employee solidarity and the commitment of employees to using the strike weapon to achieve their particular goals. Related factors include the perceived chances of success and the power balance between the parties. Decisions on strike action will be significantly influenced by contextual factors such as the business cycle, unemployment levels, and inflation. It should be noted that a decision to take strike action may involve considerable hardship for strikers through lost income and the risk of job loss. Consequently, such action is rarely taken lightly. For the trade unions strike action also represents a major dilemma: the prospects of success/failure must be weighed up together with implications for union membership, status, and finances. Despite their headline grabbing status, it is important to remember that strikes are relatively rare and many organisations have never experienced strike action.

In considering the pattern of strike activity over time, commentators can point to several factors which influence the level and nature of strike activity (see, for example, Hyman, 1989; Edwards, 1986, 1992; Brannick et al., 1997). Particularly influential factors include the level of economic activity (business cycle), unemployment (tightness/looseness of the labour market), industrial development, inflation (earnings), and unionisation. It will also be influenced by sectoral changes in employment (shifts in the employment share of agriculture, industry and services) and the nature and level of collective bargaining (particularly the incidence and nature of centrally agreed incomes policies).

Three key measures are normally used in evaluating the extent and pattern of strike activity, namely, (1) strike frequency (number of strikes), (2) workers involved (number of workers participating in strikes), and (3) working days lost (number of working days lost due to strike activity).[1] *Strike frequency* is generally seen as a valuable indicator of strike activity although it is perceived to have some deficiencies, particularly the fact that equal weight is attributed to large and small strikes (Turner, 1962). The number of *workers involved* in strike activity (often termed 'strike breadth'), while generally seen as a useful indicator, is also seen as somewhat problematic insofar as it is possible to have a drop in the number of workers involved in strikes but still have an overall increase in the numbers of working days lost (Silver, 1973; Kelly and Brannick, 1989). The number of *working days lost* due to strike activity is generally felt to be the most informative indicator of the pattern of strike activity. However,

235

analyses of strike activity are most useful where all three indices of strike activity are used concurrently.

Using these the three indicators of strike activity (frequency, breadth and working days lost), the pattern of strikes in Ireland over the period 1922–96 is summarised in Figures 7.1, 7.2 and 7.3. This review of strike activity in Ireland is based on data from University College Dublin (Brannick and Kelly, 1983; Brannick and Doyle, 1994; Brannick, Doyle and Kelly, 1997; Kelly, and Brannick, 1983, 1985, 1986, 1988, 1989) and the Central Statistics Office.

Figure 7.1 Strike frequency 1922–97

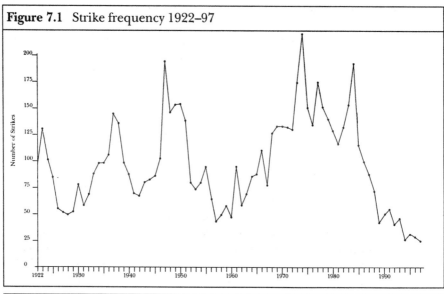

Figure 7.2 Workers involved in strike activity 1922–97

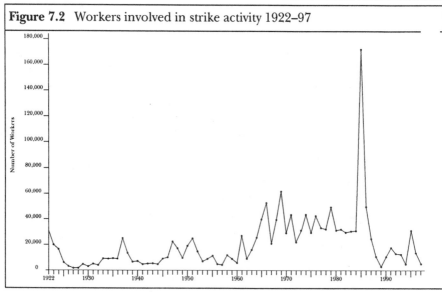

Figure 7.3 Working days lost through strike activity 1992–97

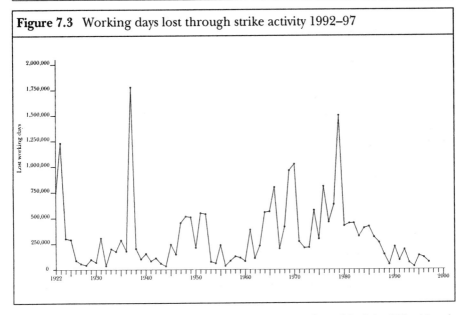

Source: UCD Database of Strike Statistics, (see references in text); Central Statistics Office (based on figures from the Department of Enterprise, Trade and Employment)
Note 1: Figures from the CSO are subject to minor fluctuations due to factors such as the carry-over of strikes from one year to another and variations in the numbers of workers participating in strike activity over the period of a particular strike. However, these minor variations do not affect overall trends in the pattern of strike activity.
Note 2: We are indebted to Teresa Brannick and her colleagues in UCD for advice and data in relation to the pattern of strike activity in Ireland.

The evidence from Figures 7.1 to 7.3 indicates a clear upward trend in strike activity in Ireland during the 1960s and 1970s, followed by a significant decline in strike activity beginning around the mid-1980s and continuing into the 1990s. This is particularly the case in relation to the key index of working days lost due to strike activity. Indeed, the period 1992–95 has recorded the lowest ever rate of strike frequency (see Brannick et al., 1997). We can also note from Figures 7.1 to 7.3 the large degree of fluctuation in the extent of strike activity from year to year. In commenting on the pattern of strike activity in Ireland over the period 1922–95, Brannick et al. (1997:310) suggest that all three indices of strike activity are:

> . . . broadly pro cyclical with respect to economic changes . . . if one examines the annual trend in the number of strikes since 1922 one can identify such a cyclical trend. For instance, the decline in strike activity experienced in the 1920s is associated with recession and stagnation in the economic environment during the decade. This was followed by an increase in strike levels during the 1930s corresponding to a period of industrialisation and so for the subsequent decades.

237

This cyclical pattern of strike activity is clearly interesting and illustrates the point that upswings in strike activity can be counteracted by periods of downswing, but, perhaps more importantly, enforces the contention that industrial disputes are an inherent part of industrial relations, and that, as Brannick et al. (1997:310) specifically comment, '. . . there is no compelling evidence of the withering away of industrial action'.

In their analysis of the pattern of strike activity in Ireland from 1960 to 1979, Kelly and Brannick (1983) identify two key trends, namely (1) the disproportionate effect of a few large strikes on Irish strike statistics, and (2) the different patterns of strike activity between the public and private sectors. In relation to the former, Kelly and Brannick note that over the period 1960–79, forty-three strikes (2 per cent of total strikes in the period) accounted for 57 per cent of all days lost due to strike activity and comment thus:

> Clearly, the Irish strike pattern is extremely sensitive to this comparatively small number of large strikes and it has been an enduring feature over the 20 year period. Indeed should these be removed from the Irish strike quantum the result would be a record which would show a comparatively strike-free nation in terms of workers involved and total man-days lost. (Kelly and Brannick, 1983:69)

More recent data point to the enduring impact of large strikes in impacting significantly on the pattern of strike activity in Ireland. If we look at Figures 7.2 and 7.3 we can generally point to the impact of one or two large strikes in contributing to the large numbers of workers involved and working days lost in particular years, including the bank dispute (1970), the post office (1979), Waterford Crystal (1990) and Dunnes Stores (1995), (Brannick et al., 1997).

Turning to strike patterns in the public and private sectors, Figure 7.4 outlines the relative pattern of strike activity in both these sectors over the period 1960–95. These data indicate that the private sector was the source of most strike activity during the decades of the 1960s and 1970s but the trend in private sector strike activity has been one of decline, particularly in relation to the numbers of workers involved in strike activity and the numbers of working days lost. This development has paralleled a marked increase in the proportion of strike activity accounted for by the public sector over the period.

In their analysis of strike trends in the public sector up to the mid-1980s, Kelly and Brannick (1985, 1986) found that the bulk of public sector strike activity was concentrated among a relatively small number of organisations. They identified nine organisations which accounted for 62 per cent of all strikes, 85 per cent of workers involved and 86 per cent of mandays lost in the public sector during the 1960–84 period. In evaluating the reasons for the increase in public sector strike activity, Brannick et al. (1997) offer a number of explanations, namely:

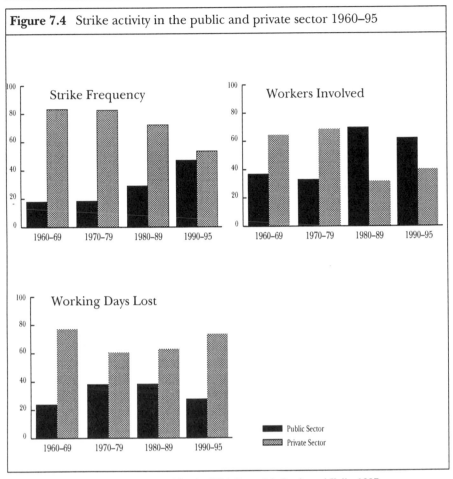

Figure 7.4 Strike activity in the public and private sector 1960–95

Source: Brannick and Doyle, 1994; Brannick, Doyle and Kelly, 1997

(1) the extension of immunities under the terms of the 1906 Trade Disputes Act to public servants in 1982 (see chapter 2);

(2) curbs in public sector expenditure and cutbacks in particular areas of the public sector, especially during the 1980s;

(3) the related development of a greater commercial ethos in the public sector; and

(4) the emergence of 'special' pay claims under centralised agreements since 1987.

Looking at trends in the private sector, Brannick et al. (1997) note the dramatic fall in the contribution of the private sector to the overall level of strike activity. However, they also point out that this has resulted primarily from a major drop in the numbers of workers involved in strike activity rather than any significant decline in the actual number of strikes. Indeed Brannick

(1997:312–3) and her colleagues point out that private sector strike frequency 'remains relatively high' and that such strikes tend to be of 'long duration'. Since employment size tends to have a very significant impact on the pattern of strike activity, notably with regard to the key indices of workers involved and working days lost, it is useful to control for the impact of organisation size in evaluating the pattern of strike activity. In so doing, Brannick and her colleagues found that both the public and private sectors witnessed a decline in strike frequency, workers involved and working days lost over the period 1960–95. However, they found considerable differences in strike patterns between these sectors, after controlling for numbers employed.

In relation to strike frequency, the data indicate a dramatic decline in the strike frequency in the private sector but strike frequency remaining quite high in the public sector. Over the period 1990–95, the public sector accounted for seven strikes per 100,000 workers, while the equivalent figure in the private sector was two strikes (per 100,000), leading Brannick et al. (1997:313) to conclude that 'in the 1990s public sector workers were three times as likely to strike than their counterparts in the private sector'. However, when we look at the average length of strikes ('strike duration') we find a different pattern, with strike duration remaining quite high in the private sector. In the period 1990–95, the average length of public sector strikes was six and a half days while in the private sector the equivalent figure was twenty-one days. However, it is the greater level of workers involved in strike activity which contributes to the generally poor record of the public sector in terms of its contribution to overall strike levels in Ireland. In summing up the situation with respect to strike trends in the public and private sectors, Brannick and her colleagues (1997:313–4) conclude as follows:

> It may be seen clearly that throughout the 1960s, 1970s and 1980s in terms of both worker involvement and work days, public sector employees were much more prone to engage in strike activity. The public sector continued to experience higher levels of worker involvement into the 1990s. However, the average strike duration was only one third that of the private sector. These different characteristics balance each other out resulting in both sectors having similar work days lost rates. In fact, the greater level of worker involvement in public sector strikes is the root cause of the sector's overall adverse performance as measured by the worker involvement and work days lost indices.

Further analysis of the UCD data allowed for a dis-aggregation of strike activity by industrial sector and revealed considerable variation in strike patterns both across different industrial sectors and sub-sectors and also within particular sectors/sub-sectors over time (Kelly and Brannick, 1988c; Brannick and Doyle, 1994; Brannick et al., 1997). This analysis identified the mining and turf sectors as the most strike prone in terms of strike frequency and working days lost over the period 1922–81. The data also identified transport and communications, and electricity, gas and water, as sectors characterised by high levels of strike frequency and working days lost. Brannick et al. (1997) note that both these sectors have high levels of public ownership. The same researchers also note the dramatic decline in strike frequency and working days lost in the building and construction sector, an area traditionally characterised by high levels of strike activity.

Turning specifically to the manufacturing sector, Kelly and Brannick (1989a and b) identify significant variations in strike patterns which, they argue, reflect both structural changes in Irish industry and the impact of economic and industrial policy developments (also see Brannick et al., 1997). Figures 7.5 and 7.6 outline the numbers of strikes and working days lost due to strike activity on an annual basis in the manufacturing sector over a seventy-year period, 1922–92.

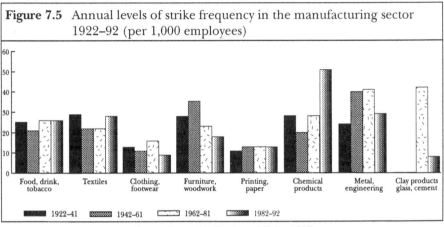

Figure 7.5 Annual levels of strike frequency in the manufacturing sector 1922–92 (per 1,000 employees)

Source: Brannick, Doyle and Kelly, 1997

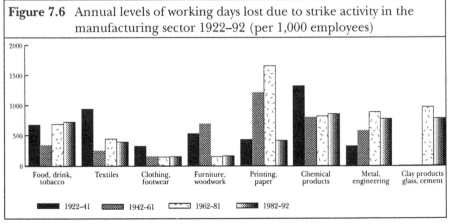

Figure 7.6 Annual levels of working days lost due to strike activity in the manufacturing sector 1922–92 (per 1,000 employees)

Source: Brannick, Doyle and Kelly, 1997

From this data we can see that certain manufacturing sectors, such as printing and paper, metals and engineering, and chemical products became increasingly strike prone, particularly in the period from the early 1940s, while others, notably textiles, and furniture and woodwork, experienced a decline in strike activity.

From the preceding analysis we see that a range of critical factors such as the level of economic activity (business cycle), unemployment (tightness/ looseness of the labour market), industrial development, inflation (earnings), and unionisation impact on the level and pattern of strike activity. In the Irish context the decline in strike activity since the 1980s is generally explained in this manner. Particularly significant factors in this regard are the low levels of economic performance for much of the decade and concurrently high levels of unemployment (see Gunnigle et al., 1995). Such macro-economic factors, together with broader developments in the social sphere, such as living standards and education levels, are widely seen as the most critical factors which significantly impact on the extent and pattern of strike activity. However, management interventions at the enterprise level also impact on patterns of strike activity. The impact of management policies and practices on patterns of strike activity is illustrated to some degree in Kelly and Brannick's analyses of strike patterns among multinational companies in Ireland (Kelly and Brannick, 1988a, b and c; 1989b, 1991). This analysis found that US companies were the most strike prone multinational sector during the 1960s but that their record improved dramatically since the 1970s to a stage where US multinationals now have a low incidence of strike activity. In evaluating the improvement of the strike record of US companies, Kelly and Brannick proffer two reasons, (1) the changed industrial composition of US multinationals: most are now high technology companies in the 'newer' industrial sectors, particularly electronics, software and chemicals (as opposed to labour-intensive companies producing standardised products in the 1960s); (2) US multinationals are predominantly based in the electronics sector which has been to the forefront in developing innovative and proactive human resource management (HRM) strategies and policies. In contrast, the strike record of UK companies has deteriorated dramatically. The reasons for this deterioration are largely attributed to product market difficulties encountered by UK-owned companies in Ireland resulting from increased competition. These difficulties prompted management initiatives to cut back on employment numbers, reduce operating costs and improve labour productivity, which in turn, it is argued, contributed to increased industrial conflict in these organisations. This latter point emphasises the significance of management philosophy and practices in developing particular industrial relations styles. In particular, it seems that the 'sophisticated unionised' or 'sophisticated paternalist' styles most closely equate to the approaches of certain US firms, many of which operate in so-called 'high technology' sectors (Purcell, 1987; McGovern, 1989a and b; Gunnigle, 1992a). Again, it is important to add a word of caution. Product market conditions are clearly an extremely influential factor, as are the age and size of establishment. Changing product market conditions can severely alter the context within which industrial relations decisions are made. High levels of volatility in some industrial sectors (such as electronics) can dramatically impact the product market conditions and other factors influencing the industrial relations style adopted in organisations, and lead to changes in style, for example, a significant decline in market share may lead to employment contraction warranting a more traditional industrial relations approach. A further issue is the potential for the development of diverse cultures in organisations requiring different industrial relations approaches or 'styles' for different workforce categories. This seems particularly likely in organisations pursuing the flexible firm route (Atkinson, 1984; Gunnigle, 1995a and b). Thus, 'soft' or benign HRM policies may be adopted with the core workforce in return for high levels of functional and task flexibility, while a more traditional adversarial industrial relations approach may be adopted in dealings with the peripheral categories (e.g., 'hard-nosed' bargaining, application of grievance/disciplinary procedures, etc.). The issue of management styles in industrial relations is considered in chapter 10.

The relative impact of official and unofficial strikes is another important issue affecting patterns of strike activity. Data on strike frequency and working days lost due to official and unofficial strikes for the period 1980–98 is outlined in Figures 7.7 and 7.8. Brannick et al. (1997) found that unofficial strikes became particularly common during the 1970s and indeed were widely seen as a major blight on Irish industrial relations during that period (Wallace and O'Shea, 1987; Wallace, 1988a and b). The prevalence of unofficial strikes in the 1970s is often associated with centralised agreements (Brannick et al., 1997). The essential argument here is that centralised agreements prescribe the levels of pay increases attainable in a given period. Since the great majority of trade unions (through ICTU) are committed to these provisions, workers wishing to secure terms above those prescribed in national agreements are highly unlikely to get official union sanction for industrial action. Consequently, if a particular work group deems that strike action is necessary, an unofficial strike is generally the only available option. However, the logic of this argument is open to question, since the most recent period of centralised bargaining, since 1987, has not seen any great resurgence in unofficial action. Again the jury is out here insofar as unofficial strike action remained subdued up to the mid-1990s but has shown some little signs of increase since then up to 1997. However, the most recent statistics indicate a major increase in unofficial strike action during the first quarter of 1998. We must await further data to assess whether this indicates a reversal of the trend in decline in the significance of unofficial strikes. Wallace and O'Shea's (1987) study of unofficial disputes noted the dramatic reduction in unofficial strikes since the early 1980s. The data presented in Figures 7.7 and 7.8 bear out this analysis.

Over the period 1980–90, approximately 40 per cent of strikes have been unofficial (29 per cent in 1987) comparing with an average of 66 per cent in the mid-1970s (Wallace and O'Shea, 1987). Looking at the distribution of working days lost, we see an even more dramatic decrease in the impact of unofficial strikes. We find that in the period 1987–97 approximately 8 per cent of the total working days lost due to strike action was attributed to unofficial strikes. Since unofficial strikes are normally of shorter duration and involve

Figure 7.7 Annual levels of strike frequency due to official and unofficial strikes 1980–98. (Note: figures for 1998 are for the first 6 months, January–June.)

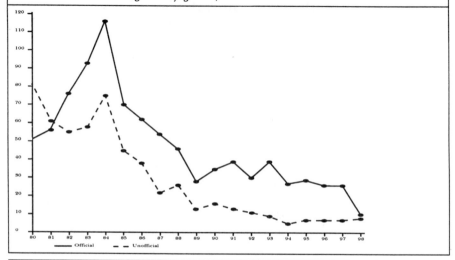

Figure 7.8 Annual levels of working days lost due to official and unofficial strikes 1980–98. (Note: figures for 1998 are for the first 6 months, January–June.)

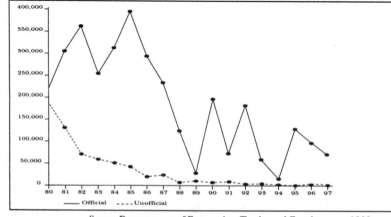

Source: Department of Enterprise, Trade and Employment 1998

244

fewer employees this means that unofficial strikes now account for quite a small proportion of working days lost due to strike activity (also see Wallace and O'Shea, 1987; Wallace, 1988a and b; Brannick et al., 1997). However, we should be cautious in making any long-term predictions since, as noted above, recent statistics point to an increase in unofficial strike activity.

A final area of interest in relation to strike activity is the actual causes of strikes. Figures 7.9 to 7.11, based on the UCD database, summarise the reported causes of strikes over the thirty-two year period, 1960–92 (Brannick and Doyle, 1994; Brannick et al., 1997).

Figure 7.9 Strike frequency by reported cause of strikes 1960–92

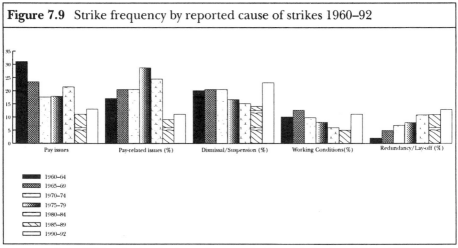

Source: UCD strike data bank; see, for example, Brannick, Doyle and Kelly, 1997

Figure 7.10 Workers involved in strike activity by reported cause of strikes 1960–92

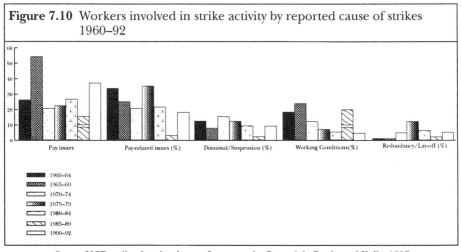

Source: UCD strike data bank; see, for example, Brannick, Doyle and Kelly, 1997

Figure 7.11 Working days lost due to strike activity by reported cause of strikes 1960–92

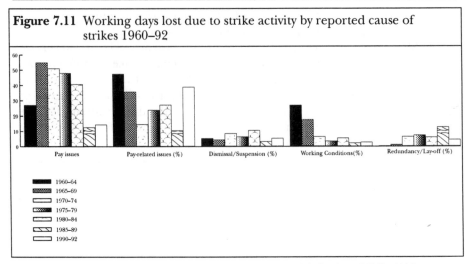

Source: UCD strike data bank; see, for example, Brannick, Doyle and Kelly, 1997

As the authors note, these data point to significant changes in the proportions of strikes which can be attributed to different causes over time. We see that pay has been a traditional source of high levels of strike activity but that its significance has declined in importance, particularly since the 1980s. Brannick et al. (1997) associate the decline in pay as a source of strike activity with the revival of centralised pay agreements in 1987. They also note that the high levels of workers involved in pay disputes in the early 1990s can be attributed to a small number of short public sector strikes. The figures also point to a recent revival in the contribution of dismissal/suspension and redundancy/lay-off issues as an important cause of strike activity in the 1990s.

7.5 CONFLICT RESOLUTION

While industrial conflict can be seen as a useful catalyst for solving organisational problems, it is important that such conflict remains within acceptable limits so that damage to organisational and national performance does not occur. All parties involved in industrial relations have an important role to play in conflict handling and resolution. For example, an integral part of the role of line managers and shop stewards is to effectively handle disputes and grievances which arise at that shopfloor level. Top management will generally have responsibility for the establishment of an organisational climate which fosters and values good management-employee relations. This role will incorporate the development of effective policies and procedures to handle conflict issues which arise in association with employees and their representative organisations. The specialist personnel/human resource function will be responsible for advising top management on optimal

246

industrial relations strategies and developing appropriate procedures and practices. It may also provide training, advice and guidance to line management in handling workplace issues. Trade unions undertake a similar role on the employee side, specifically in representing and articulating worker interests and ensuring adherence to due process. The current emphasis on partnership-based arrangements at enterprise level provides for a potentially higher level of worker and trade union involvement in sharing in the decision-making process with the firm. This latter issue is considered in greater depth in chapter 8.

As mentioned above, industrial conflict should not be viewed as having a necessarily negative impact on industrial relations. Industrial conflict can have certain positive effects. It allows employees to highlight issues of concern and facilitates change and development in the employment relationship. Possibly the most widespread response to conflict in the workplace has been the development of joint mechanisms to discuss and resolve issues of difference. Such institutionalisation of conflict involves the development of agreed practices and procedures for handling issues and is most clearly manifested in the significance of collective bargaining and trade union organisation (Jackson, 1982). The institutionalisation of conflict through the development of appropriate mechanisms and procedures reflects an implicit acceptance that conflict will arise and is characteristic of the pluralist model discussed earlier. In creating institutions (such as collective bargaining) and procedures for handling industrial relations and industrial conflict the parties involved seek to create a framework through which they can interact, argue, disagree and agree while allowing for the ongoing operation of the business. At enterprise level industrial relations institutions and procedures of various kinds have become an important feature of industrial relations in Ireland (Wallace, 1989). These can vary between organisations but will generally provide for the orderly resolution of disputes, grievances and disciplinary issues and provide an operating framework for workplace industrial relations. We now consider some of these various mechanisms, beginning with industrial relations negotiations.

In an Irish context, the significance of institutionalised industrial conflict has been highlighted by research which shows that industrial relations procedures of various kinds have over the last two decades become a permanent feature of workplace industrial relations (Wallace, 1989). Procedures can vary between organisations but will generally provide for the orderly resolution of grievances, disputes and disciplinary issues, and provide an operating framework for management/union negotiations. In addition, research has also demonstrated that personnel managers historically tended to consider industrial relations activities as the most important part of their jobs (see for instance, Gunnigle and Flood, 1988; Monks, 1992). In analysing the findings of her survey on the work of personnel practitioners in Ireland, Shivanath (1987) commented as follows:

> Industrial relations . . . [was] identified by the respondents as the most crucial area of their work. Whether the question centred around importance of activity, value to the organisation or proof of contribution, in all instances the group of activities collectively called industrial relations [was] reported to be top of the list.

It should be noted however, that writers such as Monks (1992), and Foley and Gunnigle (1994, 1995) have over the last decade detected important changes in the specialist personnel function. In essence, they have observed signs of movement away from traditional adversarial/collectivist industrial relations approaches towards more individualist ones, and have noticed that an increasing emphasis is being placed by the personnel function on the area of training and development. Nevertheless, these developments by no means constitute a disappearance of the traditional model; industrial relations activities continue to be a significant aspect of the specialist personnel role (Gunnigle et al., 1997).

Another pertinent development in relation to the institutionalisation of industrial conflict in Ireland has been the significant change in collective bargaining levels since the advent of national agreements in 1987. The four national agreements on pay and other matters have shifted the traditional focus (on multi-employer bargaining with supplementary workplace bargaining) to a higher level, but this development does not mean that collective bargaining at enterprise level has become obsolete. Indeed, local bargaining has been facilitated under recent centralised agreements which provide for the agreement of centralised pay guidelines while allowing management and employees in exceptional cases to negotiate for further changes in the rates of pay and on other issues at establishment level. Furthermore, competitive pressures and conflicts of interest unique to individual organisations continue to act as catalysts for workplace bargaining, and thus local level negotiations remain very much an integral component of industrial relations practice in Irish organisations.

Given the importance of institutionalised conflict in Irish industrial relations we now examine what are considered to be key conflict resolution mechanisms at the level of the organisation, namely, industrial relations negotiations, grievance handling and discipline administration. The area of employee participation and involvement, incorporating management-employee communications is discussed later, in chapter 10.

7.6 INDUSTRIAL RELATIONS NEGOTIATIONS[2]

When attempting to understand the dynamics of industrial relations negotiations, it is useful to have a basic perspective on the varying ways in which such negotiations have been studied.[3] Traditionally, the study of industrial relations negotiations developed in relative isolation from other areas in the field of conflict resolution theory, and was typically restricted to the observation and description of formal negotiating situations between managers and trade unions. Frequently, publications were highly prescriptive negotiation manuals, based on the limited experience of 'expert' negotiators rather than on solid research. However, as Lewicki et al. (1994) note, an interdisciplinary approach to conflict resolution has emerged over recent years, resulting in a rich body of negotiation theory with contributions from disciplines such as psychology, sociology, anthropology, political science, industrial relations, economics and mathematics. Interestingly, it appears that this cross-fertilisation of ideas was partly generated by the Cold War, which necessitated the conduct of a large amount of research on the psychology of conflict and on the practical aspects of negotiation. The benefit for the modern industrial relations negotiator is that prescriptions now tend to be grounded in more robust theory, are more versatile, and are less biased towards any particular negotiating style or theoretical discipline.

Naturally, the growth of the interdisciplinary approach has also resulted in many rather diverse definitions of negotiations, but the central thread running through most of them is that negotiation is a complex social process aimed at reaching agreement through discussion in relation to divisive issues. Hawkins (1979) provides us with what is possibly the most widely quoted definition in industrial relations circles, describing negotiation as the process of resolving conflict through compromise.

As a comprehensive examination of ways in which the negotiations process has been studied would be beyond the scope of this text, an attempt is made here to integrate some of the more commonly used methods of analysis.

Lewicki et al. (1994) provide a useful summary of approaches to studying this process, suggesting that it typically tends to be viewed from one of four mainstream perspectives. Firstly, focus is often placed on the strategies adopted during the conduct of negotiations. Alternatively, a time-series perspective which tracks the events that characterise the process is used. Another common approach is the study of key behavioural variables and sub-processes involved in negotiations, such as personality, perception, cognition, decision making, communication and persuasion. Finally, focus also tends to be placed on the key contextual factors that affect negotiations. Examples of these are factors such as the issues under dispute, the nature of the relationship between the parties involved and the power balance between them, the social and cultural context of the negotiation, the availability of alternative ways to resolve the conflict, and the physical and temporal constraints placed on the negotiations.

As there is a great deal of overlap between these mainstream approaches, the remainder of this sub-section synthesises elements of them in an effort to build a broad overview of the industrial relations negotiations process. The framework used to do this is based largely on the time-series approach, but also incorporates a fifth perspective, Walton and McKersie's (1965) model of negotiation.

Essentially, Walton and McKersie's model is based on their observations of industrial relations negotiations, and identifies two dominant forms that negotiations tend to take. Negotiations between unions and management over pay and conditions of employment are termed 'distributive bargaining', since they involve bargaining or haggling over issues where a favourable settlement for one party means an element of loss for the other. This 'win-lose' approach represents the adversarial model of collective bargaining where each party pursues its own specific objectives and hopes to yield minimal concessions to the other party. It is most obvious in pay negotiations where concessions by management inevitably represent both a quantifiable cost and a reduction in profits/dividends. However, negotiations can involve a joint problem-solving approach, sometimes referred to as 'integrative' or 'co-operative' bargaining, where both parties are concerned with finding a jointly acceptable solution resulting in mutual benefits for both sides. This is often referred to as a 'win-win' approach to industrial relations negotiations (Walton and McKersie, 1965; Chamberlain and Kuhn, 1965). Inevitably, workplace negotiations tend to involve a combination of both approaches with the 'mix' being influenced by the extent of trust and openness between the parties.

Figure 7.12 Adversarial and co-operative models of negotiation

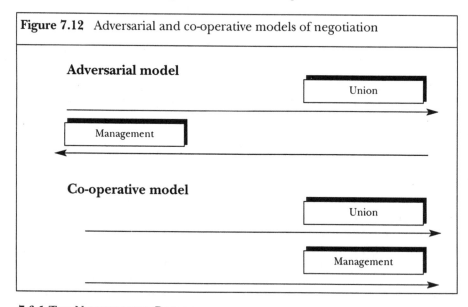

7.6.1 THE NEGOTIATIONS PROCESS

It is interesting to note that industrial relations negotiations tend to be highly ritualistic processes in which both parties engage in an elaborate game. Normally, the formal initiation of industrial relations negotiations begins with one party presenting a claim to the other, in the hope of meeting to discuss the issues raised in a specific context. Subsequent interactions generally involve the various parties bargaining and haggling over the divisive issues and reporting back to their respective constituents. These interactions may conclude either by reaching a mutually acceptable agreement on the issues raised or, possibly, a failure to agree resulting in a breakdown of negotiations. Such an impasse may be resolved through further discussion, mediation/ arbitration, or use of sanctions, such as industrial action.

Whether or not the negotiating process reaches a successful conclusion depends on a number of factors. Most importantly, issues such as the willingness to compromise, the bargaining skills of both sides (including their persuasive abilities) and ultimately, the power balance between parties will all have some impact on the final outcome of the negotiation (Hawkins, 1979). It is important to note that negotiation is an ongoing process not limited to one particular issue or time. All parties will generally be concerned with the establishment of enduring and stable relations. The long-term relationship between both parties is often treated as more important than the particular issue upon which a single negotiating process is focused. Frequently, the maintenance of this relationship takes precedence over achieving a short-term 'victory'. Indeed, bargaining 'adversaries' such as trade union officials and personnel managers can, over time, build up a close working relationship which can be very facilitative in the resolution of many troublesome issues.

The negotiating process itself will generally follow a number of predictable phases. These may be categorised as (1) preparation for negotiations (2) bargaining and (3) follow-up action as outlined in Table 7.4 and discussed below.

Table 7.4	The negotiating process
Phase	**Activities**
1. PREPARATION	Agree objectives and mandate
	Assess relative bargaining power
	Conduct relevant research
	Choose negotiating team/develop skills
	Make appropriate administrative arrangements
2. BARGAINING	Discover positions
	Expectation structuring
	Compromise and movement
3. POST-NEGOTIATION	Document agreement/disagreement
	Clarify
	Agree action plans
	Communicate
	Implement action plans
	Review

7.6.2 PREPARATION FOR NEGOTIATIONS

This phase, in which both parties prepare for the subsequent negotiations, is an essential prerequisite for success in industrial relations negotiations (Scott, 1981; Hawkins, 1979). Within the preparation phase there are several important criteria which should be satisfied. Nierenberg (1968) suggests that effective preparation involves gathering all relevant information and retaining this for use at the bargaining table as well as ensuring that any agreements/ procedures are adhered to. Such preparation requires that negotiators be familiar with the details of the case and have a clear idea of their objectives and mandate before entering the bargaining arena, i.e., negotiators should clarify what they want to achieve from the collective bargaining process in general, and each set of negotiations in particular.

For managers, the general goals might include the maintenance of good working relations with employees and their representatives, maintaining managerial prerogative in certain areas, and the avoidance of industrial conflict. Particular objectives vary according to the issue at hand and should involve specific targets, trade-off options, and resistance points. Flexible objectives are generally more appropriate than rigid ones since information may be uncovered during negotiations which can alter the substance of the management case. It is important that each party's objectives are clearly articulated and approved by constituents, particularly top management on the managerial side and trade union members/representatives on the union side. This helps ensure that each negotiating team has a clear mandate. It is also vital that objectives be agreed and communicated within the negotiating team to ensure the commitment of all members of the negotiating team to their achievement.

A central issue in agreeing negotiating objectives is deciding upon the bargaining range, including the limits or parameters within which they can be achieved. Negotiating inevitably means compromise and movement. The degree to which this is possible and consequently the scope for reaching agreement depends on the bargaining range of both parties and the degree to which these overlap. In practice this often means establishing an ideal settlement point, a realistic settlement point and also a fall-back position beyond which each party will not be prepared to reach agreement. At preparation stage, it is suggested that each party to the negotiations should establish its ideal settlement point and also its resistance point beyond which the organisation is not prepared to reach agreement (Hawkins, 1979). This process effectively prescribes the overall bargaining range and the potential area of settlement on the various issues for negotiation. This is demonstrated in the pay bargaining example as outlined in Figure 7.13. Here the process of establishing bargaining parameters facilitates the identification of bargaining objectives, deciding on trade-offs and concessions, and provides a benchmark against which to evaluate progress. In this it is clear that agreement between the management and trade union teams is only possible where resistance points (fall-back positions) overlap, that is in the 2 to 4 per cent pay range. A settlement is not possible outside this range unless one of the parties alters its position. If this does not happen then the parties are in conflict over the issue and industrial action may be used to help resolve this impasse.

Figure 7.13 Management-trade union bargaining range (pay negotiations)

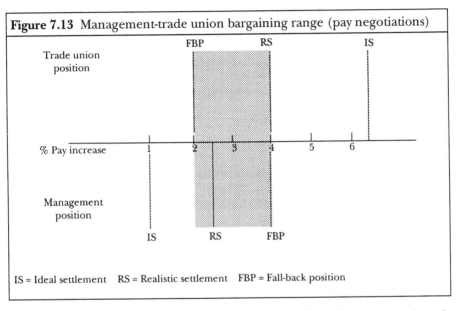

IS = Ideal settlement   RS = Realistic settlement   FBP = Fall-back position

Another key factor for parties entering industrial relations negotiations is the issue of bargaining power: it is imperative that each party have an accurate evaluation of both their own and the other party's relative bargaining power before entering negotiations. Cole (1986) suggests that bargaining power may be interpreted as the degree to which one party can achieve its negotiating goals despite the opposition of the other side. Relative bargaining power will significantly influence the outcome of industrial relations negotiations since the balance of settlement will normally favour the party with the greatest bargaining power. The amount of bargaining power which a party possesses depends on a range of factors both external and internal to the negotiations process. The general economic and business environment will have a major impact. For example, high levels of unemployment and a depressed economic climate may place trade unions in a relatively poor power position in bargaining on pay or related matters. In contrast, a full order book will favour a union claim for bonus payments as management will be keen to meet production targets. Bargaining power will also be influenced by the relative skill and ability of the negotiators and the degree to which they have prepared their case.

While it is not always easy to obtain an accurate picture of another party's resistance point or fall-back position, negotiators need to be aware that this information is important. The extent to which such information is available will often depend on the levels of trust that exist between both parties and the effectiveness of their relationship to date. It is also useful to evaluate the level of commitment of the other party and its constituents to achieving its stated objectives. Much of the negotiations process involves rhetorical arguments indicating the level of feeling on a particular issue. Much of this bluff and rhetoric is aimed at convincing the other side that one's resistance (fall-back position) is higher than it actually is to encourage the other party to make concessions. An accurate perception of actual fall-back positions indicates how far management can go without risking breakdown in negotiations. It also helps if management weigh up the advantages and disadvantages of varying concession levels.

The conduct of appropriate research is also of crucial importance when preparing for negotiations. Adequate back-up research is not only a useful tool in the assessment of relative bargaining power, but also helps to clarify realistic bargaining objectives and ensures that the presentation of a case at negotiations is well substantiated. Clearly, the extent and nature of such research will vary depending on the issues involved. Of particular relevance are indices and trends of pay increases and working conditions and comparable settlements/agreements in other organisations. Employer associations, trade union research units and some consultancy organisations provide such information. This information may also be elicited through informal contacts with other firms, trade unions or other bodies. Adequate research support helps focus negotiations on facts rather than discussing opinions or value judgments (Fisher and Ury, 1986). Preparatory research might also incorporate an evaluation of the repercussions of likely settlement options and knock-on effects of different potential outcomes of negotiations, including industrial action.

Additional criteria for effective preparation include the following: the participation of relevant team members, the development of key negotiating skills and the provision of adequate administrative arrangements.

The participation of relevant team members: Where the issue for negotiation is relatively minor the negotiating team will normally be comprised of line managers/supervisors and shop stewards/individual employees. In such instances the role of senior management and trade union officials is generally restricted to the provision of advice and guidance as required. In larger unionised organisations the personnel manager will normally represent management with the trade union official leading the union side in major negotiations. Alternatively, the leading role on the management side may be carried out by the chief executive with the personnel practitioner acting as key advisor. However, line managers and shop stewards may often be involved either individually on local issues or alongside the personnel manager and trade union official on more general issues.

The size and composition of the negotiating team largely depends on the issue for negotiation. It is generally suggested that, with the exception of quite minor issues, a negotiating team should comprise a minimum of two people, facilitate case presentation, record keeping and evaluation of progress (Nierenberg, 1968). Nierenberg, argues that using a single negotiator facilitates clarification of responsibility, speedy decision making and prevents differences of opinion. However, he also suggests that increasing the number of representatives ensures greater technical knowledge, improved planning and judgment. This facilitates the allocation of responsibilities in presenting the case, analysis of verbal and non-verbal responses, record keeping, and adequate consideration of the consequences of various settlement options and management responses. It also increases objectivity, provides a witness to the event and facilitates conclusion of the final agreement. Dealing specifically with the composition of management teams in industrial relations negotiations, Canning (1979) identifies three main tasks which need to be provided for within the management negotiating team:

(1) Spokesman/Team Leader: The role of the chief management representative is to present arguments, control strategy and tactics, and take major on-the-spot decisions. This role is often the responsibility of the senior personnel practitioner.

(2) Observer: Here the role is to evaluate progress relative to objectives, spot key reactions, identify changes in approach and advise the chief negotiator.

(3) Recorder: This involves recording key points in negotiations and documenting the final agreement.

Key skills: Negotiators should possess a sound knowledge of the organisation and the issue at hand. They also need to be flexible and articulate in presenting arguments, be good listeners and possess the analytical ability, self-discipline, patience and stamina necessary for prolonged negotiations. A spread of interests and roles facilitates the development of strategy and tactics within the team. It provides a useful source of information and allows for different negotiating styles which may result in a team member playing the potentially constructive role of a 'devil's advocate' during the process.

Adequate administrative arrangements: These should be in place before negotiations take place. This includes ensuring all parties are aware of the issues and timing of the negotiations. It also involves the provision of adequate physical facilities including the venue (spacious, free from interruptions, convenient), seating and adjournment arrangements (non-intimidating, caucus rooms) and back-up facilities (phone, fax, typing, etc.). Most industrial relations negotiations take place within the organisation. However there may be occasions when it is appropriate to move 'off-site' to provide a more neutral atmosphere, avoid on-the-job interruptions or leaks from the negotiations.

7.6.3 THE BARGAINING PHASE

STRATEGY AND TACTICS FOR INDUSTRIAL RELATIONS NEGOTIATIONS

The pre-negotiations issues discussed above will help identify and articulate each party's general approach to the subsequent negotiations. In addressing the actual conduct of negotiations a key issue for the parties involves adopting an overall negotiating strategy and selecting complementary negotiating tactics to use during the actual bargaining phase. The development of an overall negotiating strategy incorporates decisions on the general approach to be adopted in the negotiations. For instance, depending upon the nature of the relationship between parties and the problem at hand, negotiators may adopt a distributive or an integrative approach. Typically, one would expect parties to adopt a distributive strategy in an adversarial bargaining situation, while one would expect the adoption of a more integrative strategy in a co-operative situation.

Negotiating tactics refer to the various techniques which are implemented to achieve this strategy. For example, if one party wanted to achieve its particular objectives without undue confrontation, the resulting tactics might involve placing issues which are less likely to be disputed at the top of the agenda. These might then be easily agreed during the early stages of bargaining thereby establishing a conciliatory/friendly tone for the subsequent negotiations for the discussion of subsequent, more contentious issues. Clearly, there are wide ranges of tactics available under both the distributive and co-operative strategies to industrial relations negotiations. Some of the more commonly used tactics are discussed below.

TACTICS SUITED TO A DISTRIBUTIVE NEGOTIATING STRATEGY

A negotiating party's fundamental aim when adopting a distributive strategy is to maximise its 'slice' of a given 'pie'. In other words, the party is trying to minimise the opposition's slice of the pie by pushing for a settlement as close as possible to the opposition's fall-back position, or even by trying to convince the opposition to weaken its fall-back position. The two basic persuasion techniques that can be used by a negotiating party when trying to implement a distributive strategy are as follows:

(1) The party can seek to manage the flow of information during the negotiations in such a manner as to obscure its true negotiating positions.

(2) The party can attempt to probe, reveal and weaken the opposition's true negotiating positions.

A variety of tactics complement these persuasion techniques, some of which are widely seen as being acceptable in negotiating situations ('good faith' tactics) and others which are typically viewed as ethically questionable because they are intended to coerce opponents into submission ('hard ball' tactics). However, as numerous writers have noticed (see for instance Lewicki et al., 1994; Fisher and Ury, 1986), the boundary between good faith and hard ball tactics is blurred, because the degree of acceptability of any particular tactic depends on the perceptions of the individuals involved. Indeed, it is interesting to note that as perceptions are often culturally influenced, a whole genre of research has been spawned by the need to discover cross-national differences in preferences for negotiating tactics. As a general rule of thumb though, hard ball tactics are seen as Machiavellian 'dirty tricks', and are not widely recommended where negotiating parties are faced with the prospect of a long-term relationship.

GOOD FAITH TACTICS

Agenda and timing. At the very outset the structuring of the agenda may allow one side to have an advantage in negotiations. It was suggested above that either party might create a conciliatory atmosphere by placing simple, non-contentious issues at the top of the agenda and begin by making concessions on these. When a major issue is subsequently discussed the party which made the early concessions might then 'throw down the gauntlet' asking the other side to make 'similar' concessions. However, it is important to note that as management/trade union negotiations are generally expected to be tough, drawn out affairs, concessions should not be made too early/easily leading the other party to infer that even better settlement levels can be obtained.

Screening. An effective way of obscuring a negotiating position is to guide the opposition towards a 'preferred impression' of the true position (Lewicki et al., 1994). This can be achieved through the selective presentation of information, which helps to disguise a negotiating position, and also allows negotiators to only put forward facts that support their case. Unfavourable information is thus 'screened out' of the process. The use of a spokesperson or team leader can also help screening tactics, as it helps to prevent unwanted leaks of information. In addition, a technique known as 'calculated incompetence' can aid screening (Lewicki et al, 1994). This technique prevents inadvertent information leaks either by employing an agent (such as a lawyer or expert negotiator) strictly on a need-to-know basis, or by giving the agent (or negotiating team) limited authorisation to make decisions. Finally, a variation on the screening tactic is the 'kitchen sink' tactic, which entails bombarding the opposition with so many superfluous messages that the true negotiating position is obscured.

However, this tactic and the other screening activities mentioned are not without danger. They run the risk of frustrating opposition negotiators to such an extent that negotiations break down, and can also be interpreted as lies and bad faith rather than legitimate, expected attempts at concealing a position. A more ethically acceptable and potentially more effective screening activity is the exercise of control over body language and emotional reactions. Typically, instead of being seen as an effort at being economical with the truth, such control is often admired as being the sign of a tough but fair negotiator.

Bottom line: This is a tactic whereby instead of obscuring a true negotiating position, a negotiating party tries to win over the opposition party by putting forward the merits of their position, along with the benefits to the opposition of accepting the position and the serious consequences of failing to do so. An example of the tactic in use is the common management practice of outlining the implications of a union claim on factors like costs, competitiveness, survival, etc. This is often done by using financial information to demonstrate relative ability to pay or by bringing the chief executive in to the negotiators to demonstrate the strength of feeling on the issue. The danger with this technique however, is that a committed bottom line position can easily become an entrenched one, resulting in intransigence and the breakdown of negotiations, unless a face saving mechanism can be produced. It is therefore typically recommended that negotiators using the bottom line tactic prepare a secret face saving device prior to taking a committed position.

Split the opposition: This is a negotiating tactic whereby one party attempts to undermine the apparent unity of the opposition by exposing different positions or feelings on issues within the other team. Any subsequent conflict within the opposition may result in it having to withdraw, regroup its forces and reconsider its position. Non-directive, open questions are useful when trying to probe and uncover these differences. Using such questions, a team can clarify the factual basis of the other side's position, sometimes with very beneficial results. It may also be useful to question the validity of comparisons or reliability of data used by the other party. If this questioning points to weaknesses in the other party's case they may be forced to reconsider their position as discussed above. Ideally, such probing should be done sensitively so that the other party does not lose too much face and so that they don't feel 'backed into a corner', an experience that may cause them to react aggressively or irrationally. Keeping in mind that the longer term relationship must be considered, adjourning negotiations may be useful, and is sometimes necessary in order to allow for changes in position and an opportunity for one party to save face on a particular issue. This consideration is often referred to as giving the 'losing' party their 'bus fare home'.

HARD BALL TACTICS

Preconditions: Although the agenda of negotiations can be used to create a conciliatory atmosphere, it can also be used to create a more aggressive intimidatory atmosphere. For example, a crucial issue may be placed first with a stipulation that agreement must be reached on this issue before any discussions can take place on other agenda items. This approach can serve to pressurise the other party which may be more concerned with subsequent matters on the agenda. The structure of the agenda may also be used to put time pressures on the other party by placing issues crucial to them at the bottom, giving limited time for their discussion and possibly ensuring their deferral.

Bogey: The timing and nature of concessions can also be manipulated to try to produce an advantage. The bogey tactic involves tricking the opposition into believing that major concessions are being made on an issue which is actually of little or no importance, in the hope that the opposition will feel obliged to concede on the issues of real importance. The inherent danger with this tactic though is that the opposition may also be using it, with the result that both sides waste time and effort trying to outdo each other on trivial issues.

High ball/Low ball: This tactic is based on the theory that making an outrageously high or low opening offer forces the opposing party to re-evaluate and weaken its negotiating positions. However, the tactic is liable to backfire, as it is very difficult to justify an extreme position, and taking such a position can also give the opposition the impression that no agreement is possible.

The nibble: A party using this tactic introduces an extra, previously unmentioned, item for consideration just when a deal is about to be clinched. The additional item is of definite benefit to the party that introduces it, but is typically not worth losing the entire deal over, and thus puts pressure on the opposition to concede. However, the risk with the tactic is that the opposition may call the bluff, or may be motivated to seek revenge even if they do concede on the item.

Hard and soft: While the manipulation of the negotiation agenda and timing of concessions can be an effective way of asserting control over negotiations, another popular approach used is a variation of the well known good cop/bad cop police interrogation tactic. In a negotiation setting, it involves alternating between what are known as 'hard' and 'soft' approaches. This happens when different members of the negotiating team vary their style of discussion, at one stage being aggressive and at others taking a more conciliatory approach. These roles may often be divided up between members of the negotiating team with one giving no quarter while the other infers that there may be room for compromise. The objective of this tactic is to make any concessions offered by the softer partner appear more attractive than they otherwise would to the other party in the negotiations.

Chicken/Intimidation: The chicken tactic is one of many tactics which fall under the general label of intimidation, and entails pushing the negotiations as close as possible towards breakdown in the hope that the other party will lose its nerve and make concessions. However, like the dangerous driving game after which it is named, it can often result in disaster for both parties. Other intimidatory tactics include various unpleasant emotional ploys, such as aggressive or violent behaviour, or smearing the integrity of the other party (Lewicki et al., 1994). However, apart from their ethically dubious nature, the main problem with intimidatory tactics is their unproven efficacy; introducing fear into a negotiating situation often leads to a total breakdown of communication.

Fait accompli: This is a tactic which involves implementing an initiative before it has secured full agreement through the industrial relations process. A common example of this technique is when new technology is introduced by management, before such changes have been negotiated. Such an approach represents a calculated risk, the implications of which must be carefully evaluated by management in advance.

COPING WITH HARD BALL TACTICS

Although many people are phased by hard ball tactics, a number of relatively simple techniques can be used to cope with hard ball (Lewicki et al., 1994; Fisher and Ury, 1986). Often the easiest option is to ignore hard ball tactics, either by switching topics, or by calling an adjournment. Side-stepping a hard ball can give the thrower the impression that it won't be tolerated, or that it's not going to work so it's not worth the effort. Another option is to respond in kind, and thereby demonstrate that the use of hard ball tactics can be destructive, in the hope that there will subsequently be a return to more constructive methods. However, the obvious danger here is that the situation can disintegrate into chaos. A third option is 'talks about talks', i.e., discussing the ways in which the negotiations are to be conducted before the true negotiations begin. Doing this helps to concentrate the negotiations on issues rather than on the personalities of the individuals involved. Finally, befriending the opposition or co-opting them makes it more difficult for them to engage in hard ball tactics.

TACTICS FOR INTEGRATIVE BARGAINING

The fundamental aim of integrative bargaining is to create a free and honest flow of information in order to arrive at a solution that meets the needs of both sides involved. Effective information exchange allows the parties to understand each other's true objectives, and thus helps overcome the distributive tendencies of most bargaining situations and generate amicable solutions. Lewicki et al. (1994) put forward a number of tactics that facilitate integrative bargaining, some of which are discussed below.

Depersonalising the problem: In order to create a climate where an honest exchange of information can take place, the problems involved must be defined in a way that is mutually acceptable to both parties. Both parties must try to 'depersonalise' the problem by accepting that there are legitimate differences of viewpoint on the problem. This can only be done if both parties understand each other's real *interests* as opposed to just seeing each other's negotiating positions (Fisher and Ury, 1986). Interests are the underlying needs and concerns behind a negotiating position, so getting at interests involves asking the question 'why', when a party takes a particular stance.

Expanding the pie. Once the problem has been adequately defined, the search for alternative solutions can begin. When the problem revolves around a shortage of resources, a solution may be generated quite simply by both parties working together to expand the amount of resources available to them.

Logrolling. Where expanding the pie is not an option, an alternative may be to 'trade off' items under discussion, based on their relative importance to each party. This tactic is typically an iterative process of trial and error, and may require the parties to redefine problems by separating or 'unbundling' issues in order to come up with a mutually acceptable package. The danger of logrolling however, is that it can disintegrate into a typical distributive bargaining situation. Parties have to remember that integrative bargaining is not about evaluating who is 'winning' more, but rather about satisfying both sides by making sure that both are winning.

Non-specific compensation. Another integrative tactic is for one party to offer non-specific compensation in return for movement on a particular item. For instance, management may make concessions on non-monetary issues such as employee discretion over job design in return for union concessions in relation to a pay claim. Alternatively, a linked tactic is to cut the costs of agreeing to concede on a particular item. For example, unions may cut the cost of management agreeing to a pay increase by delivering a productivity increase.

Finding a bridge solution. When using this tactic, both sides aim to invent novel options which satisfy their interests. Various techniques can facilitate this process: the parties can engage in brainstorming (making spontaneous, uncensored suggestions), can split into small groups, or write down ideas as individuals (in an effort to avoid group think), or can solicit outside help.

THE BARGAINING PROCESS

The above tactics represent several of the main approaches available to negotiators during the process of bargaining. It is also important however, to examine the different phases that go to make up this process. It is generally the case that collective bargaining interactions often pass through a number of identifiable phases, namely, (1) opening; (2) expectation structuring; (3) offer, concession, movement; (4) agreement/disagreement and (5) close, as outlined in Figure 7.14.

Figure 7.14 Stages in bargaining

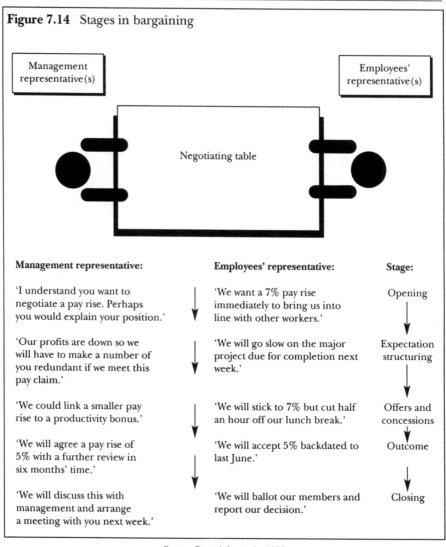

Management representative:		Employees' representative:	Stage:
'I understand you want to negotiate a pay rise. Perhaps you would explain your position.'	↓	'We want a 7% pay rise immediately to bring us into line with other workers.'	Opening
'Our profits are down so we will have to make a number of you redundant if we meet this pay claim.'	↓	'We will go slow on the major project due for completion next week.'	Expectation structuring
'We could link a smaller pay rise to a productivity bonus.'	↓	'We will stick to 7% but cut half an hour off our lunch break.'	Offers and concessions
'We will agree a pay rise of 5% with a further review in six months' time.'	↓	'We will accept 5% backdated to last June.'	Outcome
'We will discuss this with management and arrange a meeting with you next week.'	↓	'We will ballot our members and report our decision.'	Closing

Source: Gunnigle et al., 1992

When the bargaining process is initiated, management is obliged to ensure that negotiations begin and proceed in a business like way. During this initial period it is traditional for the management team to open the proceedings and then for both parties to articulate their respective positions. This may involve management referring to the subject-matter for negotiation, the details of any claim served upon them and their position on such issues. Alternatively, the union/employee team may seek to clarify or substantiate their position/claim. Either way the approach and tone adopted by the management and union/employee teams during this opening period will influence the subsequent bargaining climate. During this opening stage both parties will attempt to establish each other's positions, assess the degree to which movement and concession is possible and predict the likelihood of achieving their respective negotiating objectives.

After the initial opening stage of the bargaining process, a series of interactions known as 'expectation structuring' often takes place. During this stage both parties attempt to convince the other party as to the logic of their position and the depth of their commitment to that position while also perhaps attempting to highlight deficiencies in the other party's position. Each party to the negotiations thus attempts to structure or influence the other party's expectations and tries to convince them to accept whatever concessions are offered. For example, the management team in pay negotiations may emphasise factors like the poor economic outlook, need to retain competitiveness, danger of redundancies, etc. In so doing they attempt to shape the union's expectations by painting a bleak picture of the organisation's operating conditions, thus increasing the likelihood of their accepting a lower level of increase.

The 'offer, concession, movement' phase generally begins after both parties have attempted, at least in some way, to structure each other's expectations. This stage is where the real bargaining actually takes place. Here some initial offers and concessions may be proffered by either party. This is a crucial phase in the overall negotiating process. It is felt that correct timing is absolutely crucial in making offers/concessions and, as suggested above, it is normally advisable to take some time before making any major concessions. If such concessions are made too early in negotiations the other party may press for even greater ones during subsequent bargaining. Any movement or offer from a team's opening position should be carefully weighed up in respect of its long- and short-term implications. At this stage adjournments may be useful in order to allow both parties to evaluate progress to date. After some time it will become clear if agreement is possible, whether the parties will have to refer back to their respective constituents, or if a breakdown in negotiations is imminent. In any case the details of the issues discussed, the offers and concessions made, the agreement reached or reasons for breakdown in negotiations should be carefully recorded.

If negotiations do break down, then some channel of communication between parties should be kept open if at all possible. In the event of a breakdown, it is important that neither party walks away from the bargaining table without at least some agreement as to how communication will be re-initiated and by whom. Again, the idea that long-term relations may be more important than the issues at hand during a particular set of negotiations, is an important principle for both parties to keep in mind. For this reason the parties to negotiations should be keen to avoid damaging conflict or breakdowns and be prepared to compromise on certain issues for the benefit of that longer term perspective.

Both parties are likely to recognise when negotiations are beginning to draw to a close. This stage will generally involve finalising the agreement, issues for further negotiation, or details of breakdown. It is important that adequate time should be set aside for this stage in negotiations as there is a common tendency to rush through this closing stage in negotiations. Each party should be clear on the substance and interpretation of the agreements and on their various commitments during subsequent implementation of what was agreed during negotiations. Details of future meetings or review procedures should be clearly specified and agreed before the parties leave the negotiating table.

7.6.4 THE POST-NEGOTIATION PHASE

Once the negotiations have reached an end, the parties involved will normally report back on the outcome, the union reporting back to its members and the management team reporting back to senior and, possibly, line management. This post-negotiation stage will normally review the implementation of the agreement(s) and the overall implications of the outcome of the negotiations for industrial relations and future negotiations. The way in which the agreement is communicated to employees should also be agreed upon, as well as decisions on any administrative obligations to be carried out. It is useful to document all aspects of the negotiations carefully for further reference. Details of implementation should be worked out and responsibilities allocated. Equally, both parties may be keen to review and assess the lessons learned from the negotiations experience.

TOWARDS EFFECTIVE NEGOTIATION

The negotiations process involves interactions between people of varying personalities in different organisational contexts. Therefore, it is often impossible to predict the ways in which such negotiations will be carried out, or indeed, the kinds of outcomes to which they will give rise. Persistent problems in negotiations may arise for numerous reasons such as inflexibility and unwillingness to compromise, abrasive style and language, or poor preparation and knowledge. Such problems may be tackled by improving the competence of the negotiating team. It is always worthwhile to ensure that the members of the negotiating team have been selected carefully, are experienced and are appropriately trained. Writers have consistently emphasised the importance of negotiating skills as a means of achieving success in negotiations (Nierenberg, 1968; Scott, 1981; Atkinson, 1977). Other theorists suggest however, that problems in negotiation are not caused by incompetent negotiators so much as by inherent flaws in the process itself. It has been suggested that the entire negotiation process needs to undergo re-evaluation (Fisher and Ury, 1986). A general criticism has been the perceived dominance of distributive bargaining with its emphasis on dividing limited resources. It is sometimes felt that this approach encourages both parties to develop adversarial positions believing that any gains can only be made by inflicting losses on the other party. Distributive bargaining reflects the very essence of the traditional pluralist industrial relations model: claims, offers, bluff, threats, compromise, movement, agreement or conflict. Approaches based on more integrative/co-operative bargaining (also known as the joint problem solving approach) are often seen as a more attractive alternative (particularly from a managerial perspective) with their emphasis on a collaborative approach, exploring common ground and seeking solutions of mutual benefit to both parties.

Fisher and Ury's (1986) work on developing an alternative approach to negotiations has been one of the most influential in critically evaluating the negotiations process. They suggest that traditional haggling approaches force the parties to take opposing positions and adopt bargaining stances designed to justify and achieve that position. They feel that such 'positional bargaining' produces unwise agreements, is inefficient, and endangers the ongoing relationship. Fisher and Ury prefer a 'principled' approach to negotiations based on the merits of the case. They suggest that a move away from positional bargaining will help reduce traditional barriers to agreement and bring both parties closer to the joint solution seeking approach.

It is doubtful, however, that the traditional bargaining approaches will disappear, despite the criticism they have received. Both the conventional, adversarial approach and the more co-operative alternative tend to be appropriate in different circumstances. Given the structure of organisations and their inherent potential for the emergence of conflicts of interest, it seems inevitable that distributive bargaining will continue to be a common feature of workplace negotiations. In fact, recent research evidence suggests that the pluralist approach to industrial relations continues to characterise industrial relations practice in many Irish organisations (Roche, 1990; Gunnigle, 1991; 1993; Gunnigle et al., 1994; Turner, 1993).

7.7 DEALING WITH GRIEVANCE AND DISCIPLINARY ISSUES

While industrial relations negotiations provide an important means of dealing with many issues of conflict which arise in organisations, the parties involved must also address grievance and disciplinary matters. Grievance and disciplinary procedures are a characteristic feature of industrial relations and represent an important means of dealing with conflict at the level of the enterprise and above (see, for example, Wallace, 1989). Salamon (1998:533) defines procedure as 'an operational mechanism which defines, and may limit, the exercise of managerial authority and power through establishing a formal regulatory framework for handling specified issues'.

In respect of workplace industrial relations, one commonly finds two general types of procedure, one for dealing with grievances or disputes (normally initiated by employees), and one for handling disciplinary matters (normally initiated by management). We first consider the area of employee grievances and the handling of such matters by management.

7.7.1 GRIEVANCE HANDLING

In industrial relations, the term 'grievance' is normally used to describe a formal expression of employee dissatisfaction by either an individual employee or a small group of employees. In contrast, the term 'dispute' generally refers to collective grievances based on claims of a group of workers. In practice, both terms are often used interchangeably with any differences applying only to the level at which an issue enters the procedure (Wallace, 1989).

It is almost inevitable, given the nature of people and their workplaces, that grievances will arise from time to time. Most employees will, at some stage, encounter issues which cause them concern and which, as a result, may be voiced as a grievance. The vast majority of workplace grievances and disputes are handled at workplace level by line management and employees/employee representatives. It is particularly important that managers are aware of the importance of good grievance handling and its positive contribution to the promotion of good industrial relations. Should employees have problems which they wish to raise with management these should be handled as promptly and actively as possible. The non-handling of grievances may give rise to frustration which can permeate through to other employees and promote an uneasy working environment in which disputes and poor industrial relations can arise. Some summary guidelines for managers involved in grievance handling are outlined in Table 7.5.

Table 7.5 Management checklist for grievance handling

- Management should make every effort to understand the nature of, and the reasons for, disputes and grievances
- All levels of management should be aware of the potentially significant influence which grievance handling has on industrial relations and company performance generally.
- Management should establish a policy which sets out an orderly and effective framework for handling employee grievances.
- Line management, particularly first level supervision, should be aware of their key role in effective grievance handling.

An important initial step is for management to try and understand the nature of workplace disputes and grievances. This facilitates an appreciation of the wide variety of issues which may give rise to grievances and highlights the importance of prevention as a management strategy. A useful approach is to analyse the conditions which are most likely to give rise to grievances or disputes. These might include poor working conditions, unsafe work practices, discrimination, job insecurity, inadequate wages, and unrealistic rules and regulations. Of course the list is endless and the types of issues that do arise tend to depend on the nature of the organisation. Salamon (1998) identifies two broad types of issues which can lead to expressions of grievance or dispute (also see International Labour Office, 1977):

(1) *matters of right*, which are concerned with the interpretation and application of existing rules (for example, with respect to sick pay);

(2) *matters of interest*, which are concerned with determination of new terms and conditions of employment.

7.7.2 GRIEVANCE PROCEDURES

An important dimension in grievance handling is the establishment and application of *grievance procedures* (Thomason, 1984). Such a procedure normally outlines the stages and approaches to be followed in handling grievances in the workplace. The main advantages associated with such procedures include the following:

(1) increased clarity in industrial relations interactions;

(2) prevention of misunderstandings and arguments over interpretation;

(3) ease of communication; and

(4) increased fairness and consistency in application.

(Hawkins, 1979; also see Wallace, 1989; Gunnigle, Morley and Heraty, 1997). Grievance and disputes procedures in industrial relations usually incorporate a number of common features of which the following are particularly important:

(1) The procedure should be in writing for purposes of clarity.

(2) The grievance should be raised at the appropriate level. Usually the grievance is first discussed between employees and their immediate manager or supervisor.

(3) An appeal mechanism should be provided so that decisions can be appealed if agreement is not reached at a particular level.

(4) The procedure should be simple and rapid in operation.

(5) Time limits on each stage of the procedure should be specified. If an issue is not dealt with in the specified time the next stage of the procedure may be invoked.

(6) Employees have the right to be represented by their trade union or an employee of their choice at the various stages of the procedure.

(7) Provision should be made for issues to be referred to a third party if agreement cannot be reached 'in house'.

(8) The procedure should contain a 'peace clause' prohibiting the use of industrial action prior to all stages of the agreed procedures being exhausted.

Formal procedures generally follow an upward path from one organisational level to the next, as indicated in Figure 7.15. The main aim of grievance procedures is to ensure that issues raised by employees are adequately handled and settled fairly at, or as near as possible to, their point of origin. Such aims are based on the premise that, operated effectively, grievance procedures embrace a strong preventative dimension in helping thwart the escalation of grievance issues into more serious disputes. Most problems or complaints raised by employees should, ideally, be handled by the immediate supervisor without recourse to a formal grievance procedure. However, issues which warrant more thorough consideration may be more appropriately handled through a formal written and agreed procedure.

Figure 7.15 Grievance procedure

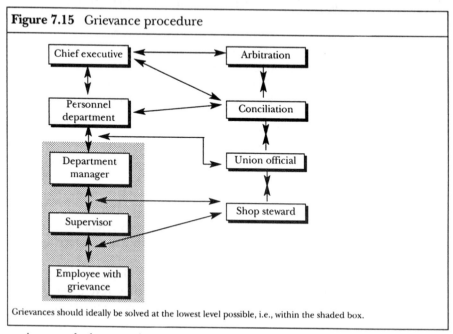

Grievances should ideally be solved at the lowest level possible, i.e., within the shaded box.

As noted above, grievance procedures should normally be in writing, simple and easy to operate, and aim to handle disputes and grievances fairly and consistently. For such procedures to operate effectively it is generally necessary that management and employees (including trade unions) are fully committed to the procedure and know how to operate and enforce it. Line managers may avail of the services of the specialist personnel/HR function in operating and interpreting such procedures while employees in unionised organisations may rely on the guidance of their shop steward or trade union official. Clearly, approaches to handling grievances and disputes may vary considerably between organisations. A sample of one company's policy guidelines on grievance handling is outlined in Table 7.6.

An example of a grievance procedure in a unionised organisation is outlined in Table 7.7. The same principles largely apply in non-union organisations. Indeed, it is possibly more important that non-unionised firms have effective grievance and disputes procedures since employees in these organisations may have less internal support in processing grievance issues. Many larger non-union companies appear to place a considerable emphasis on the rapid and effective handling of employee grievances (Toner, 1987; Foulkes, 1982; Flood and Toner, 1996; 1997).

Table 7.6 Sample company policy on disputes/grievances (pharmaceutical company)

1. The company recognises that employees have a legitimate interest in the affairs of the enterprise and thus have a right to be concerned and informed about issues which affect them.
2. Employees have a right to bring matters which concern them to the attention of management.
3. Management and employee opinions may be at variance on occasion. In such instances management will strive to understand the employee(s) viewpoint, explain the management position and seek a mutually acceptable solution.
4. Management will give consideration to matters brought to their attention by employees and action these matters in an appropriate, effective and equitable manner.

Table 7.7 Sample grievance procedure

| Stage | Nature of Grievance | Procedural Level | |
		Management	*Employees/Trade Union*
1	Issue involving local work rules or employment conditions affecting an individual worker or small work group	Immediate Supervisor	Employee(s)/ concerned
2.	(a) Any issue which has remained unresolved at Stage 1 (b) Grievance or claim where the issue has direct implications for a group of workers on a departmental or section basis	Department Manager (with relevant supervisor as appropriate)	Employee(s) concerned and shop steward or employee representative
3.	(a) Any issue which has remained unresolved from Stage 2 (b) Grievance or claim with company wide implications	Personnel/HR manager and line manager(s)	Employee(s) concerned and/or shop steward/employee reps.(inc. union official)
4.	Any unresolved issue which has been through the appropriate lower stages and remains unresolved	Third-party investigation: Rights Commissioner; Labour Relations Commission)	
5.	Any issue which remains unresolved after stage 4	Labour Court Investigation: Employment Appeals Tribunal	

Source: Gunnigle, Morley, and Heraty, 1997

As emphasised above, when such procedures are put into operation, it is generally desirable that grievance issues are handled as near to their source as possible, with a major responsibility resting with line management. Delays in handling issues can become an additional source of frustration. It is generally advisable to operate time limits which are both realistic (allowing reasonable time and opportunity to handle the issues adequately) and fair (avoiding unnecessary delay and frustration). The specialist personnel/HR function has an important role to play in establishing effective procedures, monitoring their operation, dealing with more serious issues and helping line management handle issues in their area. This involves ensuring that line managers have adequate skills and knowledge to carry out their role effectively.

7.7.3 THE GRIEVANCE INTERVIEW

The vast majority of grievance issues arise at employee-supervisor level. It is therefore important that senior management delegate adequate authority to enable supervisors and team leaders to handle issues raised at this level. Equally, supervisors must be willing and able to make decisions and act upon them at this level, thus preventing their further progression through the procedure. When an issue is raised, the initial managerial task is to listen carefully and attempt to understand the dimensions of the problem in a considered fashion. Responding impulsively or pre-judging the issue without having the full facts is, potentially, a very damaging reaction and should be avoided. Although managers may not attach as much importance to the issue as the employee(s) concerned, they should appreciate that if employees feel strongly enough to raise issues in the first place, then they equally merit that management listen, understand and take appropriate action as necessary.

Having taken the time to consider the issue, the manager concerned should take time to consult other people as necessary and respond to the employee within a reasonable period of time. Responses to employee grievances should take account of whatever implications may arise for other employees, the extent to which a precedent is being created, and consistency with company policy. If the response is negative — that is, if the manager decides that the employee has no grounds for feeling aggrieved or that, for some reason, it is impossible to solve the problem at this level — the further stages in the procedure should be outlined. The manager involved should ensure that any responses are correct in the circumstances and explain these to employees.

While grievance procedures are an important aid to management and employees in dealing with contentious issues, the importance of informality in the grievance handling process should not be overlooked. Issues will sometimes arise which need a different approach to that set down by formal procedure. For example, an employee may be reluctant to raise a personal problem with his supervisor, and may bring the matter to the attention of a more senior manager. Procedures should not prohibit these informal but useful interactions. Informality is an inherent part of workplace industrial relations and will continue to play a key role. However, such departures from procedure should be an exception and the role of the front line managers should remain central in the effective handling of the great majority of workplace issues.

Another important aspect in grievance handling is the issue of record keeping. It is generally agreed that while at the initial stages grievances are generally raised in a fairly informal manner, it is important to maintain some written records of any meetings or discussions which take place (Salamon, 1998). Record keeping needs to become more extensive in relation to issues which progress above the first stage in a procedure. Some organisations require that issues entering the procedure above the first stage must be served in writing with details of the issue and the employee(s) concerned. This helps clarify the exact nature of the claim or grievance and helps avoid misunderstandings. Such records also provide management with useful information on the extent and nature of grievances in the organisation. While record keeping is an important dimension of grievance handling, it is likely that too much record keeping creates excessive red tape and causes excessive frustration among employees. Just enough written records should be kept to provide a concise and accurate picture of the nature and procedural development of any grievance.

7.7.4 EXTERNAL REFERRAL

Since it is not always possible to resolve all grievances at enterprise level, it is generally necessary to make provision for referral of issues to an independent third party for conciliation and/or arbitration. The main third-party agencies involved in industrial relations were outlined earlier, in chapter 3.

Conciliation normally refers to the introduction of a third party who tries to guide the parties towards a solution but does not make a final decision. Arbitration involves referral to a third party who makes a final decision based on the merits of the case (Kelly, 1989). In Ireland most arbitration decisions are non-binding, though there are exceptions (e.g., certain Labour Court decisions (such as on appeal of an equality officer's decision) and in areas of the public sector). Since the 1980s we have seen some developing interest in so-called 'pendulum arbitration' (see, for example, Wood, 1985; Treble, 1986). Pendulum arbitration involves the arbitrator or arbitrating agency choosing between the final positions. This approach clearly contrasts with traditional 'open' arbitration where the arbitrator or arbitrating agency exercises 'judgement as to what is fair and equitable in the circumstances' and generally proposes a 'compromise award' (Salamon, 1998:451). Based on the premise that traditional arbitration does not encourage the conflicting parties to compromise prior to third-party referral, pendulum arbitration encourages them to take more reasonable positions, thus giving the greatest chance of winning the arbitrator's approval. However, pendulum arbitration principles are clearly at odds with the voluntarist industrial relations traditions of compromise and movement and, thus, may be difficult to accommodate within such industrial relations systems. In commenting on the UK context Salamon (1998:468) argues:

The 'winner take all' concept underlying pendulum arbitration is incompatible with the principles of compromise and flexibility underlying the negotiation and organisation experience... [and] ... suggests that it requires modification to bring it closer to conventional 'open' arbitration.

A general principle of industrial relations is that grievance issues are only referred for third-party conciliation or arbitration after all internal efforts have been unsuccessful. However, John Horgan, a former chairman of the Labour Court, has argued that the recent increased number of cases being referred externally (particularly to the Labour Court) reflects a greater reluctance on behalf of managements and unions to compromise at local level. He feels this has resulted in an over-reliance on third parties which, he suggests, is a negative development in industrial relations (Horgan, 1985).

Grievance procedures normally contain a provision that no form of industrial action be taken by either party until all stages of the procedure have been exhausted and an agreed period of notice has expired. Effectively operated, this provision helps to ensure that both parties have adequate opportunity to settle issues either through direct discussion or by opting for third-party referral. Such terms should not be used unreasonably to delay the processing of claims and grievances as this may give rise to employee frustration resulting in breaches of procedure and, possibly, unofficial action (Wallace, 1988). Lastly, it should be emphasised that workplace procedures are merely a facilitator of good industrial relations and will be of little use where the basic industrial relations climate is poor.

7.8 HANDLING DISCIPLINARY ISSUES

An inherent part of the managerial role in organisations is a desire to establish and maintain what are seen as acceptable rules and standards in areas such as employee performance, attendance and conduct at work. Inevitably, situations will arise where management seek to take disciplinary action against employees who fail to conform to these established rules or standards. Where such breaches occur, management will normally seek to take some form of disciplinary action. Such disciplinary action may range from relatively minor and informal rebukes to more serious forms such as formal warnings, suspension or dismissal.

Torrington and Hall (1998:549) define discipline as the 'regulation of human activity to produce controlled performance' and identify three broad forms of discipline:

(1) *managerial discipline*, where 'everything depends on the leader';

(2) *team discipline*, where performance is determined by mutual dependence and commitment of everybody involved; and

(3) *self-discipline*, where an individual performer is 'dependent on training, expertise and self-control'.

In industrial relations the main concern is with formal disciplinary action and related procedures. Salamon (1998:545) defines the formal disciplinary process as: 'that element of the system concerned *with formal action taken by management against an individual who fails to conform to the rules established by management within the organisation'.*

Salamon then outlines four important elements in the formal disciplinary process as follows:

(1) definition of desired standards, performance or behaviour;

(2) assessment of the employee's performance or behaviour against these standards;

(3) the disciplinary procedure ('control mechanism') used to take corrective action using sanctions;

(4) feedback on the effectiveness of any corrective action.

Thus, a critical aspect of discipline administration in organisations is the establishment of acceptable rules and standards and the utilisation of disciplinary procedures to deal with breaches of such rules/standards. *Disciplinary rules* set out the standards of acceptable behaviour expected from employees within an organisation and, importantly, the consequences of not meeting these standards. *Disciplinary procedures,* however, constitute the administrative machinery for applying these rules and executing any resulting disciplinary action.

Salamon (1998) notes that discipline administration in organisations has both punitive and corrective dimensions. The punitive (negative) dimension relates to application of particular sanctions which are designed to act as a deterrent and to penalise individuals whose actions or behaviour is found to be at variance with established rules or standards. The positive (corrective) dimension is directed towards 'rehabilitation based on a process of educative socialisation to create an attitude in which the individual not only conforms but also supports and is committed to the performance and behaviour standards' (Salamon, 1998:547).

7.8.1 THE LEGAL CONTEXT[4]

From a legal perspective, there are various guidelines and constraints on how discipline should be administered in organisations. Management's right to administer discipline stems from an employee's failure to fulfil their common law obligation to give 'faithful and honest service, using reasonable skill and care in work, obeying all reasonable orders and not committing misconduct' (see, for example, Fennell and Lynch, 1993; Salamon, 1998). The common law principles of natural justice, to which the Employment Appeals Tribunal (EAT) often makes reference, further require that:

(1) There should be a basic understanding of what constitutes a transgression: therefore company rules/standards should be clearly outlined and communicated.

(2) The consequences of breaching such rules/standards should be clear.

(3) Employees not achieving the required standards should be so informed and given opportunity to improve where possible.

(4) Employees alleged to have breached discipline are entitled to fair and consistent treatment including an opportunity to state their case, access to representation, and a right to appeal to a higher authority.

These principles, combined with the legislative framework surrounding discipline administration, indicate that organisations should have some formal disciplinary procedure in operation, ensure employees are familiar with its contents and apply this procedure in a reasonable way. The legal context for discipline administration was reviewed in chapter 3. The most significant legislative development affecting discipline administration is the Unfair Dismissals legislation (1977, 1993). This legislation provides guidelines as to what constitutes fair and unfair dismissal, outlines a mechanism for dealing with claims of unfair dismissal, and for deciding upon redress for those found to be unfairly dismissed.

7.8.2 DISCIPLINARY PROCEDURES

A disciplinary procedure is an important aspect of effective discipline administration. It is suggested that disciplinary procedures serve to establish an explicit *modus operandi* for bringing alleged offences to the notice of employees, allowing employees an opportunity to respond to such charges and facilitating the imposition of disciplinary action as necessary. Salamon (1998:557) describes the purpose of a disciplinary procedure as being '. . . to provide an acceptable mechanism within which management may exercise its control over employees when their performance or behaviour does not reach the required standards'.

As we shall see below, disciplinary procedures generally provide for comparatively minor sanctions for lesser offences and for dismissal as the ultimate form of discipline. For a particular dismissal to be held as fair, case law evidence suggests that it must normally be preceded by the application of an acceptable disciplinary procedure particularly where the offence was one which would not warrant instant or summary dismissal.[5]

To facilitate effective discipline administration the golden rules seem to suggest that disciplinary procedures should be: (1) agreed between management and employees; (2) fair; (3) understood by management and employees and (4) applied consistently (see Advisory Conciliation and Arbitration Service (ACAS) 1977; Meenan, 1994).

Disciplinary procedures should adhere to the following general objectives:
– to inform employees of offences which may lead to discipline;
– to establish a set procedure for bringing alleged offences to an employee's notice;
– to allow employees to respond to such charges;
– to discover the reason why offences occurred or why performance is inadequate;
– to impose or apply sanctions if appropriate.

7.8.3 RULES AND STANDARDS

A normal initial step in establishing a disciplinary procedure is to outline company rules and standards and the form of disciplinary action associated with breaches of these rules/standards. The establishment of explicit workplace rules helps ensure consistency in the treatment of employees. Such an outline of rules and standards should indicate: (1) those rules and standards where breaches may lead to dismissal in the first instance (e.g., theft or violence at work) and (2) those rules and standards where breaches would lead to the operation of a standard disciplinary procedure (e.g., lateness). The major responsibility for discipline administration lies with management. It is their task to establish workplace rules and standards. However, employees and their representative organisations should be consulted in this process.

Exactly how far can an organisation go in outlining rules and standards? This is not an easy question to answer. The primary consideration must be the nature of the enterprise. It would be impossible to cover all the possible transgressions that might occur. Thus, stated rules and standards can only outline general areas or deal with specific transgressions which occur frequently. This is clearly acceptable as very often rules can only be indicative of the type of offences which will lead to discipline. However, management should be as precise as possible to ensure that, as the ACAS code states, 'rules should not be so general as to be meaningless' (ACAS, 1977).

As noted above, a first and important step is to spell out those rules and standards where breaches may lead to dismissal in the first instance (summary dismissal). The offences which warrant dismissal in one organisation may be entirely different to those in another, but examples might include theft, violence, interference with clock cards, or criminal offences. Offences which might warrant summary dismissal in a particular organisation but not elsewhere should be clearly highlighted, e.g., hygiene rules in a food processing firm, or breaches of confidentiality where research and development is carried out. Case law indicates that instant dismissal (i.e., without a hearing or investigation) is extremely difficult to initiate fairly. Where a serious offence occurs, it is generally recommended that the employee be suspended pending a thorough investigation and hearing. After this investigation, appropriate disciplinary action may be initiated.

Management should also outline those rules and standards where breaches would lead to the operation of a standard disciplinary procedure (e.g., lateness, absenteeism, inadequate work performance). The details of such procedures should be given to all employees. Apart from serious misconduct, most breaches of discipline will lead to the application of a standard disciplinary procedure. A sample disciplinary procedure is outlined in Table 7.8.

Table 7.8   Sample disciplinary procedure

Preamble: The following disciplinary procedure will be used to deal with all breaches of company rules and standards except where the offences or transgression constitute gross misconduct.

The primary aim of this procedure is to help employees whose conduct or performance falls below company requirements to achieve the necessary improvements. It is desirable both in contributing to company success and the fair treatment of employees. It is company policy to apply this procedure as reasonably as possible and to ensure consistency and order in its application. It will apply to all breaches of company rules or standards not constituting gross misconduct which may typically include, but are not limited to the following:

(a) Bad time-keeping   (b) Unauthorised absence
(c) Lack of co-operation   (d) Unacceptable work performance
(e) Poor attendance   (f) Breaches of safety regulations

Disciplinary Procedure:

1. In the first instance the individual will be asked to attend a *counselling interview* by his supervisor where the employee's transgression will be made clear, the standard of performance required outlined and the employee verbally reprimanded.
2. In the second instance the employee will receive a *verbal warning* at a formal meeting with his supervisor and department manager where details of the misdemeanour and the consequences of further offences will be outlined.
3. In the third instance the employee will receive a *final written warning* from the personnel manager at a meeting with the personnel manager, the department manager and, if appropriate, the supervisor where the employee will be informed of the details of the offence, future performance standards required and that further offences will lead to suspension or dismissal.
4. In the last instance the employee will either be *suspended without pay or dismissed* (depending on the offence), notice of which will be given to the employee at a meeting with the General Manager where the offence will be outlined both verbally and in writing and the employee advised of his right of appeal.

Gross Misconduct: Gross misconduct is conduct of such a serious nature that the company could not tolerate keeping the employee in employment and it is hoped that such instances will not occur. However, for the mutual protection of the company and its workforce, any employee found guilty of gross misconduct may be dismissed summarily. Examples of gross misconduct include:

(a) Violation of a criminal law   (b) Consumption or possession of alcohol or illegal drugs
(c) Threats or acts of physical violence. (d) Theft from another employee or from the company
(c) Malicious damage to company property. (f) Falsifying company records

Before any action is taken the company will thoroughly investigate the case, during which time the employee will be suspended. After such investigation the employee will attend a meeting with company management where he will have an opportunity to state his case and be advised of his right of appeal. Should the company still feel the employee was guilty of gross misconduct s/he will be dismissed and given a letter outlining the nature of the offence and reasons for dismissal.

WARNINGS

An integral part of managerial work involves the ongoing coaching and counselling of employees. This may occasionally involve informally reprimanding employees. However, in the event of the facts of a case pointing to the need for formal disciplinary action, management should adhere to the disciplinary procedure and, where appropriate, issue a formal disciplinary warning. In issuing formal warnings the managerial emphasis approach should be remedial rather than penal, except in the most extreme circumstances (see, for example, Salamon, 1998). Thus, managers should encourage improvements in individual conduct rather than simply impose sanctions. Again, clarity is very important. Therefore, the warning should specify the way in which the employee's behaviour or performance was unsatisfactory, how performance can be improved, what the expected standard is, and what are the consequences of not improving. Management should take any reasonable measures which might facilitate improvement (such as extra training). Warnings should normally be in writing and be given to the employee and their representative, as appropriate.

For minor offences the immediate supervisor of the employee concerned will normally give an *oral warning* or equivalent. If further action is necessary or if the issue is more serious, the employee may be given a *written warning* which sets out the nature of the offence and indicates the improvement or changes required. Further misconduct might warrant a *final written warning* which should contain an unambiguous statement that any recurrence (or unsatisfactory behaviour of another kind) would lead to a specific penalty e.g., suspension, demotion, loss of seniority or dismissal as the case may be. Again, a copy of any written warning (final or otherwise) should be given to the employee and their representative. The final step in a disciplinary procedure would be the formal imposition of a disciplinary penalty, notified in writing to the employee and, as already mentioned, to his/her representative. The range of penalties available to management is broader than the obvious ones of dismissal and suspension, including transfer, loss of privileges, demotion, loss of seniority.

Warnings should remain on an employee's record for as long as is consistent with the nature of the offence and in accordance with company rules and practice. Minor warnings will obviously have a shorter time scale than those relating to more serious issues but defining specific guidelines poses difficulties. The ACAS code of practice suggests that warnings should be disregarded after a specific period of satisfactory conduct but does not suggest how long these time scales should be (ACAS, 1987). Hawkins (1977) is more specific, suggesting that verbal warnings remain on an employee's record for six months, written warnings for twelve months, and for very serious offences a period of two years or more. Many organisations do not specify limits but, in practice, allow warnings to lapse after a reasonable period of satisfactory performance.

REPRESENTATION

An important aspect of ensuring procedural fairness and equity in discipline administration is the employee's right to adequate representation (by either a fellow employee or trade union representative, as appropriate). Management should also be aware of the need for independence in discipline administration. Where issues reach a serious stage, at least two management representatives should be present to ensure correct and consistent application of rules and procedures. The personnel/HR practitioner may generally become involved at higher stages in the disciplinary procedure.

RECORD KEEPING

Accurate records should be kept of all disciplinary issues. A major onus in this area falls on management. Since the Unfair Dismissals legislation places the burden of proof primarily on the employer, companies must be able to back up reasons for discipline with adequate documentary evidence. At counselling interview stage a brief note of the issue, the individual concerned, the date and the nature of the discussion will normally suffice. At verbal, written, and all subsequent stages, records should be more elaborate. This is particularly important at and above final warning stage, where it should be clearly documented that the employee was informed of the seriousness of the issue and the fact that future offences may lead to dismissal. At each stage a written record of the nature of the issue, the date, the action taken and the reasons should be given to the employee for his retention. A copy which has been signed by the employee (as evidence that they received and understood the letter) should be placed on their personal file. A copy should also be given to the employee's representative, the trade union (if appropriate) and to the manager(s) involved. Again, much of this work will be the responsibility of the specialist personnel/HR function.

RIGHT OF APPEAL

A basic principle of natural justice is that employees subject to discipline have the right of appeal to somebody not directly involved in the case.[6] Management are obliged to investigate the case thoroughly and make a fair decision based on the facts. If an employee or his/her representative(s) are not satisfied with a decision they should have the right of appeal to a higher level of management or to external conciliation/arbitration. Indeed, management should remind employees of their right of appeal during disciplinary meetings and also the appropriate procedures for lodging such appeal. The first level of appeal will normally be the manager above the level at which the penalty was imposed. The second level of appeal may be to the highest company level — chief executive or equivalent — and the third appeal to an agreed independent third party.

7.8.4 DISCIPLINARY INTERVIEWS AND DISCIPLINE ADMINISTRATION

In disciplinary cases, there is an onus on management to thoroughly investigate the circumstances and establish the facts of the case. This means that where an employee is observed or reported to have broken rules that might warrant some disciplinary action, the supervisor or manager should first establish the facts before recollections fade. When dealing with a disciplinary matter managers need reliable information which may be derived from several sources such as work records or time sheets, as well as talking to individuals with knowledge of the situation. If, after a thorough investigation, management decide that disciplinary action is merited, a meeting should be arranged with the employee(s) concerned. Alternatively, if the offence is deemed sufficiently serious but all the facts necessary to determine the appropriate disciplinary action cannot be established, the employee may be suspended pending the outcome of further disciplinary investigation.

The purpose of disciplinary interviews is to assess culpability, decide on appropriate action and attempt to effect the desired change in employee behaviour. Salamon (1998:559) describes the disciplinary interview as the 'point at which the formal control mechanism is actually applied'. In conducting disciplinary interviews management must decide who is to carry out the interview, where the interview is to take place and establish all relevant facts about the case before the interview (see Table 7.9).

Table 7.9 Key managerial considerations in preparing for disciplinary interviews

1. *Who?* Management should decide who carries the interview (e.g., supervisor at initial levels; senior management involvement later) and consider the role of employee representatives.
2. *Where?* Interviews should generally be conducted away from the shopfloor, at an appropriate time with sufficient notice.
3. *What?* The person responsible for conducting the interview should ensure that management have established the relevant facts before the interview and have available any information pertinent to the case. Such information might include details of the employee's job and the incident, information on the employee(s) concerned (background, records etc.).

In keeping with the principles of natural justice, the disciplinary interview provides an opportunity for the employee(s) to present their point of view. In disciplinary cases, employees should be given every reasonable opportunity to explain their position and thus provide a comprehensive picture of the case and facilitate constructive discussion of the issue. Employees should be given a reasonable opportunity to explain their position. The disciplinary interview should be treated as a problem solving exercise with the objective of positively influencing employee behaviour. It is particularly important that management approach disciplinary interviews with an open mind.

Only after a thorough investigation and disciplinary meeting are management in a position to decide on appropriate action. Should the investigation and disciplinary meeting point to a need for disciplinary action, management's position should be explained to the employee(s) who should be made fully aware of their shortcomings and management's concern. The precise nature of any improvement required and the means for its achievement should be outlined, as should the consequences of future transgressions. There is an onus on management to ensure that employees fully understand the discipline imposed and their right of appeal. After the interview, the details should be accurately recorded and a copy given to the employee(s) concerned (and their representative as necessary). Any commitments entered into should be carried out as agreed at the disciplinary interview.

7.8.5 PERSPECTIVES ON DISCIPLINE ADMINISTRATION

It is generally suggested that management approach the area of discipline administration in a positive vein with the overall objective being to change employee behaviour (see, for, example, Torrington and Hall, 1998). We have already noted above that discipline administration tends to have both a punitive and corrective dimension. In this respect Salamon (1998:547) notes three key points:

(1) The positive (corrective) approach tends to be adopted only in relation to more minor transgressions while the 'ultimate sanction of dismissal is retributive or as a deterrent to others'.

(2) The extent to which a particular form of discipline constitutes 'punishment' depends very much on the perception of the person subject to disciplinary action (rather than the person(s) administering discipline). As Salamon (1998:547) comments:

> While some employees (such as those whose reward or career progression is linked to formal performance or appraisal reviews) might not like to receive a formal reprimand because of the possible effect on their career, this does not mean that other employees will place as much emphasis on such warnings — particularly those in manual or lower clerical groups, for whom there may be little, if any, career prospects.

(3) The adoption of management approaches based on 'responsible autonomy', as might be developed through delegative participation and teamworking, may serve to reduce management's need to use 'ad hoc direct formal disciplinary action'. In this approach regular performance management is used to develop a more positive corrective approach which emphasises team and self-discipline and reduces the need for managerial discipline. However, other commentators express reservations about the effectiveness of such strategies. In particular, Edwards (1994) argues that newer forms of self-discipline do not necessarily reflect increased employee

commitment and conformity but rather may reflect greater management capacity to control employee performance and behaviour. He argues that even where advanced forms of delegative participation and teamworking exist (see chapter 8), employees and work teams may be reluctant to engage in disciplinary measures against co-workers, thus leaving managers to rely on traditional forms of disciplinary action in situations where breaches of rules or standards occur (also see Salamon, 1998:547).

It should be noted that despite the elaborate procedural forms which tend to characterise discipline administration in organisations, many of the underlying concepts are quite subjective. Of particular note in this respect are concepts such as 'reasonableness', 'fairness' and 'consistency'. In their study of unofficial strikes, Wallace and O'Shea (1987) note that employees often have expectations that management will act leniently in disciplinary matters, so that the introduction of a more strict managerial approach often causes problems. This highlights the need to take consistently similar approaches in disciplinary matters so that accusations of favouritism or purges cannot be forwarded with any justification. However, a common thread in evaluations of disciplinary action is the need to take account of the unique circumstances surrounding any particular transgression: where recognised rules or standards have not been observed, it is suggested that the action taken should depend on both the circumstances and the seriousness of the offence. Thus, management are advised to bear in mind the test of reasonableness and take into account any mitigating factors. Every transgression is viewed as different: an employee may have developed a bad time-keeping record for legitimate reasons (e.g., difficult family circumstances) and management are advised to take such considerations into account in deciding on disciplinary action. However, such approaches may clearly mitigate against the need for 'consistency' so that transgressions which appear similar (e.g., poor time-keeping) may result in different forms of disciplinary action.

Turning to the impact of Unfair Dismissals legislation (in 1977) on employers, this seems to be largely favourable. There has been a fall-off level of strike activity resulting from dismissals since the introduction of the 1977 Act (Murphy, 1986, 1989). The legislation also seems to have encouraged the adoption of appropriate disciplinary procedures and practices by employers. O'Connor (1982) found that employers were now exercising greater care when recruiting, evaluating employee performance more closely and generally adopting a more systematic approach to handling discipline at work. This 'learning effect' may be partially reflected in the increased number of Employment Appeals Tribunal decisions favouring employers (see chapter 2).

Despite the growing impact of legislation in the area, collective bargaining continues to play a significant role in discipline administration in organisations (Murphy, 1989; Lennon, 1983). For example, one might argue that the poor success rate of employees in unfair dismissal cases may in part be related to the argument that, in unionised organisations, the trade union may seek to resolve most disciplinary cases through collective bargaining, leaving only weak cases to proceed to the EAT. One may also find that the EAT provides an important recourse for non-union employees who would otherwise have little means of challenging disciplinary measures instigated by management (e.g., many professional and managerial grades: see Meenan, 1985). Indeed, it seems that, by and large, the legislation has not greatly increased the job security of employees since reinstatement or re-engagement is awarded in only a minority of cases (see Lennon, 1983, and chapter 2).

Finally, it should be noted that the personnel/HR function has an important role to play in establishing disciplinary policy and related procedures and in monitoring their application throughout the organisation. In the longer term the total process should be monitored from a number of viewpoints (e.g., impact on employee behaviour, trends in disciplinary incidents, effectiveness of various forms of discipline).[7]

NOTES

1. For a more in-depth analysis of strike indices and compilation of strike statistics see, for example, Stern, R. 1987. Methodological issues in quantitative strike series. *Industrial Relations* Vol. 17: No. 1: February. The most comprehensive analysis of strike activity in Ireland has been undertaken by T. Brannick, A. Kelly and L. Doyle of University College Dublin: see references in bibliography.

2. The authors would like to acknowledge the significant contribution of Tom Dalzell in compiling this section, particularly his assistance and advice on negotiating strategies and tactics. Tom is a doctoral student at the University of Limerick and teaches collective bargaining practice.

3. For detailed treatments of the theoretical and applied aspects of industrial relations negotiations see, for example, Walton and McKersie, 1965; Warr, 1973; Atkinson, 1977; Sisson, 1977; Hawkins, 1979; Scott, 1981; Fisher and Ury, 1986; Lewicki et al., 1994.

4. This text provides a summary overview of the legal context of discipline administration and is not a legal interpretation thereof. Readers requiring more comprehensive insights into the legal context of discipline administration might refer to Fennel and Lynch (1993) and/or Meenan, F. 1994. *Working Within the Law — A Practical Guide for Employers and Employees.* Dublin: Oak Tree Press.

5. Summary dismissal means dismissal in the first instance of an offence. It will normally take place after a thorough investigation of the facts and after the employee has been given a chance to state their case and have had access to adequate representation.

6. See *National Engineering and Electrical Union (NEETU) v McConnell.* ILRM 422 1983.

7. See Note 2 above.

CHAPTER EIGHT

Employee Involvement and Participation

8.1 INTRODUCTION

Employee involvement and participation may be broadly interpreted as incorporating any mechanisms designed to increase employee input into managerial decision making. It is based on the concept that people who work in an organisation are entitled to share in decisions which affect them. It is sometimes seen as the political democratisation of the workplace insofar as it facilitates the redistribution of decision-making power within organisations (see, for example, Chamberlain, 1948; Schregle, 1974; Thomason, 1984).

We noted earlier, in chapter 5, that the structure of industrial organisations, with the support of our legal and business system, has traditionally placed decision-making power in the hands of employers. Since the foundations of this system, various initiatives have been taken to increase employee involvement and participation in managerial decision making. Such involvement may range from, for example, the relatively superficial level of management informing employees of decisions which affect them, through consultation with employees on certain decisions, to joint participation in the actual decision-making process. Such initiatives may result in a variety of institutional arrangements to facilitate employee participation and involvement at workplace level, such as suggestion schemes, joint consultative committees, works councils, quality circles, and board level participation. Employee participation can also be facilitated through the collective bargaining process which attempts to lessen the sphere of managerial prerogative and make more issues subject to joint negotiation and agreement.

8.2 FORMS OF EMPLOYEE INVOLVEMENT AND PARTICIPATION

While terms such as 'employee involvement' and 'employee participation' are often used interchangeably as above, it should be pointed out that these terms lend themselves to more precise definition. We therefore begin this chapter by describing the various forms of employee involvement and participation. Salamon (1998) identifies three broad ways in which employees can influence decision making in organisations, namely (1) industrial democracy; (2) employee participation and (3) employee involvement. These various approaches largely differ in regard to the extent of employee influence on decision making and the level of institutional 'sophistication' which is used to support each form of employee influence.

8.2.1 INDUSTRIAL DEMOCRACY

Salamon (1998:353–4) describes industrial democracy as essentially involving worker control over key decision making in the organisation. In this approach, workers exert total control over organisational decision making:

> Its central objective is the establishment of employee self-management within an organisation, whose ownership is vested in either the employees or the State and whose managerial function is exercised ultimately through a group, elected by the employees themselves, which has the authority over all decisions of the organisation, including the allocation of 'profits' between extra wages and reinvestment.

This approach is sometimes seen as the ultimate form of employee influence involving a fundamental restructuring of control and power in industrial organisations towards employees.

8.2.2 EMPLOYEE PARTICIPATION

Salamon (1998:354) argues that employee participation denotes a 'distinct evolutionary development' aimed at extending collective employee influence beyond the traditional remit of collective bargaining, and particularly into areas such as operational and strategic planning and decision making. The collectivist element is a critical aspect of employee participation since this approach involves employee influence being operationalised through representative structures such as trade unions, works councils or other forms of elected employee representatives. Salamon (1998:354) further notes the importance of power equality between capital and labour in giving effect to 'real' employee participation:

> . . . 'real' participation ideally requires both sides to have 'equal power to determine the outcome of decisions'. In the absence of such power equality, employees can only rely on management goodwill (i.e. its acceptance of and commitment to a participative philosophy or style of organisational management). There must be more than just the provision of information to employees or their representatives; there must be a genuine opportunity for employees to influence major strategic organisational decisions. (Also see Pateman, 1970.)

8.2.3 EMPLOYEE INVOLVEMENT

Over the past two decades we have seen a significant shift in the employee influence debate away from representative forms of participation and towards a greater focus on finding ways of increasing the direct involvement of individual employees in decisions of immediate work relevance. Increasing employee involvement has been a particular feature of the Human Resource Management (HRM) movement (see, for example, Beer et al., 1984), and in Ireland, has been generally associated with HR practices in larger non-union firms. Employee involvement embraces any means of increasing the direct involvement of workers in decisions affecting their work situation, such as work scheduling or quality monitoring. Salamon (1998:355) notes that some of the more common mechanisms used to operationalise employee involvement include empowerment, teamworking, briefing groups and quality circles. He further notes that employee involvement is often introduced as a means of advancing management objectives (such as quality enhancement) as well as increasing employee commitment:

> These measures have been introduced by management in order to optimise the utilisation of labour (in particular, to improve organisational quality and flexibility) and at the same time to secure the employee's identification with and commitment to the aims and needs of the organisation. Such measures may allow employees greater influence and control over decision making, but only in relation to their immediate work operations; hence the phrase sometimes used of 'task participation'.

8.3 THE EMPLOYEE INVOLVEMENT AND PARTICIPATION DEBATE — AN OVERVIEW

The movement for increased employee influence in organisational decision making has its roots in early attempts to achieve worker control dating from the Industrial Revolution period in the UK (see, for example, Coates and Topham, 1968). These initiatives were based on a rejection of the new economic order based on capitalism and wage labour (which from the Marxist perspective created worker alienation and frustration as a result of divisions of labour, the removal of discretion and responsibility from the individual worker, and the creation of hostile social classes). The movement for workers' control and self-management highlights an important element in the employee involvement and participation debate: whether it should aim at achieving a changed economic order through redrawing the decision-making mechanisms within organisations or try to bring about greater employee participation within the current structure of industrial organisations. It seems that most recent developments in the area follow the latter route:

> Industrial democracy has little currency in contemporary market-driven economies where any worker or activist concern for industrial control

has been fragmented and displaced by defensive struggles to retain individual employment and to protect employment rights. (Hyman and Mason, 1995:8)

Developments in relation to extending employee influence in organisational decision making have taken varying directions and proceeded at different paces in different countries. With the demise of the early movements for workers' control, participation achieved its most concrete form through the extension of collective bargaining as evidenced, for example, by the establishment of joint councils for collective bargaining and consultation in Britain after the First World War. More extensive developments took place in the post Second World War era with various institutional arrangements developed to further employee participation (particularly) and involvement in a number of European countries. Mulvey (n.d.) distinguishes between those countries where such arrangements were given statutory support (such as Germany) and those which were based on collective agreements (Norway, Sweden, Denmark). While these developments fall considerably short of industrial democracy as defined above, they generally entail institutional arrangements which provide for some degree of democratic control within what Salamon (1998:354) terms 'a reformist framework of limited modification of the capitalist managerial authority system rather than a fundamental restructuring (for example, co-determination through worker directors in Germany...)'.

Salamon (1998) identifies two broad pressures for the development and extension of employee participation or involvement, namely (1) socio-political and (2) industrial pressures. As noted above, industrial democracy often formed a key ideological plank of emergent labour movements in Europe during the late nineteenth and early twentieth centuries. More recently, Salamon points to significant socio-political change, including issues such as increased affluence and greater access to education. He argues that these developments heralded a change in attitudes towards 'formally constituted authority in many spheres' and placed greater emphasis on the democratisation of society and its various institutions. In the industrial arena, Salamon (1998:358) argues that these broader socio-political changes further resulted in a trend towards increased expectations and aspirations among workers while, concurrently, we also witnessed greater worker alienation and dissatisfaction with work:

In the industrial sphere these developments resulted in increased aspirations among employees — not only in terms of material rewards (wages) but also in the management of the organisation (authority). At the same time, the increased complexity of industrial organisation contributed to the alienation of employees from their work.

Salamon further argues that these developments encouraged a shift from employer and employee/union concern with the 'purely legal and economic aspects' towards the 'psychological and sociological aspects' of the employment relationship. However, there was also a more pragmatic rationale for a greater employer focus on increasing employee participation and involvement. Developments in technology, consumer demand and communications led to a change in work systems (see 8.8) involving less reliance on assembly line based mass production approaches. It became both more feasible and functional to devolve greater operational responsibility to workers. The increased pace of organisational change further required the active support of employees, and employers increasingly saw this as being most effectively achieved through some form of employee involvement and participation:

> At the same time, management recognised that technological, industrial and economic change, at the organisational level, could be carried out more smoothly, quickly and effectively with the active and full participation of the employees concerned than if it made the decision alone and then sought to implement it against the negative reaction of employees. (Salamon, 1998:359)

During the 1970s and into the 1980s, much of the focus of the employee participation and involvement debate has taken place at EU level where various policy documents have concentrated on board level participation, works councils and disclosure of financial information. In the 1970s in particular, we witnessed a burgeoning debate on diffusing forms of representative participation largely, but not exclusively, along (West) German lines. Germany has a strong tradition of representative participation dating back to post Second World War restructuring and involving two main pillars, 'co-determination' and 'works councils'. *Co-determination* normally entails the appointment of worker directors to the main (supervisory) board of companies. It should be noted that German (and many other European) corporations generally have a two-tier board structure, i.e., a supervisory board to deal with policy issues and a management board to deal with operational affairs. *Works councils* represent a method of providing formal employee representation at workplace level to facilitate consultation, discussion and information exchange between workers and management.

In evaluating developments at EU level, an important initial policy document was the so-called 'Draft Fifth Directive' (1972), designed to apply to all public limited companies employing 500 or more workers. This directive favoured a two-tier board system along German lines: a supervisory board to deal with strategy and policy, and a management board to deal with day-to-day operational matters. It provided for employee participation (worker directors) on the supervisory board. The Draft Fifth Directive met with extensive employer opposition and made little progress. The European Commission subsequently produced a Green Paper on Employee Participation and Company Structure (1975). This represented a more flexible approach and reflected widespread opposition to the imposition of structures deemed contrary to some traditional national systems. While still favouring two-tier board systems with worker directors on the supervisory board, the paper suggested that this was only one option in extending employee participation and proposed flexibility in developing transitional arrangements. The first draft of the European Company Statute (1976) also proposed a two-tier board system along similar lines. It further proposed that companies establish works councils and provided for the disclosure of certain types of company information. The Vredling Directive (1980) on employee rights to information disclosure recommended that multinational companies must consult and inform employees in subsidiaries in relation to strategic issues. Additionally, other proposals have demanded the provision of financial information through consolidated accounts.

By and large most of these proposed measures did not come into effect on any widespread basis. Rather, the general trend was for the proposals to become substantially diluted allowing Member States to adopt the approach which was seen as best suited to their particular needs/context. Thus, as Salamon (1998:361) notes, Member States could choose to adopt 'either worker directors (elected or co-opted to a supervisory board with a two-tier board structure or elected within a one-tier structure), a works council system or other consultative arrangements integrated into existing collective bargaining systems'. In Ireland the effect of the proposals was largely restricted to the appointment of worker directors to a small number of State-owned organisations (see, Kelly and Hourihan, 1997, and later in this chapter).

Recently, however, we have seen more concrete developments. Probably the most significant of these was adoption of the European Works Councils Directive (1994). This Directive provides for the establishment of Europe-wide works councils in companies which employ 1,000 or more employees and which operate in two or more EU Member States. European works councils are discussed later in this chapter.

The employee participation and involvement debate really only took off in Ireland after our entry into the then European Economic Community in 1973. Prior to this period issues of employee participation and involvement had little significance in Irish industrial relations. As Kelly and Hourihan (1997:405) state:

> Aside from collective bargaining, Irish industry had not experienced any significant institutionalised form of employee participation until 1977. Ireland was unlike many westernised countries. . . . The only opportunity to participate in Ireland was through the collective bargaining process. . . . Put simply, organisational democracy was not on the national agenda

between 1922 and 1973, either for Irish politics or for the parties to the collective bargaining process.

However, our entry into the European Community changed the situation considerably and resulted in much discussion and activity throughout the 1970s and early 1980s. This surge of interest was manifested in the passing of the Worker Participation (State Enterprises) Act 1977 which introduced board level participation to seven semi-State companies. These provisions were extended to a number of other State organisations under the terms of the Worker Participation (State Enterprises) Act 1988. Board level representation in Ireland has been largely restricted to the semi-State companies covered by the 1977 and 1988 Acts.

While national and EU-sponsored initiatives, aimed at increasing representative participation through works councils or trade unions, remain an important factor in the employee influence debate, it appears that many of the more important developments in recent years have taken place at the enterprise level. Many of these initiatives are associated with HRM approaches (see chapters 9 and 10). The reasons for this increased focus on developments at the enterprise level are treated extensively elsewhere in this text but basically relate to the increasingly competitive environment facing organisations and encouraging them to reconfigure their industrial relations approaches to achieve improvements in performance and productivity. Of particular note in this regard have been developments such as total quality management and world class manufacturing. Such approaches place a much greater emphasis on the role of the individual worker in contributing to improvements on dimensions such as product quality, unit production costs and inventory/materials management. Extending employee participation and involvement at enterprise level has thus become an increasingly critical aspect of many recent initiatives in the areas of work organisation (see, for example, Marchington and Parker, 1990; ICTU, 1993; Kochan et al., 1986; Kochan and Osterman, 1994). We now consider the various ways in which employee influence can be brought to bear on organisational decision making.

8.4 FORMS OF EMPLOYEE INVOLVEMENT AND PARTICIPATION

The preceding discussion has noted how the debate on employee participation and involvement has evolved over time. In particular, it has highlighted how the emphasis has oscillated between movements for industrial democracy (in essence, the most complete form of employee influence), a focus on representative participation (e.g., worker directors or works councils) to, most recently, initiatives to increase direct employee involvement in decisions of immediate work relevance. Clearly, these different approaches entail considerable variation in both the extent of employee influence and the means used to give effect to each particular approach: 'The paradigm of employee involvement . . . employee participation . . . and industrial democracy . . . is essentially one of ascending levels of control by employees over their work and organisations' (Hyman and Mason, 1995:18).

In particular, we can point to a difference between *direct and indirect* forms of employee influence. With the former approach, workers are directly involved in the decision-making process. Possibly the most commonly used example of direct participation is teamworking (see 8.6). In contrast, indirect forms rely on the use of employee representatives to articulate the views and input of the larger body of employees. Common examples in this regard include trade unions (through collective bargaining) and works councils. Another important area of variation in approaches to employee influence is the *level* at which such influence is exercised. We have already noted that much of the current emphasis is on increasing individual employee involvement in decisions which affect their immediate work role. However, we may also find employee influence exercised at higher levels in the organisational hierarchy, such as at business unit level (e.g., collective bargaining) or corporate level (e.g., worker directors). Another area of variation in relation to employee influence is the *scope or range* of employee input. The dimension addresses the types of issues over which employees have opportunity to influence decisions. The most commonly used categorisation in this respect is to differentiate between influence at the operational level (immediate work/enterprise level focus) and strategic level (influence on the future nature and role of the organisation).

Variations in approaches to employee participation and involvement may stem from a variety of reasons such as the structure and development of collective bargaining, the attitude of trade unions, or the political philosophy of Government. The variety of institutional arrangements adopted in different countries and by different organisations may also reflect different philosophies and approaches to employee participation and involvement. Participation and involvement may be supported by the law or may be established through collective agreements and may be minimal or extensive. We now consider the different forms of participation and involvement under two broad categories, namely representative participation and direct participation.

8.5 REPRESENTATIVE PARTICIPATION

As noted above, representative participation is an indirect form of employee influence whereby employee views and input are articulated through the use of some form of employee representation. Employee representatives are generally elected or nominated by the broader worker body and thus carry a mandate to represent the interests and views of the workers they represent. They do not act in a personal capacity but as a conduit through which the broader mass of workers can influence organisational decision making.

Representative participation is largely concerned with redressing the distribution of decision-making power in favour of employees. It thus seeks to reduce the extent of management prerogative and effect greater employee influence on areas of decision making which have traditionally been the remit of senior management. Representative participation is generally employee driven, coming from the demands of workers or their trade unions for a greater input into organisational decision making.

It is possible to identify three differing forms of representative participation, each varying in both the level and nature of participation: (1) collective bargaining; (2) works councils and (3) worker directors.

8.5.1 COLLECTIVE BARGAINING

Collective bargaining has traditionally been viewed as one of the most effective means through which employees can bring their influence to bear on organisational decision making. Earlier in this book we saw how the growth of collective bargaining in Ireland has served to extend employee influence, with trade unions acting as the principal mechanism for representing and extending employee influence in the workplace and beyond.

However, we also noted that collective bargaining in Ireland is generally adversarial in nature and, as such, has attracted the criticism that it is not an effective means of promoting more co-operative forms of management-worker participation (see, for example, Roche and Kochan, 1996; Geary, 1995). Another popular criticism of collective bargaining as a vehicle for extending employee participation is that collective bargaining agendas are often limited in the range of issues addressed. This argument refers to the trend for collective bargaining to primarily focus on pay and conditions. Collective bargaining on such 'distributive' issues tends to be adversarial by nature. It is argued that such a restricted and adversarial agenda is a limiting factor which prohibits the development of greater management-employee participation on issues outside the scope of collective bargaining. Clearly, such broader issues (e.g., product development or quality) are of considerable interest to both workers and management, and ones where employees are likely to have considerable interest in articulating their perspective. It is therefore plausible to argue that if collective bargaining is to increase its capacity to effect greater employee participation in organisations, it will become necessary to expand the scope of bargaining to incorporate broader issues of strategic and operational policy. These latter issues have traditionally been ones where management have sought to retain prerogative in decision making. In Ireland we have seen some developments in this regard, particularly in recent national agreements. Here we find that the scope of discussions between the social partners is not just restricted to pay and conditions but addresses a range of broader social and economic issues such taxation, budgetary policy and employment creation. At enterprise level we have also seen some interesting developments, many of which are discussed in the remaining sections of this chapter.

8.5.2 WORKS COUNCILS

Works councils have a long established tradition in many European countries, often enjoying legislative support and exerting considerable influence on the organisations in which they operate. Works councils are particularly associated with initiatives to extend employee participation in Germany and some other European countries, especially since the end of the Second World War. As noted earlier, they represent a method of providing formal employee representation at workplace level to facilitate consultation and discussion of enterprise related issues between workers and management. Their role is seen as primarily consultative and representing a broader range of employee opinion than trade unions alone.

This consultative role is generally seen as operating alongside collective bargaining, with councils providing a mechanism for management-worker interaction on non-distributive issues. This approach incorporates a fairly clear division between collective bargaining and works councils. This division was facilitated in countries such as Germany by the fact that collective bargaining on pay and related matters normally took place at industry level, allowing works councils to become involved in 'non-pay' issues at workplace level. Salamon (1998:380) comments that this:

> . . . apparent division allowed for the development of a more co-operative (integrative) relationship between management and employees within the organisation, with the more conflictual (distributive) wage bargaining being conducted between unions and employers' associations outside the organisation. However, in Germany for example, the trend toward decentralisation in collective bargaining has led some organisations to negotiate works agreements with their Works Councils, with the inevitable potential for change in the relationship between management and the Works Council.

In assessing the advantages of works councils, Salamon (1998) points to three main strengths:

(1) Works councils provide a mechanism through which management and employee representatives can jointly consider issues of mutual concern and thus have the potential to facilitate more co-operative management-employee relations within the enterprise.

(2) Works councils are representative of the entire workforce, not just unionised employees, and may be particularly appropriate in non-union firms (see discussion below).

(3) Works councils provide a forum through which management and employees can address both strategic and operational issues.

Works councils in Europe are generally underpinned by Statute (such as the 1959 Works Council Act in Holland or the 1972 Works Constitution Act in Germany) which generally prescribe their specific role and nature. In reviewing developments in Europe (particularly Germany), Mills (1989) identifies four types of powers of works councils:

(1) There is the *right to be informed* on certain issues, such as the current state and future prospects of the enterprise.

(2) There is the *right to be consulted* on particular matters, such as restructuring or collective redundancies.

(3) There is the *right to independently investigate* certain matters which generally involves a reciprocal obligation on management to co-operate in such investigation.

(4) There is the *right of co-determination* which means that decisions cannot be made without the agreement of the works councils. Such issues might include working hours, pay, and health and safety.

The rights of works councils will vary somewhat between countries depending on the specific legislation. We also find considerable variation in national requirements for the establishment of works councils, ranging from a requirement for the establishment of works councils in organisations employing six or more workers (Germany) to organisations employing 100 or more workers (Belgium). Based on the German experience, Mills (1989) categorises the issues over which works councils may have rights into (1) economic and (2) social issues. Economic issues relate to mergers/acquisitions, transfers, closure, expansion/contraction of operations, relocation, organisation structure, business trends and financial decisions. Social issues include redundancy/lay-offs, pay systems, training and development, pensions, profit distribution, holidays, and health, safety and welfare.

While works councils have a long established tradition in mainland Europe, this is not the case in Ireland and it is only as a result of two fairly recent developments that works councils have made their way into the vocabulary of Irish industrial relations. Firstly, we have developments at EU level which have sought to establish European works councils as part of the EU's social agenda. As Blyton and Turnbull (1994) note, increasing employee participation and involvement in workplace issues represents a 'key tenet' of the Community Charter of Fundamental Social Rights, generally known as the 'Social Charter'. An important dimension of the Social Charter was a 1991 draft Directive which proposed that all companies with over 1,000 workers which operated in two or more Member States must establish a European works council. In Ireland, this proposal reached fruition with the passing of the Transnational Information and Consultation Act 1996. This act provides for the establishment of a works council or employee forum in companies which employ at least 1,000 workers across the EU and at least 150 workers in two EU Member States. The role of these European works councils is discussed below.

A second development which has led to an increased interest in, and diffusion of, works councils relates to the establishment of such bodies in non-union firms. As discussed later, in chapter 9, the creation of such councils may often form part of a union substitution strategy, whereby

Table 8.1   Enterprise level work/employee councils and associations: some examples

---

Case 1

When Saehan Media in Sligo was originally established in 1991, many of the employees joined SIPTU, but management refused recognition. Strike notice was given at one point, although it was later withdrawn, and the issue was the subject of a Labour Court recommendation in 1993, in which the Court took the traditional pro-recognition stance.

The employee council was formed to deal with negotiations on pay and conditions and took the company to the Court on a pay claim for terms above the PCW (LCR 14866). In 1994 it negotiated 1 per cent more than the PCW increase. The following year it claimed 14.5 per cent for a one-year agreement, although the company offered 10.5 per cent over three years. At the hearing, the council showed its confidence about criticising the company, when referring to its 'paltry wage policy', which had 'increased in-house pressure from staff for trade union membership and recognition'.

Case 2

In 1996 the works committee at Pat the Baker took the company to the Labour Court on the issue of van drivers' commission payments. The committee has also been involved in a Rights Commissioner's hearing in the past — on the same issue of drivers' commission.

The Longford bakery firm's works committee had a significant role to play in the bitter *nine-month recognition dispute* of 1993 — it was in meetings between SIPTU and the works committee that the basis for a final resolution was worked out, and even though the company met SIPTU directly at the very end of the process, the works committee retains sole negotiating rights.

The committee has about a dozen members, one representing each of the six departments in the Granard plant, one for each of the depots around the country, and a chairperson. There are no management members on the committee, even from the supervisory staff. The committee meets with management once a month, and discusses matters such as changes in procedures, individual grievances and so on.

Case 3

Elan corporation's 'Representative Council' was formed about twelve months ago, a few months before a Labour Court hearing on union recognition. It has twenty-two members — four of whom are management representatives. Each department or area across the plant (and a number of R and D staff based in Trinity College) elects the employee members, and the chairperson is elected by this group of eighteen. The chair rotates on a six monthly basis, and council members are elected for a term of two years by secret ballot. Fifty per cent of the council members retire each year, so elections will be held each year in the first week of December. Each member represents a constituency of forty to fifty people. A spokesman for Elan said that the council had discussed issues such as career progression, paternity leave, productivity bonuses, and a new share option scheme. It has also been used by management as a means of communicating product and business updates. He added that the council was not seen as a body with which to negotiate agreements, as much as a way for employees to have 'an input into decisions'.

Source: Roche and Turner, 1998: 73-74 (Based on article on staff associations in
Industrial Relations News, 1996)

management seek to satisfy employee desires for formal representation while maintaining a firm's non-union status. Roche and Turner (1998) describe this development thus:

> A more direct substitute for union voice is a company based representation structure such as a staff association or works council sponsored by the company itself. How independent such structures are is often difficult to assess . . . . However, a number of cases have occurred in recent years where a staff association or works council have taken a company to the Labour Court in disputes over pay and conditions indicating some degree of independence from management control. A notable feature of each of the cases is that the development of the representative structure occurred as a measure to block union recognition.

In contrast to the specific definition and prescribed role of European works councils, the precise structure and role of works councils established as part of a union substitution strategy is difficult to establish. Indeed, the whole concept of formal employee representation in the non-union sector remains something of a 'black hole', with little available research evidence in the area. One key area of debate, as noted by Roche and Turner (1998) is the independence of such works councils, leading some critics to suggest that these councils generally remain creations of management with little capacity for independent action and are, in effect, staff associations (see discussion on the role of staff associations in chapter 4). The case examples in Table 8.1 from Roche and Turner's (1998) paper, based on an article in *Industrial Relations News*, illustrate the variation and ambiguity which exists in relation to such councils.

8.5.3 EUROPEAN WORKS COUNCILS

The European Works Councils Directive came into force in Ireland in 1996 as a result of the passing of the Transnational Information and Consultation Act of that year. The Directive also applies to thirteen other Member States of the EU (the UK being the exception), plus Norway, Iceland and Liechtenstein. However, it is noteworthy that despite the UK's 'opt-out' of the Social Chapter (including the obligation to comply with the EU's Works Council Directive), a significant number of UK companies have moved to establish some form of Europe-wide works council. The role of European works councils (EWCs) as outlined in the EU Directive is to supplement national structures to secure information and consultation rights for workers on transnational company matters.

In line with the EU Directive on EWCs, the Irish Transnational Information and Consultation Act 1996, requires the establishment of a works council or employee forum in companies which employ at least 1,000 workers across the EU and at least 150 workers in two EU Member States. In addressing the establishment of works councils, the Act outlines three ways in which 'transnational information and consultation' arrangements can be established (Kelly and Hourihan, 1997):

(1) through pre-directive agreements on information and consultation concluded before the EU Directive came into force (September, 1996);

(2) after the Act comes into force, moves to establish works councils may be initiated by employers, or alternatively, by 100 employees or their representatives. This approach requires the establishment of a 'special negotiating body' of employee representatives to negotiate the establishment of a European employees' forum or works council with management;

(3) if agreement is not reached, then employers must establish an EWC in line with the requirements of the 1996 Act. These requirements deal with composition of the EWC (minimum of three and a maximum of thirty members with membership proportional to the number of employees in each State), frequency of EWC meetings (meeting with central management at least once a year), issues for consideration at such meetings (particularly issues relating to state of enterprise, business plans, employment and financial trends, organisation structure and organisation change/new working methods, transfers of production, mergers, cut-backs/closures and redundancy).

The legislation also provides for special meetings with management in 'exceptional circumstances' (such as closure, relocation or collective redundancies). The actual expenses of EWCs or their equivalent are to be borne by management. Employees who are members of works councils are entitled to reasonable paid time off to perform their works council functions and cannot be dismissed for performing their representative duties. The legislation deals with numerous other aspects relating to EWCs such as voting and arbitration. An important employer concern in relation to works councils relates to the disclosure of commercially sensitive information. On this issue, the Irish legal context provides for the appointment of an independent arbitrator to deal with disputes over whether information being passed on or requested is commercially sensitive. Employees who disclose commercially sensitive information are subject to criminal sanctions.

In assessing progress to date, Kelly and Hourihan (1997) highlight a number of interesting developments. Firstly, in investigating the number of pre-Directive agreements, they suggest that at the time the legislation came into force (September, 1996) there were approximately eighty such agreements in Europe of which 'between twenty and thirty' affected employees in Ireland. They also note that the Act's provision for the establishment of a 'European Employees' Forum' is a unique feature of the Irish legislation. One possible reason for this to which they allude is that it is a less 'collectivist' term which may find particular favour in the non-union sector.

An issue of particular interest is the role of trade unions in both the establishment and operation of EWCs. The 1996 Act provides that trade union officials can act as nominees to the 'special negotiating bodies' which may negotiate the establishment and ground rules of works councils. Kelly and Hourihan (1997:423) point out that since the EU Directive did not prescribe who might act as employee representatives on special negotiation bodies, the Irish Act 'must be seen as affording trade unions a central role in the overall process'. The legislation also provides that trade union officials may be appointed as 'expert advisers' to these special negotiating bodies if requested by workers. Kelly and Hourihan suggest that this provision may mean that non-union companies may have to cover the expenses of trade union officials asked to act as expert advisers to their workforce. However, Kelly and Hourihan point out that such advisers would not sit on the works council once they become established. The Act provides that union officials may sit as expert advisers on special negotiation bodies but only employees of the company may sit on the works council.

Overall, Kelly and Hourihan's (1997) evaluation concludes that the Irish legislation effectively complies with the EU Directive. While cautioning that it is too early to reach any firm conclusions on the implications of this legislation, they suggest that despite significant lobbying by trade unions, the general thrust of the legislation and the Directive itself are 'widely seen as having better reflected employer priorities . . .' (Kelly and Hourihan, 1997:425). As to the initial trend of a number of prominent multinationals indicating a preference for Ireland as a base for their EWC, Kelly and Hourihan (1997:425) are sceptical of the suggestion that this indicates the Irish legislation is more 'employer friendly' than that of other countries:

> Already, a number of multinationals which have signalled a willingness to set up information and consultation arrangements, have been giving serious consideration to using Ireland as a base for the purposes of the legislation. Trade unionists may see this as proof that the Irish legislation is more employer-friendly than in other countries but it should be borne in mind that most of these companies are British or American so the fact that English is the everyday language here must also be seen as a factor explaining any such decisions.

More generally, it remains to be seen whether the establishment of EWCs in transnational firms acts as a spur to the development of similar consultation and information bodies in other organisations.

8.5.4 WORKER DIRECTORS

Possibly the most widely debated form of representative employee participation entails the election of worker directors to the board of management of an enterprise (see, for example, Kelly, 1989; Kelly and Hourihan, 1997; Rollinson, 1993; Salamon, 1998). We noted earlier that the use of worker directors became widely established in a number of mainland European countries after the Second World War. This was particularly the case in (West) Germany where the appointment of worker directors to the main (supervisory) board of companies was a critical feature of that country's system of 'co-determination' (see, for example, Visser and Van Ruysseveldt, 1996). Carley (1998:14) notes that twelve of the fifteen EU Member States have legislation or 'generally applicable collective agreements' which provide for the appointment of worker directors in at least some enterprise categories. He suggests that countries with comprehensive legislation on worker directors include Austria, Denmark, Finland, France, Germany, Holland, Luxembourg and Sweden, while countries such as Greece, Portugal and Spain are similar to Ireland in that requirements for the appointment of worker directors are confined to the State sector.

As mentioned earlier, the concept of worker directors largely emerged as an issue for debate in Ireland after joining the European Community (EC) in 1973. We also noted that the 1970s saw a number of draft proposals dealing with worker directors at EC level. The Draft Fifth Directive (1972) favoured a two-tier board system and proposed the appointment of worker directors to the supervisory board of public limited companies employing 500 or more workers. This Directive met with strong employer resistance and became substantially diluted over time. The European Commission's Green Paper on Employee Participation and Company Structure (1975) represented a more flexible approach: while retaining support for a two-tier board system with worker directors on the supervisory board, it also proposed a number of other options in employee participation and flexibility in developing transitional arrangements. The Vredling Directive (1980) proposed greater employee rights to information disclosure in multinational companies, particularly in relation to strategic issues. However, resistance to the appointment of worker directors has continued and EU level initiatives in the area became less frequent over the past decade.

Before considering the Irish situation, it is instructive to briefly review developments in the UK, particularly since the 1970s. Like Ireland, the UK does not have any established tradition of worker directors. Another similarity in this area is its use of a single board of directors (as opposed to European 'two-tier systems'). As the debate on employee participation in the EC intensified in the 1970s, the UK Government established a parliamentary Committee of Inquiry to investigate the area of employee participation, and specifically the issue of worker directors. Chaired by Lord Bullock, the Committee of Inquiry on Industrial Democracy (1977) included representatives of employers and trade unions (Bullock, 1977). The terms of the so-called 'Bullock Committee' were to identify how some form of worker representation on boards of directors could be achieved. It was not required to address the question of whether worker directors should be appointed to the boards of companies. A particular focus of the Bullock Committee's deliberations was the issue of whether worker directors should be 'an integral part of the normal management of the organisation' or whether their role should be confined to 'broad policy issues and the general overseeing of management' (Salamon, 1998:376). This debate focused on the relative advantages of retaining the prevailing single ('unitary') board structure and providing for the appointment of worker directors to this main board, or, alternatively, proposing a two-tier board structure (management and supervisory boards) with worker directors on the supervisory board only. This latter approach would have the effect of limiting worker-director input to broad policy decisions with general organisational decision making remaining a management remit through their exclusive representation on management boards. The subsequent report of the Bullock Committee (1977) contained a majority proposal which favoured the retention of the existing single ('unitary') board structure. This majority report proposed the appointment of worker directors to the main board on the following basis: boards of directors to comprise equal numbers of shareholder and employee representatives with an additional but smaller number of co-opted independent directors (the so-called '2x + y' formula). However, employer representatives on the Bullock Committee vehemently opposed the idea of worker directors on the main board and produced a minority report. This proposed a two-tier board structure with minority worker representation on supervisory boards only.

These conflicting positions are broadly representative of employer and labour positions in relation to worker representation at board level. Salamon (1998:376) notes the different perceptions of management and trade unions of the role of worker directors. Management tend to view the role of worker directors 'in terms of establishing a "coalition" between employers and management', while also making make a positive contribution to the board by articulating employee views, ensuring employee commitment to board level decisions and reducing potential conflict by increasing employee awareness of the rationale for board level decisions. In contrast, the trade union position on worker directors has been somewhat ambiguous. Certain trade unionists view the introduction of worker directors with some trepidation, fearing its capacity as an alternative power centre which may undermine the enterprise level role of trade unions and collective bargaining, in particular the capacity of unions to challenge or oppose management decisions. Others view the appointment of worker directors as a positive development which extends joint regulation and decision making in the enterprise, particularly in relation to higher level strategic decisions.

The majority report of the Bullock Committee met with widespread employer opposition and the report fell into some disrepute. The election of a Conservative Government led by Margaret Thatcher in 1979 effectively ended any Government-sponsored initiatives in relation to worker directors.

In Ireland the appointment of worker directors has been restricted to the semi-State companies covered by the worker participation legislation. The Worker Participation (State Enterprises) Act 1977 provided for the appointment of worker directors to the boards of seven semi-State companies[1] and these provisions were later extended to include Irish Steel, Bord Gais, VHI, An Post, Bord Telecom, Aer Rianta and the National Rehabilitation Board. In addition to increasing the number of organisations obliged to appoint worker directors, the Worker Participation (State Enterprises) Act 1988 provided that board level participation could be extended to other organisations without the need for further primary legislation.

The Irish worker participation legislation is designed to operate within the traditional unitary board structure. Initially, worker directors were entitled to one-third of the seats on the board of directors. More recently, it was proposed that the level of representation in non-commercial State companies should be determined by the need to retain a balance of representative interests and to ensure the board operated as an effective body (IDS/IPD, 1996). Now each case is be considered on its merits by the Minister for Enterprise, Trade and Employment who can prescribe the number of worker directors below one-third of the total board (subject to a minimum of two worker directors).

The legislation requires that candidates for election as worker directors must be nominated by a trade union or other body, such as a staff association or equivalent, which is recognised for collective bargaining purposes in the organisation concerned. The electorate comprises full-time and regular part-time employees of the organisation (and subsidiaries in particular circumstances). Once elected, worker directors hold office for a four-year term and have equal status to other directors. In 1994 it was estimated that nineteen State companies had worker directors (IDS/IPD, 1996).

In his initial review of the operation of worker directors under the terms of the 1977 Act, Kelly (1989) suggests that the experience has been broadly successful. Using the findings of some preliminary research on board level participation, he concludes that employees have positive attitudes to board level participation, and management, though harbouring some reservations about the role and contribution of worker directors, have now largely accepted their role in the senior decision-making process (see Murphy and Walsh, 1980; also see Galvin, 1980). In a later evaluation, Kelly and Hourihan (1997) noted that the new worker directors quickly settled into their roles and encountered little difficulty in becoming involved in board level activities. Kelly's (1989) analysis did not find any major conflict between the role of worker directors and the operation of collective bargaining/trade unions in the organisations studied. He found that trade unions had largely dominated the participatory process, rendering the emergence of an alternative representative mechanism to the trade union highly unlikely:

> For all practical purposes the principal trade unions . . . control the worker director initiative. In the various elections the successful candidates have been trade union activists . . . . Furthermore, the great majority of worker directors continue to hold some form of union office, which turned out to be an important linkpin in the maintenance of satisfactory relationships between the two power centres. Thus, from the

outset the prospect of an alternative, parallel and possibly competing employee voice dissolved into insignificance, and to date there is no evidence that it is ever likely to become a divisive issue. (Kelly, 1989:309)

Furthermore, it appears that worker directors go to considerable lengths to avoid involvement or interference in established union-management negotiation/consultation mechanisms. Murphy and Walsh's (1980) study suggests that worker directors place considerable weight on the need to maintain strong links between their representative role and the collective bargaining system in the organisation. As Kelly and Hourihan (1997:429) note there is no evidence of worker directors attempting to 'compete with, or compromise, the established workplace union organisation'.

The more general issue of the contribution of worker directors to promoting increased employee participation remains a matter of some debate. Salamon (1998:377) argues that the appointment of worker directors is 'unlikely to affect significantly the power and decision making of senior management'. The Bullock Committee Report (1977:72) noted that many organisations had 'developed a de facto two tier system, delegating responsibility for the formulation and implementation of policy from the main board perhaps to a management committee'. Salamon identified a number of other factors which serve to limit the extent to which worker directors can impact on management decision making, namely:
(1) the infrequency of board meetings;
(2) the exclusion of worker directors from other director and senior management meetings;
(3) the fact that the main role of the board of directors is to formally endorse senior management proposals/decisions;
(4) the fact that board level decisions rely heavily on senior management for information.

In reviewing the Irish context, Costello's (1983) study of the experience of worker directors in the seven State enterprises covered by the 1977 Worker Participation legislation found that the exclusion of worker directors from more operational management decision making served to limit the influence of worker directors. Costello's (1983:57) analysis suggested that the impact of worker directors was primarily concentrated on broader corporate objectives which effectively 'precluded worker directors from raising many of the issues which were of concern to the employees who had elected them. Most of these issues were seen to fall within management's responsibility and attempts to raise them in the boardroom were invariably ruled out of order.'

Murphy and Walsh's (1980) study also considered the views of trade union officials and shop stewards on the role and effectiveness of worker directors. It is interesting that shop stewards were generally sceptical of the capacity of worker directors to influence board level decisions because of their minority position. Stewards generally saw themselves as a more effective means of solving employee problems. While seeing benefits in the role of worker directors, shop stewards also noted certain problems, particularly in relation to the extent of feedback from worker directors. The views of trade union officials were even less supportive. Officials were particularly sceptical of the capacity of worker directors to contribute to significant improvements in industrial relations. In reviewing these study findings, Kelly and Hourihan (1997:429) noted that trade union officials were 'quick to mark a boundary separating collective bargaining issues from those concerning company policies'.

Possibly the most difficult issues for worker directors to address are those decisions which, from an employee perspective, are particularly unpalatable, such as redundancies or closures. In such circumstances, it appears that worker directors 'invariably adopt the expected trade union stance and register their opposition' (Kelly and Hourihan, 1997:429). In dealing with broader board level matters, however, the available evidence suggests that worker directors do not generally articulate and pursue the positions of their own particular union. The more general approach is for worker directors to adopt a united front which masks any differences which may exist in relation to individual union positions within the organisation.

8.5.5 SUB-BOARD LEVEL STRUCTURES

Apart from these specific developments in the State sector, the prospects for the extension of board level participation in other areas seem dim in the absence of statutory provision. Employer bodies have generally favoured the extension of participation at sub-board level on a voluntary basis, and have advocated flexibility in allowing organisations develop their own participative arrangements. The Institute of Personnel and Development have adopted a broadly similar position suggesting that employee participation may be 'attained through a wide variety of means depending on the characteristics of the organisation and the nature of its activities, structure, technology and history' (IPM/IPA, 1983).

Kelly and Hourihan (1997) considered the extent to which the legislation providing for worker directors in the Irish State sector has impacted on the development of sub-board participative structures in these organisations. They concluded that the legislation has had a 'catalytic effect' in progressing sub-board level participation. In evaluating developments in the aftermath of election of the first worker directors, Kelly and Hourihan (1997:430) argued that these new directors found themselves 'structurally expressionless'. Over time, however, a variety of sub-structure forms emerged which Kelly and Hourihan divided into two groups. Firstly, they identified organisations which had a long tradition of management-employee participation. In these organisations, the pre-existing superior sub-board level participation forum became the means by which worker directors were 'connected' with trade unions and workers. It appears that, for this first group, combining the roles of pre-existing participatory structures with the new worker directors occurred fairly painlessly and conformed to the 'developing doctrine of participation' within these organisations (Kelly and Hourihan, 1997:431). Two examples illustrate this trend. Firstly, in B & I the existing works council (established in 1972) became the mechanism for integrating worker directors into that organisation's participatory process:

> Following the first election of worker directors in 1978, the works council structure at B & I was adjusted to accommodate the worker directors. A superior sub-board participation body, known as the Policy Group, included the four worker directors and the other employee and management representatives . . . . At the Policy Group the worker directors discuss board policy issues and all relevant information is channelled through a network of sub-committees. Thus, the established sub-board mechanism, while retaining an independent purpose, became the primary back-up service and linking structure for the worker directors. (Kelly and Hourihan, 1997:431)

Secondly, in Aer Lingus the pre-existing Central Representative Council (CRC) played a similar role. CRC meetings were attended by worker directors and its deliberations included consideration of the nature and implications of board level decisions. The CRC also became the main mechanism for the articulation and representation of employee opinion to the board.

Kelly and Hourihan (1997) also identified a second group of organisations with no pre-existing sub-board participatory mechanisms. In this group two broad trends are evident. Firstly, in some organisations the appointment of worker directors acted as a stimulus for the development of sub-board structures. Examples here include the ESB, Telecom Éireann and Bord Gais. In the remainder, little progress has been achieved in this area. CIE is seen as the most prominent example of a situation where little progress has been made in the area of sub-board level participative structures.

As noted earlier, the 1988 (Worker Participation) legislation deals with the establishment of sub-board level participation. This legislation entails three basic requirements:
(1) the exchange of views and of clear and reliable information between the enterprise and employees;
(2) the communication in good time of information likely to have a significant effect on employees; and
(3) the distribution of views and information arising from the participatory process to all employees.

Apart from these specific provisions, the legislation is largely of an 'enabling' variety: it is the responsibility of management and employee representatives to develop mutually acceptable arrangements for employee involvement and participation following a request from the majority of employees. This approach reflects the voluntarist tradition. It is left to management and employee representatives to identify and implement the mode of sub-board level participation which best reflects their own particular needs and aspirations. A wide range of participative options are provided for in the legislation, including representative and direct participatory forms. The Act identifies thirty-nine companies as being suitable for the introduction of sub-board structures.

8.6 DIRECT PARTICIPATION

Direct participation encompasses any initiatives which provide for greater direct employee involvement in decisions affecting their jobs and immediate work environment. Often captured under the rubric of 'employee involvement', direct employee participation may take a variety of forms such as briefing groups, quality circles, consultative meetings and teamworking. Salamon (1998:357) argues that is normally introduced at management's behest and thus represents a form of descending employee involvement:

> This strategy may be referred to as descending involvement, in so far as management invariably initiates the development for its own purposes (involvement is offered) and, as part of the change, may transfer authority and responsibility from itself to the employees for a limited range of work-related decisions, methods of working, allocation of tasks, maintenance of quality, etc.). However, the content of the process is confined largely to the implementation phase of operational decisions already made by management. This approach is intended to motivate the individual employee directly, to increase job satisfaction and to enhance the employee's sense of identification with the aims, objectives and decisions of the organisation (all of which have been determined by management).

As such, direct participation tends to be quite an amorphous concept which may be used in organisations to describe a whole range of activities, which vary considerably in their scope and impact on industrial relations practice. In many instances, direct participation initiatives are principally confined to improving upward and downward communications with little provision for employee influence on the decision-making process. However, some direct participation initiatives clearly impact on the decision-making process and it is this dimension of direct participation which is of most interest from an industrial relations perspective. The term most widely used to describe this approach is *task participation* which Geary (1994a:637) describes thus:

> Task participation is defined as opportunities which management provides at workplace level for consultation with and/or delegation of

responsibilities and authority for decision making to its subordinates either as individuals or as groups of employees relating to the immediate work task and/or working conditions.

Task participation thus involves the devolvement of greater control over work-related decisions to employees. Employees are encouraged to become more actively involved in influencing decisions, contributing their opinions and in solving problems at the workplace level. Workers are thus required to assume greater responsibility for the general organisation and execution of work while also being expected to concern themselves with broader enterprise objectives such as improving productivity, controlling costs and general organisational efficiency:

> With TP [task participation], then, employees are granted more control over their immediate work situation and are invited to participate in decisions that relate to the organisation of work at the point of production. Thus, workers may influence the manner in which work is allocated, the scheduling of work and when to take breaks. They are also actively encouraged to seek solutions to problems and to make suggestions that will improve the organisation's efficiency. (Geary, 1998:3)

Sisson (1994a) identifies two key forms of task participation: (1) *consultative participation* whereby workers are given the opportunity to become involved in decisions and make their views known but are not involved in joint decision making; (2) *delegative participation* whereby workers are empowered to make key decisions without the need for management approval. Delegative participation thus means that individual workers assume greater autonomy in their work. Teamworking is generally seen as an advanced form of delegative task participation whereby workers are entrusted with key decisions, such as those concerning the selection of team leaders, team members, team roles, and task allocation (Geary 1994a; 1995; 1996).

Within the broad parameters of the debate on task participation, the growth of interest in *teamworking* emerges as a significant theme with significant implications for industrial relations. The concept of teamworking has its traditional roots in movements designed to improve the quality of working life (Morley, Moore et al., 1998). While these early developments met with some support in countries such as the US and Scandinavia, they had little impact in Ireland (Geary, 1996). In recent years there has been a significant increase in employer interest in work re-organisation and teamworking. However, it appears that employers are now the key instigators of teamworking (Beaumont, 1995a). This contrasts earlier initiatives in teamworking which were worker/trade union driven and designed to improve the quality of working life of employees. Teamworking is seen as an advanced form of delegative task participation whereby workers make key decisions such as those concerning the selection of team members (Geary, 1994a and b; 1995; 1996). Geary has noted that teamworking has a longer tradition in Europe than in the UK or Ireland. In his 1996 review he argues that teamworking initiatives in Ireland have been few in number and largely efficiency driven rather than quality of work life/people driven. Geary further notes that Irish developments have largely involved 'tinkering at the margins' of existing work practices and are confined to a handful of foreign-owned companies. While the progress of teamworking in continental Europe also appears modest, some of the more significant developments appear to have taken place in the automotive sector, especially in Germany (Roth, 1993; also see Womack et al., 1990). In evaluating the European experience in teamworking, Geary (1996) identifies five crucial areas:

(1) The regulation of teamwork: Geary notes that the introduction of teamworking in Europe has been achieved more through agreement with employee representatives rather than via unilateral imposition. This trend is attributed to the strength of collective employee representation (especially works councils and trade union involvement in industry bargaining) in countries such as Germany and Sweden which have led the way in the introduction of teamworking.

(2) The objectives of teamwork: Geary identifies achieving a balance between managerial goals of improved economic efficiency and worker goals of improved quality of work life as a critical issue in facilitating the successful introduction of teamworking. In particular, it appears that trade unions are more willing to engage in teamworking when it is not used solely, or primarily, to achieve managerial aims.

(3) Impact on working lives: Geary's analysis of the European experience indicates that teamworking has favoured skilled workers and that the 'gender divide' has been left relatively untouched (i.e., a major divide remains with limited opportunities for women). However, specialist categories such as engineers and accountants have been transferred to line positions. Geary further notes that employers have not relied solely on persuasion to introduce teamworking but that 'more traditional forms' of management control have also been utilised, such as increased employee surveillance and more intense work schedules and that, overall, increased skill and effort levels have been a common outcome of teamworking. However, Geary also identifies potential positive changes associated with teamworking, such as improved working conditions and job security which can lead to productive efficiencies and encourage worker acceptance of teamworking.

(4) Teamwork and management support: Geary suggests that the European experience indicates that management commitment and support is an absolute pre-requisite for the effective introduction of teamworking. He suggests that if teamworking is introduced as an 'island solution' it has little chance of success and identifies line management 'indifference and resistance' as a key impediment to the effective introduction of teamworking.

(5) Integrating teamworking with human resource management (HRM): Finally, Geary suggests that the evidence from Europe indicates that teamworking is likely to be more successful where it is integrated with complementary changes in other aspects of personnel/HR policy. In particular, a number of key policy changes are identified: (1) shift from individual-based pay to team-based pay; (2) significant investment in training and development and (3) maintenance of job security commitments.

We now consider more recent evidence on the diffusion of task participation (including teamworking) with particular emphasis on the Irish context.

8.6.1 TASK PARTICIPATION IN PRACTICE

Probably the most important source of information on the extent and nature of diffusion of task participation is the European Foundation for the Improvement of Living and Working Conditions' (EFILWC) survey conducted in ten EU Member States (see EFILWC, 1997; Sisson, 1997). Generally known as the EPOC (*E*mployee direct *P*articipation in *O*rganisational *C*hange) project, this study examined both the incidence of task participation and also the nature of such participation, particularly the scope and extent of autonomy afforded to employees. In Ireland, the EPOC study surveyed a sample of Irish companies, excluding those with less than twenty-five employees. The study achieved a response rate of nearly 39 per cent (382 organisations), which represented the highest response rate among all the countries involved in the study (EFIWLC, 1997; also see Geary, 1998).

Looking first at the diffusion of consultative participation, the EPOC study found that what Geary (1998:12) labels 'temporary groups', particularly project groups or task forces, were found in 36 per cent of firms while 'permanent groups' such as quality circles were present in 28 per cent of firms. Turning to delegative participation, the EPOC study found that team-based structures were present in 42 per cent of respondent firms. Based on these findings, Geary (1998) estimates that task participation is present in around one-third of Irish workplaces. Newly established firms seem more likely to use task participation than their longer established counterparts.

In addition to examining the incidence of task participation, the EPOC study considered the nature and intensity of such participation, particularly delegative participation (incorporating teamworking). The EPOC study utilised two measures in this regard: (1) the scope of teamworking, which measured the extent of employees' rights to solely make decisions in relation to their work; (2) the extent of autonomy afforded to employees to select team members and to decide on which issues the team should tackle (EFIWLC, 1997). The EPOC findings indicate that just 17 per cent of Irish firms which used teamworking were characterised by a high level team or group delegation.

In a further and somewhat more sophisticated attempt to identify the depth and scope of task participation, the EPOC study first distinguished between the Japanese 'Toyota' model and the Scandinavian 'Volvo' model of teamworking and then considered which was the most prevalent model among respondent organisations. In this conceptualisation, the 'Toyota' or lean production model is seen as one which places strict limits on team autonomy and where employee skills are largely of a generalist or routine kind, while the 'Volvo' model is seen as providing greater autonomy to teams and team members and where workers are comprised of a variety of skill groupings with considerable emphasis on training and development (Frohlich and Pekruhl, 1996; Geary, 1998). The EPOC findings suggest that where teamworking is used, it most closely approximates to the 'Toyota' model, with less than 1 per cent of Irish firms utilising the 'Volvo' model (Geary, 1998).

In evaluating the implications of the EPOC findings, it appears that while task participation is reasonably well diffused in Ireland, most organisations rely on predominantly traditional forms of work organisation. Of particular note is the fact that the uptake of modes of work organisation which devolve a high level of autonomy to workers and work teams is very low. This finding leads Geary (1998:14) to conclude that task participation 'of an advanced form, is a minority practice in this country'.

IMPLICATIONS FOR THE INTRODUCTION OF TEAMWORKING: THE TRADE UNION DIMENSION
Based on the European experience, Geary (1994a; 1996) suggests that a critical issue in teamworking is the development of strategies for dealing with employee representatives/trade unions. Employers commonly object to the involvement of trade unions in work reorganisation and teamworking on the grounds that it is too time consuming and serves to slow the process of organisational change. However, Geary points to the offsetting benefits of union involvement, based on the European experience: firstly, trade unions/employee representatives will have expertise which can benefit the process and, secondly, they can legitimise the 'necessity of proposed change' to their membership. An additional benefit is that such involvement forces management to integrate personnel/industrial relations considerations more centrally in their decision making than might otherwise be the case.

On this theme, Geary raises the critical question of how to involve employee representatives/trade unions in the introduction of work reorganisation initiatives such as teamworking. Since in the Irish and UK contexts such changes are normally discussed in the traditional collective bargaining arena, Geary questions whether new institutional arrangements need to be developed. In particular it is noted that in many of the European countries which have experimented with teamwork, there is an institutional separation whereby traditional collective bargaining issues are the remit of union-employer bargaining at industry level, while working arrangements are normally dealt with within the enterprise through works councils (especially in Germany and France). Turning specifically to the Irish context Geary poses a number of questions on this dilemma:

– Can the introduction of teamworking be productively discussed through traditional 'adversarial' collective bargaining arrangements?

– Is there a need for works council type arrangements?

– Are Irish managers ready for this type of joint decision making?

– Is it better if the structures used to inform employees are employee based and not strictly union based?

A final and critical concern for organisations is how can they positively facilitate such change. Geary's analysis identifies the effective 'managing of managers' as the key to successful teamworking (Geary, 1994a; 1995; 1996). He argues that employers must move beyond their traditional concern of 'getting the goods out the door and reducing costs'. Rather, he suggests that there is a need to reconcile the management of managers with the objectives of employee involvement. In particular, he argues that the reward and appraisal system for managers should reward managers who facilitate effective teamworking .

Finally, it should be noted that increased employee participation and teamworking will not mean an end to 'adversarial' collective bargaining. As Geary points out, pay issues and 'significant changes' in work organisation may still be channelled through traditional collective bargaining.

8.6.2 FINANCIAL PARTICIPATION

Financial participation is used here as a generic term to describe mechanisms through which employees can gain some form of financial or equity share in their organisations through various profit-sharing, share-ownership or similar schemes. Such schemes often have the broad based objective of increasing employee loyalty, commitment and morale through the closer identification of employee interests with those of the organisation. Financial participation is often seen as developing a sense of ownership among workers by giving them a stake in their organisation while also acting as a means of integrating employees more fully into the market economy (Salamon, 1998). However, financial or equity participation by itself will not normally allow for a substantial increase in employee influence as employees will generally represent a minority of the shareholders. Organisations such as the John Lewis Partnership in the UK and Donnelly Mirrors in Ireland have long been known for their policy of sharing profits with employees, and a number of organisations now offer share options or some other form of profit- or gain-sharing.

Salamon (1998:371) identifies two major reasons for the developing interest in financial participation: (1) it is appropriate that workers should receive a share of the profits or other positive outcomes which they have helped to create; (2) such schemes focus on organisational objectives and encourage employee co-operation with management strategies to improve performance.

We can identify two broad forms of financial participation: (1) gain- or profit- sharing and (2) employee share ownership.

(1) *Gain- or profit-sharing* arrangements essentially seek to reward employees for improvements in organisation performance. While profit-sharing is self-explanatory, gain-sharing refers to arrangements where payments to workers are contingent on some measure of improvement in organisation performance other than profits. Commonly used measures are changes in levels of productivity or value added. However, gain-sharing arrangements may also be based on less obvious measures of performance such as accident rates or scrap/re-work levels. Gain-sharing arrangements are commonly linked to management attempts to instigate particular organisational change initiatives, often embracing attempts to increase employee involvement and commitment. We can identify a number of general objectives underlying such schemes (Armstrong and Murliss, 1994):

– to encourage all employees to identify themselves more closely with the company by developing a common concern for its progress;

– to stimulate a greater interest among employees in the affairs of the company as a whole;

– to encourage better co-operation between management and employees;

– to recognise that employees of the company have a moral right to share in the profits they helped to produce;

– to demonstrate in practical terms the goodwill of the company to its employees; and

– to reward success in businesses where profitability is cyclical.

Such schemes have become particularly popular in the UK and the US and have been linked to corporate successes on such criteria as market share, profitability and quality (Hourihan, 1995; Gunnigle, Morley and Heraty, 1997).

(2) A second form of financial participation is *employee share ownership*. Employee share ownership plans (ESOPs) involve the allocation of company shares to employees according to some agreed formula. In Ireland the incidence of employee share ownership has traditionally been quite low (Long, 1988; Gunnigle, Morley and Heraty, 1997). However, some growth was initially stimulated by the Finance Acts of 1982–84 which provided a number of incentives to organisations and employees with respect to ESOPs. Subsequent Government initiatives which reduced the tax incentive value of such schemes inhibited the development of share ownership in Ireland. However, this situation was reversed in the 1995 budget which raised the tax exemption limit for buying company shares from £2,000 to £10,000. As a result we have seen some growth in ESOPs in recent years although the overall scale remains quite modest. Hourihan (1995) notes, in particular, the substantial share allocation initiatives by Guinness Ireland and Intel. More recently, trade unions and management at Telecom Eireann, together with Government representatives have been involved in developing a major ESOP which, if implemented would provide for a 14.9 per cent employee share-holding (*Industrial Relations News*, 1998c).

Table 8.2 provides some data on the diffusion of share option and profit-sharing in Ireland based on the Cranfield-University of Limerick (CUL) study. These data indicate that employee share ownership is confined to a relatively small number of organisations and to executive levels within these organisations. The CUL study also found that US and UK companies were more likely to adopt share ownership schemes for all grades in the organisation than their Irish or other European owned counterparts (Gunnigle, Morley, Clifford and Turner, 1997).

Table 8.2	Employee share options and profit-sharing in Irish organisations (%)							
	Management		**Prof/technical**		**Clerical**		**Manual**	
	1995	1992	1995	1992	1995	1992	1995	1992
Share options	23.0	22.8	13.8	13.6	11.5	9.2	9.6	8.8
Profit-sharing	19.2	15.8	13.4	12.3	12.6	10.5	10.0	10.1

Source: Cranfield-University of Limerick Study, 1992 and 1995

The CUL findings on the incidence of profit-sharing arrangements is broadly similar. Such arrangements are present in only a minority of organisations with approximately 19 per cent of managerial employees, 13 per cent of both professional/technical and clerical employees and 10 per cent of manual workers covered by such schemes. Unionisation would seem to have an effect on the presence or otherwise of a profit-sharing scheme. A higher percentage of non-union firms for all levels in the hierarchy report the implementation of such a scheme, but the difference decreases as one descends the organisational hierarchy (Gunnigle, Morley, Clifford and Turner, 1997). As was the case with share option schemes, foreign-owned organisations were more likely to have profit-sharing arrangements. UK and US companies had a far higher percentage of profit sharing for each employee grade. UK companies, particularly, demonstrated a notable increase in the use of profit-sharing.

8.6.3 COMMUNICATION

An important theme in the contemporary literature on developments in industrial relations is the suggestion that managements have shifted the focus of their communications with employees away from trade unions and towards direct communications with individual employees (see, for example, Salamon, 1998; Bacon and Storey, 1993):

> Since the early 1980s there has been a shift in the emphasis of organisational communication away from 'disclosure' of information to trade unions in support of the collective bargaining process, and towards 'dissemination' of information to employees in order to secure their

greater involvement in and identification with the organisation's interests and objectives. (Salamon, 1998:365)

In some quarters, this shift has been seen as part of a managerial strategy to adopt a more individualist 'employee' relations orientation which may concurrently involve attempts to bypass or marginalise trade unions in the communications process (Kochan et al., 1986; Blyton and Turnbull, 1994; Gunnigle, Morley and Turner, 1997). Differences in organisational approaches to communications with employees tend to focus on the nature and content of management-employee communications and the range of mechanisms used to facilitate such communications. The CUL study, carried out in both 1992 and 1995, focused on two key aspects of the debate on management-employee communications: (1) the communications fora used by management in communicating with employees and (2) the type of information communicated to employees using such fora (Gunnigle, Morley, Clifford and Turner, 1997).

In relation to communications fora, the CUL study examined trends in the modes used in the communication of major issues to employees. A particular area of interest here is the relative emphasis on collectivist and individualist fora in the communications process (McLoughlin and Gourlay, 1992; Blyton and Turnbull, 1994). Table 8.3 presents summary findings on the pattern of utilisation of three particular communications modes, namely (1) direct verbal communications; (2) direct written communications and (3) representative staff bodies, including trade unions.

Table 8.3   Changes in management-employee communications

	Increased		Same		Decreased		Not used/missing		N	
	1995	1992	1995	1992	1995	1992	1995	1992	1995	1992
Rep. Staff bodies	13%	16%	51%	48%	7%	12%	29%	4%	261	228
Verbal direct	51%	55%	42%	34%	2%	1%	5%	11%	261	228
Written direct	46%	39%	43%	42%	1%	4%	11%	16%	261	228

Source: Cranfield-University of Limerick Study, 1992 and 1995

These findings indicate a substantial increase in direct written and verbal communications with employees, a pattern which essentially replicates 1992 findings. In relation to the use of representative staff bodies, we find a relatively stable picture with over half the respondent organisations reporting no change in their level of utilisation as a communications device. Among those organisations reporting change in usage levels, a greater number reported that the use of representative bodies had increased rather than decreased. The aggregate data point to increased level of utilisation of direct communications with employees. However, this is not occurring at the expense of traditional collective lines of communication as there has been little change in the amount of communication conducted through representative bodies (generally trade unions). While larger organisations were more likely to increase all mechanisms, private sector companies were more likely to have increased direct communications, when compared with their public sector counterparts (Gunnigle, Morley, Clifford and Turner, 1997). Furthermore, the increase in direct communication mechanisms appears to be occurring at a faster pace among unionised private sector organisations.

In reviewing the actual content of management-employee communications, the CUL study explored the extent to which senior management communicated formally with employees on business strategy and financial performance (see Table 8.4). With respect to communications on business strategy, the findings indicate a high level of communications on strategy with management and professional/technical grades but a much lower level of communications with clerical and manual grades. Just over one-third (38 per cent) of organisations reported that they communicate on strategy with manual grades. A similar picture emerges when we look at the pattern of communications on financial performance. Again, we find significantly lower levels of communications on financial issues with clerical and manual grades. This result is quite low given that, as we have seen above, there is an apparent general trend of organisations increasing direct communications with their workforce. It seems that such direct communications are predominantly concerned with operational matters and not strategic or broader financial issues (Gunnigle, Morley, Clifford and Turner, 1997). In relation to explanatory factors, the CUL study found that foreign — particularly US- and UK-owned organisations — were more likely to communicate with employees on strategy and financial issues.

Table 8.4	Formal communications on business strategy and financial performance			
	FORMAL COMMUNICATIONS ON			
Employee Category	Strategy		Financial performance	
	1995	**1992**	**1995**	**1992**
Management	95.0	93.9	94.3	93.0
Professional/Technical	71.6	65.8	64.4	60.1
Clerical	50.2	41.7	50.6	41.2
Manual	37.9	39.0	39.1	36.0

Source: Cranfield-University of Limerick Study, 1992 and 1995

A number of factors may explain the increasing focus on the nature and extent of management-employee communications in recent years, notably (1) the increase in quality enhancement initiatives; (2) a move towards flatter organisation structures which facilitate greater and more informative communication at lower levels in the organisation; (3) the presence of a more educated workforce, 'a new kind of person' who desires to be involved and informed as much as possible. The impact of contemporary quality initiatives is felt to have a significant impact on the area of management-employee communications and has facilitated the passing on directly of relevant information on workplace related issues.

In evaluating these developments we can identify two broad factors which underpin management attempts to increase the extent and scope of management-employee communications. Firstly, we can point to the perceived need to inform employees of developments in relation to the business and its environment. Secondly, increased and better communications are seen as an important means of eliciting employee support for organisation change initiatives. Our earlier evidence indicates that many organisations have attempted to provide employees with more information on issues relating to organisational performance. Gunnigle's (1995a) study of employee relations in greenfield sites found a pronounced management focus on greater and more direct communications with individual employees. This study found that a significant proportion of non-union firms (generally larger US-owned firms in 'high technology' sectors) emphasised extensive management-employee communications as a means of developing a more individualist management style in industrial relations and also as a means of maintaining non-union status (see chapters 9 and 10). Much of this communication focused on keeping employees informed of the company's product market performance (see Table 8.5). For many of these companies, such information was used to emphasise issues such as market volatility, intensity of competition and requirements for high-quality and low-cost production/service. In effect, the provision of such information was used to educate employees on 'market realities' (as perceived by management). Direct communications was also seen as a means of increasing employees' sense of ownership and involvement in the organisation which, hopefully, would contribute to employee support for any change initiatives deemed necessary by management to meet the competitive challenges facing their organisations (Townley, 1994). Gunnigle's findings suggest that (at least in greenfield firms), while there is considerable emphasis on communicating relevant data to employees, the motive for such communications derives more from a commercial imperative than from any widespread desire to improve employee involvement. Thus, it appears that communications on business strategy and financial information were often used to condition employee attitudes and expectations by, for example, emphasising the need to maintain flexibility, to improve productivity, and more generally, to accept 'market imperatives'.

Table 8.5   Management-employee communications in greenfield sites

---

We place a heavy emphasis on communications but with a purpose: we emphasise volatility of the business sector and need to keep cost low. The absolute need for complete flexibility is reinforced by the use of temporary workers. At quality meetings I go through quarterly results with all employees. There is a monthly plant meeting between myself and all staff and I also meet regularly with groups of 4/5 employees. Another element is what we call 'fireside chats': here the personnel manager takes around fourteen people into a 'conference' to talk generally about any issue over coffee. All of these have a purpose: it keeps people in tune with reality and on their toes.

Chief Executive: data processing equipment

Strong communications is a key device in seeking to avoid union recognition. We are very keen to communicate on business strategy — it keeps employees in the picture. The MD gives regular communication briefings in small groups and the (US) president gets together with all employees at least once a year.

Financial Controller: electrical and instrument engineering

Source: Gunnigle, 1995a:206

In general it seems that firms with more 'sophisticated' personnel/human resource strategies tend to use a range of communications mechanisms with particular emphasis on direct communications with individual employees. Such expansive approaches seem to be quite evident in newer organisations but not near as widespread in longer established organisations. Gunnigle's (1995a) greenfield study confirms this focus on extensive direct communications with individual employees. This study suggests that the nature and scope of communications fora are more sophisticated in the great majority of US-owned firms — particularly in the computer/high technology sector. The most common approaches focus on 'cascade' mechanisms with briefings for different employee levels augmented by communications through line management, general workforce meetings and other written and oral communications. However, the majority of longer established Irish organisations seem to adopt less sophisticated approaches and rely primarily on collective bargaining, basic written communications and normal line management-employee interactions.

8.6.4 SMALLER SCALE INITIATIVES

Before considering the position of trade unions, it is worth mentioning some smaller scale initiatives which may be used to facilitate employee participation and involvement. One particular initiative which has been around for some time is the *suggestion scheme*. Many Irish organisations have operated suggestion schemes with, apparently, varying degrees of success. It has been argued that suggestion schemes can be a useful mechanism for involving employees and increasing their commitment to the organisation. However, it is unlikely that such results can be achieved without suggestion schemes being accompanied by other participation/involvement initiatives. An approach which appears to be increasing in popularity is the *attitude survey*. Opinion or attitude surveys normally involve management seeking to ascertain employees' views on the organisation, the effectiveness of communications, areas for improvement, skills and employee benefits, etc., using structured questionnaires and/or interviews. Such surveys may often be independently administered and/or validated by external consultants or institutions (such as universities). In a recent research project on industrial relations in newly established (greenfield) companies it was found that a number of non-union organisations periodically administered attitude surveys among employees to elicit information on the general industrial/employee relations climate in the organisation (Gunnigle, 1995a).

8.7 THE TRADE UNION PERSPECTIVE

A significant aspect of the debate on employee participation and involvement in Ireland concerns the role of trade unions. It appears that traditionally the Irish trade union movement did not seem particularly committed to initiatives to increase employee participation and involvement (see, for example, Morrissey, 1989). Indeed, apart from support for greater disclosure of information, the traditional trade union approach to employee participation has been marked by a considerable degree of apathy. Such apathy has strong links with the doubts many trade unionists harbour about the implications of representative participation for the union's role in collective bargaining. Salamon (1998) identifies a number of factors which may explain trade union opposition to employee participation and involvement initiatives, particularly direct participation (as discussed above):

(1) Management's tendency to emphasise the intrinsic rewards (such as increased job satisfaction) emanating from organisation change initiatives and to 'play down' the significance of extrinsic rewards.

(2) A suspicion that the primary objective of organisation change initiatives is productivity improvement and cost reduction rather than increasing employee participation and involvement, and concern that such moves may lead to downsizing.

(3) A suspicion that organisational change initiatives may lead to a dilution or removal of traditional demarcation lines between groups of workers.

(4) A suspicion that direct participation represents a management desire to undermine existing representative arrangements, with a consequent diminution in the role of trade unions and collective bargaining.

Our earlier discussion with respect to employee communications provides some support for such union reservations. For example, Gunnigle's (1995a) greenfield site study indicated that management's objectives in increasing direct communications with employees were primarily aimed at conditioning employee attitudes and expectations to appreciate 'market realities' and accept the need for high levels of flexibility and productivity. When faced with management proposals for increased employee involvement which are contingent on significant organisational change, trade unions clearly have a number of optional strategies which they can adopt (see, for example, ICTU, 1993; Bailey, 1983). Firstly, they may decide to oppose any such change and seek to retain the status quo. A second approach is that unions would enter discussions on changes in terms and conditions of employment (including pay) only, and restrict such interaction to formal negotiations on management's proposals. A third approach is for trade unions to become involved at the beginning of the organisational change process and attempt to influence the nature and direction of the resultant change initiative.

As noted earlier, a major concern for trade unionists is that 'newer' forms of representative participation (such as works councils) and certain types of direct participation may undermine and reduce the significance of collective bargaining and trade union representation. Consequently, trade unions have generally been reluctant to support the establishment of any forms of employee participation and involvement which might constitute alternative methods of employee representation at workplace level. In countries where worker directors and works councils are extensively used (such as Germany) the trade union's role primarily involves industry level negotiations. At workplace level, issues are handled through the works council. In Ireland trade unions have traditionally played a key role in workplace bargaining and are therefore keen to retain a significant role in any representative participative mechanisms. However, while collective bargaining has been a successful mechanism for extending employee participation and involvement, it has a number of limitations. Firstly, collective bargaining depends on employee organisation (such as through trade unions), employer recognition of this representative role and a degree of power balance between workers and management. These ingredients may not be present in a large number of organisations and thus collective bargaining may not be a viable route to employee participation/involvement. Secondly, collective bargaining appears to operate best at workplace level. Where the locus of management decision making is removed to a higher level, such as in many multinational organisations, the effectiveness of collective bargaining in achieving significant levels of employee influence may be severely limited.

Despite suggestions above that the traditional trade union approach to employee participation and involvement has been characterised by indifference, this position seems to have altered considerably in the recent past. The ICTU policy documents, *New Forms of Work Organisation* (1993) and *Managing Change* (1995) suggest that trade unions need to take a more proactive role in influencing the planning and implementation of new workforce management strategies (ICTU, 1993; 1995). These reports place a particular focus on task participation at enterprise level. They note the importance for trade unions of developing, and actively participating in,

317

employee involvement initiatives at workplace level: 'Involvement with management in the implementation of . . . initiatives will be the key to ensuring that the interests of . . . members are met' (ICTU, 1993).

They also identify key aspects of employee participation which trade unions need to address, particularly the joint monitoring of participation initiatives at workplace level, involvement of trade unions in the internal communications processes of organisations, access to and understanding of business information, and involvement in high level business decision making.

The trade union position with respect to financial or equity participation has also been somewhat mixed. However, this situation too appears to have changed significantly in recent times, with unions seeking a greater financial stake for employees. As noted above, a particular case in point, is the ongoing discussions on the proposed employee share ownership plan in Telecom Éireann, where the union group have been pushing for both a significant equity stake for workers and a greater role for unions/workers at a strategic level. The following comment from the General Secretary of the Communications Workers Union encapsulates the current position:

> Telecom Éireann requires major price reductions and consequential cost adjustments in order to meet the challenges posed by powerful international competitors and market deregulation. The Union Coalition [which involves the five unions representing Telecom Eireann staff] is prepared to participate actively in the speedy transformation of the company in return for a 14.9% employee shareholding with a real voice for the staff in the future of Telecom Éireann. (Mr C. Scanlon, General Secretary, CWU, *Industrial Relations News* 3: 1998)

8.8 TOWARDS A 'NEW' MODEL — PARTNERSHIP-BASED INDUSTRIAL RELATIONS ARRANGEMENTS

Much of the preceding discussion on employee involvement and participation can be traced to a general premise that while collective bargaining remains a critical institution in industrial relations it has a number of limitations and that organisations are increasingly seeking to move beyond such adversarial relations to a more co-operative approach between management and trade unions. We have earlier seen that our collective bargaining system is largely based on adversarial principles stemming from the widespread acceptance that a conflict of interests exists between management and labour. In this system collective bargaining acts as the principal means of addressing these conflicting interests through a system of mutually acceptable compromises.

The adversarial system has come in for increasing criticism in recent years, both in Ireland and abroad. A general criticism has been the perceived dominance of distributive bargaining with its emphasis on dividing limited resources (Fisher and Ury, 1986). It is argued that this approach leads the parties to develop adversarial positions believing that any gains can only be made by inflicting losses on the other party. Distributive bargaining reflects the very essence of the traditional pluralist-adversarial industrial relations model: claims, offers, bluff, threats, compromise, movement, agreement or conflict. However, it is suggested that approaches based on more integrative/ co-operative bargaining represent a more attractive alternative with their emphasis on a collaborative approach, exploring common ground and seeking solutions of mutual benefit to both parties. The so-called 'partnership approach' to industrial relations is grounded in such thinking, suggesting that employers, workers and their representative associations should seek to jointly address industrial relations problems and develop mutually beneficial solutions (see, for example, Kochan and Osterman, 1994; Beaumont, 1995a). It is expected that any shift from distributive bargaining towards more co-operative 'partnership'-based approaches requires change on behalf of both employers and trade unions (Elliott, 1984; ICTU, 1993; 1995; Salamon, 1998). Unions might be expected to move from their traditional focus on pay and conditions bargaining to actively engage with management in broader areas of organisational decision making, while employers must be prepared to shed some of their traditional prerogative and join with unions in joint decision making.

This section considers the development of partnership-based industrial relations arrangements (PBIRA).

8.8.1 THE IRISH CONTEXT[2]

This most recent sequence of centralised agreements in Ireland (1987–2000) is often characterised as representing a shift towards a more corporatist approach to industrial relations in Ireland (see, for example, O'Donnell and O'Reardon, 1996; Roche, 1997b, and chapter 6 above). Indeed, these agreements appear to meet most of the requisite characteristics of 'corporatist' arrangements, namely: (1) Government intervention in collective bargaining so that negotiations become tripartite; (2) a debate over broader issues such as economic and social policy, and (3) the existence of consensus in the national interest. However, an important criticism of this period of centralised bargaining is the failure to extend the partnership approach below national level interactions. As Roche (1995) specifically comments, the Irish model of social partnership is somewhat narrow, involving only the top levels of the union and employer bodies and has not significantly impacted on developments in enterprise level industrial relations. As a consequence, Roche (1995) describes the Irish model as 'truncated' social partnership, inferring that while a partnership orientation exists at the pinnacle of union and employer interactions, old-fashioned adversarialism characterises employer-union relations at the enterprise level.

Consequently, the development of enterprise level partnerships has been the focus of much recent debate in Ireland (see, for example, Roche and

Kochan, 1996). In particular, institutions such as the National Economic and Social Council and ICTU have pointed to the potentially significant role of enterprise level industrial relations partnerships in contributing to improvements in both management-employee relations and economic performance. At national level we have seen the establishment of a National Centre for Partnership, based in the Department of the Taoiseach, while at EU level, 1997 saw the publication by the European Commission of a Green Paper 'Partnership for a New Organization of Work'.

Why have enterprise level partnerships now emerged as a significant dimension of the debate on organisation change and employee participation? In general, one can identify two broad stimuli. Firstly, we have the increasingly competitive environment facing organisations and encouraging them to re-configure their industrial relations policies to facilitate improved performance and productivity. Secondly, we have the decline in trade union penetration which has prompted the union movement to seek mechanisms to increase their legitimacy and representativeness at both enterprise and national level (Beaumont, 1995a; Sparrow and Hiltrop, 1994). In addressing these competitive challenges many organisations have sought to improve their utilisation of human resources, particularly in seeking increased productivity and reduced labour costs. These goals are often achieved through organisation change initiatives to improve flexibility, cost effectiveness and worker performance, while concurrently seeking to increase employee participation and involvement. Most of these developments have important implications for established industrial relations traditions and practices and bring into focus the current debate on developing new industrial relations arrangements which serve to enhance enterprise level performance. This is the context of the current debate on partnership-based industrial relations arrangements.

8.8.2 PARTNERSHIP-BASED INDUSTRIAL ARRANGEMENTS — A NEW PARADIGM IN INDUSTRIAL RELATIONS?

In a 1996 paper, Professor Robert McKersie (1996:12), the eminent academic and authority on labour-management partnerships, based at the Massachusetts Institute of Technology, suggested that Ireland was an ideal location to test the premise that 'strategic partnerships, coupled with modern human resource systems' could be the basis for a new and successful model of industrial relations. We have since seen many others take up the running on enterprise level industrial relations partnerships, particularly the European Commission and, in Ireland, FORFAS, ICTU and NESC. The Commission's Green Paper Partnership for a New Organization of Work argues that improvements in competitiveness and employment can be stimulated through 'a better organization of work at the workplace, based on high skills, high trust and high quality' (European Commission, 1997:5). It goes on to invite the social partners to 'build a partnership for the development of a new framework for the modernization of work'. In Ireland, the Partnership 2000 agreement describes the probable characteristics of partnership (Government Publications Office, 1996):

> . . . an active relationship based on recognition of a common interest to secure the competitiveness, viability and prosperity of the enterprise. It involves the continuing commitment of employees to improvements in quality and efficiency; and the acceptance by employers of employees as stakeholders with rights and interests to be considered in the context of major decisions affecting their employment . . . [it] involves common ownership of the resolution of challenges, involving the direct participation of employees/representatives and an investment in their training, development and working environment.

THE ESSENCE OF PARTNERSHIP-BASED INDUSTRIAL ARRANGEMENTS (PBIRA)

We noted earlier that the proponents of partnership often point to perceived deficiencies in the adversarial industrial relations model, in particular the apparent dominance of distributive bargaining on short-term issues and its emphasis on dividing limited resources. As a result of increasing competitive pressures, not least from non-union sources, it is widely argued that there is a need for a new partnership model of industrial relations which incorporates a strong trade union role but with a more long-term strategic dimension (Kochan et al., 1986; Kochan and Osterman, 1994). It is further argued that this new model allows both sides to break out of the traditional adversarial relationship through the adoption of a partnership model based on 'mutual gains' principles as follows:
– employers recognise and facilitate worker and trade union involvement in strategic decision making;
– workers/trade unions commit themselves actively to productivity improvements;
– the gains of productivity improvements are shared between employers and workers;
– productivity improvements do not result in redundancies but rather employers actively seek new markets to keep workers gainfully employed.
The essence of this partnership thesis is that workers and trade unions actively pursue *with* management solutions to business problems and appropriate work reorganisation in return for greater involvement in business decisions and in the process of work reorganisation. It is characterised by a strong emphasis on consensual decision making using integrative rather than distributive approaches in management-union interactions/discussions.

While this model, based on voluntary employer-union interaction, is the most widely understood form of enterprise partnership it is not the only one. Cutcher-Gershenfeld and Verma (1994) identified three modes of shared decision making at enterprise level:

(1) non-union high commitment system;
(2) legislated works councils;
(3) voluntary union-management joint governance.

The non-union high commitment approach has its roots in the US and places the primary focus on facilitating direct employee involvement in operational decision making at workplace level (see chapters 9 and 10). This system does not normally encompass representative participation. In contrast, we have seen earlier that works councils normally reflect a legislated form of representative participation. In this system elected worker representatives have a right to shared decision making in prescribed areas of work organisation such as working conditions, work practices and workplace change. We have seen that while this approach is particularly associated with Germany, it also characterises a number of other EU countries. Voluntary union-management self-governance arrangements equate to management-union partnership-based industrial relations arrangements.

In assessing the characteristics of partnership-based industrial relations arrangements (PBIRA) at enterprise level, we can identify three core dimensions, (1) strategic impact; (2) role of trade unions and (3) institutional sophistication.

(1) *Strategic impact*. Employee and/or trade union involvement in the strategic decision-making process is probably *the* key element which characterises a highly developed 'strategic partnership' approach within organisations. The focus on high level strategic decisions is important and serves to differentiate 'strategic partnerships' from lower level workplace partnerships which focus on operational level decisions (such as those related to work organisation or quality). That is not to say that operational workplace issues cannot be a focus of strategic partnership arrangements but rather to indicate that the 'strategic' element refers to partnership in making long-term strategic decisions which impact on the future direction of the enterprise as a whole. As McKersie (1996:5) notes, a critical key feature of strategic partnership is union or employee involvement in key corporate decisions: 'A key feature of partnerships is that the trade union has an opportunity to challenge or confront management before a decision is made.'

(2) *Role of trade unions*. Given the critical role played by the Irish trade union movement in the four centralised agreements negotiated since 1987, the debate on partnership generally sees trade unions as integral to the development of enterprise partnerships. However, it should be noted that much of Ireland's industrial development over the last decade has been led by foreign-owned firms which are predominantly non-union. Many of these have been to the forefront in claiming to employ 'state of the art' human resource management practices. While often captured under the rubric of world class manufacturing or total quality management, many of these initiatives focus on

facilitating individual employee involvement in workplace decisions. In the burgeoning Irish non-union sector, there are many organisations which claim to have well developed management-employee partnerships. A problem here, however, is the inherent difficulty involved in establishing the existence and nature of such partnerships since most accounts are based solely on a managerial perspective. As such, these cases present difficulties in evaluating the nature and extent of employee involvement. However, it is clear that at least some of these firms provide for a reasonable level of direct employee involvement in day-to-day decision making at workplace level.

(3) *Institutional sophistication:* This dimension refers to the extent to which there are well developed institutional arrangements to facilitate a partnership approach at organisation and workplace level. The non-union high commitment system mentioned earlier (Cutcher-Gershenfeld and Verma, 1994) relies primarily on direct employee involvement through teamworking and problem solving groups and does not normally involve formal representative structures. However, to effect a high level of partnership in decision making, one would normally expect to see the development of new management-union or management-employee structures. In unionised firms these structures would normally be introduced in addition to established collective bargaining arrangements. For strategic partnership one would expect to see provision for union or worker representation at board level. An extract from a joint Bell (Canada)/Communications, Energy and Paper (CEP) Union (1993) task force paper illustrates this point:

> [Union-management partnerships need to] involve, through the corporate steering committee and other exchanges of information, appropriate union executives in planning, strategy, training, and policy formulation in areas such as quality, human resources planning, new technology, major product development and market changes, and strategic alliances with other telecommunications companies . . . Another key distinction is that *these partnerships are at the corporate level where key business decisions are made that affect the viability of the enterprise.* (Emphasis added)

To underpin well developed partnership arrangements at the operational level one might also expect to see the development of management-employee/union institutions to facilitate joint decision making. A recent Irish example is provided in the partnership agreement between Howmedica and SIPTU (*Industrial Relations News*, 1997). This provides for the establishment of a 'partnership forum' whose role is to plan, design and support implementation of the customised continuous improvement programme. However, partnership arrangements, particularly those of an operational nature, need not necessarily be underpinned by well developed institutional arrangements at enterprise level. One can point to arrangements for periodic management-employee or management briefings where the focus is on information sharing and consultation. It should be noted that such approaches do not normally provide for joint decision making: management agree to discuss issues, consider employee or union opinion but retain prerogative in decision making.

It is possible to identify two other important components which appear to form part of many industrial relations partnerships, namely gain-sharing and job security commitments. *Gain-sharing* broadly incorporates arrangements which reward workers for improvements in enterprise performance via profit-sharing, share ownership or some other reward mechanism. Such schemes are critical in giving effect to an underlying principle of partnership, namely that the gains from improved performance are shared between employers and workers. *Job security commitments* also form an important part of the partnership equation. They are particularly important in securing employee and union commitment to changes in work practices since they alleviate the fear of job losses resulting from such changes.

8.8.3 MODELS OF PARTNERSHIP

Using these core dimensions of enterprise level partnerships, we can identify two broad models of partnership.

Firstly, we can identify what can be termed *strategic partnerships*. These provide for union and/or employee involvement in top level corporate decisions. In this respect one would expect to find two variants. *Union-management partnerships* are characterised by institutional arrangements which allow for union involvement in strategic decision making while also facilitating a strong trade union role in operational decision making at workplace level. In practice this normally means union representation at board level or equivalent together with union representation in sub-board level bodies which engage in shared decision making. The second variant is *employee-management partnerships* whereby employees are represented in the highest levels of corporate decision making.

In evaluating the prospects for strategic partnerships one cannot be optimistic. Managers have traditionally been extremely reluctant to share decision-making power and, particularly so, in relation to strategic decisions. A particular instance in Europe was the widespread employer opposition to the introduction of worker directors during the 1970s and 1980s while currently we are witnessing increasing employer opposition to works councils as an institutional form of employee representation. Other factors also mitigate against the uptake of strategic partnership. The growth of larger publicly quoted organisations is a case in point. Stock markets tend to favour 'strong' executive control and the development of strategic partnerships may not be viewed positively. This may be particularly the case among 'high technology' stocks. An issue with especial resonance in Ireland is the great difficulty likely to be encountered in developing strategic partnerships in foreign-owned companies. In the great majority of such firms strategic decisions are made at corporate level — at a significant remove from the Irish subsidiary. As such, it may be particularly difficult for Irish trade unions to develop a strategic partnership arrangements in such situations.

The indigenous sector and, particularly, the public sector, is somewhat different. Here we have seen some most significant developments. Trends in the ESB, Telecom Éireann and Aer Rianta indicate that many of the appropriate institutional arrangements are in place, such as board level worker representation and reasonably well developed sub-board level structures to facilitate partnership. However, it is also clear that partnership in these organisations is at a very developmental stage and its prospects are dependent on how these organisations cope with imminent competitive challenges in their respective product markets. It is also dependent on the impact of privatisation and strategic alliances. Such developments may also mitigate against the development of strategic partnership, particularly the issue of worker directors. For example, it is questionable whether the utilisation of worker directors, as provided for in many semi-State organisations, would endure should these organisations become privatised.

A second partnership model which we can identify is what might be termed operational partnerships. Again, we can point to two possible variants. Operational union-management partnerships are normally characterised by union acceptance of change in work practices in return for participation in operational management decisions, such as those involving work organisation. In essence, the union provides a commitment to greater task flexibility and acceptance of change in exchange for greater union involvement in day-to-day decisions which affect the working of the enterprise and for greater direct employee involvement in daily operating decisions. Such arrangements may often entail some job security commitments and the introduction of gain-sharing. The second variant is operational employee-management partnerships. These partnership arrangements are to be found in some non-union firms. Many of these firms are US-owned and operate in the so-called 'high tech' sectors, particularly electronics and software. They bear all the hallmarks of union-management partnerships but exclude trade union involvement and do not normally provide for any form of representative participation. As noted earlier, such arrangements present a difficulty in evaluating the extent of employee involvement. The crucial differentiating factor between strategic and operational partnerships is that, in the latter, there is no scope for union or worker involvement in long-term strategic decision making.

It is important to point out that the extent of employee or union influence in operational partnership arrangements can vary considerably. Highly developed operational partnerships are likely to be based on joint decision-making principles whereby union/employee agreement is a requisite element of the decision-making process. Consensus is therefore a prerequisite and the approval of both parties is necessary before proposals under consideration can be proceeded with. Less well developed arrangements tend to have a more consultative focus. In this scenario, management agree to discuss upcoming decisions with employees/union(s) and share related information. Thus, employees or unions have the opportunity to influence decisions before implementation. However, there is no commitment to joint decision making and management may or may not take on board the opinions proffered.

8.8.4 THE EVIDENCE TO DATE

There is little empirical research on enterprise level partnerships in Ireland.[3] However, there are some studies which either directly, or through the use of proxy measures, throw some light on the diffusion of partnership-based industrial relations arrangements among Irish organisations. Here, we review three particular studies, namely the Irish Management Institute (IMI) pilot survey of enterprise level partnerships, the European Foundation for the Improvement of Living and Working Conditions-sponsored study on employee participation in organisational change (EPOC) and the Cranfield-University of Limerick (CUL) study of HRM practices. We also consider some other sources of information in the area.

The only specific study of partnership arrangements at enterprise level which is currently available is that conducted by the IMI in November 1997 (Hannigan, 1997). This pilot study involved a survey of participants who attended a Department of Enterprise Trade and Employment/IMI Conference on the theme Workplace 2000. This conference addressed the issue of industrial relations partnerships with particular emphasis on the EU Green Paper, the role of the National Centre of Partnership and case experiences of organisations which have undertaken partnership initiatives. Inevitably, this survey is likely to represent a biased response, as one would expect participants at such a conference to have some positive interest in developing or promoting workplace industrial relations partnerships. As such, one would expect that the survey would reveal a positive picture on partnership. Interestingly, this was not the case. The IMI survey explored a number of dimensions of partnership. Some of these might be considered direct indicators of the presence of partnership-based industrial relations arrangements while others represent more indirect or contextual variables. Respondents were asked to indicate the presence of these dimensions in their organisation on a 1 to 5 scale (low to high). The mean scores are outlined in Table 8.6.

In evaluating these findings in relation to the median value of 3, we find a reasonably clear picture. Firstly, the direct indicators of partnership-based industrial relations arrangements all score below the median value. Thus, it appears that partnership-based approaches are not well developed in the respondent firms. As the author comments: '. . . the key features of a partnership agreement, for example, employee involvement in strategic decision making and sharing in the rewards of success, are not present to any degree in this sample' (Hannigan, 1997:1–2).

Table 8.6 The diffusion partnership-based industrial relations: some initial findings

	Mean scores (range 1 — 5)
Direct Indicators of Partnership	
To what extent do you believe that partnership exists in your organisation?	2.79
Sharing in rewards of success	2.50
Employee involvement in strategic decision making	2.10
Existence of formal partnership agreement	2.05
Indirect Indicators of Partnership	
Open two-way communications	3.33
Employee involvement in decision making in work units	3.21
Top management commitment to partnership	3.07
Single status for all employees	2.95
Efficiency/Performance Indicators	
Employee responsiveness to customer requirements	3.81
Employee flexibility	3.67

Source: Hannigan, 1997

A second important trend discernible in the IMI survey, is that the variables which score highest are those which evaluate worker flexibility and responsiveness to customer requirements, i.e., indicators of employee performance/efficiency. Finally, we find that management perceptions of their commitment to partnership score higher than their evaluation of the extent to which partnership actually exists in their organisations.

The study also explored the impact of ownership (Irish private sector, public sector and foreign owned) on variations in the uptake of partnership. The overall conclusion was that the 'relative strength of each of the features of partnership does not differ greatly depending on the ownership structure of the respondent' (Hannigan, 1997:4), although public sector organisations and other Irish firms were more inclined to use the term partnership as compared to their foreign-owned counterparts.

A second important source of data is the EPOC study reviewed earlier in this chapter (EFILWC, 1997; Sisson, 1997). As we have already seen, the EPOC study focused on task participation. It found that while task participation is reasonably well diffused in Ireland, most organisations rely on predominantly traditional forms of work organisation. In particular, the study found that the delegation of high levels of autonomy to workers and work teams was very low.

A third source of data on the incidence of partnership-based industrial relations arrangements is the CUL study, also considered earlier (Gunnigle,

Morley, Clifford and Turner, 1997). It should be noted that this study did not attempt to explicitly examine the incidence of partnership-based industrial relations arrangements. We therefore rely on some proxy measure considered indicative of partnership approaches. An important pre-requisite for employee participation in management decisions is the provision of information on enterprise performance. The CUL study explored the extent to which senior management communicated formally with employees on business strategy and financial performance (see Table 8.4 above). We saw that just 38 per cent of participating organisations reported that they communicate on strategy with manual grades. This result is surprisingly low, even allowing for an expected differential in the level of communications on strategy between high ranking and low ranking employees. A similar picture emerges in relation to the extent of communications on *financial performance*. The CUL study also explored the incidence of joint consultative committees and works councils. The findings indicate that the extent to which organisations are facilitating increased employee participation through institutionalised arrangements in the form of joint consultative committees and work councils is quite modest. Just a quarter of participating organisations reported the existence of joint consultative committees or works councils. Such consultative arrangements are more widespread in the public sector with 38 per cent of organisations reporting the existence of some form of institutionalised participation, compared with 21 per cent of private sector organisations. The great majority of organisations with a works council or joint consultative committee were unionised (fifty-three of the sixty-three organisations).

An additional source of information is Gunnigle's (1995a) greenfield site, also considered earlier. This study found a similar picture to the CUL study. While there was considerable evidence of managerial attempts to introduce a modicum of individual employee involvement, partnership approaches were not a common feature of enterprise level industrial relations in these new firms.

Overall, these studies provide little or no evidence of trade union or employee involvement in strategic decision making. Rather, the predominant focus was on employee involvement initiatives aimed at facilitating the involvement of individual employees and small groups on issues of immediate work relevance. These initiatives seem to be predominantly concerned with encouraging greater employee 'voice' on workplace issues rather than employee 'influence' on higher level management decision making.

8.8.5 THE PROSPECTS FOR PARTNERSHIP

In spite of these findings on the low take-up of partnership, the 'established sector' does seem to provide potentially fertile ground for management-union partnerships. A critical area of concern for many such organisations is that of facilitating improved levels of performance on dimensions of quality and productivity. For many older, established organisations this requires extensive change in industrial relations, specifically on aspects such as (less) demarcation, (increased) task flexibility, (increased) responsibilities for workers and (reduced) staffing levels. Given their high levels of union penetration and collective bargaining traditions, such changes must normally be achieved through negotiations with trade unions. Traditionally, this would be achieved through adversarial bargaining and it is likely that this will remain the case in many organisations. However, it also likely that some companies will try to adopt a partnership approach. We can see evidence of such initiatives in the ESB and Aer Rianta in the public sector and in Howmedica in the private sector. It is instructive that the two major future challenges identified by respondents to the CUL study were: (1) efficiency, productivity and flexibility issues; (2) industrial relations (Gunnigle, Morley, Clifford and Turner, 1997). It is likely that many such organisations are attempting to change their industrial relations paradigm from an adversarial approach focused on pay and conditions to a partnership approach focused on performance and flexibility.

8.9 ACHIEVING INVOLVEMENT AND PARTICIPATION

It is widely suggested that all parties in industrial relations can benefit from increased employee participation and involvement (see, for example, Beer et al., 1984). For example, it is suggested that employers need a flexible and committed workforce who will respond to change and perform at high levels of productivity with minimum levels of supervision and that this can be achieved through employee participation and involvement initiatives. From an employee perspective, it is argued that the achievement of an input into decisions which affects their working lives is a very legitimate goal, allowing them greater control and discretion in their jobs (Hackman and Oldham, 1980). Even at the macro level, the State and the community at large may benefit from positive workplace relations based on trust, open communications, and employee satisfaction (Beer et al., 1984).

However, the achievement of real and effective participation within organisations remains problematic (Marchington and Parker, 1990; Salamon, 1998). Employer organisations may, for example, argue that business confidence and discretion in decision making must be maintained to encourage investment and expansion, while at the same time suggesting that barriers to worker involvement must be removed and employees given a worthwhile say in decision making on immediate work related issues. This perspective is commonly used to encourage employee involvement in shop floor issues while legitimising the retention of management prerogative in higher level business decision making (Gunnigle and Morley, 1993).

We have noted that while the main focus of representative participation has been on worker directors and works councils, direct participation has emphasised the involvement of employees in decisions affecting immediate work related issues. A particular concern for trade unions is the impact of these various participative forms on collective bargaining and the union role at enterprise level. We earlier noted the reservations which many trade unionists harbour in relation to employee participation and involvement. In particular, we have seen that a traditional principle of collective bargaining has been the trade union 'right and ability' to oppose management (Salamon, 1998:375). Consequently, initiatives which seek to integrate workers or trade unions in the decision-making process are often viewed with suspicion since they may serve to reduce trade union independence and capacity to oppose. Trade unions are also concerned that any participative forms complement, rather than compete with, established collective bargaining institutions. In particular, they will generally oppose approaches which are perceived to reduce or undermine the union role.

In contrast, employers often view employee participation and involvement as a means of engaging the whole workforce (not just those represented by trade unions) in organisation change initiatives aimed at improving the competitive position of the organisation. The contrast between union and management perspectives is expressed in the following quote from Salamon (1998:389):

> Management favours task-centred, direct forms of 'involvement' based on increasing the commitment of the individual employee; trade unions favour power-centred, indirect forms of 'participation' based on the established representation role of trade unions to increase employee influence in management decision making.

We have earlier seen how changes in the political, social and economic environment have led to a shift in the participation and involvement debate away from representative participation and towards direct participation (employee involvement). This shift is related to an increasing employer focus on improving organisation performance and competitiveness in dimensions such as productivity, quality levels, and customer service. At the macro level, Governments and other supra-national bodies (such as the EU) have also become preoccupied with economic and competitiveness issues, again placing a strong policy focus on organisation level and sectoral level performance. Hyman and Mason (1995) identify two optional management strategies in seeking increased productivity and performance. Firstly, management may adopt a 'coercive' approach which seeks to force organisational change and improved performance through threats of lay-offs or closure. Secondly, they may pursue an 'integrative' approach which seeks to foster common interests between workers and management using direct involvement and thus achieve improved performance through employee commitment and support.

However, the achievement of direct participation appears just as problematic as representative participation. Marchington et al. (1993) identify four common problems associated with direct participation (employee involvement):

(1) lack of continuity;

(2) absence of middle management support and commitment;

(3) adoption of inappropriate systems; and

(4) employee scepticism.

Salamon (1998) notes that middle and senior management may sometimes be a greater obstacle to direct participation than employees or trade unions (also see IRS, 1993). As much as anything, it would appear that effective participation requires a high level of commitment and positive engagement from employers, employer associations, employees and trade unions. Trust has been identified as a key factor in facilitating effective communications and information disclosure/exchange (Whelan, 1982). Indeed, it would appear that the existence of high trust relations is more important than the actual participative form or mechanism adopted.

Thus, it might be suggested that the different forms of participation and involvement described in this chapter may be viewed as options in a participative mix, any combination of which may be used in different national, sectoral or organisational contexts. Salamon (1998:389) is unambiguous in his contention that the most appropriate approach is one which combines direct and representative participation:

> The most effective structure of employee participation within an organisation is one which combines direct employee involvement in decisions relating to their immediate work situation with indirect participation at the strategic level on major organisation decisions, while not undermining the collective bargaining representational role of established trade unions.

However, the imposition of particular models has often proved problematic and the current thrust of legislative measures is to allow for a high degree of flexibility in the modes of participation and involvement to be adopted. In evaluating the merits of recent developments in relation to partnership-based arrangements between employers and trade unions, it appears that both sides face a fundamental choice on the nature of management-employee relations: should worker/trade union involvement be confined to joint consultation or extended to joint regulation? From a worker/trade union perspective, joint consultation initiatives run the risk of remaining essentially 'symbolic', whereby workers/trade unions have no real influence but become associated with decisions which they possess no right to veto. Employers may be equally reticent to enter into joint regulation initiatives because they may lead to a slowing in the decision-making process. Some of the difficulties in developing partnership approaches in the conduct of enterprise level industrial relations are apparent in recent debates in the Irish context. For example, as noted earlier, a criticism of patterns of social partnership in Ireland is that its operation is restricted to the most senior levels of employer and trade union interests with little diffusion to enterprise level (Roche, 1995).

Looking specifically at the issue of partnership based industrial relations arrangements at enterprise level, we can point to the following important trends. Firstly, the available evidence suggests that partnership approaches are not well developed in Ireland. Where partnership exists this tends to take the form of operational management-union partnerships dealing with work reorganisation. Most of these are based on a consultative basis rather than joint decision-making principles. There is, however, widespread evidence of employer initiatives to facilitate higher levels of direct employee involvement in operational decision making, particularly on issues such as work scheduling. These initiatives often form part of drives towards total quality management or world class manufacturing. Such initiatives are generally aimed at involving the individual worker and do not necessarily include trade unions. The extent and nature of employee involvement initiatives in the non-union sector is difficult to estimate. Nevertheless, it is clear that a number of non-union firms do provide for a level of direct employee involvement, particularly in relation to operational issues affecting work organisation, such as job content, scheduling, and allocation of duties. At a policy level the trade union movement has been to the fore in calling for public policy interventions to legislatively underpin partnership arrangements at the enterprise level. However, the position of employers and their representative associations is more ambiguous. While IBEC have made some encouraging noises in favour of enterprise level partnerships, their approach appears largely based on voluntarist principles. Essentially, the employer position seems based on the premise that while it would be good to have some exemplars of well developed partnerships, it is up to individual employers to decide on their chosen approach. Thus partnership is not seen as an ideal approach but rather as one of a number of options for employers (including union avoidance) for dealing with enterprise level industrial relations.

NOTES
1. Bord na Móna, CIE, ESB, Aer Lingus, B & I, Comhlucht Súicre Éireann and Nitrigin Éireann.
2. This section is largely based on Gunnigle, P. 1998a. More Rhetoric than Reality: Industrial Relations Partnerships in Ireland. *Economic and Social Review* 28: 4: 179–200.
3. A research team representing the Smurfit Graduate School of Business, University College Dublin, and the Economic and Social Research Institute have recently completed a workplace study of industrial relations and Human Resource Management. This study should provide considerable insights into the extent and pattern of utilisation of partnership-based industrial relations arrangements. This work is due for publication in late 1998/early 1999.

CHAPTER NINE

Managing Industrial Relations I: Industrial Relations, Business Strategy and HRM

9.1 INTRODUCTION

A notable characteristic of analyses of industrial relations over the past two decades has been an increasing focus on developments at enterprise level (see, for example, Kochan et al., 1986). In this regard, we find particular emphasis on management strategies and policies, often linked to the premise that industrial relations at enterprise level has undergone significant change over the period. This development is variously attributed to a 'new realism' among managers and trade unions/employees, the development of greater linkages between business strategy and personnel/human resource policies and the adoption of so-called human resource management (HRM) approaches. Of particular note is the contention that management have taken a more proactive role in stimulating change than other key 'actors' in industrial relations. Kochan et al. (1986:12) comment thus:

> One of the reasons why we place management values and strategies at the center of our analysis, however, is that since 1960 union behavior and government policy have been much slower to adapt to changes in their external environment and to changes in managerial strategies and policies.

This chapter addresses these various issues by focusing on the role of management in enterprise level industrial relations. In particular it looks at three key areas, namely, (1) business strategy-industrial relations linkages, (2) the nature and development of human resource management (HRM) and (3) the impact of HRM on industrial relations. As in previous chapters, particular emphasis is placed on the Irish context.

Before looking at these specific areas it is useful to consider the rationale for this greater focus on management's role and impact on industrial relations and, specifically, to explore the reasons why the management of enterprise level industrial relations has now emerged as a significant aspect of the debate on industrial relations change.

9.2 A CHANGING ECONOMIC CONTEXT

It is generally accepted that increased product market competition, advances in technology and changes in the composition and operation of labour markets have significantly altered the context of enterprise level industrial relations (see, for example, Kochan et al., 1986; Sparrow and Hiltrop, 1994). Of particular significance is the issue of increased competitiveness resulting from factors such as growing market competition from late industrial starters (e.g., Singapore) and greater liberalisation of trade resulting from developments under the General Agreement on Tariffs and Trade (GATT) and moves towards Economic and Monetary Union (EMU) (Turner and Morley, 1995). Piore and Sabel (1984) have argued that these developments represent a new industrial revolution incorporating a major restructuring of the capitalist order. In this vein, Marshall (1992) suggests that, increasingly, an enterprise's commercial viability depends on its ability to effectively restructure in the face of increased global competition and the fragmentation of mass markets (also see, Streeck, 1992). While the advent of a new industrial revolution is open to question, there is little doubt that we have witnessed significant change in product markets and consumer behaviour. In particular, there have been major changes in the goods and services produced, the way they are produced and in the delivery of goods and services to the market. It is evident that such developments have directly impacted on the nature of enterprise level industrial relations, and prompted management initiatives to alter traditional approaches to workforce management. These changes have generally focused on three key aspects of enterprise level performance, namely, product quality, productivity and labour flexibility (Gunnigle, Morley, Clifford and Turner, 1997). While this text does not allow for a comprehensive analysis of the factors contributing to increased market competition, some key issues which have significantly impacted on enterprise level industrial relations merit brief consideration. In this respect, we can point to a number of sources of increased market competition.

Firstly, we have witnessed the *globalisation of competition*. Since the early 1980s a key development in the macro-economic environment is the increased trend towards the greater liberalisation of world trade (Sparrow and Hiltrop, 1994). In evaluating the industrial relations implications a number of issues are important. Clearly, the trend towards greater trade liberalisation provides both opportunities and threats for firms: we have the opportunity for greater access to new markets but also the threat of increased product market competition. In the Irish context we can point to the greater competitive threat to Irish organisations from lower cost economies and the related dangers of organisations relocating from Ireland to lower cost regions (Roche and Gunnigle, 1995; Gunnigle, Morley, Clifford and Turner, 1997). On the positive side, we find that greater trade liberalisation provides increased opportunities to develop new markets. However, in order to capitalise on such opportunities in the face of greater competition it is likely that firms will have to improve their performance on dimensions such as unit production costs, speed to market, and customer support.

In addition to the globalisation of competition therefore, we can also point to the greater *intensification of competition*. Again numerous sources may be identified: in addition to traditional sources of competition such as the US and Japan, we can point to the improved performance of fast developing economies such as Singapore and South Korea and other emerging economies such as China and Mexico, some of which combine a low cost base with strong performance on dimensions such as productivity and labour skills. Nearer home, many of the countries of the former Soviet Union have undergone a period of restructuring and are likely to provide considerable competition as a result of their low cost base, industrial tradition and an educational system with a strong technical and scientific foundation (Gunnigle, Morley, Clifford and Turner, 1997).

Thirdly, we have the *changing nature of competitive strategies* as a stimulus for change in enterprise level industrial relations. In particular, key contemporary developments such as increased customisation of products and services, reduced cycle time and faster speed to market all have important implications for enterprise level industrial relations. In particular, such developments in competitive strategy often require greater flexibility in employment patterns as organisations seek to align their need for workers with the level of business demand, and greater task flexibility in terms of the variety of duties which workers may be asked to perform.

A related factor which has also served to stimulate change in enterprise level industrial relations is the changing role of trade unions. In particular, we have the decline in trade union membership and influence in many Western economies which has prompted the union movement to seek mechanisms to increase their legitimacy and representativeness at both enterprise and national level (Beaumont 1995a; Sparrow and Hiltrop, 1994). This issue was considered in some depth in chapter 4.

9.2.1 ORGANISATIONAL RESPONSES AND IMPLICATIONS FOR INDUSTRIAL RELATIONS
In responding to the challenges of increased product market competition, organisations appear to have followed two broad strategies. Firstly, we witnessed widespread rationalisation, especially in Europe during the 1980s (Sparrow and Hiltrop, 1994). Common characteristics here included redundancies, contracting out or selling 'non-core' activities, and 'de-layering', that is, reducing the number of hierarchical levels or grades in the organisation (see, for example, Gunnigle, 1998b) A second common

organisational response was a sharp increase in merger, acquisition or strategic alliance activity (Sparrow and Hiltrop, 1994). A common element in these organisational responses was an increased focus on improving workforce management at the enterprise level, specifically in seeking improvements in labour productivity and reductions in labour costs. Related enterprise level strategies included the increased use of atypical employment forms in certain sectors, improved performance management methods and initiatives to increase task flexibility. As many commentators have noted, these latter developments strike at the very heart of traditional or established industrial relations practices and bring into focus the current debate on the role of management and management strategies in seeking to develop and change industrial relations arrangements in a way which serves to enhance enterprise level performance (see, for example, Roche, 1995; Gunnigle, 1998a).

As noted earlier, we can identify three key areas of enterprise level industrial relations where the role of management is seen as particularly critical, namely, (1) business strategy-industrial relations linkages; (2) the nature and diffusion of human resource management (HRM) and (3) the likely impact of HRM on industrial relations.

9.3 BUSINESS STRATEGY AND INDUSTRIAL RELATIONS

The study of strategic management has achieved increasing prominence as organisations seek to adapt to a changing business environment. Strategic management is concerned with policy decisions affecting the entire organisation, involves major resource allocation considerations with the overall objective being to best position the organisation to deal effectively with its environment. Strategic decisions are therefore long term in nature, affect the future nature of the organisation and serve to guide subsequent decision making at lower levels. Strategic decision making incorporates strategy formulation, strategy implementation, evaluation and control; it emphasises the monitoring and evaluation of environmental opportunities and constraints as well as the strengths and weaknesses of the organisation.

Hofer and Schendel (1978) identify three levels of strategy: corporate, business and functional levels. *Corporate level strategy* is essentially concerned with the question 'What business should we be in?' *Business level (competitive) strategy* addresses the question, 'How do we compete in this business?' Finally, *Functional level strategy* focuses on how the activities of particular functions (such as personnel management/industrial relations) come together to support business level strategy. These differing strategy levels are illustrated in Figure 9.1. This conception of strategic management implies that in an organisational setting there is a hierarchy of decision choices, and that key decisions on business strategy will steer more specific operational decisions on short-term problems and issues (Thurley and Wood, 1983; Gunnigle, Morley and Heraty, 1997).

Figure 9.1 Levels of strategic decision making

Corporate strategy   *Multi-business*
(What business should we be in?)

Business/competitive strategy
(How to establish competitive advantage?)   *Single/related business(es)*

Functional strategy
(Role of component parts)

Production/operations	Marketing	Finance	Personnel/
			HRM

Corporate, business and functional strategy represent different levels of strategic decision making in an organisation. Each level involves decisions which are strategic in nature. However, decisions at higher levels, such as those at corporate or business unit level, will guide subsequent decisions on functional strategy. Purcell (1989) emphasises this point by differentiating between *upstream* (first order) and *downstream* (second/third order) strategic decisions (see Figure 9.2). Upstream decisions concern the long-term direction and nature of the organisation. Downstream decisions deal with the implications of first order decisions for organisation structure (a downstream decision). Purcell argues that personnel/human resource (P/HR) and industrial relations policy choices are made in the context of downstream strategic decisions on organisation structure. Such choices are strategic in nature since they establish the basic approach to workforce management. However, they will be heavily influenced by first and second order decisions and by broader environmental factors. Thus it is suggested that P/HR and industrial relations policy choices are third order strategic decisions.

Figure 9.2 Upstream and downstream strategic decisions

	Upstream	
		E
		N
First order	Long-term direction of the firm	V
	Scope of activities, markets, location	I
		R
Second order	Internal operating procedures	O
	Relationships between parts of the organisation	N M
Third order	Strategic choice in human resource management	E N
		T
	Downstream	

Source: Adapted from Purcell, 1989

Using UK data, Purcell examined how trends in first and second order strategies, particularly diversification and decentralisation, affect management decision making. Purcell identified the growth in size and influence of the diversified firm as giving greater prominence to decision making at the corporate level. Within this business form, portfolio planning is commonly used to, firstly, evaluate the performance of constituent business units, and, subsequently, to facilitate resource allocation and investment/divestment decisions. The portfolio planning approach views the organisation as a collection of different businesses which should pursue various strategies to suit particular market conditions. This implies that different functional strategies, including affecting industrial relations, need to be applied at business unit level to 'fit' specific business strategies.

Purcell's analysis raises an important contrast between highly *diversified* organisations operating in a variety of business sectors and *critical function* organisations whose main activities are restricted to a core industry/sector. He suggests that the firms in the latter 'core business' category are frequently characterised by a particular culture and value system which may often reflect the founder's ideology. Purcell argues that a strategic planning style, considered conducive to the development of a strategic approach to P/HR and industrial relations, is more likely to develop where there is a high level of vertical integration (interdependence between business units). However, Purcell feels that organisations which emphasise long-term strategic objectives, core values and vertical linkages are becoming less common as the trend towards diversification (multi-business organisations) gathers momentum.

We can therefore see that *first order decisions*, while not necessarily incorporating industrial relations considerations, significantly impact on industrial relations and P/HR policy and practice within particular business units. *Second order decisions* concern areas such as organisation structure, operating procedures and control of business unit performance. Purcell (1989) notes that diversified organisations tend to prefer decentralised structures with a clear differentiation between strategic and operational responsibilities. He also notes that such organisations normally view industrial relations decisions as an operational responsibility at business unit level. This implies that multi-business (diversified) organisations are likely to have considerable variation in industrial relations approaches as they seek to achieve some degree of 'fit' with their different business conditions and strategies.

Purcell concludes that in the UK and US context a short-term stock market emphasis is a primary characteristic of first order strategies. Economic values are the key yardstick, and less concrete considerations, such as industrial relations, are likely to have little influence on strategic decision making at this level. He further argues that what he terms 'strategic planning' companies with integrated human resource policies (such as IBM, Hewlett-Packard and Marks and Spencer) are the exceptions to a more general picture of little strategic consideration of industrial relations and P/HR issues.

9.3.1 THE SIGNIFICANCE OF COMPETITIVE STRATEGY

In our introduction to this chapter we identified increased competitiveness as a major reason for the greater emphasis on management's role in enterprise level industrial relations. Of particular significance in this regard has been the notion of competitive advantage, championed by Michael Porter (1980; 1985; 1987). The concept of competitive advantage addresses the means by which competing firms seek to gain market advantage over one another. Competitive advantage incorporates any factor(s) which allows an organisation to differentiate its product or service from its competitors to increase market share.

In contrast to the prominence given by Purcell to corporate decision making, Porter argues that corporate strategy has failed 'dismally' and suggests that the focus of strategic decision making should be on the development of appropriate competitive strategies at the level of individual business units. Competitive strategy is concerned with achieving sustainable competitive advantage in particular industries or industry segments. Price and quality are common mechanisms by which organisations attempt to achieve competitive advantage.

Porter identifies three generic competitive strategies:

(1) *Cost leadership*: (sometimes called *cost reduction*) involves positioning the organisation as a low cost producer of a standard 'no frills' product or service. To succeed with a cost leadership strategy it is suggested that the firm must become *the* cost leader and not one of several firms pursuing this strategy. Cost leadership requires an emphasis on tight managerial controls, low overheads, economies of scale and a dedication to achieving productive efficiency.

(2) *Product differentiation*: (sometimes called *product innovation*) requires that an organisation's product or service become unique on some dimension which is valued by the buyer to such an extent that the buyer is willing to pay a premium price. The basis for a differentiation may be the product or service itself, or other aspects such as delivery, after-sales service or brand image.

(3) *A focus strategy*: involves choosing a narrow market segment and serving this either through a low cost or a differentiation focus.

Miles and Snow (1978; 1984) have developed another commonly used competitive strategy categorisation which identifies three generic strategy types as follows:

(1) *Defenders*, who seek stability by producing only a limited set of products directed at a narrow segment of the total potential market. Within this niche, defenders strive to prevent competitors from entering the market. Organisations achieve this through standard economic actions such as competitive pricing or the production of high quality products.

(2) *Prospectors*, who are almost the opposite of defenders, since their strength is in finding and exploiting new product and market opportunities. Innovation may be more important than high profitability. The prospector's success depends on developing and maintaining the capacity to survey a wide range of environmental trends and maintaining a high degree of flexibility.

(3) *Analysers,* who try to capitalise on the best of both the preceding types. They seek to minimise risk and maximise opportunity for profit. The strategy here is to move into new products or markets only after viability has been proven by prospectors.

An organisation's choice of generic strategy specifies its fundamental approach to achieving competitive advantage in its particular market(s) and prescribes the broad context for policies and actions in each key functional area, such as industrial relations. We now consider the nature of these potential strategy-industrial relations linkages.

9.3.2 COMPETITIVE STRATEGY — INDUSTRIAL RELATIONS LINKAGES

A key thrust in the debate on competitive strategy and workforce management is the idea of 'policy fit'. Essentially, it is argued that if an organisation is to successfully pursue a particular competitive strategy, such as cost leadership or product differentiation, it must adopt and implement a comprehensive and complementary set of P/HR and industrial relations policies. Based on Porter's (1987) argument, it is expected that alternative competitive strategies need to be matched with different P/HR/industrial relations policy configurations. Of particular significance is the argued need to match employee selection, workforce profile (skills, experience, etc.) and industrial relations practices with the chosen competitive strategy. Porter (1987) also argues that different 'corporate cultures' are implied in each competitive strategy and that P/HR policy choice is a key factor in establishing and sustaining the 'appropriate' corporate cultures (also see Gunnigle, Morley, and Heraty, 1997; Morley et al., 1998).

Turning to the specific links between competitive strategy and P/HR/industrial relations policies, it is argued that organisations will experience severe problems in strategy implementation if it is not effectively linked with appropriate P/HR/industrial relations policy choices (see, for example, Galbraith and Nathanson, 1978; Fombrun et al., 1984; Fombrun, 1986). Fombrun et al. (1984) attempt to address this issue by identifying three key areas of concern for strategic decision makers in organisations:

(1) *Mission and strategy:* Identification of an organisation's purpose and plan for how this can be achieved.

(2) *Formal structure:* For the organisation of people and tasks to achieve mission and strategy.

(3) *Personnel/HR systems:* Recruitment, development, evaluation and reward of employees.

This framework is seen to differ from more traditional approaches to strategic management by incorporating workforce management considerations as an integral component of strategic decision making. Fombrun et al. (1984) suggest that an organisation's P/HR and industrial relations policies and practices symptomise managerial assumptions about employees and 'appropriate' workforce management practices. Fombrun (1986) identifies four key aspects of organisational approaches to workforce management which give valuable insights into the managerial approach to employees:

(1) *Nature of the psychological contract*: This may vary from, at one extreme, a managerial perspective which views employees in instrumental terms and emphasises high levels of control of both employees and the work environment to, at the other extreme, an approach which sees employees as intelligent and committed beings who should be afforded challenging, and meaningful work in a more benign work environment.

(2) *Level of employee involvement*: Here organisational approaches may vary from those with high levels of employee involvement in decision making to those where decisions are solely based on management prerogative.

(3) *Internal/External labour market*: This addresses the relative emphasis on internal versus external recruitment and related differences in relation to the level of investment in employee development.

(4) *Performance evaluation*: This factor addresses the relative managerial emphasis on group versus individual performance.

9.3.3 The Impact of the Product Market

An organisation's product market may be simply described as the market into which a firm supplies its goods or services. Clearly, the nature of a firm's product market has considerable significance for industrial relations. In analysing these effects, Thurley and Wood (1983) identify three dimensions along which one can evaluate a product market: (1) level of competitiveness; (2) rate of change or stability and (3) the orientation of the market. While the first two factors are self-explanatory, the last (orientation) refers to the extent to which the market is geared towards particular types of customers or suppliers (many or few; large or small) and whether it is fashion/fad orientated or subject to steady, repeat orders.

Clearly, the characteristics of an organisation's particular product market will be influenced by a variety of factors such as the cost of entry, nature of competition, technology, and the customer base. Consequently the nature of a firm's product market will be a key contextual factor influencing the choice of competitive strategy. Thurley and Wood (1983) argue that broad strategic objectives can be linked to the product market objectives, the enterprise's position in that market, the organisational characteristics and the political, social and economic influences in the community where the enterprise operates (expressed through Government policy and legislation, and interest group pressures). Kochan et al. (1986) provide a broad model of the impact of product market change on strategic decision making and on industrial relations, as outlined in Figure 9.3.

Figure 9.3 Product market change, business strategy and industrial relations

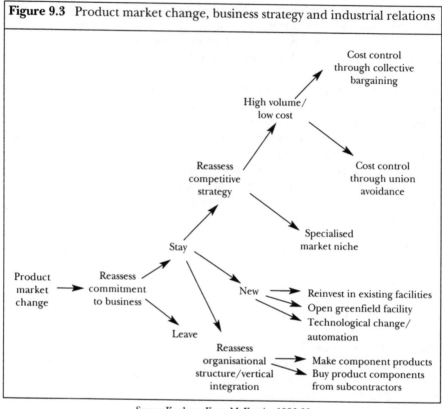

Source: Kochan, Katz, McKersie, 1986:66

This work helps to explain how changes in product market conditions can lead to critical strategic choice decisions on a number of different levels, namely:
– long-term strategy formulation at the top,
– personnel/human resource/industrial policy at the middle,
– workplace and individual-organisation relationships at the shop floor level.
From this model we can see that product market change may lead to a variety of business decisions which can profoundly affect industrial relations, such as the decision to relocate to a non-union greenfield site. In evaluating the impact of increased product market competition, Kochan et al. (1986:65) comment thus:

> When competition increases, the initial decision a firm must make is whether it wants to remain active in that line of business and compete in the new environment or withdraw and reallocate its capital resources to other opportunities. If the firm decides to remain in the market, the next decision it must make is whether to compete on the basis of low

prices (costs) and high volume or to seek out more specialised market niches that will support a price premium.

The central industrial relations effect of this increased sensitivity to prices and costs is that firms shift their priorities away from maintaining labor peace to controlling labor costs, streamlining work rules (so as to increase manufacturing efficiency) and promoting productivity. The pressure to control or lower costs is especially intense if a firm attempts to compete across all segments of its product market on the basis of low prices and high volume.

From this analysis we can see how product market context and choice of competitive strategy have important knock-on effects on P/HR and industrial relations strategies and practice, such as those relating to recruitment and training, remuneration, and job design. It is further argued that management at the enterprise level are increasingly recognising that improved utilisation of the organisation's workforce can have a significant impact on competitive advantage (Guest, 1987). Thus, we find considerable debate in the industrial relations and human resource literature on the search for appropriate P/HR and industrial relations policies to fit particular strategic types.[1]

Marchington (1990) goes somewhat further on this theme by examining the specific links between an organisation's product market position and its approach to industrial relations. Based on four detailed case studies, Marchington develops a general model to evaluate the impact of an organisation's product market circumstances on management approaches to industrial relations at the level of the enterprise. Marchington identifies two key dimensions along which to evaluate an organisation's product market position, namely that of (1) monopoly power and (2) monopsony power (also see Marchington and Parker, 1990). *Monopoly power* refers to the degree to which an organisation has power to dictate market terms to customers. High monopoly power may be the result of factors such as cartel arrangements, regulated (e.g., State) monopolies, high barriers to entry, or unique product or technology. In such situations, organisations have considerable power to dictate terms, particularly price, to customers and therefore act as 'price makers'. In contrast, *monopsony power* refers to the extent to which customers exert power over the organisation. High monopsony power may occur as a result of high levels of market competition (numerous competitors) or because of the existence of powerful customers who can exert considerable control over price and other factors (e.g., credit terms, service). In such situations, supplying organisations may be forced to accept the market terms, particularly price, dictated by customers: i.e., become 'price takers'. These relationships are illustrated in Figure 9.4.

Figure 9.4 Product market circumstances and P/HR and industrial relations policy choice

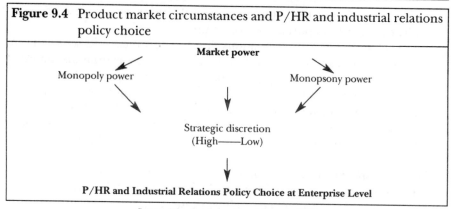

Source: Adapted from Marchington, 1990

Marchington argues that such analyses provide a measure of the power of the market over employers and, consequently, influence the degree of discretion residing with enterprise level management to make policy choices in key areas of workforce management such as industrial relations. Where monopoly power is high, top management will have considerable discretion to make broad P/HR policy choices, including those impacting on critical aspects of industrial relations such as wage levels or the extent of investment in training and development. Such favourable market conditions (high market share, growing market, stable demand) allow organisations greater scope to adopt 'investment-oriented styles', and are more conducive to the application of benign or 'soft' P/HR and industrial relations policies, such as comprehensive employee development policies, tenure commitments and gain-sharing. On the other hand, organisations operating under high levels of market pressure (high monopsony power) may have considerably less scope for choice, and a more traditional cost and labour control approach may be more appropriate.

This does not, however, imply that employers will always adopt benign P/HR and industrial relations policies in favourable product market conditions, but rather that such conditions allow management greater scope to choose from a broader range of P/HR policy choices. The actual choices made by management will be further influenced by a complex array of factors, such as the values and ideology of top management.

9.3.4 THE IRISH SITUATION

We have noted earlier in this book that, traditionally, industrial relations arrangements in Ireland were grounded in the so-called 'pluralist tradition': that is, based on an acceptance that a conflict of interests exists between management and labour and reliance on collective bargaining as the primary means of resolving these conflicting interests (Fox, 1966; 1974; Roche, 1990). Cornerstones of this approach included trade union recognition, reliance on 'adversarial' collective bargaining and some degree of procedural formalisation. There is now little doubt that the pluralist industrial relations model has come under increasing challenge in recent years (Kochan et al., 1986). There is also general agreement that developments in the wider economic and political environment have been the main catalyst in stimulating changes in enterprise level industrial relations (Beaumont, 1995b). In evaluating Irish developments, Roche and Gunnigle (1995:3) comment thus:

> Never before has the analysis of industrial relations practices and policies been so closely tied to an appreciation of commercial and national and international political pressures. In the past the worlds of industrial relations practitioners and academics alike tended to be much more introverted and preoccupied with the internal dynamics of industrial relations systems, agreements and procedures . . . . Currently, these concerns, though not altogether displaced, often take second place to such issues as company performance, the union's role in contributing to business success, mission statements and quality standards, business units, employment flexibility and so on.

The most widely accepted explanation of these changes is the increasingly competitive nature of product and service markets. The main sources of increased competitiveness are well treated in the literature and include: the liberalisation of European and world trade; associated deregulation in product, service and capital markets; improved communications and transport infrastructures; developments in information technology and greater market penetration by emerging economies (Beaumont, 1995b; Roche, 1995; Roche and Gunnigle, 1995). These developments have significant ramifications for Ireland, particularly as a result of its status as a small, open economy which is heavily reliant on international trade, especially export performance. It seems that the result of these increased competitive pressures has been to focus management attention on both cost *and* product innovation/quality as critical aspects of enterprise level performance which significantly impact on their firm's competitiveness. It further appears that these pressures serve to create a 'flexibility imperative' whereby more and more organisations have to be increasingly responsive to consumer demand on dimensions such as cost, customer service and quality. It is argued that the implication of these developments has substantially diluted the premise that companies compete on either a price (low cost) or a product differentiation (premium price) basis (Gunnigle, Morley, Clifford and Turner, 1997; Marchington and Parker, 1990). Increasingly, it appears that the great majority of firms, not just those which compete primarily on a low-price basis, must strive to tightly control their cost structures to ensure they remain 'price competitive'. It is significant that these competitive trends are increasingly penetrating the State sector (Hastings, 1994; Hourihan, 1997). Clearly, a major reason is the erosion of State monopolies as a result of developments at EU level. An early example of an Irish State-owned company having to deal with increased competitiveness is Aer Lingus. In this case, deregulation in the airline industry meant that the company faced increased competition on key routes, most notably from low cost competitors such as Ryanair. Resultant restructuring led to significant changes in employee numbers, employment patterns and reward systems. The ESB, Aer Rianta and Telecom Éireann are now faced with EU-sponsored initiatives aimed at deregulating their respective markets. It is likely that these will have profound effects on industrial relations strategies, policies and practices in these companies.

9.4 HUMAN RESOURCE MANAGEMENT

The preceding analysis has noted the marked increase in interest in linkages between business strategy and industrial relations. It is widely argued that this emphasis on a strategic perspective of P/HR and industrial relations will continue because human resource considerations have been the most neglected area of strategic management and because of its central role in implementing organisational change (see for example, Beer et al., 1984; Fombrun et al., 1984). In this respect, the emergence of what has come to be termed human resource management (HRM) is probably the most important development identified in the contemporary literature. In particular, we find the contention that HRM-based approaches are increasingly being adopted by employers and significantly impacting key aspects of enterprise level industrial relations, such as the argued decline in the importance of collective bargaining and the growth of non-union approaches (see, for example, Kochan et al., 1986; Mooney, 1989; Beaumont, 1995a).

9.4.1 THE NATURE OF HRM

Human resource management (HRM) refers to the development of a strategic corporate approach to workforce management (Beer et al., 1984; Armstrong, 1995; Guest, 1987). As Sparrow and Hiltrop (1994) specifically note, while HRM as a generic concept has been around for many years, it was the movement to more closely align workforce management and strategic decision making which essentially differentiated HRM from 'traditional' personnel management:

> In order to achieve this tighter link between 'people management' and business transformation, the need to integrate HRM considerations into strategic planning systems was also widely argued . . . . *It was this linkage of 'people management' issues and strategic planning processes that was seen to differentiate HRM from personnel management.* (Sparrow and Hiltrop, 1994:6) (Emphasis added)

In spite of this differentiation, there remains considerable confusion as to the distinctive characteristics of HRM, its applicability to organisations, and contrasts with 'traditional' personnel management. This section attempts to outline the key characteristics of HRM as the field has developed since the early 1980s. It points to the emergence of particular conceptions of HRM, which identify a greater strategic role for HRM and emphasise a closer alignment between business strategies and HRM policies and practice. We later consider the nature and diffusion of HRM in Ireland.

HRM has its academic roots in two, primarily distinct, sources of literature, both originating in the US. The first source emanates from the 'human resource' literature and is based on the *human capital approach* of the Harvard Business School model (Beer et al., 1984; 1985). This model is the basis for the 'soft' or benign approach to human resource management whereby senior management acknowledge that people are the organisation's 'most valuable' resource which management must nurture and develop to maximise its contribution to the organisation. The Harvard Business School model approach suggests that management adopt a coherent range of pro-employee ('soft') human resource policies to ensure the attraction, retention and development of committed, competent and high-performing employees.

The second literature source advocating increased strategic consideration of HR issues emanates from broader *business strategy literature,* specifically the work of Fombrun et al. (Fombrun, Tichy and Devanna, 1984), discussed earlier in this chapter. This approach suggests that organisational performance can be substantially improved by integrating HR and industrial relations considerations into strategic decision making to ensure that HR policies complement business strategy. In contrast to the Harvard model, this approach does not prescribe either a hard or soft approach to workforce management. Rather, it suggests that top management adopt the policies which best suit their particular circumstances and complement their business strategy. In spite of this, we often find that this literature base is most often linked to the adoption of what has come to be termed 'hard' HRM .

These contrasting models are summarised in Table 9.1. We consider the Harvard model in greater depth below.

Table 9.1   The nature of HRM

Human Resource Management	*Human Resource* **Management**
HR Strategy as:	HR Strategy as:
Series of policy choices	Fit to corporate/business strategy
Total HR/Management philosophy	Emphasis on alignment and coherence
General Management Perspective	Key to strategy implementation
Multiple stakeholders	
Evaluation through commitment, competence, congruence and cost effectiveness	
Primary emphasis on management philosophy not situational contingencies	*HR as strategic resource and source of competitive advantage*

Source: Adapted from Sparrow and Hiltrop, 1994:7

9.4.2 THE HARVARD MODEL

Possibly the most influential work on HRM has been the Harvard model (Beer et al., 1984). This model presents a broad causal map of the determinants and consequences of HRM policy choices as outlined in Figure 9.5. Beer et al. (1984: 1) describe HRM in generic terms as 'involving all management decisions and actions that affect the nature of the relationship between the organization and its employees — its human resources'. Thus, those in top management, and particularly the chief executive, are seen as having the primary responsibility for aligning business strategy and P/HR policy choice. Four key components comprise the Harvard model, namely (1) stakeholder interests; (2) HRM policy choice; (3) HRM outcomes and (4) long-term consequences.

Figure 9.5 Harvard model of human resource management

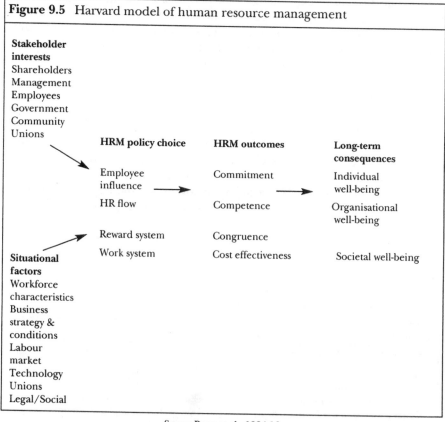

Source: Beer et al., 1984:16

A central contention of the Harvard model is that personnel and industrial relations outcomes are affected by the policy choices made in four key areas:
(1) the reward system (financial and non-financial);
(2) human resource flow (recruitment, selection, training, development, deployment, etc.);

(3) work system (job/work design, supervisory style, etc.) and

(4) employee influence (employee involvement in decision making).

Each of these policy areas is seen as a key element of strategic choice which profoundly impacts upon employee behaviour and attitude towards the organisation. Decisions made in these policy areas are seen as affecting personnel and industrial relations outcomes in the area of employee commitment, congruence of employee and management interests, employee competence, and cost effectiveness. These outcomes are also seen as having broader long-term consequences for individual employee well-being, organisational effectiveness and societal well-being.

9.4.3 REASONS FOR THE EMERGENCE OF HRM

Numerous reasons are given for the upsurge of interest in human resource management, many of which can be sourced to increased market competition since the early 1980s. One such factor is the quest for *competitive advantage* through improved quality and performance. The notion of competitive advantage was considered earlier. For an organisation to achieve competitive advantage it needs to orient and utilise its various resources towards the achievement of this goal. Beer et al. (1984) argue that human resources are often under-utilised within organisations by comparison with the attention paid to resource utilisation in the finance and technology areas. They also argue that by virtue of this under-utilisation, organisations which have a coherent strategy to utilise their human resources will often achieve advantage over competitors who do not optimally utilise their human resources. Similarly, if an organisation aims to compete largely on price, the extent to which employees contribute to cost control of raw materials, avoidance of wastage and so on, will again have a major bearing on their organisation's competitive position.

HRM has also been closely associated with the *excellence* literature of the 1980s (Peters and Waterman, 1982; Goldsmith and Clutterbuck, 1984; Kanter, 1984). This suggested that certain organisations demonstrate 'excellent' characteristics, notably in their corporate culture. It was argued that by identifying and copying these characteristics, organisations could improve performance via greater innovation, flexibility, and quality consciousness. The excellence literature gave particular prominence to the employment practices required to establish and sustain a strong organisation culture. An organisation's culture is the system of shared beliefs, norms and attitudes within an organisation regarding the legitimacy or otherwise of its objectives and the practices pursued in their achievement (Flood, 1989). When an organisation's members do not share a common set of beliefs or adhere to a common set of norms it is often described as a 'weak' culture, usually characterised by the presence of numerous sub-cultures which may often compete with each other.

Another reason proffered for the emergence of HRM is the suggestion that *more traditional approaches to workforce management have failed*. A common

349

criticism of traditional industrial relations practice in organisations is that it was essentially reactive in nature, overly bureaucratic and proceduralised and, increasingly, the responsibility of personnel specialists (see, for example, Fombrun et al., 1984; Beer et al., 1984; Guest, 1987). As a consequence, it was suggested that this traditional model had failed to promote a strategic awareness of human resource considerations at top management level. In the US context, Miles and Snow (1984) argued that the personnel and industrial relations area has lagged behind developments in management strategy and structure. In particular, they contended that traditional workforce management approaches were too 'technique oriented' with the emphasis on making incremental improvements in current practice rather than adopting a strategic role in evaluating policy options and subsequent implementation. In contrast HRM was seen as being based on a more generalist managerial perspective which placed a strong emphasis on devolving the practice of personnel and industrial relations to line management. This train of thought is captured by Michael Beer and his colleagues' comment, in their highly influential text *Managing Human Assets* (1984), that HR policy decisions are 'too important' to be left to personnel specialists and need to be incorporated into mainstream management activities, with strategic human resource decisions vested in top management (Beer et al., 1984).

Other reasons for the emergence of HRM include financial market preferences for *decentralised organisational structures* involving the devolution of greater autonomy to business unit management, *shifting employment patterns,* particularly the growth of so-called 'knowledge' workers, and *declining trade union power* encompassing a reduction in the significance of collective bargaining and the pluralist industrial relations model.

9.4.4 HRM IN EUROPE

On this side of the Atlantic, Guest's 'soft-hard, loose-tight' framework of HRM is possibly the most widely referenced and is outlined in Figure 9.6 (see, for example, Guest, 1987; 1989a and b). The 'soft-hard' dimension in Guest's framework refers to a continuum ranging from a resource-based ('soft') managerial perspective characterised by benign pro-employee policies to a more calculative ('hard') management perspective where personnel and industrial relations policy choice is driven by the need to complement business strategy and meet financial criteria. The 'loose-tight' dimension refers to a continuum ranging from HRM merely involving a retitling of traditional industrial relations/personnel management ('loose') with no real change in personnel practice, to HRM becoming a clearly defined and articulated approach to workforce management with an explicit and strong ('tight') theoretical underpinning.

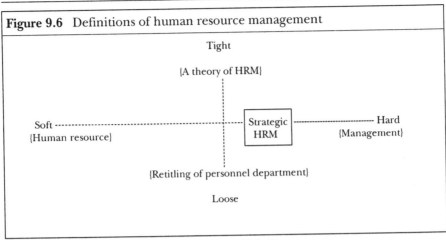

Figure 9.6 Definitions of human resource management

Tight

{A theory of HRM}

Soft -------------------------------- ------- | Strategic | ------------------------- Hard
{Human resource} | HRM | {Management}

{Retitling of personnel department}

Loose

Source: Guest, 1989:49

Guest proceeds to develop a theory of HRM which identifies four key HRM goals, namely: (1) strategic integration; (2) employee commitment; (3) flexibility and (4) quality. He suggests that these HRM goals can be optimally achieved through coherent HRM policy choices in the areas of organisation/ job design, management of change, recruitment, selection and socialisation, appraisal, training and development, rewards and communications. He identifies five conditions necessary for the effective operation of HRM:

(1) corporate leadership (to ensure the values inherent in HRM are championed and implemented);

(2) strategic vision (to ensure the integration of HRM as a key component of corporate strategy);

(3) technological/production feasibility (Guest suggests that if heavy investment has taken place in short cycle, repetitive production/assembly equipment, this mitigates against the job design principles and autonomous teamworking necessary for HRM);

(4) industrial relations feasibility (here Guest suggests that multi-unionism, low trust management-employee relations and an adversarial industrial relations climate mitigates against the implementation of HRM);

(5) ability of personnel specialists to implement appropriate HRM policies with the assistance of top and line management.

Guest's theory of HRM is outlined in Table 9.2

Table 9.2 A theory of human resource management

HRM policies	HR outcomes	Organisational outcomes
Organisation/job design		High job performance
Management of change	Strategic integration	High problem solving, change and innovation
Recruitment, selection and socialisation	Commitment	
Appraisal, training, development	Flexibility/adaptability	High cost effectiveness
Reward systems	Quality	Low turnover, absence, grievances
Communications		
	↑ **Leadership/Culture/Strategy** ↑	

Source: Guest, 1989a:49

An important contrast between the HRM debate in the US and that in Europe is the greater US focus on the need for organisations to tailor their HR policies to fit the business strategy. This emphasis on 'strategic fit' is a dominant theme in the US debate and contrasts with the European perspective which places much greater emphasis on the broader socio-economic context of organisations, in particular, the need to achieve a balance between business goals and broader social policy.

In the industrial relations area in particular, we find significant contrasts in the perspectives and approaches adopted between the US and Europe. In general, we find that approaches to issues such as collective bargaining and employee involvement are determined by different perspectives on the role of the nature of management and organisations in Europe and the US, and underpinned by different values held by the various 'actors' involved (see, for example, Sparrow and Hiltrop, 1994). Some of these differences are outlined in Table 9.3.

Table 9.3 Differences between HRM in Europe and the US

In the debate on HRM in Europe we tend to find:

- More restricted employer autonomy
- Less emphasis on market forces
- More collectivist, less individualist
- More emphasis on workers than managers
- Greater role for social partners
- Greater Government intervention in many areas of HRM
- Greater industrial relations and trade union influence

Source: Adapted from Sparrow and Hiltrop, 1994

9.5 HRM v Traditional Personnel Management

When HRM is contrasted with more traditional personnel management, as in Table 9.4, a number of key differences emerge. Firstly, it is argued that personnel/industrial relations considerations are fully integrated with strategic decision making in the HRM model, whereas in the traditional personnel management model the HR input is less pronounced and issue specific. A second contrast is that HRM is seen as essentially proactive and long term while traditional personnel management/industrial relations is more reactive and adopts a shorter term perspective. In terms of the desired mode of psychological contract, HRM is seen as facilitating greater employee commitment to the organisation, while personnel management is seen as a mode of managerial control over employees. A specific difference in the industrial relations sphere is that HRM is seen as essentially unitarist in perspective, involving no apparent conflict of interests between employers and employees. In contrast, traditional personnel management is grounded in the pluralist tradition and essentially concerned with the adversarial relationship between employers and workers. A related factor is that HRM is seen as focusing on the individual and relations between (line) management and the individual worker, while the traditional model is seen as operating primarily through collectivist relations between management and employee representatives. Another area of contrast is that HRM is seen as operating most effectively in organic, fluid organisation structures, while traditional personnel management is felt to characterise more bureaucratic and rigid organisational forms. As we have seen, HRM is seen to operate primarily through line management while in the traditional model primary responsibility for workforce management is vested in the specialist personnel function. The final difference relates to the criterion utilised to evaluate effectiveness. HRM is seen as being essentially focused on the maximum utilisation of human resources through policies which seek to release individual potential and to ensure the optimal contribution to organisational effectiveness. In contrast, personnel management is seen as having somewhat more pragmatic objectives, namely the maximisation of cost effectiveness.

Despite these perceived contrasts between HRM and personnel management, Guest (1987; 1989a and b) cautions that this does not necessarily infer that HRM is better than traditional personnel management and should be adopted by organisations in general (as might be inferred from some of the 'excellence' literature). Rather, he suggests that traditional approaches may be more appropriate in certain organisational contexts, such as large bureaucratic or heavily unionised organisations, while HRM may be appropriate in organisations with more organic structures and characterised by more individualist high trust management-employee relations.

Table 9.4   Personnel management and human resource management compared

	PERSONNEL MANAGEMENT	HRM
Input into Corporate Planning	Issue Specific	Integrated
Time & Planning Perspective	Short-Term; Reactive; Marginal	Long Term; Proactive, Strategic
Psychological Contract	Compliance	Commitment
Industrial Relations	Pluralist; Collective Low trust; Adversarial	Unitarist; Individual; High-trust
Organisation Structures/	Bureaucratic; Mechanistic;	Organic; Fluid;
Systems	Centralised; Formal defined roles	Devolved; Flexible roles
Principal Delivery Mechanism	Specialist personnel management function	Line management
Aims	Maximise cost effectiveness	Maximise HR utilisation

Source: Adapted from Guest, 1987

9.5.1 CONTRADICTIONS AND INCONSISTENCIES IN HRM

Several authors have identified a number of inherent contradictions and inconsistencies in HRM, particularly the 'soft' variant advocated by the Harvard model (Legge, 1989; Keenoy, 1990; Blyton and Turnbull, 1992; Cradden, 1992). For example, Legge (1989) highlights the apparent paradox between the traditional commodity status of labour under capitalism and the essentially unitarist perspective of HRM which sees no inherent conflict of interests between management and employees. It has generally been accepted that under the capitalist system there is an inherent conflict of interest between management and employees over the price of labour. Indeed this conflict of interest is the very basis for the existence of industrial relations as a key concern of workers and management. However, the HRM perspective appears to ignore the 'inherency' of a conflict of interests but rather focuses on the achievement of congruence of management and employee interests, and on developing high levels of employee commitment to the organisation and its business goals. For example, Flood (1989) argues that HRM-based approaches require that organisations focus on satisfying both the extrinsic and intrinsic needs of employees and, in so doing, develop high levels of employee commitment. Similarly, Walton (1985) encourages firms to adopt

354

HR policies which emphasise the mutuality of employer and employee interests so as to increase employee commitment to organisational goals.

This focus on increasing employee commitment not only seems incongruent with a pluralist perspective of the organisation but also appears to conflict with another basic tenet of HRM, namely that HR policies should complement ('fit') business strategy. Clearly many decisions which complement business strategy may not serve to increase employee commitment. Consider, for example, the instance of an organisation where the key business objective is to maximise short-term return on investment. Clearly, such a business strategy may well entail decisions which do not enhance employee commitment, such as replacing labour with technology, increasing the pace of work, contracting out certain tasks and/or making employees redundant. A related issue on this theme is the suggestion that HRM involves the simultaneous achievement of high levels of individualism and teamwork. These twin goals clearly have tremendous potential for conflict. For example, the utilisation of performance-related pay systems tied to measures of individual employee performance may indeed prohibit teamwork, by encouraging workers to perform in their own self-interest rather than for the overall good of the group or team (Gunnigle, Turner and D'Art, 1998 BJIR). This issue is further considered later in discussing the relative management emphasis on individualist and collectivist approaches to industrial relations.

High levels of organisational flexibility are seen as a core objective of HRM. Guest (1987; 1989a) suggests that increased flexibility involves the creation of structural mechanisms in organisations to ensure responsiveness to changing environmental conditions. Guest suggests that such flexibility should encompass both functional (task) and numerical (head-count) flexibility. However, several authors have noted the difficulties in achieving congruence in different flexibility forms, viz. numerical, functional and financial flexibility. It is clearly difficult to achieve high levels of functional flexibility (e.g., multi-skilling) where employees have a tenuous relationship with the organisation, as may result from attempts to improve numerical flexibility, such as through temporary or part-time working (Blyton and Morris, 1992; Gunnigle, 1992a). The issue of flexibility is considered later in this book.

A related contradiction in the HRM argument touches on job security. A prominent theme in the literature is that for HRM to be effective, employers must provide job tenure guarantees for employees (Beer et al., 1984; Guest, 1987, 1989b; Walton, 1985). For example, it is often argued that job tenure commitments are a necessary precondition for developing the key HRM goal of a 'mutuality' of management and employee interests (Beer et al., 1984; Walton, 1985; Guest, 1989b). However, it is patently evident that high levels of competition and volatility in product markets have made job security increasingly more difficult to achieve. Indeed, job security may itself be incompatible with broader business goals attributed to HRM, such as increased numerical flexibility in responding to rapid changes in demand. In practice, it seems that many organisations seek to enhance organisational flexibility by policies which actually reduce job tenure commitments — for example, by using subcontracting, part-time and temporary working. In evaluating the practicality of job tenure commitments as a core element of HRM, Blyton and Turnbull (1992:10) comment as follows:

> This [job security] is particularly problematic in highly competitive or recessionary conditions where the 'needs of the business' are likely to undermine any internal 'fit' with ('soft') HRM values : shedding labour for example will severely challenge, if not destroy, an organisation's HRM image of caring for the needs and security of its employees.

Another apparent inconsistency in HRM is the focus on achieving greater individualism in management-employee relations. As we have seen, industrial relations in the Republic of Ireland have traditionally been characterised by reliance on collectivism, as manifested in high levels of trade union density, widespread use of collective bargaining and low trust management-employee relations (Whelan, 1982; Roche, 1990). The 'soft' HRM approach, as represented in the Harvard model and also in Guest's (1987; 1989a) inter-pretation, places the managerial focus on developing high trust relations between management and employees. Little or no emphasis is placed on the role of the representative groups such as trade unions or employer organisations. Indeed, the HRM literature seems to reflect a clear preference for non-union approaches. Within the 'soft' HRM model, high trust relations are pursued via managerial initiatives to increase individual employee commitment and involvement through the adoption of specific HR practices such as task participation, performance appraisal and performance-related pay. Thus, HRM appears to reflect a managerial desire to develop closer management-employee ties and to break down the traditional 'them and us' management-worker dichotomy, of which collective bargaining is seen as the principal manifestation. As Guest (1989b:43) comments:

> HRM values are unitarist to the extent that they assume no underlying and inevitable differences of interest between management and workers . . . . HRM values are essentially individualistic in that they emphasize the individual-organization linkage in preference to operating through group and representative systems. . . . These values underpinning HRM leave little scope for collective arrangements and assume little need for collective bargaining. HRM therefore poses a considerable challenge to traditional industrial relations and more particularly to trade unionism.

Such an approach clearly reflects a singularly unitarist management perspective which has considerable potential for conflict with the pluralist 'collectivist' perspective, traditionally seen as characteristic of enterprise level industrial relations practice in Ireland.

9.6 HRM AND INDUSTRIAL RELATIONS IN IRELAND

We earlier noted that industrial relations practice in Ireland has traditionally been associated with a strong pluralist orientation. As such, management approaches to industrial relations were seen as essentially reactive, dealing with various problematic aspects of workforce management (see, for example, Shivanath, 1987). This emphasis is generally linked to a historical preference for a collectivist approach to management-industrial relations involving collective bargaining with trade unions (Roche, 1990). We have also noted that, since the early 1980s, industrial relations at enterprise level appears to have undergone some considerable change. In particular, we have seen an increasing focus on the utilisation of HRM approaches by foreign-owned, non-union organisations in the high technology sector. Many of these firms are subsidiaries of US organisations which espouse a particular philosophy of workforce management emphasising employee commitment and loyalty, and high levels of quality and performance.

In this section we consider how HRM might potentially impact on industrial relations. Specifically, we consider the potential interaction between HRM and collective bargaining, with particular emphasis on the effects on trade unions. We firstly consider available evidence on the impact of HRM-based approaches on trade unions. We then consider more general evidence on the impact of HRM on industrial relations.

9.7 TRADE UNIONS AND HRM

In a review of US literature, Beaumont (1992) found that the chief, or at least most frequently cited, components of HRM were: a relatively well developed internal labour market (in matters of promotion and employee development); flexible work organisations; contingent (performance-related) compensation practices; individual and group participation in task-related decisions and extensive internal communications arrangements. We have earlier seen that HRM, specifically the 'soft' variant represented by the Harvard model, is aimed at increasing the identification and commitment of the employee to the organisation. As such HRM is frequently seen as being incompatible with the collectivist ethos of trade union recognition and collective bargaining (Beer et al., 1984; Guest, 1987; 1989a and b). For example, Fiorito et al. (1987) argue that HRM practices are often part of attempts by employers to either substitute for, or avoid, trade unions. Using a comprehensive index of twelve measures of HRM practices, Fiorito et al. (1987) concluded that such practices do inhibit unionisation but that the impact of specific policies varies considerably, with those in the area of communications and participation having the greatest adverse impact on union organising success. However, Milner and Richards (1991) found a significant positive association between companies which recognised unions and the greater use of employee involvement techniques such as quality circles, joint consultative committees, suggestion schemes and a regular newsletter. They suggest that recognising a union can facilitate the introduction of employee involvement by providing a ready-made organisational structure and, more importantly, an authority structure among employees which can be utilised to increase the chances of employee involvement techniques succeeding. Thus, we find a significant contrast in perspectives on the impact of HRM on trade unions. On the one hand, it is widely argued that HRM mitigates union penetration in organisations (Fiorito et al., 1987), while, on the other hand, it is said that unionisation can be both compatible with, and supportive of, trade unions (Storey, 1989; Milner and Richards, 1991).

9.7.1 UNION SUBSTITUTION AND UNION SUPPRESSION

In evaluating the specific implications for industrial relations, it appears that the adoption of HRM approaches presents an explicit challenge to collective bargaining, and specifically trade unions (Guest, 1987; Storey, 1989, 1992). The essence of such challenge is the potentially reduced emphasis on collective bargaining and management-trade union interactions. Indeed, an area of major importance in evaluating the impact of HRM and industrial relations is the issue of trade union recognition. The term 'union substitution' seems to have achieved widespread notoriety as a result of its association with non-union greenfield sites in the US. Probably the most widely known exemplar in this regard was the Topeka plant in Kansas, as described by Walton (1982). This plant was seen to have two particular distinguishing characteristics: it was established on a non-union basis, and located outside a traditional urban/industrial centre. Beaumont and Townley (1985) suggest that work practices in this and similar greenfield companies, such as fewer job grades, greater task flexibility, teamworking arrangements and extensive communications and grievance handling systems, restrict the recruitment opportunities of trade unions and constitute a 'union-substitution effect', producing a strong employee-organisation identification process that limits the development of job dissatisfaction, widely seen as precursor to unionisation (see Beaumont and Townley, 1985; Foulkes, 1980; Kochan et al., 1986).

Here in Ireland, the past two decades have witnessed significant growth in non-union approaches, particularly among US-owned firms (McGovern, 1989a; Gunnigle, 1995a and b). It is likely that at least some of these firms adopt a 'union substitution' strategy, involving the adoption of HRM policies designed to eliminate employee needs for collective representation by, for example, extensive line management training in industrial relations, prompt handling of employee grievances, good terms and conditions of employment, and a facilitative supervisory style (Foulkes, 1980; Kochan et al., 1986;

Beaumont and Harris, 1994; Guest and Hoque, 1994a). As such, a union substitution strategy is characterised by a high level of HR policy co-ordination and sophistication. Union substitution is seen as significantly different to what has been termed 'union suppression'. This latter approach is characterised by outright opposition to union recognition using tactics based on fear and coercion, such as dismissals, related sanctions, and threats to close the firm and transfer operations elsewhere. Thus, union substitution is primarily associated with sophisticated HR policies and high employment standards while union suppression is associated with low employment standards and little HR policy sophistication.

Flood and Toner (1997) suggest that a union substitution strategy is based on removing so-called 'triggers' to unionisation through a combination of 'soft' HRM practices. Commentators have identified a range of reasons why workers join trade unions, some of which are based on pragmatic considerations, such as dissatisfaction with the work environment or a critical incident (e.g., dismissal), others may be more ideological in nature, such as a deeply held belief in collective representation and solidarity, while still others may relate to issues such as peer pressure (see, for example, Flood and Toner, 1996). Brett (1980) identifies two broad reasons why workers join trade unions:
(1) dissatisfaction with working conditions but feeling powerless to change these conditions;
(2) belief in the concept of collective action *and* the ability of trade unions to provide positive rather than negative outcomes for workers.

Freeman and Medoff (1984) point to the benefits of union membership in providing an effective 'voice' for employees which, in turn, can contribute to improved worker morale and motivation, reduced rivalry between employees, and a greater sense of equity through the establishment of effective procedures for handling issues such as grievances and discipline. Clearly, such developments can also be beneficial from an employer perspective. To successfully effect a union substitution strategy, employers must effectively ensure that most of these benefits, associated with union recognition, still accrue in the non-union environment. Toner's work (1987) on non-union companies in Ireland identifies a range of HR practices which may be used to effect a union substitution strategy and develop shared interests between workers and management. These include lifelong employment, single status, merit pay, regular communications, gain-sharing, internal promotion and continuous development of employees. In a similar vein, Roche and Turner (1998) suggest that large non-union companies with sophisticated HRM policies can effectively substitute for union voice by providing particular HR processes. Such processes include substantial information exchange on issues such as company strategy and performance; high levels of expenditure on training and development; pay and employment conditions which are above the industry/sectoral norm and job tenure commitments. They also noted that the utilisation of in-house employee representative structures, such as staff associations or works committees/councils, can form an important part of a union substitution strategy. These mechanisms may often be used to create a semi-independent voice mechanism for employees and also to block any moves towards union recognition. However, we have little research data on the nature and operation of in-company representative fora.

From an employer perspective, a key issue informing the approach to the issue of union recognition is the advantages and disadvantages, both substantial and perceived, of union recognition. In this regard, much of the international literature has focused on the impact of unionisation on firm performance and specifically on issues such as profit levels, labour productivity and return on investment (see, for example, Freeman and Medoff, 1984; Belman, 1992; Huselid, 1995). In evaluating this literature, Roche and Turner (1998) find the results on the impact of unionisation on productivity inconclusive but argue that the evidence from the manufacturing sector, particularly in the US, indicates that unionisation serves to reduce firm profitability. Thus, it is argued that non-union firms have a sound economic rationale for pursuing a union substitution strategy. However, there are also potential costs with such a strategy. In the Irish context, Flood and Toner's (1997) analysis identified a number of disadvantages associated with union and non-union approaches. These findings are based on Toner's earlier study of industrial relations in union and non-union firms, specifically in soliciting the views of supervisors on the issue of unionisation (Toner, 1987) and summarised in Table 9.5.

Table 9.5 Disadvantages of union substitution and union recognition strategies

Disadvantages of union substitution	Disadvantages of union recognition
• Need to provide pay and employment conditions at least on a par with those in similar unionised companies	• Unions make changes in work organisation more difficult
• Management is reluctant to enforce discipline	• Unions give rise to demarcation problems and impose restrictions on production
• Absence of adequate structure to deal with grievances (particularly collective issues)	• Unions impose higher manning levels
• Fear of unionisation is a constant concern	• Unions protect unsatisfactory workers
• The supervisors are monitored too closely	• Unions inhibit individual reward systems
• Management in non-union firms must work harder at communications	• Unions promote adversarial industrial relations climate and can cause industrial action
• Need for expensive, well-resourced personnel function	• Unions encourage the pursuit of trivial grievances
	• Unions make communication with employees more difficult

Source: Flood and Toner, 1997

The disadvantages associated with union substitution are categorised by Flood and Toner (1997) as a 'catch-22' situation, whereby firms pursuing a union substitution strategy cannot take advantage of their non-union status, by, for example, reducing pay and employment conditions or disciplining/dismissing unsatisfactory workers, due to the fear that such action will lead to union recognition. This leads the authors to conclude that the major advantages of union substitution lie not in clear economic 'cost-benefit' criteria but rather in allowing the firm greater scope to develop a unitary company culture and to foster 'warm personal relations' between management and employees (Flood and Toner, 1997:270; Toner, 1987; Roche and Turner, 1998). While we do not have sufficient empirical evidence to substantiate this argument, there is conclusive evidence of a substantial growth in popularity in non-union approaches, particularly among firms which have established new facilities in Ireland since the early 1980s.

9.7.2 PATTERNS OF HRM-INDUSTRIAL RELATIONS INTERACTION

There is little empirical investigation of the impact of HRM practices on industrial relations and trade unions in Ireland. However, research by Turner (1993) and Roche and Turner (1998) provides some interesting insights. Turner's (1993) analysis considered the diffusion of HRM practices in Ireland and their impact on union penetration. Turner's analysis concluded that HRM practices did not significantly influence union density. He also found few significant differences between union and non-union firms in the use of HRM practices.

While information on the application of particular HRM policies and the impact on union penetration provides useful insights on the diffusion of HRM in Ireland, it is possibly more interesting to consider evidence on the emergence of particular HRM-industrial relations patterns. Of particular benefit in this regard is the categorisation of HRM-industrial relations effects developed by Roche and Turner (1998) who outline three ways through which HRM policies impact on trade unions and collective bargaining, namely:
(1) the adoption of HRM as a union substitution strategy;
(2) the unco-ordinated adoption of HRM policies in parallel with 'adversarial' industrial relations;
(3) the adoption of HRM policies as part of a 'partnership' strategy.
These three modes of HR-industrial relations interaction are discussed below.

(1) UNION SUBSTITUTION

Roche and Turner (1998) argue that a union substitution strategy is most likely to emerge in larger firms which operate in the more profitable sectors of the economy. In such instances, firms have the financial wherewithal to provide the levels of pay, employment conditions and general working environment necessary to underpin such a strategy. This is in line with our earlier discussion on the impact of product market context, where Marchington (1990) argued that firms with high monopoly power had greater scope to choose from a wide range of human resource and industrial relations policy options. In contrast, a union suppression strategy is seen as most likely to emerge where there is little threat of unionisation (as might be the case in sectors characterised by high levels of competition); where most firms are quite small; where work is predominantly low skilled; and where there is an unfavourable legal framework for trade unions (Roche and Turner, 1998).

In reviewing the empirical evidence on union penetration, we noted earlier that aggregate levels of union membership and recognition in Ireland are quite high, but also that there is a significant trend of union avoidance in new 'greenfield firms'. However, union de-recognition, has not emerged to any great extent in Ireland although it has become an issue of some significance in the UK. Finally, it is important to note that what is often termed 'union marginalisation', that is reducing the impact of trade unions in enterprise level industrial relations, has indeed emerged as an important, if under-researched, development in Irish industrial relations. Roche and Turner (1998) suggest that union substitution strategy can form part of either a union avoidance or a union marginalisation approach.

As numerous commentators have noted, a union substitution strategy is most commonly associated with large multinational subsidiaries whose industrial relations approaches are generally characterised by good pay and conditions, influential and well-resourced P/HR departments and utilisation of a comprehensive range of sophisticated P/HR policies which are designed to enhance employee satisfaction and commitment and remove any desire or moves by workers to join trade unions (Foulkes, 1980; Kochan et al., 1986; Roche and Turner, 1998). Household names in this regard include Intel, Hewlett Packard, IBM, and Motorola. As we have noted above, there is considerable evidence to suggest that such firms have been successful, both in avoiding unionisation and in meeting employee needs for voice and equity at work (Toner, 1987; Flood and Toner, 1996, 1997). However, there is some need for caution in this regard as there is a tendency to generalise on practice in non-union firms on the basis of a small number of exemplar companies. Gunnigle's (1995a and b) study of greenfield companies found that the bulk of non-union firms did not utilise what could be termed as comprehensive or sophisticated HRM policies. Rather, it appeared that union avoidance was achieved through 'harder' HR practices such as outsourcing, subcontracted labour and other forms of atypical employment (Gunnigle, Morley and Turner, 1997). This finding is in line with UK evidence which suggested that commonly used exemplar firms, such as Marks and Spencer, Motorola and IBM, are the exception rather than the rule, and that the majority of non-union firms 'do not *need,* nor could they the majority *afford,* to adopt a substitution strategy' (Blyton and Turnbull, 1994:252; also see Roche and Turner, 1998). These issues are further considered in chapter 10.

(2) THE UNCO-ORDINATED ADOPTION OF HRM POLICIES IN PARALLEL WITH ADVERSARIAL INDUSTRIAL RELATIONS

This second mode of HRM-industrial relations interaction identified by Roche and Turner (1998) refers to the adoption of HRM policies in an ad hoc and unsystematic fashion within a tradition of adversarial relations between management and unions. As many commentators have noted, the empirical evidence on the adoption of HRM suggests that it is most commonly adopted in this fashion (see, for example, Gunnigle et al., 1994). Ireland is no exception in this regard:

> Much the most common practice in Irish companies to date, the evidence suggests, has been for managements to adopt HRM policies in an essentially piecemeal or fragmented manner, without any attempt to use these policies to promote union substitution, co-ordinate these policies with collective bargaining or to involve unions in their uptake or implementation. Unions, for their part, at local or plant level appear often to have been predisposed to watch management innovations from the wings, adopting an unenthusiastic, vigilant or defensive posture. (Roche and Turner, 1998:76–7)

To support this contention, Roche and Turner (1998:78) point to a number of studies which indicate that Irish firms have tended to adopt HRM policies 'selectively and opportunistically', with little perceptible 'concern with the overall coherence of those policies' (also see Gunnigle et al., 1994; Roche and Turner, 1994, 1997). They conclude that is unusual to find firms which have adopted consistent sets of HRM policies 'across the spectrum of HRM policy innovations' but, rather the more widespread pattern was the utilisation of selected HRM policies in one or a limited number of HR areas. They further argue that the uptake of HRM policy innovations was lowest in areas traditionally regulated through collective bargaining, particularly issues such as payment systems and pay increases. Rather, HRM approaches were more commonly adopted in areas such as communications and recruitment/ deployment. In attempting to explain such variation in the uptake of HRM policies, Roche and Turner (1998:79–80) identify constraints emanating from Ireland's industrial relations and collective bargaining traditions:

> Managements show greatest conservatism in adopting HRM innovations in the areas of pay and work organisation as these in practice tend to be most heavily regulated by trade unions. A significant change in these areas is likely to run into strong union resistance, or to require the active co-operation of trade unions. In contrast, unions are likely to be least resistant to management innovations in areas like communications, provided that they are not seen to threaten collective bargaining. In such areas management may enjoy scope to press ahead without

engaging unions in their new policies. The same broadly holds for innovations in 'flow' policies. Unions have not traditionally tended to negotiate over such areas as selection policies and techniques, other than perhaps by seeking to defend established recruitment channels. Nor have they attempted to negotiate over performance appraisal systems, other than possibly by trying to regulate the use to which appraisal records are put.

In evaluating these findings, Roche and Turner conclude that the Irish evidence of fairly widespread but gradual change in the uptake of HRM approaches is similar to evidence on prevailing patterns of change in Europe and the US. They also note that such changes are most often implemented without trade unions being accorded a central role (see, for example, Roche and Kochan, 1996). It thus appears that trade unions have not generally played a prominent role in the diffusion of HRM. As such, Roche and Turner suggest that union attitudes to HRM reflect high levels of mistrust and the adoption of 'traditional adversarial' postures. This reaction most probably reflects union fears that HRM approaches constitute a management driven agenda for significant organisational change and present a major threat to the role and influence of trade unions within the enterprise (see, for example, Gunnigle, 1998a).

As we have seen earlier in this chapter, an important tenet of HRM is that its impact on performance is contingent on 'coherency' and 'fit': the extent to which HRM innovations positively impact on performance depends on the degree to which a coherent and complementary set of HRM policies are implemented across the full range of HR policy choice areas ('coherency'), and also the degree to which such policies complement business strategy ('fit') (Fombrun et al., 1984; Beer et al., 1984). A second important tenet, identified by Roche and Turner (1998:83-4) is the argument that HRM policies should complement and 'build new and more co-operative relations with (trade) unions' (also see Kochan et al., 1986; Kochan and Osterman, 1994). Roche and Turner point to empirical evidence from the US and UK to support both these propositions (see, for example, Huselid, 1995; Guest and Hoque, 1996; Ichniowski, et al., 1996). However, one must interpret these findings on strong causal linkages between particular sets of HR policies and improvements in organisational performance with considerable caution. Clearly, many and complex factors impact on the effectiveness or otherwise of P/HR policies and also on measures of company performance, such as profitability or return on investment. While there certainly is some strong evidence that comprehensive sets of HR policies which complement business strategy can positively impact on company performance, it is also likely that smaller scale HRM innovations which do not necessarily fit with, for example, established industrial relations traditions, can also have a positive impact on company performance. As Roche and Turner (1998:86) note:

Cases can be found of high performance companies which emphasise direct staff involvement in HRM-type initiatives and policies, but choose to maintain traditional arms-length adversarial relations with unions. The viability of such an approach, and in particular the degree to which it impairs the effectiveness of HRM initiatives, is likely to be moderated by a number of factors. Among the most important of these will be the level of union organisation at workplace level, the level of attachment of employees to unions and the degree of influence unions have exercised over areas of employment central to HRM policies and innovations. The higher the level of union organisation, the greater the level of employees' attachment to unions and the more influence or control unions have gained over areas of employment which HRM policies and innovations seek to address, the greater the likelihood that such policies and innovations will be at best ineffective if they are not co-ordinated with collective bargaining.

(3) The adoption of HRM policies as part of a strategy of promoting 'partnership'
This third mode of HRM-industrial relations interaction identified by Roche and Turner (1998) refers to the attempts by management and trade unions to actively co-operate in the implementation of HRM and related change initiatives. Generally captured under the rubric of 'partnership'-based industrial relations arrangements, these normally involve joint management-trade union initiatives designed to substantially change aspects of work organisation and as such inevitably involve the utilisation of HRM policies.

The nature and diffusion of partnership-based industrial relations arrangements at enterprise level was discussed in depth in the previous chapter. Of particular significance for a management and trade union perspective is the relationship between HRM initiatives and established collective bargaining arrangements. As we have seen, the adoption of partnership-based approaches requires considerable change in the role and postures of both employers and trade unions.

From an employer perspective a key concern appears to be the extent to which partnership allows the organisation to substantially change aspects of work organisation, such as work practices, manning levels and use of atypical employment forms. Such changes are often accompanied by the introduction of particular HRM policies, particularly performance management and performance appraisal, performance-related pay, and more extensive and direct communications with employees. For trade unions, a critical concern is the extent to which they are given a more extensive and meaningful role in influencing key decisions on the nature of workplace change and reorganisation. As such, they will be concerned that HRM policies are effectively co-ordinated with established collective bargaining and collective representation mechanisms and do not serve to undermine or diminish the role of trade unions and collective bargaining in the enterprise (Roche and Turner, 1998).

9.8 SUMMARY AND CONCLUSIONS

This chapter has considered recent developments in enterprise level industrial relations. It has placed particular emphasis on the management's role and reviewed some of the principal reasons why employers appear to have taken a proactive role in initiating change in enterprise level industrial relations. We have reviewed the emergence of a greater strategic perspective on the linkages between business strategy and human resource management. Specifically, we have focused on the industrial relations implications, particularly the linkages between business strategy and industrial relations, the nature and development of HRM and the issue of HRM-industrial relations interaction.

In the Irish context there has been limited investigation of the linkages between business strategy, product market conditions and developments in industrial relations. In evaluating current developments in industrial relations in Ireland, there is a danger in confusing prominent examples of 'soft' HRM with the widespread pervasiveness of such approaches. In the UK context Blyton and Turnbull (1992) note that empirically it is difficult to find examples of organisations that adopt coherent HRM approaches and that when firms attempt to implement HRM they run up against some key inherent contradictions and inconsistencies between the theory and practice of HRM, reviewed in this chapter. This analysis points to the significance of contextual factors in interpreting the diffusion and evaluating its impact on industrial relations. We have seen that much of the evidence and support for HRM approaches emanates from the US. However, the context of such developments in the US is considerably different from that in Ireland and it is inappropriate to simply extrapolate from the US experience and infer similar trends here. Differences in industrial and employment structure and trade union density are some of the unique factors influencing organisational approaches to industrial relations in Ireland.

Nevertheless, our review of available research points to a significant diffusion of HRM in Irish organisations and also to the fact that it is having a considerable impact on industrial relations practice. The latter section of this chapter points to the different emergent patterns or typologies of HRM-industrial relations interactions. This analysis illustrates the range of management approaches or styles which employers may seek to adopt in their approach to enterprise level industrial relations. It is to this issue of management styles in industrial relations that we turn in the next chapter. This analysis also considers the nature and diffusion of HRM in greater depth.

NOTE

1. This discussion of business strategy and industrial relations draws heavily on material in Gunnigle, P., Morley, M. and Heraty, N., 1997. *Personnel and Human Resource Management: Theory and Practice in Ireland.* Dublin: Gill & Macmillan.

CHAPTER TEN

Managing Industrial Relations II: The Significance of Management Styles in Industrial Relations

10.1 INTRODUCTION

The previous chapter has highlighted the marked increase in emphasis on developing linkages between business strategy, personnel/human resource (P/HR) management and industrial relations. A critical aspect of this debate is the contention that greater strategic significance is being accorded to P/HR and industrial relations considerations, manifest in managerial initiatives to develop particular industrial approaches or styles at enterprise level. Such approaches or styles can of course vary, on dimensions such as the absence or presence of trade unions, the application or otherwise of particular human resource management techniques and the impact of industrial relations considerations on strategic decision making. Despite this persuasive debate, there remains considerable confusion, and indeed doubt, about the degree to which managements consider P/HR and industrial relations issues in strategic decision making and choose complementary strategies and policies. Beyond some prominent examples of strategic approaches to workforce management, there remains a reservation that the great majority of organisations do not exercise any degree of strategic choice in P/HR or industrial relations management and consequently their approach may be variously characterised as reactive, opportunist or, to use the old cliché, 'fire-fighting'.

This chapter considers the issue of management styles in industrial relations in the context of changing patterns of industrial relations. It examines the nature of management styles in industrial relations, the possible determinants of style, the dimensions along which management styles in industrial relations may differ and the alternative styles that may be adopted in organisations. It also considers recent Irish and international research evidence in this field. Building upon the preceding chapter, this analysis seeks to shed further light on the diffusion of HRM-based approaches among Irish organisations.

10.2 MANAGEMENT STYLES IN INDUSTRIAL RELATIONS

In industrial relations the concept of management style has been principally used to categorise and explain management's overall approach to industrial relations (Fox, 1966, 1974; Purcell and Sisson, 1983; Poole, 1986; Purcell, 1987; Marchington and Parker, 1990). In this vein, Rollinson (1993:92) describes management style in industrial relations as referring to 'management's overall approach to handling the relationship between the organization and its employees'. Thus, we can conceive of management styles in industrial relations as incorporating the distinctive approaches, policies and practices which management adopt in their approach to industrial relations with the enterprise (see Figure 10.1 below). As such, management style in industrial relations is a dynamic concept which may be refined and changed over time in the light of changing needs and circumstances. The influence and mediating effect of environmental variables on industrial relations styles is considered later in this chapter.

10.2.1 STRATEGIC CHOICE AND MANAGEMENT STYLES IN INDUSTRIAL RELATIONS

In a previous chapter we considered how employers may choose to organise into representative employer associations for industrial relations purposes. While employer associations clearly play an important role in industrial relations, individual employers are primarily responsible for the development and implementation of industrial relations policies and practices within their particular enterprise. Consequently, employer and management approaches to industrial relations are a critical determinant of the nature of enterprise level industrial relations.

In our review of employer objectives in industrial relations in chapter 5 we noted that economic criteria, such as profitability and return on investment, are the major yardsticks for evaluating corporate performance. We have also noted that management objectives are primarily identified with owner interests. Since control is associated with ownership, the power to exercise control over work is exercised by the owners of an enterprise through their representatives in the workplace, namely the management team. This link between ownership and the legitimacy of management authority is a critical characteristic of organisational life, despite the fact that management must also be responsible to other interest groups, such as employees and their trade unions. Consequently, management (and particularly senior management) exercise considerable power and influence by virtue of their scope to take strategic decisions.

Purcell (1987) notes the tendency to identify and contrast organisations according to their employment policies and practices and suggests that differences which arise cannot be wholly explained by structural variables such as size, product markets and technology. Rather, Purcell identifies strategic choice (exercised by senior management) as a key factor explaining differences in management styles in industrial relations. Strategic choice in industrial relations addresses the degree to which management (1) possess and (2) exercise, strategic choice in developing industrial relations policies and practices. The notion of strategic choice infers that senior management possess some room for manoeuvre and, while environmental factors may constrain the range of choice, they retain considerable power in making decisions on 'appropriate' styles and policies.

Employer approaches to workforce management are often seen as operating between two extreme positions: one emphasising managerial control, the other allowing greater employee control and autonomy. Friedman (1977) highlights these contrasting positions in identifying two major types of workforce management strategy: (1) responsible autonomy and (2) direct control. Responsible autonomy involves giving employees status and authority and allowing them scope to undertake challenging work which benefits both themselves and the organisation. Direct control seeks to reduce employee power and authority via coercive supervisory approaches and minimising employee discretion. The particular approach adopted will depend substantially on the decision and preferences of senior management, although other factors will influence managerial choice such as product and labour market conditions.

Senior management can therefore use their resources and power to make strategic choices which both influence environmental factors and affect particular management styles in industrial relations. Management styles in industrial relations should therefore be evaluated in terms of the interplay between environmental factors, managerial ideology/values and strategic choice. As Marchington and Parker (1990:99) state:

> Choice should be viewed as both a cause and a consequence of environmental influences . . . that is, managements have some influence over the kind of markets in which they choose to operate, and in some cases over the structure of the market itself, as well as having some choice over the way in which they respond to environmental pressures.

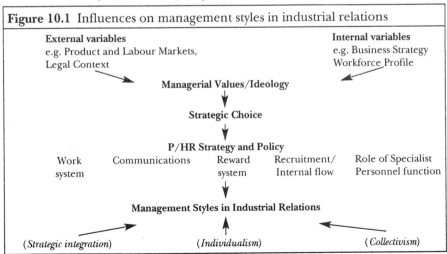

Figure 10.1 Influences on management styles in industrial relations

External variables
e.g. Product and Labour Markets, Legal Context

Internal variables
e.g. Business Strategy Workforce Profile

Managerial Values/Ideology

Strategic Choice

P/HR Strategy and Policy

Work system   Communications   Reward system   Recruitment/ Internal flow   Role of Specialist Personnel function

Management Styles in Industrial Relations

(*Strategic integration*)   (*Individualism*)   (*Collectivism*)

Often the impact of strategic decisions on industrial relations will be indirect. For example, an organisation may decide to terminate a particular product line because of financial and market considerations. However, this decision may mean redundancies and detrimentally affect morale and ultimately industrial relations. Management may also take strategic decisions which directly influence industrial relations, such as a decision on whether or not to deal with trade unions.

As noted earlier, the question of whether senior managements actually do take strategic industrial relations decisions remains a matter for debate. A traditional view has been that senior management concentrate their strategic decision making on 'primary' business areas, such as investment or production, and any attention devoted to industrial relations is secondary and somewhat incidental to the main thrust of such strategic decision making (Purcell, 1987). However, there is evidence to suggest that some organisations adopt a particular industrial relations style or approach and take well thought out strategic decisions to establish and sustain this style (Beer et al., 1984; Kochan et al., 1986; Guest, 1987). Indeed, practice would seem to vary widely from a general approach of 'incidentalism', characterised by little or no strategic decision making in industrial relations, to a more planned approach involving a series of key strategic decisions taken to effect a particular desired management style in industrial relations. This variation is illustrated in Figure 10.2 as a continuum along which employers may adopt a variety of positions ranging from 'incidentalist' to 'planned' approaches to industrial relations management.

Figure 10.2 Continuum of strategic decision making in industrial relations

'Incidentalism'   **Planned Employee**
                                                                  Relations Approach

No consideration of industrial   *Key strategic decisions taken*
relations considerations in   *to achieve/advance a particular*
strategic decision making   *desired industrial relations approach*

It is also possible to identify a range of issues on which employers may choose to make conscious decisions which, either directly or indirectly, impact on industrial relations at enterprise level. These are outlined in Table 10.1.

10.2.2 CONTEXTUAL INFLUENCES

To identify and explain variations in management styles in industrial relations in different organisations we need to examine the interplay of a diverse range of external and internal factors which may influence and constrain managerial choice and practice in industrial relations. Kochan et al. (1986) place particular emphasis on the external environment (such as product and labour markets), management values, business strategy and historical factors as key

Table 10.1 Indicative strategic decisions impacting on industrial relations

Decisions	Impact on Industrial Relations
Location of Plant	Influences nature of labour force, labour costs and related issues such as unionisation
Size of Plant	Influences span of managerial control, communications, leadership/managerial style
Recruitment	By deciding on the nature of the workforce, management may directly and indirectly influence industrial relations (e.g., propensity of workers to join trade unions)
Training and Development	Nature and extent of training and development can influence management and employee approaches and attitudes to industrial relations
Union recognition	In a greenfield situation management may be able to decide on whether to deal with trade unions or not, a decision which will have a significant impact on the subsequent nature of enterprise level industrial relations
Employer Association	Deciding whether to join an employer association may influence subsequent industrial relations decisions
Procedural Formalisation	The extent and nature of formalisation of industrial relations procedures will impact on enterprise level industrial relations
Use of HRM Policies Techniques	By introducing techniques such as performance appraisal and performance-related pay to aid decisions on issues such as pay, management can limit the scope of trade unions in influencing such decisions

triggers in stimulating change in industrial relations. It is argued that changes in environmental conditions affect decisions on business strategy and ultimately industrial relations. Such decisions will be conditioned by the managerial values and constrained by historical factors and current practice in industrial relations.

The *external environment* exerts a major influence on organisational decision making. Trends in the external environment such as levels of *economic performance, public policy* and *cultural/societal values* will impact upon business strategy and management practice. Economic performance and public policy, as manifested in areas such as levels of economic activity, State intervention and control, and approaches to organised labour, clearly have an important impact on management style in industrial relations. For example, it might be argued that the anti-union policies of successive Conservative Governments in the UK during the 1980s gave legitimacy and support to 'macho' management styles and policies designed to undermine the role of trade unions in the workplace. These factors are particularly important at an aggregate level in explaining variations in national approaches to industrial relations. Poole (1986) identifies the role of Government and centralised control ('challenge from above') as a key constraining influence on managerial prerogative/

discretion in decision making at enterprise level. This line of argument suggests that the greater the level of centralised control (corporatism) the more limited the scope of management to develop atypical industrial relations styles and, particularly, non-union approaches. Conversely, it may be argued that low levels of central intervention in industrial relations allows management greater discretion in industrial relations and renders more likely the emergence of industrial relations styles which diverge from the traditional pluralist-adversarial model.

Developments in *technology* is another key external environmental factor affecting managerial styles in industrial relations. Technology, seen in generic terms as the equipment used to perform particular tasks in the organisation and the way it is organised, is a major influence on approaches to managing industrial relations (Beer et al., 1984). In the previous chapter we noted Guest's (1987) analysis which identified technological/production feasibility as a requisite condition for the successful implementation of HRM type styles and his suggestion that the utilisation of short cycle, repetitive, assembly line technology mitigates against the job design principles and autonomous team working characteristic of 'soft' HRM. Technology also affects cost structure and consequently impacts upon key aspects of industrial relations such as reward systems. Marchington (1982) suggests that in labour intensive sectors, where labour costs are high, organisations may be more constrained in developing 'soft' HRM type management styles. However, in capital intensive sectors, where labour costs constitute a small proportion of total costs, organisations may have greater scope to adopt more benign management styles in industrial relations, incorporating, for example, attractive rewards and employee development policies.

The *labour market* is a particularly important influence on industrial relations, especially in relation to recruitment, employee development and reward systems. Poole (1986) notes the modifying effect of labour market conditions on management styles in industrial relations. In particular high unemployment clearly impacts on the power balance in labour-management relations and can facilitate more autocratic or directive forms of management decision making. Looking at the Irish labour market the most notable developments include the progressive decline of agricultural and industrial employment and the growth of the service sector as an employer. Other notable characteristics of the Irish labour market are its relatively young age profile, increased female participation rates and the growth of 'atypical' employment forms. A particularly important development in recent years has been the rapid fall in unemployment and the consequent tightening of the labour market, particularly among certain skilled categories. These developments clearly affect industrial relations. For example, low unemployment and a 'tight' labour market places a premium on workforce retention. It also exerts upward pressures on wages and affects other aspects of industrial relations, such as labour turnover and power relations in collective bargaining.

An organisation's *product market* is seen as possibly the most significant influence on strategic decision making and has a significant impact on management styles in industrial relations, as discussed in the preceding chapter. This analysis suggested that organisations which operate from a strong product market position (e.g., high market share, growing market, stable demand) have greater scope to adopt sophisticated human resource policies in areas such as employee development, job tenure commitments and communications which, in turn, can positively contribute to a more co-operative industrial relations climate. In contrast, firms under high levels of market pressure (contracting market share; high levels of price competition) may have considerably less scope for choice and be forced to adopt a more traditional cost and labour control approach which may contribute to a more adversarial industrial relations climate.

While factors in the external environment will serve to guide management decisions on industrial relations, factors in an organisation's *internal environment* will determine unique organisational responses to external factors. Such factors include managerial ideology, business strategy and organisation size/structure.

Organisation size and structure is clearly an important factor impacting on management styles in industrial relations. Numerous studies in the UK have noted that trade union recognition and greater specialisation in personnel management are positively correlated with organisation size. In the Irish context, Gunnigle and Brady (1984) found that managements in smaller organisations veer towards a unitarist frame of reference and adopt less formality in industrial relations than their counterparts in larger organisations. In relation to organisation structure, Purcell (1992) argues that senior (corporate) management in highly diversified organisations are primarily concerned with financial issues, with the result that P/HR considerations (including industrial relations) are not a concern of corporate decision making but rather an operational concern for management at the business unit level. A corollary of this argument is that 'core business' organisations whose operation relies on a narrow product range are more likely to integrate human resource issues into strategic planning, whereas highly diversified organisations are more likely to adopt differing P/HR and industrial relations policies suited to the needs of different constituent divisions and establishments. Several writers identify the locus of industrial relations strategy formulation as a key issue influencing the nature of establishment industrial relations including the presence or absence of trade unions (Purcell and Sisson, 1983; Kochan et al., 1986; Poole, 1986). Poole (1986: 53) argues that the growth of conglomerate multinational enterprises presents management with the opportunity to develop industrial relations policies at corporate level 'where they are relatively unrestricted by intervention by government or by plant-level agreements with labour'. Of course, such discretion is dependent both on public policy (e.g., in relation to trade union recognition) and the distribution of power between the various parties in industrial relations.

Another important internal factor impacting upon industrial relations style is *business strategy*. Again, this issue was discussed at some length in the preceding chapter. Here, we noted that business strategy occurs at the level of the individual business unit and is concerned with achieving sustainable competitive advantage in a particular industry or segment. Depending on the particular business strategy chosen, it is likely that management will take steps to configure their P/HR policies, including industrial relations, in a way which aids strategy implementation.

Other important internal factors which impact on management styles in industrial relations include *workforce profile* and *established P/HR and industrial relations practices*. These factors will be particularly important in impacting upon the effectiveness of change initiatives in areas such as employee involvement. We may find, for example, that in a particular organisation workers may react differently to particular employee involvement or job enrichment initiatives. A case in point here is Hackman and Oldham's (1980) research which found that all employees may not react favourably to their suggestions for enriching jobs or increasing their involvement in management decision making. Rather, it was found that only those workers with a strong desire for achievement, responsibility and autonomy are expected to be motivated by such job redesign initiatives. These traits may in turn have been conditioned by traditional P/HR and industrial relations policies and practices. For example, if internal mobility and individual initiative have traditionally been discouraged it may be difficult to quickly implement a comprehensive employee development and promotion policy. At a more general level, we have seen that industrial relations practice in Ireland has traditionally been associated with a strong collectivist, industrial relations emphasis and consequent reliance on collective bargaining as the main vehicle for managing industrial relations at enterprise level. Over time these traditions have led to the institutionalisation of established or accepted industrial relations practices which reflect both the roles and influence of the major actors, and custom and practice on how key issues in industrial relations are handled. The significance of these industrial relations traditions is clearly a factor whose impact differs significantly between established and new companies. Specifically, newly established greenfield firms are felt to have considerably more scope to choose from a range of alternative approaches to industrial relations while management approaches in established companies will be circumscribed by past practice and the established industrial relations system. In the absence of severe crisis it is likely that change in industrial relations in established companies will comprise incremental variations on the established system (see, for example, Gunnigle, 1995a; Gunnigle, Morley, Clifford and Turner, 1997; Roche and Turner, 1998).

10.2.3 MANAGERIAL VALUES AND IDEOLOGY

Managerial values and ideology are seen as a particularly significant variable impacting on management styles in industrial relations. They incorporate the deeply held beliefs of senior management which guide decisions on various aspects of workforce management (Poole, 1986; Purcell, 1987; Gunnigle, 1995a). It is clear from our earlier discussion that managerial values and ideology are critical factors in interpreting developments in the external and internal environment and influencing management decisions on the organisation's overall approach to industrial relations (Purcell and Sisson, 1983; Purcell, 1987; Rollinson, 1993). It was also noted earlier that management's desired approach will closely reflect their underlying values but may not necessarily translate into practice or behaviour because of the mediating effect of environmental variables (Poole, 1986; Rollinson, 1993; Salamon, 1998). Thus a critical issue in the study of management styles in industrial relations is the interaction between management values, environmental variables, strategic choice, and industrial relations style.

In relation to managerial values, Kochan et al. (1986:18) argue that these have a tremendous impact upon industrial relations styles and strategies, acting as a 'lens' through which 'managerial decision makers weigh their options for responding to cues from the external environment'. Thus, options that are inconsistent with accepted values are discounted or not consciously considered, and organisational responses in industrial relations will conform to managerial choices which in turn reflect managerial values in industrial relations. Friedman (1977; 1984) also places the role of management at the centre of his analysis of developments in industrial relations suggesting that the primary 'dynamic influence on the organisation of work is normally exerted through the initiatives of managers'. Friedman (1977:180) relates this dominance to the structure of capitalist societies: '. . . the fundamental structure of property rights in capitalist societies means that those with a primary claim of possession of the means of production will normally take the primary initiatives in the organisation of productive activity.'

Friedman argues for the primary consideration of managerial roles rather than structural factors on the basis that managerial responses to particular environmental contexts cannot be predicted merely from an examination of structural factors, and because different styles and strategies may be chosen in response to particular contexts. Salamon (1998:230) identifies organisational and managerial structures as exerting a significant influence on management styles in industrial relations, and suggests that during the 1980s it was:

> . . . senior managers, with their strategic concern for the competitive performance of the organisation, who have been the major impetus for changing the style of industrial relations management, developing HRM strategies and linking these changes directly with the achievement of business objectives.

Clearly, all organisations are characterised by particular values and philosophies with respect to industrial relations. In some organisations such values may be explicit, as demonstrated in statements of corporate mission or philosophy. In others they may be implicit and inferred from management practice in areas such as supervisory style, reward systems and communications. Two cases may be highlighted to emphasise the key role of management values in impacting on industrial relations style. Firstly, in a number of organisations the role of influential founders has had a determining influence on their organisation's corporate values and industrial relations style. Prominent international examples include Marks and Spencer, Hewlett-Packard and Wang. The influence of entrepreneurial founders is also prominent in Irish indigenous firms and the industrial relations styles adopted over time in organisations such as Dunnes Stores, Superquinn and Ryanair seem to be heavily influenced by the values and philosophy of particular chief executives. A second instance of the impact of managerial values on management styles in industrial relations is the notion that managerial ideology is related to broader ethnic and cultural values. Of particular significance is the suggestion that managerial opposition to pluralism and particularly unionisation is characteristic of the value system of US managers whereas certain HRM type approaches which emphasise individual freedom and initiative, direct communications and merit-based rewards are very much in line with this value system (Bendix, 1956; Kochan et al., 1986). This interpretation is very significant in Ireland where our economy is heavily dependent on foreign investment and where the bulk of such investment comes from the US. In analysing the broad links between ideology and style Poole (1986) finds support for the suggestion that managerial ideologies differ between countries, particularly in relation to the achievement of control over labour, and suggests that these have led to the emergence of different management styles in industrial relations. In relation to Japan, Poole (1986:47) suggests that while culture is not solely responsible for 'benevolent paternalism' in the Japanese system of industrial relations, the 'modified Confucian world-view which prevailed in the late nineteenth century' was a significant influence in encouraging 'employers to evoke moral appeals to authority and to stress the efficiency of benevolence'. Poole argues that it also helped 'shape personal objectives (the desire of private industrialists and managers to be good moral citizens) and economic goals (such as public reputation *as well as* greater profits and efficiency and faster expansion)' (also see Dore, 1973). Poole argues that in the US context, the effects of values and ideologies are most obviously manifest in union avoidance practices, a pronounced 'unitary' perspective and deployment of sophisticated HRM approaches. Both Poole and Kochan et al. (1986) note that while managerial preferences have fluctuated over time, many US employers have embraced a non-union approach against a more general trend in the developed world towards a tacit acceptance of trade unions.

Several writers identify the origins of this approach with the concept of 'individualism' in the wider US culture, coupled with prevalent private enterprise commitments (Rothenberg and Silverman, 1973; Foulkes, 1980; Poole, 1986; Guest, 1989b).

10.3 PERSONNEL/HUMAN RESOURCE (P/HR) POLICY CHOICE AND MANAGEMENT STYLES IN INDUSTRIAL RELATIONS

Along with looking at the factors which will influence management styles in industrial relations, it is important to consider the areas where variations in style may become manifest. Of particular significance in this regard is the issue of P/HR policy choice: namely, the key areas of P/HR activity where different policy options may be chosen which contribute to the establishment of a particular management style in industrial relations.

The manifestations of managerial preferences will be evident in key areas of P/HR policy choice, particularly the work system, communications, rewards, recruitment/internal flow policies and the role of the specialist personnel function (for greater detail see Gunnigle, Morley and Heraty, 1997). P/HR policy choice in these areas will both reflect and reinforce preferred management styles in industrial relations styles which are seen as the outcomes of personnel policy choice as guided by managerial preferences and conditioned by external and internal environmental factors. These relationships were summarised in Figure 10.1, and are discussed below.

The *work system* incorporates the way the various tasks in the organisation are structured and impacts on issues such as organisation structure and job design (Beer et al., 1984). Decisions on the work system are primarily a management responsibility. Over the past decade or so, the increasing emphasis on improving quality, service and overall competitiveness has led to work redesign initiatives aimed at restructuring work systems to increase employee autonomy, motivation and performance. Much of the focus of work system redesign has been on restructuring organisations and jobs to incorporate greater scope for intrinsic motivation and to facilitate greater employee involvement.

A second important area of P/HR policy choice which has a significant impact on industrial relations is the area of *communications*. In recent years we have seen an increasing managerial emphasis on more extensive and direct communications with employees (Gunnigle, Morley, Clifford and Turner, 1997). This approach is seen to contrast traditional management-employee communications in unionised organisations where collective bargaining is the main communications device. Evidence from the US indicates that supplementary communications mechanisms may be used in addition to traditional collective communications, giving the approach both a collectivist and individualist dimension (Kochan et al., 1986). The nature of management-employee communications, the presence or absence of particular communications mechanisms and the relative emphasis on collective and individual communications fora represent key areas in which differences in management styles in industrial relations are manifest.

Reward systems represent a third key area of P/HR policy choice and a traditionally core aspect of industrial relations interactions in organisations. As with the design of the work system, an organisation's reward system is a powerful indicator of organisational philosophy and approach to industrial relations management. High or low pay, the range of fringe benefits and the mechanism for determining reward levels provide valuable insights into desired employer approaches to industrial relations.

A fourth area of personnel policy choice is the *recruitment and internal flow system*. This area incorporates the nature and sophistication of both recruitment and employment practices. The latter dimension embodies the management and deployment of workers once they have taken up employment, and incorporates key P/HR issues such as employee development, succession planning, appraisal, and career counselling.

10.3.1 THE ROLE OF THE SPECIALIST PERSONNEL FUNCTION

It is widely accepted that workforce management is a key aspect of the role of managerial work. Generically termed personnel management or human resource management, this *generalist* responsibility constitutes an important aspect of the job of everyone with managerial responsibilities. All managers, supervisors and team leaders have important P/HR management responsibilities, such as those dealing with the selection, deployment, development and motivation of staff. Many of these roles incorporate a significant industrial relations dimension, for example, staff supervision, reward management and grievance handling. However, we must also acknowledge the critical role played by P/HR or industrial relations *specialists*. Generally employed in medium to large organisations, P/HR specialists usually undertake particular responsibilities in key areas of workforce management such as developing and monitoring P/HR strategies and providing expert advice and assistance to line managers in handling particular issues such as selection testing or interpretation of employment legislation. This role is often manifested at enterprise level in the establishment of a specialist personnel function with responsibility for P/HR areas, including industrial relations.

INDUSTRIAL RELATIONS AS THE KEY PERSONNEL ACTIVITY

An important theme emerging from a review of the historical development of the specialist P/HR function in Ireland is the dominance of industrial relations as *the* most significant area of personnel activity (see, for example, O'Mahony, 1964; Shivanath, 1987; Gunnigle and Flood, 1990; Monks, 1992). It is argued that the growth of an industrial relations emphasis in personnel work was a direct result of the increasing influence of trade unions whereby employers sought to engage specialist practitioners to deal with industrial

378

relations matters at enterprise level. It is further argued that the significance of industrial relations within the personnel role reflected the widespread acceptance of the pluralist industrial relations model:

> For the personnel function, industrial relations became *the* priority with personnel practitioners vested with the responsibility to negotiate and police agreements. Industrial harmony was the objective and personnel specialists through their negotiating, inter-personal, and procedural skills had responsibility for its achievement. This industrial relations emphasis helped position the personnel function in a more central management role, albeit a largely reactive one. (Gunnigle 1996:32)

As we will see later, a number of developments have occurred since the early 1980s which have impacted on the role of the P/HR function. For example, it is argued that a key feature of HRM based approaches is that the major responsibility for managing human resources be assumed by line managers rather than P/HR specialists. Recognising the considerable differences that may arise in the role which the P/HR function may play in organisations, Tyson and Fell (1986) developed three broad models of the personnel function, as outlined in Table 10.2 (also see Tyson, 1987).

Table 10.2 Models of the specialist personnel function

(a) **Clerk of Works:** Within this model personnel management is a low level activity operating in an administrative support mode to line management. It is responsible for basic administration and welfare provision.

(b) **Contracts Manager:** Within this model personnel management is a high level function with a key role in handling industrial relations and developing policies and procedures in other core areas. The role is largely reactive, dealing with the personnel management implications of business decisions. This model incorporates a strong 'policing' component where the personnel department is concerned with securing adherence to agreed systems and procedures.

(c) **Architect:** Within this role personnel management is a top level management function involved in establishing and adjusting corporate objectives and developing strategic personnel policies designed to facilitate the achievement of long-term business goals. Personnel management considerations are recognised as an integral component of corporate success with the Personnel Director best placed to assess how the organisation's human resources can best contribute to this goal. Routine personnel activities are delegated allowing senior practitioners adopt the broad strategic outlook of a 'business manager'.

Source: Tyson and Fell, 1986

In a 1987 study of the role of P/HR practitioners in Irish organisations, Shivanath evaluated the applicablity of this typology. In looking first at the *clerk of works model*, the survey evidence found that while the majority of Irish personnel practitioners surveyed were not limited to this role, their work incorporated a significant administrative dimension. Thus, personnel departments were concerned with routine clerical/administrative tasks but most of these tasks were delegated allowing senior practitioners deal with higher level issues. The description of the personnel practitioner within the *contracts manager* model seemed to most accurately reflect reality in the Irish organisations studied. Industrial relations was identified by the majority of personnel practitioners as the most important aspect of their work. The study also found that the *architect model* was prominent in a number of organisations, with a significant number of senior P/HR practitioners involved at a more strategic level.

While more recent research points to a continuing emphasis on industrial relations as an important aspect of the P/HR work there is also evidence of significant change in the role played by the P/HR function. In particular, we can point to an increasing strategic role for senior P/HR practitioners in some organisations, particularly in the area of change management (see, for example, Monks, 1992). We are also witnessing a shift away from a traditional pluralist industrial relations emphasis to a more individualist approach or style, as discussed earlier in this chapter. There is further evidence of an increasing emphasis on other areas of personnel activity, particularly recruitment and selection and employee development (Heraty et al., 1994).

In evaluating these developments, Gunnigle (1998b:17) argues that up to the late 1970s the development of the personnel function in Ireland was characterised by *convergence* to a common model which he terms 'industrial relations orthodoxy' but that since then a range of environmental changes have both questioned the appropriateness of this model and led to the proliferation of alternative models of the P/HR function:

> In tracing the development of the personnel function in Ireland over recent decades one can identify a predictable pattern of evolution. From somewhat humble beginnings, the specialist personnel function developed to a stage where it became accepted as an integral part of the management structure of larger organisations. This pattern of evolution saw convergence to a *prevailing orthodoxy* of the role of the personnel function. This orthodoxy was grounded in the belief that *the* key employer concern in workforce management was the establishment and maintenance of stable industrial relations . . . . While more reactive rather than strategic, this *industrial relations* role was nonetheless significant: it served to both define what personnel work involved and position the personnel management function as an important aspect of the managerial infrastructure.

Table 10.3 Organisational context-personnel/human resource function models

The commitment model: Generally associated with a 'soft' HRM style, this was the first P/HR model to seriously challenge industrial relations orthodoxy. It is characterised by a resource perspective of employees incorporating the view that there is an organisational pay-off in performance terms from a combination of 'sophisticated' HR policies designed to develop employee commitment and emphasise the mutuality of management and employee interests. In this model, the P/HR function is high powered and well resourced with a significant change in agent role. This model appears to characterise core business organisations whose competitive strategy is based on a product differentiation/premium price approach, often on a 'first to market' basis. Such organisations may employ significant numbers of highly trained technical and engineering staffs whose development and retention are critical to organisational success. This model generally relies on a *union substitution* premise, although organisations with union recognition but where the union role is essentially peripheral also fall within this category.

The transaction cost model: While the commitment model has received much attention, its viability has increasingly come under scrutiny in recent years. In particular, exemplars of the commitment model (e.g., Wang and Digital) experienced intense competitive pressures from low cost producers. The transaction cost model places the workforce management emphasis on minimising operating costs. Thus, outsourcing becomes an important strategy, particularly in using contracted labour and other forms of 'atypical' employment. This approach is also associated with intensification of the pace of work flow and an increased range of work tasks. This model may rely on a *union suppression* premise: often linked to the (management) suggestion that unions inhibit the development of necessary flexibility levels to ensure competitiveness. In this model the key role of the P/HR function is cost-effective labour supply. The role is essentially reactive: dealing with the operational workforce management consequences of a low cost competitive strategy.

The traditional adversarial model: This model equates to 'industrial relations orthodoxy' discussed earlier and was traditionally the predominant P/HR function type in Ireland. It is grounded in low trust management-employee relations and primary reliance on adversarial collective bargaining. It equates to Tyson's contracts manager model.

The partnership model: We have earlier noted that the development of union-management partnerships has been the focus of much recent debate in Ireland [see chapter 7]. The rationale for partnership is based on so-called 'mutual gains' principles whereby workers and trade unions actively pursue *with* management solutions to business problems and appropriate work reorganisation in return for greater involvement in business decisions and in the process of work reorganisation. Within this model, the P/HR function becomes an important strategic lever in developing the partnership agenda. It also assumes an important role in implementing a range of HR policy initiatives to underpin this new orientation: specifically in areas such as reward systems, management-employee communications, job design and employee development.

Source: Gunnigle, 1998b:18–19

Gunnigle argues that this role reached its 'heyday' in the 1970s and that by the early 1980s *industrial relations orthodoxy* as the prevailing model of the P/HR function began to unravel. As noted earlier, this transformation can be traced to numerous sources but most particularly to the increased competitive pressures on organisations. It therefore seems that the past decade has seen the emergence of a range of alternative P/HR function types so that as Paauwe (1996:227) states 'it is almost impossible to speak of *the* personnel function'. Gunnigle (1998b) thus argues that 'contingency approaches' are now the order of the day with the role of P/HR function influenced by a variety of factors such as industrial sector, managerial philosophy and market context. He outlines four *organisational context-P/HR function* models: (1) the commitment model; (2) the transaction cost model; (3) the traditional adversarial model; and (4) the partnership model as outlined in Table 10.3.

10.4 CATEGORISING MANAGEMENT STYLES IN INDUSTRIAL RELATIONS

The preceding discussion has attempted to outline the main factors which impact on variations in management styles in industrial relations. This section examines alternative typologies of management styles in industrial relations and considers their relevance for Irish industrial relations. We begin by revisiting Fox's (1966; 1974) work on unitarist and pluralist approaches to industrial relations.

10.4.1 MANAGERIAL FRAMES OF REFERENCE

In his seminal work, Fox (1966) argues that management approaches to industrial relations are largely determined by the frame of reference adopted by managers. A frame of reference is defined by Thelen and Withall (1979) as 'the main selective influences at work as the perceiver supplements, omits and structures what he notices'. Fox suggests that a manager's frame of reference is important because: (1) it determines how management expect people to behave and how they think they should behave (i.e., values and beliefs); (2) it determines management reactions to actual behaviour (i.e., management practice) and (3) it shapes the methods management choose when they wish to change the behaviour of people at work (e.g., strategies/policies). Fox identified two alternative frames of reference to help evaluate management approaches to industrial relations. These were termed the *unitarist* and *pluralist* frame of reference (also see chapters 1 and 7). The key features of these two approaches are summarised in Table 10.4.

Table 10.4 Unitarist and pluralist frames of reference

Unitarist	Pluralist
Emphasises the dominance of common interests Everyone – management and employees – should strive to achieve the organisation's primary business goals since everyone will benefit	The organisation is viewed as composed of different interest groups with different objectives but linked together instrumentally by their common association with the organisation
There is only one source of authority (management) and it must command full loyalty	Management's role is to achieve some equilibrium satisfying the various interest groups, thus helping achieve the organisation's goals
Anyone who does not share these common interests and does not accept managerial authority is viewed as a dissenter/agitator	A certain amount of conflict is inevitable since the objectives of the parties will clash on occasion
Since dissenters endanger organisational success they must either fall into line, appreciate the overriding importance of corporate goals and accept managerial authority, or risk elimination from the organisation	Management must expect and plan for conflict so that it can be handled successfully and not endanger the achievement of the organisation's primary objectives
	Management should not seek to suppress conflicting interests, but rather aim to reconcile them in the organisation's interests

Source: Fox, 1966; 1974

These contrasting frames of reference represent dominant industrial relations orientations which may be adopted by management. In practice, one finds that managers do not strictly adhere to one of these approaches but may adopt different approaches in different situations and/or change their approaches over time. Nevertheless, the frames of reference approach provides a useful framework for evaluating management approaches to industrial relations at enterprise level. To this end, Marchington (1982) analysed how management approaches to industrial relations might differ depending on the particular frame of reference adopted.

In first evaluating management approaches to *trade unions*, Marchington (1982) argues that managers holding a unitary perspective see no role for trade unions. Such managers would see unions as 'encroaching on management's territory', making unreasonable demands, prohibiting change, flexibility, and, therefore, competitiveness (also see Gunnigle et al., 1995). As a consequence trade unions would be viewed as an externally imposed force which introduces conflict into the organisation and prohibits the development of 'good' industrial relations. Furthermore, workers associated with the promotion of trade unionism would be seen as disloyal, agitators or troublemakers. In contrast, managers adopting a pluralist perspective would see a legitimate role for trade unions in representing and articulating employee views in the workplace.

A second area where Marchington identified different approaches was in relation to *managerial prerogative*. Managerial prerogative refers to areas of decision making where management see themselves as having sole decision-making authority. Marchington suggests that managers adopting a unitary frame of reference would be unwilling to accept any reduction of management prerogative as a result of trade union organisation. They would see management as the legitimate decision-making authority. Against that, managers adopting a pluralist frame of reference would acknowledge the legitimacy of other interest groups in the organisation, such as trade unions. They would therefore accept the need to allow trade unions a role in decision making and consequently accept some reduction in managerial prerogative.

The final area where management approaches may differ is in relation to *industrial conflict* (also see chapter 7). Marchington suggests that managers adopting a unitary frame of reference would view the enterprise very much along 'team'/'family' lines with everyone working together to achieve company objectives. In this context, conflict is seen as something of an aberration, only occurring as a result of a breakdown of communications or the work of troublemakers. By contrast, managers adopting a pluralist frame of reference would accept that some degree of industrial conflict is inevitable because the interests of management and labour will clash on occasion. Since the pluralist perspective accepts the legitimacy of conflict, managers adopting this frame of reference will tend to plan for it by, for example, agreeing grievance, disputes and disciplinary procedures.

10.4.2 TYPOLOGIES OF MANAGEMENT STYLES IN INDUSTRIAL RELATIONS

Moving beyond Fox's unitarist-pluralist dichotomy, several commentators have attempted to develop categorisations of management styles in industrial relations to explain differences in organisational approaches to industrial relations. Earlier we introduced and explored the idea of identifiable patterns or styles of industrial relations management and attempted to distinguish between organisations which develop some kind of strategic approach to industrial relations from those which managed industrial relations in a more reactive or ad hoc manner. Several writers have attempted to move beyond this crude distinction to develop ideal-typical styles of industrial relations management and classify them according to specific criteria.

While the unitarist/pluralist classification discussed above is useful in evaluating the approach of individual managers to industrial relations it is of limited benefit in considering different organisational approaches or styles in industrial relations (Purcell and Sisson, 1983). Recognising this, Fox (1974) developed a typology of industrial relations styles which was subsequently modified by Purcell and Sisson (1983) to provide a five-fold categorisation of 'ideal-typical' management styles in industrial relations. This typology is outlined in Table 10.5 and is based on variations in management approaches to trade unions, collective bargaining, consultation and communications.

Table 10.5 Management styles in industrial relations

Management Style	Characteristics
Traditionalist	'Orthodox unitarism': oppose role for unions; little attention to employee needs
Sophisticated Paternalist	Emphasise employee needs (training, pay, conditions etc.); discourage unionisation; demand employee loyalty and commitment
Sophisticated Modern (Two variations)	Accept trade unions' role in specific areas; emphasis on procedures and consultative mechanisms **Two variations:** (a) *Constitutionalists*: emphasise codification of management-union relations through collective agreements; (b) *Consultors*: collective bargaining established but management emphasises personal contact and problem-solving, playing down formal union role at workplace level
Standard Modern	Pragmatic approach; unions' role accepted but no overall philosophy or strategy developed: 'Fire-fighting' approach

Source: Purcell and Sisson, 1983

This categorisation of management styles in industrial relations provides a useful conceptual map with which to evaluate differing management approaches to enterprise level industrial relations. However, it is necessary to examine actual evidence on variations in management styles in industrial relations to evaluate the extent to which such categorisations provide a valid reflection of the realities of enterprise level industrial relations. To this end, Deaton (1985) attempted the first major empirical study of management styles using evidence from the UK Workplace Industrial Survey. Using data from some 1,400 organisations, Deaton (1985) sought to empirically evaluate the appropriateness of Purcell and Sisson's typology. He attempted first to classify management styles in unionised companies as either 'sophisticated' or 'standard moderns'. However, he found it difficult to distinguish between these two types of management styles, suggesting that it is rather tenuous to classify firms recognising trade unions into either of these groupings. He also attempted to categorise management styles in non-union companies into 'paternalist', 'anti-union', and 'sophisticated paternalists'. Here, he found greater evidence of organisations conforming to Purcell and Sisson's typologies. He found that 'sophisticated paternalists' and 'anti-union' organisations emerged as polar opposites while 'paternalist' organisations took the middle ground (having some characteristics common to both 'anti-union' and 'sophisticated paternalist' organisations). He concluded that attempts to classify firms into a small number of ideal styles were problematic and that, while the distinction between organisations which recognise trade unions and those which do not is crucial, it may not be possible to subdivide styles further in organisations where unions are recognised. However, he felt that there was a greater tendency in organisations which do not recognise trade unions to adopt the 'identikit' styles suggested above.

Using more anecdotal evidence to examine variations in management styles in industrial relations Poole (1986) did not focus on particular identikit styles but rather suggested that the evidence points to the existence of 'a progressively rich array' of hybrid styles, rather than any convergence towards particular predominant styles or patterns. Other research studies have also identified the development of particular management styles in industrial relations. We find, for example, a number of studies which point to the significance of styles designed to develop and sustain employee commitment (Walton, 1985; Edwards, 1987), while others have identified the development of neo-pluralist styles (Batstone, 1984) and 'sophisticated' non-union styles (Foulkes, 1980).

10.5 INDIVIDUALISM AND COLLECTIVISM AS DIMENSIONS OF MANAGEMENT STYLES IN INDUSTRIAL RELATIONS

More recent analyses of management styles in industrial relations have tended to focus on key dimensions of management styles in industrial relations rather than 'ideal-typical' style categorisations. John Purcell (1987) provides us with two widely accepted dimensions of management styles in industrial relations, namely individualism and collectivism.

Collectivism in industrial relations incorporates the extent to which management acknowledge the right of employees to collective representation and the involvement of the collective in influencing management decision making (Purcell, 1987; Sisson, 1987; 1994c; Storey and Sisson, 1994). This dimension addresses both the level of democratic employee representative structures and the extent to which management legitimise their representational and bargaining role. Thus conceived, the collectivism dimension spans a continuum from a unitarist perspective incorporating management opposition to employee representation, through a middle ground of adversarial or reluctant collectivism, to a co-operative perspective (Purcell, 1987; Marchington and Parker, 1990). Thus, high collectivism is manifested in the establishment, recognition and incorporation of mechanisms for employee representation, particularly trade unions, as a vehicle in the conduct of establishment level industrial relations, while at the other extreme, low collectivism is manifested in managerial opposition to collective employee representation (see Figure 10.3).

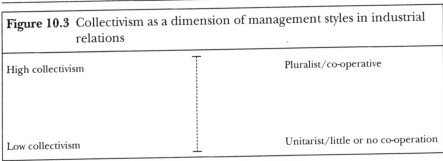

Figure 10.3 Collectivism as a dimension of management styles in industrial relations

High collectivism	Pluralist/co-operative
Low collectivism	Unitarist/little or no co-operation

Source: Adapted from Purcell, 1987

Individualism as a dimension of management styles in industrial relations is described by Purcell (1987:536) as:

> . . . the extent to which the firm gives credence to the feelings and sentiments of each employee and seeks to develop and encourage each employee's capacity and role at work . . . . Firms which have individualistically-centred policies are thus expected to emphasise employees as a resource and be concerned with developing each person's talents and worth.

The extant literature identifies an increased management emphasis on the development of an individualist orientation in industrial relations as one of the most important developments in industrial relations over the past two decades (Beaumont, 1985, 1991; Beaumont and Townley, 1985; Gunnigle, Morley and Turner, 1997; Kochan et al., 1986; Guest, 1989b; Storey, 1992; Bacon and Storey, 1993). However, beyond Purcell's (1987) and Bacon and Storey's (1993) attempts to explore the discrete components of individualism, it remains quite an amorphous concept. The most popular conception of high individualism identified in the literature incorporates a strong human capital perspective whereby workers are seen as a critical resource (Beer et al., 1984; Walton, 1985). It is argued that managements pursuing this style will seek to develop this 'critical resource' through a combination of individualist policies in areas such as training, job design and reward systems (Kochan et al., 1986; Purcell, 1987; Beaumont 1992, 1993). It is further suggested that management styles which emphasise lower levels of collectivism in industrial relations may often be counterbalanced by higher levels of individualism (Poole, 1986; Purcell, 1987; Gunnigle, Morley and Turner, 1997). Critical manifestations of higher levels of individualism include the use of performance-related pay systems linked to formal employee appraisals and increased direct management-employee communications (Roche and Turner, 1994). Purcell argues that high individualism is characterised by managements recognising the resource value of employees and adopting comprehensive employee development policies. In contrast, low individualism conceives of employees in utility terms within the overriding goal of profit maximisation. Thus, the management emphasis is on tight management control, minimisation of labour costs and little concern for broader human resource issues such as job satisfaction, employment security or employee commitment (see Figure 10. 4).

Figure 10.4 Individualism as a dimension of management styles in industrial relations

High individualism		Employees as a resource; comprehensive employee development emphasis
Low individualism		Employees as commodities; no employee development

Source: Adapted from Purcell, 1987

10.5.1 SOME IRISH EVIDENCE

In an Irish study of recently established (greenfield) companies operating in the manufacturing and internationally traded services sectors, Gunnigle (1995) attempted to evaluate management approaches to industrial relations on the dimensions of collectivism and individualism (also see Gunnigle, Morley and Turner, 1997). To this end a number of indicators were developed to evaluate the relative management emphasis on individualism and collectivism in industrial relations. These indicators were further combined to produce overall composite measures of individualism and collectivism in industrial relations: see Table 10.6.[1]

While the findings only apply to recently established firms, they provide some interesting insights into management styles in industrial relations in Ireland. We have already noted that high levels of collectivism, and specifically trade union recognition, membership and influence, are integral to the traditional pluralist model, considered characteristic of industrial relations in Ireland (Roche, 1994a; Brewster and Hegewisch, 1994; Roche and Turner, 1994; Hillery, 1994). Thus, findings on the levels of collectivism, and particularly trade union recognition, are seen as critical indicators of change in management styles in industrial relations (Beaumont, 1985; 1992). An important issue in evaluating the relative emphasis on collectivism and individualism is the extent to which greenfield organisations adopt what have been termed 'dualist' styles in industrial relations: namely, the utilisation of a range of individualist HRM policies within a collectivist industrial relations context (see, for example, Storey 1992).

Table 10.6 Indicators of collectivism and individualism

Measures of Individualism

1. *Sophistication of the Employment and Socialisation System*: measured through an evaluation of the degree of sophistication and relative emphasis on individualism in the management of human resource 'flows'

2. *Direct Communications*: based on an analysis of the level, nature and sophistication of management-employee communications

3. *Performance-Related Pay*: measured through an analysis of the incidence of performance-related pay systems and the utilisation of formal performance appraisals to aid performance-related pay decisions among non-managerial/white collar grades

4. *Employee Involvement*: measured through an analysis of the extent to which management utilises explicit techniques to facilitate employee involvement in decision making

5. *Employee Autonomy*: measured through an analysis of the extent to which management seek to facilitate/promote employee autonomy.

Measures of Collectivism

1. *Trade union presence*: measured through an analysis of levels of trade union recognition and trade union density

2. *Pattern of trade union organisation*: measured though an examination of the nature of trade union recognition and impact of trade unions on workplace industrial relations

3. *Role of trade unions and other employee representative bodies*: measured though an examination of role of trade unions and other employee representative bodies in management-employee communications/interactions

4. *Employer association membership and utilisation*: measured through an examination of the extent to which greenfield companies are in membership of employer associations and of the patterns of utilisation of employer association services

---

Source: Gunnigle, 1995b; Gunnigle, Morley and Turner, 1997

In attempting to interpret and explain the interplay of collectivism and individualism as dimensions of management styles in industrial relations in Irish greenfield sites, Gunnigle, Morley and Turner (1997) developed two broad hypotheses. Firstly, they drew on the 'non-union' literature to hypothesise that *high individualism will counterpoise low collectivism* (Foulkes, 1980; Kochan et al., 1986; Beaumont, 1991; Beaumont and Harris, 1994; McLoughlin and Gourlay, 1992). In this model, which was termed the *countervailing hypothesis*, it might be expected that greenfield firms characterised by low collectivism will adopt highly individualist industrial relations styles which seek to mitigate the need for collective employee representation (Beaumont, 1985; Beaumont and Harris, 1994; McLoughlin and Gourlay, 1992; Guest and Hoque, 1994). A second and contrasting hypothesis, termed the *dualist hypothesis*, stated that 'high individualism will complement high collectivism'. This implies that greenfield firms will concurrently adopt high levels of collectivism and individualism and employ what are termed 'dualist' industrial relations styles (also see Purcell, 1987;

Storey, 1992). It might be argued that dualist styles are appropriate where there is a strong tradition of collective employee representation (Kochan et al., 1986). In the Irish context it might plausibly be suggested that the dualist approach is the most likely pattern for industrial relations given the strong legitimacy of trade unions and collective bargaining (Gunnigle et al., 1994; Roche and Turner, 1994).

The findings on the indicative measures of collectivism and individualism are outlined in Table 10.7. This evidence suggests that we should accept the 'countervailing hypothesis'. On almost all of the measures there is a negative relationship between individualism and collectivism. This negative relationship is most pronounced in the area of performance-related pay. This variable measured the extent to which firms used performance-related pay (PRP) systems based on formal appraisals of individual employee performance. The inverse relationship between PRP and collectivism is most pointed in relation to measures of trade union recognition and density ('presence') and the role of trade unions/other employee representative bodies in communications ('collective communications'). It is clear that PRP systems are most likely to be employed where there are low levels of union recognition and membership and where there is little or no role for collective employee representation.

Table 10.7 Measuring collectivism and individualism in greenfield sites

		Individualism				
		Employee autonomy	Direct Communications	Employment System	Employee involvement	Performance- Related Pay	Individualism (composite measure)
	Trade Union Presence	ns	–	–	ns	–	–
Collectivism	Trade Union Organisation	ns	ns	ns	ns	–	–
	Collective Communications	ns	–	–	ns	–	–
	Employer Organisation	ns	ns	ns	–ns	–	–
	COLLECTIVISM (composite measure)	ns	–	ns	ns	–	–

ns = no significant relationship; – = significant and negative relationship

Source: Adapted from Gunnigle, Morley and Turner, 1997

As outlined earlier, 'dualist' industrial relations styles are characterised by high levels of collectivism and individualism. The data from greenfield sites provides little evidence of a positive relationship between collectivism and individualism. Thus, it appears that dualist industrial relations styles are not common in Irish greenfield companies.

This study also sought to establish the main explanatory factors impacting upon variations in management styles in industrial relations in the firms studied. This analysis found that company ownership, and specifically US ownership, was the most significant explanatory variable. On the collectivism dimension company ownership exerted the greatest impact. Levels of collectivism were positively associated with European ownership and negatively associated with US ownership. This was particularly the case in relation to trade union presence. Non-union companies were predominantly US owned, while, in contrast, all of the European companies recognised trade unions. On the individualism dimension, US ownership emerged as the most significant factor positively impacting on levels of individualism. The critical impact of ownership is illustrated in Table 10.8 which presents the mean and standard deviation scores on the dimensions of collectivism and individualism disaggregated by ownership. This table clearly illustrates the considerable contrast between US and other companies on the dimensions of collectivism and individualism. US companies score highest on the individualism measures and lowest on collectivism measures. Conversely, European-owned companies score highest on measures of collectivism and lowest on individualism.

Table 10.8 Company ownership, collectivism and individualism

Nationality	Collectivism (1–3)*		Individualism (1–3)	
	Mean	Standard Deviation	Mean	Standard Deviation
US	1.30	0.87	2.30	0.54
ASIAN	1.86	0.90	1.86	0.38
IRISH	2.09	0.67	1.46	0.69
EUROPEAN	2.88	0.35	1.25	0.46

* 1=low; 2=medium; 3=high

As noted earlier, this study found that most significant indicators of high levels of individualism were performance-based pay systems tied to individual employee appraisals and greater direct communications with employees. An increased management focus on more extensive and direct communications with individual employees was an important feature of industrial relations management in many of the greenfield companies studied. In particular, many companies put an especially strong emphasis on communicating information on company performance to employees. In many of these companies, such information was used to emphasise issues such as market volatility, intensity of competition and requirements for high quality and low cost production/service. The other critical indicator of individualism identified in the greenfield study was the extent of utilisation of performance-related pay (PRP) systems based on formal appraisals of individual employee performance (Gunnigle, 1995a and b; Gunnigle, Turner and D'Art, 1998). This research data points to significant differences between new and longer established ('brownfield') companies in the extent of utilisation of PRP systems based on formal appraisals among non-managerial/white collar grades. The role of appraisal in aiding PRP decisions among non-managerial/white collar grades is a crucial differentiating factor since the use of more traditional PRP systems among these grades is nothing new. However, traditional PRP systems (e.g., measured day work) were based on quantitative evaluations of employee performance and were normally the subject of collective bargaining. As such, quantitative PRP systems were very much integral to the collectivist tradition of Irish industrial relations. In contrast, performance appraisal is essentially an individualist management tool (Beer et al., 1984). By linking performance appraisals to incremental pay decisions, managements in greenfield sites are posing a challenge to collectivism in industrial relations. The collectivist tradition implies that incremental pay decisions are achieved through collective bargaining and, once agreed, apply 'across the board' to all relevant employee categories. In contrast, PRP decisions based on performance appraisal are normally the subject of a management review of individual employee performance. Consequently, incremental pay decisions are made by management rather than through collective bargaining and vary according to individual appraisals rather than applying equally to all through a collective agreement. Thus, individualism replaces collectivism at two critical phases: (1) the process of appraisal is individualist rather than collectivist (individual appraisal rather than collective bargaining); and (2) the outcome takes the form of varying PRP decisions among individual employees rather than a fixed amount which applies equally to all employees.

Another indicator of increased individualism identified in the literature is the adoption of sophisticated and highly individualist employment systems to effectively manage 'human resource flows', particularly in the areas of selection and employee development (Foulkes, 1980; Beer et al., 1984). A further important indicator of high individualism in the extant literature is the incidence of extensive mechanisms to facilitate employee autonomy and involvement (Lawler, 1978; 1982; Beer et al., 1984). It was interesting that Gunnigle's study of Irish greenfield companies did not find widespread evidence of sophisticated employment systems or mechanisms to facilitate employee involvement or autonomy in the majority of greenfield companies studied (Gunnigle, 1995a and b).

In considering these results it can be argued that while individualism appeared to be an important and significant aspect of management styles in industrial relations in greenfield companies, this did not necessarily imply that managements in greenfield companies adopt a 'resource perspective' on employees (see, for example, Purcell, 1987). This Irish study found little evidence of a shift from a utility perspective to a resource perspective in greenfield companies. The aggregate evidence suggests that while there is a greater emphasis on individualism in greenfield companies than has traditionally been the case with longer established companies, this does not equate to high levels of individualism. Rather, it appears that managements in greenfield sites are adopting more individualist approaches in selected aspects of industrial relations but are not moving towards a wholly individualist approach equating to the 'soft' HRM model.

10.6 STRATEGIC INTEGRATION AS A DIMENSION OF MANAGEMENT STYLES IN INDUSTRIAL RELATIONS

We have already considered the extent to which industrial relations and P/HR management issues are a concern for strategic decision makers in organisations. In this section we develop this theme by examining the concept of strategic integration in industrial relations. Strategic integration, as a dimension of management approaches to industrial relations, refers to the extent to which industrial relations considerations impact on strategic decision making. Thus, 'high' strategic integration is characterised by the integration of industrial relations considerations into the business plan to facilitate the establishment and maintenance of competitive advantage. Such policies need not necessarily be employee centred, but may be either 'hard' or 'soft', depending on the chosen route to competitive advantage. In contrast, the traditional 'pluralist-adversarial' approach is seen as largely reactive in nature. Consequently, industrial relations considerations are not a concern of strategic decision makers, but rather an operational issue only given priority when problems arise.

We noted earlier that a traditional perception of strategic decision making is that it concerns 'primary' business issues (such as finance) and any attention devoted to industrial relations issues is secondary and somewhat incidental. However, it is evident that some organisations incorporate human resource issues in the strategic process and take well thought out, strategic decisions to establish a particular industrial relations style. In practice the idea of strategic integration as either total or absent does not adequately reflect the complexities of P/HR and industrial relations policy choice in organisations. A more useful analysis is provided by Wood and Peccei (1990) who differentiate between *strategic human resource management*, where human resource issues are fully integrated into the strategic planning process and *business led human resource management* where human resource policies are linked to the commercial imperatives of the organisation. Differences between these two approaches lie in the level of strategic consideration of P/HR and industrial relations issues. In relation to strategic HRM, P/HR and industrial relations issues are integral to strategic planning and form part of the organisation's long-term business strategy. In business led HRM, P/HR/industrial relations policies and practices are very much a lower order strategic activity but are linked to higher order strategic decisions in areas such as product development or market penetration. This model differs significantly from the traditional industrial relations model where human resource considerations are not a significant top management concern but rather a peripheral operational responsibility. Consequently, they are not strategic in nature but rather ad hoc, piecemeal responses to immediate issues. These alternative approaches are represented in Figure 10.5.

Figure 10.5	Strategic integration as a dimension of management styles in industrial relations	
High strategic integration	Strategic HRM	Industrial relations and P/HR issues form an integral component of the organisation's long-term strategy and mission.
	Business-led HRM	Industrial relations and P/HR issues are dependent upon but linked to higher order decisions on corporate mission and objectives.
Low strategic integration	'Traditional' industrial relations/ personnel management	Industrial relations and P/HR issues are a peripheral management concern and handled in an essentially reactive fashion.

Factors encouraging greater strategic integration in industrial relations include: (1) increased competition and greater emphasis on achieving competitive advantage; (2) organisation restructuring to devolve more responsibility to strategic business units; (3) increasing importance of culture and mission in focusing management effort and guiding decisions on resource allocation; (4) quality rather than price as a dominant route to competitive advantage (Carroll, 1985; Kelly and Brannick, 1988b; Toner, 1987; Storey and Sisson, 1990). However, there is considerable debate on the nature of these developments, and factors mitigating against greater strategic integration include the traditionally low level of consideration of P/HR issues in strategic decision making, the embeddedness of pluralist industrial relations traditions and the probable growth in organisation size and diversity in the next millennium. A further limiting factor is the suggestion that comprehensive 'soft' HRM initiatives are confined to a limited number of foreign-owned organisations (Storey and Sisson, 1990). In Ireland most notable examples of such approaches have been in foreign-owned, particularly US, organisations (Toner, 1987).

10.6.1 SOME IRISH EVIDENCE
Despite the widespread emphasis on the strategic role of industrial relations in the international literature, there have been few attempts to investigate the

actual extent of strategic integration in industrial relations. Consequently, the nature and extent of strategic integration of industrial relations considerations into top-level management decision making remains unclear. This is most probably related to the inherent difficulties in identifying acceptable measures of strategic integration. Strategic decision making is a notoriously difficult area for researchers to analyse. Researchers often develop proxy indicators of strategic integration. This is a useful approach but requires the identification of an adequate range of robust indicators. In the Irish context, the study of management styles in industrial relations in greenfield firms examined the extent of strategic integration (Gunnigle, 1995a and b; Gunnigle and Morley, 1998; Gunnigle, Turner and Morley, 1998).

To evaluate the nature and extent of strategic integration as a dimension of management styles in industrial relations, Gunnigle and Morley (1998) developed a number of variables regarded as indicative of strategic integration in industrial relations as follows:

(1) *Impact on location*: assesses the impact of industrial relations considerations on location decisions of greenfield-site facilities;

(2) *Formal strategy development*: addresses the capacity to engage in business strategy and whether such capacity follows through into a capacity to formulate P/HR and industrial relations strategy;

(3) *Role of P/HR/industrial relations function*: assesses the incidence and role of a specialist P/HR and industrial relations function;

(4) *Impact on business policy*: measures the impact of P/HR and industrial relations considerations on business policy decisions at establishment level.

Such measures are clearly useful insofar as they lend themselves to empirical investigation. However, they are obviously limited in their ability to precisely measure the actual level of strategic integration in industrial relations. Given this important caveat, it is useful to briefly consider the research findings on strategic integration in Irish greenfield sites insofar as they provide a broad guide rather than a precise measure of the extent and direction of strategic integration as a dimension of management styles in industrial relations.

Using the measures of strategic integration outlined above, Gunnigle, Morley and Turner (1998) attempted first to assess the extent of strategic integration of industrial relations. They then examined the relationship between strategic integration and the other two key dimensions of management styles in industrial relations discussed above, namely collectivism and individualism. The study findings on the overall levels of strategic integration in Irish greenfield sites are outlined in Table 10.9.

Table 10.9 Strategic integration in greenfield sites

Variables	Mean (range 1–3*)	Standard deviation
Location	1.87	0.59
Formal strategy development	2.08	0.76
Impact of IR on business policy decisions	1.74	0.65
Role of P/HR/industrial relations function	2.23	0.87
Composite measure of strategic integration based on combination of the four variables above	1.91	0.69
* 1=low; 2=medium; 3=high		

Source: Adapted from Gunnigle, Morley and Turner, 1998

These findings indicate that the extent of strategic integration is just below the mid point of the range with the composite indicator receiving a mean score of 1.91. However, there is considerable variation in the four constituent measures which comprise the overall composite measure. The highest scoring indicator was that measuring the incidence and role of the specialist P/HR/industrial relations function. The second highest scoring variable was that measuring the level of formal strategy development. This variable measured the extent of sophistication in the development of formal mission statements, corporate strategy and P/HR/industrial relations strategy. In contrast, the lowest scoring variable was that measuring the impact of P/HR and industrial relations considerations on major business policy decisions. The variable measuring the impact of industrial relations on the decisions of where to locate a new greenfield site facility also scored below the average. The standard deviation scores are quite high indicating considerable disparity in the levels of strategic integration in the study population.

The relationships between the study findings on strategic integration and levels of individualism and collectivism are outlined in Tables 10.10 and 10.11.

Table 10.10 Individualism and strategic integration in industrial relations

		INDIVIDUALISM					
		Employee autonomy	Direct Communications	Employment System	Employee involvement	Performance- Related Pay	Individualism
STRATEGIC INTEGRATION	Location	ns	ns	+	+	ns	+
	Formal strategy development	ns	+	+	+	ns	+
	Impact on business policy	+	+	+	+	ns	+
	Role of IR function	ns	+	+	+	ns	+
	Strategic Integration	+	+	+	+	+	+
ns = no significant relationship; + = significant and positive relationship							

Source: Adapted from Gunnigle, Morley and Turner, 1998

Table 10.11 Collectivism and strategic integration in industrial relations

		Collectivism				
		Trade union presence	Trade union organisation	Collective communications	Employer organisation	Collectivism
Strategic Integration	Location	–	ns	–	ns	ns
	Formal strategy development	–	–	–	ns	–
	Impact on business policy	ns	ns	–	ns	ns
	Role of IR function	–	ns	ns	ns	ns
	Strategic Integration	–	ns	–	ns	–

ns = no significant relationship; – = significant and negative relationship

Source: Adapted from Gunnigle, Morley and Turner, 1998

These study findings suggest that there is a positive relationship between individualist management styles in industrial relations and levels of strategic integration. This relationship is particularly strong when one considers the overall composite indicator ('strategic integration') and also the variable which measures the level of sophistication of the employment and socialisation system ('employment system'). These findings clearly suggest that management styles which are characterised by a strong strategic focus are also most likely to adopt a discernible individualist orientation. This finding is also interesting insofar as it indicates that if, as much of the literature suggests, there is a trend towards an increasing strategic focus in industrial relations, this may lead to increasingly individualist management styles in industrial relations and a concomitant diminution in collectivism.

Turning to the relationship between collectivism and levels of strategic integration, the findings in Table 10.11 suggest that where companies integrate industrial relations considerations into strategic decision making, this is most likely to be associated with management styles characterised by low levels of collectivism and, more particularly, low levels of trade union recognition and density. These findings indicate an extremely weak or a negative relationship between levels of strategic integration and collectivism. Overall, it appears that the greater the strategic consideration afforded to industrial relations issues, the greater the likelihood that this will be associated with individualist industrial relations styles which exclude trade union recognition.

In relation to explanatory factors, the research findings indicate that company ownership and specifically US ownership is the most significant variable, positively impacting on levels of strategic integration. Strategic integration was also positively associated with size, and location in advanced industrial sectors. The only factor which impacted negatively on levels of strategic integration was market location in predominantly indigenous/local markets.

10.7 MANAGEMENT STYLES IN INDUSTRIAL RELATIONS IN IRELAND — AN OVERVIEW

Ever since Fox (1966) first articulated his unitarist and pluralist frames of reference, numerous attempts have been made to develop 'ideal-typical' categorisations of management styles in industrial relations. It is important to note the limitations associated with ideal-typical style categorisations. Previous studies have identified problems in placing many firms within ideal-typical management style categorisations (Deaton, 1985; Salamon, 1998). Ideal-typical style categorisations are inherently limiting and may not reflect organisational reality in the sense that there may be an absence of a clear and preferred management style in some companies or, indeed, companies may be in transition between styles. However, given these caveats, such style categorisations are useful in indicating dominant management orientations, and therefore represent a useful analytical tool for evaluating management approaches to industrial relations and explaining variations in approaches. Style categorisations are also useful in distinguishing between companies which consciously pursue coherent industrial relations styles and those which do not. Based on our review of typologies of management styles in industrial relations and the key dimensions of such styles, we are now in a position to outline a broad categorisation of management styles in industrial relations which draws on the available research evidence and which is considered appropriate in the Irish context. This categorisation of management styles in industrial relations in Ireland is outlined in Table 10.12 and is a variant of that developed by Purcell and Sisson (1983), which in turn, was based on the work of Fox (1966; 1974). This typology identifies six major management styles with differences deriving from varying positions on the benchmark dimensions of strategic integration, individualism and collectivism and gauged through personnel policy manifestations in relation to work systems, communications, reward systems, employment patterns and role of the specialist P/HR function.

Table 10.12 Proposed typology of management styles in industrial relations

1. **Anti-union style**: Organisations in this category are characterised by a commodity view of labour. In relation to the dimensions of management style in industrial relations, such firms are characterised by low strategic integration, low collectivism and individualism. Manifestations of this approach include a preoccupation with retaining managerial prerogative; rejection of any role for trade unions or other modes of collective representation and open hostility to unions; little or no attention to P/HR/industrial relations except where absolutely necessary; no, or at best a low level P/HR function; absence of procedures for communicating or consulting with employees; authoritarian management control, poor rewards and low levels of job security. The available research evidence suggests that 'anti-union' styles are predominantly confined to indigenous companies established and managed in the classic 'small firm/entrepreneurial' mode but may also be found in some foreign-owned, particularly US-owned, firms.

Table 10.12 Proposed typology of management styles in industrial relations
contd.

2. **Paternalist style**: In this style top management prioritise a need to 'look after' employees. The characteristics of this approach are a benevolent, welfare-oriented approach to employees. However, as in the 'anti-union' style, the management view of the organisation is essentially unitarist. Little attention is paid to employee representation, involvement or development. Divergent opinions from those of management are seen as indicative of disloyalty and potentially damaging to the fabric of employer-industrial relations. Indeed, the paternalist style may incorporate a high level of management complacency about the perceived closeness of management and employee interests and expectations. In relation to the benchmark dimensions of management style, the paternalist style is felt to be characterised by little strategic integration, medium individualism (i.e., caring approach to employees but few mechanisms to enhance employee involvement or commitment) and low collectivism. P/HR policy manifestations include a caring supervisory style but a work system which limits employee involvement and discretion, limited communications mechanisms, an external labour market and extrinsic rewards emphasis, and a P/HR function whose role is of an administrative support nature.

3. **Traditional industrial relations style**: The 'traditional IR' style equates to the traditional pluralist perspective characterised by adversarial industrial relations, primary reliance on collective bargaining and employer association membership and utilisation. It is characterised by low strategic integration, low/medium individualism and medium to high collectivism (of an adversarial nature). This style has many of the characteristics of Purcell and Sisson's 'sophisticated modern-constitutionalist' style — particularly in the conception of industrial relations in terms of 'conflictual terms and conditions of employment and the codification and limiting of collective bargaining arrangements' (Purcell and Sisson, 1983; Salamon, 1998). The main manifestations are trade union recognition (often incorporating multi-unionism) and reliance on collective bargaining. Management-union relations may sometimes be formalised in a procedural agreement regulating relations between the parties and encompassing issues such as union recognition (including closed shop), disciplinary, grievance and disputes procedures. However, other organisational arrangements may not be formalised in a comprehensive written agreement and are largely a product of custom and practice. Other manifestations include a bureaucratic organisation structure, tightly defined jobs, limited and top-down communications, external and internal labour market emphasis, extrinsic rewards and a 'contracts manager' type P/HR function whose primary role is to handle industrial relations (Tyson and Fell, 1986). Information sharing and consultation are not common in these companies. In Ireland it appears that this style is most common among long established and larger indigenous organisations and many European-owned firms. This style is seen as particularly characteristic of organisations in the State and semi-State sector.

4. **'Soft' Human Resource Management style**: The 'soft' HRM style is characterised by a resource perspective on employees, and a desire to create an organisational climate where individual employee needs are satisfied through a combination of positive employee-oriented policies designed (in part) to render collective representation unnecessary. This style equates to what has been termed 'union substitution' (see chapter 9). This style is grounded in the unitarist perspective and is normally associated with pronounced preference for non-union status. Manifestations of this style include: competitive pay and employment conditions; extensive management-employee communications; mechanisms to facilitate direct employee involvement in work-related decisions and procedures to handle grievance and disciplinary issues. Other manifestations include an internal labour market emphasis, availability of intrinsic and extrinsic rewards (at least partially based on merit), and a highly developed and influential P/HR function. The hallmarks of this management style are high individualism (resource perspective on employees), high strategic integration and low to medium

Table 10.12 Proposed typology of management styles in industrial relations *contd.*

collectivism: however, the latter is achieved through non-union fora such as consultative committees, quality circles, etc. In the greenfield site study discussed earlier, it was found that seven of the fifty-three companies studied adopted all the hallmarks of 'soft' HRM (Gunnigle, 1995a and b; Gunnigle, Morley and Turner, 1997). All but one of these companies was US-owned and all were manufacturing companies operating from strong market positions. This seems to reflect a common consensus that 'soft' HRM approaches are most common in US-owned firms operating in high technology sectors.

5. **'Hard' Human Resource Management style**: In the 'hard' HRM style the management of the company's human resources (incorporating not only employees but also subcontracted labour) is largely focused on transaction costs (see also Storey, 1989; Blyton and Turnbull, 1992). Thus, the management objective is to source and manage labour in as cheap and cost effective a fashion as possible to ensure achievement of the organisation's 'bottom line' objectives. This style equates to what has been termed 'union suppression' incorporating low employment standards and is in contrast with 'union substitution' or high standard non-union companies ('soft' HRM). The greenfield site study found that this style was particularly common among US-owned information/data processing services and electronics assembly companies operating in a subcontracting mode to major manufacturers. On the benchmark dimensions this style is characterised by high strategic integration, low/medium collectivism and low individualism. Manifestations of this style are most obvious in the adoption of 'atypical' employment forms, particularly extensive use of subcontracting and temporary/part-time employees, to improve cost effectiveness while meeting required performance standards and in the use of performance management techniques designed to achieve maximum return on the organisation's investment in human resources. Storey (1992:46) describes this approach as '. . . calculative, business-like treatment of labour with the accent upon it as a resource like any other to be deployed and disposed of in an economically rational way and with impatience towards institutional arrangements or procedures which interfere in that process'.

6. **Dualist style**: The 'dualist' style is characterised by an acceptance of the legitimacy of collective employee representation but supplemented by a strong individualist emphasis. Companies adopting this style are seen to differ from the 'soft' HRM firms on the collectivism dimension but otherwise pursue broadly similar policies. Union recognition would generally be formalised in a procedural agreement specifying management and union rights and collective bargaining arrangements. At shop floor level, management will seek to keep formality to a minimum. The management focus is placed on minimising the extent of collective bargaining especially that of an adversarial/distributive nature and on emphasising more integrative/co-operative bargaining and on direct dealings with employees. This style might be termed 'neo-pluralism', involving the use of selected HRM techniques, such as sophisticated selection, extensive direct communications with employees and performance-related pay systems, alongside established collective bargaining procedures. In the greenfield study the 'dualist' style was extremely rare and in its 'pure form', (high levels of collectivism, individualism and strategic integration) was confined to only one of the fifty-three greenfield companies studied. On the benchmark dimensions, this style is characterised by high strategic integration, high individualism and high collectivism. Manifestations include an organic organisation structure, broadly defined jobs, extensive communications fora, internal labour market emphasis, extrinsic and intrinsic rewards and a well developed and influential P/HR function. Further characteristics may include careful selection and extensive employee development; employees encouraged to deal directly with management on issues of concern; line management trained in industrial relations and backed up by a well developed P/HR department which, on the one hand, co-ordinates collective bargaining with the trade unions

The typology is considered indicative of the predominant styles that might be adopted by Irish organisations. There will obviously be overlap in management styles where companies adopt practices/policies which are common to two or more style categories. Given our earlier caveats on the limitations of 'ideal-typical' style categorisations and reflecting on the Irish situation, the most striking feature of this typology relates to the 'soft' HRM, 'hard' HRM and 'dualist' styles. These styles are significant because they indicate a planned and co-ordinated approach to industrial relations management in contrast to the other styles which are indicative of a more 'incidentalist' approach. The 'traditional' IR style equates to the pluralist-adversarial model and has been the most pervasive style in the majority of medium and large organisations in Ireland (Hillery, 1994; Roche, 1990). However, the 'anti-union' and 'paternalist' styles reflect opposition to the pluralist model as manifested through forthright attempts to curb or eliminate moves towards collective employee representation. It has traditionally been argued that these styles were confined to smaller organisations and that in the event of growth they would over time succumb to the 'traditional pluralist' model (Gunnigle, 1989; Roche, 1990). However, the available evidence indicates considerable change in enterprise level industrial relations in Ireland. In terms of management styles, such developments are characterised by the increased adoption of HRM-based styles ('hard' or 'soft' variants). Such developments suggest a strengthening of the unitarist ideology among the management of Irish greenfield organisations and, particularly, greater opposition to union recognition, the emergence of a strong non-union sector and a fall in union density. Unlike the 'dualist' style (which is essentially a variant of traditional pluralism), both the 'hard' and 'soft' HRM styles contrast significantly with the traditional pluralist model and are essentially unitarist in character.

10.8 Summary

This chapter has explored the issue of management styles in industrial relations. It has examined the nature of managerial choice in industrial relations and specifically the context, dimensions and key areas of choice. It has also presented a typology of management styles in industrial relations considered relevant to the Irish context.

NOTE
1. For greater details on the construction of these measures see Gunnigle, Morley and Turner (1997).

CHAPTER ELEVEN

Contemporary Developments in Industrial Relations

11.1 INTRODUCTION

This chapter considers some contemporary developments in Irish industrial relations. In particular, it reviews some important contextual developments and looks at areas of particular significance, notably the impact of technological change, quality enhancement initiatives and the role of the EU. We begin by reviewing the macro-economic and labour market context.

11.2 THE IRISH ECONOMY — A SUMMARY

Some general data on the Irish economy were presented in chapter 1. There we saw that Ireland is a late developing economy, its population being predominantly rural and agriculture based until the 1960s. The late 1950s witnessed a major change in Irish industrial policy, moving from a protectionist stance to a more open economy. Because of the country's historically weak industrial base, this was achieved by what has been termed 'industrialisation by invitation'. Essentially, the Government provided various incentives to encourage foreign-owned companies to establish facilities in Ireland.

The 1960s was a period of significant growth and development in the Irish economy. This began to taper off during the 1970s and by the early 1980s the economy was in a dreadful financial state. Economic growth during the first half of the 1980s was very low, unemployment and inflation were rising steadily, and the country's fiscal debt was unsustainable. Substantial employment decline was recorded during this recessionary period when unemployment rose from less than 8 per cent to almost 17 per cent of the labour force and resulted in the resumption of large scale emigration. As public debt and unemployment reached record proportions, the economy became locked in deep recession.

The period since the late 1980s has seen a remarkable turnaround in the Irish economy. Initial fiscal rectitude and subsequent economic growth have made Ireland the OECD's fastest growing economy and have earned it the label of 'Celtic Tiger', emphasising economic performance at or above the levels of most of the world's high growth economies. Since 1994 the expansion of the Irish economy has been impressive, with the growth rate of real GDP averaging out at approximately 8 per cent per year, making Ireland one of the world's fastest growing economies. In 1995, Ireland replaced the UK as the favoured site for US electronic hardware overseas investment — Ireland now attracts approximately one-quarter of all US direct investment in the EU, a remarkable statistic given that Ireland accounts for just 1 per cent of the population of the EU. In terms of international competitiveness, the 1997 World Competitiveness Report ranked Ireland as the fifteenth most competitive world economy, achieving particularly strong scores on education, Government, and technological capacity (World Economic Forum, 1997).

Unemployment, a persistent problem in Ireland, has also fallen significantly. Employment growth reached record levels in recent years while the long-term trend is favourable (falling from 17 per cent in 1986 to just over 9 per cent in 1998). Economic forecasts suggest that GDP is expected to grow strongly with further increases in employment. The only dark cloud appearing on the economic horizon is the trend towards increasing inflation.

11.3 INDUSTRIAL RELATIONS AND PUBLIC POLICY[1]

We have seen that industrial relations in Ireland has traditionally been associated with a strong pluralist orientation. This pluralist tradition is manifest in comparatively high levels of union density and recognition, a reliance on adversarial collective bargaining and industrial relations as the key human resource priority within organisations.

In evaluating Irish industrial relations, three particular aspects of public policy are noteworthy: (1) support for trade unions and collective bargaining and promotion of centralised 'social partnership' agreements; (2) a strong emphasis on attracting direct foreign investment; and (3) constitutional support for freedom of association.

Historically, Irish Governments have, over recent decades, supported the principle of collective bargaining and accepted the legitimacy and role of trade unions at enterprise and national level. Traditionally, Government approaches to industrial relations were grounded in the voluntarist tradition, essentially characterised by a 'hands off' approach with a minimal legislative and procedural framework to underpin collective bargaining. This approach was largely an historical legacy of the UK voluntarist tradition. However, in the early 1980s the industrial relations approaches of the UK and Irish Governments pursued markedly contrasting routes.

In the UK, Conservative Governments during the 1980s took progressive steps, both legislative and otherwise, to reduce union power and ensure that wage levels and other industrial relations outcomes were determined by market forces.

In Ireland, the voluntarist tradition has also become diluted in recent years. In contrast to the UK, however, this change has taken the form of greater centralisation of industrial relations. Recent Governments have been strong advocates of centralised agreements on pay and other aspects of economic and social policy, involving negotiations between the 'social partners'. Since 1987 Ireland has had four centralised agreements with the current agreement (Partnership 2000) scheduled to expire in 2000. These agreements deal not only with pay, but with a range of economic and social policy issues such as welfare provision, employment creation and tax reform.

Another important aspect of Irish Government policy is the attraction of direct foreign investment through incentives to multinational companies (MNCs) to establish facilities in Ireland. There are now over 1,000 overseas companies operating in Ireland which employ over 100,000 people, with a particular focus on electronics, pharmaceuticals, software and internationally traded services. Employment in MNCs accounts for roughly one-third of the industrial workforce. These foreign-owned companies account for 50 per cent of manufactured output and some three-quarters of industrial exports. The main sources of direct foreign investment in Ireland are the US (almost 50 per cent), the UK, and Germany. US-owned firms have a particularly strong presence in Ireland: over 400 such firms employ around 50,000 people. In 1995 Ireland was the ninth most important global location for US direct investment (sixth most important in Europe; third in 1994). Ireland has also been the most profitable European location for US companies, providing a return on investment of 24 per cent over the period 1983–1994 or almost three times the EU average.

The major advantage of Ireland's policy of attracting foreign MNCs has been their contribution to employment creation, technology transfer, and export growth. Some of the potential downsides include the following: many are located in very volatile sectors (it is estimated that 15 per cent of Irish electronics jobs are 'high risk' and many more are 'medium risk', McGowan, 1996); transfer pricing and high profit repatriation; many are confined to low level activities which are quite 'footloose'; there is a low R&D component and many have weak linkages into the domestic economy. On the industrial relations front, MNCs have been an important source of innovation in management practices, particularly in the application of new human resource management approaches and in expanding the role of the specialist personnel/HR function. However, it would also seem that MNCs pose particular and unique challenges in the industrial relations sphere, particularly in their ability to switch the locus of production and also to adopt industrial relations styles which challenge or, indeed, undermine the traditional pluralist model. In Ireland we have seen a dramatic growth in non-union approaches over the past decade. This is particularly the case in the manufacturing sector where we find that the great majority of new large firms are non-union (see later discussion on freedom of association).

A critical aspect of Irish public policy in industrial relations is constitutional support for the concept of freedom of association. Article 40.6.1. of the Irish Constitution provides for the right of individuals to form or join associations or unions. We have seen that this provision has also been interpreted to include an implied right not to join trade unions where individuals do not wish to do so. However, beyond this constitutional guarantee of freedom of association, there is no statutory provision for trade union recognition in Ireland. This means that although workers have constitutional support to join trade unions, there is no legal obligation on employers to recognise or bargain with such unions (see chapter 4).

We have also seen that Ireland is characterised by comparatively high levels of trade union density. It is estimated that approximately 43 per cent of the Irish workforce are trade union members (Roche, 1997a). Although longitudinal data indicate some decline in union density, especially during the 1980s, it appears that union density has held up comparatively well by international standards and indeed aggregate union membership increased in the early 1990s.

While national statistics provide us with an overall picture of trade union density, it is necessary to look at union membership levels at organisation level to gain insights into the operational role and impact of trade unions. The Cranfield-University of Limerick (CUL) study investigated human resource management practices in a representative sample of Irish organisations (Gunnigle, Morley, Clifford and Turner, 1997). Figures for 1995 indicate that the level of trade union density in Irish organisations is quite high, with over two-thirds of organisations reporting that 50 per cent or more of their employees were trade union members (see chapter 4). Union penetration is greatest in the public service and 'traditional' manufacturing. Levels of union density are particularly high in the public sector.

As noted above, despite Ireland's high level of union density, there are no specific statutory provisions to govern the process of trade union recognition. The extent of trade union recognition is therefore an important indicator of employer approaches to industrial relations, since the granting of such recognition is largely an issue of management prerogative. Evidence from the CUL study suggests a healthy picture of trade union recognition in Ireland: almost 80 per cent of participating organisations recognised trade unions for collective bargaining purposes. Overall, this evidence indicates that trade union penetration in Ireland remains quite robust with high levels of union recognition and union density characterising most of Ireland's larger organisations. This evidence might lead one to conclude that there is a high level of congruity between public policy, which supports trade unions and collective bargaining, and actual practice, which indicates that trade unions play an active part in both national level and organisation level industrial relations.

A more in-depth analysis of available data suggests otherwise. Since union penetration is strongest in the public service and 'traditional' manufacturing, it is appropriate to look outside these sectors for a more reliable indicator of the changing role of trade unions. In chapter 4 we noted that studies of more recently established firms point to a high and increasing incidence of non-unionism, especially in manufacturing and internationally traded services. Non-union approaches appear particularly common among US-owned firms in 'high technology sectors'. These findings point to a significant trend of union avoidance in greenfield site companies. In a period when direct foreign investment in Ireland is at an all time high, it appears that these new companies are increasingly choosing the non-union route.

From a research perspective, Ireland presents a somewhat unique context for examining the relationship between public policy and industrial relations. In particular, the industrial relations environment is quite different to those of the US and UK, whence much of the contemporary literature emanates. The most explicit manifestations of this difference include the widely accepted legitimacy of trade unions in Irish society, the maintenance of comparatively high levels of trade union density, high levels of centralisation of decision making on pay and other aspects of economic and social policy, and the absence of a strong anti-union ideology among any of the major political parties (see, for example, Gunnigle, 1995a and b; Roche, 1997b; Roche and Turner, 1994). These factors contribute to a social, political and economic context considered conducive to the sustenance of the pluralist industrial relations model.

However, despite this apparently supportive context we have seen that trade unions and collective bargaining are facing particular challenges, principally in Ireland's new growth industries.

11.4 LABOUR MARKET DEVELOPMENTS

The most notable changes in the Irish labour market over the past twenty years have been the dramatic fall in numbers employed in agriculture and the consistent growth in employment in the services sector which now accounts for over 60 per cent of all employees (see Figure 11.1). Much of this service sector growth in recent years has been concentrated in private services. In the period 1975–89 there was a significant increase in employment in financial and business services (42 per cent), professional services (21 per cent) and personal services (16 per cent) (Dineen, 1992).

While the proportion of the workforce employed in industry has remained relatively constant, there has been significant change in the sectoral distribution of industrial employment. In particular, the period since the 1970s has seen a substantial fall in the numbers employed in older indigenous

Figure 11.1 Employment changes by sector 1961–97

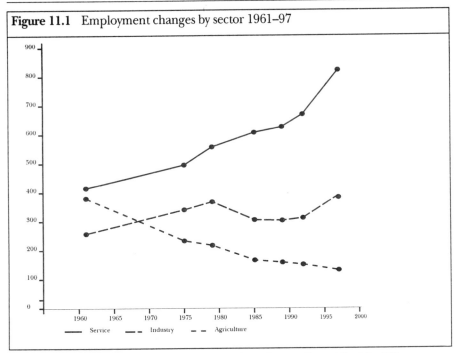

Source: Census of Population and Labour Force Surveys, Central Statistics Office

manufacturing involving a large reduction in the numbers employed in the textiles, clothing and footwear sectors. In the same period there were substantial increases in employment in foreign-owned firms, particularly in chemicals and engineering. Generally, job losses in the manufacturing sector tended to be concentrated in labour intensive industries catering for the home market while companies (largely foreign-owned) in more capital intensive export-oriented sectors fared much better.

Unemployment increased dramatically over the 1980s and in early 1993 reached over 300,000 or almost 20 per cent of the workforce. The onset of economic recession in the early 1980s combined with the rapid growth in numbers joining the labour force caused major problems for employment creation. Total numbers at work fell by almost 7 per cent in the 1979–85 period and unemployment increased dramatically over the period. Dineen (1992) suggests that the reasons for this dramatic growth in unemployment are part supply driven (population growth and increased labour force participation rates) and part demand driven (weak international demand abroad and fiscal rectitude at home).

However, since 1994, the strong performance of the Irish economy has seen significant growth in employment, leading to a remarkable transformation in the debate on labour issues: from a concern with escalating unemployment and a brain drain (through emigration) to an increasing concern about labour

407

shortages. The numbers at work are growing by almost 4 per cent a year and the standardised unemployment rate has fallen below the EU average and currently stands at approximately 9 per cent. The economy is witnessing particularly strong growth in private sector non-agricultural employment. Between 1980 and 1996, non-agricultural employment growth at 26 per cent exceeded that of the EU 12 (7 per cent) and the US (15 per cent) (ESRI, 1997:39). Of the current Irish labour force, 10 per cent are employed in agriculture, 29 per cent in industry and 61 per cent in services.

During 1995 and 1996 the largest share of employment creation was accounted for by the expansion of the services sector with increases of 48,000 and 43,000 recorded respectively. This pattern was reversed somewhat in 1997 when employment creation was largely attributed to the industrial sector and particularly to the manufacturing sector (growth in employment of approximately 17 per cent) and to the building and construction sector (10,000 job increase), although employment in the services sector did also increase by 14,000. Latest EU (1997) estimates suggest there is a danger that the Irish economy is approaching full capacity and there are already bottlenecks and skills shortages appearing in certain sectors. In evaluating recent changes in the Irish labour market, Heraty and Morley (1998) identify a number of developments which underpin recent employment growth:

(1) Female labour force participation has risen dramatically in recent years. Expressed as a proportion of the total female population of working age, the number of females in the labour force has increased from 34.1 per cent in 1992 to 39.2 per cent in 1997 (Central Bank, 1997; Baker et al., 1997). If one adopts a longer term perspective, female participation in the labour force has increased by more than 40 per cent since 1980 (European Commission, 1997b). Speculation on the causes of this increased participation has focused on factors such as smaller family sizes, changing structure of employment demand, institutional factors, and improvements in educational attainment. While female participation continues to increase in Ireland, the current degree of participation remains lower than that in other EU Member States and OECD countries.

(2) Significant changes are evidenced in the age structure of the population: in 1981, 30 per cent of the Irish labour force was aged fifteen to twenty-four; the corresponding figure in 1997 is less than 19 per cent.

(3) Economic buoyancy has resulted in a reversal of external migration; it is estimated that, in the absence of external migration, the Irish labour force has the capacity to expand by between 20,000 and 25,000 persons each year (1.5 per cent of the total labour force).

11.4.1 THE GROWTH OF 'ATYPICAL' EMPLOYMENT

It would appear that shifts in employment structure, competitive pressures on organisations and the currently buoyant economic environment have led to greater variation in forms of employment, with a discernible trend towards more 'atypical' forms of employment. Indeed, one of the most visible changes in employment practices in Ireland has been the growth of atypical employment forms. Atypical employment is defined as any form of employment which deviates from the full-time, permanent format. Analyses of atypical employment have primarily focused on part-time, temporary and self-employment although broader definitions include areas such as the black economy and tele-working (Dineen, 1992; Cordova, 1986).

The latest European Commission's (1997) study on the Irish labour market indicates that while the incidence of part-time work, as a proportion of total employment in the Irish economy, is relatively low when compared with other EU countries, it has increased significantly in recent years. From 1983–93, virtually all employment creation related to part-time work which is, perhaps, reflective of the shift to service sector employment, particularly evidenced in 1995 and 1996. The current proportion of part-time work in Ireland is 12.3 per cent (comparable figure for 1992 was 9 per cent), but is as high as 20 per cent for females. Almost 50 per cent of females engaged in part-time work are to be found in service type occupations, with a further 20 per cent engaged in clerical work. It appears that the majority of workers in part-time employment are there out of choice (Wallace and Clifford, 1998).

In spite of a growth in part-time employment, it is important to point out that, since 1993, the unprecedented growth in the Irish economy has resulted in the creation of mainly full-time jobs (see Tables 11.1 and 11.2). Indeed, the available data indicate an increase in both part- and full-time working:

> Data from the Labour Force Survey in Ireland shows an increase in the use of part-time contracts . . . over the period 1986 to 1996 *with corresponding stability in the level of full-time, secure, permanent employment* . . . Although the level of full-time jobs reached a high of 79.9 per cent in 1990 and a low of 75.2 per cent in 1993, the figure in 1996 is almost exactly as it stood in 1986. This indicates that *although there has been an increase in the use of part-time contracts in the same period, this has not affected the proportion of full-time jobs*, which stood at 78 per cent of all jobs in 1996. (Wallace and Clifford, 1998:5) (Emphasis added)

The increase in full-time working may be as a result of the expansion of manufacturing employment and the current 'boom' being experienced in the building and construction industry and in many areas of the services sector. Overall, the increased propensity towards part-time employment may be indicative of improved flexibility in the Irish labour market. However, part-time working remains exceptionally low by EU standards and there is considerable scope for an upward trend to continue (see Table 11.3). Temporary work, as a proportion of overall employment, currently stands at just 7 per cent.

Table 11.1 Employment categorisation of economically active individuals 1986–96

	1986	1988	1990	1991	1992	1993	1994	1995	1996
Full-time	77.9%	77.1%	79.9%	78.3%	77.3%	75.2%	75.6%	77.3%	78%
Part-time (not underemployed)	3.9%	5.1%	5.7%	5.7%	6.2%	7.4%	7.9%	8.8%	8.6%
Part-time (underemployed)	1.2%	1.4%	1.2%	1.4%	1.4%	1.7%	1.7%	1.8%	1.6%
Seeking full-time Employment	15.1%	14.7%	11.5%	12.9%	13.5%	14.0%	13.0%	10.5%	10%
Seeking Part-time Employment	2.0%	1.6%	1.7%	1.9%	1.6%	1.7%	1.7%	1.6%	1.8%
N (thousands)	1321.7	1328.5	1326.2	1345.3	1369.8	1399.1	1424.9	1449.5	1494.4

Source: Labour Force Surveys, 1986–96, Central Statistics Office

Table 11.2 Employment changes 1986–94 (in thousands)

	1986	1994	Change '86–'94
Full-time employment	1029	1077	+ 48 (+4.7%)
Part-time employment	66	137	+ 71 (+108%)
Total employment	1096	1214	+119 (+11%)

Source: Labour Force Surveys, Central Statistics Office

Table 11.3 Part-time Workers in selected EU Member States

	As a share of total employment 1985 (%)	Average Annual Increase* 1994 (%)	1985–94 (%)
Denmark	24.3	21.2	-1.6
Greece	5.3	4.8	-0.5
United Kingdom	20.9	23.8	1.8
Spain	5.8	6.9	3.5
Ireland	**6.4**	**10.8**	**9.3**
Netherlands	22.4	36.4	12.5
*EU 15** *	*12.5*	*15.3*	*3.7*

* Countries ranked according to average annual increase.
** 1985 data excludes new German Lander; 1994 data includes new German Lander.
Figures for 1994 include 1993 data for Austria and Sweden

Source: European Commission, Employment in Europe, 1995

Of those 137,000 part-time workers in 1994, some 98,000, or over seven in ten, were women. In absolute figures, this indicates that over one in every five women in employment were working part-time: the comparable figure for men was just over one in twenty. The sectoral changes in the structure of Irish employment and the concomitant increase in female participation rates are inextricably linked with changes in atypical employment (see Table 11.4). Sectoral shifts in employment are favourably biased towards greater female employment with women proportionately over represented in the expanding sectors. However, as noted above, overall female participation rates remain low by European standards.

Table 11.4 Job categorisation by gender 1991–96

	1991	1992	1993	1994	1995	1996
Regular full-time:						
Male	63.3%	61.8%	59.7%	58.8%	58.2%	57.9%
Female	28.1%	29.1%	28.6%	28.9%	28.7%	29.8%
Regular part-time:						
Male	1.9%	2.1%	2.4%	2.5%	2.6%	2.5%
Female	5.1%	5.6%	6.5%	6.9%	7.6%	7.4%
Occasional full-time:						
Male	0.2%	0	0.5%	0.7%	0.6%	0.5%
Female	0.2%	0.1%	0.4%	0.4%	0.4%	0.3%
Occasional part-time:						
Male	0.4%	0.4%	0.7%	0.7%	0.7%	0.5%
Female	0.8%	0.9%	1.2%	1.1%	1.0%	1.0%
N(thousands)	1147.4	1159.9	1177.5	1214.1	1267.5	1316.8

Source: Labour Force Surveys, 1991–96, Central Statistics Office

Despite some growth in atypical employment, it must be emphasised that the majority of workers in the non-agricultural sector (almost 80 per cent) still work in typical employment. Thus, while there is a definite trend towards atypical employment, the change is a gradual one and must be viewed in the context of broader economic and (particularly) labour market change. In sectors where we find some substitution of atypical for typical employment forms, such as in the public sector, this appears largely an expedient and reactionary measure taken in response to competitive pressures facing these organisations. This situation may indeed change as the labour market tightens and workers become more reluctant to take up atypical employment offers. However, it is plausible to argue many of these changes in employment patterns will pertain in the longer term, at least in part, due to the financial attractions to employers of lower wage levels, reduced employment-related overheads (such as pensions, holidays) and increased numerical flexibility (Hakim, 1991). This latter issue is discussed below.

11.5 The Flexibility Debate[2]

An associated development with important implications for industrial relations is the contention that the flexible firm model as advocated by Atkinson (1984) and characterised by the planned development of a core/periphery employment model is emerging in Irish organisations (Flood,

1990). Within this scenario the 'core' is composed of full-time staff enjoying relatively secure, challenging jobs with good pay and employment conditions, while the 'periphery' is composed of an amalgam of temporary, part-time and contract groups enjoying much less favourable pay and employment conditions, and less job security or training and promotion opportunities. The flexible firm scenario is based on the planned development of a 'core-periphery' employment model incorporating increased flexibility in three key areas:

(1) *numerical flexibility*, incorporating the use of non-standard employment forms, which allows the organisation to take on or shed labour flexibly in line with business demands;

(2) *functional flexibility*, which is defined as the expansion of skills within a workforce or the ability of organisations to reorganise the competencies associated with jobs so that the job holder is willing and able to deploy such competencies across a broader range of skills (often described as 'multi-skilling');

(3) *financial flexibility*, whereby pay rates are linked to labour and product market conditions and pay increases for individual employees are variable and contingent on some measure of performance.

Atkinson (1984) proposed that the implementation of each of these flexibility forms simultaneously within an organisation would allow that organisation to cater for, and adapt to, changing economic circumstances. However, a number of weaknesses and limitations have been identified in relation to the flexible firm scenario (see, for example, Pollert, 1987, 1988a and b; Brewster, et al., 1994:188; Morley and Gunnigle, 1994). The debate has centred on a number of key issues, not least of which is the extent to which organisations are pursuing a planned strategic approach to incorporating various forms of flexibility in order to improve organisational performance. Research evidence to date has not confirmed this argument. Rather it has held that 'despite the appeal of the flexible firm scenario in some quarters, the research evidence to date suggests that change in this area would appear to be more closely aligned with gradual incrementalism rather than with a radical post-industrial futurology' (Morley and Gunnigle, 1994:109). Indeed Atkinson himself, in a later paper with Meager (1986:26), commented that:

> Although the observed changes were widespread, they did not cut very deeply in most firms, and therefore the outcome was more likely to be marginal, ad-hoc and tentative, rather than a purposeful thrust to achieve flexibility.

In the Irish context it is instructive to briefly consider the development of numerical, functional and financial flexibility.

11.5.1 NUMERICAL FLEXIBILITY
Current Irish evidence indicates a definite trend towards greater numerical flexibility (Suttle, 1988; Flood, 1990). Developments in numerical flexibility

were discussed above in the context of growth in 'atypical' employment forms. Looking at enterprise level developments, the Cranfield-University of Limerick (CUL) study examined whether the use of non-standard forms of employment had changed over recent years. It is important to note that the actual extent of any such changes in flexible work practices is not indicated in the study, so it may be inaccurate to draw too heavily on the findings in relation to this question. Non-standard employment contracts are divided into three broad categories: (1) those which are normally associated with the core workforce of the organisation, such as shift work, overtime, annual hours, job sharing, flexible working time and weekend work (time flexibility); (2) those associated with the periphery workforce of the organisation, such as part-time work, temporary or casual work, fixed term contracts and subcontracting (numerical flexibility); and (3) newly emerging forms of flexibility which are not yet widely used in Ireland, such as tele-working and home based work.

The CUL study indicates a general increase in organisational usage of most forms of atypical employment in Ireland (see Tables 11.5 and 11.6). Shift work and overtime appear to be the most stable forms of flexible work arrangements, with over 40 per cent of respondents reporting that there had been no change in the levels of either since 1992 (see Table 11.5).

However, it should be noted that these forms of non-standard employment practices most often occur in the core workforce, and are seldom considered in discussions on atypical employment. Against that, there seem to be substantial increases in the number of organisations reporting the use of forms of atypical employment which are associated with the peripheral workforce, as outlined in Table 11.6. The most significant increase is the utilisation of temporary/casual work. The findings also indicate that there has been no major change in the percentage of organisations reporting non-utilisation of these flexible work arrangements since 1992. Thus, while a high proportion of organisations already using subcontracting, part-time, temporary and fixed term work have sought to increase their use, the overall number of organisations adopting these flexible work methods has not changed significantly (Gunnigle, Morley, Clifford and Turner, 1997).

Table 11.5 Change in organisational use of flexible work arrangements — core workforce (1992–95)

	Increased	No Change	Decreased	Not Used	N
Weekend work	25(60)	40(94)	5(13)	27(71)	238
Shift work	24(57)	44(106)	2(5)	30(72)	240
Overtime	24(60)	44(111)	25(63)	6(16)	250
Annual hours	5(11)	15(34)	4(9)	76(168)	222
Job sharing	29(68)	15(34)	0	56(131)	233
Flexible working time	25(56)	31(70)	1(2)	43(97)	225

Source: Cranfield-University of Limerick Study 1992 and 1995

Table 11.6 Change in organisational use of flexible work arrangements — peripheral workforce (1992–1995)

	Increased	No Change	Decreased	Not Used	N
Part-time work	40(97)	29(69)	6(15)	25(59)	240
Temporary/casual	49(120)	35(85)	6(15)	10(24)	244
Fixed term contract	47(109)	29(67)	2(5)	23(53)	234
Subcontracting	41(98)	23(54)	2(5)	34(80)	237

Source: Cranfield-University of Limerick Study 1992 and 1995

Tele-working and homebased work are the least popular forms of non-standard contract (see Table 11.7), with 77 per cent and 74 per cent of organisations, respectively, reporting that they do not use these flexibility types.

Table 11.7 Change in organisational use of flexible work arrangements (1992–95)

	Increased	No Change	Decreased	Not Used	N
Home based work	6(13)	5(11)	.5(1)	89(193)	218
Tele-working	6(13)	3(6)	0	91(201)	220

Source: Cranfield-University of Limerick Study 1992 and 1995

The CUL study also explored what proportion of an organisation's workforce was employed on non-standard contracts. The results are quite surprising in the context of available research evidence which points to an increased use of flexible working practices across Europe. While 73 per cent of organisations which responded to the CUL (1995) survey use part-time employees, approximately half employ less than 1 per cent of their workforce on such contracts (see Table 11.8). However, since 1992 the number of organisations reporting between 1 and 10 per cent of the workforce on part-time contracts has increased slightly. The same trend can be identified in the use of temporary and fixed term contracts. Annual hours contracts, while accepted as a cost-effective way of dealing with excessive amounts of overtime, and having taken a firm foothold in countries such as Germany, Finland, The Netherlands and the UK, are not as yet popular methods of flexible working in Ireland.

Table 11.8 Proportion of the workforce on non-standard contracts

	<1%		1–10%		11–20%		>20%		N	
	1995	1992	1995	1992	1995	1992	1995	1992	1995	1992
Part-time	49	51	43	37	3	6	5	6	242	186
Temporary	28	29	55	54	14	11	3	6	243	197
Fixed term	51	52	33	27	4	5	11	16	237	181
Home based	98	99	0.5	1	0.5	0	1	0	206	106
Tele-working	95	—	4	—	1	—	0	—	208	
Shift working	42	—	18	—	10	—	31	—	220	
Annual hours	90	—	4	—	1	—	5	—	209	

Source: Cranfield-University of Limerick Study 1992 and 1995

By and large, these findings point to some increase in the use of atypical employment forms. However, the adoption of flexible work practices is occurring at a gradual, incremental pace. Managerial motives for using flexible work arrangements include reduced costs, speed with which they can be recruited, administrative ease, and as a 'buffer' to cope with market uncertainty (Pfeffer, 1994:23–4). Thus, flexibility could be considered as an ongoing strategy to deal with environmental uncertainty, rather than a long-term strategic approach to human resource planning. It seems that different organisations are utilising different employment types (e.g., part-time, temporary workers) and practices (e.g., shift work, weekend work), and that such uses of flexible work practices appear to be more in response to cost and competitive strategies than deliberate flexibility strategies.

11.5.2 FUNCTIONAL FLEXIBILITY

Functional flexibility was defined above as the expansion of skills within a workforce or the ability of firms to reorganise the competencies associated with jobs so that the job holder is able and willing to deploy such competencies across a broader range of tasks. This process can mean employees moving into either higher or lower skill areas or a combination of both. It is often referred to as multi-skilling.

The CUL study examined whether 'major change' had been introduced in people's jobs which served to make them 'more specific or flexible' (Gunnigle, Morley, Clifford and Turner, 1997). The findings as outlined in Figure 11.2 indicate a general trend towards wider, more flexible jobs. While the majority of respondents report no change in their job specifications, a greater percentage of jobs in all categories have been made wider to encompass broader duties and responsibilities.

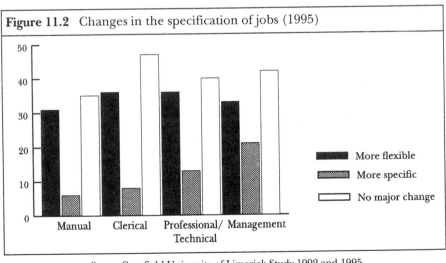

Figure 11.2 Changes in the specification of jobs (1995)

Source: Cranfield-University of Limerick Study 1992 and 1995

415

When compared to the results of the 1992 survey, it is clear that a significantly greater number of respondents in 1995 feel that jobs have become more flexible for all categories of workers in their organisations. However, when the figures are disaggregated to determine the effect of ownership on the degree of functional flexibility, it was found that indigenous Irish organisations were more likely to have made no changes whatsoever to the specification of jobs for all employee categories. Conversely, US-owned organisations tend to expand job specifications for all levels of the hierarchy, with the exception of clerical workers. Similarly, 68 per cent of UK-owned organisations had broadened job specifications. Change was less likely to take place in public sector organisations across all job categories. A greater proportion of jobs have been made more flexible in private sector organisations. The overall picture that emerges from the data is one of change in the private sector and stability in the public sector.

The CUL findings pertaining to job changes and trade union recognition were interesting. It has been argued that the existence of trade unions can inhibit flexibility and change, a factor often considered to be the rationale behind an organisation's decision to have non-union status (Flood and Toner, 1996, 1997; Gunnigle, 1995a and b). However, the CUL study revealed that change is more likely in unionised organisations. Similarly, a greater percentage of jobs for all categories, particularly manual and clerical, have become wider/more flexible in unionised organisations. Conversely, a greater number of jobs have become more specific in organisations that do not recognise trade unions. This finding is in line with a recent study of collective bargaining and flexibility in Ireland which suggests that levels of flexibility are as high in unionised as in non-union firms (Wallace and Clifford, 1998). This study indicates that Irish employers are generally satisfied with levels of flexibility in their organisations (also see Hannigan, 1997). It further suggests that centralised agreements have been a positive force in promoting greater flexibility at workplace level.

We noted above that the use of functional flexibility is often seen as encompassing 'multi-skilling' (see, for example, Suttle, 1988). Some larger organisations have taken a number of initiatives in this area, such as the ESB in the semi-State sector and Krups Engineering and Aughinish Alumina in the private sector. Case study evidence suggests that 'add-skilling' or 'extra-skilling' are more accurate descriptions of these developments than multi-skilling. This conclusion is based on the evidence that functional flexibility among skilled workers largely involves those categories receiving training in, and agreeing to undertake, a quite limited range of extra tasks in addition to their traditional trade, for example, fitters undertaking some electrical/instrumentation work (Gunnigle and Daly, 1992). There is, of course, evidence of organisations claiming to have total functional flexibility in their operations. However, such flexibility would appear to only pertain in unskilled or low skilled work where there is a minimal training requirement and it is thus relatively easy to deploy workers across a large range of (simple) tasks as required (Gunnigle, 1992b).

11.5.3 FINANCIAL FLEXIBILITY

Financial flexibility consists of two elements. Firstly, it encourages the introduction of merit/performance-related reward systems whereby employees are paid at a rate dependent on their performance, using an assessment based system or payment related to their level of skills acquisition (often termed 'contingent pay systems'). Secondly, it incorporates the ability of organisations to align basic wage rates to reflect product and labour market conditions. One may often find that financial flexibility is used to encourage functional flexibility (Keenan and Thom, 1984).

It is difficult to identify a clear picture in the area of financial flexibility. Findings from the Cranfield-University of Limerick (CUL) study (Table 11.9) suggest an evident trend towards greater financial flexibility, particularly in the increased incidence of variable pay systems (Gunnigle, Morley, Clifford and Turner, 1997). However, in examining the application of performance-related pay systems to different employee categories, we find a much more traditional picture. Here, the survey evidence points to merit or performance-related pay as largely confined to managerial and professional categories with a lower, but increasing, level of utilisation among clerical and manual grades (see Table 11.10). In relation to the second aspect of financial flexibility, namely basing pay level to market conditions, there have been two prominent examples of 'two-tier' pay systems in Bank of Ireland and Aer Lingus (Flood, 1989). Both of these involved the introduction of a new entry grade at pay levels considerably below that pertaining for those who traditionally carried out such work. While we saw some evidence of increasing utilisation of this form of financial flexibility in the early 1990s — a prominent example being Waterford Glass — the current 'tightening' of the Irish labour market may serve to mitigate trends in this direction (see later in this chapter).

Table 11.9 Change in reward systems

	Increased		Decreased		Same	
	1992	1995	1992	1995	1992	1995
Variable pay	32%	26%	4%	4%	56%	60%
Non-money benefits	19%	13%	2%	6%	67%	68%

Source: Cranfield-University of Limerick Study 1992 and 1995

Table 11.10 Utilisation of merit/performance-related pay (PRP)

	utilisation of merit/PRP	
	1992	1995
1. Among managerial grades	49%	51%
2. Among professional grades	42%	45%
3. Among clerical grades	29%	37%
4. Among manual grades	13%	15%

Source: Cranfield-University of Limerick Study 1992 and 1995

Overall, it appears that while there have been increases in all forms of flexibility, the aggregate picture does not point to the widespread emergence of the flexible firm model. Suttle's (1988) examination of ninety-six Irish companies which had introduced some form of flexibility found that none of these firms had attempted to combine numerical, functional and financial flexibility. Indeed it seems that, while flexibility is on the increase, this is occurring in a somewhat piecemeal fashion, often in reaction to labour and product market conditions rather than reflecting the planned emergence of the flexible firm. Nevertheless, such apparently expedient responses to environmental conditions may well be sustained in the longer term as organisations seek to retain the advantages of certain flexibility forms (Hakim, 1991).

11.6 TECHNOLOGICAL CHANGE

Technological change is of central relevance to industrial relations. It influences the power position of employers and employees, via its impact on the general demand for labour and on specific job types. New technology concurrently boosts and eliminates the demand for a plethora of skills. The relevance of technological developments to industrial relations is evident from the fact that an ICTU survey discovered that more than two-thirds of trade union officials had been involved in technology related negotiations in the course of the previous two years (ICTU, 1989a).

Technology involves the use of any implement, equipment or machinery which assists work. It took on a major significance during the Industrial Revolution of the eighteenth and nineteenth centuries. The harnessing of steam power and the subsequent generation of electricity led to dramatic economic and social change. Over the past twenty-five years the speed and extent of change has increased significantly. It is often argued that we are experiencing a new industrial revolution, based upon microprocessor developments and bio-technology. In contrast with the past, where new developments were interspersed between periods of relative stability, change today is apparently more rapid and continuous. For example, a new generation of computers now hits the market at least annually, whilst scientific advances allow the introduction of totally new processes and materials affecting practically every branch of industry and the services. This has massive implications for blue and white collar workers, and for the methods of production of goods and services. For the blue collar worker these developments have created the spectre of robotic factories, maintained by a small number of multi-skilled technicians. Many white collar workers have also seen their jobs deskilled and — as a consequence — their differential treatment become more difficult to defend.

11.6.1 THE LABOUR MARKET IMPACT

There is no consensus as to what the overall impact of technological advances has been on employment levels in the economy. Whilst they have served to obliterate and revise some jobs, they have also created both new jobs and industries, and expanded existing jobs. For example, in Ireland, the positive effects are evident from the growth of the electronics sector, which up to the beginning of the 1990s, had provided about 15,000 new jobs, with another 3,000 or so employed in the software industry. In 1995 there were just under 50,000 employed in the electrical/electronics sector. By 1997 this had risen to over 60,000. Against this however, process technology tends to lead to job losses. The St. James' Gate brewery of Guinness, for example, reduced its workforce by half, over a five-year period, as a result of technological modernisation. Reviewing the British scene, Gennard (1992) concludes that:

> There is no doubt that in some industries, such as coal mining, shipbuilding, railways, steel manufacture, docks and textiles, technology has been a factor in accounting for the long run decline in their employment levels. However it has also been a factor in the growth of employment in such industries as air transport, chemicals, financial services and public utilities such as gas, water and electricity.

It is clear that the technological revolution has contributed to the relative decline of employment in many areas of the industrial sector, and to its growth in the services sector. This is particularly evident in those jobs which involve the generation, processing or transmission of knowledge or information e.g., the media, telecentres, data processing, research, education and training.

In terms of the occupational impact there has been a definite decline in the availability of some job types e.g., in manual work. This has been compensated for somewhat by the new employment opportunities created by the 'high tech' industries which supply the computers, micro-chips and new technical systems. In addition, technological change has dramatically altered the nature of work in some industries (e.g., communications). It has also significantly reduced the bargaining power and employment opportunities of workers in many instances (e.g., printing, paper and textile manufacture), whilst strengthening the position of others (e.g., computer manufacture and electronic media). Furthermore, the application of new technologies has obliterated many demarcation lines and boundaries between previously separated trades and industries (e.g., between mechanics, electricians and fitters, in newspaper production and in the printing industry).

As to the actual impact on job skill levels, the broad debate on whether new technology results in deskilling or enskilling remains inconclusive. Whilst instances of both have been detected, Ramsay et al. (1992) argue that 'the evidence on skill is largely indeterminate', as 'jobs are often just different, gaining and losing skill elements in ways that are not readily commensurable'.

It is interesting in this regard however, to note the findings of an ICTU survey of its membership, which discovered that sizeable majorities of males, and (to a lesser extent) females, reported an increase in their skill requirements as a result of technological change (ICTU, 1989a and b). Furthermore, a majority of those surveyed felt that their working conditions remained the same as a result yet an overwhelming majority of the respondents reported an increase in stress levels following the introduction of the new technology.

EMPLOYER AND TRADE UNION PERSPECTIVES

Whilst the speed and applicability of technological change varies somewhat across sectors and organisations it is, nevertheless, persistent. Naturally the faster the pace of change the more difficult it is for both employers and trade unions to adapt. Employer motives with regard to new technology tend to be driven by the opportunities presented to consolidate or increase product market competitiveness and to improve productivity levels. By and large, the trade union position seems to be based upon a recognition of 'market realities' and tends therefore to support the employers' aspirations, where they are based upon 'change by agreement' policies. As ICTU(1989c) puts it: 'To attempt to embargo change puts the unions in a confrontation with management in which they appear to be adopting a Luddite stance.'

Trade union aspirations in regard to new technology are therefore concerned with ensuring that its introduction is the subject of negotiation. Accordingly, they attempt to influence the form of the new work arrangements and to ensure that the benefits to be derived from such change are reflected in the terms and conditions of its membership, and in the maintenance or expansion of employment levels. The preference for a 'joint regulatory' approach is reflected in the trade union recommendation that 'a common approach is clearly desirable from the adversarial approach generated by traditional collective bargaining' (ICTU, 1989a). That is, as the issues of mutual interest are addressed in a joint working party, the demands for protected employment levels, improved terms and conditions of employment and a better work environment can be pursued in the bargaining arena.

Of course particular difficulties are posed in this arena where technological advances jeopardise the demand for the skills of particular groups. Against this, many workers may also see the prospect of a better working environment (e.g., via computer aided manufacture and design), greater job security and enhanced terms and conditions of employment, as attractive. However, such developments constitute a particular threat to those trade unions that normally organise their recruitment along occupational or skill lines and base their power on exclusive representation of specific occupations or crafts. This reality has undoubtedly prompted a number of small trade unions to amalgamate or join up with larger unions (e.g., the merger of the Automobile, General Engineering and Mechanical Operatives Union with SIPTU). Allied to this is the fact that job losses and reduced employee control are most evident amongst semi-skilled manual groups in manufacturing and clerical/administrative work generally — both categories with a traditionally high level of trade union membership. This threat is accentuated by the many employment opportunities created by technological advances in areas characterised by low unionisation levels e.g., amongst professional categories and in 'high tech' non-union policy establishments (Bell, 1983).

11.6.2 IMPLEMENTING TECHNOLOGICAL CHANGE

Employer approaches to the introduction of new technology may be classified into two broad categories: the 'joint' and the 'unilateral'. The joint approach involves negotiation with the relevant trade union(s), thus enabling workers' insecurities to be allayed and/or compensated for. That is, worker co-operation and commitment (as opposed to confrontation), in the implementation of the new technology is sought. This approach is often based on the premise that change can be brought about more effectively via active staff participation, than if management attempt to impose change unilaterally in the face of negative employee reaction. For example, in 1991 the Department of Finance reviewed the high-tech command and control system, which was being operated by the Garda Síochána in Dublin. The review was prompted by the fact that the system was not apparently being used to anything near its full potential. The department's review attributed this failure exclusively to the system's lack of acceptance by the gardaí and their representative associations. According to McMahon (1996), so 'effective' was this resistance that the departmental review concluded, '. . . in all our research it became clear that the introduction of the Command and Control system has resulted in a net increase in the administrative work to be carried out in Garda stations'.

In contrast, it may be argued that by involving staff in those decisions which impinge upon their working lives, and by drawing upon their knowledge and experience, a direct improvement in working practices and operations, together with a more committed workforce may emerge. Such an approach is supported by research work undertaken by the European Foundation for the Improvement of Living and Working Conditions (1985). According to the Foundation, however, trade unions face real difficulties in making an effective contribution to strategy formulation when entering into such arrangements, due to a lack of expert support and training in the relevant areas. This experience is, in fact, being repeated with the plethora of 'quality' and 'new forms of work organisation' initiatives in evidence as: 'One of the key issues identified by workplace representatives is their urgent need for greater guidance and support from their unions in responding to the initiatives' (ICTU, 1993).

In contrast to the joint approach many employers prefer to introduce new technology 'by stealth', or unilaterally (Bell, 1982). This route assumes automatic and/or eventual employee support for the initiative and, it may, therefore, be introduced on a piecemeal basis. It may also take the form of securing the support of a traditionally 'loyal' group of staff in the hope that as their colleagues see the benefit of the initiative potential resistance will evaporate. Of course, both strategies have in instances led to industrial action by workers opposing such changes. The available evidence indicates that the depressed economic climate for much of the 1980s and early 1990s favoured employers from an industrial relations perspective, and consequently enabled them to implement change peacefully and on terms more favourable to themselves (Gennard, 1992). Trade unions have been left to negotiate from a position of weakness, as they recognise their common interest with the employer — that the enterprise must survive in the longer term, or be replaced by more competitive (perhaps non-union) employers, who have adapted to the necessary technical changes. Allied to this is the belief that these technological revisions render jobs considerably less amenable to employee control and consequently strengthen management's position. In contrast, however, the upsurge of total quality management (TQM) and world class manufacturing (WCM) type initiatives — examined below — may serve to redress this swing somewhat.

11.6.3 TECHNOLOGY AGREEMENTS
In 1991 the European Commission published a 'Joint Opinion', agreed by the social partners, on the introduction of new information technologies in firms. In the document the social partners:

> . . . recognised the need to make use of the economic and social potential offered by technological innovation in order to enhance the competitiveness of European firms and strengthen economic growth, thus creating one of the necessary conditions for better employment and, taking particular account of progress in the field of ergonomics, for improved working conditions. (Commission of the European Communities, 1991)

The social dialogue led to a double agreement on new technologies (covering training and motivation, and information and consultation) in European enterprises. However to date, this has produced limited results, and has contributed to a demand for such Joint Opinions to be made binding on the parties (Gill, 1992). This failure to secure a consequential agreement between employers and trade unions on technological developments is nothing new. For example, during the late 1970s and the early 1980s trade unions devoted considerable resources to the procurement of technology agreements. Such agreements ought to be differentiated from the productivity agreements more commonly found in the 1960s and 1970s. These productivity agreements usually involved revised working practices, with employees doing the same or similar work, albeit more flexibly and effectively. In contrast, technology agreements are designed to protect workers' interests in the event of significant revisions brought about by technological advances. However, according to Benson and Lloyd's (1983) review of new technology agreements in the UK:

> Health and safety is the most strikingly precise of the issues agreed: the others, such as job security, consultation and disclosure, and sharing benefits — are usually either tentative or vague, and all depend heavily on the maintenance of considerable strength and vigilance on the part of the unions.

This view is accentuated by James (1980) who concluded that trade unions rarely receive an assurance from management that change will be introduced via prior negotiation and agreement, or that full information on costs will be made available to them. Daniel (1987) agrees, having discovered in the UK that in only 10 to 15 per cent of cases is the introduction of technological change in unionised establishments negotiated. According to Brewster (1992) this failure, on the part of trade unions, is attributable to the fact that:
– it is frequently difficult to distinguish agreements on new technology from agreements on changing working practices or pay;
– new technology is a blanket term, and in reality every situation is different, thus rendering general trade union guidelines inappropriate and/or difficult to follow;
– economic circumstances, allied to management confidence, have allowed trade unions to be bypassed on the introduction of technical change.

Of course, it is difficult to reach a definitive conclusion on whether trade unions have been able to secure financial compensation for their members, as such compensation may be 'buried' in an overall wage round award or accommodated in a local bargaining clause under a national agreement. However, given the employer's general reluctance to provide relevant cost-benefit estimate data, when introducing new technology, it is somewhat ambitious to talk of a 'distribution of benefits' resulting from such change. Indeed, even in those instances where trade unions have had recourse to the Labour Court to secure compensation on behalf of their membership for new technology initiatives, it is striking to observe the preponderance of relatively modest once-off lump sum cash award settlements.

Related to this is the fact that, in general, interested parties have supported the implementation of technological change at work. Research indicates that there is often little worker resistance to the introduction of new technology (Blennerhasset and Haskins, 1985; Daniel, 1987 and 1990). For example, a survey of the 'general attitude' of trade union members toward technology revealed a majority in favour (ICTU, 1989a). However, where the advent of such technology threatens employment prospects, the resolution of differing group interests is much more likely to be protracted. Yet in general, the paucity of technology-related conflict can stand alongside: '. . . the often low wage settlements, the abortive industrial actions, the often hopeless factory occupations and mass redundancies as evidence of trade union weaknesses' (Benson and Lloyd, 1983).

Despite this apparent coalescence however, it is interesting to note the apparent failure of one of the major corporate panaceas of the 1990s, namely 'business process re-engineering'. This idea, of improving efficiency and profit levels by redesigning work structures, seemed a simple and obvious approach. Too often, however, such initiatives left employers with more complex work processes, increased costs and an alienated workforce (Mumford and Hendricks, 1996). Yet according to Taylor (1996), an examination of national level agreements since 1987 suggests that rather than constraining management, the PNR, the PESP and the PCW have assisted in the introduction of flexible work practices and new forms of technology via their local bargaining clauses. However, as the 'Celtic Tiger' wields its influence in a burgeoning economy, it is hardly surprising to now see the largest trade union in Ireland (SIPTU) warning employers that if they want changes in work practices or productivity they must agree to pay more than is provided for in the Partnership 2000 agreement (Sheehan, 1997).

11.6.4 EVALUATION

From the vast array of research work undertaken across Europe in recent years (Bratton and Gold, 1994), it is clear that technological change is, and will continue to be, widespread. Furthermore, it will present new opportunities for co-operation, together with potential for conflict, between management and staff. In this regard it is interesting to note the UK experience, which has revealed that where the personnel/HR specialists were involved in the change process, they have had a positive impact. That is, 'their involvement was associated with a stronger level of workers' support for change' (Daniel and Millward, 1993).

This conclusion has important implications, both for the personnel/HR function and the Irish economy. With an imminent statutory national minimum wage restricting the scope for reliance on a low wage competitive strategy, the focus must be on efforts to remain competitive via new technology. Again, the British experience is particularly insightful in this regard:

> . . . for many inefficient, low productivity enterprises low wages and low social charges have become a precondition for survival . . . over time low wages and low productivity have become self-reinforcing . . . the weaker has been the incentive for firms to innovate and modernise, in other words to reduce costs by implementing more efficient technologies. At issue is the difference between an organisational and economic environment which is conducive to a virtuous circle of high productivity and high levels of remuneration and an environment characterised by a vicious and self-perpetuating spiral of low wages, low morale and low productivity. (Nolan, 1989)

Given that Ireland has the highest proportionate level of low pay in the European Community (McMahon, 1992), the case for a progressive attitude toward technological change is strong and, fortunately, at least from an industrial relations perspective, apparent (ICTU, 1993).

11.7 NEW WORK ORGANISATION AND QUALITY INITIATIVES

For some years now the term 'Japanisation' has been used to describe many of the organisational changes taking place across Europe and North America. Just as North America itself has influenced the practice and language of human resource management, so has the Japanese experience driven the adoption of total quality management (TQM) techniques. Put simply, the proponents of 'Japanisation' describe it as a coherent and distinctive managerial strategy seeking to enlist employees' ingenuity, initiative and co-operation at the point of production or service provision. It also entails a range of human resource management policies designed to promote this high degree of worker commitment and to minimise the likelihood of industrial action. TQM-type initiatives involve such practices as 'lean production', cellular manufacturing and teamwork, autonomous work groups and self-inspection, total preventative maintenance, statistical process control and just-in-time (JIT) systems of production and service provision (see chapter 8). 'Lean production' is reflected in organisational and work structures which facilitate flexible working arrangements, JIT inventory levels and staff-management collaboration. In contrast with 'Taylorism', and the specialised machinist operating one machine at one particular work station, there is now a generalised, skilled machinist with flexible job boundaries. Under a JIT system waste is minimised in a 'hand-to-mouth' mode of manufacturing, which aims to produce the necessary components, in the required quantities, to quality specifications on demand.

With TQM, responsibility for quality production is assigned to the worker. It is concerned with continuously improving customer satisfaction by quality-led company-wide management (Wilkinson, 1992). In its ideal conception, the genuine TQM company is one which practices TQM without thinking about it, as quality is a way of life which permeates every part and aspect of the organisation's existence. This involves the abandonment of efficiency in favour of effectiveness, with an emphasis on customer satisfaction rather than quality control specifications. Indeed some would say that quality initiatives now focus on 'customer delight' rather than 'customer satisfaction' (Pearson, 1991)! If customers are in fact 'delighted', the implications for an expanding market share are self-evident. Accordingly, quality is transformed from being a single aspect of corporate affairs to one of strategic importance. The competitive pressures for the adoption of this orientation come mainly from:
– the need to increase productivity and reduce unit costs;
– the need to guarantee quality to customers;
– the need to have more flexible and adaptable operations.

There is some evidence to suggest that organisations which have successfully introduced TQM find that the costs incurred during implementation are outweighed by the eventual savings (Hogg, 1990). One would, of course, expect reduced physical costs in terms of lower inventory, reduced recalls and fewer corrections or replacements. Lower labour costs may also ensue if organisations are discovering ways of increasing production, or of improving the service, with fewer employees. Certainly the traditional inspection team would no longer be required and complaints departments could be scaled down. TQM is also attributed with a sizeable motivation impact, via the provision of employees with increased control over their own work and greater opportunities to train and experiment. One could also expect greater levels of motivation where a unifying theme — a commitment to total quality — pervades all transactions in the organisation, including those between different levels in the hierarchy. The benefit of having a workforce which now comes to work 'mentally' (or intellectually), as opposed to just physically, offers rewards for all concerned.

An initial import from Japan (though the original idea stemmed from the US) was the quality circle (QC). It is estimated that there are now over ten million workers involved in one million such quality circles in Japan. The quality circle actively encourages employee involvement in decision-making, albeit at task level and within specified boundaries. Its objective is to improve decision making and to iron out problems at the earliest possible opportunity. Additional beneficial by-products of such arrangements are adjudged to be improved organisational morale, the development of a range of employees' skills and superior company quality and profitability. In many instances quality circles have either been replaced by, or incorporated into, a TQM program. Given a failure rate for QCs of over 20 per cent in the UK, and 50 per cent in the US, it is felt that TQM schemes have more chance of success and continuity as they resolve some of the organisational and strategic problems that QCs by their nature, could not (Cressey, 1991).

The main distinguishing features of the TQM organisation are that quality is seen as a strategic issue rather than an operational one (see, for example, Deming, 1982; Juran, 1986; Ouchi, 1981). It extends to both horizontal and vertical improvements in organisational attitudes and practices (i.e., with regard to outside customers and internal (co-worker) ones). The impetus and drive toward TQM comes from senior management, as reflected by their approach, priorities, attitudes and resource allocations. In fact, the ideal corporate culture of the TQM company is seen as one of open communication, multidisciplinary teamwork, employee involvement, high trust relations, the internalisation of quality and responsiveness to customers. In short, TQM is not something that applies for one hour out of the forty in the working week, rather it is transformative in its effect on the complete organisation culture (Cressey, 1991).

Interest in this quality orientation is reflected in the fact that, for example, by early 1999, about 1,500 companies operative in the Republic of Ireland had been registered to the ISO 9000–2 (an international quality standard), by the National Standards Authority of Ireland. In 1993, the Irish Quality Association (IQA) — now Excellence Ireland — had conducted 1,500 system audits for the purpose of assessing the adequacy of companies' quality assurance programs. In 1997 about 400 inspections in respect of the 'Q' mark were undertaken. This interest is fuelled by national survey findings which reveal that 'people regard quality as the most important feature when buying a product' (IQA, 1994), and is reinforced by separate survey findings across a sample of Irish service companies which show that 'quality significantly overshadowed price (86 per cent versus 14 per cent) in competitive pressures' (IQA, 1994).

11.7.1 WHY DOES TQM FAIL?

Though the interest in the Japanese model is clearly more than a passing fad, it is nevertheless notable that where applied, the overwhelming majority of organisations appear to have cherry picked from the range of possible TQM and WCM initiatives (Jurgens, 1989). That is, there are hardly any organisations in the UK or Ireland that adopt a total approach to TQM (Wilkinson, 1992; Brewster, 1992). Furthermore, only 8 per cent of UK managers rate their quality initiatives as totally successful — the majority claim only a moderate degree of success or are neutral about such practices (Wilkinson et al., 1993). The main reasons for this are attributed to the challenge which TQM poses to existing corporate culture. According to Wilkinson (1992) this is reflected in a preoccupation with:

(1) short-termism,
(2) organisational structure,
(3) a lack of management support, and
(4) a lack of employee support.

Short-termism refers to the emphasis on short-term performance indicators rather than on longer term objectives. For example, the focus is still on current sales quantities as opposed to the quality of sales, and the consequent building of market share, together with the development and exploitation of more effective new technologies and work methods. The quantity rather than quality-driven preoccupation is therefore reflected in short-term quantitative controls rather than longer term qualitative experimentation. This is also evident from the surge in popularity of merit/performance-related pay systems. In the opinion of Deming, the leading 'guru' in the field, quality is incompatible with 'annual or merit rating and . . . management by objectives' (Brewster, 1992). For the complete TQM package to apply, however, it is argued that workers must be free to experiment, take risks and make mistakes, and should not be restrained by pre-established targets. In contrast, however, for merit pay to work it may be argued that effective, tight, pre-established targets are required, against which performance can be evaluated.

The organisational structure barrier arises from the anti-expert or specialisation orientation of TQM. That is, TQM emphasises that all workers can and should contribute to quality. This, however, has implications for power sharing and its delegation to both customers and the workforce. If the customer and the subordinate are to be allowed to influence the 'expert' then the 'expert' surrenders power. This approach often goes against both human nature and organisational power culture.

Top management support may also be suspect on occasion, given that TQM requires new propensities, abilities and attitudes from management. Consequently, the teamwork or participative 'language' may be widespread, but the actual practice sparse. Many corporate cultures still emphasise compliance over commitment, with low trust levels and considerable inter-departmental rivalry. Some managers may also see TQM initiatives as another costly fad, fashion or flavour of the month. For example, in contrast with the Japanese experience with QCs, UK research suggests that most of their QC initiatives have been 'less than successful because of a lack of commitment from managerial grades' (Atkinson and Naden, 1989). Research indicates that this experience is being repeated with the other ingredients of the quality package (Wilkinson et al., 1993).

Employee support may also be lukewarm, given that working relationships between 'superiors and subordinates' have traditionally been the battleground for disputes over payment schemes, productivity, demarcation, work practices and staffing levels. Increased employee involvement may also be viewed as greater responsibility and pressure for workers without extra pay. Put bluntly, it is one thing for workers to be encouraged to come up with ideas, it is another that they be expected to do so! The move toward 'gain-sharing' type arrangements in some companies is often designed to overcome this limitation (see chapter 8). Where top management have adopted an elitist approach via prioritised car parking, the segregation of staff facilities, and other differential terms and conditions of employment, the implications for participative forms of management along the lines prescribed by TQM are apparent. Related to this is the Volkswagen experience with the 'quality' initiative:

> Resistance is particularly strong where change has been implemented from the top without involving those affected. It is also strong where management takes account of only the quantifiable benefits and excludes issues where no quantifiable advantage is evident. In such cases, the labour force rapidly withdraws its support and stops raising issues, thus bringing about the collapse of the whole project (Marciniak, 1991).

Consequently, it is hardly surprising that instances of failed initiatives with 'quality' and 'new forms of work organisation' have been identified where 'relationships were characterised by low trust and a traditional adversarial approach' (ICTU, 1993). It shall be interesting then to monitor the progress of the Irish Government's most recent attempt to introduce these ideas to the public sector — via the Strategic Management Initiative — with its emphasis on a more responsive and efficient service to the 'customer', through performance-related pay and devolved accountability and responsibility to the 'point of contact' with the customer.

11.7.2 THE INDUSTRIAL RELATIONS DIMENSION

Trade unions are often sceptical about mechanisms perceived to compete with or bypass them. The pressures created by JIT and TQM, involving lower staff levels and more intensive work systems, demand a more active and co-operative workforce. It is most pertinent then that: 'A mere work-to-rule or overtime ban could be as disastrous for a company operating a JIT system as could a strike for a company not doing so' (Oliver and Wilkinson, 1989).

For example, given the absence of buffer stocks in the JIT environment, and the continuous improvement focus under TQM, there is effectively a management dependency on labour co-operation. This dependency was less evident when (higher) stock levels protected management from short-term production disruptions, or when the same product (or service) could be produced (or supplied), in the same way for years on end, without any real fear of losing market share to higher quality or more effective competitors (Turnbull, 1988; Wilkinson and Oliver, 1990).

Consequently, though such terms as 'worker empowerment' and 'mutual dependency' accompany the quality initiative, some commentators argue that real autonomy for the workforce is largely cosmetic, as the production decisions and quality targets are effectively jointly determined by management decrees and customer preferences. Workers end up experiencing TQM as a 'low trust' activity (Klein, 1989), and as a system of 'information and control' rather than genuine participation (Taylor et al., 1991; Sewell and Wilkinson, 1992). According to Delbridge and Turnbull (1992):

> Responsibility is devolved to the shopfloor but not control, which remains highly centralized in the hands of management. Employees are only required to participate in incremental improvements to product quality and process efficiency, which simply incorporates workers in the projects of capital without extending any real control or collective autonomy to the workforce.

The response of the trade union movement to these new forms of work organisation appears to be based on a general acceptance of their inevitability. Consequently, they have generally endeavoured to avail of such opportunities to address many of their own traditional concerns about improving the quality of work life. To date, Irish trade unions have largely had minimal involvement in the formal organisational structures that implement such initiatives. However, given that such initiatives are expected to deepen within existing companies, spread to indigenous manufacturing companies and to be introduced in service and public sector organisations, ICTU has categorised three possible (trade union) responses to these developments (ICTU, 1993; also see previous chapters):

(1) *Opposition,* on the assumption that such initiatives represent a move toward a non-union environment;

(2) *Pragmatic scepticism,* accepts that change is permanent and responds accordingly by advising and guiding its membership;

(3) *Shaping the agenda,* accepts that change is permanent and endeavours to actively influence the quality of worker participation in all of the enterprise's affairs.

Reviewing these responses, it concluded that the 'opposition' route would not meet the needs of its membership, and would do little to enhance the union's perception and credibility. Accordingly, it concluded that the most effective trade union response should entail the development of a:

> . . . flexible and supportive approach while seeking to optimise the outcome for both their members and the companies they are employed within. Moving from an adversarial role which concentrates on pay and conditions to the new role envisaged will require a new orientation at all levels of union organisation.

11.8 THE EUROPEAN UNION AND DEVELOPMENTS IN INDUSTRIAL RELATIONS

It would be difficult to dispute that Ireland's membership of the EU has had and will continue to have a significant impact on the conduct of industrial relations in this country. The EU has emerged as an important agent in the operating environment of Irish organisations and exerts a growing influence in the Irish industrial relations system.

In many ways the most tangible influence of the EU on Irish industrial relations has been the considerable increase in employment legislation particularly in the 1970s, in response to EU social policy. Accession to the EC in 1973 committed Ireland to implementing in full the legislative and social policy changes already adopted by the Community since 1958, and equally obliged the State to adopt a programme of European and legislative initiatives advocated by the Council of Ministers in January 1974. As a result, many pieces of Irish labour legislation considered in chapter 2, for example, the Anti-Discrimination (Pay) Act 1974 and the Employment Equality Act 1977, owe their intellectual parentage to this social action programme and to the directives emanating from Brussels.

Ongoing EU developments in social policy, whose immediate origin lie in the signing of the Single European Act in 1987, have equally led to the modification of the existing labour law framework. The Single European Act, which aimed to strengthen economic cohesion in the EU by removing all barriers to competition between Member States, was centred on the issue of integration of social policy throughout the EU. In 1989, a Charter of

Fundamental Rights of Workers, the Social Charter, containing twelve articles (see Table 11.11) was signed in Strasbourg by the Member States except the UK. The Social Charter was drafted in response to the objectives set by the Single European Act of harmonising working conditions in the EU, and is a non-binding largely aspirational document. The Social Charter which was subsequently renamed the Social Chapter has an attendant Social Action Programme (see Hourihan, 1994) agreed in 1990, which comprises forty-nine legally binding directives and recommendations designed to realise the aims of the Social Chapter. The attainment of the rights set out in the Social Chapter was agreed by the Irish Government, trade unions and employers as signatories of the PESP, which commits Ireland to 'support Community action geared to promoting social cohesion' (PESP, 1991) Many of the provisions of the Social Chapter though, already exist under Irish employment law.

Table 11.11	The provisions of the Social Chapter
Article 1	Freedom of Movement Workers have the right to work in any Member State and are entitled to the same working conditions and social protection as nationals in that country.
Article 2	Employment and Remuneration The freedom to choose an occupation and the right to be fairly remunerated.
Article 3	Improvements in Living and Working Conditions Workers have the right to improved working and living conditions.
Article 4	Social Protection Each worker has the right to social protection.
Article 5	Freedom of Association and Collective Bargaining Workers have the right to join or not to join trade unions. Workers and employers' organisations have the right to engage in collective bargaining.
Article 6	Vocational Training Each worker has the right to vocational training.
Article 7	Equal Treatment for Men and Women Men and Women have the right to equal treatment.
Article 8	Information, Consultation and Participation Workers have the right to information, consultation and participation.
Article 9	Healthy Protection, and Safety at the Workplace All workers have the right to health protection and safety at work.
Article 10	The Protection of Children and Adolescents The minimum employment age should be not lower than fifteen years and young persons should receive equitable remuneration in accordance with national practice.
Article 11	Elderly Persons Elderly persons have the right to a decent standard of living.
Article 12	Disabled Persons All disabled persons are entitled to measures designed to improve their social and professional integration.

The EU has long viewed the social dimension as a crucial part of the single European market. The rationale for this, as Rollinson (1993) explains, lies in the fact that there are considerable differences in the levels of prosperity among the different member countries, and unless employment rights and conditions are levelled up, the single market could create a situation which would give some States an unfair advantage over others. This, some would argue, was central to the UK decision to seek an opt out clause from the Social Chapter prior to the ratification of the Maastricht Treaty. To date considerable progress has been made on many of the points contained in the Social Action Programme, with the most important developments occurring in the adoption of Directives covering working time, the protection of pregnant workers, the protection of young workers, health and safety, employment contracts and on information and consultation.

Setting aside the issue of social policy, the EU has also influenced Irish industrial relations in a number of other areas of importance. Hourihan (1994) argues that membership of the EU has contributed to a shift in the focus of industrial relations away from an adversarial model of industrial relations inherited from the UK to the adoption of European models of corporatism as evidenced by the return to centralised bargaining in 1987 and the evolving nature of the Irish model of social partnership. The completion of the internal market and the removal of technical barriers have exposed organisations in this country to new levels of competition due to increased market access, which has undoubtedly had implications for company level personnel and industrial relations policies. It can be argued that the competitive pressures resulting from the free movement of goods and the completion of the internal market have helped to structure union expectations in pay bargaining and have contributed to the pay discipline that, by and large, has been maintained under the national wage agreements.

Undoubtedly, the most significant EU development in recent years has been movement towards Economic and Monetary Union (EMU). EMU was agreed by the Maastricht Treaty, or the Treaty on European Union, in 1992, which declared the intent of the signatories to proceed with the planned introduction of a single European currency by January 1999. The initial participating countries will be locked into a fixed exchange rate and will introduce new euro notes and coins in 2002. EMU will have far-reaching implications for all aspects of Irish life, including the nature and conduct of collective bargaining and industrial relations.

The Maastricht Treaty set out a number of convergence criteria for admission to EMU, the most notable being a low rate of inflation (2.7 per cent), low budget deficit (-3 per cent), Debt/GDP ratio of 60 per cent or less and low interest rates (7.1 per cent). Meeting these criteria for admission has formed the core of Irish macro-economic policy throughout the 1990s. These disciplines imposed from Brussels have underpinned budgetary policy and have been to the fore of the Government's agendas in the negotiations for national wage agreements with the other social partners. The control of public expenditure has been a principal policy instrument utilised by the Government in its efforts to limit inflation. As a major proportion of public expenditure is taken up by public sector pay, managing the public sector pay bill has assumed a critical importance in recent years. Successive administrations have contended that the continuation of the social partnership which re-emerged in 1987 has been the most appropriate response for attaining the economic stability required for admittance to EMU. The modest pay increases largely offset by tax concessions by the Government, agreed by the social partners in programmes such as the Programme for Competitiveness and Work, and Partnership 2000, have been cognisant of the Government strategy to meet the EMU criteria. As such, it is apparent that in recent years the EU has had, and continues to have, a considerable influence on the process of collective bargaining and pay determination in Ireland.

There has been much debate in recent years amongst economists as to the merits of Ireland's entry into EMU. The principal concerns of a number of economists centre on the probability of a devalued sterling in the wake of the single currency and the threat that this would pose to those companies exporting to the UK market. John Dunne, Director General of IBEC estimates that between 40,000 and 50,000 jobs might be at risk from this scenario. Many economists argue that increased labour market flexibility is one of the few mechanisms that may deal with the economic adjustments following the adoption of the single currency, and complain of the rigidities that centralised wage agreements impose in this context.

Little attention has been given to the potential effects on the relationship between the social partners. Wallace et al. (1998) have recently conducted a survey of the perceptions of employers and unions on the likely impact of EMU on Irish industrial relations and in particular on the centralised bargaining process. The study, carried out at the Department of Personnel and Employee Relations at the University of Limerick, concludes that Irish entry to EMU is unlikely to significantly alter the present approach to wage bargaining in this country. The following are the principal findings of the survey:

– 97 per cent of those surveyed were favourably disposed to entry to EMU even in the absence of the UK;
– all employer respondents believed that joining EMU would be generally beneficial to Irish business;
– trade union respondents believed that the EMU will have no appreciable effect on the Irish or European trade union movements;
– 73 per cent of those surveyed felt that the most appropriate way of dealing with the challenges posed by EMU is to continue national centralised bargaining;
– there was general support that EMU is likely to promote the continuation of centralised agreements;

– EMU is likely to make it more difficult for the social partners to reach agreement in future negotiations;

– the majority of the employers surveyed did not see wages as being bargained upwards as a result of workers comparing wage rates across Europe but a majority of union respondents believed that this could happen;

– few employer and union respondents believed that as a result of EMU Europe-wide centralised bargaining would replace the Irish system of national bargaining within ten years;

– flexibility in wage determination is not favoured by the majority of employer respondents, who prefer certainty rather than flexibility in pay determination.

11.9 THE STATE OF IRISH INDUSTRIAL RELATIONS — A CONCLUDING EVALUATION

Industrial relations remains a critical dimension in both the management of individual enterprises and in relation to the economy at large. However, there is clear evidence that the nature of industrial relations has undergone considerable change over the past two decades. In evaluating such developments it should be noted that analyses of change in industrial relations are fraught with danger. A particular problem is the tendency to focus on evidence of change while failing to highlight areas of stability in industrial relations (Dastmalachian et al., 1991).

There is a widespread view that industrial relations practice in Ireland has undergone significant change over the past decade and that the pluralist model is undergoing some modification, involving either a variant of traditional pluralism (neo-pluralism), or a unitarist (neo-unitarism) perspective involving a range of HRM policies designed to eliminate employee needs for collective representation(Flood, 1989; Hannaway, 1987, 1992; Kelly and Brannick, 1988). The most significant aspects of such change have focused on a reduced role for collective bargaining and trade unions and a growth in non-union systems. In Ireland, we find that the proportion of the workforce who are trade union members has fallen from a high of 55 per cent in 1980, to a current level of approximately 43 per cent. However, we have also seen that this level of union penetration still compares favourably with density in other countries. For example, it is estimated that union density in the UK is now approximately 40 per cent while in the US union density is only 16 per cent. In evaluating recent developments in Irish industrial relations it is clear trade union recognition has become an issue of considerable debate. Indeed, we have seen conclusive evidence of increased management opposition to unionisation in recent years, particularly among multinational organisations.

11.9.1 A PERSPECTIVE ON CONTEMPORARY INDUSTRIAL RELATIONS IN IRELAND
In this book, we have seen that the Irish system of industrial relations is hugely influenced by political, economic and social history. The UK origins of the

system are still clearly visible in the collective legal framework, trade union structures and traditions, employer preferences, bargaining tactics, industrial relations 'third party' institutions, terminology and the presence of UK based unions (Von Prondzynski, 1998). While the system still displays many of the inherited characteristics of the UK model, recent years have also seen it develop its own distinguishing features. For example, the impact of foreign capital has seen many multinational companies establish subsidiaries, deploying human resource management techniques and non-union policies, often on greenfield sites in non-traditional industrial areas. Furthermore, the EU influence has seen the system move more toward economic integration and a stronger social policy, characteristic of the Germanic system of industrial relations.

The Irish system of industrial relations is built on the basic premise that it be regulated by voluntary collective bargaining as opposed to legal regulation. Most workers have their terms and conditions of employment settled by collective agreements, and there has traditionally been long-term public policy support for this approach. Bargaining tends to occur predominantly at workplace, enterprise and national levels. For example, over the past several years basic pay rises have been determined through centralised agreements made at national level. The 'special' increases, justified on grounds such as productivity, changed work practices and relativities, tend to be settled at firm level. Given the pattern of historical development of the trade union movement, this ambivalence toward legal intervention in the process is not surprising (see chapter 4).

In many respects the system is driven by the assumption that the interests of employers and employees are in conflict. Characteristic of the pluralist industrial relations system, this conflict is addressed via the practice of collective bargaining, and where this fails, by the institutions of the State (e.g., the Labour Relations Commission, the Labour Court, Employment Appeals Tribunal). These 'institutions of the middle ground' tend to be State-sponsored, providing dispute resolution and advisory facilities. The persistence of the antagonistic or adversarial union-employer relationship may also have been aided and abetted by the lack of pervasive formal worker participation structures and practices at plant level. This contrasts with the national level where, for example, since 1971, almost all pay agreements, encompassing the national labour force, have been centrally negotiated, or followed national pay norms.

In mid-1998 trade unions, employer associations and Government are concerned about the durability of Partnership 2000 — the latest in a series of national economic and social agenda (including pay) deals, dating back to 1987. By the late 1990s the impact of the 'Celtic Tiger' had become apparent in the industrial relations arena. Though much of Ireland's industrial development over the decade has been led by foreign-owned firms which are predominantly non-union, and industrial disputes have been thin on the ground, the climate shows evidence of some change. Trade unionists are witnessing a prosperous economy which many workers feel owes them more than it is delivering. This was apparent in such incidents as the militancy displayed, and pay rises secured by the nurses and the Garda Síochána towards the end of 1990s, which were adjudged by many to be in breach of the national agreements. The demand for the 'right to representation' or trade union recognition disputes, like the infamous Ryanair strike in 1998, also reflect the potential resurgence of industrial conflict in industrial relations, as an *Irish Times* editorial cautioned:

> . . . the Ryanair dispute has even more worrying ramifications. In recent months we have seen groups like the Gardaí, train drivers, craft workers in the health services and bricklayers, embark on highly disruptive industrial action with impunity . . . . The striking Ryanair employees did everything by the rules for nine weeks and were largely ignored . . . we are in danger of creating a two-tier industrial relations system in this State. One tier is for the compliant, who keep the rules, and the other is for groups ready to flex their industrial muscle. (*Irish Times* 16 July 1998)

Nevertheless, the endurance of such national agreements confirms Ireland as a country in which industrial relations are still influenced by corporatist tendencies. As Von Prondzynski (1998) contends 'the traditional industrial relations model is one of a conservative, rigid, pluralistic and antagonistic system, characterised by powerful institutions and widespread restrictive practices'.

Strike statistics are a useful indicator of the state of industrial relations in any jurisdiction. For example, during 1997 a total of 74,508 days was lost in industrial disputes. This was a reduction of over 40,000 on the previous year. Overall, fewer days have been lost in industrial disputes in the 1990s than in previous decades. In the 1970s an average of 584,000 days per year was lost while during the 1980s the equivalent figure was 314,000 days per year. Up to the end of 1997, however, the average number of days lost per year was approximately 113,000. This represents a significant improvement, reflecting a downward movement in this important barometer of the health of Irish industrial relations in recent years. Whether the occasional bouts of industrial unrest, particularly in the public sector, which tend to disturb the trend periodically, serve to undermine it, and the corporatist model with it, remains to be seen. Undoubtedly, economic cycles are a very significant influence on strike trends, with a weakened trade union movement and more confident management during times of recession (e.g., the mid to late 1980s), and more confident trade unions during growth periods (e.g., the 1970s, mid to late 1990s).

11.9.2 A DIMINUTION OF INDUSTRIAL RELATIONS ORTHODOXY?

Our consideration of the historical development of Irish industrial relations in this book suggests that we can point to a relatively predictable pattern of evolution towards what might be termed 'industrial relations orthodoxy' (Gunnigle, Morley, Clifford and Turner, 1997). This approach is based on accepting that a fundamental conflict of interest exists between capital and labour and that the optimal means of managing such conflict is through collective bargaining between employers and trade unions. The main characteristics of this approach are trade union recognition, distributive collective bargaining and a degree of procedural formalisation. In this model the management role is often akin to that of a 'fire-fighter', reacting to problems as they arise in a largely adversarial environment.

In assessing contemporary developments, it might plausibly be argued that we have witnessed some diminution of 'industrial relations orthodoxy' over recent years (see, for example, Roche, 1995; Gunnigle, 1996). Using data based on the Cranfield-University of Limerick (CUL) study, Gunnigle, Morley, Clifford, and Turner (1997) identified two broad areas of change with respect to industrial relations:

(1) A decline in the significance of industrial relations as the dominant activity area in personnel/human resource (P/HR) management, and in industrial relations orthodoxy as the dominant paradigm of workforce management at enterprise level. Increasingly, it appears that other aspects of P/HR management are becoming more significant, such as recruitment/ retention, training and development and payment systems, although, of course, many of these areas have significant industrial relations dimensions.
(2) It seems that for a number of organisations the P/HR role is increasingly concerned with broader strategic issues such as organisational restructuring and productivity improvements.

In evaluating these developments the authors question whether the apparent reduction in 'industrial relations orthodoxy' represents a long-term trend of decreasing importance of industrial relations and, particularly, a reduced emphasis on trade unions and collective bargaining. Evidence from the CUL study indicates that trade unions and collective bargaining remain integral to the conduct of enterprise level industrial relations in Ireland. However, trade union penetration also tends to be greatest in the public service and 'traditional' manufacturing. In contrast, other studies have noted a significant diminution of trade union penetration in certain sectors. In particular, recent research on greenfield firms finds a high incidence of union avoidance. It has been suggested that the last decade may therefore be typified as a period of both 'continuity and change' for industrial relations and P/HR management in Ireland (Gunnigle, Morley, Clifford and Turner, 1997; also see Monks, 1992). The continuity element is manifested in the continuing emphasis on collective bargaining and 'adversarial' industrial relations, especially in the public sector and 'traditional' manufacturing. The change component is evident in the growth of non-union approaches and a shift from traditional industrial relations to more individualist approaches, a greater focus on training and development and an increase in atypical employment forms.

In evaluating the implications for industrial relations in Ireland, it could be argued that we are witnessing the emergence of two fairly distinctive approaches to enterprise level industrial relations, one which is based on industrial relations orthodoxy or variants thereof, and one which is based on non-unionism. In older and larger organisations, we have the classic components of traditional pluralism: high levels of union penetration and a strong focus on collective bargaining. In many newer private sector organisations (particularly 'high tech' manufacturing and internationally traded services) we see the growth of non-union or 'low-union' systems characterised by more individualist HRM policies such as performance-related pay and direct communications. However, even in the 'established sector' we find that, at least in some organisations, industrial relations is taking on an increasingly proactive orientation. In particular, it is clear that an increasing and critical area of concern is that of facilitating improved levels of organisational performance on dimensions such as quality levels and productivity. For many older, established organisations this requires extensive change in industrial relations, specifically in aspects such as (less) demarcation, (increased) task flexibility, (increased) responsibilities for workers and (reduced) staffing levels (Gunnigle, 1998a). Given their high levels of union penetration and collective bargaining traditions, such changes must normally be achieved through negotiations with trade unions. It is instructive to note that when respondents to the CUL survey were asked to identify areas of 'major challenge for personnel/HR management of over the next three years', the most important areas identified were (in order of priority): (1) efficiency, productivity and flexibility issues; (2) training and development; and (3) industrial relations. It is likely that many such organisations are attempting to change their industrial relations paradigm from a traditional approach focused on pay and conditions to a partnership approach focused on performance and flexibility.

In the greenfield sector industrial relations is also an important area of HR activity. However, it is not as dominant as in the established sector and other HR activities tend to receive equal or greater priority. Two HR paradigms are apparent in this sector. One paradigm focuses on employee commitment. This approach encompasses many of the characteristics of what has been termed 'soft' HRM. Essentially, it is based on the resource perspective of employees incorporating the view that there is an organisational pay-off in performance terms from a combination of 'sophisticated' P/HR policies designed to develop employee commitment and emphasise a mutuality of employer and worker interests. This approach encompasses the non-union HR model most often referred to in the 1980s debate, and associated with organisations such as IBM, Digital and Wang. This model generally relies on a union substitution premise, although organisations which recognise trade unions but where the union role is essentially marginal also fall within this category (see chapters 9 and 10). The second paradigm evident in the greenfield sector equates to what we have termed the 'transaction cost model'. This approach is heavily focused on minimising HR costs. It is associated with extensive outsourcing, particularly in the utilisation of contracted labour and other 'atypical' employment forms. It is also associated with the intensification of the pace of work flow and an increased range of work tasks. This approach is generally based on union avoidance which is normally achieved through union suppression rather than union substitution (see chapter 9).

In general, it appears that for Irish industrial relations many of the basic features of traditional pluralism are alive and well. However, we also find evidence of a growing range of industrial relations and P/HR activities and an increasing emphasis on strategic dimensions. An area of particular focus is organisation change, specifically the adoption of organisation and management structures which are more cost efficient, flexible and responsive to change. This now appears as the area of most critical challenge in industrial relations as we begin a new millenium.

NOTES

1. For a more detailed review of the interaction of public policy and industrial relations in Ireland, see Gunnigle, P. 1998. Paradox in Policy and Practice: Trade Unions and Public Policy in the Republic of Ireland. *Review of Employment Topics* (in press).
2. This section draws heavily on Gunnigle, P., Morley, M., Clifford, N. and Turner, T. 1997. *Human Resource Management in Irish Organisations: Practice in Perspective.* Dublin: Oak Tree Press.

Bibliography

Adams, R.J. 1998. What's at stake in the battle over Australia's ports? *The Globe and Mail.* Toronto. 30 April.

Advisory Committee on Management Training 1988. *Managers for Ireland: The case for the development of Irish managers.* Dublin: Government Publications Office.

Advisory Conciliation Arbitration Service [ACAS] 1977. Disciplinary practices and procedure in employment. Code of Practice No.1. London: HMSO.

— — —. 1987. Discipline at work: The ACAS advisory handbook. London: HMSO.

Allen, V. 1971. *The sociology of industrial relations.* London: Longman.

Anthony, P.D. 1980. *The conduct of industrial relations.* London: Institute of Personnel Management.

Appelbaum, S. and Shapiro, B. 1991. Pay for performance: Implementation of individual and group plans. *Journal Of Management Development.* 10: 7.

Argenti, A. 1976. Business policy. In Kemper, T. (ed.) *A handbook of management.* London: Penguin.

Argyris, C. 1964. *Integrating the individual and the organization.* New York: Wiley.

Armstrong, M. 1987. Human resource management: A case of the emperor's new clothes. *Personnel Management:* August.

— — —. 1995. *A handbook of personnel management practice.* London: Kogan Page.

— — — and Murliss, H. 1994. *Reward management: A handbook of remuneration strategy and practice.* London: Kogan Page in association with the Institute of Personnel Management.

Armstrong, P. 1988. The personnel profession in the age of management accountancy. *Personnel Review.* 17:1.

Ashton, P. 1984. *Management in the organisation: Analysis and action.* London: Macmillan.

Atkinson, A.J. 1984. *Flexible manning: The way ahead.* London: Institute of Manpower Studies.

Atkinson, G. 1977. *The Effective Negotiator.* London: Quest Research Publications.

Atkinson, P. and J. Naden. 1989. Total quality management: Eight lessons to learn from Japan. *Management Services:* March.

Atkinson, J. 1984. Manpower strategies for flexible organisations. *Personnel Management:* August: 28–31.

— — — and Meager, N. 1986. Is flexibility just a flash in the pan? *Personnel Management:* September: 26–29.

Bacon, N. and Storey, J. 1993. Individualization of the employment relationship and the implications for trade unions. *Employee Relations.* 15: 1: 5–17.

Bailey, J. 1983. *Job design and work organisation.* London: Prentice Hall.

Bain, G. S. 1970. *The growth of white collar unionism.* Oxford: Clarendon Press.

— — — 1966. The growth of white collar unionism in Britain. *British Journal of Industrial Relations:* IV:3.

— — — and Price, R. 1983. Union growth: Dimensions, determinants and destiny. Bain, G.S. (ed.) *Industrial Relations in Britain.* Oxford: Blackwell.

— — — and Elias, 1985. Trade union membership in Great Britain: An individual level analysis. *British Journal of Industrial Relations.* 23.

— — — and Elsheikh, F. 1979. *Union growth and the business cycle.* Oxford: Blackwell.

— — — and Elsheikh, F. 1980. Unionisation in Britain: An inter-establishment analysis based on Survey Data. *British Journal of Industrial Relations.* xviii.

Baker, T.J., Duffy, D. and Shortall, F. 1997. *Quarterly Economic Commentary.* Dublin: The Economic and Social Research Institute. December.

Balkin, D. and Gomez–Mejia, L. (eds) 1987. *New Perspectives On Compensation.* London: Prentice Hall.

Barbash, J. 1984. *The elements of industrial relations.* Madison: University of Wisconsin Press.

Barret, S. 1991. A case of national misunderstanding. *Business and Finance.* January.

— — — 1993. Don't try another PESP. *Sunday Independent.* 9 May.

Barrington, D. 1982. *Report of the commission of inquiry on safety, health and welfare at work.* Dublin: Pl. 1868: Government Publications Office.

Barrow, M. and Loughlin, H. 1992. Towards a learning organisation: 1. the rationale. *Industrial and Commercial Training.* 24: 1.

Bassett, P. 1986. *Strike free.* London: Macmillan.

Batstone, E. 1984. *Working order.* Oxford: Blackwell.

— — — Boraston, I. and Frenkel, S. 1977. *Shop stewards in action.* Oxford: Blackwell.

Bean, R. 1976. Industrial Reactions. Cohen, E. and Studdard, G. (eds). *The bargaining context.* London: Arrow.

Beaumont, P. 1980. The success of white collar recognition claims. *Employee Relations.* 2: 4.

— — — 1983. The future for trade union recognition in Britain. *Columbia Journal of World Business.* 18: 2: Summer.

— — — 1985. New plant work practices. *Personnel Review.* 14: 5: 15–19.

— — — 1987. *The decline of trade union organisation.* London: Croom Helm.

— — — 1990. *Change in industrial relations: The organization and the environment.* London: Routledge.

— — — 1991. Trade unions and HRM. *Industrial Relations Journal.* 22: 4: 300–308.

— — —. 1992. The US human resource management literature: A review. In Salaman, G. (ed.). *Human resource strategies.* London: Open University/Sage.

— — —. 1993. *Human resource management: Key concepts and skills.* London: Sage.

— — —. 1995a. *The future of employment relations.* London: Sage.

— — —. 1995b. The European Union and developments in industrial relations. In Gunnigle, P. and Roche, W.K. (eds). *New challenges to Irish industrial relations.* Dublin: Oak Tree Press in association with the Labour Relations Commission.

441

— — — and Harris, R. 1989. The north south divide in Britain: The case of trade union recognition. *Oxford Bulletin of Economics and Statistics*: 51.

— — —, Cresey, P. and Jakobsen, P. 1990. Key industrial relations: West German subsidiaries in Britain. *Employee Relations*: 12: 6.

— — — and Gregory, M. 1980. The role of employers in Britain. *Industrial Relations Journal*: XI: 5.

— — — and Harris, R. 1988. Non-union establishments in Britain: The spatial pattern. *Employee Relations*:10: 4.

— — — and Harris R. 1991. Trade union recognition and employment contraction, 1980–1984. *British Journal of Industrial Relations*: 29: 1.

— — — and Harris, R. 1992. 'Double-breasted' recognition arrangements in Britain. *International Journal of Human Resource Management*: 3: 2: 267–83.

— — — and Harris, R. 1994. Opposition to unions in the non-union sector in Britain. *International Journal of Human Resource Management*: 5: 2: 457–71.

— — — and Townley, B., 1985. Greenfield sites, new plants and work practices. In Hammond, V. (ed.). *Current research in management*. London: Frances Pinter.

Becker, B.E., and Olson, C.A. 1986. The impact of strikes on shareholders' equity. *Industrial and Labour Relations Review*: 39: April .

— — —. 1987. Concession bargaining: The impact on shareholders' equity. *Industrial and Labour Relations Review*: 40: January.

Beer, M., Spector, B., Lawrence, P.R., Quinn-Mills, D. and Walton, R.E. 1984. *Managing human assets: The groundbreaking harvard business school program*. New York: The Free Press: Macmillan.

— — —, Spector, B., Lawrence, P., Mills, D. and Walton, R. 1985. *Human resource management: A general manager's perspective*. New York: The Free Press.

Bell, A. 1982. Computer in the office: The I.R. implications. *Industrial Relations News*: 14 January.

— — —. 1983. The non-union company approach to I.R. The computer industry. *Industrial Relations News*: 4 February.

Belman, D. 1992. Unions: The quality of labour relations and firm performance. In Mishel, L. and Voos, P. (eds). *Unions and economic competitiveness*. New York: Sharpe Economic Policy Institute.

Bendix, R. 1956. *Work and authority in industry*. New York: Wiley.

Benson, I. and Lloyd, J. 1983. *New technology and industrial change*. London: Kogan Page.

Berridge, J. 1992. Human resource management in Britain. *Employee Relations*: 14: 5.

Bevan, S. and Thompson M. 1991. How are companies interpreting performance management? *Personnel Management*: November.

Blackburn, R. A. and Mann, D. 1979. *The working class in the labour market*. London: Macmillan.

Blennerhassett, E. and Haskins, J. 1985. Technological developments and the public service: Impact on the general public and employees. Consolidated Report. Dublin: Institute Of Public Administration: June.

Blyton, P. and Morris, J. 1992. HRM and the limits of flexibility. In Blyton, P. and Turnbull, P. (eds). *Reassessing human resource management*. London: Sage.

— — — and Turnbull, P. (eds) 1992. *Reassessing human resource management*. London: Sage.

— — — and Turnbull, P. 1994. *The dynamics of employee relations.* London: Macmillan.

Bonner, K. 1987. Industrial relations and the law: What next? In *Industrial Relations in Ireland.* Dublin: University College Dublin. 1989.

— — —. 1989. Industrial relations reform. In *Industrial relations in Ireland.* Dublin: University College Dublin. 1989.

Booth, A. 1986. Estimating the probability of trade union membership, a study of men and women in Britain. *Economica:* 53.

Bowey, A. 1974. *A guide to human resource planning.* London: Macmillan.

— — — and Thorpe, R. 1986. *Payment systems and productivity.* London: Macmillan.

Boyd, A. 1972. *The rise of Irish trade unions 1729–1970.* Tralee: Anvil.

— — —. 1984. *Have trade unions failed the north?* Cork: Mercier Press.

Brannick, T. and Kelly, A. 1983. The reliability and validity of Irish strike data and statistics. *Economic and Social Review.* 14: 249–58.

— — —, Doyle, L. and Kelly, A. 1994. Industrial conflict. In Murphy, T.V. and Roche, W.K. (eds). *Irish industrial relations in practice.* Dublin: Oak Tree Press.

Bratton, J., and Gold, J. 1994. *Human resource management: Theory and practice.* London: Macmillan.

Breen, R., Hannon, D., Rottman, D. and Whelan, C. 1990. *Understanding contemporary Ireland.* Dublin: Gill and Macmillan.

Brett, J.M. 1980. Why employees join unions. *Organizational Dynamics:* Spring: 53–4.

Brewster, C. 1989. *Employee relations.* London: Macmillan.

— — —. 1992. Managing industrial relations. In Towers, B. (ed.). *A Handbook of industrial relations practice.* London: Kogan Page.

— — — and Bournois, F. 1991. Human resource management: A European perspective. *Personnel Review.* 20: 6.

— — — and Connock, S. 1985. Industrial relations: Cost-effective strategies. London: Hutchinson.

— — — and Hegewisch, A. 1994. *Policy and practice in European human resource management: The Price Waterhouse Cranfield Survey.* London: Routledge.

— — — Hegewisch, A. and Mayne, L. 1994. Flexible working practices: The controversy and the evidence. In Brewster, C. and Hegewisch, A. (eds). *Policy and practice in European human resource management: The Price Waterhouse Cranfield Study.* London: Routledge.

Briscoe, T. 1992. Accident statistics make grim reading. *Occupational Health and Safety Newsletter.* Dublin: Federation of Irish Employers.

Brown, C. and Medoff, J. 1978: Trade unions in the production process. *Journal of Political Economy.* 86: 3 June.

Brown, G. 1977. *Sabotage.* Nottingham: Spokesman Books.

Brown, W. 1981. (ed.) *The changing contours of British industrial relations: A survey of manufacturing industry.* Oxford: Blackwell.

Bullock, Lord. 1977. *Report of the committee of inquiry on industrial democracy.* London: HMSO.

Business and Finance. 1987. Dilemmas all round in tripartite talks. July 30.

Butler, J. E. 1988. HRM as a driving force in business strategy. *Journal of General Management.* 13: 4.

Butler, P. 1986. Employer organisations: A study. Unpublished BBS project. Limerick: NIHE.

Buzzell, R.B. and Gale, B.T. 1987. *The PIMS principles, linking strategy to performance.* New York: The Free Press.

Callan, T. and Farrell, B. 1991. *Women's participation in the Irish labour market.* Dublin: National Economic and Social Council.

Calmfors, L. and Drilfill, J. 1988. Bargaining structure, corporatism and macro-economic performance. *Economic Policy* 6.

Canning, L. 1979. Negotiating in industrial relations. Unpublished paper. Dublin: Irish Management Institute.

Cappelli, P. and McKersie, R. 1987. Management strategy in the redesign of work rules. *Journal of Management Studies* 24: September.

Carley, M. 1998. Irish worker directors in a European perspective. *Industrial Relations News* 19: 14 May: 14–17.

Carroll, C. 1985. *Building Ireland's business: Perspectives from PIMS.* Dublin: Irish Management Institute.

— — — and Byrne, R. 1992. EC requirements on safety and health at work: An update. *Industrial Relations News* 25 June.

Carruth, A. and Disney, R. 1988. Where have two million trade union members gone? *Economica* 55.

Central Bank of Ireland. 1997. Dublin: Winter Report. CBI.

CEP/Bell Canada. 1993. (Communications, Energy and Paperworkers Union of Canada(CEP)). Workplace reorganization: Shaping the future, balancing the system. Toronto. (August.).

Chamberlain, N.W. 1948. *The union challenge to management control.* New York: Harper.

Chamberlain, N. and Kuhn, J. 1965. *Collective bargaining.* New York: McGraw-Hill.

Chandler, A.D. 1962. *Strategy and structure.* Boston: MIT Press.

Child, J. 1972. Organisation structure, environment and performance: The role of strategic choice. *Sociology* 6: 1.

Chubb, B. 1992. *FIE: Federation of Irish Employers 1942–1992.* Dublin: Gill and Macmillan.

Clarke, E. 1984. Unionisation and firm performance: The impact on profits, grown and productivity. *American Economic Review* 24: 4 July.

Clarke, K. and Clarke, K. 1991. Personnel management, defence, retrenchment, advance? *Personnel Review* 20: 1.

Clarke, P. 1989. Payment by result schemes: A review of trends. *Industrial Relations News* 8: 23 February.

Clegg, H. A. 1975. Pluralism in industrial relations. *British Journal of Industrial Relations*: November.

Clegg, H. 1976. *Trade unionism under collective bargaining, a theory based on comparisons of six countries.* Oxford: Blackwell.

Coates, K. and Topham, A. (eds). 1968. *Industrial democracy in Great Britain.* London: McGibbon and Kee.

Cole, G.A. 1988. *Personnel management: Theory and practice.* London: DP Publications.

Cole, R.E. 1982. Diffusion of participatory work structures in Japan, Sweden and the United States. P.S. Goodman (ed.). *Change in organisations.* San Francisco: Jossey Bass.

Commission of the European Communities. 1991. *Joint Opinions*. European Social Dialogue Documentary Series. Brussels: EC.

Commission on Industrial Relations. 1972. Employers' organisations and industrial relations. Study 1. London: HMSO.

Conniffe, D. and Kennedy, K.A. 1984. Employment and unemployment policy for Ireland. Dublin: ESRI.

Connolly, R.A., Hirsch, B. and Hirschey M. 1985. Union rent seeking, intangible capital, and market value of the firm. Mimeo. University of North Carolina at Greensboro.

Cook, D. and Ferris, G. 1988. Strategic human resource management and firm effectiveness in industries experiencing decline. *Human Resource Management* 25: 3: Fall.

Cooke, R. and Armstrong, M. 1990. The search for strategic HRM. *Personnel Management*: December.

Cordova, E. 1988. From full-time wage employment to atypical employment: A major shift in the evolution of labour relations. *International Labour Review* 125: 6.

Costello, M. 1983. Ireland's experiment with worker directors. *Personnel Management*: October.

Cox, B. and Hughes, J. 1989. Industrial relations in the public sector. In *Industrial relations in Ireland*. Dublin: University College Dublin. 1989.

Cradden, T. 1992. Trade unionism and HRM: The incompatibles. *Irish Business and Administrative Research*: 13: 37–48.

Cressey, P. 1991. Total quality management and worker participation. In M. Gold (ed.) *Total quality management and worker particiipation*. European Foundation for the Improvement of Living and Working Conditions 2. Dublin: European Foundation.

Croke, N. 1993. Trade union membership participation in centralised bargaining. *Industrial Relations News* 2: 14 January.

— — —. 1996. A decade of centralised bargaining under scrutiny. *Industrial Relations News* 23: 13 June.

Crouch, C. 1982. Trade unions: The logic of collective action. London: Fontana.

Curran, J., and Stanworth, J. 1979. Self selection and the small firm worker, a critique and an alternative view. *Sociology* 13: September.

— — — and Stanworth, J. 1981a. The social dynamics of the small manufacturing enterprise. *Journal of Management Studies* 18: 2.

— — — and Stanworth, J. 1981b. Size of workplace and attitudes to industrial relations in the printing and electronics industries. *British Journal of Industrial Relations* 14.

— — — and Downing, S. 1989. The State and small business owners: An empirical assessment of consultation strategies. London: National Small Firms Policy and Research Conference.

Curson, C. 1986. *Flexible Patterns of Work*. London: IPM.

Cutcher-Gershenfeld, J. and Verma, A. 1994. Joint governance in North American work-places: A glimpse of the future or the end of an era? *International Journal of Human Resource Management* 5: 3: 547–80.

Dahrendorf, R. 1959. *Class and class conflict in industrial society*. London: Routledge and Kegan Paul.

Dáil Éireann, 1963, 1970, 1977, 1981. Dáil debates collections. Dublin: Government Publications Office.

445

Daly, A. 1989. *Pay and benefits in Irish industry.* Dublin: Federation of Irish Employers.

Daniel, W. 1987. Workplace industrial relations and technical change. DE/ESRC/Policy Studies Institute/ACAS. London: Heinemann.

— — — and Hogarth, T. 1990. Worker support for technical change. *New Technology, Work and Employment* 5: 2: Autumn.

— — — and Millward, N. 1983. Workplace industrial relations in Britain: The DE/PSI/SSRC survey. London: Heinemann.

Dastmalachian, A., Blyton, P. and Adamson, R. 1991. *The climate of workplace relations.* London: Routledge.

Deaton, D. 1985. Management style and large scale survey evidence. *Industrial Relations Journal* 16: 2: 67–71.

Deaton, D.R. and Beaumont, P.B. 1980. The determinants of bargaining structure: Some large scale survey evidence. *British Journal of Industrial Relations*: 18: July.

Deery, S. and De Cieri, H. 1991. Determinants of trade union membership in Australia. *British Journal of Industrial Relations* 29: March.

Delbridge, R. and Turnbull, P. 1992. Human resource maximisation: The management of labour under just-in-time manufacturing systems. In P. Blyton and P. Turnbull (eds). *Reassessing Human Resource Management.* London: Sage.

Deming, W. 1982. *Quality production and competitive position.* Cambridge, Mass: MIT Press.

Department of Labour. 1983. Discussion document and 1985 on industrial relations law reform. Dublin: Department of Labour.

— — —. 1986. *Employers' perception of the effect of labour legislation.* Dublin: Government Publications Office.

— — —. 1988. Proposals on industrial relations reform. Dublin: Department of Labour.

— — —. 1991. A guide to the Industrial Relations Act 1990. Dublin: Department of Labour.

— — —. 1991. Keynote address by Minister for Labour B. Ahern to the Institute of Personnel Management Annual Conference, Killarney. Dublin: Department of Labour.

— — —. 1991a, 1992. Annual reports. Dublin: Department of Labour.

— — —. 1991b. Speech by the Minister for Labour. Seminar on The Industrial Relations Act 1990. Irish Society for Labour Law. 13 July. Dublin: Government Publications Office.

Department of Public Services 1987. Estimates. Dublin: Government Publications Office.

Deutsch, M. 1973. *The resolution of conflict.* New Haven, Conn.: Yale University Press.

Dineen, D.A. 1988. Changing employment patterns in Ireland: Recent trends and future prospects. Limerick: University of Limerick.

— — —. 1992. Atypical work patterns in Ireland: Short-term adjustments or fundamental changes. *Administration* 40: 3: Autumn.

— — — and Wallace, J. 1991. An Overview of Irish Labour Market Issues. Paper presented at the Université Catholique de Louvain. Louvain.

Disney, R. 1990. Explanations of the decline in trade union density in Britain, an appraisal. *British Journal of Industrial Relations* 29: 2.

Doeringer, P. and Piore, M. 1971. *Internal labour markets and manpower analysis.* Lexington, Mass.: D.C. Heath.

Donovan, Lord. 1968. Royal commission on trade unions and employers' associations, 1965–1968. CMND 3623: HMSO.

Dore, R. 1973. *British factory–Japanese factory.* London: Allen and Unwin.

Drew, E. 1987. New structures of work: An Irish perspective. *International Journal of Manpower* 6: 2.

Dubin, R., A. Kornhauser and A. Ross (eds). 1954. *Industrial conflict.* New York: McGraw-Hill.

Duffy, K. 1993. Industrial Relations Act 1990 — the trade union experience. *Irish Industrial Relations Review* January.

Dunlop, J. 1958. *Industrial relations systems.* Carbondale: Southern Illinois University Press.

— — —. 1993. *Industrial relations systems.* Southern Boston: Harvard Business School Press.

Dunne, J. 1996. The John Dunne interview. *Industrial Relations News* 19: 16 May.

Economic and Social Research Institute (ESRI). 1997. *Medium term review: 1997–2003.* Dublin: ESRI.

Economist Intelligence Unit (EIU). 1997. Ireland country report — third quarter. UK:EIU.

Edwards, P.K. 1985. Managing labour relations through the recession: The plant and the company. *Employee Relations* 7: 2: 3–7.

— — —. 1986. *Conflict at work: A materialist analysis of workplace relations.* Oxford: Blackwell.

— — —. 1987. Factory managers: Their role in personnel management and their place in the company. *Journal of Management Studies* 24: 5: September: 479–501.

— — —. 1992. Industrial conflict: Themes and issues in recent research. *British Journal of Industrial Relations* 30: 361–404.

— — —. 1994. Discipline and the Creation of Order. In Sisson, K. (ed.) *Personnel management: A comprehensive guide to theory and practice in Britain.* Oxford: Blackwell. 1989.

Edwards, R. 1979. *Contested terrain.* New York: Basic Books.

Eichel, E., and Bender, H. 1984. *Performance related pay, a study of current techniques.* American Management Association.

Elger, T. 1991. Flexible futures? New technology and the contemporary transformation of work. *Work, Employment and Society* 1: 4.

Elliott, J. 1984. *Conflict or co-operation: The growth of industrial democracy.* London: Kogan Page.

Emery, F. 1980. Designing socio-technical systems for 'greenfield' sites. *Journal of Occupational Behaviour* 1: 1.

Employment Appeals Tribunal (EAT). 1985–1996. Annual reports. Dublin: EAT.

Employment Equality Agency (EEA). 1983. *Code of practice: Equality of opportunity in employment.* Dublin: EEA.

— — —. 1986. *Transitions to equal opportunities at work: Problems and possibilities.* Dublin: EEA.

— — —. 1991. *A model equal opportunities policy.* Dublin: EEA.

447

Enderwick, P. 1982. Labour and the theory of the multinational corporation. *Industrial Relations Journal* 13: 3.

— — —. 1986. Multinationals and labour relations: The case of Ireland. *Irish Business and Administrative Research* 8: 2.

EOLAS. 1993. Concluding statement of the board — 15 December.

European Commission. 1997a. Partnership for a New Organization of Work. European Commission Green Paper, Supplement 4/97. Brussels: Bulletin of the European Union.

— — —. 1997b. *Labour market studies: Ireland.* Series 1. Brussels: European Commission.

European Foundation for the Improvement of Living and Working Conditions 1985. *The role of the parties involved in the introduction of new technology.* Dublin: European Foundation for the Improvement of Living and Working Conditions.

— — —. 1991. *Hygeia: A newsletter for the European Year of Safety, Hygiene and Health at Work* 3. Dublin: European Foundation for the Improvement of Living and Working Conditions.

— — —. 1997. *New Forms of Work Organisation: Can Europe realise its potential?* Dublin: European Foundation for the Improvement of Living and Working Conditions.

Farnham, D. and Pimlott, J. 1990. *Understanding industrial relations.* London: Cassell.

Federated Union of Employers (FUE). 1987. FUE Annual report 1986. Dublin: FUE.

— — —. 1984. Profit sharing. *FUE Bulletin.* Dublin: FUE.

Federation of Irish Employers (FIE). 1991. Accident rate is too high. *FIE Bulletin* May. Dublin: FIE.

Fennell, C. and Lynch, I. 1993. *Labour law in Ireland.* Dublin: Gill and Macmillan.

Fiorito, J., Lowman, C. and Nelson, F.D. 1987. The impact of human resource policies on union organising. *Industrial Relations* 26: 2, Spring: 113–126.

Fisher, R. and Ury, W. 1986. *Getting to yes.* London: Hutchinson.

Fitzpatrick, D. 1977. *Politics and Irish life 1913–21.* Dublin: Gill and Macmillan.

Flanders, A. 1967. *Collective bargaining: Prescription for change.* London: Faber and Faber.

— — —. 1968. *Trade unions.* London: Hutchinson.

Flood, P.C. 1989. Human resource management: Promise, possibility and limitations. Mimeo. College of Business: University of Limerick

— — —. 1990. Atypical employment: Core-periphery manpower strategies — the implications for corporate culture. *Industrial Relations News* 9 and 10.

— — — and Garavan, T. 1989. HRM, industrial relations and the implications for unions. *Industrial Relations News* 12: 23 March.

— — — and Toner, B. 1996. Managing without unions: A pyrrhic victory? In Flood, P.C., Gannon, M.J. and Paauwe, J. (eds). *Managing Without Traditional Methods: International Innovations in Human Resource Management.* Wokingham: Addison-Wesley.

— — —. 1997. How do large non-union companies avoid a Catch 22? *British Journal of Industrial Relations* 35: 2: 257–77.

— — —, Gannon, M.J. and Paauwe, J. (eds). 1996. *Managing Without Traditional Methods: International Innovations in Human Resource Management.* Wokingham: Addison-Wesley.

Fogarty, M.P., Egan, D. and Ryan W.J.L. 1981. Pay Policy for the 1980's. Dublin: Federated Union of Employers.

Foley, K. and Gunnigle, P. 1993. Organisational reward practices in Ireland. Dublin: Department of Enterprise and Employment.

Fombrun, C. 1986. Environmental trends create new pressures on human resources. In Rynes, S.L. and Milkovich, G.T. (eds). *Current Issues in Human Resource Management: Commentary and Readings.* Plano: Business Publications Inc.

— — —, Tichy, N. and Devanna, M. 1984. *Strategic Human Resource Management.* New York: Wiley.

Forde, M. 1992. *Employment Law.* Dublin: Roundhall Press.

FORFAS. 1996. *Shaping our Future: A strategy for enterprise in Ireland in the 21st Century.* Dublin: Forfas.

Foulkes, F. 1980. *Personnel Policies in Large Non-Union Companies.* Englewood Cliffs: Prentice Hall.

Fowler, A. 1988. New Directions in Performance Pay. *Personnel Management.* November.

— — —. 1990. Performance Related Pay. *Personnel Management Plus.*

Fox, A. 1966. Industrial sociology and industrial relations. Research Paper 3 to the Royal Commission on Trade Unions and Employers' Associations: HMSO.

— — —. 1973. Industrial relations: a social critique of pluralist ideology. In J. Child (ed.). *Man and Organisation.* London: Allen and Unwin.

— — —. 1974. *Beyond contract: Work, power and trust relations.* London: Faber and Faber.

— — —. 1975. Collective bargaining: Flanders and the Webbs. *British Journal of Industrial Relations* 13: 2.

Frawley, M. 1991. Large increase in sexual harassment cases reported by E.E.A. *Industrial Relations News.* Dublin: 12 September.

— — —. 1992. Sexual harassment enquiries leap by 350%. *Industrial Relations News.* Dublin: 5 November.

Freeman, R. and Medoff, J. 1979. The Two Faces of Unionism. *Public Interest* 57: Fall.

— — — and Medoff, J. 1984. *What do unions do?* New York: Basic Books.

— — — and Pelletier, J. 1990. The impact of industrial relations legislation on British union density. *British Journal of Industrial Relations* 28.

Freidman, A. 1977. *Industry and Labour.* London: Macmillan.

— — —. 1984. Management strategies, market conditions and the labour process. In Stephen, R. (ed.). *Firms, Organisation and Labour.* London: Macmillan.

Frohlich, D. and Pekruhl, U. 1996. *Direct participation and organisational change, fashionable but misunderstood?* Luxembourg: Office for Official Publications of the European Communities.

Galbraith, J. and Nathanson, D. 1978. *Strategy Implementation: the Role of Structure and Process.* St Paul, MN: West Publishing.

Gallie, D. 1978. *In search of the new working class.* Cambridge: Cambridge University Press.

Galvin, D. 1980. Worker participation survey. Unpublished BBS Dissertation. Limerick: University of Limerick.

Garavan, T. 1990. Strategic human resource development: Characteristics, conditions and benefits. *Journal of European Industrial Training.* August.

Geary, J. 1994a. Task participation: Employee's participation — enabled or constrained. In Sisson, K. (ed.). *Personnel management.* Oxford: Blackwell. 1989.

— — —. 1994b. New forms of work organisation: Implications for employers, trade unions and employees. Working Paper 9. Graduate School of Business: University College Dublin.

— — —. 1995. World class manufacturing and the implications for industrial relations. In Gunnigle, P. and Roche, W.K. (eds). 1995 *New challenges to Irish industrial relations*. Dublin: Oak Tree Press in association with the Labour Relations Commission.

— — —. 1996. Working at restructuring work in Europe: The case of team-working. *Irish Business and Administrative Research* 17: 44–57.

— — —. 1998. New work structures and the diffusion of teamworking arrangements in Ireland. Paper presented at the Sixth Annual John Lovett Memorial Lecture: University of Limerick: 2 April.

Gennard, J. 1976. Multinationals: Industrial relations and the trade union response. Occasional Papers in Industrial Relations 1. Universities of Leeds and Nottingham.

— — —. 1992. Industrial relations and technological Change. In Towers, B. (ed.) *A handbook of industrial relations practice*. London: Kogan Page. (3rd edn.)

Geoghegan, F. 1996. IBEC expert defends PCW. *Sunday Business Post* 30 August.

Gill, C. 1992. British Industrial Relations and the European Community. In Towers, B. (ed.) *A handbook of industrial relations practice*. London: Kogan Page.

Gill, D. 1973. Performance appraisal in perspective, a study of current techniques. London: Institute of Personnel Management.

— — —. 1977. Appraising performance: Present trends and the next decade. London: Institute of Personnel Management.

Gladstone, A. 1984. Employers' associations in comparative perspective: Functions and activities. In Windmuller, J.P. and Gladstone, A. *Employers' associations and industrial relations: A comparative study*. Oxford: Clarendon.

Golderberg, V. 1980. Bridges over contested terrain, exploring the radical account of the employment relationship. *Journal of Economic Behavior and Organisation* 1.

Goldsmith, W. and Clutterbuck, D. 1985. *The Winning Streak*. London: Penguin.

Goldthorpe, J. 1974. Industrial relations in Great Britain: A critique of reformism. *Politics and Society* 44.

Goold, M. and Campbell, A. 1987. *Strategies and styles: The role of the centre in managing diversified corporations*. Oxford: Blackwell.

Goss, D. 1991. *Small Business and Society*. London: Routledge.

Gouldner, A.W. 1954. *Wildcat Strike*. New York: Harper.

Government Publications Office. 1996. *Partnership 2000 for inclusion, employment and competitiveness*. Dublin: Government Publications Sales Office.

Government Social Survey. 1968. *Workplace Industrial Relations* SS4OZ. London: HMSO.

Grafton, D. 1988. Performance related pay: Securing employee trust. *Industrial Relations News* 17 November.

Green, G. 1990. *Industrial Relations*. London: Pitman.

Guest, D. 1987. Human resource management and industrial relations. *Journal of Management Studies* 24: 5. 503–21.

— — —. 1988. Human resource management: A new opportunity for psychologists or another passing fad. *The Occupational Psychologist* February.

— — —. 1989a. Personnel and HRM: Can you tell the difference? *Personnel Management* January 48–51.

— — —. 1989b. Human resource management: Its implications for industrial relations and trade unions. In Storey, J. (ed.). *New perspectives on human resource management*. London: Routledge.

— — —. 1990. Human resource management and the American dream. *Journal of Management Studies* 27: 4. 377–97.

— — —. 1992. Right enough to be dangerously wrong: An analysis of the in search of excellence phenomenon. In Salaman, G. (ed.). *Human resource strategies*. London: Sage/Open University Press. 1992.

— — — and Hoque, K. 1994a. Employee relations in non-union greenfield sites: The good, the bad and the ugly. *Human Resource Management Journal* 5: 1: 1–14.

— — — and Hoque, K. 1994b. Yes, personnel does make a difference. *Personnel Management* November 40–44.

— — — and Hoque, K. 1996. Human resource management and the new industrial relations. In Beardwell, I. (ed.). *Contemporary industrial relations: A critical analysis*. Oxford: Oxford University Press.

— — — and Rosenthal, P. 1992. Industrial relations in greenfield sites. Mimeo. London: Centre for Economic Performance: Industrial Relations Conference: March.

Gunnigle, P. 1989. Management approaches to industrial relations in the small firm in University College Dublin. *Industrial Relations in Ireland*. Dublin: University College Dublin. 1989

— — —. 1992a. Changing management approaches to employee relations in Ireland. *Employee Relations* 14: 1: 17–32.

— — —. 1992b. Human resource management in Ireland. *Employee Relations* 14: 5: 5–22.

— — —. 1992c. Ireland. In Brewster, C., Hegewisch, A., Holden, L. and Lockhart, T. (eds). *The European Human Resource Management Guide*. London: Academic Press.

— — —. 1995a. Management styles in employee relations in greenfield sites: Challenging a collectivist tradition. Unpublished PhD Thesis. Cranfield: Cranfield School of Management.

— — —. 1995b. Collectivism and the management of industrial relations in greenfield sites. *Human Resource Management Journal* 5: 4: 24–40.

— — —. 1996. The personnel management function in Ireland: Models and prospects. *Irish Business and Administrative Research* 17: 32–43.

— — —. 1997. Industrial relations and HRM in Ireland: Current trends and a perspective on the future. *Industrial Relations News* 46: 4 December.

— — —. 1998a. More rhetoric than reality: Industrial relations partnerships in Ireland. *Economic and Social Review* 28: 4: 179–200.

— — —. 1998b. Human resource management and the personnel function. In Roche, W.K., Monks, K. and Walsh, J. (eds). *Human Resource Management Strategies: Policy and Practice in Ireland*. Dublin: Oak Tree Press.

— — —. 1998c. Paradox in policy and practice: Trade unions and public policy in the Republic of Ireland. *Review of Employment Topics*: in press.

Gunnigle, P. and Brady, T. 1984. The management of industrial relations in the small firm. *Employee Relations* 6: 5: 21–24.

— — — and Daly, A. 1992. Craft integration and flexible work practices. *Journal of Industrial and Commercial Training* 24: 10: 10–17.

— — — and Flood, P. 1990. *Personnel management in Ireland: Practice, trends and developments.* Dublin: Gill and Macmillan.

— — — and Foley, K. 1993. *Pay determination and collective bargaining in Ireland.* Dublin: Department of Enterprise and Employment.

— — — and Morley, M. 1993. Something old, something new: A perspective on industrial relations in the Republic of Ireland. *Review of Employment Topics* 1: 1: 114–142.

— — — and Morley, M. 1998. Strategic integration and industrial relations in greenfield sites. In Skinner, D., Mabey, C. and Clark, T. (eds). *Experiencing Human Resource Management.* London: Sage.

— — —, McMahon, G.V. and Fitzgerald, G. 1995. *Industrial relations in Ireland: Theory and practice.* Dublin: Gill and Macmillan.

— — —, Morley, M. and Heraty, N. 1997. *Personnel and human resource management: Theory and practice in Ireland.* Dublin: Gill and Macmillan.

— — —, Morley, M. and Turner, T. 1997. Challenging collectivist traditions: Individualism and the management of industrial relations in greenfield sites. *Economic and Social Review* 28: 2: 105–134.

— — —, Morley, M., Clifford, N. and Turner, T. 1997. *Human Resource Management in Irish Organisations: Practice in Perspective.* Dublin: Oak Tree Press.

— — —, T. Garavan and G. Fitzgerald, 1992. *Employee Relations and Employment Law In Ireland.* The Open Business School-PMTC University of Limerick.

— — —, Turner, T. and D'Art. 1997. Counterpoising collectivism: Performance related pay and industrial relations in greenfield sites. *British Journal of Industrial Relations* 36 4: 565–79.

— — —, Turner, T. and Morley, M. 1998. Strategic integration and industrial relations: The Impact of Managerial Styles. *Employee Relations* 20: 2: 115–31.

Hackman, J.R. and Oldham, G.R. 1980. *Work redesign.* New York: Addison-Wesley.

Hakim, C. 1991. Impact of changing employment patterns on manpower policy. Paper presented to Institute of Public Administration. Dublin: Conference on industrial relations outlook and new employment patterns.

Hannaway, C. 1987. New style collective agreements-an Irish approach. *Industrial Relations News* 13.

— — —. 1992. Why Irish eyes are smiling. *Personnel Management* May.

Hannigan, K. 1997. Partnership Survey. Unpublished findings of Irish Management Institute pilot survey on partnership conducted among participants at IMI/Department of Enterprise, Trade and Employment Conference, Workplace 2000. Dublin: Irish Management Institute.

Harbison, F. 1966. *Industrial relations: Challenges and responses.* Toronto: University of Toronto Press.

Hardiman, N. 1988. Pay, politics and economic performance in Ireland 1970–1987. Oxford: Clarendon Press.

Hastings, T. 1994. *Semi-states in crisis: The challenge for industrial relations in the ESB and other major semi-state companies.* Dublin: Oak Tree Press.

— — —. 1996. All sides hail new style national deal. *Irish Independent* 21 December.

Hawkins, K. 1972. *Conflict and Change: Aspects of Industrial Relations.* London: Holt, Rhinshart and Winston.

— — —. 1977. *A handbook of industrial relations practice.* London: Kogan Page.

Henderson, J., and Johnson, B. 1974. Labour relations in the smaller firm. *Personnel Management* December.

Hendry, C. 1988. Changing patterns of human resource management. *Personnel Management* November.

— — — and Pettigrew, A. 1990. Human resource management: An agenda for the 1990s. *International Journal of Human Resource Management* 1: 1.

— — —, Pettigrew, A. and Sparrow, P. 1988. Changing patterns of human resource management. *Personnel Management* November.

Heraty, N. and Morley, M. 1998. Training and development in the Irish context: Responding to the competitiveness agenda? *Journal of European Industrial Training* 22: 4/5: 190–204.

— — —, Morley, M. and Turner, T. 1994. Trends and developments in the organistion of the employment relationship. In Gunnigle, P. et al. (eds). *Continuity and change in Irish employee relations*. Dublin: Oak Tree Press.

Higgins, C. 1997. IT sector sees rises of up to 31%. *Industrial Relations News Report* 25: 26 June.

Hillery, B. 1979. Necessary changes in Irish industrial relations. *Journal of the Statistical and Social Inquiry Society of Ireland* xxiv: Part 1.

— — —. 1985. Ireland's strike record: The manifestation of change in industrial relations. Paper presented to the Annual Conference of the Institute of Personnel Management. Galway, Ireland.

— — —. 1989. An overview of the Irish industrial relations system. In *Industrial relations in Ireland*. Dublin: University College Dublin. 1989.

— — —. 1994. The institutions of industrial relations. In Murphy, T.V. and Roche, W.K. (eds). *Irish industrial relations in practice*. Dublin: Oak Tree Press.

Hirsch, B.T. 1980. The determinants of unionisation, an analysis of inter-area differences. *Industrial and Labour Relations Review* XXXIII.

— — — and Berger, M. 1984. Union membership determination and industry characteristics. *Southern Economic Journal* 1.

— — — and Addison, J.T. 1986. The economic analysis of unions, new approaches and evidence. London: Unwin.

HMSO. 1968. Royal commission on trade unions and employers' associations. London.

Hoevemeyer, V. 1989. Performance based compensation, miracle or waste. *Personnel Journal* July.

Hofer, C. and Schendel, D. 1978. *Strategy formulation: Analytical concepts*. St Paul: West Publishing.

Hogg, C. 1990. *Total quality*. Institute of Personnel Management Factsheet 29: May.

Hood, H. and Young, S. 1982. *Multinationals in retreat: The Scottish experience*. Edinburgh: Edinburgh University Press.

Horgan, J. 1985. The future of collective bargaining. Paper presented to the Annual Conference of the IPM. Galway, Ireland.

Horwitz, F.M. 1990. HRM: An ideological perspective. *Personnel Review* 19: 2.

Hourihan, F. 1990. I.R. Bill 1989 — Dáil debate raises serious issues. *Industrial Relations News* 12 April.

— — —. 1995. Profit-sharing — the means to 10% greater productivity. *Industrial Relations News* 30: 3 August: 13–15.

— — —. 1996. The Labour Court — fifty years on. *Industrial Relations News* 12: 21 March.

— — —. 1996. Non-union policies on the increase among new overseas firms. *Industrial Relations News* 25: 4 January: 17–23.

— — —. 1997. The European Union and industrial relations. In Murphy, T.V. and Roche, W.K. (eds). *Irish Industrial Relations in Practice: Revised and Expanded Edition.* Dublin: Oak Tree Press.

Huczynski, A.A. and Buchanan, D. A. 1991. *Organizational behaviour: An introductory text.* London: Prentice Hall.

Huselid, M.A. 1995. The impact of human resource management practices on turnover, productivity, and corporate financial performance. *Academy of Management Journal* 38: 3: 635–72.

Hyman. R. 1976. Industrial relations: A marxist introduction. London: Macmillan.

— — —. 1989. *Strikes.* London: Macmillan.

— — — and Mason, B. 1995. *Managing Employee Involvement and Pariticipation.* London: Sage.

Ichniowski, C. 1986. The effects of grievance activity on productivity. *Industrial and Labour Relations Review* 40: October.

— — —, Kochan, T.A., Levine, D., Olson, C. and Strauss, G. 1996. What works at work? *Industrial Relations:* 35: 3: 299–333.

Incomes Data Services. 1991. European Report 360: December.

— — —. 1992. *Pay and Benefits.* London: IPM.

— — —. 1996. *Industrial Relations and Collective Bargaining.* European Management Guides. London: Institute of Personnel and Development.

Industrial Participation Association (IPA)/Institute of Personnel Management (IPM). 1983. *Employee involvement and participation: Principles and standards of practice.* London: IPA/IPM.

Industrial Relations News. 1991. Labour law society reviews IR Act 1990. *Industrial Relations News* 28: 18 July.

— — —. 1996. Staff associations — how are they organised? *Industrial Relations News* 46: 17–20.

— — —. 1997. Howmedica and SIPTU conclude partnership agreement. *Industrial Relations News* 40: 23 Oct.

— — —. 1997. Post budget votes swung majority decisively in favour of partnership 2000. *Industrial Relations News* 6: 6 February.

— — —. 1998a. Draft proposals on union recognition likely to face trenchant opposition. *Industrial Relations News* 1 and 2: January: 3–5.

— — —. 1998b. Union recognition formula points to limit of partnership approach. *Industrial Relations News* 3: 15 January: 16–18.

— — —. 1998c. Telecom — breakthrough as talks get underway. *Industrial Relations News* 3: 15 January.

Institute of Public Administration (IPA). 1989. *Personnel and industrial relations directory.* Dublin: IPA.

International Labour Office (ILO). 1960. *Collective bargaining: A workers manual.* Geneva: ILO.

— — —. 1973. *Collective bargaining in industrial market economies.* Geneva: ILO.

— — —. 1975. *Collective bargaining in industrialised market economies.* Geneva: ILO.

— — —. 1977. *Grievance arbitration: A practical guide.* Geneva: ILO.

Irish Business and Employers' Confederation (IBEC). 1993. *IBEC: An Introduction.* Dublin: IBEC.

— — —. 1996. *Prosperity through competitiveness: IBEC's strategic policy framework.* Dublin: IBEC.

— — —. 1984–98. Annual Reports. Dublin: IBEC.

Irish Congress of Trade Unions (ICTU). 1975–97. Annual Reports. Dublin: ICTU

— — —. 1989a. *Technology: Who Decides?* Dublin: ICTU.

— — —. 1989b. *Technology: New Hazards.* Dublin: ICTU.

— — —. 1989c. *Technology And Work.* Dublin: ICTU.

— — —. 1993. *New forms of work organisation: Options for unions.* Dublin: ICTU.

— — —. 1995. *Managing Change.* Dublin: ICTU.

— — —. 1996. *Minimum Standards for Atypical Work.* Dublin: ICTU.

Irish Industrial Relations Review. 1993. Trade union organisation in the Republic. *Irish Industrial Relations Review* 2: 7: July.

Irish Productivity Centre. 1986. *A guide to employee shareholding through profit sharing.* Dublin: Irish Productivity Centre.

Irish Quality Association. 1994. *The value of marked improvements.* Dublin: Irish Quality Association.

Irish Small and Medium Enterprises (ISME). 1997. Annual Report. Dublin: ISME.

Irish Times. 1998. The Ryanair Dispute. Editorial. *The Irish Times* 16 July.

IRS Employment Trends. 1993. Employee involvement — the current state of play. *IRS Employment Trends* 545: October.

Jackson, M. P. 1982. *Industrial relations: A textbook.* London: Kogan Page.

— — —. 1987. *Strikes: Industrial conflict in Britain, USA and Australia.* London: Wheatsheaf.

James, B. 1980. The trade union response to new technology. Internal Papers in Economics 5. Middlesex: Polytechnic.

Jensen, V. 1956. Notes on the beginnings of collective bargaining. *Industrial and Labor Relations Review* 9: 2: January: 230–32.

Juran, J. 1986. The Quality Trilogy. *Quality Progress* 19: 8: 19–24.

Jurgens, U. 1989. The transfer of Japanese management concepts in the international automobile industry. In S. Wood (ed.). *The Transformation of Work?* London: Unwin Hyman.

Kahn-Freund, O. 1977. *Labour and the Law.* London: Stevens.

Kamoche, K. 1991. Human resource management. A multi paradigmatic analysis. *Personnel Review* 20: 4.

Kanter, R. 1984. *The Change Masters.* London: Allen and Unwin.

Katz, H.C., Kochan, T. A. and Weber, M. 1985. Assessing the effects of industrial relations systems and efforts to improve the quality of working on organizational effectiveness. *Academy of Management Journal* 28: September.

Kavanagh, R. 1987. *Labour from the beginning — 75 years.* Dublin: The Labour Party.

Keating, M. 1989. Personnel management in Ireland. In *Industrial Relations in Ireland:* Dublin: University College Dublin. 1989.

Keenan, J. and Thom, A. 1988. The future through the keyhole: Some thoughts on employment patterns. *Personnel Review* 17: 1.

Keenoy, T. 1990. HRM: A case of the wolf in sheep's clothing? *Personnel Review* 19: 2: 3–9.

Kelly, A. 1975. Changes in the occupational structure and industrial relations in Ireland. *Management* 2.

— — —. 1979. The nature of worker participation in Ireland: The incongruity of European and Irish industrial relations structures. Paper presented at the National Conference on Industrial Relations: Galway Regional Technical College.

— — —. 1989a. The worker director in Irish industrial relations. In *Industrial relations in Ireland.* Dublin: University College Dublin. 1989.

— — —. 1989b. The Rights Commissioner: Conciliator, mediator or arbitrator. In *Industrial relations in Ireland.* Dublin: University College Dublin. 1989

— — — Undated. In support of the new working class thesis: The case of the Irish white collar worker. Working paper. Dublin: Department of Industrial Relations: University College Dublin.

— — — and Bourke, P. 1979. *Management, labour and consumer.* Dublin: Gill and Macmillan.

— — — and Brannick, T. 1983. The pattern of strike activity in Ireland, 1960–1979. *Irish Business and Administrative Research* 5: 1: 65–77.

— — — and Brannick, T. 1985. Industrial relations practices of multinational companies in Ireland. *Irish Business and Administrative Research* 7: 1.

— — — and Brannick, T. 1986. The changing contours of Irish strike patterns: 1960–1984. *Irish Business and Administrative Research* 8: 77–88.

— — — and Brannick, T. 1988a. Explaining the strike proneness of British Companies in Ireland. *British Journal of Industrial Relations* 26: 1: 37–57.

— — — and Brannick, T. 1988b. The management of human resources: New trends and the challenge to trade unions. *Arena: Journal of the Irish Institute of Training and Development* August: 11–15.

— — — and Brannick, T. 1988c. Strike trends in the Irish private sector. *Irish Business and Administrative Research* 9: 87–98.

— — — and Brannick, T. 1989a. Strikes in Ireland: Measurement, indices and trends. In *Industrial Relations in Ireland.* Dublin: University College Dublin. 1989

— — — and Brannick, T. 1989b. The changing contours of Irish industrial conflict. Paper presented to the International Polish-Irish Conference: University of Warsaw.

— — — and Brannick, T. 1991. The impact of new human resource management policies on US MNC strike patterns. Mimeo. Dublin: Department of Business Administration: University College Dublin.

— — — and Roche, W. 1983. Institutional reform in Irish industrial relations. *Studies* Autumn.

— — — and Hourihan, F. 1997. Employee Participation. In Murphy, T.V. and Roche, W.K. (eds). *Irish Industrial Relations in Practice: Revised and Expanded Edition.* Dublin: Oak Tree Press.

Kerr, A. 1989. Trade Unions and the Law. In *Industrial Relations in Ireland*. Dublin: University College Dublin. 1989.

— — —. 1987. Maternity protection — The spectre of legalism. *Industrial Relations News* 5 March.

— — —. 1989. Trade unions and the law. In *Industrial relations in Ireland*. Dublin: University College Dublin. 1989.

— — —. 1991a. *Irish current law statutes annotated*. London: Sweet and Maxwell.

— — —. 1991b. Irish industrial relations legislation consensus not compulsion. *Industrial Law Journal* 20: 4: December.

— — —. 1997. Collective labour law. In Murphy, T.V. and Roche, W.K. (eds). *Irish Industrial Relations in Practice*. Dublin: Oak Tree Press.

— — — and Whyte, G. 1985. Irish Trade Union Law. Dublin: Professional Books.

Kiberd, D. 1996. Partnership 2000 falls far short of real public sector reform. *Sunday Business Post* 29 December.

Kinnie, N. 1985. Changing management strategies in industrial relations. *Industrial Relations Journal* 16: 4.

— — —. 1986. Patterns of industrial relations management. *Employee Relations* 8: 2.

— — —. 1983. Single employer bargaining: Structures and strategies. *Industrial Relations Journal* 14: 3.

Klein, J. 1989. The human cost of manufacturing reform. *Harvard Business Review* March-April.

Kleiner, M. 1990. The role of industrial relations in industrial performance. In Fossum, J. A. (ed.). *Employee and Labour Relations*. Washington: Bureau of National Affairs.

Kochan, T. 1980. *Collective bargaining and industrial relations*. Homewood: Irwin.

— — — and Chalykoff, J. 1987. Human resource management and business life cycles: Some preliminary propositions. In Kleingartner, A. and Anderson, C. (eds). *Human resources and high technology firms*. Lexington, Mass.: Lexington Books.

— — — and Katz, H.C. 1988. *Collective bargaining and industrial relations* Homewood: Irwin.

— — —, Katz, H.C. and McKersie, R.B. 1986. *The transformation of American industrial relations*. New York: Basic Books.

— — —, McKersie, R. and Capelli, P. 1984. Strategic choice and industrial relations. *Industrial Relations* 23.

— — — and Osterman, P. 1994. *The mutual gains enterprise*. Cambridge, Mass.: Harvard Business School Press.

Kreckel, R. 1980. Unequal opportunity: Structures and labour market segmentation. *Sociology* 14: 4.

Labour Court. *Explanatory handout*. Dublin: Labour Court.

— — — Forty-second annual report. Dublin: Government Stationery Office.

— — — Third annual report. Dublin: Government Stationery Office.

— — — Thirty-first annual report. Dublin: Government Stationery Office.

Labour Relations Commission. 1992. Labour relations commission annual report. Dublin: Government Stationery Office.

— — —. 1997. Annual Report 1996. Dublin: Government Publications Office.

Larkin, E. 1965. *James Larkin: 1876–1947 — Irish labour leader*. London: Routledge and Kegan Paul.

Lash, S. and Ury, J. 1988. *The end of organised capitalism.* Cambridge: Polity press.

Lawler, E. 1978. The new plant revolution. *Organisational Dynamics* Winter.

— — —. 1988a. Human resource management, meeting the new challenge. *Personnel* January.

— — —. 1988b. Pay for performance: Making it work. *Personnel* October.

— — —. 1982. Increasing worker involvement to enhance organisational effectiveness. In Goodman, P.S. (ed.). *Change in organisations.* San Francisco: Jossey Bass.

Leddin, A. and B. Walsh. 1997. *The macro-economy of Ireland.* Dublin: Gill and Macmillan.

Lee, J. 1980. Worker and society since 1945. *Trade unions and change in Irish society.* D. Nevin (ed.). Dublin: Mercier/RTÉ.

Legge, K. 1978. *Power, innovation and problem-solving in personnel management.* New York: McGraw-Hill.

— — —. 1989. Human resource management — A critical analysis. In Storey, J. (ed.). *New perspectives on human resource management.* London: Routledge. 1989.

Lehmbruch, G., Schmitter, F. and Philippe, C. 1982. Patterns of corporatist policy making. London: Sage.

Leiserson, W. 1922. Constitutional government in American industries. *American Economic Review* 12: 21.

Lennon, P. 1983. The Unfair Dismissals Act 1977 — a critical evaluation. *Industrial Relations News* 21.

Lewiki, R.J., Litterer, J.A., Minton, J.W. and Saunders, D.M. 1994. *Negotiation.* Burr Ridge: Irwin.

Locke, E. and Schweiger, D. 1979. Participation in decision making: One more look. In Shaw, B. and Cummings, L. (eds). *Research in Organisational Behaviour.* Greenwich, CT.: JAI Press.

Lockwood, D. 1989. *The black coated worker.* Clarendon: Oxford.

Long, P. 1988. A review of approved profit sharing: Trust schemes in Ireland and the UK. Unpublished Dissertation. Dublin Institute of Technology.

MacInnes, J. and Sproull, A. 1989. Union recognition and employment change in Scottish Electronics. *Industrial Relations Journal* 20: 1: Spring.

Mackay, L. 1987. Personnel: changes disguising decline. *Personnel Review* 16: 5.

— — — and Torrington, D. 1986. *The changing nature of personnel management.* Institute of Personnel Management.

Madden, D. and Kerr, A. 1990. *Unfair dismissal: Cases and commentary.* Dublin: Federation of Irish Employers.

Marchington, M. 1982. *Managing industrial relations.* London: McGraw-Hill.

— — —. 1990. Analysing the links between product markets and the management of employee relations. *Journal of Management Studies* 27: 2: 111–132.

— — — and Parker, P. 1990. *Changing patterns of employee relations.* Hemel Hempstead: Harvester Wheatsheaf.

— — —, Wilkinson, A. and Ackers, P. 1993. Waving or drowning in participation? *Personnel Management* March: 47–9.

Marciniak, F. 1991. VW circles as a component in total quality management. *P+ total quality management and worker participation.* European Foundation for the Improvement of Living and Working Conditions: 2. Dublin: European Foundation.

Marsden, D. 1990. Institutions and labour mobility, occupational and internal labour markets in Britain, France, Italy and West Germany. Brunetta, R. and DellAringa, C. (eds). *Labor relations and economic performance*. Basington: Macmillan.

Marsh, A.I. 1973. *Managers and shop stewards: Shop floor revolution*. London: Institute of Personnel Management.

Marshall, R. 1992. Work organisation, unions and economic performance. In Mishel, L. and Voos, P.(eds). *Unions and Economic Competitiveness*. New York: ME Sharpe Inc.

McBeath G. & Rands, N. 1989. *Salary administration* (4th edn). London: Gower.

McCall, B.1989. Labour law — all changed. *Management* 35: 11.

McCarthy, C. 1975. *The decade of upheaval*. Dublin: Institute of Public Administration.

— — —. 1977. *Trade unions in Ireland: 1894–1960*. Dublin: Institute of Public Administration.

— — —. 1982. Reform: A strategy for research. In Pollock, H. (ed.). *Reform of industrial relations*. Dublin: O'Brien Press.

— — —. 1984. *Elements in a theory of industrial relations*. Dublin: Trinity College Dublin.

— — — and Von Prondzynski, F. 1982. The reform of industrial relations. *Administration* 29: 3.

McCarthy, W.E.J., O'Brien, J.F. and O'Dowd, V.G. 1975. Wage inflation and wage leadership. Paper 79. Dublin: Economic and Social Research Institute.

McGinley, M. 1989a. Pay in the 1980's: The issue of control. *Industrial Relations News* 30: August.

— — —. 1989b. Pay increases between 1981–1987. *Personnel and Industrial Relations Directory*. Dublin: Institute of Public Administration.

— — —. 1990. Trade union law — look back in anguish. *Industrial Relations News* 16: 26: April.

— — —. 1997. Industrial relations in the public sector. In Murphy, T.V. and Roche W.K. (eds). *Industrial relations in practice*. Dublin: Oak Tree Press.

McGovern, P. 1988. Increasing opposition to unionisation in the 1980s. *Industrial Relations News* 45: 24 November: 15–18.

— — —. 1989a. Union recognition and union avoidance in the 1980s. *Industrial Relations in Ireland*. Dublin: University College Dublin. 1989.

— — —. 1989b. Trade union recognition — five case studies. *Industrial Relations News* 6: 9 February: 12–16.

McGowan, K. 1996. Address to the Cork Electronics Association. *Irish Times*. 6 November.

McInnes, J. 1988. The question of flexibility. *Personnel Review* 17: 3.

McKersie, R.B. 1996. Labor-management partnerships: US evidence and implications for Ireland. *Irish Business and Administrative Research* 17: 2: 1–13.

McLoughlin, I. and Gourlay, S. 1992. Enterprise without unions: The management of employee relations in non-union firms. *Journal of Management Studies* 29: 5: 669–691.

McMahon, G. 1987. Wage structure in the Republic of Ireland. *Advances in Business Studies* 1: 1. Dublin: Dublin Institute of Technology.

— — —. 1987a. Selection interviewing and the employment decision: A recipe for discrimination. *Industrial Relations News* 2 July.

— — —. 1988. Rush the recruitment — Rue the results. *Management* February.

— — —. 1989. Low pay and the joint labour committee system. *Industrial relations in Ireland*. Dublin: University College Dublin. 1989.

— — —. 1990. Multinationals: The labour relations experience in Ireland. *Advances in Business Studies* 2: 2.

— — —. 1992. Pay inequality in the 1990s: An evaluation of strategic alternatives. *Administration* 40: 2, Summer.

— — —. 1996. Claim by the garda representative association for a pay increase. Dublin: Garda Representative Association/Dublin Institute of Technology.

— — — Neary, C. and O'Connor, K. 1988. Multinationals in Ireland — Three decades on. *Industrial Relations News* 6.

McNamara, G. and Williams, K. and West, D. 1988. *Understanding trade unions: Yesterday and today.* Dublin: O'Brien Educational Press.

McPartlin, B. 1997. The development of trade union organisation. In Murphy, T.V. and Roche, W.K. (eds). *Irish Industrial Relations in Practice.* Dublin: Oak Tree Press.

Meenan, F. 1985. A survey of unfair dismissal cases 1977–1984. *FUE Bulletin Supplement:* June. Dublin: FUE.

— — —. 1991 'Industrial Relations Act 1990 — A commentary on the trade disputes provisions part 1 and part 2. *Industrial Relations IR Data Bank* 9: 207 and 208: February.

— — —. 1994. *Working within the law — A practical guide for employers and employees.* Dublin: Oak Tree Press.

Metcalf, D. 1990. Union presence and labour productivity in British manufacturing, a reply to Nolan and Marginson. *British Journal of Industrial Relations* 28: 2.

Miles, R.E. and Snow, C.C. 1978. *Organizational strategy, structure and process.* New York: McGraw Hill.

— — —. 1984. Designing strategic human resources systems. *Organisational Dynamics* Spring: 36–52.

Miller, P. 1984. Strategic HRM: What it is and what it isn't. *Personnel Management* February: 1984.

Mills, D.Q. 1989. *Labor-management relations.* New York: McGraw-Hill.

Millward, N. and Stevens, M. 1986. *British workplace industrial relations: The DE/PSI/ESRC survey.* Aldershot: Gower.

— — —, Smart, D. and Hawes, W. 1992. *Workplace industrial relations in transition: The DE/PSI/ESRC survey.* Aldershot: Gower.

Milner, S. and Richards, E. 1991. Determinants of union recognition and employee involvement, evidence from the London docklands. *British Journal of Industrial Relations* 29: 3: 377–90.

Miner, J.B. and Miner, M.G. 1977. *Personnel management and employee relations: A managerial approach.* New York: Macmillan.

Monks, K. 1992. Personnel management practices: Uniformity or diversity? Evidence from some Irish organisatons. *Irish Business and Administrative Research* 13: 74–86.

Mooney, P. 1980. An inquiry into wage payment systems in Ireland. Dublin: ESRI/European Foundation for the Improvement of Living and Working Conditions.

— — —.1989. From industrial relations to employee relations in Ireland. Unpublished PhD Dissertation. Dublin: Trinity College Dublin.

Morley, M. and Gunnigle, P. 1994. Trends in flexible working patterns in Ireland. In Gunnigle, P., Flood, P., Morley, M. and Turner, T. *Continuity and change in Irish employee relations: Irish studies in management.* Dublin: Oak Tree Press.

460

— — —, Moore, S., Heraty, N., and Gunnigle, P. 1998. *Principles of organisational behaviour*. Dublin: Gill and Macmillan.

Morrissey, T.J. 1989. Employee participation at sub-board level. In *Industrial Relations in Ireland*. Dublin: University College Dublin. 1989.

Mowday, R.T., Porter, L.W. and Steers, R.M. 1982. Employee-organization linkages: The psychology of commitment, absenteeism and turnover. New York: Academic Press.

Mulligan, H. 1993. The Unfair Dismissals Act — day to day reality. *Industrial Relations News* 4 March.

Mulvey, C. (n.d.). Industrial democracy: A report by the Federated Union of Employers and the Confederation of Irish Industry. Dublin: FUE/CII.

Mulvey, K. 1991a. The potential role of the Labour Relations Commission. Paper presented to the Irish Association of Industrial Relations: 16 April. Dublin: The Labour Relations Commission.

— — —. 1991b. The Labour Relations Commission. Paper presented to the Mid-West Chapter of the IPM: November. Dublin: The Labour Relations Commission.

Mumford, E. and R. Hendricks. 1996. Business process re-engineering RIP. *People Management* 2 May.

Munns, V.G. 1967. The functions and organisation of employers' associations in selected industries. Employers' Associations Research Paper 7. Royal Commission on Trade Unions and Employers' Associations. London: HMSO.

Murphy, T. and Walsh, D. 1980. *The worker director and his influence on the enterprise: Expectations, experience and effectiveness in seven Irish companies*. Dublin: Irish Productivity Centre.

Murphy, T.V. 1986. The dismissal issue in industrial relations: Employers and trade unions show improved performances since 1977. *Industrial Relations News* 29: 24 July.

— — —. 1989. The impact of the Unfair Dismissals Act, 1977 on workplace industrial relations. In *Industrial Relations In Ireland*. Dublin: University College Dublin. 1989.

— — — and Roche, W.K. (eds). 1994. *Irish industrial relations in practice*. Dublin: Oak Tree Press.

— — —. 1997. *Irish industrial relations in practice: Revised and Expanded Edition*. Dublin: Oak Tree Press.

Murray, S. 1984. *Employee relations in Irish private sector manufacturing industry*. Dublin: Industrial Development Authority.

Myers, M. 1976. *Managing without unions*. Wokingham: Addison-Wesley.

National Economic and Social Council (NESC). 1986. *A strategy for development 1986–1990*. Dublin: NESC.

— — —. 1988. *Building On Reality 1985–1987*. Dublin: Government Publications Office.

— — —. 1996. *Strategy into the 21st century*. Dublin: NESC.

Neumann, G. 1980. The predictability of strikes: Evidence from the stock market. *Industrial and Labour Relations Review* 33: July.

Newby, H. 1977. *The deferential worker*. London: Penguin.

Nierenberg, G.I. 1968. *The art of negotiating*. New York: Cornerstone.

Nolan, P. 1989. Walking on water? Performance and industrial relations under Thatcher. *Industrial Relations Journal* 20: 2.

461

Norman, D. 1983. How a new plant made Pilkington reflect on its IR structure. *Personnel Management* 5: 8: August.

O'Brien, J.F. 1981. *A study of the national wage agreements in Ireland.* Dublin: Economic and Social Research Institute.

— — —. 1989. Pay determination in Ireland. In *Industrial relations in Ireland.* Dublin: University College Dublin. 1989.

— — —. 1989. The PNR in perspective — another round? Eighth annual industrial relations guest lecture. Limerick: University of Limerick.

O'Connor, K. 1982. The impact of the Unfair Dismissals Act, 1977 on personnel management and industrial relations. *Irish Business and Administrative Research* 5: 2.

O'Donnell, R. and O'Reardon, C. 1996. Irish experiment: Social partnership has yielded economic growth and social progress. Mimeo. Dublin: National Economic and Social Council/Economic and Social Research Institute.

O'Grada, C. 1997. *A rocky road: The Irish economy since the 1920s.* Manchester: Manchester University Press.

O'Hagan, J. 1987. *The economy of Ireland: Policy and performance* (5th edn). Dublin: Irish Management Institute.

O'Hara, B. 1981. *The evolution of Irish industrial relations: Law and practice.* Dublin: Folens.

O'Mahony, D. 1964. *Industrial Relations in Ireland.* Dublin: Economic and Social Research Institute.

O'Shea, F. 1983. Neo-corporatism. Mimeo. Limerick: University of Limerick.

Oechslin, J.J. 1985. Employers' organisations. Blanpain, R. (ed.) *Labour law and industrial relations.* Deventer: Kluwer.

Oliver, N. and Wilkinson, B. 1989. Japanese manufacturing techniques and personnel and industrial relations in Britain: Evidence and implications. *British Journal of Industrial Relations* 27: 2.

— — —. 1988. *The Japanization of British industry.* Oxford: Blackwell.

O'Malley, E. 1983. Late industrialisation under outward looking policies: The experience and prospects of the Republic of Ireland. Unpublished Ph.D. Thesis. Sussex: University of Sussex.

Organisation for Economic Co-operation and Development (OECD). 1979. *Wage policies and collective bargaining developments in Finland, Ireland and Norway.* Paris: OECD.

Osterman, P. 1982. Employment structures within firms. *British Journal of Industrial Relations* November.

Ouchi, W. 1981. *Theory Z: How American business can meet the Japanese challenge.* Reading, Mass.: Addison-Wesley.

Paauwe, J. 1996. Personnel management without personnel managers. In Flood, P., Gannon, M.J. and Paauwe, J. (eds). *Managing without traditional methods: International innovations in human resource management.* Wokingham: Addison-Wesley.

Parker, P.A.L., Hayes, W.R. and Lumb, A.L. 1971. *The reform of collective bargaining at plant and company level.* London: HMSO.

Pateman, C. 1970. *Participation and democratic theory.* Cambridge: Cambridge University Press.

Pearson, R. 1991. *The human resource.* New York: McGraw-Hill.

Perlman, S. 1936. The principle of collective bargaining. *The Journal of the American Academy of Political and Social Science* March: 154–9.

Peters, T. and Waterman, R.H. 1982. *In search of excellence: Lessons from America's best run companies.* New York: Harper and Row.

Pettigrew, A., Sparrow, P. and Hendry, C. 1988. The forces that trigger training. *Personnel Management* December.

Pfeffer, J. 1994. *Competitive advantage through people: Unleashing the power of the workforce.* Boston: Stanford Graduate School of Business: Harvard Business School Press.

Pfeffry J. and Cohen, Y. 1984. Determinants of internal labour markets in organisations. *Administrative Science Quarterly* 29.

Phelps Brown, E.H. 1971. Collective Bargaining Considered. London: Athlone Press.

— — —. 1986. *The origins of trade union power.* Oxford: Oxford University Press.

Pierson, P. 1961. Cited in Sisson, K. 1987. The management of collective bargaining — an international comparison. London: Blackwell.

Piore, M. and Sabel, C. 1984. *The second industrial divide.* New York: Basic Books.

Pollert, A. 1987. The flexible firm: A model in search of reality or a policy in search of a practice? *Warwick Papers in Industrial Relations* 19: December.

— — —. 1988a. Dismantling flexibility. *Capital and Class* 34: Spring: 42–75.

— — —. 1988b. The 'flexible firm': Fixation or fact? *Work, Employment and Society* 2: 3: September: 281–316.

— — —. 1991. *Farewell to flexibility?* Oxford: Blackwell.

Pollock, H. and O'Dwyer, L. 1985. *We can work it out: Relationships in the workplace.* Dublin: O'Brien Educational Press.

Poole, M. 1980. Management strategies and industrial relations. In Poole, M. and Mansfield, R.(eds). *Managerial roles in industrial relations.* London: Gower.

— — —. 1984. *Theories of trade unionism.* London: Routledge and Kegan Paul.

— — —. 1986. *Industrial relations: Origins and patterns of national diversity.* London: Routledge and Kegan Paul.

— — —. 1987. Managerial strategies and styles in industrial relations: A compartative analysis. *Journal of General Management* Autumn.

— — —, Mansfield, R., Blyton, P. and Frost, P. 1981. *Managers in focus.* London: Gower.

— — —, Mansfield, R., Blyton, P. and Frost, P. 1992. Managerial attitudes and behaviour in industrial relations: Evidence from a national survey. *British Journal of Industrial Relations* 20.

Porter, M. 1980. *Competitive strategy: Techniques for analysing industries and competitors.* New York: The Free Press.

— — —. 1985. *Competitive advantage: Creating and sustaining superior performance.* New York: The Free Press.

— — —. 1987. From competitive advantage to corporate strategy. *Harvard Business Review* May–June: 43–59.

— — —. 1990. *The competitive advantage of nations.* New York: Free Press.

Purcell, J. 1982. Macho managers and the new industrial relations. *Employee Relations* 4: 1.

— — —. 1983. The management of industrial relations in the modern corporation: Agenda for research. *British Journal of Industrial Relations* 21.

— — — and Gray, A. 1986. Corporate personnel departments and the management of industrial relations: Two case studies in ambiguity. *Journal of Management Studies* 23: 2: 205–23.

— — —. 1987. Mapping management styles in employee relations. *Journal of Management Studies* 24: 5: 533–48.

— — —. 1989. The impact of corporate strategy on human resource management. Storey, J. (ed.). *New perspectives on human resource management.* London: Routledge.

— — —. 1992. The Impact of corporate strategy on human resource management. In Salaman, G. (ed.). *Human resource strategies,* London: Sage/Open University.

— — —, Marginson, P., Edwards, P., and Sisson, K. 1987. The industrial relations practices of multi-plant foreign owned firms. *Industrial Relations Journal* 18: 2 Summer.

— — — and Sisson, K. 1983. Strategies and practice in the management of industrial relations. In Bain, G. (ed.). *Industrial Relations in Britain.* Oxford: Blackwell.

Rabbitte, P. and Gilmore, E. 1990. Bertie's Bill. Dublin: The Workers' Party.

Rainnie, A. 1989. *Industrial relations in small firms: small isn't beautiful,* London: Routledge.

— — — and Scott, M. 1982. Industrial relations in the small firm. In Curran, J., Stanworth, J., and Watkins, D. (eds). *The survival of the small firm: Volume 2.* London: Gower.

Ramsay, H., Pollert, A., and Rainbird, H. 1992. A decade of transformation? Labour market flexibility and work organisation in the United Kingdom. *New directions in work organisation: The industrial relations response.* Paris: OECD.

Reed, M. 1989. *The sociology of management.* Hemel Hempstead: Harvester Wheatsheaf.

Report of the Commission of Inquiry of Industrial Relations. 1981. Dublin: Government Stationery Office.

Reynaud, J.P. 1978. Problems and prospects for collective bargaining in the EEC member states. Commission of the European Community Document no. V/394/78-EN. Brussels: European Commission.

Ridgely, P. 1988. How relevant is the FUE? *Irish Business* February.

Robbins, S.P. 1983. *Organizational theory: The structure and design of organizations.* New Jersey: Prentice Hall.

Robinson, O. 1984. Part-time employment and industrial relations developments in the EEC. *Industrial Relations Journal* 15: 4: Spring.

Roche, W.K. 1989. State strategies and the politics of industrial relations in Ireland. *Industrial Relations In Ireland.* Dublin: University College Dublin.

— — —. 1990. Industrial relations research in Ireland and the trade union interest. Paper presented to the Irish Congress of Trade Unions Conference on joint research between trade unions, universities, third level colleges and research institutes. Dublin.

— — —. 1991. The future of trade unions — SIPTU seminar examines the issues. *Industrial Relations News* 25 April.

— — —. 1992a. Modelling trade union growth and decline in the Republic of Ireland. *Irish Business and Administrative Research* 13: 1: 86–102.

— — —. 1992b. The liberal theory of industrialism and the development of industrial telations in Ireland. J. Goldthorpe and C. Whelan (eds). *The development of industrial society in Ireland.* Oxford: Oxford University Press.

— — —. 1994a. Pay determination, the state and the politics of industrial relations. In Murphy, T.V. and Roche, W.K. (eds). *Irish industrial relations in practice.* Dublin: Oak Tree Press.

— — —. 1994b. The trend of unionisation. In Murphy, T.V. and Roche, W.K. (eds). *Irish industrial relations in practice.* Dublin: Oak Tree Press.

— — —. 1995. The new competitive order and employee relations in Ireland. Paper presented to the Irish Business and Employers Confederation Conference on human resources in the global market. Dublin (November).

— — —. 1997a. The trend of unionisation. In Murphy, T.V. and Roche, W.K. (eds). *Irish industrial relations in practice.* Dublin: Oak Tree Press.

— — —. 1997b. Pay determination, the state and the politics of industrial relations. In Murphy, T.V. and Roche, W.K. (eds). *Irish industrial relations in practice: Revised and expanded edition.* Dublin: Oak Tree Press.

— — — and Larragy, J. 1986. The formation of the Irish trade union movement and organisational developments since 1945. Working Paper. Dublin: Department of Industrial Relations, University College Dublin.

— — — and Larragy, J. 1989a. The trend of unionisation in the Irish Republic. *Industrial relations in Ireland.* Dublin: University College Dublin.

— — — and Larragy, J. 1989b. The determinants of the annual rate of trade union growth and decline in the Irish Republic: Evidence from the DUES membership series. Dublin: University College Dublin.

— — — and Larragy, J. 1990. Cyclical and institutional determinants of annual trade union growth and decline in Ireland: Evidence from the DUES data series. *European Sociological Review* 6.

— — — and Geary, J. 1994. The attenuation of host-country effects? Multinationals, industrial relations and collective bargaining in Ireland. Working Paper. Business Research Programme. Dublin: Smurfit Graduate School of Business: University College Dublin.

— — — and Geary, J. 1996. Multinational companies in Ireland: Adapting to or diverging from national industrial relations and traditions? *Irish Business and Administrative Research* 17.

— — — and Turner, T. 1994. Testing alternative models of human resource policy effects on trade union recognition in the Republic of Ireland. *International Journal of Human Resource Management* 5: 3: 721–53.

— — — and Turner, T. 1997. The diffusion of the commitment model in the Republic of Ireland. *Review of Employment Topics* 3: 108–51.

— — — and Turner, T. 1998. Human resource management and industrial relations: Substitution, dualism and partnership. In Roche, W.K., Monks, K. and Walsh, J. (eds). *Human resource management strategies: Policy and practice in Ireland.* Dublin: Oak Tree Press.

— — — and Kochan, T.A. 1996. Strategies for extending social partnership to enterprise and workplace levels in Ireland. Report Prepared for the National Economic and Social Council. Dublin.

465

— — — and Ashmore, J. 1997. The changing shape of trade union membership in the Republic of Ireland: 1990–1996. Working Paper. Dublin: Smurfit Graduate School of Business: University College Dublin.

— — — and Gunnigle, P. 1997. Competition and the new industrial relations agenda. In Murphy, T.V. and Roche, W.K. (eds). *Irish industrial relations in practice: Revised and expanded edition.* Dublin: Oak Tree Press.

Rollinson, D. 1993. *Understanding employee relations: A behavioural approach.* Wokingham: Addison-Wesley.

Roth, S. 1993. Lean production in German motor manufacturing. *P+: European Participation Monitor* 1: 5: 35–39. Dublin: European Foundation for the Improvement of Living and Working Conditions.

Rothenberg, H. I. and Silverman, S.B. 1973. *Labor unions: How to avert them, beat them, out-negotiate them, live with them, unload them.* Elkins Park: Management Relations Inc.

Ruback, R. and Zimmerman, M.B. 1984. Unionization and profitability: Evidence from the capital market. *Journal of Political Economy* 6 December.

Rynes, S.L. & Milkovich, G.T. 1986. *Current issues in in human resource management: Commentary and readings.* Texas: Business Publications Inc.

Salamon, M. 1992. *Industrial relations: Theory and practice.* (2nd edn) London: Prentice-Hall.

— — —. 1998. *Industrial relations: Theory and practice.* (3rd edn) London: Prentice-Hall.

Schregle, J. 1974. Labour relations in Western Europe: Some topical issues. *International Labour Review* Jan.–June.

Schuler, R. 1987. Personnel and human resource management choices and organizational strategy. *Human Resource Planning* 10: 1: 1–17.

— — —. 1987. *Personnel and human resource management.* St Paul (MN): West Publishing Company.

— — —. 1989. Strategic human resource management. *Human Relations* 42: 2: 157–84.

— — —. 1992. Strategic human resource management: Linking the people with the strategic needs of the business. *Organisational Dynamics* 21: 1: 18–31.

— — —, Galante, S.P. and Jackson, S.E. 1987. Matching effective HR practices with competitive strategy. *Personnel* September: 18–27.

Schuler, R and Jackson, S. 1987. Linking competitive strategies with human resource management practices. *Academy of Management Executive* 1: 3 August: 209–13.

Scott, B. 1981. *The skills of negotiating.* London: Gower.

Sewell, G. and Wilkinson, B. 1992. Employment or emasculation? Shopfloor surveillance in a total quality organisation. In P. Blyton and P. Turnbull (eds). *Reassessing human resource management.* London: Sage.

Sheehan, B. 1989. Industrial relations reform. *Industrial Relations News* 42: 9 November.

— — —. 1991. Social consensus and incomes policy: Has centralised bargaining served the country well? *Industrial Relations News*: 26: September.

— — —. 1992. SIPTU analysis of national agreements shows real increases in take home pay. *Industrial Relations News* 36: September.

— — —. 1993. Attley predicts difficult pay bargaining climate for trade unions. *Industrial Relations News* March.

— — —. 1996. Ahern says consensus could collapse, blames taoiseach. *Industrial Relations News* 9: 29 February.

— — —. 1996b. Spectre of return to '70s style deal raised in report. *Industrial Relations News*: 9 29 February.

— — —. 1996c. Agenda for talks emerges as SIPTU's tax demands receive boost. *Industrial Relations News* 35: 19 September.

— — —. 1997. Employers must pay for change says SIPTU vice-president. *Industrial Relations News* 14: 10 April.

Shivanath, G. 1987. Personnel practitioners 1986: Their role and status in Irish industry. Unpublished MBS Thesis. Limerick: University of Limerick.

Silver, M. 1973. Recent British Strike Trends: A Factual Analysis. *British Journal of Industrial Relations*, 11–1: 66–104.

Silverman, J. 1970. *The theory of organisations*. London: Heinemann.

Sisson, K. 1977. *Negotiating in Practice*. London: Institute of Personnel Management.

— — —. 1983. Employers' organisations. In Bain, G. (ed.). *Industrial relations in Britain*. Blackwell: Oxford.

— — —. 1987. *The management of collective bargaining: An international comparison*. Oxford: Blackwell.

— — —. 1989. *Personnel management in Britain*. Oxford: Blackwell.

— — —. 1991. Industrial relations: Challenges and opportunities. *Employee Relations* 13: 6.

— — —. 1994a. Workplace Europe. Direct participation in organisational change: Introducing the EPOC project. Presented to the International Industrial Relations Association Fourth European Regional Congress on transformation of European industrial relations: Consequences of integration and disintegration. Helsinki.

— — —. 1994b. *Personnel management: A comprehensive guide to theory and practice in Britain*. Oxford: Blackwell.

— — —. 1994c. Paradigms, practice and prospects. In Sisson, K. (ed.). *Personnel Management*. Oxford: Blackwell.

— — —. 1997. Towards new forms of work organisation — can Europe realise its innovative potential? An interim report of the results of the EPOC questionnaire survey of direct employee participation in Europe. Luxembourg: European Foundation/Office for the Official Publication of the European Communities.

Smith, A. 1970. *The wealth of nations*. London: Pelican.

Smith, P. and Morton, G. 1993. Union exclusion and the decollectivisation of industrial relations in Great Britain. *British Journal of Industrial Relations* 31: 1: 97–114.

Sparrow, P.R. and Hiltrop, J.M. 1994. *European human resource management in transition*. London: Prentice Hall.

Sproull, A. and MacInnes, J. 1987. Patterns of union recognition in Scottish electronics. *British Journal of Industrial Relations* 25: 3.

Steers, R.M. and Mowday, R.T. 1987. Employee turnover in organisations. Steers, R.M. and Porter, L.W. *Motivation and work behaviour*. New York: McGraw-Hill.

Stevens, C.M. 1963. *Strategy and collective bargaining negotiations*. McGraw Hill: New York.

Storey, J. 1989. (Ed.). *New perspectives on human resource management*. London: Routledge.

— — —. 1992. *Developments in the management of human resources*. Oxford: Blackwell.

467

— — — and Sisson, K. 1990. Limits to transformation: Human resource management in the British context. *Industrial Relations Journal* 21: Spring: 60–65.

— — — and Sisson, K. 1994. *Managing human resources and industrial relations.* Buckingham: Open University Press.

Streeck, W. 1992. Training and the new industrial relations: A strategic role for unions? In Regini, M. (ed.). *The Future of Labour Movements.* London: Sage.

— — —. 1997. The end of the new industrial relations? Presentation at congress seminar, Fifth International Industrial Relations Association European Regional Congress. Available on video from Smurfit Graduate Business School, University College Dublin.

Suttle, S. 1988. Labour market flexibility. *Industrial relations News* 38.

Sweeney, P. 1998. *The celtic tiger — Ireland's economic miracle explained.* Dublin: Oak Tree Press.

Tansey, P. 1994. Pay deal scuppers budget. *The Sunday Tribune* 13 February.

Taylor, B., Elger, T. and Fairbrother, P. 1991. Work relations in electronics: What has become of Japanisation in Britain? Paper presented to the Ninth Annual Labour Process Conference: University of Manchester Institute of Science and Technology.

Taylor, G. 1996. Labour market rigidities, institutional impediments and managerial constraints: Some reflections on the recent experience of macro-political bargaining in Ireland. *Economic and Social Review:* Economic and Social Studies. Dublin: ESRI.

Teague, P. 1995. Pay determination in the Republic of Ireland: Towards social corporatism? *British Journal of Industrial Relations* 33: 2: 253–73.

Thelen, H.A. and Withall, J. 1979. Three frames of reference: The description of climate. *Human Relations* 2: 2: 159–76.

Thomas, S. and Kleiner, M. 1989. Two-tier collective bargaining arrangements and shareholder equity. Unpublished Manuscript. University of Minnesota.

Thomason, G. 1984. *A textbook of industrial relations management.* London: Institute of Personnel Management.

Thurley, K. and Wood, S. 1983. (Eds). *Industrial relations and management strategy.* Cambridge: Cambridge University Press.

Tiernan, F. 1993. Sexual harassment in the workplace. *I.P.M. News* February.

Tiernan, S., Morley, M. and Foley, E. 1996. *Modern management: Theory & practice for Irish students.* Dublin: Gill and Macmillan.

Toner, B. 1985. The unionisation and productivity debate: An employee opinion survey in Ireland. *British Journal of Industrial Relations* 23: 2.

— — —. 1987. Union or non-union-employee relations strategies in the Republic of Ireland. Unpublished PhD thesis. London School of Economics.

Torrington, D. and Hall, L. 1991. *Personnel management: A new approach.* London: Prentice Hall.

— — — and Hall, L. 1998. *Human resource management.* London: Prentice Hall.

Traxler, F. 1998. Employers and employer organisations. In Towers, B. and Terry, M. (eds). *Industrial Relations Journal: European Annual Review 1997.* Oxford: Blackwell.

Townley, B. 1994. Communicating with employees. In Sisson, K. (ed.). *Personnel Management.* Oxford: Blackwell.

Treble, J.G. 1986. How new is final offer arbitration? *Industrial Relations* 25: 1.

Turnbull, P. 1988. The limits to 'Japanisation' — just-in-time, labour relations and the U.K. automotive industry. *New Technology, Work and Employment* 3: 1.

Turner, D. and D'Art, D. 1998. A review of centralised wage agreements in Ireland 1987–1997. Paper presented to the international seminar for the Federation of Israeli Economic Organisations on industrial relations and labour law. Limerick: University of Limerick.

Turner, H. 1962. *Trade union growth, structure and policy*. London: Allen and Unwin.

Turner, T. 1988. Wage bargaining in Ireland: Future strategies. *Industrial Relations News* 27: July.

— — —. 1993. Unionisation and human resource management in Irish companies. *Industrial Relations Journal* 25: 1: 39–51.

— — —. 1994. Internal labour markets and employment systems. *International Journal of Manpower* 15: 1.

— — —, Morley, M. and Gunnigle, P. 1994. Developments in industrial relations and HRM in the Republic of Ireland. *Irish Business and Administrative Research* 15: 1: 76–92.

— — — and Morley, M. 1995. *Industrial relations and the new order*. Dublin: Oak Tree Press.

— — —, D'Art, D. and Gunnigle, P. 1997. US multi-nationals: Changing the framework of Irish industrial relations? *Industrial Relations Journal* 28: 2: 92–102.

Tyson, S. 1985. Is this the very model of the modern personnel manager? *Personnel Management* May.

— — —. 1987. The management of the personnel function. *Journal of Management Studies* 24: 5: 523–32.

— — —. 1992. Business & human resource strategy. *Irish Business and Administrative Research* 13: 1. 1–5.

— — — and Fell, A. 1986. *Evaluating the personnel function*. London: Hutchinson.

— — —, Witcher, M. and Doherty, N. 1994. *Different routes to excellence*. Cranfield University School of Management: Human Resource Research Centre.

University College Dublin (UCD). 1989. *Industrial relations in Ireland: Contemporary issues and developments*. Dublin: Department of Industrial Relations: University College Dublin.

Van De Vliert, E. 1985. Escalative intervention in small groups. *Journal of Applied Behavioural Science* 12: 1: 19–36.

Visser, J. 1991. Trends in union membership. *OECD Outlook*. Paris (July).

— — — and Van Ruysseveldt, J. 1996. Robust corporatism, still? Industrial relations in Germany. In Van Ruysseveldt, J. and Visser, J. (eds). *Industrial relations in Europe*. London: Sage.

Von Prondzynski, F. 1982. Operating a disciplinary procedure — the essential requirements. *Industrial Relations News* 45: 26 November.

— — —. 1985. The Death of the Pay Round. *Industrial Relations News* 16 (November).

— — —. 1988. Social partnership in Ireland and Austria. In Matthews, A. and Sagarri, A. (eds). *Economic performance in two small European economies: Ireland and Austria*. Dublin: Trinity College Dublin.

— — —. 1989a. *Employment law in Ireland*. London: Sweet and Maxwell.

— — —. 1989b. Collective labour law. In *Industrial Relations in Ireland*. Dublin: University College Dublin. 1989.

— — —. 1992. Ireland between centralism and the market. In Ferner, A. and Hyman, R. (eds). *Industrial relations in the new Europe*. Oxford: Blackwell.

— — —. 1998. Ireland: Corporatism revived. In Ferner, A. and Hyman, R. (eds). *Changing industrial relations in Europe*. Oxford: Blackwell.

— — — and Richards, W. 1994. *European employment and industrial relations glossary: Ireland*. London: Sweet and Maxwell / Luxembourg: Office for Official Publications of the European Communities.

— — — and McCarthy, C. 1989. *Employment law in Ireland*. London: Sweet and Maxwell.

Wallace, J. 1982. *Industrial relations in Limerick city and environs*. Employment Research Programme. Limerick: University of Limerick.

— — —. 1987. Selected aspects of employment legislation. Mimeo. Limerick: University of Limerick.

— — —. 1988a. Unofficial strikes in Ireland. *Industrial Relations News* 8: 15 February.

— — —. 1988b. Workplace aspects of unofficial strikes. *Industrial Relations News* 9: 3 March.

— — —. 1988c. A review of proposed reforms of trade disputes legislation in Ireland. *Advances in Business Studies* 1: 2.

— — —. 1989. Procedure agreements and their place in workplace industrial relations. In *Industrial Relations in Ireland*. Dublin: University College Dublin. 1989.

— — —. 1991a. The Industrial Relations Act 1990 and judicial constructivism: A threat to neo-corporatism in Ireland? Paper presented to University of Cardiff conference on the future of employment relations: International comparisons in an age of uncertainty. University of Cardiff.

— — —. 1991b. Selected aspects of employment legislation. Mimeo. Limerick: University of Limerick.

— — —. 1991c. The Industrial Relations Act 1990 and other developments in labour law. Paper presented to the Mid-West Chapter of the Institute of Personnel Management. University of Limerick.

— — —. 1994. Industrial relations: An economic, social, political and legal perspective. Mimeo. University of Limerick.

— — —. 1997. Back to the future? The Irish Industrial Relations Act 1990. In Meenan (ed.). *Legal perspectives — the juridification of the employment relationship. Proceedings of the fifth European regional industrial relations conference of the International Industrial Relations Association*. Dublin: Oak Tree Press.

— — — and O'Shea, F. 1987. *A study of unofficial strikes in Ireland*. Dublin: Government Publications Office.

— — — and Clifford, N. 1998. Collective bargaining and flexibility in Ireland. Labour law and labour relations programme. Working Paper. Geneva: International Labour Office.

— — —, Turner, T. and McCarthy, A. 1998. EMU and the impact on Irish industrial relations. In Kauppinen, T. (ed.). The impact of EMU on industrial relations in Europe, Finnish Labour Relations Association. Publication 9. Helsinki: Finnish Labour Relations Association.

Walton, R.E. 1982. The topeka work system: Optimistic visions, pessimistic hypothesis and reality. In Zager, R. and Rosow, M. (eds). *The innovative organisation*, New York: Pergamon.

——. 1985. From control to commitment in the workplace. *Harvard Business Review* March–April: 77–84.

—— and McKersie R.B. 1965. *A behavioural theory of labor negotiations*. New York: McGraw-Hill.

Warr, P. 1973. *Psychology and collective bargaining*. London: Hutchinson.

Watson, T. 1987. *Sociology, work and industry*. London: Routledge.

Webb, S. and Webb, B. 1920. *The history of trade unionism*. London: Longman.

Wedderburn, Lord. 1986. *The worker and the law*. London: Penguin.

Whelan, C. 1982. Worker priorities, trust in management and prospects for worker participation. Paper 111. Dublin: Economic and Social Research Institute.

Whitaker, A. 1986. Managerial strategy and industrial relations: A case study of plant relocation. *Journal of Management Studies* 23: 6.

Wickens, P. 1987. *The road to Nissan: Flexibility, quality, teamwork*. London: Macmillan.

Wilkinson, A. et al. 1992. Fitness for use? Barriers to full T.Q.M. in the U.K. *Management Decision* 29: 8.

——, Redman, T. and Snape, E. 1993. *Quality and the manager*. London: Institute of Management.

Wilkinson, B. and Oliver, N. 1990. Obstacles to Japanization: The case of Ford U.K. *Employee Relations* 12: 1.

Windmuller, J.P. 1984. Employers' associations in comparative perspective; Organisation, structure and administration. In Windmuller, J.P. and Gladstone, A. (eds). *Employer Associations and Industrial Relations*. Oxford: Clarendon.

Womack, J.P., Jones, D.T. and Roos, D. 1990. *The machine that changed the world*. New York: Rawson Associates.

Wood, S. 1978. Ideology in industrial relations theory. *Industrial Relations Journal* 9: 4.

—— and Pecci, R. 1990. Preparing for 1992? Business-led versus strategic human resource management. *Human Resource Management* 1: 1: 63–89.

Wood, J. 1985. Last offer arbitration. *British Journal of Industrial Relations* 20: 3: 414–24.

World Economic Forum. 1997. *The world competitiveness report, 1997*. Geneva: World Economic Forum.

Worsley, P. 1977. *Introducing Sociology*. London: Penguin.

Yeates, P. 1993. Personnel managers favour a new PESP. *Irish Times* 21 December.

——. 1997. Pay agreement criticised by trade union leader. *Irish Times* 17 January.

——. 1998. Jobless rate of 5 percent forecast. *Irish Times* 2 October.

Index

absenteeism, 231, 232, 234
acquired rights, 56
Adams, R.J., 233
Adoptive Leave Act 1995, 50
Advisory Conciliation and Arbitration
  Service (ACAS), 274, 275, 277
advisory service, LRC, 93–4
Aer Lingus, 303, 346, 417
Aer Rianta, 299, 325, 329, 346
agriculture, 11, 17
Ahern, Bertie, 64, 66, 210, 212
Alarm Association of Ireland, 152
Allen, V., 226
Amalgamated Engineering and Electrical
  Union (AEEU), 117
Amalgamated Society of Engineers, 116
Amalgamated Society of Railway Servants,
  59
Amalgamated Transport and General
  Workers' Union (ATGWU), 144, 210,
  218–19
Amsterdam Treaty, 23
analysers, 340
Anthony, P.D., 179, 184
Anti-Discrimination (Pay) Act 1974, 42,
  43–4, 430
  Equality Officers, 98–100
  Labour Court, 84
appeal, right of, 278
arbitration, 271–2
architect model, 380
Armstrong, M. and Murliss, H., 310
Armstrong, M., 346
Association of Landscape Contractors of
  Ireland, 152
Association of Pharmaceutical
  Manufacturers of Ireland, 152

Association of Scientific Technical and
  Managerial Staffs (ASTMS), 119
Association of Secondary Teachers of
  Ireland (ASTI), 119
asylum seekers, 20
Atkinson, G., 264
Atkinson, J. and Meager, N., 412
Atkinson, J., 243, 411, 412
Atkinson, P. and Naden, J., 428
attitude surveys, 316
Attley, Bill, 205, 212, 219
'atypical' employment, 19, 412–15, 438
Aughinish Alumina, 416
Austria, 78, 298
authoritarianism, 28
Automobile, General Engineering and
  Mechanical Operatives Union
  (AGEMOU), 420
autonomy, 159–60, 164

B & I, 303
Bacon, N. and Storey, J., 311, 387
Bailey, J., 317
Bain, G.S. and Elsheikh, F., 136
Bain, G.S. and Price, R., 134, 136
Bain, G.S., 112
Baker, T.J. et al., 408
bank dispute, 94, 238
Bank of Ireland, 15, 417
bargained corporatism, 76–7
bargaining power, 253–4
Barret, S., 208, 209
Barrington, D., 47
Batstone, E., 386
BATU v G & T Crampton, 69–70
Bean, R., 230
Beaumont, P. and Harris, R., 135, 359, 389